THE WEISSENHOFSIEDLUNG

THE WEISSENHOFSIEDLUNG

Experimental Housing Built for the
Deutscher Werkbund, Stuttgart, 1927

Karin Kirsch

*Drawings from architects' final plans
by Gerhard Kirsch*

RIZZOLI NEW YORK

To whom?
Gerhard Kirsch, Konrad, and Valentin

To whom, besides?
Gustaf Stotz

First published in the United States of America in 1989 by
RIZZOLI INTERNATIONAL PUBLICATIONS, INC.
300 Park Avenue South, New York, NY 10010

Originally published in Germany under the title
Die Weissenhofsiedlung in 1987 by Deutsche Verlags-Anstalt

Copyright © Deutsche Verlags-Anstalt GmbH, Stuttgart

English-language copyright © 1989 Rizzoli International Publications, Inc.

Library of Congress Cataloging-in-Publication Data
Kirsch, Karin.
    [Weissenhofsiedlung. English]
    The Weissenhofsiedlung : Experimental housing, 1927 : from
the Exhibition Die Wohnung, organized by the Deutscher Werkbund,
Stuttgart / Karin Kirsch.
        p.   cm.
    Translation of: Die Weissenhofsiedlung.
    Bibliography: p.
    ISBN 0-8478-1107-7
    1. Architecture, Domestic—Germany (West)—Stuttgart.
2. Architecture, Modern—20th century—Germany (West)—Stuttgart.
3. Stuttgart (Germany)—Buildings, structures, etc.   4. Interior
decoration—History—20th century.   5. Furniture—History—20th
century.   6. Deutscher Werkbund.   7. Werkbund-Ausstellung "Die
Wohnung" (1927 : Stuttgart, Germany) I. Kirsch, Gerhard.
II. Werkbund-Ausstellung "Die Wohnung" (1927 : Stuttgart, Germany)
III. Deutscher Werkbund.   IV. Title.
NA7351.S7K5713   1989
728'.0943'4715—dc20   89-42784
                                                          CIP

Translated from the German by David Britt
Page layout by Mary McBride
Typeset by David E. Seham Associates, Metuchen, New Jersey
Printed and bound by Dai Nippon Printing Company, Tokyo, Japan

Contents

PREFACE

Our work is experimental; but experiment is often more important than the safe way. We are well aware of the deficiencies in our work, and we can safely say that we have learned much from it.[1]

Ever since I took up a teaching post at the Fachhochschule für Technik, the Stuttgart Institute of Technology, I have been discussing the Weissenhofsiedlung—the neighborhood built for the 1927 Stuttgart architectural exhibition—in my classes. This seems all the more natural because I myself studied very close to Weissenhof, at the Akademie der bildenden Künste, under Herbert Hirche; and he in turn was a student of Ludwig Mies van der Rohe's. Yet neither of these factors is the origin of this book. We were studying in a period that had no sense of history: we were within the tradition of early twentieth-century Modernism, but we made no analytical study of its products. Like early Modernism itself, we set out to start from scratch," finding solutions to our problems entirely out of our own resources. More or less as a matter of principle, this precluded any examination of the products of Modernism, because of the risk of imitation.

A changing intellectual climate and an increasing tendency to condemn the leading figures of Modernism, their works and their theories, induced me to take an interest in their original intentions. My preparations for classes on the subject, for a seminar on Weissenhof and its architects, and finally for a further seminar on the interiors of the Weissenhof houses, brought me step by step closer to the theme. The idea of a book on the 1927 Deutscher Werkbund exhibition, *Die Wohnung* (The Home), did not emerge until I realized just how little material there was for me to put into my students' hands. I set out to contact the eye-witnesses: Mia Seeger, who with Werner Graeff had run the exhibition press office in 1927; Heinz Rasch, who had known Mies van der Rohe in Berlin, and who had accompanied him on his first on-site inspections in Stuttgart; Bodo Rasch, who founded the Society of Friends of the Weissenhofsiedlung in 1977; Alfred Roth, who was resident architect at Weissenhof for Le Corbusier and Pierre Jeanneret; Max Berling, who was resident architect for Hans Poelzig; Ferdinand Kramer and Oscar Heinitz, who worked on interior installations, as did the Rasch brothers; Sergius Ruegenberg, who was then working in Mies van der Rohe's office; Margarete Schütte-Lihotzky, inventor of the Frankfurt Kitchen"; and Walter Boll, who would—if allowed—have owned a house at Weissenhof by Adolf Loos, and who eventually owned one by Victor Bourgeois. All of them encouraged and supported me in every conceivable way, and I am extremely grateful to them. Thanks to the information and the contacts they gave me, I have been able to trace the heirs of many of the architects and interior designers who were involved

in 1927.

As I worked in the Stadtarchiv in Stuttgart, in the Mies van der Rohe Archive at The Museum of Modern Art, New York, in the Bauhaus-Archiv, the Werkbund-Archiv, and the archives of the Akademie der Künste in Berlin, in the Fondation Le Corbusier in Paris, and in the smaller personal archives of those concerned, I grew increasingly familiar with the theme and the people involved at Weissenhof, and I marveled all the more at the extent of the gaps in the existing published record. As my starting point had been the individual dwellings and their furnishings, I naturally looked everywhere for details, furnishing plans, furniture designs. Often, instead of what I was looking for, I came across a clue to some other aspect of the Weissenhof enterprise. I was astonished at the abundance of material that had never been studied.

It may have been something of an advantage that, as an architect specializing in interior design, I am familiar with the thought processes, the design processes, and the everyday routine of construction work. I could not believe that an architect like Ludwig Mies van der Rohe would have put forward flexible floor plans without previously satisfying himself that they were furnishable; in New York I found his preliminary drawings. Equally, I could not imagine that Paul Bonatz would have worked out the first overall layout plan for the Weissenhofsiedlung, only to allow a comparatively obscure architect like Mies to be brought in over his head to make a new plan. I was able to correct this misconception, with many others. The pursuit of details, the quest for facts, however dry and banal they may sometimes have been, had its importance in making the situation in Stuttgart in the late 1920s concrete and comprehensible. Very often, such extraneous factors as a shortage of city funds, or the conscientious scruples of city councilmen had a decisive influence on the development of the project.

At the outset the perceived problem was one of shortage of information; by the time I concluded my researches, the problem was one of superabundance. I soon realized that I was going to have to select one point in the existence of the Weissenhofsiedlung at which to describe it. I decided to concentrate on the time of the 1927 Werkbund exhibition itself: to convey the impression that a visitor to that exhibition would have had, and the information that might notionally have been available at the time concerning the genesis of the idea, the local Stuttgart context, the choice of architects and their intentions, and the new features of this four-part exhibition on "The Home."

This decision led to the decision to redraw the architects' final plans, as submitted to the building office, as a record of their final intentions. It became apparent that designs had subsequently been modified by the superintendent, Richard Döcker, and structural features and building materials changed without reference to the architects; the building of Mart Stam's houses provides a particularly gross example.

Comparatively little space has been devoted to the fate of the Weissenhof development after 1927—its vilification in the years of the Third Reich, its disfigurement after World War II, its repair, and the restoration of its color scheme. Where the written sources supply contradictory information, or none, I have said so; and everywhere I have given precedence to the accounts of those who were personally involved in 1927.

I have constantly found myself regretting that I can only quote letters, minutes, and interviews in part: even in these dry, factual documents—even in the files at City Hall—individual temperaments find expression. These individuals—some of whom are among the master architects of the twentieth century—have been a fascinating study. Full of curiosity, suspense, and growing affection, I have traced their interrelationships, the ways in which they approached their problems, and the processes by which, in their early years, they set about making their mark.

Alongside the eye-witnesses already named, I must first and foremost thank my husband for his redrawing of the plans and his readiness to talk, and Nora von Mühlendahl for her sympathetic work as editor. My thanks are also due to the many relatives, executors,

and trustees of those involved; to my students of Semester 8, 1983-84; and to all those who have given me the benefit of their advice and practical assistance. I would like to mention, in particular, the contributions, some of them indirect, that have been made by the following individuals:

Pierre Adler, Till Behrens, Karl-Georg Bitterberg, Bernard Colenbrander, Claudia Colombini, Magdalena Droste, Herbert Eilmann, Dieter Faller, Peter Faller, Carla Fandray, Ludwig Glaeser, Ursula Graeff-Hirsch, Carmela Haerdtl, Peter Hahn, Eugen Helmlé, Jörg Herkommer, Frank Herre, Rainer Hildebrandt, Herbert Hirche, Jürgen Joedicke, Felicitas Karg-Baumeister, Robert Knoll, Karl H. Krämer, Lore Kramer, Miroslav Kunštát, Jörg Lachenmann, Richard Lisker Jr., Dirk Lohan, Arnulf Lutz, Otakar Máčel, Egidio Marzona, Christine Mengin, Hans Oud, J.M.A. Oud-Dinaux, Christian Plath, Anne Rotzler, Christian Schädlich, Egon Schirmbeck, Matthias Schirren, Julie Schneider, Kathinka Schreiber, Heike Schröder, Franz Schulze, Peter C. von Seidlein, Eckhard Siepmann, Johannes Spalt, the staff of the Stadtarchiv Stuttgart (Frau Bayer, Herr Blank, Frau Mahlmeister, Frau Scharf), Olga Stam, Donatus Stotz, Alexander H. Volger, Andrew Weininger, Eva Weininger, Achim Wendschuh, Klaus Wilhelm, Marion Winter, Dietrich Worbs.

Stuttgart, April 1987   Karin Kirsch

I THE CLIMATE AFTER WORLD WAR I

POLITICS AND SOCIETY

In the preamble to the Weimar Constitution of 1919, we read

> In the wake of the revolution that followed the horrors of World War, the German nation was confronted by the urgent need of a new constitution which would maintain its political and cultural identity by setting its existence as a State on a new legal foundation. Now that all the old sources of power had collapsed, reconstruction could take place only on a basis of total equality, embracing all sections of the people, without regard to occupation or wealth, sex or local origin: and thus on a basis of pure democracy. To this end, only a few weeks after the Revolution, the decree of November 30, 1918, was issued, providing for elections to a National Constituent Assembly. This convened in Weimar on February 6, 1919. . . .
>
> The name of Weimar means for every German, transcending all the vicissitudes of history, the memory of a time when that city witnessed the richest and freest development of German intellectual life.[1]

Elections took place in Württemberg on January 12, 1919, and in the Reich as a whole on January 19. In the Württemberg capital, Stuttgart, the task of forming a government fell to a member of the Social Democratic Party of Germany (SPD), Wilhelm Blos. His counterpart in the government of the Reich as a whole was Friedrich Ebert, another Social Democrat; the same "Weimar Coalition" was in power nationally and locally.

In Württemberg, where the departing king had taken care, as one of his last public acts, to arrange for the old civil service to be taken over intact by the new State, the restoration of order went more smoothly than in the rest of the Reich. There existed a revolutionary council (or soviet) of workers and soldiers, and even a "brain-workers' soviet" whose members included the architects Bernhard Pankok and Paul Bonatz.

An initial optimism soon succumbed to an inflation to this day remembered with horror. At its climax, in 1923, no price remained stationary for more than a few days or even hours. Every citizen suffered a financial body-blow. The main sufferers were the middle class, the wage and salary earners, and the unemployed. The situation was stabilized by the introduction of the Rentenmark (exchanged for the existing paper currency at the rate of 1 to 1 trillion, on and after October 23, 1923) and later (from August 30, 1924) the new Reichsmark. A brief interlude of peace and reconstruction in the economy, in housing, and in politics made possible the building of an experimental housing project at Weis-

senhof, in Stuttgart—the Weissenhofsiedlung.

This was a time of seeming stability in Germany, starting with a shift of about two million votes from the extremist parties to the SPD during 1924 (when there were two Reichstag elections); nor was there any great change for the following three-and-a-half years, after which the Socialists again increased their vote. The Mark remained steady, thanks largely to American investment following the Dawes Plan, and there was a high level of public spending.[2]

Architecture and design in Germany had been crippled by the war years. Either the architects went off to war, like other sections of the population, in a mood of patriotic enthusiasm, or else they totally rejected the war and anything connected with it—as did Bruno Taut, who so weakened his body through hunger that the medical board had no alternative but to classify him as unfit to serve. This status, once achieved, had to be maintained: Taut took on a job as resident architect in a munitions factory, and then an office job in a factory making furnaces, to make sure that he was not just "unfit" but "engaged in essential work."[3]

Instead of silver spoons and luxury flatware, the factory owned by the champion of modern design and chairman of the Deutscher Werkbund, Peter Bruckmann, was making grenades, which were then shipped in packing-cases made in the workshops of the "Pope of Furniture," Karl Schmidt, at Hellerau.[4] The few commissions forthcoming at the end of the war went to established architects. The "young" were deprived of work, although not of ideas; the resulting enforced theoretical activity lasted almost halfway through the 1920s.

Military equipment and its spare parts, the assembly of prefabricated components in improvised workshops, exactness of fit, and truth to materials were the essential wartime lessons that sparked off a rethinking of the building process: "standardization, normalization, rationalization, puritanism, constructivism, functionalism" was Emanuel Margold's summary of the "slogan mania" that now set in.[5] The enthusiasm for forms derived from structure (or apparently derived from structure and from clearly definable function) was summarized by Le Corbusier:

> Our eyes are constructed to enable us to see forms in light.
> Primary forms are beautiful forms, because they can be clearly appreciated.
> Architects today no longer achieve these simple forms.
> Working by calculation, engineers employ geo-

metrical forms, satisfying our eyes by their geometry and our understanding by their mathematics; their work is on the direct line of good art.[6]

The automobile, the ocean liner, and the airplane as the signs of a new spirit—signs which would be industrially produced—led Le Corbusier to reflect on the problem of the house, speaking for his own generation:

> The airplane is the product of close selection.
> The lesson of the airplane lies in the logic which governed the statement of the problem and its realization.
> The problem of the house has not yet been stated. Nevertheless there do exist standards for the dwelling house. Machinery contains in itself the factor of economy, which makes for selection. The house is a machine for living in.[7]

Was this standardization, as Hermann Muthesius had used the term? Certainly, no slogan did more to inflame the imagination and to promote the debate about new ways of building, and of living, than did Le Corbusier's phrase, "a machine for living in."

THE CULTURAL SITUATION IN STUTTGART

The history of the Weissenhofsiedlung project is also the story of individuals. For many, their part in this project was a decisive event in their careers.

The exhibition *Die Wohnung*, held in Stuttgart in 1927, represented the climax of Peter Bruckmann's longstanding commitment to the Deutscher Werkbund and its work for German design. He was involved at the very beginning: at the age of forty-two, vice president and prospective chief of the family silverware firm of P. Bruckmann & Söhne, Heilbronn, he spoke as the representative of industry at the founding ceremony of the Werkbund in Munich in 1907. All his life, Bruckmann upheld the objectives of the Werkbund: to couple excellence in design with commercial success; to enhance the prestige of Germany; and to give precedence to the expressive resources of the present day over the imitation of past forms.

From 1908 to 1909, Bruckmann was deputy chairman of the Deutscher Werkbund; from 1909 to 1919 chairman; from 1919 to 1926 deputy chairman again; and from 1926 to 1932 once more chairman, before becoming honorary chairman. But these were not his only public offices; he was a city councilman in his native Heilbronn, and a member of the Württemberg legislature (the Landtag) representing the German Democratic Party, which he helped to found, and whose chairman he became after the death of Conrad Haussmann. He was an honorary Doctor of Engineering of the Technische Hochschule, Aachen (1920, cited for "services to German quality workmanship"), and of the Württembergische Technische Hochschule, Stuttgart (1924, cited for his pursuit of "ideal and cultural objectives" and his selfless work for the ideals of the Werkbund).

Gustaf Stotz, once an apprentice in the Bruckmann flatware factory, is a background figure who tends to go unmentioned; a street in the Weissenhofsiedlung is named after Peter Bruckmann, but none after Gustaf Stotz. Yet without Stotz the project would never have come to fruition. His boyhood friend, the future West German President Theodor Heuss, was to call him a "propagandist for others";[8] Mia Seeger has called him a "key figure."[9]

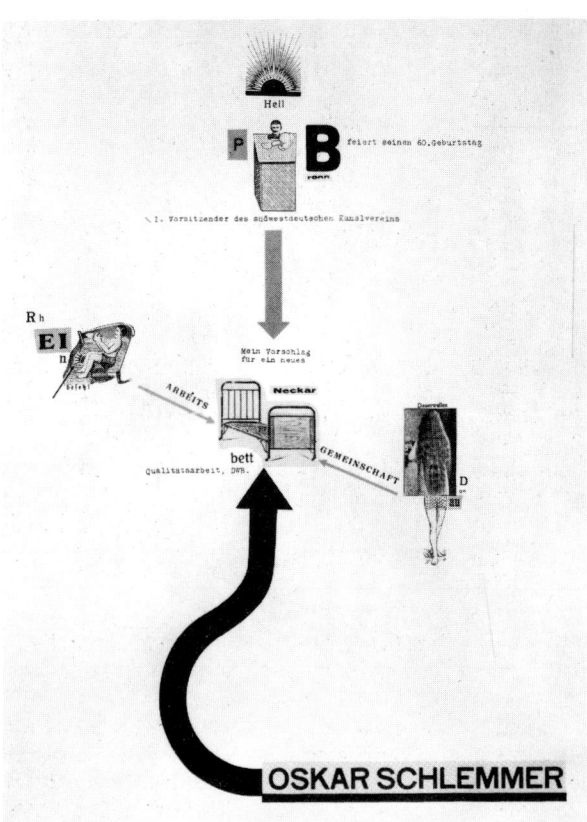

Oskar Schlemmer: collage for Peter Bruckmann's sixtieth birthday, January 13, 1925

As the history of the Weissenhofsiedlung is closely tied to individual personalities, it is also inseparable from the story of the Deutscher Werkbund and from that of the Südwestdeutscher Kanalverein (Southwest German Canal Union). A number of the most important individuals involved in them were the same.

Bruckmann, as has been said, was chairman of the Werkbund for many years. In 1915, while a member of the German Progressive Party, he committed himself to the canalization of the River Neckar. The Südwestdeutscher Kanalverein was set up in 1916 at Maulbronn (a small town in the Kraichgau district that had a fine Benedictine monastery but no access to the Neckar). Bruckmann became chairman of the working committee. From 1919 until well after the Weissenhof project was completed, the Stuttgart addresses of the Kanalverein and the Deutscher Werkbund (or rather its Württemberg section) were identical—at Neckarstrasse 30 until 1919, then on Geiss-Strasse, and then at Eberhardstrasse 3. In 1921, the Kanalverein, as the organization with overall responsibility, set up an incorporated joint-stock company to execute the canal project. Thus there were three organizations at one address;[10] the chairman of two of them was Bruckmann; and the administrator of both the Kanalverein and the Württemberg section (*Arbeitsgemeinschaft*) of the Werkbund was Stotz.

Among those with whom the Südwestdeutscher Kanalverein had to deal were the elected representatives of the city of Stuttgart, Mayor Dr. Karl Lautenschlager, and Building Commissioner Dr. Daniel Sigloch. It was Lautenschlager who presented Bruckmann on his sixtieth birthday with a painting by Reinhold Nägele of the Neckar canal works, with all the working structures involved. (The same artist was to paint a view of the Weissenhofsiedlung in 1927.)

In the course of the 1920s, the Württemberg section of the Werkbund mounted a succession of exhibitions in Stuttgart. In February and March of 1922, the *Werkbundausstellung Württembergischer Erzeugnisse* (Werk-

Peter Bruckmann
Gustaf Stotz
Karl Lautenschlager

bund Exhibition of Württemberg Products) at the Staatliches Ausstellungsgebäude, part of the preparatory work for a Munich Trade Show, was intended both to show what Württemberg artists were capable of and to solicit the participation of those who had previously been too diffident or too uncommitted to come forward.[12] In May of 1922, the exhibits finally selected for showing in Munich were collected together. Exhibitions of liturgical objects and of indigo textile printing and garments followed and led to the exhibition *Die Form*, mounted in the newly founded Stuttgarter Handelshof, the former crown prince's palace at Königstrasse 32, as part of the summer art festival, the *Stuttgarter Kunstsommer*, of 1924.

This exhibition, which ran from June 29, 1924 through the end of July, was a kind of dress rehearsal for the larger undertaking of 1927. On a comparatively small scale, it held the nucleus of the idea of the Weissenhof project. A printed "Invitation to Participate in the Werkbund Exhibition *Die Form*" laid down the following principles:

The Deutscher Werkbund has charged its Württemberg section with the execution of the exhibition *Die Form*, which is to include only those objects from the realm of the applied arts which bear no ornament whatsoever. This exhibition will include works from all over Germany and German Austria, which will demonstrate the extraordinary wealth of expression that can be embodied in pure form without the addition of any ornament.[13]

Alongside examples of "technical form," the show also included examples of "primitive form":

The "primitives" are almost all women. And the outstanding examples of technical form stem from men. This seems right: technology has hitherto remained an exclusively male concern. But, just as it takes man and woman together to constitute the true, complete human being, it takes technical and primitive form, seen as one, to give us the true, complete image of our time. . . . Salvation lies only in the Either/Or of technical and primitive form.[14]

Die Form subsequently went on tour to four other Ger-

man cities,[16] and was an unqualified success. But one event connected with the 1924 exhibition was to have its repercussions in 1927. Adolf Loos, the high priest of Modernism, visited the exhibition and had an altercation with those responsible on the grounds that his own contribution to the formulation of the show's central idea had not received sufficient credit. Nor, indeed, had it been mentioned at all. As Stotz was to tell Mia Seeger, the story was soon all over Stuttgart and beyond;[15] in consequence, when the Weissenhofsiedlung project came along and architects had to be selected, it was felt that life was going to be difficult enough without Adolf Loos. He was kept out.

It was in the summer of the 1924 *Die Form* exhibition that the government building advisory service (Staatliche Beratungsstelle für das Baugewerbe) organized the first major building exhibition in Germany since the war, *Bauausstellung Stuttgart 1924*.[17] The leading Stuttgart architect in charge of the exhibition, Hugo Keuerleber, had enlisted as his administrator a City Hall accountant, Carl Hagstotz, who was to play an important part behind the scenes at Weissenhof in 1927; and the show included a wide spectrum of building trade products as well as prefabrication systems and a group

Richard Herre: poster for Werkbund exhibition, *Die Form*, 1924

11

of show houses. Among the architects involved who re-appear in the Weissenhof story were Richard Döcker, Adolf Gustav Schneck, Franz Krause (who designed the cafeteria in 1924), and Heinz Rasch (press officer).

It is not known who had the idea of combining the ideas of *Die Form* and the *Bauaustellung,* or when, but the idea may have emerged when Ludwig Mies van der Rohe came from Berlin to visit the latter. Stotz had Willi Baumeister throw a studio party in Mies's honor, "with mattresses and phonograph" and dancing, although Mies, according to Rasch, did not dance much.[18]

Early in 1925, the Württemberg Werkbund took part in the international exhibition of arts and crafts at Monza, near Milan. In the fall of that same year, preparations began for "the Werkbund exhibition of 1927, *Die Wohnung,* planned in association with the city administration."[19]

The "climate" of a city is made up of its politics, its economy, its institutions, and its individuals—but above all its art. A city like Stuttgart, with its decided sense of provincial isolation, might seem unsuited to play host to so splendid and ambitious an undertaking as the 1927 exhibition. In a centrally organized state like France, it would have gone without saying that the place for such an enterprise was Paris. But, as a building trade periodical explained in 1930, on the occasion of the tenth anniversary of the Werkbund in Württemberg,

> In Germany, since the war, and in spite of the most zealous efforts, it has proved impossible to concentrate culture in a national capital. Quite the reverse. The keen rivalry between the major German cities has played its part in keeping cultural endeavor alive. Cities like Munich, Stuttgart, Frankfurt, or Cologne are a program in themselves. They have identities of their own, which have often had a fructifying influence on what happens in the capital of the Reich.[20]

A festschrift was published in which Bruckmann wrote:

> The economic structure of the country [Württemberg], with its highly developed processing and refining industries, and its excellent workshops, provided fertile soil for the development of Werkbund thinking and Werkbund practice, as also did the Swabian mind, with its happy combination of sober practicality in money matters, far-reaching idealism, and great intellectual openness.[21]

Nobody thought to mention the artistic atmosphere, the necessary basis for the appearance of new visions, changed views, and added insights. There was, first of all, the circle which had gathered around the painter Adolf Hölzel, and in particular his students, with their "varied gifts and temperaments."[22] Hölzel himself had retired by the mid-1920s, when the idea of the Weissenhofsiedlung project first came up. His pupils, Oskar Schlemmer, Willi Baumeister, Ida Kerkovius, and Lily Uhlmann (who married the art historian, Hans Hildebrandt), carried on his work and formed centers of their own. They were joined by a number of architects, including Richard Döcker, Richard Herre, and Camille Graeser, some of whom also painted and had artistic leanings. The group met in the house of Lily and Hans Hildebrandt, as well as in the studio of Willi Baumeister.

Baumeister remembered his circle as "innocently convivial in studio gatherings, on excursions, in cafés, or in swimming parties."[23] Surviving postcards (see the

In Willi Baumeister's studio, left to right: Richard Döcker, Richard Herre, unknown, Willi Baumeister

chapter on Le Corbusier and Pierre Jeanneret) prove that, as they grew older, their sense of fun did not disappear. They all traveled together to the Paris Exposition of 1925 (*Exposition internationale des arts décoratifs et industriels*) and visited Le Corbusier in his studio.

Well before the Weissenhof project got underway, and in the absence of any architects from "outside," sharp contrasts of attitude were already manifest in Stuttgart in the persons of Paul Schmitthenner and Richard Döcker: *Stuttgarter Schule* (or Stuttgart School) on one side, *Neues Bauen* (New Architecture, or Modernism) on the other. At a symposium on "The Architecture of the Future of Architecture" (1981) Julius Posener said that "the Weissenhof people liked to think of themselves as radical innovators; the Schmitthenner people liked to see themselves as defenders of a core tradition."[24]

The fact that the Werkbund opted for Modernism, and that it was in Stuttgart that the necessary initiative and enterprise were found, was a consequence of the catholicity of the city's much-invoked "climate."

THE DEUTSCHER WERKBUND

Not all, but most, of the architects involved in the Weissenhofsiedlung were members of the Deutscher Werkbund. Many of them were also members of Der Ring, the Novembergruppe, and the Arbeitsrat für Kunst, or Art Soviet. (Their opponents, in turn, would eventually form themselves into a group called Der Block, although not until the Weissenhofsiedlung exhibition had closed.) Here I attempt to sketch the individual groups within the array of talents whom Paul Bonatz called the *Weissenhöfler.*

Bruckmann recalled on the occasion of the Werkbund's silver jubilee in 1932 that

> it was in 1907 that the architect Hermann Muthesius, a privy councillor in the trade ministry in Berlin, made a speech at the new business school in Berlin in which he solemnly warned German craftsmen and industrialists, in the field of the so-called arts and crafts, of the superficiality of the so-called styling of the objects they made. He prophesied a massive economic setback if they continued to design their objects by thoughtlessly and unscrupulously pillaging the formal repertoire of previous centuries. He invited them to consider whether modern life, new habits, and new everyday needs, did not in themselves de-

mand a new spirit, a formal penetration, and a new design.[25]

Muthesius put his case forward in a succession of lectures and speeches, and his appeal to craftspeople and industrialists aroused strong public opposition. The trade association, Verband für die wirtschaftlichen Interessen des Kunstgewerbes (Union for the Economic Interests of the Arts and Crafts), thus felt impelled to place "the Muthesius affair" on the agenda at its convention in June of 1907. This meeting, which was attended by Peter Bruckmann among others, led to contacts among the advocates of a fresh start in design:

Dr. Wolf Dohrn from the Dresdner Werkstätte, and Josef August Lux, the "arts and crafts" writer. Dohrn stood up on the spur of the moment and declared that his organization was leaving the "Union for the Economic Interests of the Arts and Crafts," whereupon Lux announced the withdrawal of the firm of Karl Bertsch, Munich, and of Royal Nymphenburg Porcelain, and declared that he was now a member of a new association which was being formed to protect artistic interests.[26]

The Deutscher Werkbund was founded at a meeting held, in the absence of Muthesius, in Munich on October 6, 1907. "No one who was there will ever forget the sheer power of the hope and faith that people invested in the victory of the Werkbund idea."[27]

In 1910 the Werkbund described its objectives:

The Bund seeks to make a choice of the best talents working in art, industry, craft, and commerce. It seeks to bring together all that is best in quality and in aspiration in craft work. It forms a rallying point for all those who regard the crafts as a part—and a not insignificant part—of the work of culture in general; who want to create for themselves and for others a focus which will represent their interests while maintaining an exclusive concern with quality. The objective of the Bund is therefore "the advancement of craft work in collaboration between art, industry, and craftsmanship, through education, propaganda, and a united approach to vital issues" (article 2 of Werkbund constitution). The Werkbund, as a representative body, thus works toward a cultural objective which, although it transcends immediate occupational interests, is nevertheless in the interests of craftsmanship as such.

The Werkbund seeks its collaborators primarily in those areas where craftwork proves susceptible of advancement through artistic ideas of form. Its scope of interest includes the whole of manufacturing industry, and in particular craftwork itself.[28]

The founding document of October 1907 was signed by or for twelve artists and twelve companies.[29]

At its inception, the Werkbund's activities were directed largely toward a revitalizing of design in decorative art; but soon the emphasis widened to include design in general. The twenty-four founder members were soon joined by a constantly growing roster of leading architects, artists, and industrial and craft companies. The Werkbund never saw itself as a trade association or an occupational grouping, but as an elite assembly drawn from many separate areas of activity.

The Werkbund was run by a chairman and deputy chairman (or first and second chairmen, as they were known); a governing board; and committees formed ad hoc to undertake specific tasks. The business side was under the control of an administrator (during the Weissenhof period this was Otto Baur; later it was to be Theodor Heuss), and in the individual states of the Reich, on the initiative of the local membership, there were formed sections (Arbeitsgemeinschaften or working groups) such as the one in Württemberg. As Bruckmann's example shows, the local chairmen often stayed in office for long periods; in his case at least, this was a sign of his considerable skill in getting people to work together.

"The Werkbund," said the architect Hans Poelzig, "must become the conscience of the nation. . . . People must believe in it; they must be convinced that it promotes all that is good and forward-looking."[30] The Werkbund wanted to set an example: to show exemplary work in an exemplary way. It had a catalogue or Warenbuch which showed selected objects and gave the addresses of makers and suppliers. The aim was to lead the willing buyer by the hand, to educate him away from the horrors of kitsch.

The most spectacular Werkbund exhibition before World War I was undoubtedly the Werkbund-Ausstellung Coeln 1914, which nearly led to the breakup of the Werkbund itself. Muthesius proclaimed that standardization was the order of the day; Henry Van de Velde spoke up for artistic freedom and intuition. Bruno Taut and Walter Gropius took Van de Velde's side.[31] Muthesius lost, and left the Werkbund. He was replaced as deputy chairman in 1916 by Poelzig; Bruckmann remained chairman.

The history of the Werkbund from the end of World War I to the building of the Weissenhofsiedlung is dominated by the changes in its leadership and by the new groupings that appeared after the war. The Werkbund coexisted, and to a large extent shared its personnel, with the Arbeitsrat für Kunst and Der Zehnerring (which became Der Ring). There was even talk at one time of a merger between Werkbund and Arbeitsrat für Kunst,[32] although this came to nothing. Bruno Taut, founder chairman of the Arbeitsrat, was a Werkbund member, and so was his successor, Gropius; another member of both groups was the painter, César Klein, who in turn was one of the founders of the Novembergruppe.[33]

The first annual convention of the Deutscher Werkbund after World War I took place in Stuttgart in 1919. At the board meeting that followed, Poelzig and Bruckmann changed places: Poelzig became chairman and Bruckmann deputy. Even before that Stuttgart meeting, however, there were signs within the movement that the times were changing, a conflict between the younger ("emerging") and more conservative forces. Some believed passionately in the ideal of socialist internationalism; others preferred to see German problems solved on a nationalist basis.

At the Werkbund convention held in Bremen on June 20–24, 1925, Ludwig Mies van der Rohe and Walter Gropius were elected to the board. Bruckmann reported that an exhibition was "planned in Stuttgart in the course of the next year on the 'modern home.'" He asked the conference to commission the Werkbund's Württemberg section to organize the exhibition, and to appoint Mies and Walter Curt Behrendt as artistic consultants. This was agreed.[34] Gustaf Stotz was present, as were Richard Lisker, Adolf Meyer, Bernhard Pankok, Edwin Redslob, Hans Scharoun, Adolf Schneck, and Lilly Reich. The leading members of the Stuttgart School, Bonatz and Schmitthenner, were absent when the decision was taken to hold the Stuttgart exhibition; they thus missed an opportunity of making contact with Mies, and in the subsequent development of the exhibition they were neither consulted nor informed.

The final, public shift of power in the Württemberg section took place on June 12, 1926; the national Werkbund followed suit in Essen on June 23. Bruckmann became chairman of the Deutscher Werkbund, and Mies became his deputy. According to the minutes of the board meeting

Richard Riemerschmid expressed the view that it was important for the movement and for the structure of the Werkbund that younger talents should test themselves in leading positions, and that positions on the board should not remain in the same hands for too long. It was his own intention to make way for someone younger.[35]

It would seem, in fact, as if the election took place in an atmosphere of harmony, free of rivalries and subliminal tensions: Riemerschmid voluntarily resigned, and Bruckmann wanted to follow suit, but changed his mind when Mies announced that he would not accept office unless Bruckmann stayed on. In the evening session that day, Bruckmann stressed that he had no intention of acting as a "figurehead" but would carry out his duties to the best of his ability.[36]

However, the background to this election is worth emphasizing. Six weeks earlier, on May 14, 1926, the board of the Werkbund's Württemberg section had met to consider the action of the excluded Stuttgart School architects, Bonatz and Schmitthenner, in publishing abusive articles in the local press concerning the conduct of the Weissenhofsiedlung exhibition project; on the same day, the building committee of the city council had met to confirm the appointment of Mies as artistic director of the exhibition. Once Mies's position had been confirmed in this way, the Deutscher Werkbund had no alternative but to give him its support. Mies thus emerged in a position of strength from every point of view. Bonatz vacated his position on the Werkbund board by lot; an apparently fateful coincidence, except that he was reelected that same evening.[37] He remained a powerful presence both in Stuttgart and in Berlin, and there was no public breach.

THE REVOLUTIONARY GROUPINGS OF NOVEMBER 1918: ARBEITSRAT FÜR KUNST AND NOVEMBERGRUPPE

At the end of World War I, established organizations such as the Deutscher Werkbund or the Bund Deutscher Architekten (BDA, Federation of German Architects) embraced too great a variety of opinions to be in any position to take up and articulate the revolutionary moods of the day. The "young" wanted to have their say, to exert influence, and to control developments. Many of these radicals, whether literally young or young at heart, were later to work on the Weissenhofsiedlung or to have some connection with it; the focus here will remain on them. How did these architects come to know each other, and how did these individuals and not others come to be involved in the project?

A further question, and one which has an importance of its own, is that of the origin of the principles embodied in the Weissenhofsiedlung project. If we assume that these, like social conditions in general, had an organic growth, then the past of the people involved and the groups to which they belonged deserve study.

The Novembergruppe took its name from the revolution of November 1918 which overthrew the Kaiser and ended the war. Its embryonic stages, early in 1918, were described by Karl Jakob Hirsch:

November storms, November group. It all began when we were still running around Berlin in the dark in tattered army greatcoats; when we were standing on ladders in the rain and painting the word *Aktion* in red, white, and blue on the front of the new bookstore in the Kaiserallee, until a cop in a spiked helmet came bustling up and ordered us to desist, because in a "ceremonial thoroughfare" no advertising signs were permitted; when the deep nocturnal peace of the Royal Aviation Inspectorate was disturbed by a top secret telegram which read: "Danger of Revolution—all personnel to be confined to quarters."

It all began in the office of the Royal Inspectorate of Military Aviation, more like a studio, really, in which painters dressed up as soldiers were set to draw illustrations of airplanes; but under the tables were revolutionary drawings for the intrepid Pfemfert's *Die Aktion*,[38] drawn on Royal Prussian paper with Royal Prussian india ink. Then . . . many a Red Rooster was hatched. We let our eyes express our sympathy with the workers demonstrating in January 1918, then sat and waited for the hour of liberation; for the light shone from the east!

It started! We were inwardly ready to cast away everything, all that was old, the ballast. . . .

What was form, to us? "Content" was all. And Content was a given quantity: Liberty, Equality, Fraternity. The important thing was not to paint the flagstaff neatly, but to convey the message of the fluttering cloth.[39] In the Novembergruppe, true enthusiasts found each other; in Hirsch's words, "Doubters were ostracized." The members of the Novembergruppe met with the editors of the magazine *De Stijl*, in Holland in November 1918 to formulate the group's first manifesto. Point 7 of this reads,

The artists of the present day all over the world, impelled by one and the same consciousness, have united in a World War of the mind, against the dominance of individualism and personal whim. They therefore sympathize with all those who fight, mentally and materially, for the creation of international unity in life, art, and culture.[40]

The first revolutionary art group to constitute itself, in November of 1918, was the Arbeitsrat für Kunst, or Art Soviet. At Christmas it issued its first flyer, *Das Architektur-Programm*, by Bruno Taut, which appeared in a second edition early in 1919.

Taut's program begins with the words "Art! That is something! When it is there. At the moment this art does not exist."[41] It goes on to call for a union of all idealistic talents among architects; for the pursuit of Utopian ideas; for a piece of ground, a test lot, where architects could try out new ideas (such as the use of glass as a building material, always a preoccupation of Bruno Taut's); for a say in the training of architects, and in the distribution of commissions; for the building of new housing developments; and for the holding of exhibitions to help disseminate the new ideas of architects and artists.

It is worth paying particular attention to the idea of the test lot, where architects would have a chance to carry out their ideas at full size (1 : 1), and that of the housing project—or *Siedlung*—which was to be planned under the unifying control of an architect, "in such a way that one architect sets out extensive guidelines and later scrutinizes all the projects and the buildings, without interfering with personal freedom in matters of detail. This architect would have a power of veto."[42]

Mies's planning and artistic role in the Weissenhof project must surely have been entirely congenial to those architects who signed the Arbeitsrat program. Several of them, indeed, were at one stage or another to be involved in the project: Otto Bartning, Walter Gropius, Ludwig Hilberseimer, Hans and Wassili Luckhardt, Gustav Lüdecke, Erich Mendelsohn, Adolf Meyer, Hans Poelzig, and Bruno and Max Taut.[43]

An abridgment of the same program appeared in *Die Bauwelt* and other trade papers in December, 1918. It began with these words:

Art and People must be one. Art must no longer constitute an enjoyment for a few, but happiness and life for the masses. Unity of the arts, beneath the sheltering wings of a great Art of Building, is the objective. Henceforward, the artist alone, as the one who gives form to the people's sensibility, is responsible for the visible garb of the new State. He must determine the design, from the city to the coin and the postage stamp.[44]

The signatories were Heinrich Tessenow, Max Taut, Walter Gropius, Hans Poelzig, Otto Bartning, Bruno Taut, Richard L.F. Schulz, Adolf Meyer, Walter Curt Behrendt, and—surprising though it may seem, in view of later developments—Paul Schmitthenner.

The Novembergruppe was formally constituted, shortly after the Arbeitsrat für Kunst, by the painters Max Pechstein and César Klein; its first meeting took place on December 3, 1918. Both Pechstein and Klein had signed the Arbeitsrat für Kunst program. Others who belonged to both groups were Otto Bartning, Walter Gropius, Ludwig Hilberseimer, Hans Luckhardt, Wassili Luckhardt, Erich Mendelsohn, Bruno Taut, and Max Taut. They were joined in the Novembergruppe by Alfred Gellhorn, Ludwig Mies van der Rohe, and Hugo Häring. The Novembergruppe turned down an invitation from the Arbeitsrat to take up a group membership.[45]

The Novembergruppe stayed in being until 1933, and organized—or contributed collectively to—nineteen exhibitions. It promoted and supported not only architecture but painting, music, and experimental filmmaking.[46] In 1925, Mies's friend Heinz Rasch wrote in the BDA magazine, *Die Baugilde,*

The "Novembergruppe" has won through. That is, it now has the public on its side. Partly out of conviction, and partly out of weariness with obsolete forms and modish zigzags. Partly from that favorable predisposition that comes so easily to a human being, whether from fellow-feeling or from vanity, when confronted with something "daring."[47]

By this time the groundwork seemed to have been done, and the Novembergruppe exhibits no longer gave anyone "palpitations." The early days had been very different. At one show in 1919—according to a story in *Volk und Zeit*—the art of the "Novembrists" had been met by the public with downright hilarity:

It seems to regard it [the Novembergruppe section] as a joke shop. Flappers bent double with laughter dig each other in the ribs, shrieking, in front of sculptures that look like a mountain of whipped cream and are actually intended to represent "Rapture."[48]

Or, a year or so later:

The rooms set aside for the Novembergruppe in the great Berlin Exhibition are one big joke shop. The naive public holds its sides or finds nothing in the works but a cue for more or less witless jokes.[49]

The Novembergruppe agreed with the Arbeitsrat für Kunst in its principal objective, which was to present a comprehensive program for the emergence of a new society:

The aim is not to help each other along within a small circle, to lend each other artistic, moral, and financial support, but to join in and build, where a whole people has taken the decision to reshape its life from its very foundations. . . .
This is an association of radical artists, not an association to protect economic interests: it expects to have its say in questions of artistic form, in questions of architecture, in the redesign of art schools, in the rearrangement of museums, in the allotment of exhibition spaces, and in legislation on art.[50]

This program did not really differ from that of the Arbeitsrat. Perhaps the Novembergruppe was able to be more effective because its regular exhibitions offered concrete opportunities for members to work together and strengthen their solidarity. These were exhibitions in which all members were entitled to the same amount of floor or wall space, and there was no jury.

Membership in the Novembergruppe and participation in its debates soon ceased to be an indication of a particular political allegiance. The Nazis were more convinced that this was a "left-wing" organization than the dogmatic Communists ever were.[51] The Novembergruppe began its career in a spirit of optimism and hope for the betterment of conditions in Germany; and, although political compromise and the rise of reaction soon led to disillusionment, the group never relapsed into being just an "exhibition society." The opportunities for debate and discussion that it afforded, and its unequivocal commitment to modern art and architecture, were—if we remember who its enemies were—political acts.

The Novembergruppe had around 120 members: documentation is unreliable and incomplete.[52] Of those who either exhibited with the group or are listed as members, the following were associated at some stage with the Weissenhof project: Otto Bartning, Willi Baumeister, Peter Behrens, Theo van Doesburg, Alfred Gellhorn, Walter Gropius, Hugo Häring, Ludwig Hilberseimer, Arthur Korn, Hans Luckhardt, Wassili Luckhardt, Erich Mendelsohn, Adolf Meyer, Ludwig Mies van der Rohe, J.J.P. Oud, Hans Poelzig, Adolf Rading, Mart Stam, Bruno Taut, Max Taut, and Heinrich Tessenow.[53]

DER ZEHNERRING AND DER RING

The Novembergruppe represented a fruitful combination of all "radically minded" practitioners of painting, sculpture, architecture, theater, music, and literature; Der Zehnerring (The Ring of Ten), on the other hand, which emerged out of meetings hosted by Mies and Hugo Häring in 1923 and 1924,[54] consisted in fact of nine architects only: Bartning, Behrens, Häring, Mendelsohn, Mies, Poelzig, Walter Schilbach, and Bruno and Max Taut.[55] The name "Der Zehnerring" was adopted only when the group went public in order "to topple the city building director [of Berlin], Ludwig Hoffmann, who blocks everything that is new, and to help Martin Wagner to succeed to his office and his position." This was successfully accomplished, and by 1926 it seemed right to allow other architects of Modernist sympathies, all over the Reich and in Austria, to join an expanded group under the name "Der Ring."

In 1955 there was an attempt to refound Der Ring. This time there really were ten architects, who met in Württemberg at the Hotel zum Goldenen Rad in Biberach an der Riss. The initiative had been taken by Richard Döcker, in Stuttgart, who had invited Gropius to return from the U.S. for the occasion. Gropius wrote back on May 2, 1955, that it was "a very tempting thought," but that he could not come. He went on to say of Der Ring as it was founded in 1926:

> I think we can feel some satisfaction that we really made a beginning with our work in Der Ring, and I remember how surprised we were that the mere fact of the formation of our little group was enough to take the BDA by storm. The victory of the New Architecture is now an accomplished fact in every civilized country.[56]

In 1926 the first secretary of Der Ring was Hugo Häring. It had an office in Berlin, and the trade journal *Die Bauwelt* gave it a monthly supplement. Der Ring was supposed to be more of a collective—or a lodge—than an institution, and there was to be no inner committee. The members undertook to help each other in any way they could, and new members were selected with great care: acceptance had to be unanimous, and a court of honor ruled on expulsions.

It was the task of the secretary to formulate a position on "the building problems of the present day" and on "governmental and official building policies and the construction industry." The archive for information of interest to the member architects was to be the Bauhaus in Dessau; Der Ring thus formed a kind of exclusive information service for the exchange of technical information and for debate.

The vital factor in the relationship between Der Ring and the Weissenhof project was the secretary's public stand on issues affecting architecture and architects. Accordingly, Häring protested in the summer of 1926 when the city of Stuttgart set the fees for Weissenhof too low; but Mies—whose concern, like that of Gustaf Stotz, was above all to get the project built—told Häring that Der Ring had no business to interfere. (More on this in Chapter III, under the heading "The Selection Process").

Most, but not all, of the Weissenhof architects were members of Der Ring. In 1925, when the first shortlists of architects were drawn up in Stuttgart, Der Ring did not yet exist in its extended form: this was first proposed in April of 1926, and constituted itself on June 5 of that year.[57] Of the twenty-seven members of the enlarged Ring, twenty-one were involved in one way or another with the 1927 Stuttgart exhibition: Otto Bartning, Walter C. Behrendt, Peter Behrens, Richard Döcker, Walter Gropius, Hugo Häring, Ludwig Hilberseimer, Arthur Korn, Hans Luckhardt, Wassili Luckhardt, Ernst May, Erich Mendelsohn, Adolf Meyer, Ludwig Mies van der Rohe, Hans Poelzig, Adolf Rading, Hans Scharoun, Bruno Taut, Max Taut, Heinrich Tessenow, and Martin Wagner.[58]

As work on the 1927 exhibition proceeded, it became apparent that the egalitarian constitution of Der Ring did not preclude personal rivalry or forthright criticism: the Döcker-Mies confrontation, the departure of Häring and Mendelsohn from the shortlist, and Mies's final resignation from Der Ring in August of 1927 illustrate the limits of group solidarity.

DER BLOCK

The last grouping that calls for discussion here is Der Block, formed early in 1928 more or less as a counterweight to Der Ring. Its members were architects who felt an affinity of "cultural approach" and desired to "give expression to this in their works": a new approach to building was possible only by "taking into account the outlook of one's own nation and the given facts of the nature of the land." They set out to take "heritage" and "existing achievements" into account, and to avoid "excessive haste in promoting fashionable creations at the expense of a healthy future evolution." Their talk of "People, Homeland, Blood, and Soil" and their call for a "healthy" architecture find expression in a manifesto which bears the signatures of Bestelmayer, Blunck, Bonatz, Gessner, Schmitthenner, Schultze-Naumburg, Seeck, and Stoffregen.[59] Der Block "stresses the value of tradition, of inheritance. It wants evolution, not revolution."[60]

"Is Der Block going to smash Der Ring, or is Der Ring going to encircle Der Block?"; would the entirely reputable members of Der Block "really find a good line of march of their own" through a gesture seen as motivated by resentment over their exclusion from Weissenhofsiedlung? The answer to this was expected to be provided in Stuttgart itself by a second Werkbund housing development masterminded by Schmitthenner—the Kochenhofsiedlung. In 1928 it still looked as if Kochenhof would be completed in the autumn of that year.[61]

Alongside all these groups, there were other centers of communication in the German architectural world. The practices of Peter Behrens, Bruno Paul, Theodor Fischer, Karl Moser, and Paul Bonatz, even those of Schmitthenner and others, served as centers where professional contacts took place.

II THE WERKBUND EXHIBITION

THE AIMS OF THE 1927 EXHIBITION

From the outset, the hardest task that faced the promoters of the Stuttgart Werkbund exhibition, *Die Wohnung*, was to define what they had in mind. This they set out to do in a number of memoranda, declarations of intent, and programmatic speeches. The first policy document, jointly signed by Karl Lautenschlager, mayor of Stuttgart, and by Peter Bruckmann, dates from June 27, 1925. It declares the housing problem to be one of the most pressing current issues:

> The rationalization that has affected every area of our life has extended to the housing problem also. The economic circumstances of our time forbid any extravagance; they demand that the greatest ends be attained with the smallest means. For house building, and for home economy itself, this entails the use of such materials and such technical installations as will reduce the cost of the building and administration of housing, simplify housekeeping, and improve living conditions. A systematic pursuit of these objectives signifies an improvement of conditions in large cities, and of the quality of life in general; it thus serves to strengthen our national economy.

To this end it was agreed that a neighborhood of modern specimen houses, the Weissenhofsiedlung, would be built in Stuttgart with public money; the houses were to remain city property.

> As it is intended to give as comprehensive a picture as possible of the finest technological, hygienic, and artistic achievements, and this cannot be done through the construction of dwellings alone, the existing halls of the Exhibition and Conference Center will contain a complementary exhibition surveying the areas allied to the program.
> The categories planned for this are as follows:
> (a) building materials;
> (b) technical installations;
> (c) furnishings;
> (d) products required in fitting out homes, such as textiles, wallpapers, floor coverings, etc.;
> (e) color in construction and in the home;
> (f) international exhibition of models of contemporary housing structures;
> (g) architectural sculpture and mural art;
> (h) "simple household utensils" (organized by the Union for the Promotion of Popular Education).

All these groups are to be presented, not in the spirit of a building trade fair, but in accordance with the program of the Deutscher Werkbund, with quality as the basis of selection, which means that inclusion in the exhibition is a distinction in itself.[1]

At this stage, it was intended to work in conjunction with a local housing trust, Bau- und Heimstättenverein, and the exhibition scheduled for 1926. However, the exhibition venues were already established: the Weissenhof site for the houses, and in the center of Stuttgart the Gewerbehalle and the exhibition halls adjoining the Schlossgarten for the accompanying exhibits.

Initially, and throughout the negotiations with Bau- und Heimstättenverein, the houses were to be occupied by manual and white-collar workers, including minor civil servants—a class which corresponded to the membership structure of that organization. When City Hall and the Werkbund came to the conclusion that the project should be carried out without Bau- und Heimstättenverein, the target group changed: at a meeting with Württemberg representatives of women's organizations, the Werkbund's Gustaf Stotz talked of catering for "modern urban humanity." Mies was later to brief Le Corbusier to build "houses for the educated middle class," but was glad to find that at least one other architect, J.J.P. Oud, did propose to build housing on the Weissenhofsiedlung for the original working-class and lower middle-class groups.

In January 1926, the Württemberg Werkbund sent out a second policy paper under the title "Housing for a New Age" which essentially tallied with that of June 1925, but was now intended for a wider public and the press. Parts of the earlier document were taken word for word, but its Werkbund authors additionally stressed

> that there can be no question of putting up "exhibition buildings" or luxury homes. The dwellings here will be built with an eye to the City of Stuttgart's most urgent housing needs, which is to say for families of low and middle income levels. . . . The Deutscher Werkbund knows, and emphasizes, that so ambitious an undertaking can be successful and influential only if the solutions it offers are both technically irreproachable and architecturally strong and forward-looking.[2]

The accompanying exhibitions listed are those contained in the earlier "provisional plan," but the "international exhibition of models of contemporary housing structures" receives greater prominence.

Finally, in December of 1926 an information sheet was sent out announcing the Werkbund exhibition, *Die Wohnung*, Stuttgart 1927 (Appendix A).

A close study of the text reveals that in November (when this was drafted) and December of 1926 the main stress was still on basic housing: "Small dwellings, in particular, need to be designed with great care, because here the resources available are most limited."[3]

This is surprising for two reasons: Mies had already issued his instructions to the individual architects, and indeed some had already sent in their designs to Stuttgart; and everyone concerned, including the members of the city council's building committee, had seen and agreed on his list of building types (Appendix B). At a city council meeting in the summer of 1926 Councilman Krämer, for the People's Party, had commented that "a six-room dwelling, with bathroom and maid's room, undoubtedly falls into the category of upper-class accommodation."[4] And a Communist, Councilman Müllerschön, had declared that

> as long as in one place human beings are crammed together like a flock of sheep, and elsewhere the few are living in the lap of luxury, far away from the so-called mob which toils day in, day out, and is very largely workless and homeless; so long as this rigid class segregation is imposed, we can have no part of it.[5]

In May of 1927 the left-wing paper Die Rote Fahne published a piece which declared that

> the distinguished architects who have gathered here seem for the most part never to have heard of such a thing as a housing crisis. Ten-room houses are being built as models for large-scale housing developments. . . . The Deutscher Werkbund, at a great cost in money and labor, has undertaken an extensive program of experiments, from which we hope that good architects have

learned precisely how not to do it. Of course, none of this does much to ease the housing crisis.[6]

The instructions given to the participating architects were already criticized in 1926; and they are still criticized today. Ultimately, those responsible had failed to define their goals with sufficient clarity.

As for the considerations of hygiene stressed in the early policy papers, the text issued in December of 1926 does not lay any particular stress on them. In the houses themselves hygiene seems to have been taken for granted, as a preassumed standard.

THE OPENING

> May our efforts here serve the German people and its welfare. There will of course be faults, here and there, which we as a Werkbund cannot conceal. But one thing must emerge from it all: the serious will, the serious intent, to contribute to the solution of one of the gravest problems of modern times.[7]

With these words Peter Bruckmann, chairman of the Werkbund and "spiritual originator of the exhibition,"[8] concluded his speech on the evening of opening day, July 23, 1927. The opening ceremony was the hard-won culmination of a process which had begun in 1925; every effort had been directed toward completing the indoor exhibitions, and above all the dwellings at Weissenhof, on time. But as with any exhibition on a comparable scale, not everything was ready for the opening. Despite valiant efforts, the time lost from various causes could not all be made up, and it was impossible to present the first visitors to the show with a

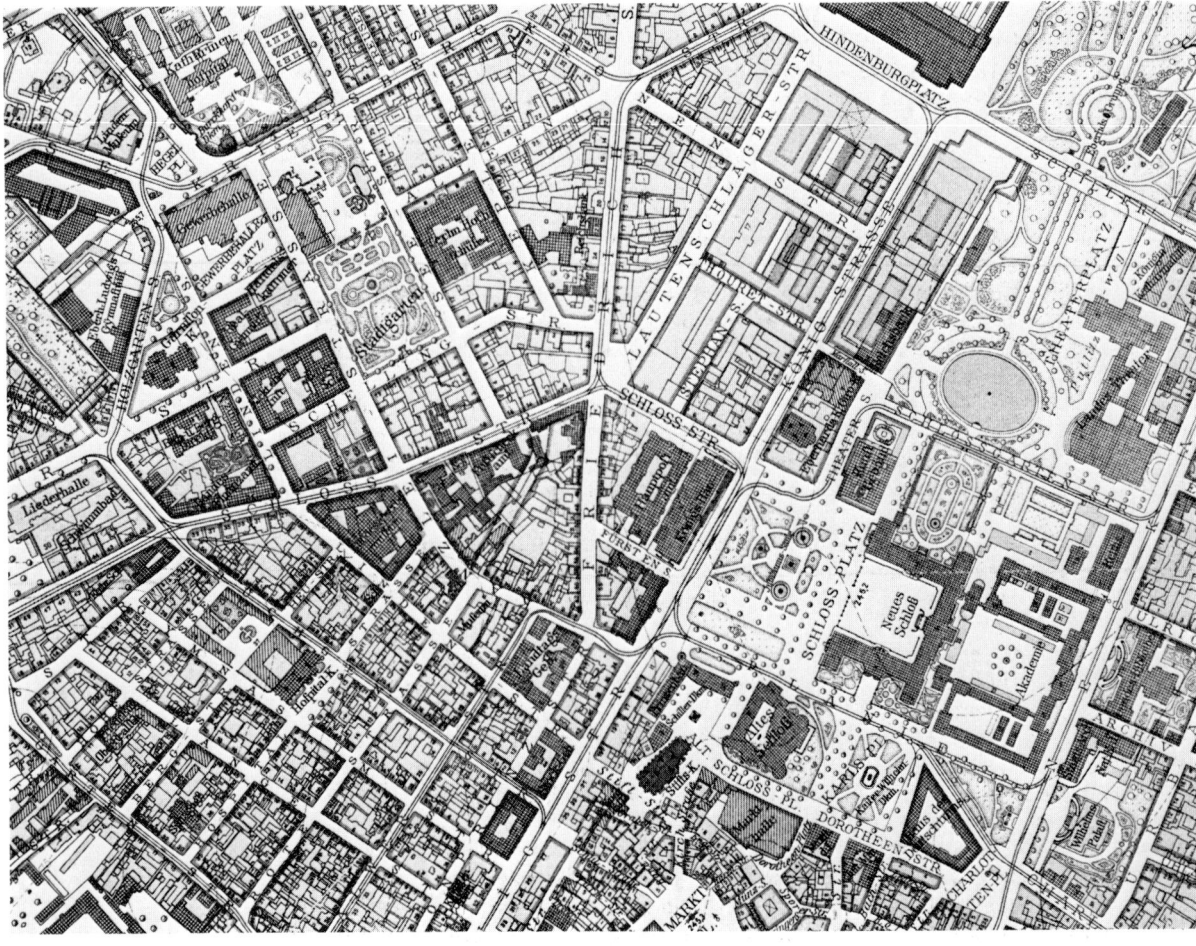

Downtown Stuttgart, c. 1924, showing Gewerbehalle (top left) and [Interims]theaterplatz (center right)

perfect and complete piece of work.

The night before the opening itself, a thunderstorm made it necessary to abandon the idea of holding the inaugural ceremony in the open air, in the former royal private garden. The guests from Germany and beyond were therefore received in the hall of the Städtisches Ausstellungsgebäude, the city exhibition building on the Interimstheaterplatz, which Bernhard Pankok had built in 1925.[9]

> The whole [Württemberg] state government, led by President Bazille; representatives of the Reich, of the other German states, and of foreign governments; personalities from commerce and industry, and senior officials, in great numbers; a number of south German municipalities; representatives of the chambers of commerce, of the university, the Technische Hochschule, the museums and art collections; and artists and architects from all over Germany, had gathered in the great hall. Foreign countries, especially Switzerland and the Latin countries, were also strongly represented.[10]

Dr. Karl Lautenschlager, who had been Mayor of Stuttgart since 1911, began the proceedings by saying,

> This exhibition departs markedly from outworn traditions. The idea behind it has sprung from the urgent needs of the present day: it is intended to serve immediate, practical ends, and to show, through drawings, models, furnishings, everyday utensils, and completed, permanent buildings, how by using simple means and taking up a minimum of space a comfortable, practical home can be achieved, satisfying every need; and how, in particular, the harassed housewife can maintain her home with ease in the absence of unnecessary

ornament, trinkets, and cumbersome furnishings.[11]

Ludwig Mies van der Rohe, the deputy chairman of the Werkbund and artistic director of the 1927 Werkbund exhibition as a whole, was brief and to the point. After thanking his collaborators,[12] he went on to repeat the words he had prefixed to the catalogue:

> The problems of the New Home are rooted in the altered material, social, and mental structure of our time; and it is only from this standpoint that those problems can be understood. The degree of structural change determines the character and the extent of the problems. There is nothing arbitrary or personal about them. They cannot be solved with slogans; nor are slogans of any use in the continuing debate on them.
>
> The issue of rationalization and standardization is only part of the real issue. Rationalization and standardization are no more than means to an end; they must never become an end in themselves. The problem of the New Home is ultimately a problem of the mind, and the struggle for the New Home is only one element in the great struggle for new forms of living.[13]

Bruckmann, the Werkbund chairman, in his speech also expanded on the fundamental objectives of the exhibition, the continuing work of the Werkbund (which was celebrating its twentieth anniversary in the same year), and the far-reaching importance of the pursuit of new approaches to the exhibition's theme, "The Home":

> It has become apparent that the concern with housing is not only a German issue but a concern for the whole world; for us in Germany, there can be no question of going our own way. We must

approach the urgent issue of present-day housing in common with all peoples. This realization has led us to invite architects from other countries and nations to this exhibition in Stuttgart.[14]

There were three posters for the exhibition: two showed rooms filled with useless clutter, and the third was a photomontage of bright, smooth, contemporary apartments and houses from the Weissenhofsiedlung, represented by models and photographs. The intention was to point out the contrast between the modern home and the overcrowded and unhealthy apartments of previous generations, with their pernicious effect on female nerves and domestic peace; but the first two posters provoked criticism and some strong emotion. The members of the exhibition committee (a joint body made up of representatives of City Hall and the Werkbund) themselves considered that the representation of old-fashioned rooms was too detailed.[15] The influential critic of the *Berliner Tageblatt*, Fritz Stahl, considered that it was beyond the "widest limits of permissible propaganda":

> A thick red cross cancels out what is presented to the public as the old-fashioned home which these innovatory geniuses have relegated to the past. And what sort of a home is it? Dark, stuffy, with elaborately carved furniture, an interior dating from 1900. No doubt such a thing does still exist, here and there, as a relic—or it may even be installed afresh, by newly rich people whose ideas stem from that period. But anyone who claims that it is now necessary to campaign against such an interior is telling a brazen untruth. That kind of apartment went out twenty years ago. Present-day homes look completely different. But then, of course: if they had illustrated a room by Bertsch, Pankok, Riemerschmid—I could name many, many others, but those names are on the Committee of Honor of the present exhibition—if such a room had been illustrated, there would have been a risk that the public would turn against the most modern designs and prefer the one that is destined to be eliminated.[16]

Another objector was Professor Gustav E. Pazaurek, "curator of the collections of the Landesmuseum in Stuttgart, and a well-known campaigner over many years for the improvement of standards of taste in the arts and crafts,"[17] who considered the poster misleading and badly designed and said that as the room showed mixed "antiquarian tendencies with Art Nouveau excesses" it represented something that, if not entirely extinct, was the product of an outworn period.[18]

The official catalogue, printed in an edition of 20,000,[19] was an important adjunct to the exhibition; as a guide to its three widely separated sites it was quite indispensable on opening day. It very nearly came out without Mies's contribution. On July 18, 1927, five days before the opening, the exhibition subcommittee (made up of party representatives from the city council, a representative of the union of Württemberg women's organizations, and professors from the Staatliche Kunstgewerbeschule [School of Arts and Crafts] and the Höhere Bauschule [College of Building], together with Commissioner Sigloch) resolved to go to press with only the article by Bruckmann unless Mies's article came in by 7 A.M. the following day.[20]

Mies, however, finally met his deadline; his text serves to set the slogan words Rationalization and Standardization in the overall context of the "struggle for

Karl Straub: poster design for Werkbund exhibition *Die Wohnung*, 1927

new forms of living."[21] For the Werkbund, Bruckmann contributed an article in which he stressed the exemplary nature of the exhibition and its permanent housing, but also its closeness to related endeavors in America, Holland, and Austria.[22]

Alongside the programmatic contributions by Mies and Bruckmann—and such practicalities as opening times, a ban on photography, membership lists of all committees, company addresses, descriptions of halls, and precise data on individual houses at Weissenhof—the catalogue contains an announcement of a lottery with 100,000 one-mark tickets, each of which would either win "nothing" or a prize of from two to five hundred marks.

Additionally, a summary guide in several languages was printed, as well as banners, plaques, and two million adhesive stamps or seals which were sent on correspondence all over the world as "silent advertising."[23]

The building committee of the Stuttgart city council, which, after the representatives of the city hall administrative departments, was the Werkbund's most important partner in the exhibition enterprise, tried to arrange a special issue of 5 and 10 pfennig postage stamps, to be designed by Willi Baumeister, but they were never printed. The Werkbund had given the commission to Baumeister without advertising for a designer or holding a public competition.[24]

Together with Karl Straub, Baumeister was also responsible for all the printed matter for the exhibition,[25]

Willi Baumeister: designs for 5 and 10 pfennig stamps, 1927

and designed and saw through the press both of the official Werkbund books on the Weissenhofsiedlung, *Bau und Wohnung* and *Innenräume*, as well as Alfred Roth's pamphlet on the houses by Le Corbusier and Pierre Jeanneret.[26] These important books were not, however, ready for the opening of the exhibition.

It was announced at the opening that the Stuttgart School of Bonatz and Schmitthenner was to be given the opportunity to make its own practical contribution to the debate on home design and building in general. At a location known as Kochenhof—about half a kilometer, or one-third of a mile, to the west of Weissenhof—Schmitthenner was to supervise the construction of a development of one hundred dwellings, with the object of "establishing the best economic, constructional, and residential solutions for dwellings of different sizes."[27]

The Kochenhof project was not completed until 1933; but before that happened Schmitthenner backed out and went to build another development in the Stuttgart area (Auf dem Hallschlag, Bad Cannstadt); the Werkbund restarted the project without him in 1932; and it was returned to Schmitthenner after the Nazi takeover in 1933 (see Chronology).

On the evening of July 23, 1927, the inaugural festivities took their course:

> In the later after-dinner speeches there were many more expressions of appreciation and thanks: by Privy Councillor Riemerschmid, of Cologne, to the press; by Professor Dr. Fuchs, of Tübingen—who was unable to summon up any enthusiasm for the flat roof, but who described the exhibition as a highly interesting practical experiment—to Privy Councillor Dr. Bruckmann; by the latter to the collaborators from Germany and abroad; and by Consul Suter, of Switzerland, on behalf of the visitors from abroad, to the Werkbund and to the City of Stuttgart.[29]

The official record sounds rather dry and unexciting by comparison with the account given by Kurt Schwitters, who reveals that the right-wing conservationists of *Heimatschutz*, Homeland Protection, had their say:

> Here in Stuttgart, at the official dinner, the opposition of official circles comes to light when the

aged representative of the University of Tübingen, in his capacity as a *Heimatschutzmann*, as he calls himself, gets up and mentions that Stuttgart is not actually in Holland or California, and flat roofs do not belong here. . . . Finally, the worthy Protectionist was restrained from uttering any more platform-roof platitudes, because the whole flat subject was not on the agenda, and most of his fellow diners were talking so loudly that no one could hear what he was saying . . . I then raised a glass to Herr Mies van der Rohe, because I was so sorry for him, what with no one letting him build flat roofs anymore, but he took it terribly well and laughed his head off. It is a long time since I have seen him laugh so much. But you want to know why I am telling you all this. Well, the fact is that this spirit is the source of the whole exhibition and the whole Weissenhofsiedlung itself.[29]

THE INTERNATIONAL EXHIBITION OF MODERN ARCHITECTURE: DESIGNS AND MODELS

The transfer of the opening ceremonies to the exhibition hall of the Ausstellungsgebäude (on Interimstheaterplatz, adjoining the Schlossgarten, the garden of the old royal palace) had one advantage, at least: no one had far to go to begin looking at the exhibition. The guests found themselves sitting in the first room of *Internatio-*

President Bazille of Württemberg (left) is given a conducted tour by Mies van der Rohe

nale Plan- und Modellausstellung Neuer Baukunst (International Exhibition of Modern Architecture: Designs and Models), an important component part of the Werkbund exhibition as a whole; they must have had a chance to take a look around before the proceedings began, and even while they were going on.

In this part of the exhibition examples of modern buildings from Europe and America were assembled, as in an imaginary museum, to demonstrate the related and interdependent forms taken by contemporary architecture. A local critic wrote, "One thing that will have been made clear straight away, by the exhibition in the Schlossgarten, is that the flat roof is not the whim of any one architect in particular; it has been used everywhere almost simultaneously."[30]

In his speech at the opening, Mies pointed out that the buildings of the Weissenhofsiedlung were not by any means a modish phenomenon, or restricted to Germany, but the expression of a worldwide intellectual movement. The exhibition of drawings and models was presumably intended to convey this message to the visitor from the very outset, and before he saw the buildings themselves. In all its undertakings, the Werkbund had always had an educational purpose.

The exhibition made its point: it was understood as a coherent whole, "an image of modern world architecture,"[31] supporting and confirming the work of Modernist architects and delivering a polemical riposte to the assaults of the embittered traditionalists. It left no doubt as to where the avant-garde was to be found.

In the official catalogue, 531 designs are listed (including those which had not yet arrived when the catalogue went to press) from Germany, Czechoslovakia, the U.S.S.R., the U.S., Switzerland, Italy, France, Belgium, and Austria. Great Britain and the Scandinavian countries were not represented.[32]

In the collection of valuable material for the Internationale Plan- und Modellausstellung, the exhibition directorate has enjoyed, inter alia, the support of those listed below:
— in Belgium, Henry van de Velde, Professor at the University of Ghent, and Director of the College of Decorative Art, Brussels;
— in France, Le Corbusier, Geneva and Paris;
— in Holland, J.J.P. Oud, city architect, Rotterdam;
— in Italy, Professor Papini and Baron von Bülow, Rome;
— in Austria, Professor Dr.-Ing. Josef Frank, Vienna;
— in Switzerland, Professor Karl Moser, Zürich;
— in the United States of America, Friedrich [Frederick] Kiesler, architect, New York.[33]

In listing those responsible for selection, the directorate forgot to mention that Ludwig Hilberseimer had designed the exhibition itself. The list of selectors reflects the situation on opening day. Previously, there had been discussions with others: Richard Neutra, in Los Angeles, and Knut Lönberg-Holm, in Detroit, had been discussed as possible U.S. selectors, along with El Lissitzky for Russia and Pol Henningsen, of Copenhagen, for the Scandinavian countries.[34]

Not all the selectors felt any great commitment to ensuring an adequate representation of their compatriots. It may be that many felt like Le Corbusier, who wrote to Werner Graeff, the head of the exhibition press office, to say that he had been out of town and unable to look

for possible candidates: "But I beg you to recognize that in Paris a fierce individualism prevails, and that we are all separated from each other by jealousies, rivalries, differences of approach, unbridled passions."[35]

Le Corbusier nevertheless supplied seven names: Auguste Perret, Tony Garnier, Robert Mallet-Stevens, M. Baugé, M. Boyer, Djo Bourgeois, and André Lurçat (in that order), and asked Graeff to write to them direct. In the final exhibition, only Djo Bourgeois, André Lurçat, and Mallet-Stevens were represented.[36]

For Austria, the choice was made by Josef Frank. It is surprising that neither he himself nor any of the other really important Austrian architects submitted anything. Austria was represented by A. Z. Ulrich, with models and a perspective view of a row housing project and a model neighborhood or Siedlungstype,[37] and Ph. Ginter with a country house project.[38] Quite apart from the question of Loos, the scanty representation of Austria is hard to understand; the minutes of the exhibition committee reveal that it had intended to devote a whole room in this section of the exhibition to the achievements of the city of Vienna in the field of public housing. There is no record of what transpired.[39]

Henry Van de Velde's contribution was equally meager: just three Belgian architects showed their works, although Van de Velde had written of an extraordinary interest on the part of "the circle of young Belgian architects."[40] Victor Bourgeois—who also built a private house on the periphery of the Weissenhof site, listed as House 10 of the Weissenhofsiedlung—submitted his own controversial Siedlung development, the Cité Moderne in Brussels (1921–22), and a living room;[41] J. C. Eggericz sent in a house; and Huib Hoste, from Bruges, sent an office building, a house, and the North Sea Hotel at Knokke-sur-Mer.[42]

The contributions from Czechoslovakia, on the other hand, were extraordinarily numerous. No less than thirty architects and groups—the highest total after that from Germany—exhibited in Stuttgart, although the catalogue does not name anyone as a local intermediary or selector.

Victor Bourgeois: Cité moderne, near Brussels

Clockwise:
Le Corbusier with Pierre Jeanneret: Stein-De Monzie house, Garches, 1927, isometric view showing main entrance

Ludwig Mies van der Rohe: country house in brick, 1924

Ludwig Hilberseimer: project for Tempelhofer Feld, Berlin, 1924

Ludwig Hilberseimer: row houses, 1927

L.C. van der Vlugt with Mart Stam: Van Nelle tobacco factory, Rotterdam, 1927

J.J.P. Oud: Oud-Mathenesse housing, Rotterdam, 1922–24

Ludwig Mies van der Rohe: glass and concrete office building, 1923

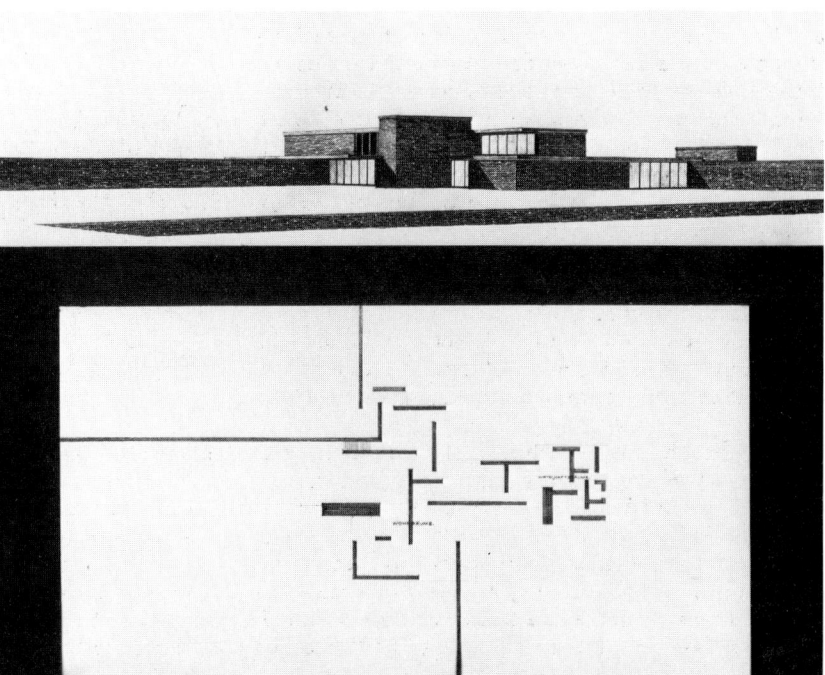

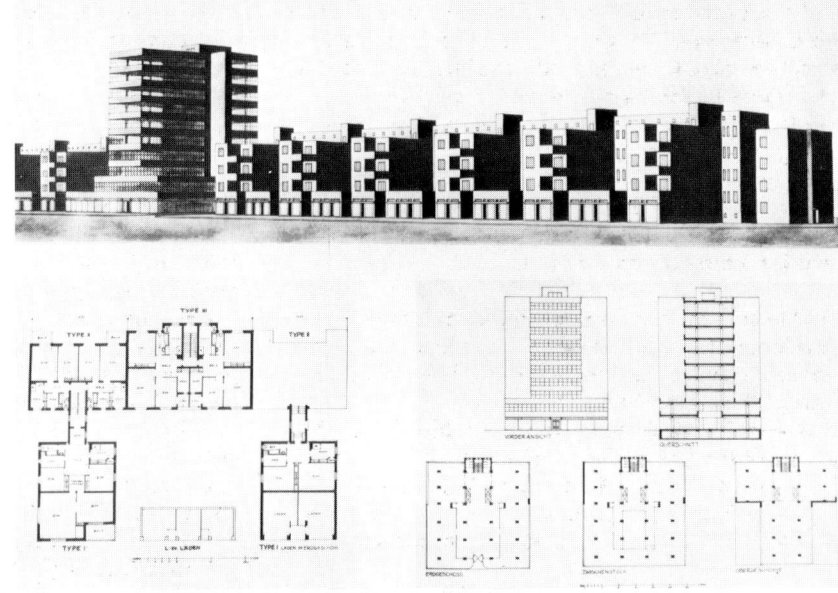

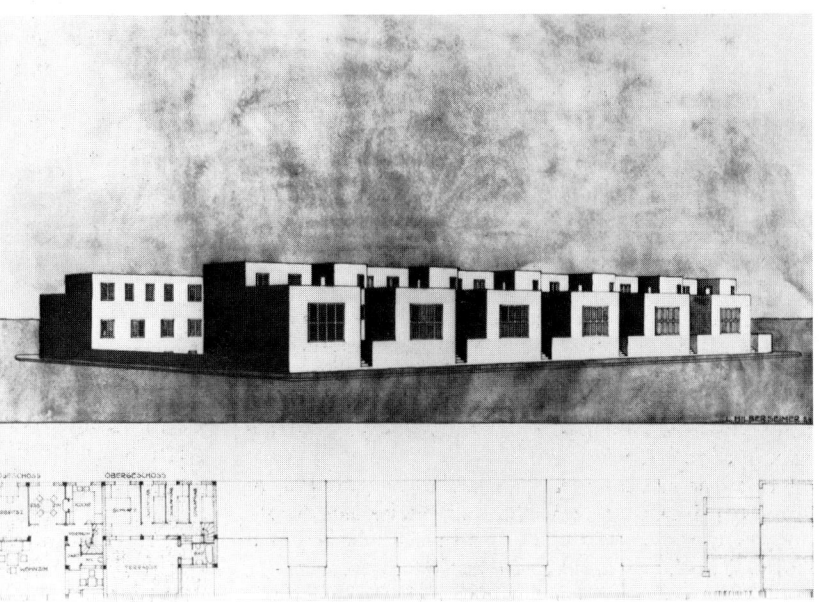

The press reaction to the exhibit was generally favorable. The Swiss periodical *Das Werk* did, however, point out that almost without exception no actual floor plans were shown: "A survey of a purely pragmatic form of architecture," the Swiss critic observed, "ought really to consist exclusively of working drawings rather than exclusively of perspective drawings; or is it, here as elsewhere, ultimately the face that counts?" The same magazine judged the Russian contribution to be absolutely consistent in "its grim determination to avoid even the slightest echo of czarist formalism."[43] The absence of Britain and Scandinavia led the *Stuttgarter Neues Tagblatt* to conclude that "there the most modern architectural style has made next to no headway."[44]

In this part of the exhibition the Weissenhof architects could see themselves as part of a worldwide architectural movement which made it clear what they were fighting and working for: the decisive factor in their work was no longer to be the facade, or the preconceived formal intention, but the nature of the problems embodied in every individual piece of work, which carried within itself its own solution through the application of new building methods, new structural features, and new materials. And so this concentration of new work, the largest to date, was seen as a "view of a generation of architects, who honestly and straightforwardly adhere to the new architecture."[45]

All the Weissenhofsiedlung architects, but Behrens and Frank, showed projects or completed buildings.

The *Internationale Plan- und Modellausstellung* remained open until the end of the Werkbund exhibition itself on October 31, 1927. In November of 1927 Stotz went to Berlin "to sort out the business of the drawing and model exhibition, once and for all."[46] The outcome of his visit was that the panels from Stuttgart traveled as a touring show to seventeen cities.[47] Even before the Stuttgart opening there had been approaches from Holland and from the Swiss cities of Basel and Zürich for a transfer of the exhibition; but the Werkbund committee responsible decided that, although a transfer was favorably looked upon, no mention of it should be published before the Stuttgart exhibition closed.

INDOOR EXHIBITIONS: GEWERBEHALLE AND STADTGARTENUMGANG

Whereas the *Internationale Plan- und Modellausstellung* was intended as a complement to the Weissenhof project itself and as an introduction to the new language of architecture, the other indoor exhibitions were subsidiary presentations of furnishings, fittings, and technical installations.

There was no suitable hall near Weissenhof itself (the Killesberg exhibition center, which now stands nearby, was not built until after World War II). It was at first intended to use the new Stadthalle on Neckarstrasse, opened in 1926.[48] Stotz sent Mies drawings of the hall in January 1927 and asked him to think about the exhibition design. Mies responded

> I think it will be useful to mask the entrance by way of the big staircase, so that the visitor coming up does not take in the whole hall at once, but has to walk through a covered space from which he will then get a view of the main part of the exhibit—and from which he can enter the living rooms to left and right.
>
> The sides of the living rooms, facing out toward the hall, should I think be fronted with small,

enclosed, yard-like spaces, finished as verandas or gardens, with garden furniture in them. On the far sides of the living rooms there could be lobbies, or bathrooms, and what not, which will need artificial lighting, because they lie under the gallery. This yard-like space, enclosed by the two rows of living rooms, ought to contain the ornamental part of the exhibition, let's say textiles, wallpapers, and so on. The semicircular end beyond ought to contain large-scale exhibition spaces. Have you forgotten about glass and china, by the way? All the little stuff, like windows, door furniture, and so on, I would arrange on the upper gallery . . .[49]

Mies thus intended to show complete interiors in the exhibition, as in the Weissenhof houses. In the event, however, the exhibition was organized by Lilly Reich according to categories of objects.

The exhibition directorate was never happy with the initial choice of the Stadthalle as a venue, because it was so far away from Weissenhof and from the city center. When the Gewerbehalle, with subsidiary halls on Stadtgartenumgang, became free—on March 14, 1927, it was announced that Haus für Technik und Industrie (Hati) would vacate the Gewerbehalle and the Stadtgartenumgang halls by July 1, and the gallery of the Gewerbehalle as early as May 1[50]—the planning start-

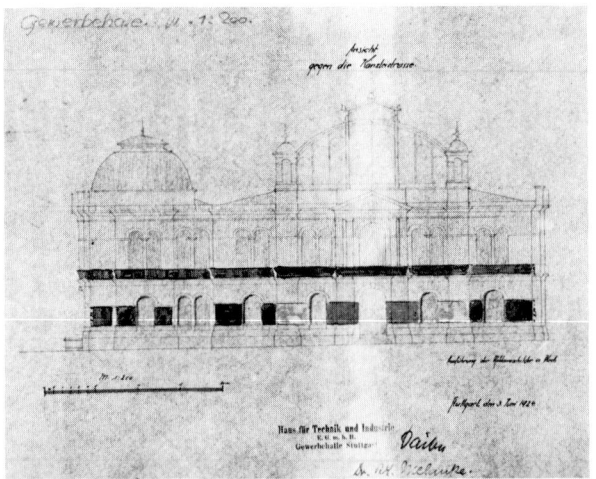

Kanzleistrasse elevation of Gewerbehalle, Stuttgart

Gewerbehalle (Hall 1): domestic equipment

ed over again, despite information sent out to prospective exhibitors at the beginning of the year specifying the Stadthalle as the venue.[51]

As Mies's designs for the Stadthalle were now superseded, he asked for photographs of the Gewerbehalle, so as to work on "a new color scheme for the facade."[52] Unfortunately none of these designs have been preserved. Soon after this, in mid-April, Lilly Reich, whose friendship with Mies had developed in the course of the preliminary work for the Stuttgart exhibition, was asked to take over the design of the halls. At a meeting of the exhibition committee on April 25, Mayor Lautenschlager proposed her appointment, stressing that although he had no qualms whatever about the appointment, and although it was definitely desirable to find an artistic personality to work on the design, he did not want to appoint "a Berlin lady" entirely on his own responsibility, because "there is bound to be resentment."[53]

The organizational problem that faced Lilly Reich was eased by the published conditions for exhibitors: not everyone who chose to exhibit might do so, but only those companies that had been selected for the quality of design shown in their products. Sketches and drawings had to be submitted in good time for the exhibition design work to be done, and would require the approval of the artistic and technical directorate:

> Existing signboards (including the address of the firm) may be used only with the approval of the exhibition directorate. The principal of uniformity in design is strictly enforced for the benefit of the exhibitors themselves. The cost of the signboard is borne by the exhibitor.[54]

Lilly Reich set out to design the separate halls in a uniform style and to use a single typeface. It was not to be a matter of renting individual stands: groups related by content would share particular halls.

On the whole, the exhibitors were glad of the rigorous selection process to which firms and their products were submitted and the proposal to organize the various halls according to product groups, distinguished by what would now be called color coding.[55] Conscious of the distinction conferred by admission to the show, a number of firms afterward asked whether they could be given a certificate. City hall did send out "confirmations," although the Werkbund tended to the view that being chosen for the exhibition was honor enough.[56]

The demand for stands was so heavy that it soon became clear that all the spaces in the Gewerbehalle would be needed, leaving no space for the *Internationale Plan- und Modellausstellung*. Mies had been against the use of the Stadtgartenumgang halls from the start as not impressive enough, but they were pressed into service.[57]

The look of the halls was to be extremely simple. So that the goods could speak for themselves, Lilly Reich painted the walls white and avoided decoration of any kind apart from the meticulously designed, striking, and colorful lettering by Baumeister. All the structures and stands left over from previous exhibitions were torn out, making a clean sweep of the halls; people who knew the space were struck by its new beauty. The Gewerbehalle became a "showpiece" in itself.[58]

The issue of kitchen design and domestic economy loomed large in the organizers' thoughts, with their commitment to rationalization and standardization. The kitchen was the part of the home which could most immediately, and most conspicuously, be organized in ac-

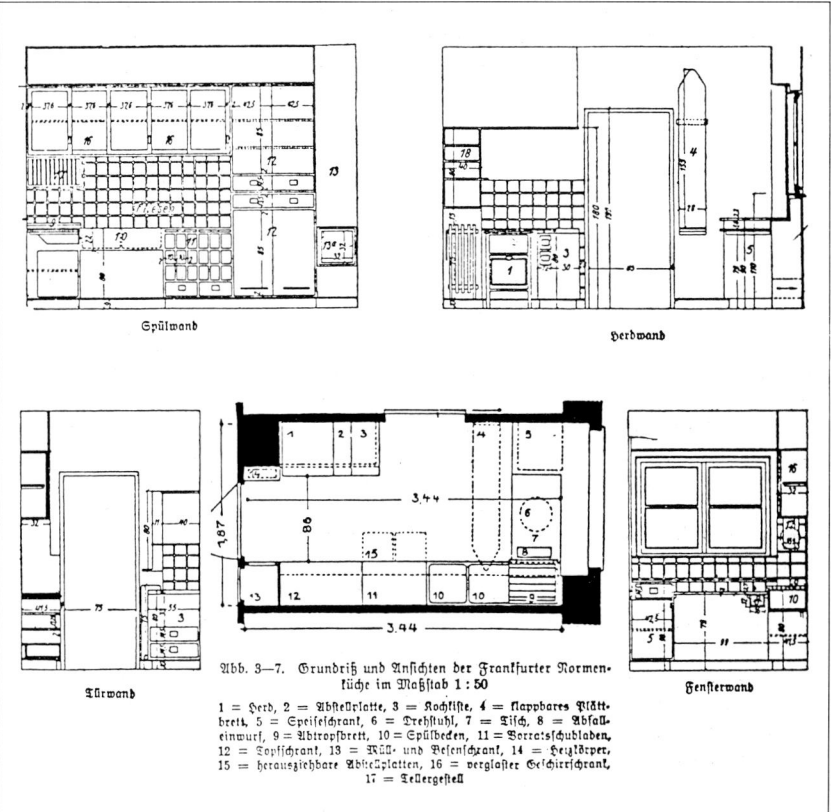

Abb. 3—7. Grundriß und Ansichten der Frankfurter Normenküche im Maßstab 1 : 50

1 = Herd, 2 = Abstellplatte, 3 = Kochliste, 4 = klappbares Plättbrett, 5 = Speiseschrank, 6 = Drehstuhl, 7 = Tisch, 8 = Abfalleinwurf, 9 = Abtropfbrett, 10 = Spülbecken, 11 = Vorratsschubladen, 12 = Topfschrank, 13 = Müll- und Besenschrank, 14 = Heizkörper, 15 = herausziehbare Abstellplatten, 16 = verglaster Geschirrschrank, 17 = Tellergestell

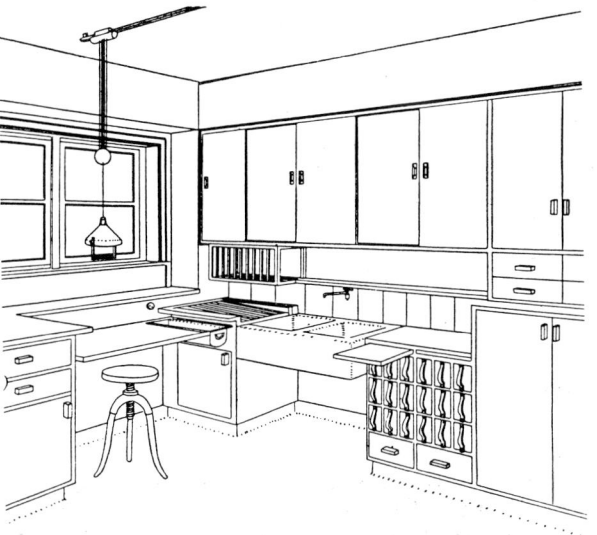

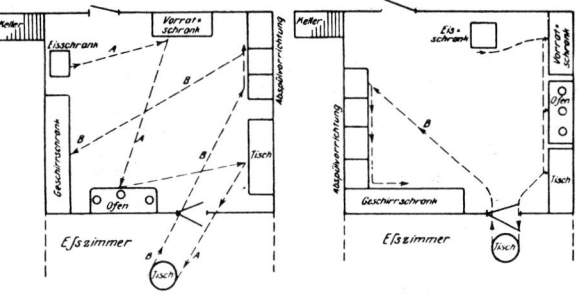

Margarete Schütte-Lihotzky: plan and elevations of the Frankfurt Kitchen

Margarete Schütte-Lihotzky: isometric view of the Frankfurt Kitchen

After Christine Frederick: (left) "Badly grouped kitchen equipment"; (right) "Efficient grouping of kitchen equipment"

cordance with the principles governing an industrial workplace. An American housewife, Christine Frederick, had been the first to apply the methods of time and motion study, first devised by F. W. Taylor (1856–1915), to the tasks of housekeeping. Her book, *Scientific Management in the Home*, was eagerly taken up in Germany when it appeared there in a translation by Irene

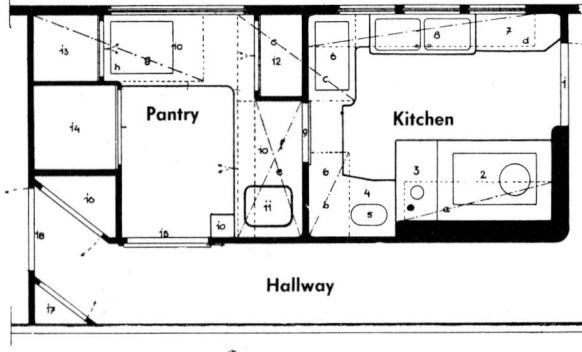

Kitchen
1. door
2. stove
3. sink
4. coalbox beneath counter
5. chimney
6. worktable
7. worktable with shelf
8. double sink
9. hatch between kitchen and pantry

above and below the countertops
a) platewarmer
b) warm water boiler
c) freezer
d) supply cabinet with sliding doors; Ceiling hooks for cooking utensils

Pantry
10. work table covered with bronze plates
11. sink to rinse glasses
12. closet for china and silver with two drawers and three shelves
13. linen closet with three shelves
14. large freezer with ten drink trays
15. sliding door to hall

above and below the tabletops
e) cupboard
f) cupboard
g) freezer

Hallway
16. coat closet for personnel
17. closet, below hamper for used table linen
18. entrance to the dining room

The height of the work tables is 34 inches above the floor; the upper ledge of the windows is 70 inches above the floor. There are ventilator domes with ventilators in the kitchen ceiling. Also the well-known turnable lights.

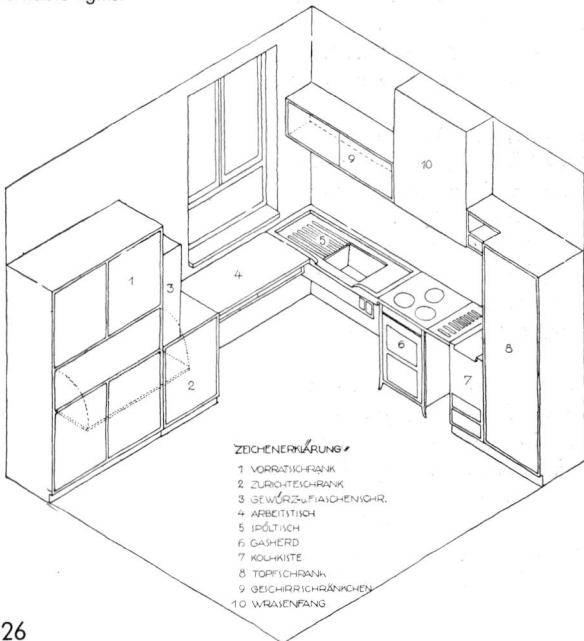

Margarete Witte, an SPD member of the Reichstag,[59] in 1922. Fredericks demonstrated, by contrasting "wrong" and "right," or "before" and "after," just how many unnecessary trips the housewife makes in a badly organized kitchen. As Taylor and his school had set out to use "efficiency engineering" to plan workplaces and working processes to combine maximum productivity with minimum risk to the worker's health, Mrs. Frederick subjected the kitchen, the laundry, and the other equipment of the home to the same scrutiny.

An important model for the rethinking and rationalization of the kitchen was the design of kitchens in express trains. Pullman dining cars had been patented in 1869,[60] and had since been used in Europe, in similar or improved form, by the Mitropa company (Mitteleuropäische Speisewagengesellschaft). A Mitropa kitchen was on show at the exhibition alongside the modern-looking "Frankfurt Kitchen" designed for Ernst May's industrialized public housing program in Frankfurt am Main by Margarete Schütte-Lihotzky and inspired by those traveling kitchens:

> The amount of work that is done in restaurant-car kitchens only gets done because the kitchen is so small. As a result of the closest observation of the working routines involved, everything is so arranged for cooking and preparation that it is within arm's reach for the person who is doing the work. Time-wasting walks are impossible. In a kitchen and a pantry neither of which is even 2 meters square (197 × 183 cm [$77\frac{1}{2}$ × 72 in]),[61] approximately 182 lunches, 60 breakfasts, 60 dinners, apart from incidental orders, are readied for well over 400 customers. An ordinary-sized kitchen normally requires twice the space for one-tenth of the work.[62]

Le Corbusier once coined the phrase "one-fortieth of a cook."[63]

Visitors to Hall 4, originally intended for wallpapers, were in for a unexpected visual treat.[64] Lilly Reich and Mies van der Rohe (named in that order in the official catalogue) turned it into a Hall of Mirrors. The exhibition designers, Reich and Mies, not the mirror glass company Verein Deutscher Spiegelglasfabriken GmbH, had the idea of walling a room with plain, tinted, and frosted mirror glass. Gustaf Stotz reported, at a meeting of the exhibition subcommittee, that "Herr Mies van der Rohe and Frau Reich . . . have produced a very interesting design for a hall of mirrors for Hall 4." He knew the costs, too: "The setting and assembly would cost around 2,600 marks." A quick decision was necessary, he said, for the room to be there on opening day; and it was, although not quite complete when the show opened. The furnishings, and thus the color scheme, were not finished until after August 12.[65] It can now be seen as a dry run, a sort of prototype, for Mies's Barcelona Pavilion of 1928–29.

On entering the room the visitor walked straight toward a mouse-gray mirror wall. If he turned right (after the furnishings were in, that is), he saw a writing desk with chair, and a wall-wide bookcase with books casually and decoratively arranged next to the uprights. Apart from its decorative value, such an arrangement ensures that even when the shelves are too long they do not sag.

The desk—spartan, plain veneer, closed sides—looks like Lilly Reich's R 50 design. If it was that design—impossible to confirm simply from the photograph—it had three shallow drawers built into the

"Dust traps: things that are no trouble to clean if they are not there in the first place" (Erna Meyer)

Plan of train kitchen

Isometric view of the Stuttgart Small Kitchen, designed for housewives' organization by Erna Meyer and Hilde Zimmermann

plinth. Unfortunately, we have no information on the veneers used for the shelves and the desk.

The floor covering seems to have been plain linoleum. Lilly Reich is known to have ordered some bright red linoleum samples from Deutsche Linoleum-Werke (DLW). She was sent two samples in "not very widely differing tones," with a request for telegraphic confirmation of her selection; "We return your color guide herewith, but it looks to us as if it is rather faded."[66] The date of the letter coincides with the design work on Hall 4 (mirror hall) and Hall 5 (DLW hall).

The flooring of the mirror hall is described in the Werkbund book, *Innenräume*, as "white, black, and red linoleum by Deutsche Linoleum-Werke AG, Bietigheim." As the only photographs available are in black and white, it is rather speculative to sort out the red from the black; but it is certain that the floor coloring was related to that of the adjacent Hall 5, into which the visitor could walk directly from the mirror hall.

Let us assume for the moment that the floor in the reception area of the mirror hall was red, the glazing of the walls mouse-gray and transparent, the desk chair black, and the wooden parts perhaps mahogany or macassar: it would then come as a harmonious surprise, if, in line with the glass partition, a junction between red and white linoleum were to show the visitor that there was another space beyond to be entered. There, on white linoleum, stood a large, simple table on full-width supports inset from either end. It was flanked on two sides by partitions of mirror-glass panels: frosted on both sides toward the seating area; frosted on one side toward the lobby leading on to the DLW hall; and transparent toward the niche containing Wilhelm Lehmbruck's sculpture, *Torso of a Girl, Turning*.[67] The girl's head looked away from the visitor toward the left—not without cause, as we shall see. The material of the table can be assumed to be that of the desk and of the low table in the seating area; at any rate, we can assume that choice veneers were used here, as on the room-high plywood panels which make up the outer wall.

The visitor was then led, as if by an invisible hand, to follow the white floor around into the seating area, turning back along the inner side of the first gray mirror-glass partition. Too far, and he would come up against an olive-green mirror and see an array of plants behind clear mirror panes. The seating zone, sharply delineated from the white passage area by its floor color, which on this assumption would have been black, repeated the white of the implied dining area in its neat row of white wash-leather club armchairs. The tables were low, as before, but now there was a solitary, contrasting (red or black leather?) club chair.

"Herr Mies also asks you to install the balance of the seating for the mirror hall (the desk chair and the black and the red leather club chair) as soon as possible, as our office now tells us that the rest of the furniture for this hall has now been delivered," Mies's secretary wrote to the Knoll chair company at Feuerbach near Stuttgart on August 12.[68] The club chair might have been black, which would have created a more restful and serious atmosphere; or red, but in a darker, more subdued shade subtly echoing the coloring of the entrance area. The transitional area leading to the DLW linoleum display in Hall 5, which brought the visitor face to face with the *Torso of a Girl* behind mouse-gray mirror glass, would then have been black: rather a somber impression.

In fact, however, if one looks at Hall 4 in conjunction with Hall 5, one is forced to the conclusion that the linoleum in the entrance lobby of the mirror hall was defi-

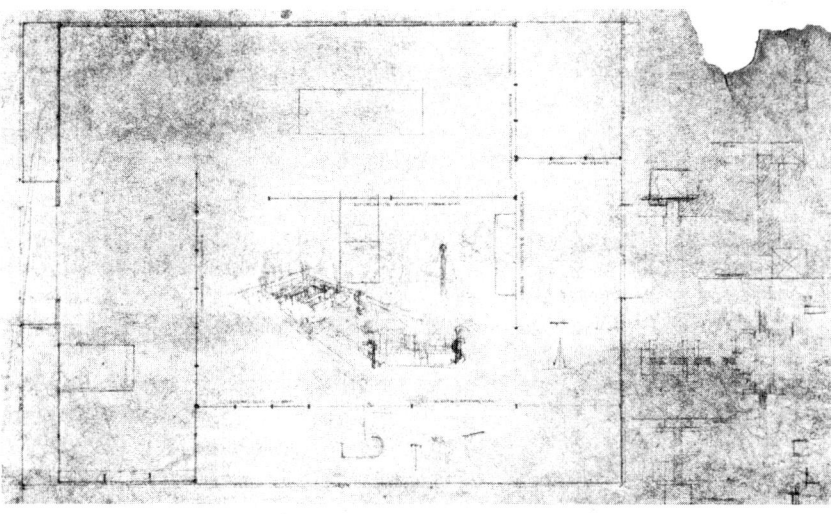

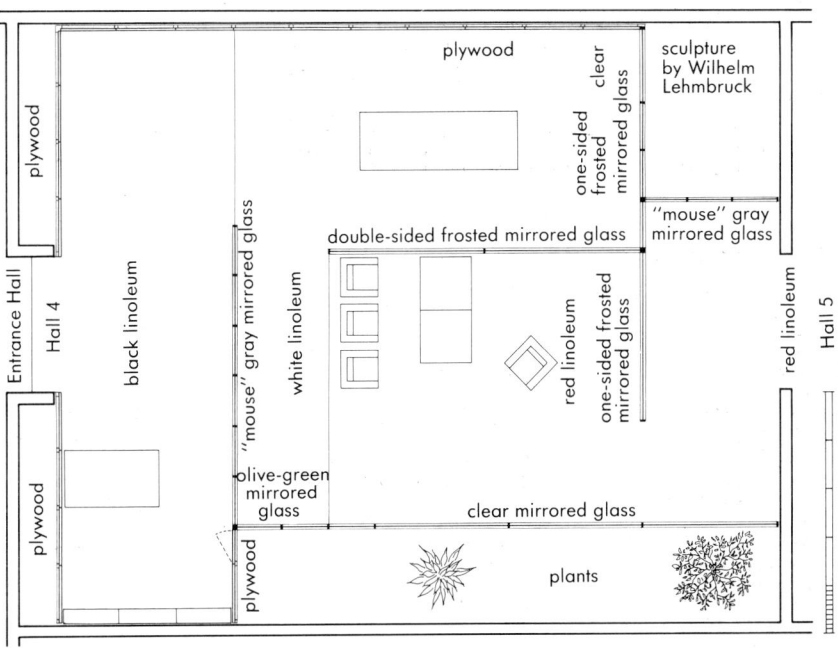

nitely not red at all but black, contrasting sharply with the white of the implied dining area; that this white floor led on to a central seating area floored in bright red; and that the red led on to the face-to-face encounter with the sculpture, and to the DLW hall, where it contrasted once more with the black, white, and green floor of the reception area. The single club chair must have been black.

Sergius Ruegenberg has said that Mies "discovered" the idea of the "volte-face"[69]—leading the observer along to the end of a partition and back along the other side—in Le Corbusier's single-family House 13 at Weissenhof, and that he then took it up for the Barcelona Pavilion in 1928. It is clear, however, that he had already invented a 90-degree turn of his own, and that Le Corbusier's example supplied him with, at most, the 180-degree version.

The lighting in the mirror hall was diffuse. Above the wall panels (probably around 2.5 meters [8 feet] high) there was a translucent ceiling, probably of strips of white cloth,[70] concealing from view the ingenious top lighting devised for the Gewerbehalle annexes by their designer, Hugo Keuerleber, in January of 1925. The structural members of the glass walls were probably nickel-plated steel profiles. Unfortunately, neither the

Lilly Reich and Ludwig Mies van der Rohe: Plan of mirror hall; reconstruction of plan

official catalogue nor the Werkbund book *Innenräume* gives more detailed information.

Looking back from the DLW hall into the mirror hall, only a single bright, matt mirror surface and a glimpse of the plants in the sparsely planted, glazed area to the left could be seen.

The color schemes devised by Mies and Reich for Halls 4 and 5 are inseparable. Hall 5, adjoining the mirror hall, was designed for the German linoleum industry, which in 1926—with the exception of one firm at Bedburg in the Rhineland[71]—had amalgamated into a single company, DLW. Linoleum consists of pure natural ingredients: a jute base and a surface consisting of a mixture of linseed oil (Linoxyn), resins, pigments, and powdered cork. Its widespread use in Modernist interior design is unsurprising if one considers its properties: resistant to bacteria, easy to clean, jointless, sound-absorbent, warm to the touch, and decorative. The design of a special display of linoleum in Hall 5 can be thus be regarded as complementary to the use of the material as a floor covering in all sections of the exhibition. The postcard-sized advertising leaflet designed for DLW by Baumeister and Straub extols the qualities of linoleum—economical and durable even in low thicknesses—and mentions that "rooms of all kinds in the dwellings built at Weissenhof" were floored with linoleum, much of it colored.

Up to this point, the industry had produced linoleum only in somber, marmoreal shades "which for decades one saw only in hospitals and institutions"; now it launched into pure colors, "in every tone imaginable, bounded by the brutal contrasts of red, white, and black. Nor is that all: it means to displace stone slabs and tiles from kitchens and bathrooms, and is bringing linoleum out in tile form."[72]

The photographs of the stand show the terse and factual information content and the didactic idea imposed by the exhibition directorate. The exemplary cooperation between DLW and the designers, Reich and Mies, was widely praised. The DLW management was the first to respond: three days after the exhibition opened, the board sent Mies and Reich a check for 2,000 marks as a token of thanks for "the great interest that you have shown in the effective presentation of our products."[73]

After press and customer reactions began to come in, the firm's Berlin office wrote again to thank Mies for the

totally unprecedented achievement on the part of yourself and Frau Reich, in assembling our various types of linoleum and the new plain-colored Lincrusta into a sensitively conceived, harmonious symphony of colors.

We are glad to take this opportunity of expressing our deep appreciation of the design of the stand, and of the success of the exhibition enterprise as a whole.[74]

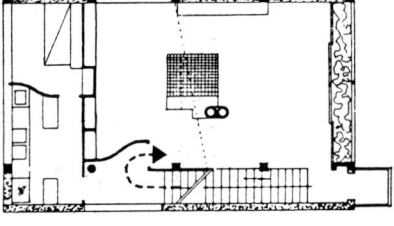

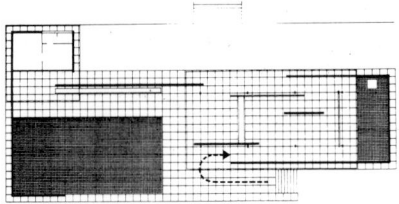

Two views of Hall 5, Deutsche Linoleum-Werke

The exhibition, which is a small one, is fundamentally different from anything that the Werkbund has customarily shown in this area. The companies have obviously been allowed to show anything they may have done, with or without the participation of the leading Werkbund artists. I do not mean this as a criticism. But the overall look of the exhibition is definitely not a unified one. Each of the firms has one outstanding piece or another on show; and all of them show some beautiful things. But one cannot escape from the feeling that one is not in an exhibition but in a very select furniture store.[79]

The wallpaper section, Hall 9a, was designed by Lilly Reich, and she achieved a selection that conveyed a restful sense of cool objectivity, or *Sachlichkeit*. The papers were hung on long stands, and sample books were there to complete the selection.

It was not, however, until one reached the hall devot-

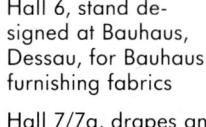

Hall 6, stand designed at Bauhaus, Dessau, for Bauhaus furnishing fabrics

Hall 7/7a, drapes and curtains: Indanthren fabrics by IG Farben

An uncommon experience for designers and architects: payment for success, the only instance of this in the whole Werkbund exhibition! In almost every other case the architects, and Mies in particular, were rewarded for their pains with criticism, and often insults, from every side. The mirror glass combine might well have joined DLW in thanking Mies and Reich, but no documents have survived. The new product mentioned in the DLW letter, Anker-Lincrusta, had been developed in conjunction with the architects of Der Ring.[75]

> Even one who has reservations about some of the colors in this superb piece of exhibition design will concede that this hall is a model of how colors and color effects can be studied . . . and that it is not inferior, in this respect, to the hall of I.G. Farben.[76]

Hall 7, occupied by the dyestuff manufacturers I.G. Farben, was directly accessible from Hall 5 (linoleum), as also was Hall 6, textiles. The view that offered itself as the visitor left Hall 5 was "a feast for the eyes," gushed a contributor to the Swiss trade paper *Das Werk*.[77] The visitor had the choice of first examining the textiles in Hall 6, or Halls 7 and 7a, with drapes and the I.G. Farben display. All were designed by Lilly Reich, and all sent the critics into ecstasies.

"The Home," after all the title of the exhibition, generally suggests furniture, but this did not appear until the visitor reached Hall 8, where it was presented in a space designed by Bernhard Pankok with a rather curious ground plan. Like Reich, Pankok avoided the traditional exhibition stand. The furnishings made by the individual Stuttgart firms—Behr was an exception—were integrated with each other like "an enfilade of interconnecting rooms."[78]

This hall seems to have felt the lack of Lilly Reich's acute critical eye. Perhaps Pankok was less rigorous in his selection:

THE WEISSENHOF TEST LOT

On the test lot at the Werkbund exhibition the whole range of experimentation . . . was brought together and offered to the critical scrutiny of the still wary visitor. Much is still developing, and not yet ready. But, by and large, people went away with the impression that a new technology is beginning to blossom, and that the old must sooner or later give way to it.[81]

Like all the parts of the Werkbund exhibition, the presentation of building methods and materials on the test lot adjoining the Weissenhofsiedlung was in accordance with the policy of the exhibition directorate: constructional techniques and solutions to problems of detail were shown alongside building materials of the most varied kinds: roofing papers; plywood sheets weatherproofed with asbestos (Xylotekt), Feifel cavity blocks and chimneys, all invented by the versatile Albert Feifel from Schwäbisch-Gmund;[82] Fonitram woodwool panels, as used in House 20 at Weissenhof by Hans Poelzig; Thermos building panels, made on the Pohlmann system; cavity ceilings; angle beads for rendered walls; windows; paving slabs for pathways and lobbies; and much besides, including hollow blocks in pumice concrete from the Neuwied Basin, whose comparative lightness in economic sizes made them a popular building material.[83] The brick and tile industry, rather left out in the Weissenhofsiedlung itself, made efforts on the test lot to show "that the material of brick, too, can attain a more useful and more economic form."[84]

Alongside these individual building materials complete houses were on show: the "Single-Family Row House according to the Frankfurt Prefabrication Method of City Architect May," and constructed and exhibited by the city architectural office of Frankfurt am Main;[85] the "Country House on the Urban-Kersten construction, system," a steel building system;[86] and a weekend cottage in corrugated steel, designed by the Stuttgart architect Erich Leistner. There is no photographic material to show what either the Urban-Kersten or the Leistner design looked like.

ed to lighting that the "Werkbund Idea," whatever that may have been, became apparent:

> The Werkbund Idea has banished, as a matter of principle, all those fantasy light fittings, tinkling glass, silk, and ruches. These things are not, it is true, to be eradicated without trace. This is shown by the selection that the jury has made here. But the scene is dominated by lights conceived in technological terms, which nakedly and forthrightly reveal their structure, and which were previously seen less in private homes than in purely functional buildings.[80]

Fluorescent tubes were a new development; but the greatest impression was made by the light fittings created in the Bauhaus metal workshop by Marianne Brandt and Hans Przyrembel, and by Adolf Meyer's work for Zeiss-Ikon-Werke of Berlin. Meyer's mass-produced lamps had flexible tubular metal pendants, white opalescent glass shades, and glass reflectors, and were plated with real silver. The lighting made by the Danish firm of Poulsen—and still on the market today—was designed by Pol Henningsen; mass-produced, it even had price tags. Also still in production is the wall light with a swiveling arm made of "Elektron," by Max Ernst Haefeli, of Zürich, which was used in the Swiss Werkbund apartments in House 4 of Mies's Weissenhof apartment building. Other mass-produced light fittings were those by Gispen of Rotterdam, with their clear overall form and well-conceived detailing—also very competitive in price when bought without extras—and by Adolf Meyer.

The vertically adjustable overhead lights designed by the brothers Heinz and Bodo Rasch were an ingenious variation on the "bowl" fittings common at that time, which had the disadvantage of offering large surfaces for the accumulation of dust. Dust was the enemy, whether on bibelots or on lights; undraped windows, bright lights, and light-colored carpets brought the battle right out into the open.

On Stadtgartenumgang in the building materials section of the show, Baumeister designed a very interesting stand for the Siegle company, with colored pseudo-architectural structures; color samples were displayed on wall shelves and tables that seemed almost to hang unsupported.

Ceiling light by Louis Poulsen

Wall-mounted light by Rasch brothers

The *Plattenhaus*, by Ernst May and the Frankfurt city architectural department, under construction on the test lot at Weissenhof

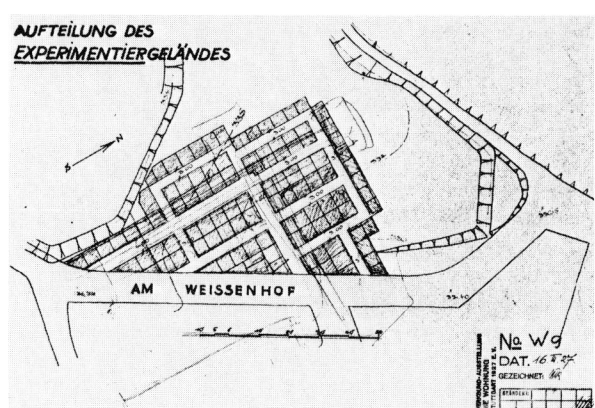

Nor do we know the state of completion in which the Frankfurt prefabricated house was exhibited.[87] Made up of panels and known as the *Plattenhaus*, this was "brought to the lot by road and assembled straight off the truck. A small, two-story house takes one to two days to assemble."[88] In Stuttgart, perhaps because of the distance from home base, construction seems to have taken five days: "the first floor completed and even furnished, the upper floor left unplastered, so that the seeker after truth can really take stock of the much-discussed rationalization of building and the scope for mass production."[89]

However, neither the architect, Ferdinand Kramer, who had been assigned to furnish and equip the dwelling when finished, nor Margarete Schütte-Lihotzky, who supervised the construction, could recall any completed living accommodation inside the Frankfurt *Plattenhaus*.[90]

The photograph of the house built in Stuttgart shows, as the major accessory to the building process, a crane: the symbol of the New Architecture. In Behne's foreword to the Rasch brothers' book, *Wie Bauen?*, a systematic survey of the building materials and methods used in the Werkbund exhibition,[91] he pointed out, "a crane is not the right tool for attaching acanthus leaves and bead moldings. The modern building lot has no room for thirty different styles. All that counts is the construction—and a new beauty."

Margarete Schütte-Lihotzky in front of the *Plattenhaus*, Stuttgart, 1927

Block plan of the test lot, to the west of the Weissenhofsiedlung, Stuttgart, 1927

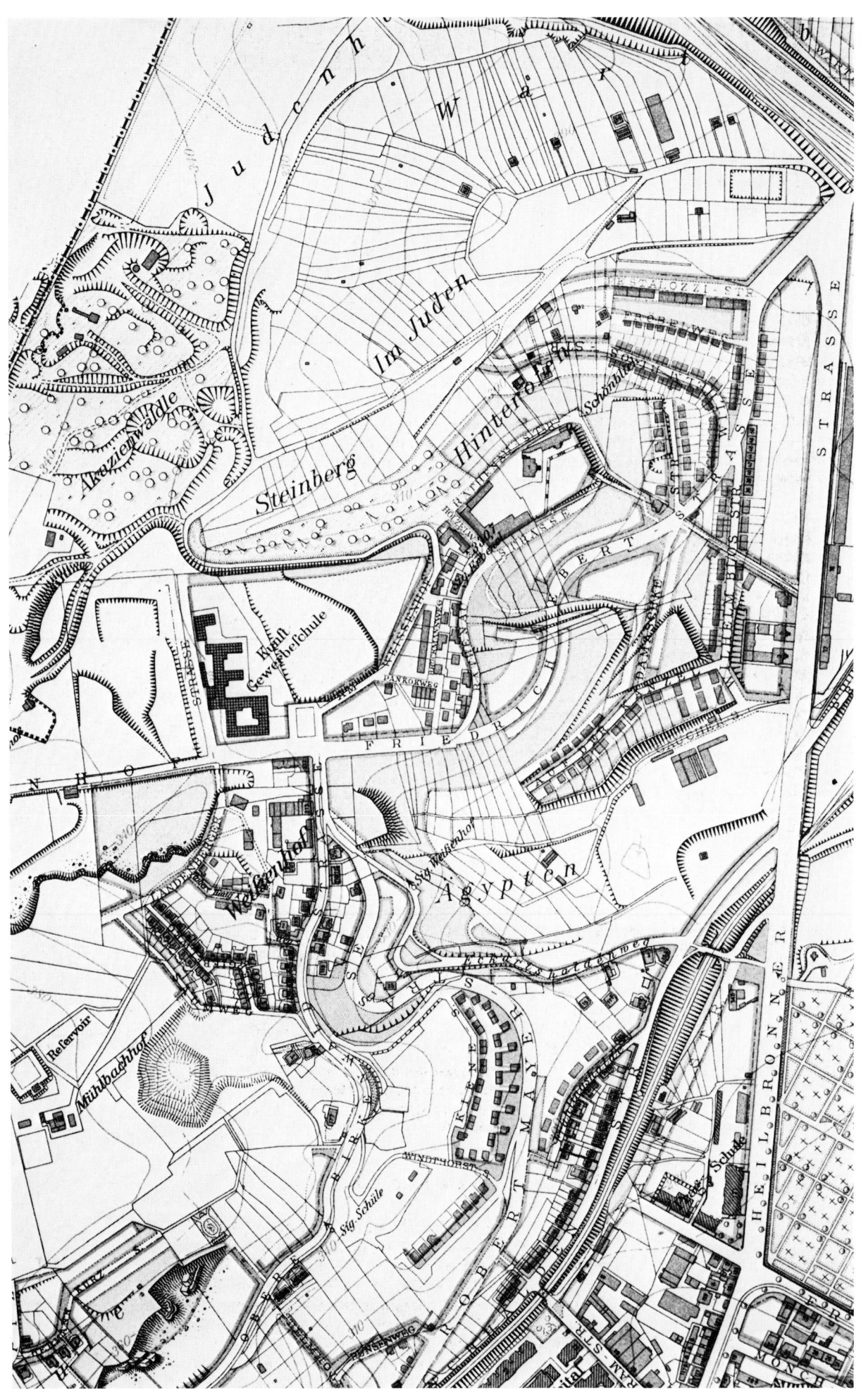

Section of Stuttgart
city map, 1928; north
is top right

III THE WEISSENHOFSIEDLUNG

PROLOGUE

In Stuttgart nowadays, anyone who mentions Weissenhof is more likely to hear about the famous tennis club of that name than about the architectural monument that is the subject of this book—a monument with an eventful history, and a highly individual character.

In 1927, twenty-one structures were built by seventeen different architects and fitted out by fifty-five different interior designers and architects, from Germany and abroad. Idiosyncratic artists built on the same piece of land as strict, functional, objective revolutionaries; but all were harbingers and prophets.

The uniqueness of the monument was as a strain of architectural evolution documented at a given point in time, captured and preserved as a record of work in progress. What was shown here was not an end but a beginning: not something finished but impulses toward the Real Thing, the true form. "The problem of the New Home is ultimately a problem of the mind," Mies van der Rohe said at the opening, "and the struggle for the New Home is only one element in the great struggle for new forms of living."

As I examined all of the individual houses and apartments in turn it became evident that every one of the architects put into the work a great deal of himself and of his own long-cherished design preoccupations. This is perhaps clearest in the case of Bruno Taut, who had been dreaming since 1919 of setting a colored house against white snow, and who now, in 1927, set down his brightly painted House 19 in the middle of a discreetly off-white *Siedlung*. "Anyone today who looks deeply into the matter will realize that what impelled the minds of that group was none other than the pursuit of the New Form," Julius Posener said in 1981, adding that the social content of the project was, "let's say, undefined."[1]

The assignment with which the architects were presented, to design homes for "inhabitants of big cities," is as vague as one can imagine: there is, after all, no population so heterogeneous as that of a big city. So the organizers sensibly restricted the remit by excluding both social extremes, of wealth and of poverty, and leaving the architects with as much scope as their many and varied preoccupations required. The "Struggle for the New Home," in all its aspects, was to be taken stock of, interpreted, and presented by seventeen individual architects. And so it transpired that some of them were concerned, ultimately, not with "The Home," as such, or with new methods of building, or even with society, but with the use of color or the battle against tuberculosis.

Neither the exhibition directorate nor the architects themselves ever mentioned the idea of building housing for the oppressed, exploited German people. In the eyes of committed Socialists and Communists, they remained "salon Marxists," to a man.

In one respect the Weissenhof architects truly failed in their duty: the maid's room. In almost every dwelling this is so small as to impel a protest—even more as it was taken for granted that the servant would wash herself in the laundry.

Viewed from a left-wing standpoint, the architects of the Weissenhofsiedlung thus gave little sign of commitment to social progress or to the cause of the working class. Seen from the right, however, from the traditionalist viewpoint of the *Heimatschutz* movement, they looked alarmingly subversive, not to say revolutionary. The Nazis had no difficulty in identifying them with the extreme left and regarded it as a historic duty to fight against all *Baubolschewisten* or Bolshevik Builders. A number of the Weissenhof architects were to go into exile; others were forbidden to practice. One, Richard Döcker, became a student of biology in the hope of escaping from unemployment. There were, of course, a few "Weissenhöfler" who conformed and even prospered under the Nazis, and their houses need to be seen in the light of this fact.

Weissenhof's status was from the very start as a kind of interim progress report on German Modernism. On the evening of the Württemberg Werkbund meeting of June 12, 1926, Bruckmann referred to the "plan to hold an International Werkbund Exhibition in Germany in 1930, to demonstrate, in competition with all nations, that our creative energy is unimpaired."[2] The preparations for this ambitious undertaking went on alongside the work on Weissenhof; and one of the reasons for Mies van der Rohe's election as deputy chairman of the Werkbund was that he lived in Berlin and could start to set things going for 1930. Mies's commitment to the 1930 project was partly responsible for his tendency to deliver his Weissenhof drawings late and his allegedly insufficient interest in Stuttgart, compounded by the chronic dilatoriness and indecision mentioned in all first-hand accounts of Mies. As a result of the world-wide economic catastrophe, however, the Werkbund exhibition did not take place until May 6 through August 3 of 1931, and then on a much smaller scale than had been envisaged in 1926.

CHOICE OF SITE AND EVOLUTION OF SITE LAYOUT

At a very early stage in the planning process for the Stuttgart Werkbund exhibition, as recorded in the minutes of a meeting on May 7, 1925, the mere fact that an organization dedicated to low-cost housing, the Bau- und Heimstättenverein, was included in the discussions confirms that the parcel of city-owned land at Weissenhof—or more precisely the upper part of the so-called Gauchergelände, between Weissenhof and Schönblick—was destined for public housing: the "erection of multistory apartment houses for rent, along with a number of type dwellings for neighborhood developments [*Siedlungstypen*]."[3]

The building committee of the city council, meeting on July 24, 1925,[4] had before it a first site plan, drawn up by the urban expansion department (Stadterweiterungsamt), and showing forty-three dwellings divided among twenty-nine single-family houses and one building of fourteen apartments. The interest of this plan lies in the street layout, which marks the boundaries of the area in a way that was never materially changed; in the existence of a rectangular building to the west, where Mies was to place his apartment house; and in the hint of a small open space at the junction of the streets that are now Bruckmannweg and Pankokweg.

The land extended between the existing Friedrich-Ebert-Strasse, the new line of the existing street Am Weissenhof, and the gently curving street, following the contour, which was then known as Strasse XVIIIb, and which later became Rathenaustrasse. Together with the straight section of Am Weissenhof, this was a determinant factor in the eventual design.

After several urgent reminders, Mies finally submitted his own 1 : 200 sketch layout plan in September of 1925. He told Stotz,

> I have based myself on the idea of striving for as coherent a layout as possible, partly because I consider this to be artistically right, and partly because this way we shall not be so dependent on the individual contributors.... The layout is not at all meant to be final, because it will ultimately depend on the individual ground plans; but it does show what we are aiming for, and I believe it will be entirely adequate for negotiating purposes.[5]

While the urban expansion department was working on a 1 : 200 scale model, a draft contract for the architects, and a more specific program of dwelling sizes, Mies and Häring in Berlin were working out some provisional ground plan types and reassessing the adequacy of the preliminary layout. Häring wrote to Stotz, on Mies's behalf, that what was at stake was

> not isolated buildings, but the combination and coordination of twenty individual views into an overall plan.... Our task also ... naturally extends to the execution. And for this we issue completely uniform standards: for instance, the same materials for all buildings; doors, windows, floor and ceiling constructions, flat roofs, kitchen installations, heating, and so on. This amounts to commissioning the development as a whole, according to individual lots, but not house by house.
>
> There is total freedom when it comes to the interiors of the houses; we reserve only the right to criticize. That sums up the division of labor and the mode of operation. There is no alternative, either in practical terms, or in view of the undertakings that have been given. It goes without saying that Stuttgart not only can but must make its wishes clear; but specific decisions must remain with the artistic director: that is, with Mies. This must now be regarded as final.[6]

In October, 1926, Häring sent the urban expansion department a

study of the ground plans for the exhibition. I must, however, expressly ask you not to regard these as definitive plans, but simply as preliminary layout sketches to clarify, in particular, the interlocking of the individual houses.[7]

Stuttgart now had a block plan by Mies (and Häring) on a scale of 1 : 200, and studies of the ground plans of the individual houses. It remained for City Hall to prepare the model and a finished 1 : 500 plan. These are based on Mies's first sketch. No preliminary drawings have yet been found.

The houses in this design interlock loosely, spreading wide and low along the slope with a strong horizontal emphasis; they are dominated by a kind of acropolis. "The whole thing a sculpture!" said Sergius Ruegenberg, Mies's associate, defining the central design concept.[8] And there is an undeniable kinship, in the interlocking and overlapping forms and in the tension of the spatial composition, with Mies's memorial to Rosa Luxemburg and Karl Liebknecht.

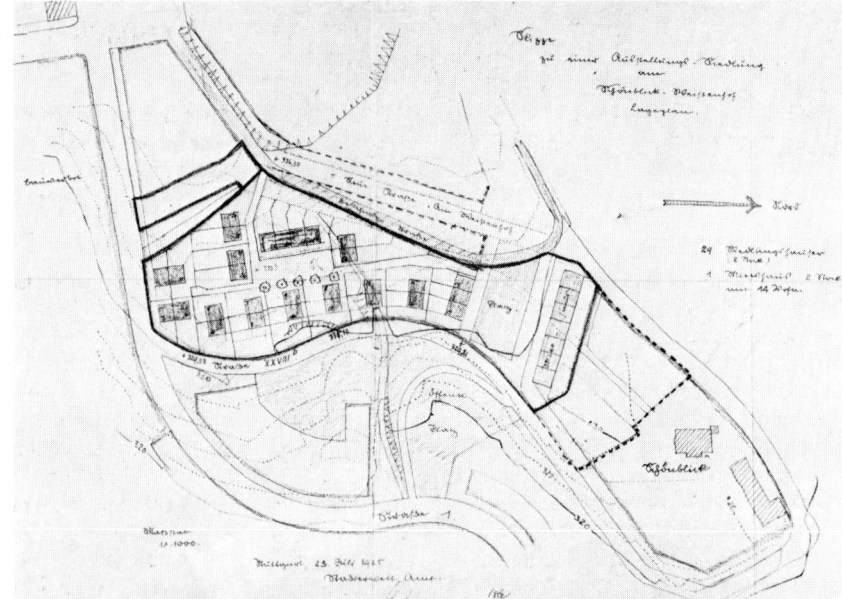

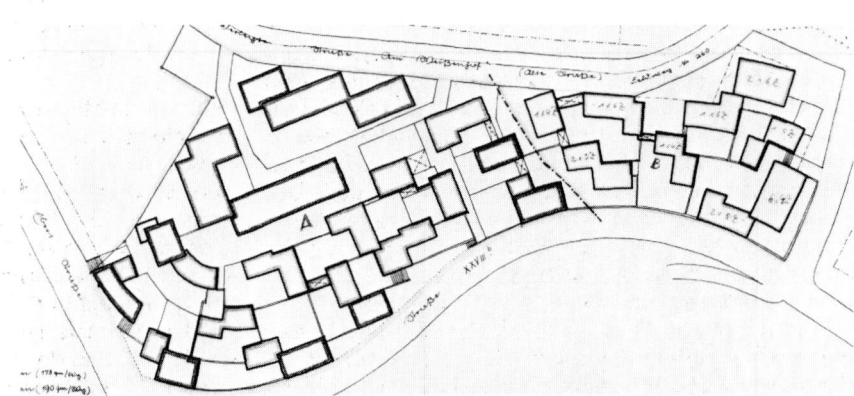

Above, block plans by Stadterweiterungsamt (urban expansion office), July 23 and October 14, 1925

Model based on Mies van der Rohe's first sketch

The officials of the urban expansion department must have been delighted by the density of the building; on a site smaller than originally envisaged, they calculated that there would be more living space than ever envisaged: an extraordinarily high population density of 129 dwellings in buildings of one, two, and three stories. On the basis of this layout the city architectural department worked out a first realistic estimate of costs, which amounted to "around 1.3 million marks,"[9] exclusive of site clearance. This estimate was based on a total of 56 dwellings. Recalculated to cover 61 dwellings, this gives a sum of 1.4 million marks, inclusive of site costs, which is very close to the final figure as calculated by the same office in 1928: 1,492,436 marks.[10]

For the moment, however, all these estimates, however encouraging or however realistic, were of no help. An unforeseen obstacle now stood in the way. The Socialist (SDP) members of the building committee, who had close political ties with the Bau-und Heimstättenverein, were reluctant to vote for the Weissenhof land to be made available for the Werkbund project. This had the consequence—as council elections were due in Decmber, 1925—of damping the enthusiasm of other members of the committee. By this time, however, the date of the exhibition had been moved to 1927, and time was no longer so short.[11]

The debate on Mies's layout began. The first comments reflect differences of attitude within the executive departments and in the building committee. The daybook of the urban expansion department casts light on some aspects of the debate. By October 15, 1925, it had been agreed that

the most modern endeavors in the field of urban planning and housing forms must find expression here. From an urban planning point of view, the objective is to break with the traditional way of organizing buildings in rows and to bring the structures into a relationship that is no longer uniform and static but strong, spatial, animated. This emphasis on a line that shifts in three dimensions leads to a form of building which is abstract and identical from all directions: the cube.

Diagonal planes, such as the traditional roof, would interfere with the desired expressive effect. The characteristic of this form of building is therefore the absence of roofs.

This form of building represents a total break with tradition, and its abstract form means that it must be defined as an international art. It is therefore understandable that this form of building has enjoyed a rapid dissemination all over the world. In Germany, Holland, Scandinavia, and France, and also in South America, some remarkable buildings and housing developments have been constructed in this style. . . .

It is therefore also understandable that the Werkbund wants to involve architects of international reputation in the proposed development, artists who have considerable experience in building in this style. In the execution of the artistic idea, to allow these architects to compete with each other while conforming to the overall masses defined by the models, would undoubtedly lead to a pioneer architectural achievement.[12]

The building committee, unlike the urban expansion department, did not consist of architects and building specialists but of councilmen from a motley assortment of trades and professions, including a few architects, who were united only by a common interest in building. On the following day it received a presentation of the plan from the head of urban expansion, Dr. Paul Otto. According to the official record,

On first hearing of the plan, just before he went on vacation, he too had initially reacted against it. But on careful consideration he had come to the conclusion that the whole plan was excellently conceived. He was in no doubt that this undertaking, if carried out, would attract attention from all over the Continent. It would be no exaggeration to regard the architectural concept as the expression of an entirely new sense of style, which was surfacing with the same rightness and inevitability as past styles of architecture such as the Gothic, the Renaissance, etc.[13]

Bold, prophetic words. The completed project, however, retains only a fraction of the tight, coherent overall structure on which the initial layout idea was based. It seems that this unity, which sprang from the interlocking forms and the close proximity of the individual buildings, and which would have imposed a strict discipline on each of the participant architects, sprang from the initial concept and the influence of Hugo Häring. The evidence for this lies in something Häring himself wrote in 1951: "I had done all the preliminary work for Stuttgart, but I didn't agree with Mies; he left everything to the other architects, and that is why I then withdrew."[14]

In the Weissenhof context, Mies's conduct—his personal behavior pattern—emerges much more clearly than that of Häring, who left the project early on, and whose papers include no documents on the period. It was just like Mies to leave "everything to the other architects": any restriction on the individuality of his professional colleagues would have been unwelcome to him. If we look at the circumspection that Mies showed in inviting architects to participate, and the reserve he always showed in personal relationships, Häring's assertion can certainly not be dismissed out of hand.

Ludwig Mies van der Rohe: monument to Rosa Luxemburg and Karl Liebknecht, Berlin, 1926

Leaving everything to the other architects can have its negative as well as its positive side; but at least it does not smack of arrogance and authoritarianism.

The reactions to the layout plan were by no means all so positive as that of Dr. Otto's department: in fact, his response was the only one that was positive. The senior man in the architectural department (Hochbauamt) was Oberbaurat Franz Cloos, a more influential figure than Otto. His account of the plan to the building committee was very different:

> The ground plan, which was to be regarded only as a sketch of an idea on the architect's part, departed from the hitherto customary manner of construction. Flat roofs, wide passages, and the lack of a cellar seemed to be the dominant characteristics ... The layout would necessitate a number of small retaining walls, the cost of which had not been taken into consideration.[15]

It was as if Cloos had breached a dam: the members of the committee were confirmed in their hitherto unspoken negative reactions. "Building homes without cellars" seemed inconceivable to one right-wing speaker; a Communist had reservations of his own, although he was "sympathetic" on the whole. It was the elected building commissioner, Dr. Daniel Sigloch, who let everyone off the hook by proposing that before the proposal was accepted there should be another site inspection by the whole committee.[16] This took place on November 15, 1925. One of the SPD committee members present was Karl Beer, who was also the house architect to the Bau- und Heimstättenverein, and who was in overall charge of building on the Gauchergelände land which surrounded Weissenhof.

A written record was made of this visit, and the layout plan was reworked; after that, all minds were concentrated on the December city council elections, in which half the members came up for reelection. It was some time before anyone found leisure to discuss the Werkbund project, and there was resentment when the Werkbund side pushed for a press announcement to be made—and actually made one, only to agree under city hall pressure to ask the press not to publish for the time being.[17]

And so Bruckmann's press conference of January 22, 1926, was not published in the daily press until March, together with "appraisals by authoritative architects" including Behrens, Gropius, Oud, Poelzig, Riemerschmid, Theodor Fischer, Josef Hoffmann, and Bruno Taut. The statement contained some detailed information on the development, and an utterly nonsensical sketch of the project by that same Dr. Otto of the urban expansion department who had spoken such fine words on the initial idea to his colleagues and to the building committee. From this time onward, the press showed a lively interest in the Werkbund's project.

On April 21 Bruckmann addressed the building committee at his own request and the ice was broken. An initial sum of 15,000 marks was voted on April 24, for preliminary work.[18] It was now necessary to conciliate or confront the local architectural interests, represented within the Werkbund by the Stuttgart School headed by Paul Bonatz and Paul Schmitthenner. Bruckmann arranged a meeting between Mies and Bonatz for May 5.

On that very day, however, the major Stuttgart daily papers ran articles by Bonatz and Schmitthenner in which Mies's proposals were condemned in violent language. Bonatz dismissed the layout as "impractical, arty-crafty, and amateurish."[19] He was the first, but by no means the last, to liken it to patterns found in more southerly countries: "an assemblage of flat cubes swarms up the slope in a succession of horizontal terraces, looking more like a suburb of Jerusalem than dwellings in Stuttgart."[20] Schmitthenner was reminded of Italian hill villages; [the exhibition] may represent anything else you like, but not ... 'the rationalization of the housing question.' " In his view, the international twentieth-century style was being "reduced to formulas."[21]

The articles caused a furor. City hall was no less offended than the Werkbund. The committee of the Württemberg section met on May 14. Mies was not present, but his archive contains a copy of the record, in which the speeches by Bonatz and Schmitthenner are marked "Uncorrected" in red pencil.[22] This 48-page document reveals that Bonatz had known of the Werkbund's intentions from a very early stage, although he had never officially been asked to take part. Bonatz, who was a committee member of the Württemberg Werkbund, and Schmitthenner, who was actually its deputy mayor for urban design, had been getting their information not from their Werkbund friends but from the city executive officers concerned. The fact that this meeting took place at all proves that the Württemberg Werkbund was anything but a conspiratorial unity.

At the meeting the reasons for the hostility of the Stuttgart School were made abundantly clear. Bonatz and Schmitthenner took open exception to the appointment of Mies van der Rohe, an architect entirely unknown in Stuttgart, to direct the Werkbund exhibition, and to his unconventional initial proposal for the layout of the project:

> We have kept our doubts to ourselves, and we would have continued to do so, if it had not been for the Mies van der Rohe plan. This plan goes far beyond our worst fears. . . . The whole thing is so impractical, entirely based on decorative considerations, and in practical terms impossible to execute. The utilities, retaining walls, terracing, and so forth, would be roughly doubled, by comparison with building two simple rows of houses.

It was presumably these and other, related arguments that inspired Stotz to do the sketch marked "Roughly as proposed by Bonatz," which is also in Mies's archive.[23] Neither that archive nor that of Bonatz himself, nor the memory of eye-witnesses such as Heinz Rasch, affords any other reference to an alternative proposal from Bonatz; the sketch was probably never meant to be taken seriously.[24]

So what were the main reasons for Bonatz's and Schmitthenner's hostility to Mies's proposal? There was the accusation of lack of professionalism, closely linked with a second argument: their own position as instructors at the Technische Hochschule in Stuttgart and their responsibility for the attitudes of the architectural students. Then there was their own resentment at not being asked. To all this was added the argument that the taxpayers' money was being squandered, although this was certainly a subordinate consideration.

Schmitthenner called for an "experienced architect"

Dr. Paul Otto: sketch of the Weissenhofsiedlung

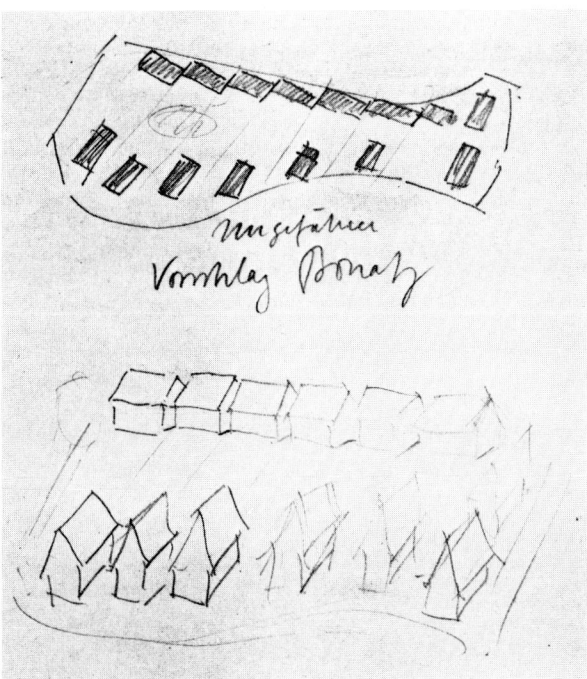

to be brought in; meanwhile, Bonatz was expecting to be consulted:

I kept waiting for the discussion to take place, but I had the feeling that what was wanted was to create a *fait accompli* before anyone came to me. The outcome of the discussion between Herr Stotz and Deputy Mayor Sigloch was that I should be asked to act as superintendent architect in charge of building the project. But to put it in that way is to give the impression that the person concerned—in this case myself—is totally in agreement with what was being done, and that I have declared my readiness to go along with it. . . . Herr Stotz knows very well that I am not about to build a house under the supervision of Mies van der Rohe. . . .

When I have a conviction that nothing but amateurism is shown by a man of whom I know nothing but a drawing of a skyscraper, when I have the impression that the plan is being handled in a completely impractical way, then I as an instructor at the Hochschule regard it as my duty to protest and to fight against it with all due force.

In the course of the meeting, Bonatz enlarged on his criticisms of the proposed layout:

The whole thing has not been approached in a practical way at all. Here is one house, there is another. Nobody has an uninterrupted view; everyone looks into someone else's bathroom window. Everything is scattered, nothing aligned. Here's someone who is hemmed in like a convict. No one enjoys any free space. It will cost about four times as much for terracing as is necessary. The Werkbund is always talking about rational building. And that means taking technical factors into consideration. If you rationalize, then for instance you need only one sewer line for all the soil pipes. And it's the same thing here with every technical aspect. It is the opposite of what a reasonable person does when he builds a housing development. . . .

This initial plan inevitably arouses the acutest misgivings.

Another Werkbund committee member, Adolf Schneck, defended Mies on the grounds that the layout had been drawn as a first sketch, without preliminary work, because Mies had been told at the Bremen Werkbund convention to "just do a general plan" as a basis for discussion.

Schmitthenner expressed his own reservations:

This is a part of the Stuttgart city expansion plan: it's a town plan. This is something that calls for organization, in many different respects. If you look at the plan, it's a slap in the face for all that. Everything is artistic, picturesque, aesthetic; delightful in a movie-house or in an exhibition; but this is stupid stuff. It throws years of patient evolution straight out the window. . . .

Evolution, not innovation, is what really counts. You hear a lot of slogans. To create a noble form out of machines, material, construction: that's the way. That's just what we intend to do. The form must be worked out by using the resources that industry provides. But here the form comes first. Anyone who's a real professional knows how wrong that is. This plan is a slap in the face for all that, and you are not going to tell me that there are no serious people who have taken a serious look at the economic problems of urban expansion. You have no right to ask those people to turn round and say, Yes, this is another way of doing it. That would be tantamount to branding themselves as idiots.

The meeting ended with another exchange of verbal fisticuffs between Stotz on one side and Bonatz and Schmitthenner on the other. It was moved that "two competing designs should be worked out in Stuttgart, by [Richard] Döcker and [Wilhelm] Jost." The motion was carried by seven votes to three; Bruckmann and Stotz abstained.

By this time, however, the die was cast: the city council building committee debated Bonatz's proposal "to enlist three architects to work on the elaboration of the overall plan of the project," and concluded (as the minutes tell us) that "undoubtedly three outstanding pieces of work" would be produced, but that "because their artistic attitudes are so different they would not be directly comparable, so that a decision as to which of the three was the best would be virtually impossible," and so the committee would first await Mies's reworked layout design.[25]

On May 17, 1926, the mayor's office informed Bonatz of the decision, and on June 5 the Werkbund replied by confirming Mies in his position as the person responsible for the artistic direction of the exhibition, and described the course of action proposed by Bonatz as "not feasible."[26]

The May 14 committee meeting of the Württemberg Werkbund had concluded (off the record) with a decision that the committee would resign "en bloc."[27] On June 2, at a general meeting of the membership, the committee's composition changed almost completely. Stotz reported to Mies: "We have a new committee, in which the previous majority consisting of Bonatz, Schmitthenner, and supporters has been booted out."[28]

Bonatz kept his seat on the committee, but Schmitthenner, Jost, and others were replaced by such people

Gustaf Stotz: "Bonatz's proposal, roughly," probably sketched during a meeting

37

Ludwig Mies van der Rohe: elevation of Weissenhofsiedlung, July 1, 1926

Variants of block plan, July 1, 1926, and thereafter

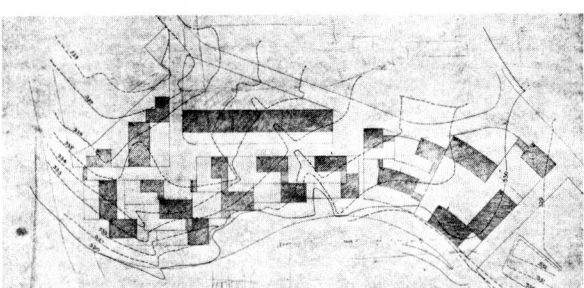

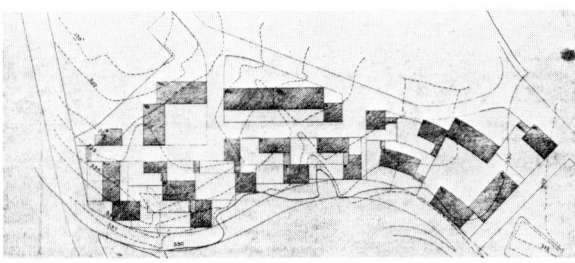

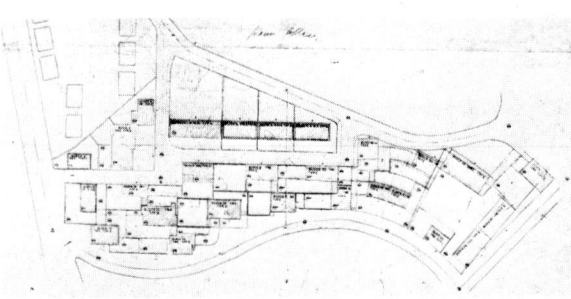

as Döcker, Schneck, and Hans Hildebrandt.[29] This change at the top of the section was the prelude to the reshuffle at central Werkbund board level in Berlin, in which Mies became deputy chairman and Bruckmann chairman.

A truce followed: Bonatz and Schmitthenner kept their criticisms to themselves until the 1927 exhibition was over. But it must have been at this time that Carl Hagstotz, administrator of the Württemberg Werkbund, proposed that the anti-Weissenhof party should undertake a rival project of their own—the germ of what became the Kochenhofsiedlung.

Now that the air was cleared, lines of command established, and hostilities laid aside, the city architects produced exact reference drawings and models, and these were sent to Mies in Berlin. Meanwhile, Mies and Döcker came up against each other for the first time. Döcker, as the representative of the "left wing" of the Stuttgart School, told Stotz—in ignorance of the City Hall decision of May 17—that, "for the sake of the project," he was not prepared to produce a design to compete with that of Mies.

He then proceeded, still with the best of intentions, to offer his services to Mies in the preparation of a detailed, regular layout plan. He told Mies that Bonatz had shown him the layout and that he had been "very startled" by it, but that he had told Bonatz that he "could see that there was something in it . . . that this was in any case only a rapid preliminary sketch, which would certainly lead to a solution."[30]

Döcker went on to offer to show Mies a proposal that would be "realistic, practical, achievable, economic and organic." His objection to the old plan was—and here his arguments agreed with those of his teacher, Bonatz—that the way the land was divided, and the relationships of the blocks to each other, were "often so capricious that some rooms would never get either light or air."[31]

Mies's counterblast was more like a manifesto; a clear rebuff for Döcker, it marked the beginning of the difficulties the two men were to have during the building process. Mies wrote,

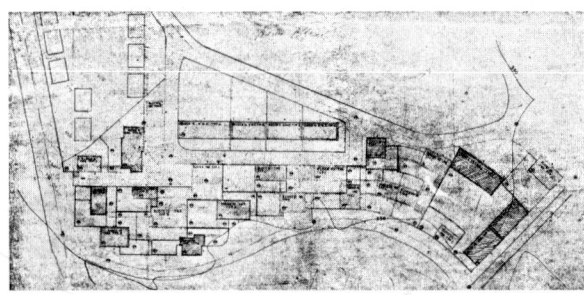

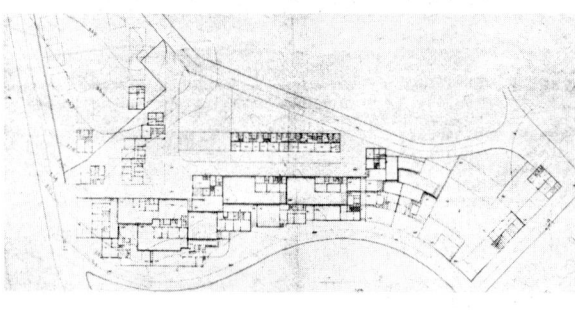

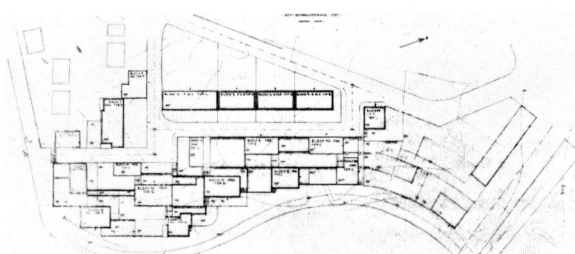

My dear Herr Döcker,
I have received your letter of the 18th, and I must tell you that I am sincerely glad of its candor, but that I am no less alarmed by the lack of understanding of my objectives which it reveals. For this reason, I must decline your kind offer of help. But I also want to make it clear that I was simply making a solid representation of a general forming principle, from which it would be possible to deduce the type and character of the development, but emphatically not such things as house sizes. Talk of a building plan is therefore nonsense. I was in no position to think of such a thing, if only because the volume requirements were not given to me until the middle of May.

Did you seriously suppose it possible that I would build rooms without light or ventilation, or that I would not give the buildings the right aspect to the sun? You clearly regard a building layout as a site plan in the old sense, with neatly outlined lots and regular house types.

At Weissenhof I consider it necessary to embark on a new approach, because I believe that a New Home will extend beyond four walls. This is not a matter of producing a layout as a pattern, in the old way; here, as also in the building, I want to break new ground. This, for me, is the point, the only point, of our work.

All the rest we could safely have left to Herr Bonatz and Herr Schmitthenner. These two have made it all too clear how they define a building problem. I would not waste an hour of my time on such work. Twenty years ago I took pains to build good, clean, reasonable houses. Since then my ambitions have changed. Building to me is a thing of the mind: it is creative, not in details but in essentials.

With kind regards . . . [32]

After a number of queries on both sides concerning sewer levels, numbers of rooms, state of subsoil, Mies worked out his first full layout proposal, which he was asked to expound to a meeting of the Württemberg Werkbund committee before it went any further.[33] On July 1, 1926, in Stotz's presence, Mies presented his plan to the representatives of the city executive departments.[34] On July 22 the costings were ready. The target figure of 900,000 marks was exceeded only by 26,152

marks.[35] The new plans—with variants—were just what the city wanted: neatly drawn, complete with contours, definition by housing types, and a "1:200 sketch model assuming flat roofs."[36]

The plan was redrawn at City Hall and sent out, together with ideas for ground plans and comparative drawings, to the city council members in advance of the full council meeting of July 28. By comparison with the plan which Mies called an "idea sketch," this one looked much more realistic and, with its steps and pergolas, realizable without loss of freshness and charm.

The accompanying comparative floor plans were intended to contrast conventional domestic designs with those proposed by the Werkbund. The latter show a reduction in the areas set aside for circulation in favor of larger living rooms, smaller individual rooms, and a clear distinction between living and sleeping areas. The comparisons of available floor space always work out in favor of the Werkbund principles: a more functional division of the house improves the ratio of living space to ground area.

When a meeting of the building committee on July 24, 1926, failed to agree on the overall layout, they decided to refer the fate of the Weissenhofsiedlung to a meeting of the full council, set to open on July 28.[37] And so the curious situation arose whereby the elected representatives of a whole city would take a vote on Mod-

Block plan of Weissenhofsiedlung based on Mies van der Rohe's designs, July 25, 1926

Comparative floor plans drawn by Städtisches Hochbauamt (city architectural department), July 1926, to compare conventional designs with entrance lobbies with Werkbund floor plans in which the functions of the rooms are clearly defined and the lobby area is added to the living room, thus affording a better ratio of living space to ground covered

Ludwig Mies van der Rohe: *Siedlungstypen* (housing types), undated (for translation see Appendix B)

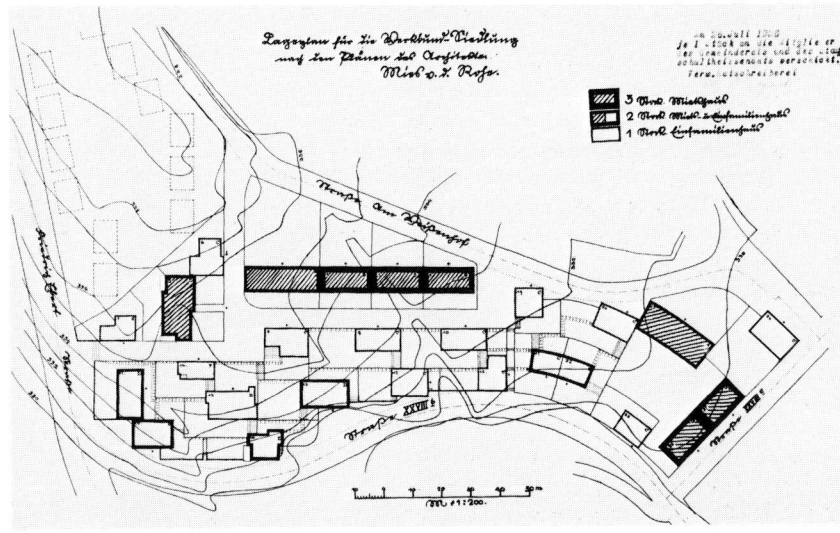

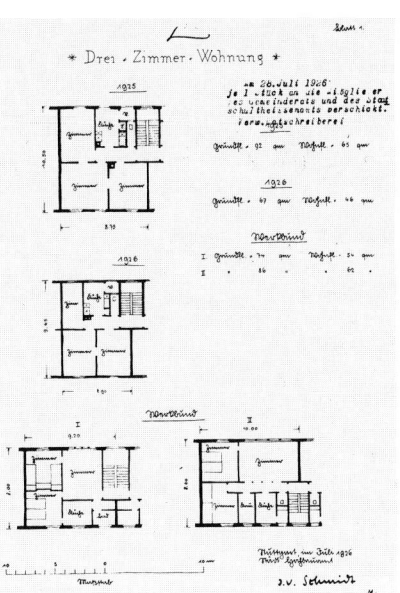

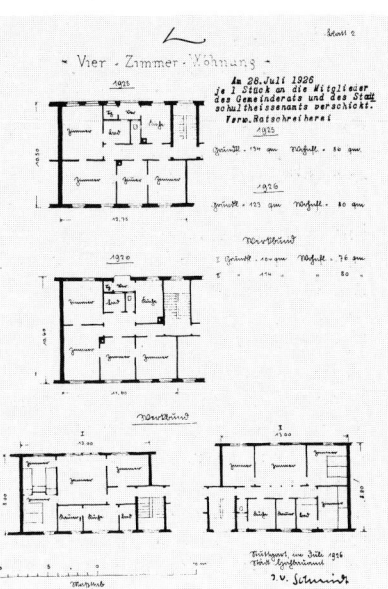

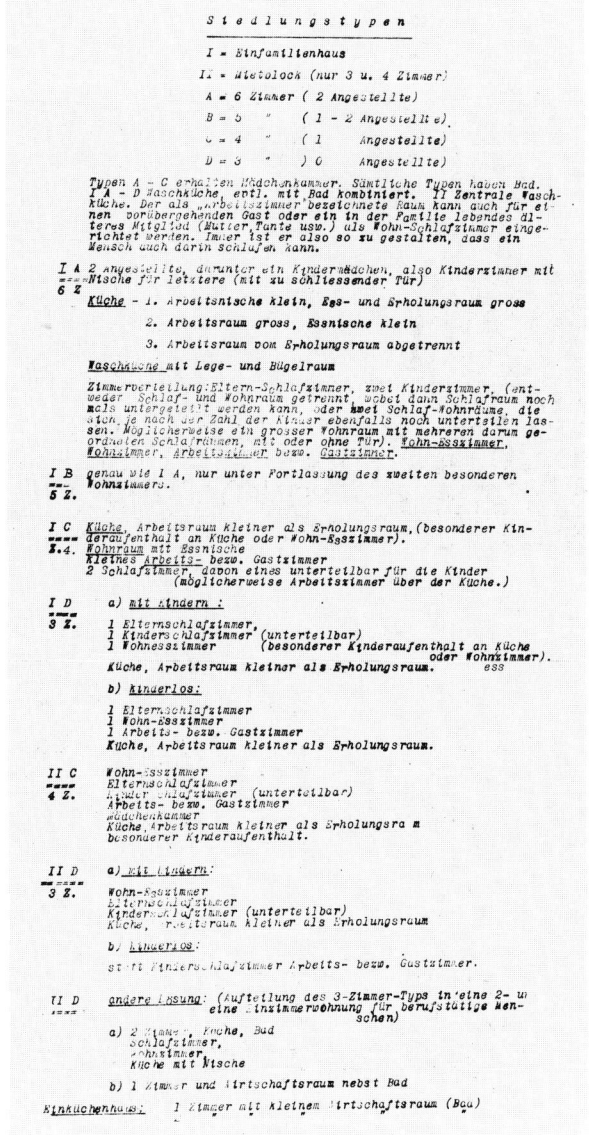

ernist architecture and on its representatives, the architects proposed by the Werkbund. In roll call vote, the council voted in favor with eight votes from the Democrats, nine from the Socialists, four from the Zentrumspartei two from the German Nationalists, and one from the German People's Party: twenty-five Ayes, eleven Noes, and six abstentions.

The Communists were the only party to vote against the Werkbund project as one. Their arguments are worth mentioning, because Mies was after all trying to enlist "left-oriented" architects to join him in the work. On the second day of the debate, July 29, a Communist councilman found it significant that

in one place there is to be meager housing for proletarians, and in another a very different kind of building for the well-off and the well-situated. . . . This is the lesson in attitudes that the population of the city of Stuttgart is receiving from the building of the Werkbund project. At the Eiernest [a development of basic housing for the poor] we have 36 square meters of usable living space for an average gross area of 50 square meters. The cost of a dwelling here is 7,000 marks; for the Werkbund project the average cost is to be 15,000 to 20,000 marks. If we take into account that there are going to be some detached villas at Weissenhof, then one of these units will probably come to 20,000 to 25,000 marks. The building costs will be higher than those provided for in the housing program which is intended to remedy the housing shortage. We cannot agree to this Werkbund development under any circumstances, much though it pains us for the sake of modern architecture and of the endeavor to create something new. We must decline to regard the Werkbund development as connected in any way with the public housing construction proposals. . . .

The building of villas is something that we may safely leave to private capital, or in other words to those who want to live in them. We cannot agree to experimental building within the framework of the public housing program, paid for by city funds. . . . We therefore propose . . . that the monies set aside for the Werkbund project be used in their entirety for the provision of 120 dwelling units at a cost of 10,000 marks each, and that these dwellings be placed on the housing market without delay. This would be an answer to the needs of the overwhelming majority of those in Stuttgart who are seeking homes. And above all we would be relieved of the odium of building villas for the affluent and banishing the underprivileged to a separate neighborhood.[38]

The Communist amendment was negatived by twenty-three votes to nineteen—a close call. However, the 23-11 vote on the main motion augured rather better for the Weissenhof project. From July 29, 1926, onward, the project could—for the time being—be regarded as safe.

At the beginning of September of 1926 Mies assigned the lots or "blocks" to the individual architects: Döcker, Gropius, Häring, Hilberseimer, Le Corbusier, Mendelsohn, Mies, Oud, Rading, Schneck, Stam, Taut, Max, Tessenow.[39] He invited each of them to design one or more units in association with the fellow-architects whose names were inscribed on the plan. The units assigned were classified into types according to a list

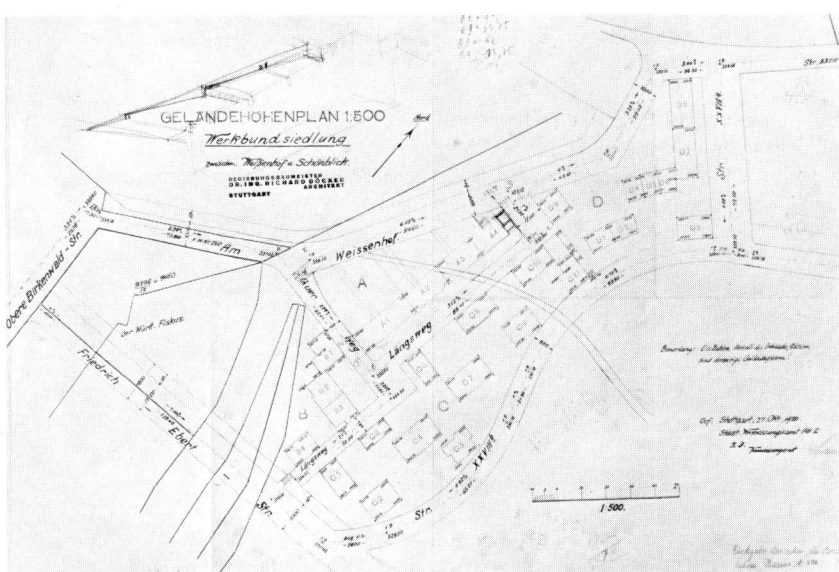

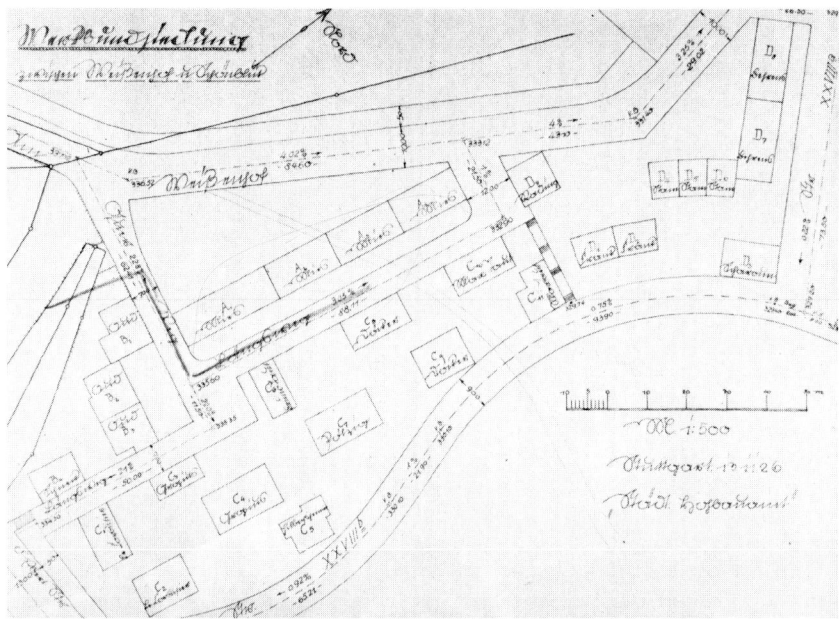

Plan showing spot levels, by Städtisches Vermessungsamt (city survey office), October 27, 1926

Plan of the Weissenhofsiedlung, showing architects' names, drawn up by Städtisches Hochbauamt, November 13, 1926

Two views of the Weissenhofsiedlung model made shortly before the opening of the 1927 exhibition

drawn up by Mies, one copy of which is illustrated here; its text is translated at the end of this book as Appendix B.

In October of 1926 the city surveyor's office (Vermessungsamt) prepared a plan with spot heights for the streets and this was sent to all the participating architects. Even so, Le Corbusier and Pierre Jeanneret got their particular lot so wrong that the entry to the finished building is through the furnace room in what should have been the cellar, and not, as planned, in the supposed first floor at ground level.

The final placing of the houses and assignment to individual architects were settled by November 13. The project had now reached its definitive stage. All the architects fitted their designs to the building lots assigned to them; but the forms of the houses themselves were to change by comparison with the plan of November 13. The model of the Weissenhof project which was shown in the *Internationale Plan- und Modellausstellung Neuer Baukunst* in 1927 showed all the houses in their final form.

THE SELECTION PROCESS
"As a basic principle, only those architects must be asked to participate who work in the spirit of progressive artistic form, in keeping with present-day conditions, and who are familiar with the equipment appropriate for home building."[40] With these words, in September of 1925, Bruckmann defined for the benefit of the Werkbund's national leadership the criteria to be observed in selecting architects for the Weissenhof project. It was a clear decision to opt for "the Young."

Mies was even more forthright. "I have the audacious idea," he wrote to Gustaf Stotz in the same month of September, 1925, "of attracting all left-wing architects, and from an exhibition point of view that would be extraordinarily successful."[41] Häring, still at that time working with Mies, offered a caveat: "Let's look at the intellectual, not the political aspect,"[42] he replied when Bruckmann asked him about Henry Van de Velde's political past. No other letter or publication exists in which political allegiance is mentioned as an argument for or against the choice of a particular architect; it is a stroke of luck that we do have Mies's view stated here so clearly.

The broad lines of the selection process were set. The to and fro of details, disagreements and discrepancies, the reasons for rejections, and the genesis of the selection list itself followed.

The nomination of the architects was the joint responsibility of the Württemberg Werkbund and city hall. A "provisional plan for the execution" of the 1927 exhibition[43] prepared in June of 1925 states that "invitations shall be extended to the architects selected to design the buildings by the Werkbund, and the construction contracts shall be placed by the City"; in practice, however, city hall always sought, and obtained, a say in the choice of architects.

Whether Häring or Mies most influenced the initial conceptions of the Weissenhof project is not absolutely clear. Häring wrote to Stotz, enclosing the second list of architects he and Mies worked out, that

bringing twenty or so architects under one umbrella means working with them all the time. What is involved is not individual buildings, but combining and working twenty individual intentions into a coherent plan . . . And so Stuttgart has nothing at all to do with the individual architects themselves; that is a matter for Berlin.[44]

It is no exaggeration to describe Häring's idea of coordination as an idealistic one. It may have become clear to Mies very early on that it would not be possible to control twenty architects "under one umbrella"; the distance in itself would have posed an insuperable problem. It remains to be considered whether Mies's and Häring's first list (List II below) was conceived in this collaborative spirit.

List I was compiled by Gustaf Stotz in Stuttgart and sent to Mies in Berlin. As the text of the covering letter reveals, it had emerged from discussions between Stotz and Mies, and between Stotz and Bruckmann: it did not represent Stotz's own personal opinion alone. (The successive lists are quoted here with the original variations in the spelling of names.)

List I, September 24, 1925 (Stotz)
1. Behrens—Berlin
2. Tessenow—Dresden
3. Taut
4. Gropius—Dessau
5. Mies—Berlin
6. Häring—Berlin
7. Hilberseimer—Berlin
8. Döcker—Stuttgart
9. Herre—Stuttgart
10. Keuerleber—Stuttgart [handwritten addition: Van de Velde?]
11. Schneck—Stuttgart
12. Kramer—Frankfurt
13. Adolf Loos—Vienna
14. Dr. Frank—Vienna
15. Oud—Rotterdam
16. Corbusier—Paris
17. Stam—Zürich
18. Poelzig—Berlin
19. Mendelsohn—Berlin
20. Doesburg
21. Bonatz—Stuttgart[45]

Deletions on List I might be the work of Mies's sharp pen; Van de Velde has been added by Stotz.

List II, September 26, 1925 (Mies and Häring)
1. Berlage
2. Behrens
3. van de Velde
4. Pölzig
5. Tessenow
6. Taut
7. Bartning
8. Corbusier
9. Oud
10. Doesburg
11. Gropius
12. Hilberseimer
13. Stam
14. Kramer
15. Schneck
16. Mendelsohn
17. Korn
18. Döcker
19. Herre
20. Luckhardt
21. Gelhorn
22. Scharoun

To these should be added 23 Mies and 24 Häring.
It is as yet not at all clear whether we shall be able to come to terms with all of the above. We have to expect, too, that there will often have to be changes of plan when it comes to the individual projects.[46]

On October 8, 1925, after further discussions with Mies (Stotz had asked him to dinner in Stuttgart, together with Mayor Lautenschlager and his wife, Bruckmann, and Schneck), Stotz gave the mayor's office the first official Werkbund list.

List III, October 8, 1925 (Werkbund)
1. Prof. Behrens, Berlin—Vienna
2. Le Corbusier, Geneva, currently in Paris
3. Government Architect Dr. Richard Döcker, Stuttgart
4. Theo van Doesburg, Holland, currently in Paris
5. Dr. Frank, Vienna
6. Professor Walter Gropius, Dessau
7. Hugo Häring, Biberach, currently in Berlin

8. Richard Herre, Stuttgart
9. Ludwig Hilberseimer, Karlsruhe
10. Baurat Hugo Keuerleber, Stuttgart
11. Ferdinand Kramer, Frankfurt
12. Mies van der Rohe, Aachen—Berlin
13. J.J.P. Oud, city architect, Rotterdam
14. Professor Ad. G. Schneck, Stuttgart
15. Professor Tessenow, Dresden

Additionally:
16. Dr. h. c. Otto Bartning, Weimar
17. Government Architect Dr. Alfred Gellhorn, Berlin
18. Arthur Korn, Breslau
19. W. Luckhardt, Berlin
20. K. [Erich] Mendelsohn, Berlin
21. Prof. Hans Poelzig, Potsdam
22. Sigmund, Stuttgart
23. Mat. Stam, Zürich
24. Bruno Taut, Königsberg
25. Henry van de Velde, Brussels—Hague (Holland)
26. Prof. Hans Scharoun, Akademie, Breslau[47]

Among the first fifteen names on this third list, nine actually built houses on the Weissenhof; Nos. 16–26 include four more. Three others, Kramer, Herre, and Korn, were eventually involved with interior design.

List IV, April 1926 (Werkbund)

List IV was submitted by the Württemberg Werkbund.[48] In it, the names are not arranged alphabetically, as in List III, but according to location:

From Stuttgart (two-fifths): (1) Bonatz, (2) Döcker, (3) Sigmund, (4) Schneck, (5) Gutschow, (6) Herre. = 6
From outside (two-fifths): (7) Mies van der Rohe, (8) Gropius, (9) Häring, (10) Behrens, (11) Mendelsohn, (12) Hilberseimer. (Reserve list: Kramer (16), Tessenow (17), Luckhardt (18), Taut (19), Scharoun (20).) = 6
From abroad (one-fifth): (13) Oud, (14) Corbusier, (15) Dr. Frank. = 3

If we compare this official list with the previous ones, it is apparent that the Stuttgart names are markedly more numerous; and every one of them, including Schneck, had studied under Paul Bonatz! Keuerleber's name does not appear. (He was probably in the course of being appointed professor of material studies at the Technische Hochschule, an appointment which he took over in 1927.)[49] The number of foreigners was halved, and Doesburg, Stam, and Van de Velde had disappeared.

In April of 1926 the political prospects were uncertain. The members of the city council, half of whom were newly elected, had little enthusiasm for the Weissenhof project on ideological grounds. Even further proposed changes in the list, replacing three Stuttgart names (Sigmund, Gutschow, and Heere) with four others (Professors Wetzel and Wagner, plus Herkommer and Hoffmann), did not help.

In these circumstances Deputy Mayor Sigloch invited Bruckmann to address the building committee of the city council on the aims, ideology, and objectives of the Werkbund, which he did on April 16. He told the committee he was assuming that Bonatz would take over "the supreme authority," and that Mies would become a kind of associate: "I am of the opinion that they will

be able to work very well together, as the one is perhaps more familiar with the local conditions in Stuttgart, while the other is most familiar with the precise thing we want to show, namely the new techniques and new processes."[50]

Bruckmann's words found favor with the members of the building committee—the minutes of the meeting were distributed to the members of the full council and to the city executive departments, and a preliminary project was approved. Bruckmann's silver tongue presented the previously unknown figure of Mies van der Rohe as a man of integrity and competence; an architect "who is the son of a stonemason in Aachen, and who has served an apprenticeship and worked as a stonemason," a man whom he had known for a long time, who was "a thoroughly practical, workmanlike architect," entrusted with "carrying out the preliminary work and visiting the site."

Alongside these official moves in City Hall there were other, unofficial ones. Stotz asked Mies to have the Soviet mission in Berlin write a letter of recommendation to the Stuttgart caucus of the Communist Party,[51] and in September of 1926, when further difficulties were in the wind, he asked Max Taut to put in a word with an influential Social Democrat who was a client of his.[52]

The publication of the anti-Mies articles by Bonatz and Schmitthenner[53] precipitated the withdrawal of the Stuttgart professors and a clear confirmation of Mies's position as artistic director. The provisional compromise reached by Bonatz and Bruckmann to reconcile the interests of the Stuttgart architects and the Württemberg Werkbund—according to which three architects (Mies, "from the Stuttgart School left wing, say, Döcker, and from the Stuttgart School right wing, say, Schmitthenner") should work together—was disowned by city and Werkbund alike.[54] Carl Hagstotz, one of the administrators of the exhibition, later made it known that he had encouraged the rival Stuttgart architects to consider building a project of their own, creating the germ of the Kochenhof project as early as May of 1926.[55]

List V, July 20, 1926 (Werkbund)

This list, sent out by the administrator of the Werkbund central office in Berlin, Otto Baur, contains a few surprises.[56]

Fifteen names on the short list; five on the reserve list. Loos—absent since Stotz's very first list—reappears,

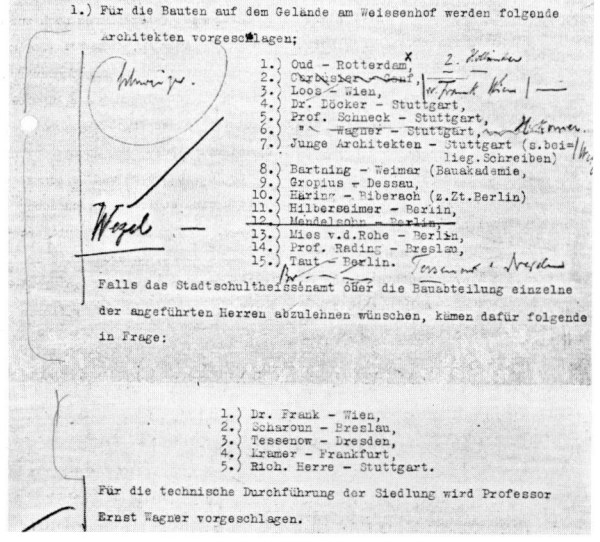

but fleetingly: he is omitted from List VI, drawn up only four days later. No. 7 on this list, "Young Architects—Stuttgart (see letter herewith)," refers to a letter which five architects, Gerhard Graubner, Rudolf Schroeder, Albert Kluftinger, Hans Seytter, and Paul Stotz (perhaps the brother of Gustaf Stotz, who also bore the name of Paul), wrote to the Württemberg Werkbund on June 17, 1926, asking it "to release at least a small part of the building for a competition open to young architects, and then to entrust the execution to the winners."[57]

Ernst Wagner, an instructor at the Staatliche Höhere Bauschule in Stuttgart,[58] is proposed as superintendent only on this list. In 1927, like Adolf Schneck and Victor Bourgeois, he built a house on adjoining land belonging to the State Württemberg which was included in a number of the Weissenhof plans; unlike those of Schneck and Bourgeois, however, this house—for a Dr. Christ—receives no mention in any of the accompanying Werkbund publications.

Of the Stuttgart architects mentioned in List IV, Friedrich Sigmund, a Stuttgart architect and a member of Döcker's circle, disappears along with Konstanty Gutschow and Richard Herre. The correspondence shows that at this stage these men did not even know they were being considered. By publicly enquiring about their chances, Sigmund, Herre, and others thus damaged rather than improved them.[59]

One new name in List V is that of Adolf Rading, of Breslau; the Luckhardt brothers are absent.

List VI, July 24, 1926 (City Hall)

This list was produced at the meeting of the city council building committee which resolved not to approve the Weissenhof project but to refer the decision back to a meeting of the full council. In discussion, Ernst Wagner was once more proposed as superintendent (as was Baurat Dr. Schmidt, of the city architectural department), but his name does not appear in the list that emerged.[60] In this, the Werkbund's twenty names are reduced to fourteen:

```
      Nach Vorschlägen des Vorsitzenden, Bürgermeisters Dr.Sigloch
 und Gemeinderats Beer beschliesst die Abteilung, folgende Architek-
 ten zu wählen:
                    1.) Oud - Rotterdam,
                    2.) Dr.Frank - Wien,                2. Wien
                    3.) Dr.Döcker-Stuttgart,
                    4.) Prof.Schneck - Stuttgart,
                    5.) Architekt Herkommer,
                    6.) Prof. Wezel - Stuttgart
                        (falls er annehmen sollte),        ... Wils
                    7.) Bartning - Weimar,
                    8.) Gropius - Dessau,                   Tessenow
                    9.) Häring - Biberach (z.Zt.Berlin),
Corbusier          10.) Hilberseimer - Berlin,
                   11.) Mies van der Rohe - Berlin,
                   12.) Prof.Rading - Breslau,
                   13.) Taut - Berlin,
                   14.) Tessenow - Dresden.

      Neben Oud - Rotterdam soll noch ein weiterer Holländer und für
 Corbusier - Genf ein anderer Schweizer Architekt zugezogen werden.
                                    dass
      Die Bauabteilung wünscht, die Namen der Architekten bis zur Ge-
 meinderatssitzung bekanntgegeben werden.
```

The record of the meeting, and the letter from the Werkbund incorporating List IV, bear handwritten additions which suggest a lively debate. The name "John Wils" is written in the margin; the name "Corbusier" (whom it was decided to replace with "another Swiss architect") is written in several times, once in a penciled box; on the Werkbund letter (List V) someone has scored out the name of Ernst Wagner, added that of Heinz Wetzel, canceled Taut, and added Tessenow. List VI also includes Wetzel (with, in parenthesis, "if he were to accept") and mentions the addition of "another Dutch architect."

From this time onward Adolf Loos's name disappears from the lists and from the files of the city and of

the project. A private patron, Dr. Walter Boll, was to contact him late in the autumn of 1926 with a view to having him design a house (see the chapter on Victor Bourgeois, below).

The plenary session of the council took place on July 29. After some heated exchanges, the choice of architects for the Weissenhofsiedlung was referred back to the building committee.

The list which Deputy Mayor Sigloch sent to Bruckmann on August 24, 1926, and which he then forwarded to Mies in Berlin, is identical to List VI (except for the omission of the parenthesis following Wetzel's name). Mies and the Werkbund responded immediately by asking for the restoration of Le Corbusier and Sigloch laying this request before the building committee at its next meeting, on August 27. The response beggars belief: "When the matter was put to the vote, the selection of the architect Corbusier, who is from the West of Switzerland, was rejected on national grounds."[61]

Extract from minutes, Bauabteilung des Gemeinderates (city council building committee), August 27, 1926: Le Corbusier is voted out

This official rejection seems to have been less final than it appears. Mies gave Stotz some more names, including that of Anton Brenner, a Viennese whom Heinrich de Fries had recommended "because of his excellent work in building small apartments for the city of Vienna, and especially for the exemplary interior finish of those units." From Holland, he suggested Johannes B. van Loghem, or Mart Stam; from Switzerland, Hannes Meyer, if that were not too many.[62] Stotz proposed, "Instead of Professor Wetzel, let Wagner and Wetzel have the commission jointly. They have often worked together before, and they will accept. Herkommer is impossible: Corbusier takes his place. If it turns out to be possible to issue another commission, then let Mendelsohn be brought in."[63]

An architects' meeting was arranged for September 14 and 15, for which invitations went out to some architects from Mies and to others from the Württemberg Werkbund. Several of the recipients of Mies's invitations (including Tessenow and Schneck) were also invited to visit Weissenhof.[64]

On September 14 there was a fruitful encounter between City Hall representatives, Stotz, and Mies, at which the choice of superintendent, the vexed question of fees, and the selection of participants were discussed again. Mies asked to replace Bartning with Mendelsohn because "this is more a matter of a consortium of individuals than of representatives of individual schools." (Bartning had succeeded Gropius at the former Weimar Bauhaus.) The minutes record Mies as saying,

43

Without Mendelsohn there would be a lacuna: the fact that he had a hotel under construction here was irrelevant, as the Weissenhof project was not all about making money. Herr Herkommer and Herr Wetzel were definitely to be replaced by others, because they had no inner affinity whatsoever with the ideals embodied in Weissenhof and would therefore only be able to imitate. It was unthinkable to do without Le Corbusier: this would damage the whole project; his name would carry a lot of weight, especially abroad. His book, which enjoyed a great reputation everywhere, had actually been published by a Stuttgart house. The Dutchman, Van Lochem [Loghem], ought to be included as well.[65]

After the Stuttgart meeting, the refusals began to come in. The first was from Tessenow:

If the Werkbund project were to be built in Berlin, where I—as you probably know—shall be permanently based from October onward, then I would join in without hesitation; but taking on the job envisaged for Stuttgart would either increase my workload out of all proportion or else destroy my peace of mind, and so I am afraid I must decline the offer of participation. I beg you not to take my refusal amiss, and I hope we shall be able to talk the matter over very soon.[66]

Now that the city council had finally agreed to the project, there were many decisions to be taken, the architects' contract to be worked out, and the superintendent to be appointed. The second half of September 1926 was a time of busy optimism; no one foresaw complications which would stem from the architects themselves. The trouble probably began when the building committee decided to negotiate the contract not with Gropius and Häring, the elected secretary of Der Ring, but with Gropius and Max Taut. From the correspondence, and from the transpositions of names and other clues contained in the selection lists, the following sequence of events emerges.

On Friday, September 25, 1926, Mies met in Stuttgart with City Hall representatives, probably including the members of the building committee, and with the representatives of the Württemberg Werkbund. He wanted the financing of Weissenhof, and thus the question of the architects' fees, to be kept separate from the finances of the exhibition as a whole; the architects to be paid their traveling expenses; and, if necessary, his own separate fee as artistic director to be paid by the Werkbund and from exhibition funds. The city had agreed to a global sum of 50,000 marks for architects' fees, which Mies wanted to distribute among the architects equally, irrespective of the size of their individual contributions. The shareout would thus depend, not on the cost of each specific building, but on the number of architects taking part. Otherwise, Mies might have had the lion's share for himself, and Bruno Taut, for example, would have received only a proportion corresponding to his small house. This was the negotiating position that Mies adopted—without, of course, making the mistake of giving away his own minimum demands too soon.

On September 28, he wrote to Adolf Rading, "I have just come back from Stuttgart, and, predictably, hard though we tried, the city has turned us down."[67] He, Schneck, and Döcker had written a letter "to the gentlemen who were with us in Stuttgart . . . the resistance of those in Berlin, which means principally Herr Häring, is

not entirely based on objective considerations."[68]

The mention of Häring in this context is surprising. On September 22 Mies had told Gropius that Häring would probably not be able to go to Stuttgart because of lack of money.[69] Even Mies's own trip was not a certainty at this stage, and Max Taut stayed in Berlin.

Why were the architects dissatisfied? They quite properly wanted the terms of the BDA standard contract to apply. They were quite prepared to remit 40 percent of the total fee calculated according to these terms "in view of the special circumstances of this commission." But the 50,000 marks allotted by the city was supposed to be all-inclusive (including expenses, superintendent, etc.). This they resisted on the grounds that the superintendent alone, with his staff, could be expected to cost 20,000 marks, and that every trip to Stuttgart was going to cost the out-of-town architects around 200 marks. Mies costed out the fee element at a total of 80,545 marks, and the architects were prepared to bear their own expenses up to a figure of 1,600 marks.

When the city turned this down flat, a number of the architects (Max Taut was one) took the view that there must be no giving in, and that they must insist on their just demands. Häring, in his Der Ring capacity as a representative of architects' interests, was particularly insistent and expressed his views both verbally and in writing. The evidence shows that at the end of September Häring must have sent Mies, Döcker, and Schneck an answer to the letter written by the three of them after the breakdown of the talks in Stuttgart. Mies's response was an angry one. He told Stotz,

I shall write Häring straight away to say that I strongly object to his imagining that as secretary of Der Ring he can dictate to me in the management of the exhibition. I have no desire to submit to this kind of treatment any more. We did not form Der Ring in order to make Herr Häring a dictator, but in order to give effective external representation to the interests of the modern movement.[70]

Then he wrote to Häring himself, with a copy to Stotz:

Dear Häring,
I gather from your letter of September 30 that you regard the Stuttgart undertaking as a matter for Der Ring. I take the liberty of pointing out to you that it is and will remain a Werkbund matter.
    Regards. . . .[71]

Mies did nothing to avoid a breach with Häring. Two days before the date of Häring's letter he had told Rading,

I am determined to carry the exhibition through, and I would be prepared, if I were forced to it, to regroup the participants, supposing that one or another decides not to take part. The attitude that prevails here, which is that we are in a position to dictate to the Stuttgart city authorities, is childish and mischievous. At the very least, it reveals a total misreading of the situation.[72]

Stotz wrote in similar terms to Max Taut, revealing the strength of his own commitment to the Weissenhof project. He begged Taut not to see the matter in terms of

"What have we not yet achieved?" but, on the contrary: "How much we have already got done in Stuttgart. . . . I close this letter with a personal appeal to you to give us your support in carrying on the enterprise, and to join with a will in the great battle that is being fought here, not for Stuttgart alone but for the whole Reich and beyond.[73]

Imperfect though the terms on offer undoubtedly were, Rading, Max Taut, Gropius, Poelzig, and Hilberseimer signed. Häring withdrew; so did Mendelsohn. Häring's confidant and biographer, Heinrich Lauterbach, described his departure: "After initially participating in the project, Häring withdrew from it because he had different ideas about the nature of the task. Peter Behrens took his place."[74]

Meanwhile, with the project still in some jeopardy from this disagreement, the city council building committee confirmed, on the basis of the discussions with Mies and Stotz, a new selection of architects:

The following was decided by a majority vote:
1. To add the architects Le Corbusier and Mendelsohn, and (at the instance of Councilman Beer) Ma[r]t Stam, to the list of those engaged for the Weissenhof project.
2. To exclude the architect Herkommer (on the grounds that he already has a commission from the city . . .).
3. To exclude the architect Professor Wetzel.
4. To reject the list of replacements proposed by the Werkbund.[75]

List VII, October 1, 1926 (city hall)
1. Oud—Rotterdam
2. Dr. Frank—Vienna
3. Dr. Döcker—Stuttgart
4. Prof. Schneck—Stuttgart
5. Gropius—Dessau
6. Häring—Biberach
7. Hilberseimer—Berlin
8. Mies van der Rohe—Berlin
9. Prof. Rading—Breslau
10. Max Taut—Berlin
11. Prof. Tessenow—Dresden
12. Corbusier—Geneva
13. Mendelsohn—Berlin
14. Stam—Hague[76]

As may be clear already, this list was so much waste paper before it was even drawn up.

Der Ring held a meeting on October 7 in which current issues were discussed. Stotz offered to give the member architects "a detailed verbal report on the bases and the evolution of our plans for the exhibition." He described Häring's letter as "shameless" and told Mies that he hoped Häring would draw the proper consequences from Mies's letter.[77]

While attempts were thus being made in Berlin to make it possible for the representatives of the New Architecture to work together, the "marking out" of the Weissenhof site was in full swing.[78] Mies went ahead with the invitations to Le Corbusier and Josef Frank, and accepted a request from Max Taut. "I have been talking with Max Taut," he wrote Stotz; "he is willing to come in, of course. He pointed out that it was not right to pass over his brother entirely, especially as he has so expressly committed himself to the redesigning of the home. "I'll think about how and where we can find a place for him."[79]

List VII is the first one in which Max Taut is given his first name: one is tempted to suspect that, all along,

Mies had been talking about Max while the members of the building committee had been thinking of the better-known Bruno.

The meeting healed rifts in Der Ring; Schneck wrote Mies, "The cracked Ring is in one piece again."[80] But while Häring did indeed draw "the proper consequences," Mendelsohn was still resentful. Stotz and Mies tried to placate him by showing him evidence that he had been on all the Werkbund lists, and that Mies and Stotz had both made particular efforts to induce the city authorities to accept him.[81] Nevertheless Mendelsohn declined to reconsider, saying that he had now taken on new work and that he would therefore not have time to take part in the Weissenhof project: "This is the main reason why I must, I am afraid, say no. The other reasons, which you know, are not crucial in themselves, but I wish that they had never arisen among members of Der Ring."[82]

Meanwhile, even after the withdrawal of Häring, Tessenow, and Mendelsohn, Stotz was still reporting on project finances and the state of negotiations to a central committee meeting of the Werkbund in Berlin as if nothing had happened.[83]

List VIII, October 16, 1926 (Werkbund)
1. Oud—Rotterdam
2. Dr. Frank—Vienna
3. Dr. Döcker—Stuttgart
4. Prof. Schneck—Stuttgart
5. Gropius—Dessau
6. Häring—Biberach
7. Hilberseimer—Berlin
8. Mies van der Rohe—Berlin
9. Prof. Rading—Breslau
10. Mendelsohn—Berlin
11. Max Taut—Berlin
12. Prof. Tessenow—Dresden
13. Corbusier—Geneva
14. Stam—Hague[84]

This list contains the same names as List VII in a slightly different order. If Stotz had named any other names than those approved by the building committee he would certainly have been accused of high-handedness.

The Werkbund did, however, have a number of new names in mind. Bruno Taut we know about; from Vienna, Peter Behrens wrote his former assistant, Mies, that as he had heard that Mies was in charge of the Werkbund's Stuttgart project he wondered "whether it might not be possible to realize the idea of my terraced block."[85] Mies probably invited Scharoun and Poelzig by word of mouth: there is nothing on file. Bourgeois was the last; he was included—probably not until 1927—on Van de Velde's recommendation.

On November 12, 1926, the city council building committee discussed the list of architects and the replacements for Häring, Tessenow, and Mendelsohn. The names of Bruno Taut, Hans Poelzig, Hans Scharoun, and Peter Behrens were approved, and the houses to be built (classified into Types A through D; see Appendix B) were assigned to individuals.

List IX, November 12, 1926
The distribution of the buildings produces the following list:

A1, A2, A3, A4	1. Mies van der Rohe
B1, B2, B3	2. Oud
B4	3. Schneck
C1 + C2	4. Le Corbusier

C3 + C4	5. Gropius
C5	6. Hilberseimer
C6	7. Taut, Bruno
C7	8. Poelzig
C8 + C9	9. Döcker
C10 + C11	10. Taut, Max
[D1 + D2	Dr. Frank]
D3	11. Scharoun
D4, D5, + D6	12. Stam
D7 + D8	13. Behrens
D9	14. Rading.[86]

Only one name, that of Hans Scharoun, was separately put to the vote at the insistance of the architect and SPD floor leader, Karl Beer, on the grounds of what Beer is reported to have called "the particularly idiosyncratic attitude of this architect in artistic matters." Scharoun was accepted by six votes to one, with three absten-tions.[87] The absence of the name of Josef Frank from the list was an oversight.

The publication of the fifteen names in the *Süddeutsche Zeitung* on December 10, 1926, brought the selection process to an end. Döcker was appointed superintendent.[88] When Baurat Dr. Schmidt of the city architectural department, on behalf of his chief, Commissioner Sigloch, asked Döcker what were the principles on which the commissions had been distributed, Döcker did not venture on a personal interpretation but consulted Mies, who replied,

Please tell Herr Baurat Schmidt that the architectural commissions were distributed on a basis of appropriateness, and above all with an eye to the greatest possible unity of the project. What else am I supposed to say?[89]

Ludwig Mies van der Rohe

HOUSES 1, 2, 3, 4
Design: Mies van der Rohe, architect
Berlin W 35, Am Karlsbad 24

*Rental apartment building consisting of four row houses
each containing six apartments of varying sizes: cellar,
first story, second story, third story, roof story with roof
garden, laundries, and in Houses 3 and 4 drying rooms
and attics.*
*Construction: iron frame filled with single-tier brickwork,
4 cm [1½ in] of Torfisotherm insulation. Plastered to interior and exterior. Ceilings in hollow structural tiles between iron joists. Internal partitions in pumice concrete
blockwork, Celotex board, Fulgurit, or plywood.[1]*

Economic considerations today, in the building of
rental units, demand rationalization and standardization of production. The constantly growing diversity of our housing needs, on the other
hand, demands great flexibility in the use of the
accommodation. In future it will be necessary to
do justice to both considerations. Skeleton construction is the most appropriate building system
in this case. It permits a rationalized production
process and affords every possible scope for varying the internal divisions. If the architect limits
himself to treating the kitchen and the bathroom
as constants, because of their plumbing, while
partitioning the remaining living area with movable walls, I believe that by these means it is possible to satisfy every reasonable dwelling need.[2]

In these terse words Mies described his Weissenhof
apartment building in *Bau und Wohnung*. The formula,
with its structural system derived from industry—skeleton construction—dates back to the genesis of his first
layout plan. The first model, and the first layout sketch,
show a structure of several stories, at the highest point
of the development, which seems to be holding the
smaller buildings together. As Mies never put anything
in writing about the allocation of the buildings to individual architects, it is impossible to be quite sure that he
always kept this particular lot in mind for himself; but
any alternative supposition would be even more speculative.

The form of the structure underwent a succession of
changes from parallel, staggered cubes to the ultimate
simplification, a large, wide rectilinear building with
windows neatly fitted, almost flush, into a facade articulated only by door canopies and French-looking balconies.

Mies, as his own artistic director, did not enter into
correspondence about his building until the time came
to start building, when he had dealings on the subject
with Döcker, as superintendent, and with city hall. The

earliest letter on file concerning the design of Mies's
building is actually from Schneck, offering the services
of his own students as "cheap labor" to prepare plans
and working drawings. Schneck particularly praised
the skill of Rudolf Frank.[3] Mies declined the offer with
thanks, saying that he first wanted to work "the thing"
through himself; later, however, it might be time to discuss the offer. And, a little later, he does seem to have
accepted the offer of assistance.[4]

Schneck was not the only one who offered help:
Döcker did the same. With the best of intentions, he
wrote Mies, "For your designs, I would recommend
drawing sections and basement and roof-level plans,
as well as front and rear elevations corresponding to
the lie of the land."[5] Eventually, in exasperation, he
gave up; Mies's answers were patronizing, not to say
brusque.

Mies, who kept his public utterances terse, left it to
the visitors to the exhibition to extract from his laconic
explanatory text the quintessence of his design concept—the flexibility of apartment plans according to
size of family and individual requirements. It was not
the first time he had concerned himself with the problems of flexible floor plans. In 1921, in his project for an
office building on Friedrichstrasse, Berlin, he avoided
static divisions. "The only fixed points in the whole
plan," he told the readers of Bruno Taut's magazine,
Frühlicht, "are the stair and elevator shafts. All other
subdivisions are to be adapted to individual requirements and constructed in glass."[6]

In Stuttgart he demonstrated the wide variety of possibilities by enlisting twenty-nine architects and interior
designers (including the thirteen Swiss members of a
Schweizer Werkbund collective) to design the interiors
of his twenty-four apartments, not before investigating
the furnishability of the dwellings from every angle and
taking advice from Erna Meyer in matters of cooking
and domestic economy. We owe to his correspondence
with her—as we do in the cases of Le Corbusier and
Oud—some essential statements of planning principle:

As you know, I intend to try out the most varied
plans in this apartment house. For the time being,
I am building only the outside and common walls,
and inside each apartment only the two piers that
support the ceiling. All the rest is to be as free as
it possibly can be. If I could contrive to get some
cheap plywood partitions made, I would treat
only the kitchen and the bathroom as fixed spaces, and make the rest of the apartment variable,
so that the spaces could be divided according to
the needs of the individual tenant. This would
have the advantage that it would make it possible
to rearrange the apartment whenever family circumstances changed, without spending a lot of

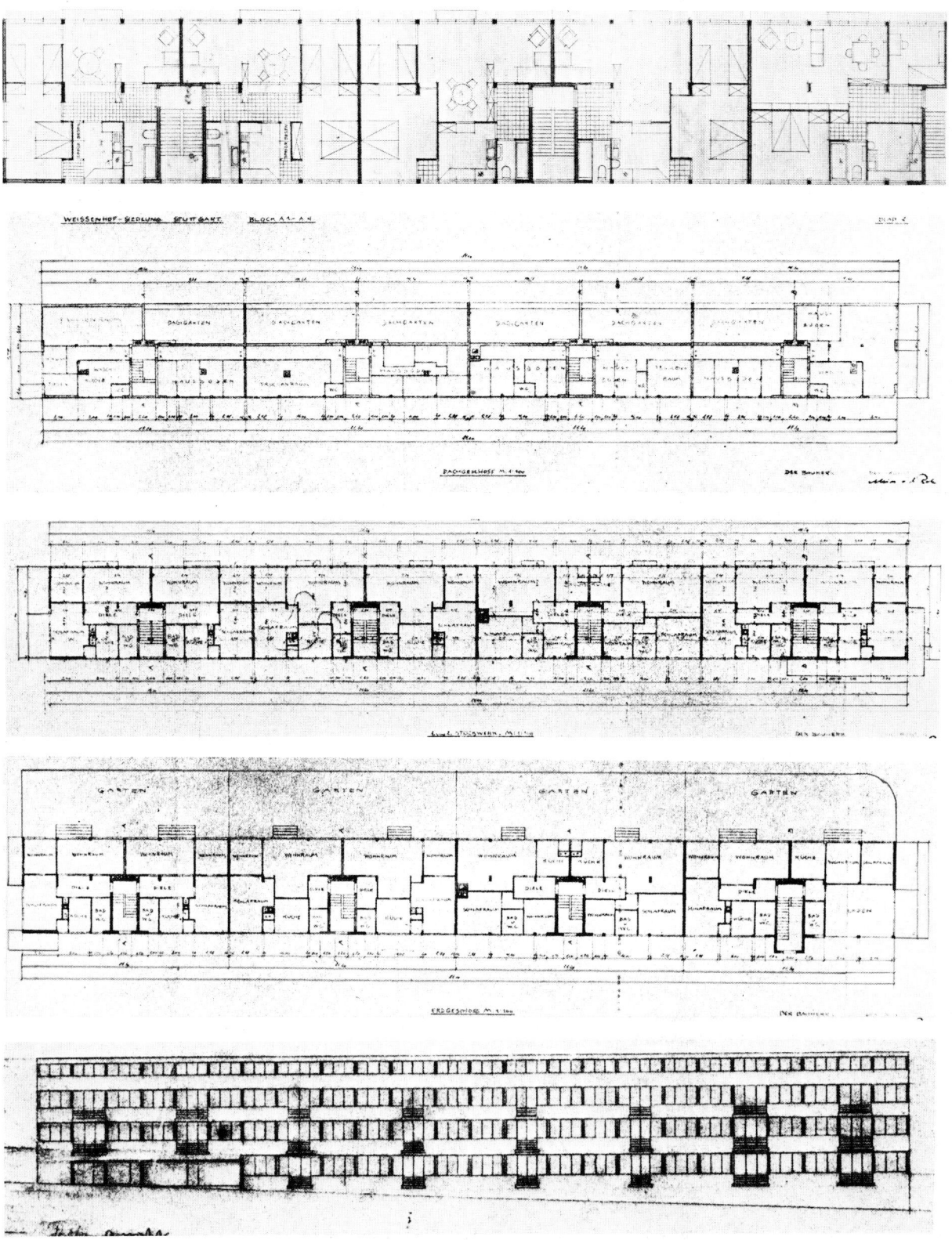

Ludwig Mies van der Rohe: first version of Houses 1–4

Floor plan study, showing an entrance lobby to each apartment, and various versions of the kitchen balcony demanded by Erna Meyer

Plan of roof level, showing roof garden and drying and storage rooms, undated, probably December 1926

Plan of upper (second or third) floor showing paired identical floor plans within each house and kitchen balconies

Plan of first floor with same floor layout as second and third floors, but with a retail unit at the south end of the block

Elevation of garden (east) front, undated

money on a conversion. Any carpenter, or any practically minded layman, would be able to shift the walls.[7]

The first version of the design as shown to city hall and the exhibition directorate differed in external and internal form, and in overall dimensions, from the building as it was finally built. Four houses, organized in mirror-image pairs, added up to a considerable length of 84 meters [275½ feet]. The apartments were not, in this first design, partitioned flexibly, but with fixed, although light, partitions. The living room differed from the other rooms only in size. The idea of using it for access to

other parts of the apartment was manifested in only one way—but this quickly attracted criticism, as he told Erna Meyer. Döcker asked Mies how "getting from the parents' and children's bedrooms to the toilet by way of the living room" was going to work; and it really was the case in this plan (House 3), that the way from the bedroom to the bathroom (which contained the toilet) was either through the living room or via the kitchen balcony and the kitchen.

In 1927 it became necessary to shorten the building by 12 meters [40 feet] to save costs,[8] and the organization of the plan changed. The principle of twinned houses was kept, but the mirror symmetry of the apartments within the houses was abandoned so that larger and smaller apartments faced each other across each stairwell.

Houses 1 through 4 are described in the official catalogue as a "Rental apartment building consisting of 4 row houses." A surviving account of the building by Mies furnishes precise information on the hot-water central heating system, the radiators, the installation of the pipes in the apartments, the design of the ceiling-high internal doors, apartment entrance doors, and external doors, the equipment of the kitchens and bathrooms, with sanitary fittings and gas cooker, and the electrical wiring: "Each room will have a light pendant and a receptacle."[9]

The contract for the work was placed on March 5 with the firm of Stephan, jointly with Stuttgarter Baugeschäft, for a price of 263,000 marks. Döcker's final accounts as superintendent, dated December 30, 1927, show the total net building cost as 310,085.63 marks.[10] Such a large increase in building costs was bound to cause unpleasantness. Mies, who had specified a price of 35 marks per cubic meter for all the prospective participant architects, found himself in the awkward position of having to depart from his own original design because of cost overruns. Worse, although his design changes were repeatedly—and urgently—asked for, they did not arrive in Stuttgart until too late. The excavations for the foundations were already complete: as a result, all work had to be halted and workers let go. The contract was at a standstill—four months before opening day.

This began a tale of woe with consequences even on a personal level; the tension between Döcker and Mies came into the open to such an extent that Döcker eventually refused to act as superintendent for this part of the project.

Not only were the excavations far advanced when the new drawings arrived, the whole planning of the project was called into question by the excessive structural loads involved. The foundations had to be reinforced; on the side facing south, toward Oud's row houses, a concrete raft was laid to bed the house firmly in the back-filled soil on which it was built. Mies had asked the city authorities for exact information on the soil structure but did not get a final answer until the middle of March, 1927, by which time a Berlin civil engineering firm had already done all the calculations.[11] Things were made worse by Mies's slowness in sending the necessary drawings; Döcker sent endless imploring cables. Mies did give instructions and send answers, but not enough to keep the work progressing briskly.[12]

When Ludwig Hilberseimer returned to Berlin in April, 1927, after spending a few days in Stuttgart, what he told Mies spurred him to action. Mies wired the exhibition directorate in Stuttgart:

Herr Hilberseimer, who has been in Stuttgart for a few days, has reported to me on the state of the works on the Weissenhof land and describes the situation as simply deplorable. In the four days of his stay he observed virtually no progress on his own house and found the speed of work on the other buildings to be equally unsatisfactory. It is his impression that the necessary steps are not being taken to ensure the punctual completion of the works, but that on the contrary progress is being blocked by passive resistance, and he has observed that my buildings appear to be singled out for particular attention in this respect. This report

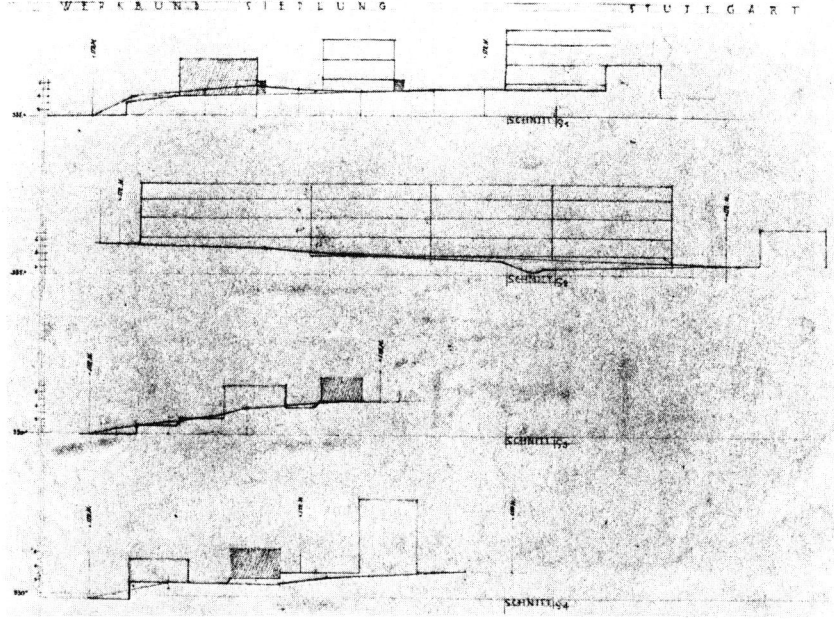

Sections, undated

Wire from Mies van der Rohe in Berlin to the exhibition directorate in Stuttgart, April 24, 1927 (for translation see text)

49

confirms my own impressions, which I have not wished to voice hitherto, in order to avoid controversy which might make matters worse. Now the situation forces me to lay such constraints aside, to make clear to you the seriousness of the situation, and to press for immediate remedial action. Herr Hilberseimer considers it absolutely essential that for every three or four buildings an additional resident architect, to be nominated by the [participant] architects, be appointed to assist Herr Döcker. Also that the architects be allowed additional visits to Stuttgart. I can only concur with these proposals and propose that funds for this purpose, which I estimate at approximately 10,000 marks, be made available. Please consider that the size of this sum bears no relationship to the damage that would result from a delay in the opening of the exhibition, and that the inadequate financial resources granted for the exhibition have already often impaired the progress of the work. I would also emphasize that I am not kept adequately informed as to the status of dealings between the city and the contractors or the practicalities of construction work on individual projects. The same goes for the architects. Thus, Stam complains forcefully that major alterations are being made to his building without his knowledge and without consultation; Poelzig and Scharoun complain that they have received no answer to repeated enquiries. A further obstacle, it seems to us, is that our intentions and our work are systematically disparaged and undermined in a way that to us seems incomprehensible. You yourselves have repeatedly been in a position to observe this. I have no alternative but to appoint, with effect from Thursday of this week, a resident architect for my own building, who will devote all his efforts to ensuring that work proceeds unhindered and according to schedule.[13]

The representative whom Mies sent to Stuttgart, to save the situation and expedite the work, was Ernst Walther. On arriving, Walther's initial reaction was that "all concerned have done their best to further the work," and that the main trouble was a shortage of building materials in southern Germany.[14] He was very soon disabused, and found himself blocked at every turn. He was refused any responsibility for the building. Deputy Mayor Sigloch came along in person and told him that he was not recognized as resident architect, and that he was to do nothing on his own authority. Walther was to work through the existing resident management—the same management that Mies had so sharply criticized in his telegram. Walther wrote to Mies: "Since the last wire the gentlemen here have not a good word to say for Herr Mies, or for Herr Hilberseimer either."[15]

The contractor, Stephan, gave an entirely different account of the reasons for the slow progress of the building work, especially the work on Mies's building. He wrote to the city architectural department:

I must stress once more that I very much regret that, on this highly important project, "rapid construction" is turning out to proceed so very slowly. If the choice of materials had been left to me, the shell of the structure would be up and roofed by now. The partitioning and the other work which Herr Mies van der Rohe wants incorporated in the completed shell would have been entirely preserved. . . . I have the impression, increasingly,

that these so-called rapid construction methods are actually techniques for building more slowly.[16]

Stephan's comment, which was echoed by his fellow contractor Gustav Epple in connection with Gropius's houses, reflects the conflict that has smoldered ever since the Renaissance between the architect who designs and the craftsman or contractor who executes. The builder is expected to follow instructions exactly, but would prefer, in the light of experience, to do things differently; the architect will not allow it. Thus, Mies strongly resisted Stephan's attempts to alter the construction of the staircases because he could not accept so wide a deviation from his plans. Over less important details such as the smoke flue or the cellar walls he did give in—even when it came to so manifest an impairment of his design as the use of single glazing in the windows in place of double glazing.[17]

At Weissenhof Walther wrestled with contractors, foremen, building code officials, and the superintendent's office, and reported back to his "Herr Bau-meister" almost daily on the progress of the work, the on-site conflicts, and his own efforts. Walther's enquiries revealed that the situation had been unclear and unsatisfactory from the very start; that Stephan's firm had subcontracted the ironwork to Stuttgarter Baugeschäft, and all concerned had been out of their depth because it was the first steel skeleton construction they had ever done and because the designs of a detail fanatic like Mies made no allowances for the robust, profit-oriented pragmatism of time and the existence of often contradictory pressures from every side. Walther wrote Mies,

It always comes to the same thing: there is always one who was never told, and one who doesn't want to know. . . . There ought to be a resident engineer in the team. . . . I hear that even one of Dr. Döcker's assistants said . . . "Let's give the man from Berlin some say in what happens; he must know best, he did do it in the first place."[18]

Walther—a pleasant man, according to Max Berling, Poelzig's resident architect—was surely one of the high-spirited volunteer firefighters who rushed to Mies's building when sunlight reflected from the red wall of Bruno Taut's house opposite appeared to set it alight.[19] No doubt, too, he was one of those resident architects who went to Mies's aid and set him free when he got struck in the narrow passageway in Le Corbusier's two-family house.[20]

Apart from the miscalculation of the load on the foundations of Mies's building, many difficulties were caused by the arbitrary changes made to the construction by the various contractors. Mies had prescribed diagonal braces to give rigidity to the skeleton, where the contractor wanted to use masonary infilling: familiar problems which were more acute then than they are now because skeleton construction in residential building was new. The column anchors were not installed as instructed:

Instead of our anchors, which pass right down into the foundations, there are only bolts, 42 cm [16½ in] long, concreted in. . . . No checking has yet begun, because contractors have not supplied the materials on which we based the load calculations asked for by the city engineer's office, but different ones. Hence the constant objections, because Dr. Schnittmann [city engineer] rightly doubts the correctness of the structural calculations.[21]

Walther's reports are richly informative, but they also betray a resigned acceptance of his own impotence. All this was to change radically when, after an on-site inspection on May 2, 1927, the city authorities agreed to appoint the additional resident architects requested by Mies. The city paid them through mid-July, although some—including Walther and Le Corbusier's resident architect, Alfred Roth—stayed on until September.[22]

Mies's relations with Döcker's team became increasingly strained, especially Mies's wire to the directorate. Mies and Döcker continued to correspond on matters of detail, and drawings were passed to and fro, but on Mies's fairly frequent visits to Stuttgart the two men avoided each other. Franz Krause, who worked in Döcker's office, seems to have taken over part of the task of dealing with Mies—and also a considerable proportion of Döcker's duties as superintendent of the project as a whole.[23]

Döcker sent out copies of Mies's wire to the other participant architects, with his own comments on its implicit accusations:

As for Herr Mies's own building, on April 21, 1927, I received the further load calculations which are important for the execution of the iron construction, but which were returned to me by the city building control office on the grounds that they were incomplete and too complicated for so simple a structure.

As Herr Mies's wire, if read between the lines, mainly consists of criticisms of me, I would like to say something about the expression "passive resistance." If my own office had not done some of the drawing work for the Mies building, the building would not be so far advanced as it now is. I feel that the less said about the drawings received for the Mies building the better.[24]

Döcker was not the only one who criticized the way Mies interpreted his position as artistic director of the exhibition: the relevant officials in City Hall, from Sigloch on down, felt the same way. Such was the mood that there was serious thought of taking the job away from Mies and giving it to Döcker. Messages to this effect reached the architects in circulars, and Mies in letters from city hall. He was accused of neglecting his responsibilities and of being far behindhand both with his own building and with the supervision of the other architects, and told that his complaints about City Hall and the superintendent were "sheer hallucinations," and that he would be held responsible for additional costs occasioned by his own dilatoriness.[25] Sigloch considered canceling the contract with Mies, and, in accordance with normal practice, took the matter up with the city attorney, Dr. Waldmüller.[26]

Feelings against Mies were still running high after the site visit on May 2, which led to a review of projected completion dates. It was now clear that neither Mies's apartment building nor Behrens's would be ready for opening day (still at that time set for July 1). Councilman Krämer, one of the council representatives on the main exhibition committee, remarked that this meant that 50 or 60 percent of the project would not be ready to go on show.[27]

When Döcker replied that at least the most interesting parts of the project, the single-family houses, would

be ready—although some had not yet even been begun—Krämer remarked that his understanding had been that "the primary idea in the whole project had been to provide cheap, modern, and large-scale housing, not houses for single families."[28] Döcker mollified him somewhat by saying that Mies's building was in four parts, and that one of these could certainly be completed in time.

The disagreements, the criticism to which Mies was subjected, and the proposal to put Döcker in instead of Mies as artistic director prompted Stotz to interpose "that Herr Mies van der Rohe has already made great sacrifices out of idealism," and that he would be making more in the future. Mies had "traveled far and wide, and gone to great expense, to obtain modern and practical constructional methods for his apartment building."[29] The main cause of all the delays, he said, lay in the tardiness of the city departments responsible in dealing with the whole matter, added to by the constant rain.

To remedy the delays the builders worked double shifts, and all the architects were asked to appoint resident associates of their own choice to supervise the work.[30] Walther and Roth, who were already at work, were confirmed in office and had their pay backdated.

The unedifying and damaging quarrel between Döcker and Mies was laid to rest on May 13, 1927, by a letter from Bruckmann to all the architects and to the city administration:

As chairman of the Deutscher Werkbund I am anxious to clarify the situation by stating the following facts:

Herr Mies van der Rohe is charged with the direction of the Werkbund exhibition. In this respect nothing has changed. At the meeting on May 3, Dr. Döcker was confirmed in the authority and the duty previously conferred on him, as superintendent architect in charge of building operations for the Weissenhof project, to set up a technical office on the site and to engage further representatives of the participating architects to assist him, in order to make it possible to finish the projected buildings punctually. There has been no change whatever in the authority or the responsibilities involved. Herr Mies van der Rohe is now, as before, in overall charge.[31]

Among Mies's papers there are a number of drafts for this letter of Bruckmann's; all are in Mies's own handwriting.

The division of responsibility had been reaffirmed, but feelings still ran high. Döcker disowned any responsibility for Mies's apartment building; and City Hall was in no mood to do Mies any favors whatever, as the disagreements over its painting were to make only too clear.

Mies now received an ultimatum to submit an overall design for the outdoor works on the Weissenhof development for city approval by June 10, failing which—or

Handwritten draft by Mies van der Rohe for Bruckmann's letter of May 13, 1927

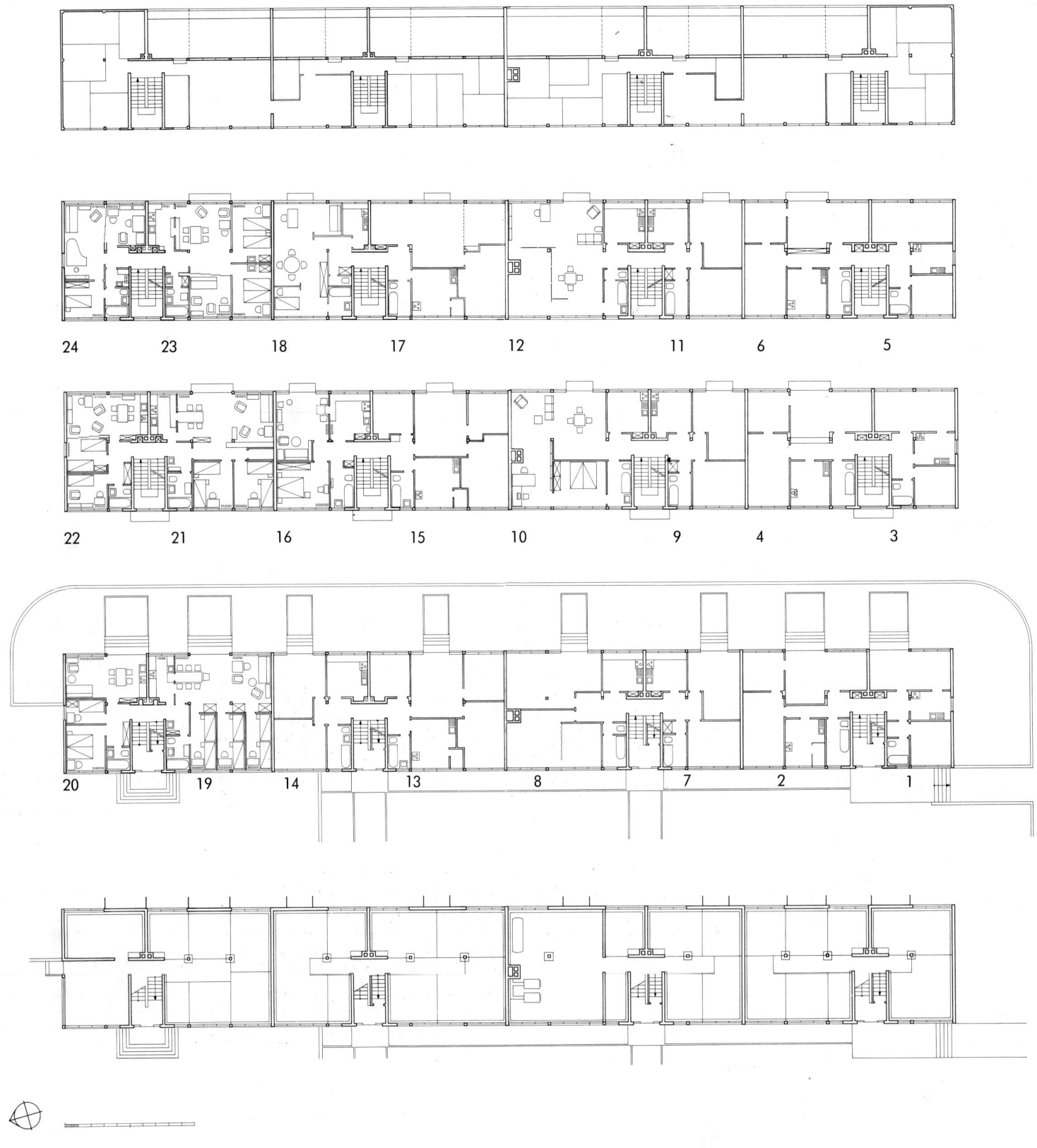

24   23   18   17   12   11   6   5

22   21   16   15   10   9   4   3

20   19   14   13   8   7   2   1

Houses 1, 2, 3, 4
Architect: Ludwig
Mies van der Rohe
Plans and elevations
drawn from the archi-
tect's building code
submissions of March
22, 1927

Roof level with roof
garden, lofts, laun-
dries, drying rooms

Third floor with interi-
ors by (left to right):
(24) Schweizer Werk-
bund, (23) Schweizer
Werkbund, (18) Rasch
brothers, (17) Arthur
Korn, (12) Mies, (11)
Mies (empty), (5) Fer-
dinand Kramer, (6)
Ferdinand Kramer

Second floor with in-
teriors by: (22) Sch-
weizer Werkbund,
(21) Schweizer Werk-
bund, (16) Franz
Schuster, (15) Adolf
G. Schneck, (10)
Mies, (9) Erich Dieck-
mann, (4) Adolf Mey-
er (empty), (3) Adolf
Meyer

First floor with interi-
ors by: (20) Schweizer
Werkbund, (19) Sch-
weizer Werkbund,
(14) Camille Graeser,
(13) Max Hoene (Bay-
erische Hausratshil-
fe), (8) Lilly Reich, (7)
Rudolf Frank, (2)
Richard Lisker,

(1) "Apartment of the
Professional Wom-
an" by Hans Zimmer-
mann (kitchen),
Reinhold and Marga-
rete Stotz (bedroom),
Walter Schneider (liv-
ing room)

Cellar floor with retail
unit and ancillary
rooms (north end),
store cellars and
heating

This page: elevations
from north, south,
east, west

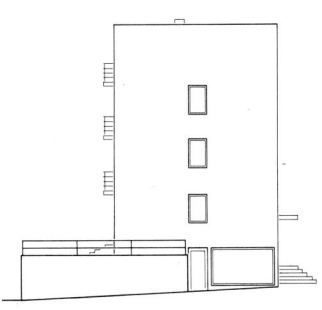

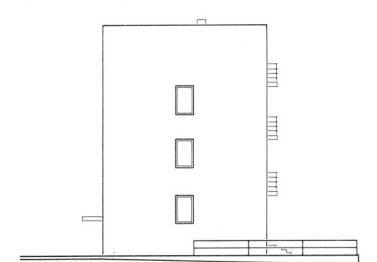

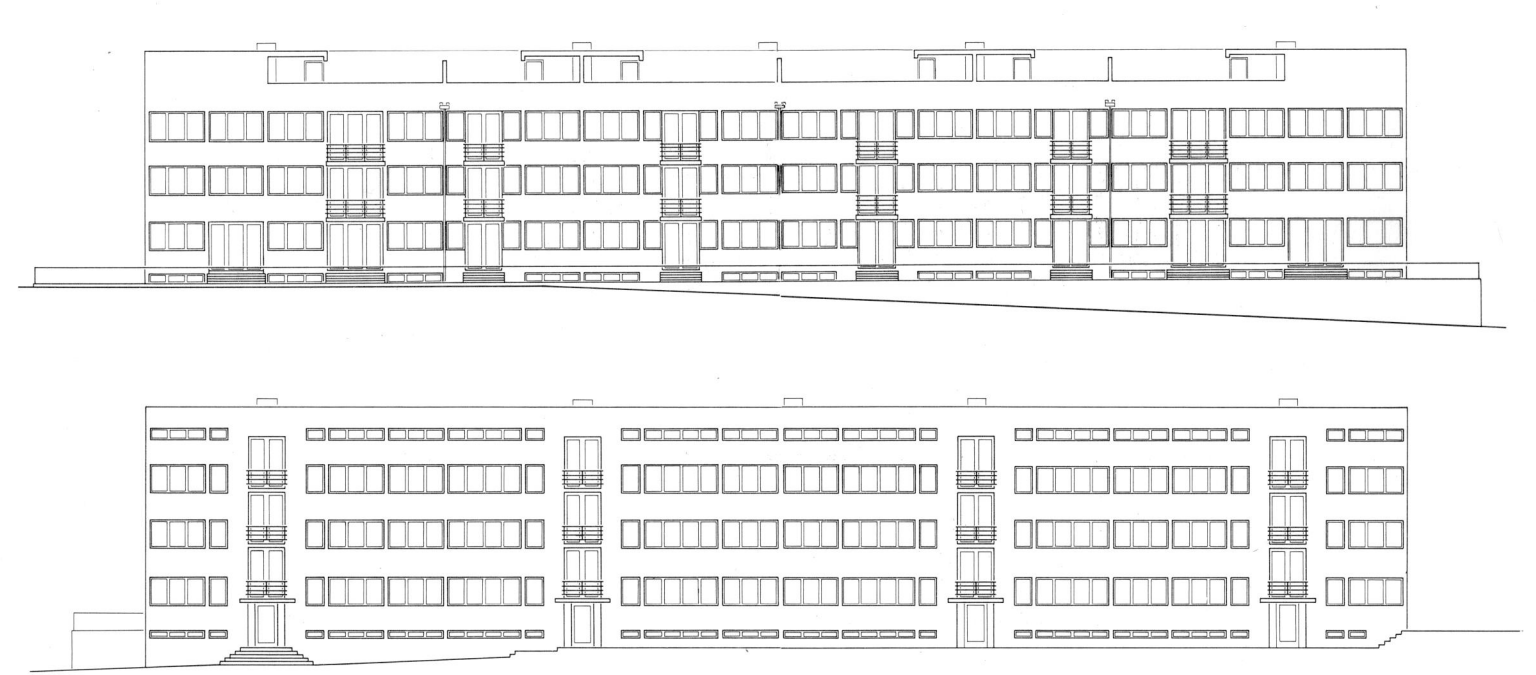

53

if the plan were to be too expensive—the city as ultimate client for the project would make its own decision on who should make the design, and how.[32] No secret was made of the fact that the person whom City Hall had in mind for this was Döcker.

As far as City Hall was concerned, Mies failed the test. He did send a letter in due time, on June 9, in which he gave information on the overall color scheme for the project, and mentioned some outdoor features; but otherwise he limited himself to a brief account of his own on-site work on landscaping. Mies wanted to explain himself on the spot; but City Hall, and Döcker, wanted plans. A senior official of the city architectural department, one Baurat Faerber, wrote on the margin of the letter: "Drawing required! So this is the plan requested for 10th inst. for the environmental works, terracings, boundary and retaining walls, landscaping, and color scheme. Please advise whether Herr Döcker is now to be commissioned to draw up the plans."[33]

What were Mies's instructions as to the color scheme? The answer will amaze anyone who has lived through the long debates in recent years over color in the Weissenhof project, and who now goes to look at them in their renovated (not "restored"!) state. Mies instructed "that all the buildings in the Weissenhof project except those of Max Taut and Bruno Taut be painted off-white. . . . I have arranged for sample patches to be painted on, and when I am next there, in the course of the coming week, I shall make a final choice."[34]

Whether Mies rethought the colors in conjunction with the architects in mid-June, and whether the various tints added to the white were suggested, supervised, or approved by him, is not known. One thing that is certain, however, is that his own building was not painted at all. Mies's surviving papers and the meticulous records kept by the city of Stuttgart reveal that two or three weeks after opening day (July 23, 1927) Mies's building was still not ready, that the final stages of the work were overrunning, and that Döcker's refusal to take responsibility for this building as he did for the others was a contributory cause of the delay.

In mid-August, Mies wanted to have his building scaffolded in order to apply the paint. It must have come as a great surprise to find how unanimously the city side closed ranks to frustrate him. Dr. Waldmüller, the city attorney, wrote in person to the exhibition directorate: "I have expressly forbidden it [the painting work], because I would regard it as a positive catastrophe for anyone to see scaffolding on this building now, even if only on one part of it."[35] This and the orders of Deputy Mayor Sigloch were enough to quash Mies's proposal to scaffold the four houses one at a time for painting.[36] The city council building committee confirmed the decision: it resolved "No Painting."[37]

All this sounds very like revenge—among other things, for the obduracy with which Mies had refused to grant permission to the tenant of the neighboring Schönblick Restaurant (built for the Bau- und Heimstättenverein by an architect, Karl Beer, who was also the SPD leader on the council and a member of the building committee) to run a line of telephone posts the length of Mies's apartment building. When posts were erected, Mies had them torn down so that from the beginning of August onward the restaurant was cut off. The matter was not cleared up until September, 1927, when the exhibition directorate announced that a telephone line had been installed.[38]

Over the matter of the painting of the walls, City Hall remained implacable; but by patient attention to detail Walther was able to deal with a number of Mies's other complaints. The wrong windows had been delivered, and details of the interior fittings did not conform to the plans: they were replaced.

On September 6, 1927, Mies's building, together with a number of other buildings, was declared "ready for exhibition." On September 9, Walther sent to Berlin some first reactions from visitors: "The general reaction of visitors to Houses 1 through 4 is good. The floor plans are very much liked . . . as for practical experience, I will report in Berlin."[39]

In 1986, when Mies van der Rohe would have been one hundred years old, Deutsche Bundespost brought out a postage stamp in his honor, and all over the world he was commemorated as a great twentieth-century architect. But in 1927 the overall direction of the Werkbund exhibition was very nearly taken away from him and handed over to Richard Döcker. Stotz and Bruckmann—with some others—stood by Mies, preventing

what now seems like an act of blasphemy.

From his holiday retreat on the island of Sylt, Mies let City Hall know what was on his mind:

> The whole trouble with this exhibition is that our work was initially delayed because people without sufficient professional knowledge found fault with our decisions.
>
> I reserve the right to publish in the architectural press the constructional decisions which we took, and which you presume to criticize, as well as the way in which the matter has been dealt with in practice in Stuttgart.[40]

THE INTERIORS OF MIES'S APARTMENT BUILDING

Mies had declared it his policy to satisfy the requirements of rationalization, standardization, and freedom in the internal division of space through the use of a steel skeleton constructional system with panel walls and continuous window bands; but true flexibility remained to be demonstrated in the detail of the interiors, through the floor plans and furnishings of the individual apartments.

Limited in this only by the fixed position of the stairwells and of the kitchen and bathroom in each apartment, he set out to realize his own concept of "freedom of use," which resided in the combination of maximum flexibility in the interior with a strictly articulated, well-proportioned overall external form. The Mies building as a whole, which from a planning point of view served as the backbone of the whole Weissenhofsiedlung, worked internally as an ordering, unifying force: multiplicity in unity, and multiplicity also beyond that unity.

Once Mies had made up his mind to build a large-scale structure with varied internal plans, and satisfied himself that his conception would work, he needed to prove that the internal partitions could be intelligently resited, not only by him but by any other architect or interested person. Eschewing long-winded explanations, Mies let visitors enter his very austere-looking building and experience for themselves the variety of interior design possibilities that existed within it.

The work was done by architects and interior designers of Mies's choice, working either individually or collectively on one or more apartments. The largest collective was the thirteen-strong Schweizer Werkbund group, which designed six apartments; the smallest was a group of three designers, commissioned by the Commission of Stuttgart Housewives, who did one room each: the kitchen, living room and bedroom of Apartment 1, "The Apartment for a Professional Woman."[41]

Mies assigned the jobs, specified materials, supplied technical data, and passed on to the designers the guidelines supplied by Erna Meyer and the Stuttgart housewives' organizations. Only a few of these sets of instructions have survived, but we may assume that each designer received his or her own. Individual licence was forestalled, partly by the choice of designers, and partly by Mies's excellent advice to use "furniture off the peg." In four cases designers included furniture that they themselves had previously designed "for the low-cost home" or for issue by local and regional government bodies. Mies's word for all this was Konfektion: ready-made. He himself did the interior design for two apartments, and left a third unfurnished to demonstrate his system of movable partitions.

Not all the interior designs for the building can now be visualized; some of them seem to have been decidedly unattractive, so much so that no photographs exist. However, the official catalogue contains precise specifications of design and furnishing work. All the designers are listed, with the work they did, and so are all the suppliers.

With the exception of those in House 4, designed by the Schweizer Werkbund, all the internal doors go right up to the ceiling. When Deputy Mayor Sigloch asked Mies why this was so, Mies is said to have answered, "That's the way I do it. You can do it some other way."[42]

The process of selecting the interior designers—as we shall call them here, for simplicity's sake, although not all of them would have described that as their principal occupation—was a much less dramatic story than that of selecting the Weissenhof architects, although it was not without its bruised feelings and its displays of temperament. The designers were chosen partly from the local Stuttgart membership of the Werkbund and partly from Mies's own circle of friends and professional acquaintances in Berlin. In making his choice, Mies set out to demonstrate some of the exemplary efforts toward simplicity in interior design that had been made in various parts of the Reich, and how good-looking simple furniture could be.

Mies himself avoided trying his hand at designing "low-cost articles of furniture"; however hard he might have tried to keep them modest, they probably would have come out looking like luxury articles. He wanted to show furnishings for the simple life, but he did not want to design them. Perhaps, too, he knew only too well that the clean lines of these designs, many of them by highly creative designers like Ferdinand Kramer, actually postulate users who are familiar with creative thought processes, rather than people who know themselves to be disadvantaged and who tend to resent, as patronizing, any attempt to deny them a touch of Chippendale or German Renaissance. But Mies cannot fairly be accused of abdicating his responsibilities in the interior design of the twenty-four apartments in his building.[43] Here he let others do their part of the work in their own different ways, precisely in order to show that his part had been well done.

The interior designers were chosen considerably later than the participant architects, at a stage when there was something to be seen of most of the houses, if only from the shape of the scaffolding. As a basis for their work the designers were sent, together with the invitations, details of intended materials, the decor, and drawings for each apartment. Erna Meyer's practical guidelines for kitchen and bathroom were also enclosed. Designs were to be sent to Stuttgart, where Gustaf Stotz took the decisions on what was to be accepted and what was not.

Not all the interior designers whom Mies approached for his building actually took part. In some

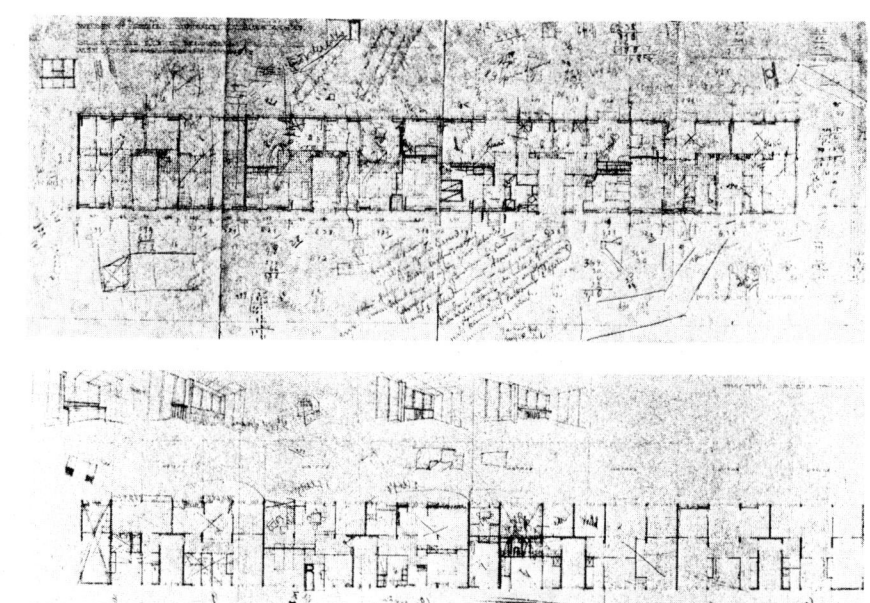

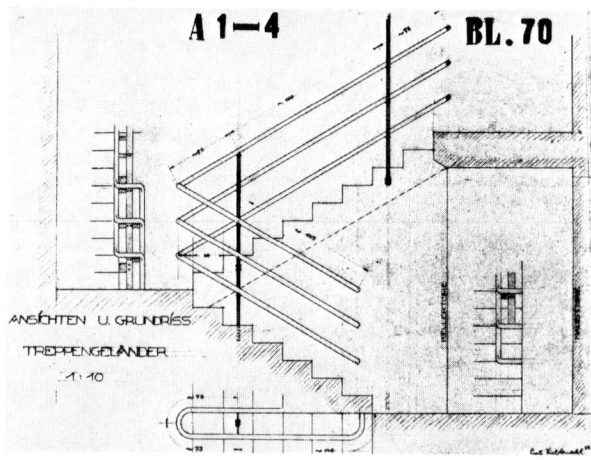

Ludwig Mies van der Rohe: floor plan sketches

Details of stairs

Interior perspective

Furniture studies

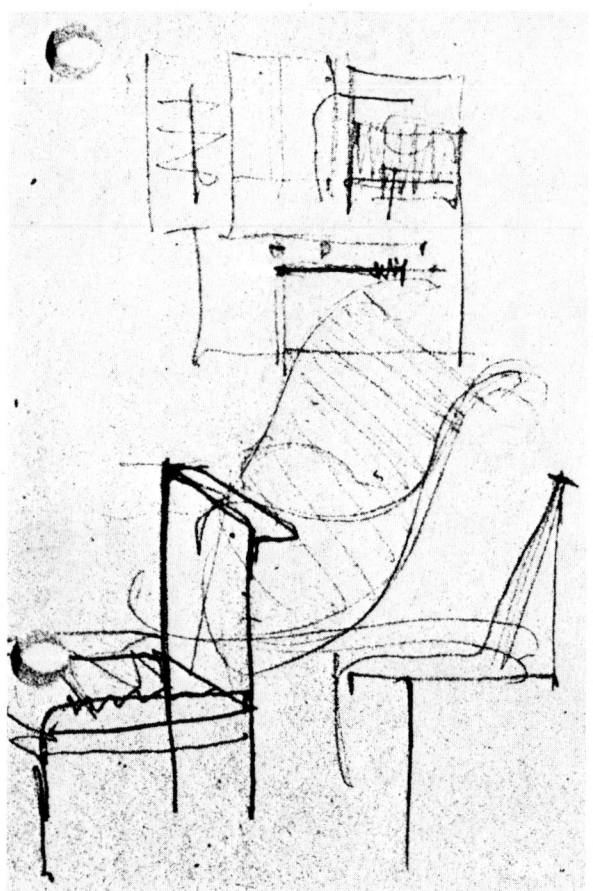

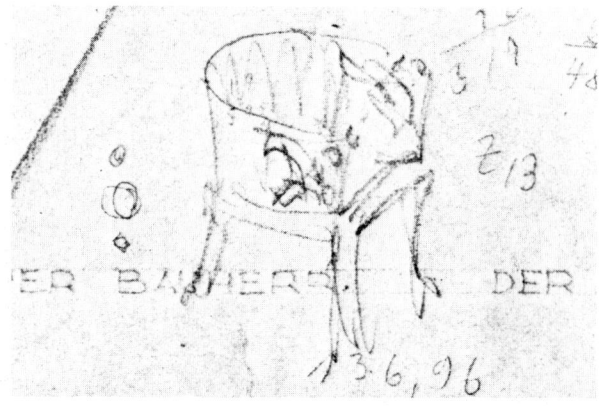

well-known cases the grounds for their refusal are of some interest, as there has been speculation about the reasons for their absence from the Weissenhof project as a whole. The brothers Wassili (1889–1972) and Hans (1890–1954) Luckhardt shared an avowedly Modernist architectural office in Berlin with Alfons Anker. Their names had appeared on Lists II, III, and IV of possible architects for Weissenhof houses, though far down the list, between No.18 and No.20. On April 11, 1927, their names appeared, assigned to Mies's building, on the list of interior designers that Mies sent to A&T, the Stuttgart exhibitions and conventions office;[44] there is no indication of which apartment was assigned to them, although the correspondence shows that it was to have three rooms.[45]

The negotiations reached the stage of looking for a maker for the Luckhardts' furniture designs; but they rejected every firm that was suggested. The failure to find the right manufacturer may have been one reason for their withdrawal. Another could well have been a lack of commitment on the Stuttgart side; or maybe the Luckhardts found something better to do. On May 30, 1927, they sent back the drawings "with kind regards."[46]

Martin Wagner, an old comrade-in-arms of Mies's since the days of Der Zehnerring and now city architect in Berlin, was another who was invited to participate. He declined on the grounds that he had no suitable work to hand over at the moment.[47] Another who was invited, Richard L. F. Schulz, a member of the Deutscher Werkbund since 1908 and a former board member, accepted and then withdrew. Walther asked him to return the drawings, but no further correspondence is to be found.

Another architect selected for the work was Gustav Lüdecke. When Mies wrote to ask him for details of internal walls and floor coverings, Lüdecke wrote back, "I have to tell you that as far as I am concerned the commission to design the apartment interiors is at an end, in that I have been notified by the exhibition directorate that my proposals are rejected. The question of further wall and flooring details consequently does not arise."[48] Stotz subjected everything to relentless scrutiny, and Mies accepted his decisions.

HOUSE 1, MIES VAN DER ROHE BUILDING

Apartment 1, first floor right

The interior design of the "Apartment for a Professional Woman" has been assembled by the representatives of the Professional Women and of the Housewives' Commissions from designs by the architects Hans Zimmermann, Stuttgart (kitchen), R. & M. Stotz, Kirchheim unter Teck (bedroom), and Walter Schneider, Stuttgart (living room).
The accommodation comprises: kitchen, bathroom, one bedroom, one living room.[49]

Hans Zimmermann—the brother of the kitchen expert, Hilde Zimmermann—was someone who might have seemed destined for greater things. He had worked under Bonatz, Bruno Paul, Behrens, Taut, and Hoffmann;[50] and Le Corbusier had recommended him to a prospective client in Stuttgart.[51] No photographs of the kitchen, or of the bedroom—designed by two former students of Schneck's, Margret and Reinhold Stotz—have survived. Both Walter Schneider and Reinhold Stotz had previously been noticed as designers of add-on furniture,[52] so objects of this kind were presumably used through-

out the "Apartment for a Professional Woman."

The flooring material throughout, including the kitchen, appears to have been "a light yellow linoleum that shows every mark . . . a nuisance for the housewife," according to the survey of residents' opinions published in 1929.[53]

Apartment 2, first floor left

Interior design: Richard Lisker, Frankfurt am Main, Bockenheimer Landstrasse 101.
The accommodation comprises: kitchen, bathroom, living room, two bedrooms.[54]

Richard Lisker, a member of the Werkbund since 1912, holds a special position among the interior designers connected with Weissenhof. He was a painter by training who had specialized in the design and making of blue-ground printed fabrics, and had founded workshops for two-dimensional design, textile printing and batik. In 1924 he was appointed to a teaching post at the Städelschule, the Frankfurt college of applied arts, and worked at Haus Werkbund—an annual design show at the Frankfurt Trade Fair—alongside Lilly Reich, who proposed him for the design of an apartment in the Mies building.

After Reich moved from Frankfurt to Berlin in the fall of 1926, she stayed in touch by letter. Writing to Lisker's wife about a carpet design for Mies's Wolff house in Guben, she added,

Mies has just asked me to ask Lisker whether he would not like to do the interior design, furnish-

Apartment 1:
Living room by Walter Schneider

Apartment 2:
Bedroom by Richard Lisker

ings, etc., for one of the small apartments in the Mies apartment building. It is a rush job, but the floor plans are very nice, and there wouldn't be much furniture.[55]

Lisker accepted. It was presumably the exhibition directorate that passed on his furniture designs to the firms of Hermann Maier (for the bedrooms) and M. Kohler (for the living room and chairs).[56]

This apartment was described in a retrospective survey of the Weissenhof project that appeared in the *Frankfurter Zeitung* on November 10, 1927. After the well-known cry of "We want a home to live in, not a machine room," the writer inserted just one qualification:

> To be fair to the exhibition: among the many different interior designs that were shown in the Mies van der Rohe apartment building, there was *one* first-floor apartment (by a Frankfurt interior designer, Richard Lisker) that in its unpretentious way did show something of what we mean. Here was some hint of a desire for (let us not be afraid of using the simple-minded, but tried and tested, word) *Gemütlichkeit.*[57]

This interior was not Lisker's only contribution to the 1927 Werkbund exhibition. At the request of the exhibition's press officer, Werner Graeff,[58] he contributed an article on fabrics and wall-coverings to the latter's Werkbund book on Weissenhof interiors, *Innenräume.* After describing the predilection of "modern architects" for white or monochrome walls and monochrome textiles, Lisker went on:

> This form of expression is limited by its nature and represents only a fraction of the possibilities that surface design offers as an expressive resource and as a component of spatial design. The use of large plywood wall panels, with their beautiful figure; the breaking up of the smooth paint surface; and the preference for interesting weaves in textiles, show that there is a gradual tendency to return to the intimate charm of surface patterns.[59]

Apartment 3, second floor right

Interior design: Professor Adolf Meyer, architect, Frankfurt am Main, Neue Mainzer Strasse 47.
The accommodation comprises: kitchen, bathroom, bedroom, living room.

Apartment 4, second floor left

Room layout: Professor Adolf Meyer, architect, Frankfurt am Main, Neue Mainzer Strasse 47.
The accommodation comprises: kitchen, bathroom, living room, two bedrooms.[60]

Adolf Meyer, best remembered as Walter Gropius's partner, was a former student and associate of Behrens and an instructor at the Weimar Bauhaus. When the Bauhaus moved from Weimar to Dessau in 1925, Meyer did not follow; but contacts were maintained. He became a planning architect (Baurat) at the Frankfurt city architect's department, and in 1927 he took charge of the structural engineering class at the Städtische Technische Hochschule in Frankfurt.

When he was invited to work at Weissenhof,[61] he tried to get Oskar Schlemmer to paint one wall in his three-room apartment, the unfurnished Apartment 4. Schlemmer agreed in principle, but asked about the fee. Meyer wrote Mies,

> Now it all comes down to the cost, as Herr Schlemmer cannot afford to be out of pocket. Might it be possible for the Werkbund exhibition to find some money, and what kind of sum can we assume? I would regard Schlemmer's participation as an enrichment of the exhibition, and I would be very glad if you could find a way to make the work possible.[62]

Mies replied by return of post,

> Money for painting the walls of the rooms is not available. Nor is there any prospect of making any funds liquid for this purpose. I am sorry not to be able to give you a better answer.[63]

So Schlemmer never got a chance to contribute to the Weissenhofsiedlung. Even if his mural painting had been short-lived, it would have been recorded in photographs, and these would thus have afforded us a glimpse of the room spaces laid out by Meyer in Apartment 4, which have now vanished without trace.

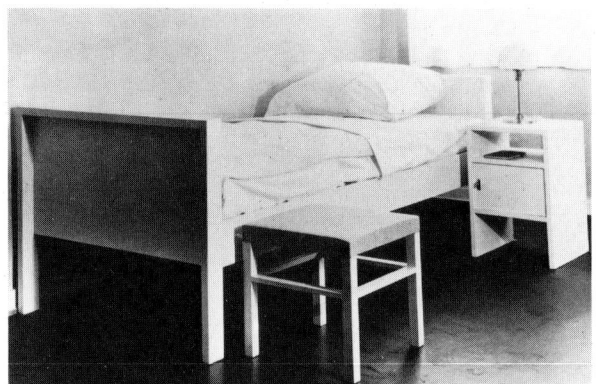

Apartments 5 and 6:

Standard bed, stool, and bedside table, by Ferdinand Kramer

Living room with extending table, chairs, and adjustable ceiling light, by Ferdinand Kramer

No designs for Meyer's furniture are available—none, at any rate, that can be ascribed with certainty to his work for Weissenhof.

Apartment 5, third floor right

Interior design: Dipl.-Ing. F. Kramer, architect, Frankfurt am Main, Oppenheimer Strasse 44.
The accommodation comprises: kitchen, bathroom, bedroom, living room.

Apartment 6, third floor left

Interior design: Dipl.-Ing. F. Kramer, architect, Frankfurt am Main, Oppenheimer Strasse 44.
The accommodation comprises: kitchen, bathroom, living room, two bedrooms.[64]

As late as 1968, Ferdinand Kramer was gratified to discover that he had been seriously considered for the list of "building architects" for Weissenhof: among the top 14 in Lists I through III, dropping to 16 in List IV and to 19 in List V. His astonishment at having been included, however briefly, in the inner circle of Weissenhof architects proves how secret the selection process was kept, and how few people were involved in the compilation of the successive lists.

Having—for whatever reasons—not invited Kramer to build a house of his own, Mies and Stotz were all the more anxious to secure his participation in the interior design. One of Oud's houses, and two apartments in the Mies building, were entrusted to him. He also contributed to the demonstration of the Frankfurt *Plattenhaus* on the test lot adjoining Weissenhof.

Kramer's furniture for the house by Oud was made in Frankfurt by the same firm that made Grete Schütte-Lihotzky's Frankfurt Kitchen; but the pieces in Kramer's Mies apartments were mostly made to his designs by firms in Stuttgart or elsewhere in Württemberg.[65] He wrote of his furniture designs for Hausrat GmbH, a city-run project for the unemployed,

> In 1925 I had won a competition organized by Hausrat GmbH to furnish a three-room apartment, kitchen, bedroom, and living room, with standardized furniture. This was chest furniture in plywood, a material with which Karl Schmidt of Hellerau, the "Goethe of Woodwork," had experimented after World War I, in which it had been carried to a peak of perfection in aircraft building. Light, movable pieces, able to be combined as the need arose, and low in cost, instead of the solid wood suites that had previously been customary as status symbols.[66]

In 1927 Paul Renner wrote an account of Kramer's furniture for the Werkbund periodical, *Die Form:*

> With intense concentration, he thinks through the issues of practicality and of potential innovations in material and technique. His furniture represents the last word in comfort. But his head is free of Mondrian, free of all the narcotics that emanate from the intellectual contortions of the theorists. His thinking does not stop at thought, but is completely absorbed by the object of that thought, the concrete piece of work—and no veil comes between that work and his artist's eye. The resulting forms are classics in a contemporary vein. Kramer's furniture is the best domestic equipment imaginable for the simple, cubic, reliefless rooms of the modern house, with the flush plywood panels of its doors; they are instinct with the modern sense of style with which the occupants of these houses clothe their own fit, athletic bodies.[67]

Unfortunately, the apartment floor plans which Kramer drew up for Mies have not survived, but we have a record of the decisions he made in planning the interior design:

> Those are all the changes I have made, except for the kitchen in the two-room apartment [6], which I have widened to a minimum width of 2 meters [6½ feet]. I prefer one door to the lobby and one to the living room. Please specify the internal measurements of the doorways. My kitchen cabinet is 55 centimeters [21½ inches] deep. The power and light receptacles are visible. Please build the electric lights into the ceilings using sockets flush with the upper surface of the ceiling. As this is a multistory building, cannot the gas meter be put on the stairs? By when do you need the details of the treatment of the walls?[68]

The furniture in the children's room was painted in gray-white lacquer; the table was covered with linoleum, the extending table was made of oak, and the chairs had rush seats.[69]

In 1933, Kramer resigned from the Deutscher Werkbund, of which he had been a member since 1920. Its administrator, Otto Baur, who remained in his post after the Nazi takeover, wrote back to ask for "the reasons that have led to this decision" and signed his letter "With a German salute."[70]

HOUSE 2, MIES VAN DER ROHE BUILDING

This house contained a communal laundry incorporating an automatic water heater, a hand-operated washing machine, an electrically powered spin-dryer, and a wall-mounted ironing assembly. The exhibition directorate told the mayor of Stuttgart that the special feature of House 2 was the demonstration of movable partitions.[71]

Apartment 7, first floor right

Interior decoration: Rudolf Frank, architect, Stuttgart, Kunstgewerbeschule.
The accommodation comprises: kitchen, bathroom, bedroom, living room.[72]

The invitation to Rudolf Frank came from the exhibition directorate—that is, from Gustaf Stotz—at the prompting of Stotz's friend Schneck. Frank had been an assistant of Schneck's, and an instructor at the Kunstgewerbeschule, since 1924.[73] His name was one of those that Schneck had already mentioned in connection with the building, in the letter he wrote to Mies to recommend a number of his own students, "among them Herr Frank, whose competence is already known to you."[74]

Rudolf Frank designed a two-room apartment of which, sadly, no record remains, either in photographs or in drawings. Only the information in the official catalogue reveals the names of the firms involved, and the fact that Frank designed the lighting fitments himself.

The position of the apartment designed by Frank

corresponds to that mentioned in the anecdote of the apartment that was believed to be on fire when it caught the reflection of the sun from Bruno Taut's red wall.

Apartment 8, first floor left

Interior design: Lilly Reich, Berlin W 35, Genthinerstrasse 40.
The accommodation comprises: kitchen, bathroom, two living rooms, one bedroom.[75]

Lilly Reich was the most important of the women concerned with the Weissenhof project and the indoor exhibitions. (Another woman involved in the interior design was Margret Stotz; Else Oppler-Legband was assigned an apartment in Behrens's building, but for unknown reasons she did not do the work.)

Lilly Reich was a member of the Werkbund from 1912 onward. She was a national board member for many years, and together with Richard L. F. Schulz she ran the Werkbund's trade fair showplace in Frankfurt, Haus Werkbund. Ferdinand Kramer was to recall,

Lilly Reich was put forward by the Deutscher Werkbund as a selector to pick out "Werkbundworthy" artifacts from the objects on show, and to diplay them for the benefit of producers and consumers at Haus Werkbund: it was an experiment in aesthetic education that stemmed from the catalogue, *Deutsches Warenbuch*, published in 1916 on the initiative of Karl Schmidt of Hellerau. Haus Werkbund had a street frontage with display windows in which the selected goods were arranged by Lilly Reich, by R.L.F. Schulz—a member of the Werkbund from Berlin—and by myself. I found it absorbing work, and I learned a great deal from both of them.[76]

Lilly Reich's sure taste, instinctive appreciation of quality, and decisive choices were the reason why she was chosen to design the indoor part of the 1927 Werkbund exhibition in Stuttgart. She clearly was a fascinating, self-assured, intelligent woman, "emancipated by nature" at a time when women's equality was beginning

to be recognized. She did pioneer work, achieved professional recognition, and worked with men on equal terms. One year older than Mies, Lilly Reich would have been 100 years old in 1985; but no articles were written, no commemorative events arranged. She has always been regarded mainly as Mies's collaborator and lover, his alter ego, a vine entwined around the figure of a great man.

Mies, who was not a member of the Werkbund until the early 1920s, had met Lilly Reich at various committee meetings, exhibitions, and receptions. Stotz once tried to get him along to a garden party by promising that Reich would be there.[77] That was during the preparatory work for the 1927 exhibition, when Mies and Reich got to know one another better; they thenceforth worked side by side, both on joint and separate projects. (Mies had been separated from his wife since the early 1920s.) Apart from designing the exhibitions in the Gewerbehalle and subsidiary halls, Lilly Reich did the interior design for one apartment in Mies's building and helped Mies with the design of the apartment that he himself designed.

On August 27, 1927, four weeks after the exhibition opened, Lilly Reich wrote Gustaf Stotz's wife (a former singer, Erna Elmenreich) a letter which gives an idea of the division of labor between her and Mies, and the way in which color schemes and matters of detail were decided in the course of work on the interior design of the apartments:

Enclosed, as promised, the sketches for the furnishings of our apartments. I hope you can make sense of them. In my apartment everything is clear, because the furniture is already there; all that is still missing is the Thonet [bentwood] chairs, which will be here within the next ten days. All that is still missing is the big cheval mirror and the glass-topped table in the dressing room, but I hope that Arnold [of Schorn-dorf] will let me have the stand for the mirror. Reisser has already promised me the mirror itself, and I'll ask Schorn-dorf for the little table. For a desk chair, put a black Thonet chair in for the time being, or else a Rockhausen chair out of the exhibition; I hope to

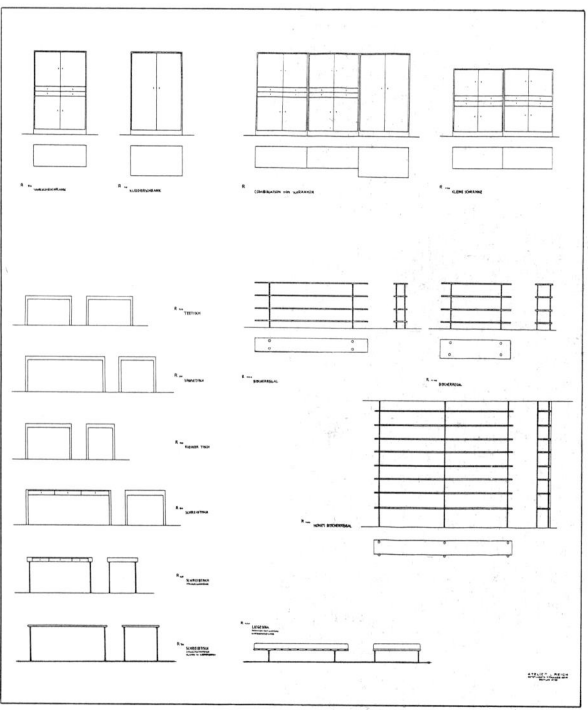

Lilly Reich: table and closets, undated

Apartment 8: Living room by Lilly Reich with MR chairs

Apartment 8:

Living room by Lilly Reich with "writing desk 150 × 70 cm [59 × 27½ inches], Net price 85 marks; tea table 70 × 45 cm [27½ × 18 inches], fumed oak, net price 48 marks"

Dressing room by Lilly Reich, seen from bed alcove: "MR Stool, white linoleum, white velvet drapes, yellow armchair. Large bed alcove separated from dressing room only by drapes"

Dining alcove by Lilly Reich

61

be able to put in a metal chair later on. For the lighting, BZ are letting me have 3 Poulsen lamps and a ceiling light with a nickel rim. In the little lobby there will be a big wall mirror by Reisser, and pegs for clothes.

Mies's second-floor apartment [10] is also complete except for the Thonet chairs; however, they go with the desk, because the one I looked at can't be used, so I hope Arnold will make us one of the tables instead; he has the drawings already. Then one of the new metal chairs will go with it. The books are also important; I would like some for my apartment too, please, and also for the [Mies] apartment on the third floor.

On the third floor there is another difficulty. I don't think there will be room in the bedroom for the chests of drawers, in which case they will have to be omitted altogether, or you must try to fit them in along the window wall behind the dining table.

There may also be difficulty in finding room for the two closets. If it's really too cramped, then make it just one. The writing desk and chair for this apartment should be the metal furniture from Schorndorf, likewise the dining chairs.[78]

Among Lilly Reich's papers—which, fittingly, are united with Mies's in The Museum of Modern Art, New York—there is a drawing juxtaposing a number of tables and closets, which might well be contemporary with the Weissenhof project. Unfortunately, it is not dated, so that it is impossible to be certain. The tables in the drawing correspond to those in the photographs, but the closets do not. No metal writing desks were exhibited.

Whether Lilly Reich was concerned in the design of Mies's furniture must be left for a later, detailed consideration. It seems unlikely, however, that a woman like Lilly Reich would have written "MR Stool" on the back of a photograph of her dressing room if—as has been alleged—the stool in question were not by Mies at all but designed by her, together with the whole accompanying range of tubular steel furniture. The question "Was it Lilly?"[79] went around the world in 1977, was indignantly negatived, and was as firmly answered in the affirmative.

The mood that emerges from the color indications for the dressing room is subtle and distinguished, based on exquisite materials: the "MR Stool," the full-length mirror, and the long, low closet in choice veneer are set off by a white linoleum floor, white velvet drapes, and a yellow chair. It can be assumed that the walls were white, so that the yellow chair—possibly in leather—stood as the only color accent in a white varied only by differences in texture and lighting. Lilly Reich was known for her sensitive use of materials, especially textiles.[80]

Then there was the arrangement of mirror, shelf, and pegs, used in Lilly Reich's entrance lobby, but manufactured for bathroom use by the Stuttgart firm of Reisser, "wholesalers and manufacturers of hygienic installations" (still existent today). Using a form of alienation, she diverted objects from the realm of sanitary engineering where form already followed function, to give them different functions in the context of an elegant interior design. Mart Stam, too, built his first cantilever chair out of gas piping!

In a newspaper article published in 1927, Siegfried Kracauer wrote, "The precise little faucet, which was far ahead of the world it was made for, now finds whole houses that live up to it; and bathtubs no longer put dining rooms to shame."[81] Accordingly, Lilly Reich, who

was collecting bathroom objects for the exhibition halls, aimed for the unity between technical form and living environment, between the precise function of an object and the equally precise design of a modern apartment—and exemplified it by a hallway and its pegs, mirror, and glass shelf.

The last word may be left to Lilly Reich herself, who ended an article on "Questions of Fashion" thus: "How the way to the New Form is to be found, who can say? Anything worthwhile takes time; the vital thing, here as elsewhere, is to give expression to the mentality of the kind of woman who wants to be what she is, rather than to seem what she is not."[82]

Apartment 9, second floor right

Interior design: Erich Dieckmann, architect, Staatliche Hochschule für Handwerk und Baukunst, Weimar.
The accommodation comprises: kitchen, bathroom, bedroom, living room.[83]

It was Adolf Meyer who suggested to Mies that he invite Erich Dieckmann to design an apartment. Mies's letter is dated June 11, 1927, two months later than the invitations which went out to other interior designers; the date coincides exactly with the negative replies from Lüdecke and the Luckhardt brothers.

Dieckmann was sent a ground plan, to a scale of 1:10, and a view of the living room, looking toward the windows, plus the information that the height of the window sills in the bedroom and in the living room was the same.[84] Mies completely forgot to tell him that the building was designed by himself, and neglected—or considered it unnecessary—to send him pictures of the outside. Dieckmann, for his part, attached great importance to both factors. He wrote back: "What is the character [of the building]? Who designed it?"[85] His idea of planning an apartment involved knowing something about the building it was in. He also wanted to know how far the building had progressed; what had been agreed with regard to colors, materials, and display objects; and how to interpret the alcove in the kitchen which forms a void on the lobby side; "What is the material of the closet with drawers, built in between the living room and the bedroom, whether painted or natural wood, etc."[86]

Dieckmann's question makes it clear that not all the interior designers had equal scope to alter the floor plans of their apartments; which also explains why a number of floor plans appear more than once.

The furniture that Dieckmann put into Mies's preordained plan consisted of types that he had designed at the Hochschule für Handwerk und Baukunst, Weimar, and which had been made under his supervision for submission to the German Industrial Standards Institute (DIN) as standard furnishings for small apartments.[87] It was paid for by the school in Weimar,[88] in which Dieckmann was an instructor in interior design and furniture;[89] like Adolf Meyer he had remained behind when the Bauhaus left its Weimar building and moved to Dessau in 1925.

The combined living and dining room suite may be in oak, stained in two colors, or in cherrywood, natural and stained. The bedroom woodwork is painted in an ivory lacquer. The linings of the closets are all gabon and mahogany; like the outsides, they are of course made of plywood.

Now for the prices: the small living and dining room . . . costs 385 marks, the larger version . . .

725 marks; there is a third price in between (without the sewing cabinet and the divan) of 565 marks. The price of the bedroom is 580 marks including the patent mattresses.[90]

Dieckmann's chairs, too, were the outcome of exact research, and he achieved both a strict overall form and a high degree of comfort. The chair is assembled from separate components; even to a lay person, it conveys an impression of clarity and comprehensibility.

Apartment 10, second floor left

Interior design: Mies van der Rohe, architect, Berlin W 35, Am Karlsbad 24.
The accommodation comprises: kitchen, bathroom, bedroom, living room.

Apartment 11, third floor right

Interior design: Mies van der Rohe, architect, Berlin W 35, Am Karlsbad 24.
The accommodation comprises: kitchen, bathroom, 2 bedrooms, living room.

Apartment 12, third floor left

Interior design: Mies van der Rohe, architect, Berlin W 35, Am Karlsbad 24.
The accommodation comprises: kitchen, bathroom, 2 bedrooms, living room.[91]

Mies did the interior design for three of the twenty-four apartments in his own building. He used the two-room Apartment 11 to demonstrate the flexible partitioning. In this apartment, left unfurnished, he presented the principle, intended for all of the apartments, of using movable partitions to alter the interior shape of the apartment in accordance with the residents' changing needs.

> To this end, it was originally intended to make the ceilings and partitions in plywood. The ceilings were to be divided into panels, 1 meter square, and the wall units were fully movable plywood sheets. Once the ceilings were plastered, either plasterboard partitions were used, or some other structural solution had to be found.
> The partitions consist of plywood panels, 1 meter wide. These stand on the floor in a nickel-plated metal shoe in which they can be raised and lowered with the aid of a pair of screws. In this way the partitions are braced between floor and ceiling and stand fast. Strips of felt seal the joints.[92]

The idea of bracing the partition against the floor and ceiling (which became popular again in the 1950s) brings with it the danger of material fatigue. For this reason, Mies attached his partitions to each other at right angles, so that no bracing was necessary except to ensure an airtight fit.
In the small Apartment 11 Mies set forward his principle; in the two three-room apartments, 10 and 12, he showed its application. More demarcation than spatial division, more offer than *diktat*, his apartments show exact definition of function only in the entrance area, with kitchen and bathroom. Elsewhere the layout is free, with flowing, doorless spaces that lay no onus on the occupants except the need for constant order and tidiness.

Apartment 9:
Study corner by Erich Dieckmann

Erich Dieckmann: simple chairs in straight squared wood

Erich Dieckmann: the Bed, basic types

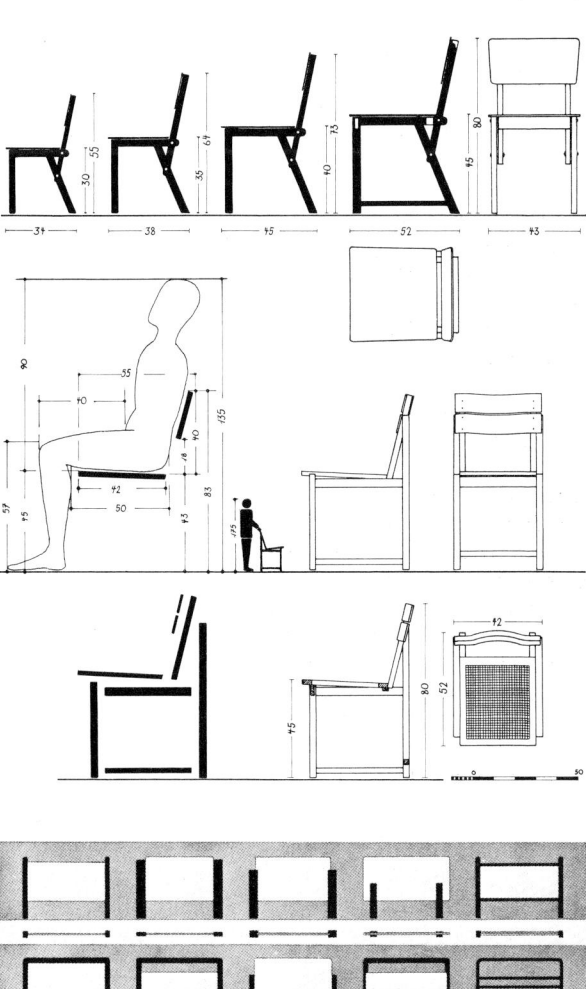

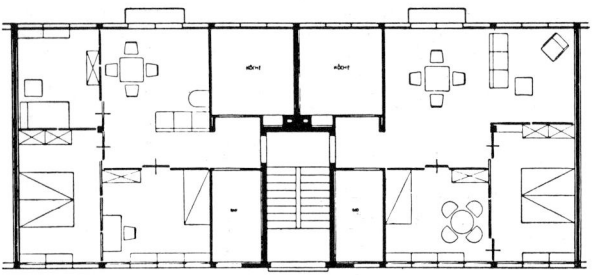

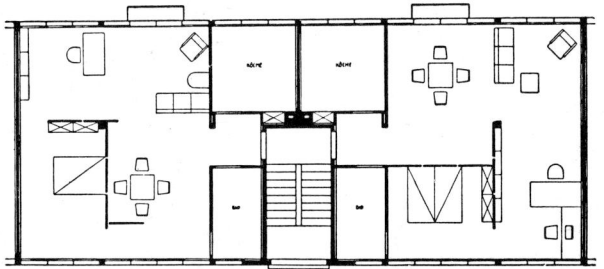

Variations on the lay-
out of Apartments 10
and 12 (no fireplace),
by Mies van der
Rohe. Left, enclosed;
right, open

Apartment 10:
Movable partitions by
Mies van der Rohe

These were definitely places to live in without children—ideal apartments for a single person or a couple
from the "educated middle classes" with artistic leanings. Books and somewhere to work, tea table and wing
armchair, tubular steel furniture, designed specially for
these apartments—it all has an exclusive air; generosity
and spaciousness in social housing.

It seems certain that this is exactly what Mies was
setting out to prove: in contrast to all the earnest and
necessary efforts to create low-cost housing, he sought
to show that it could be done with a touch of class while
"avoiding any hint of the salon," as he had written in
his invitations to prospective interior designers. Avoid
any hint of the salon, by all means, but also avoid the
look of poverty: that is the message of the Mies apartments. As he once told Heinz Rasch, he was building
homes and not tin cans.

The simplicity of Mies's apartments and his aspiration to achieve "perfection to the point of inconspicu-
ousness," both in plan and in furnishings, makes them
a paragon of generosity in spatial design. They are calculated to distance themselves from all petty-bourgeois
concerns; the living-room closet and sideboard are no
longer to look like monuments but to be made up of
additive components. The stale aroma of the nine-
teenth-century is banished, once and for all.

In his essay, "Concerning My Block," Mies said of
these movable partitions that "by these means any reasonable accommodation needs might be satisfied."[93]
Discussing the apartments in the Werkbund periodical
Die Form he went further:

> In taking on this work, it was clear to me that we
> would have to execute it in a way contrary to
> ideas generally current, because everyone who
> has concerned himself seriously with the problem
> of home-building has become aware of its com-
> plex character. The slogan, "Rationalization and
> Standardization," and also the call for an eco-
> nomic home building industry, touch only on par-
> tial problems, which are highly important in
> themselves but take on a real importance only
> when seen in proportion. Alongside or rather
> above these requirements, there is the spatial
> problem, *the creation of a New Home*. This is a
> problem of the mind, one that can be solved only
> through creative power, not by mathematical or
> organizational means . . .
>
> We were entirely free only in dealing with the
> spatial problem: the truly architectural issue.[94]

"Creative power," an "architectural issue," a "problem
of the mind," "the creation of a New Home": all these
self-imposed objectives were not, for Mies, to be
lumped together in generalized terms, but to be held
in the architect's mind throughout, in the layout of the
apartments and through all the details of structural
components and furniture. In the Weissenhofsiedlung,
Mies did what he set out to do, however hard a time

he may have given to the men from City Hall, or to the
superintendent architect. His ideas seldom fitted in with
their expectations.

Unfortunately, little is known in detail about the color
schemes or the precise choice of materials inside the
apartments. The partitions were macassar plywood
panels;[95] the seats, bent steel tubing with leather seats
and backs. These were described by their makers, Berliner Metallgewerbe Joseph Müller of Neukölln, Lichten-
rader Strasse 32, as MR Chairs, or, to be precise,
"MR-Stühle D.R.P. und A.P.a." The designation may
look unremarkable; but it conceals the genesis of a
Modernist classic, the chair of the century.

Mies had his tubular steel furniture made in Berlin;
Mart Stam, after some experiments in Holland, had his
made by the firm of Arnold, at Schorndorf, near Stuttgart. The question of priority naturally arises. There can
be no doubt that Stam was the first to design a tubular
steel chair, but Mies pursued the idea, extended it, and
added the flexibility that gives the seat its bounce.
Stam's chair was rigid; Mies made use of the possibilities of his material, the elasticity of the steel tubing from
Mannesmann. Mies's tubular steel chair was rendered
unmistakable and formally autonomous by the semicircular shape imparted to the front of the frame, with the
intention of improving the bounce; a spatially expansive
gesture which predestines the chair to stand alone. The

Apartment 12:

Living room by Mies van der Rohe with wing chair

Living room by Mies van der Rohe (later state, with glass table)

armrests, added with equal generosity, reinforce the impression of an exclusive object which is free of any niggardly subordination to mere function: once more, typical of Mies.

The same series included the round glass-topped table on crossed frames, floating as if insubstantial, light-filled, enlarging the airy space of the living room: the expansion of space as a method of design. Then there was its utter antithesis, the wing armchair: massive and compact, a bastion against drafts and against all life's ills, a refuge from wide open spaces and from too much transparency, softly upholstered and enveloping.

Then there was a tea table in the same palisander veneer[96] as the tables in Lilly Reich's apartment. Bookshelves were of the simplest kind, then unthinkable except for cheap paper-covered editions—it was inconceivable to place lavish publications such as *Weltall und Menschheit*, or *Andrés Weltatlas*, on such shelves. Their place was in a proper bookcase, behind glass—in other words, in the nineteenth century. In both of his furnished apartments Mies used bookshelves to articulate the space. In Apartment 10, the ceiling-high, wall-length bookcase marks the transition into the study, effortlessly incorporating a necessary structural pier; in Apartment 12, a low strip of bookshelves links the living room with the bedroom and visually reduces the great depth of the chimney piece.

Apart from a desk lamp of unknown provenance, Mies steered clear of the general craze for designing light fittings: these apartments of his grew dark as night fell. This was arguably a correct decision, in the context of this exhibition: it always closed before dusk, around 6:30 P.M.[97]

HOUSE 3, MIES VAN DER ROHE BUILDING

This house contained a gas-fired laundry incorporating a Vaillant automatic washing machine, a spin-dryer, and a wall-mounted ironing board. Whether Mies and the exhibition directorate had intended to set aside his House 3 entirely for the nonprofit *Hausratgesellschaften*

or "household goods societies" is impossible to determine; but if so, Kramer's work ought to have been here too.[98]

Apartment 13, first floor right

Interior design: Max Hoene, architect, Munich, in association with Bayerische Hausrathilfe Gemeinnützige GmbH, of Munich, Nuremberg, Ludwigshafen, and Regensburg, a member of Verband der Gemeinnützigen Deutschen Hausratgesellschaften e.V. The accommodation comprises: two bedrooms, two living rooms, bathroom and kitchen.[99]

Max Hoene was a sculptor by profession, a specialist in memorials and fountains, and is listed as such in all the reference books (a fact which did nothing to assist the research for the present work).[100] From the early 1920s onward, he designed items of mass-production furniture for Bayerische Hausrathilfe. They consisted of a basic cupboard unit which could be combined and transformed by such separate add-on elements as glazed cabinets or little bookcases or map chests; the idea was to meet the needs of people "whose financial means do not entitle them to have anything specially made for them," but nevertheless attach value to a certain individuality, to being different from their neighbors.[101] The attempt was made to meet this requirement not only through the additive combination of components, but also through surface treatments, such as differently colored stains and lacquers. The furniture had initially been constructed in a frame and panel system using softwood; a further degree of rationalization in machine production was achieved through the use of economical plywood, sold with a ready-finished surface.[102]

Hoene was not invited by Mies, or by the exhibition directorate in Stuttgart, but nominated by Bayerische Hausratshilfe at the request of its parent body.[103] His relationship with Mies and with the exhibition directorate was not an easy one: communications on the matter of deadlines do not seem to have been very precise.[104]

According to contract, Hausrathilfe dispatched the furniture by truck to Stuttgart punctually in time for installation to begin two days before opening day, without realizing that the building which was to contain the furniture was still a shell and would not be ready to be furnished before September.

Hausrathilfe provided its own fixtures for the apartment: kitchen closet and serving hatch between living room and kitchen (612 marks); wash basin enclosure for bedroom (450 marks); window ledges with chests of drawers and folding tables in bedroom, children's room, and guestroom (166, 236, and 236 marks). Additionally, a closet was built in and offered to the city of Stuttgart for cash sale. When City Hall did not respond, the closet was simply dismantled and shipped out, together with the other furniture, before the exhibition closed.[105]

Apartment 14, first floor left

Interior design: Camille Graeser, architect, Stuttgart, Landhausstrasse 10.
The accommodation comprises: kitchen, bathroom, bedroom, living room.[106]

Camille Graeser—a member of the Werkbund since 1918, a master student under Bernhard Pankok in Stuttgart, and a private student with Adolf Hölzel—concerned himself in the first half of his life with product and interior design, as well as with painting. He was a member of the group of Stuttgart interior designers who saw fit to write Mies complaining of discrimination against them in the allocation of contracts for Weissenhof. Mies's answer made it plain that, although there had been no blanket ban on their work as such, an aesthetic criterion had been applied: "For our exhibition the only interiors that can be considered are those that deal in an entirely objective [*sachlich*] fashion with the problems defined by us."[107]

Camille Graeser, at least, knew himself to be entirely in agreement with Mies. In a newspaper article the previous year, he had written,

Modern man cares what kind of rooms he lives in, whether he lives within his own four walls surrounded by junk inherited from our fathers' time, or whether he surrounds himself exclusively with the creations of this century. Modern man demands logic and consistency, and involves himself with the events of the world.

Modern man loves only absolute necessity. He shuns all unnecessary objects, has no time for sentiment, and makes no concessions in assembling an interior; he loves only perfect purposefulness and clarity, which combine to produce a closed, tranquil form and at the same time contain a wealth of new beauties within themselves.[108]

When Mies invited Graeser to participate in the Weissenhof project as an interior designer, he intended him to design an apartment in Behrens' building.[109] Graeser thanked him politely but enquired whether Mies had "a more interesting commission, viz. the plan of an apartment in your own building" for him.[110] Mies did not, because all those apartments had already been assigned;[111] but a month later things changed, and the Luckhardt brothers, Schulz, Martin Wagner, and Lüdecke were eliminated or eliminated themselves. So Mies was able to offer Graeser an apartment in his own building after all, even though Graeser, under time pressure from the contractors, had already asked for the Behrens drawings.[112]

Graeser made one change to the layout of his apartment: the partition between bedroom and living room was moved forward into the living room by 60 cm (2 feet) to give him an alcove in the bedroom for a closet. The book *Bau und Wohnung* shows the change; and Graeser's sketch gives us the additional information that, in his apartment—if not throughout the building—the partitions consisted of panels 8 cm (3 in) thick. In the living and dining area, there was a "combination sideboard, bookcase, bureau, and seat," designed by Graeser.[113] The light fittings and carpets in the living room and bedroom were also designed by him.[114]

Apartment 13:
Nursery furniture by Max Hoene

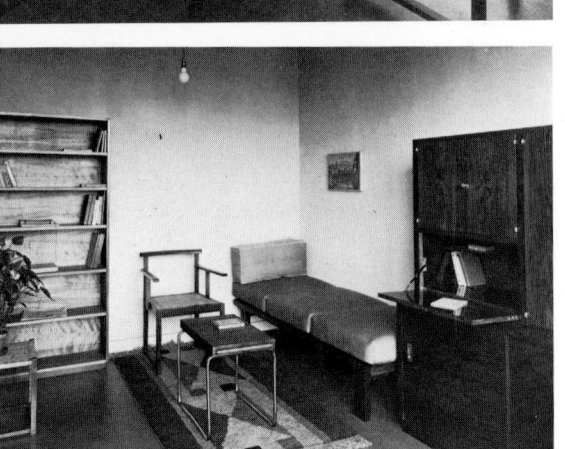

Apartment 14:

Dining suite by Camille Graeser

Living room by Camille Graeser

Apartment 15, second floor right

Interior design: Professor Ad. G. Schneck, Staatliche Kunstgewerbeschule, Stuttgart.
The accommodation comprises: two bedrooms, living room, kitchen, bathroom.[115]

It was for Weissenhof that Adolf Schneck developed his own industrial furnishing range, "Die billige Wohnung," which he used to design the interior of Apartment 15 in Mies's building. The two houses that he himself built, Houses 11 and 12, have furnishings executed individually by firms from Stuttgart and elsewhere—to his designs, naturally.

Schneck had made a systematic study of the possibilities of industrial production of furniture. This went back many years: simplified furniture by him had been shown in the Werkbund exhibition *Die Form* in 1924, and also at Monza in 1925. Early in 1926 he wrote to Oud,

> At last I can now send you the promised booklet on the Monza exhibition. At the same time I am giving you a short essay on the making of simplified furniture, which is being published by Baurat Keuerleber. These models cater for the small furniture maker who has no veneer presses and has to make all of his large components in frame and panel construction. The models will be assembled into whole rooms by the spring of this year; the finish is stained and varnished. At the moment I am working on types for rational factory production. I will send you the patterns when they are ready.[116]

Whether this letter entitles us to assume that Schneck had already developed the models for Weissenhof, spent much time working out production details, and timed the preproduction process so consummately that Deutsche Werkstätten, of Hellerau, were ready on opening day with a new and spectacular range, is a question that we need not answer here. Perhaps it was just a fortunate coincidence: Deutsche Werkstätten had given Schneck a commission to design simplified furniture which fitted perfectly into the Weissenhof concept of standardized furniture, and was enabled to derive maximum publicity from that fact.

Schneck's furniture did not draw down on him the fury of those who labeled other architects "Bolshevik Builders" and hounded them out of Germany: in fact, "he remained a full professor in Stuttgart until he acquired emeritus status in 1949. He went on teaching without interruption during the years of the Third Reich. The 'success' of Schneck's department of furniture remained unquestioned."[117]

The commission for the interior design of Apartment 15 was given to Schneck by Mies: "I enclose the drawings for the apartment you are going to furnish with D[eutsche] W[erkstätte] furnishings. Please talk it through with Herr Walther right away, so that he can arrange the partitions and lighting points."[118] The letter is dated June 4, 1927, although the apartment had been assigned to Schneck on April 11.[119]

On the subject of standardized and mass-produced furniture, Schneck wrote:

> The question of standardization is not a matter for the artist alone. It can only be resolved in close collaboration with the architect and the man of business.

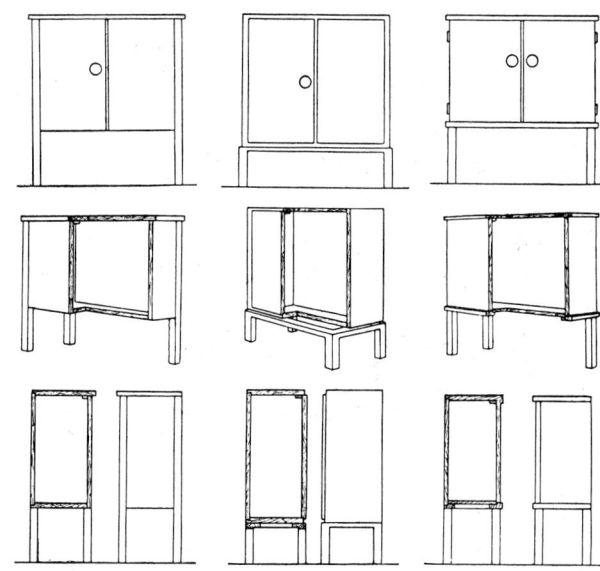

Apartment 15:

Adolf G. Schneck: standard furniture types

Dining suite by Adolf G. Schneck

> Standardization is the same thing as mass production. Mass production presupposes mass sales, and mass sales can only be attained if the execution is of the highest quality.
>
> Standardization is possible only for those items of furniture that one absolutely must have in one's home. More than 90 percent of consumers can no longer buy any more furniture for their homes than they absolutely need.
>
> And why should they buy more? The less furniture, the less ballast. There have been attempts in the recent past to standardize items of furniture that are not absolute necessities.
>
> Any item of furniture that is not an absolute necessity is a luxury article. And a luxury article that is standardized is what we call kitsch.[120]

Apartment 16, second floor left

Interior design: Professor Franz Schuster, architect, Frankfurt a. M., Myliusstrasse 60.
The accommodation comprises: bedroom, living room, kitchen, bathroom.[121]

In September of 1926, Stotz drew Mies's attention to the work of the Austrian architect, Franz Schuster, and suggested that he might be incorporated in the list of architects as a possible reserve choice.[122] He never appeared on that list, but Mies did ask him to furnish an apartment in his building. Schuster readily agreed, was sent the guidelines drawn up by the housewives'

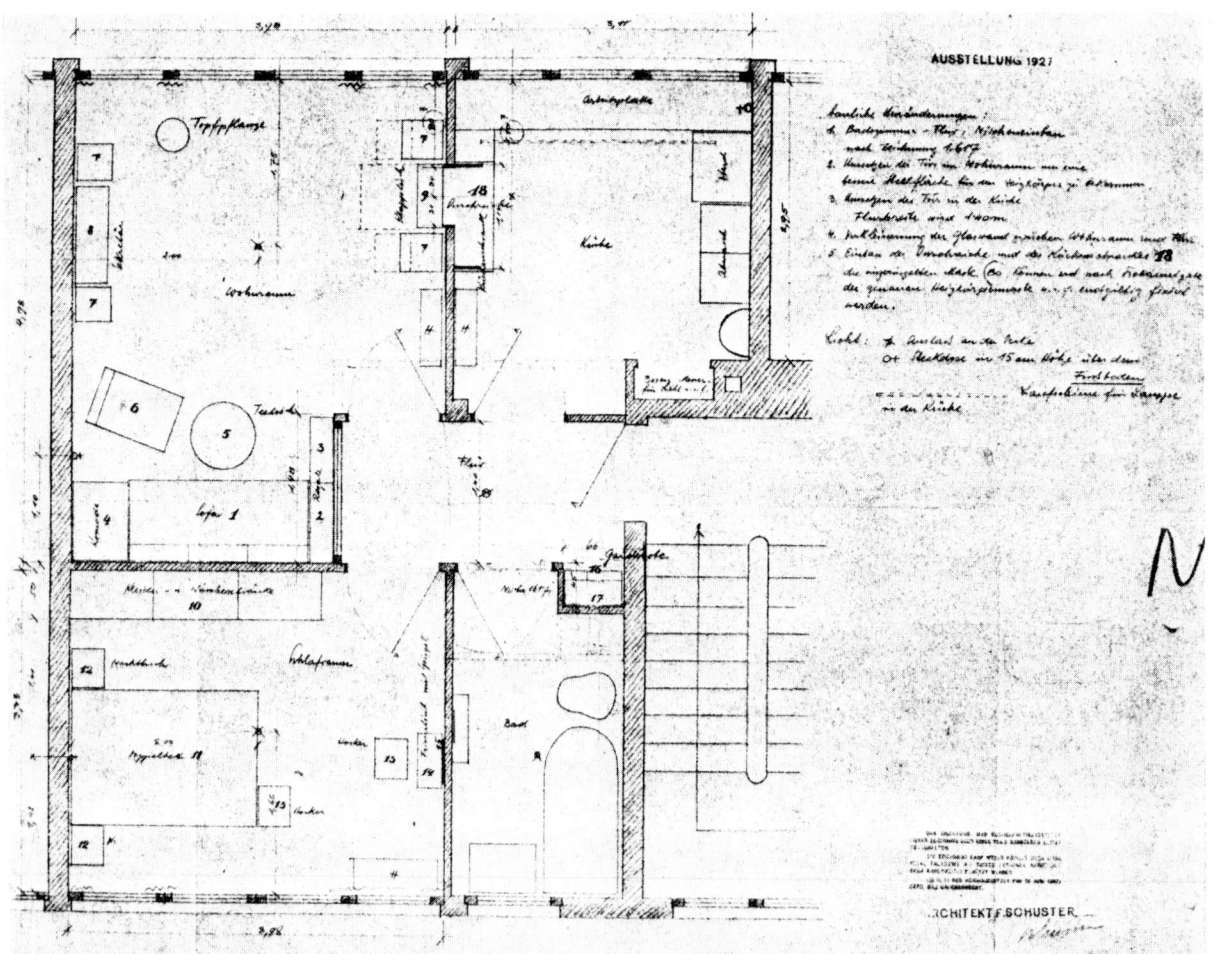

Apartment 16:
Franz Schuster: sketch
plan of apartment for
a childless couple

organizations and by Erna Meyer, and promptly submitted his drawings, first to Mies, who proposed some
changes, and then, together with suggestions for modifications, direct to Stuttgart.[123]

The design description for the two-room Apartment
16 was "Apartment for a Childless Couple."[124] Schuster
had some questions for Mies:

> Above all, to improve the closet provision in the
> bedroom, it would be necessary to give up on the
> highboy proposed between bedroom and living
> room; additionally, this makes it possible to have
> a corner sofa with a tea table in the living room.
> In positioning the heater in the living room, it must
> be remembered that the dining table must be next
> to the serving hatch, so that the wife can put the
> food on the tray in the kitchen and then, in the
> dining room—because there is no maid—sit at the
> table, take it all through the hatch, and remove it
> from the tray. In the bedroom, the heater has to
> be positioned so that the door can be opened
> wide. Door to bathroom—if any—a narrow slid-
> ing door (30 cm [1 foot]) wide on bath side). In
> the plan that was sent to me, the toilet is in the
> bathroom; I think the separate toilet space pre-
> viously specified can be dispensed with, as the
> three doors (closet door) are very awkwardly
> placed anyway. This would make it possible to
> put a small recess into the lobby for coats, in
> which I could very well accommodate the wall
> closet that is supposed to be by the door. In the
> kitchen it would be advantageous to keep the
> drain outlet where it was first meant to be in the
> drawings, so that a kitchen cabinet can be built

> around it . . .
> Why is the width of the doorways 107 cm [42
> in] clear? Wouldn't 80–85 cm [31½–33½ in] be
> enough?[125]

Mies's answer came four days later and is characteristic of his way of dealing with other people's designs,
criticizing, leading, and articulating common ground: it
is worth quoting at length, as this is one of the few cases

Extending table and
chairs by Franz
Schuster

in which the correspondence on the interior design of one of these apartments has survived.

As to your designs themselves, I would suggest making the glass wall shorter and moving the door back so that it is not obstructed by the heater. I agree to the omission of the highboy against the bedroom wall. I am afraid the sliding door to the bathroom is not covered by the cost estimates. Please reconsider whether you really attach great importance to it, and if so I would try to have it included. But in any case I don't think it would be any inconvenience to have to go from bedroom to bathroom by way of the lobby. There is no provision for a bidet in the specifications, but here, too, it might in certain circumstances be possible to do it.

The change to the cloakroom can be done. The kitchen outlet cannot be put where you now want it, because the plumbing in the other apartments has to stay where I planned it. So in this case please follow my layout, especially as there is not enough room for the gas meter in that little recess. I must repeat that the balcony door in the big room is so constructed that it opens back flat against the adjoining window.

The saving in space you hope for in taking the garbage can out of the corridor seems to me so slight as not to justify the additional work. Please also give this some more thought.

As I am now sending your drawings back, please let me have your final version. . . .

I have sent the furniture designs to Stuttgart today . . .

My suggestions for changes are:
1. A closet alcove in the lobby with a door to the bathroom (see drawing).
2. Move living room and kitchen doors forward to make lobby 1.1 meters [43 inches] wide, which seems plenty for so small an apartment and makes it easier to position the heaters in the two rooms.
3. A serving hatch built into the kitchen cabinet, which means that the intended cabinet may require some changes (I have seen no drawings of it thus far).
Drain outlet remains as you planned, bathroom door from bedroom omitted.[126]

The photographs of the serving hatch with a gateleg table show a checkered floor pattern, whereas the table itself was photographed against a plain floor covering. There is no further information to clarify this. The detail of the kitchen cabinet with its serving hatch to the living room reveals not so much a reduction to basics as an attachment to tradition. It would have been easy to continue the working surface under the window along as far as the heater; and yet the kitchen cabinet has become a sort of hybrid sideboard, although with some indication of an upper and a lower compartment.

In an article published in the following year, Schuster considered women's role in home and society:

A woman no longer wants to spend the whole day cleaning the house and doing meaningless chores: she wants to involve herself in the things that matter today; she must be able to hold her own in the economic struggle and can no longer afford to waste her mental and physical energy

Apartment 17: Living room by Arthur Korn

on trivia. For, whether as a wife and mother or fending entirely for herself, she has a valuable part to play in the struggle for a new age. She must therefore expect her home—as we expect everything else—not to hamper but to promote the evolution of our best and most vital powers: and no one is going to say that dusting, cleaning, and brushing furniture have any major contribution to make in that direction. So the age itself demands the new household equipment.[127]

Apartment 17, third floor right

Interior design: Arthur Korn, architect, Berlin W 15, Uhlandstrasse 175.
The accommodation comprises: bedroom, living room, kitchen, bathroom.[128]

Arthur Korn was a long-standing member of the Novembergruppe in Berlin, whose secretary he was for a short time (late 1923 through early 1924). He participated in many of the group's exhibitions, and in 1926 he joined the enlarged Der Ring.[129] There is no evidence that he ever belonged to the Werkbund, although he does seem to have been a member of the BDA. In List II of prospective architects for Weissenhof he appears as No. 17, but he is not mentioned thereafter.

On April 11, 1927, Mies named him in his letter to the city exhibition and conventions office as one of those who were to design an apartment in Mies's building. On May 9 Korn sent Mies his drawing of a three-leaf sliding door and promised furnishing plans, which have unfortunately not survived. All that can be found is a photograph taken in the apartment of the tubular steel furniture by Korn which was manufactured by Arnold, of Schorndorf, until the 1930s.[130]

Apartment 18, third floor left

Interior design: Rasch Brothers, architects, Stuttgart, Paulinenstrasse 3.
The accommodation comprises: kitchen, bathroom, bedroom, living room.[131]

The brothers Heinz and Bodo Rasch have maintained their connection with the Weissenhofsiedlung to this day: from the preparatory phase, including the Stuttgart *Bauausstellung* of 1924, by way of the interior design of two apartments at Weissenhof and the accompanying book, *Wie bauen?*, to the renovation phase of the 1970s and 1980s.

It was Heinz Rasch who accompanied Mies from Berlin to Stuttgart in the preparatory period of the 1927 exhibition, acting as his guide, audience, chronicler and interpreter. He records one conversation—or rather monologue—in particular, on the subject of space and communications, which was occasioned by a lecture given by Häring. Mies told Rasch,

Backs and soles of feet are the basic surfaces; hands and eyes grasp the space in front by swinging in semicircles. Two zones: one above and three-dimensional, one below and one-dimensional. Organically curved, like the course of a stream, is how the tracks would be in nature, and the line of the walls ought ideally to be governed by these curves. But what two people will ever make the same curve, or what single person will repeat the same curve? It can't be done, even with a pencil. Curves are individual expressive forms. Footprints are not points of departure; they are the places where somebody putters, sits, or sleeps. The armchair, the meal table—rear walls, alcoves, concave forms inside and outside—and in between is empty space. . . .

Of course, any lengthwise form can be subdivided by partitions, props, frameworks, and then the cross walls become the back walls. All that counts is the intervals between. But nothing is gained by making a curve instead of a right angle. It's hard to furnish a round, too, it all has to be done to measure. And construction—anyone who has ever done it is cured for life. With right angles, everything is simplified. Bricks are rectangular, beams are straight. You can walk in any curve you like. Basically, all that is left is a passageway with rooms opening off from it, a lengthwise track with transverse walls, corresponding to the position of a human being with the legs straight ahead, the arms left and right, the same situation at every step. This also corresponds to the normal positioning of supports. It is naturally tempting to express the direction. Like a plant, for instance, or a tree, slanting walls and ceilings ought to correspond better to the way we perceive; but what happens then is that the space and the construction become secondary; and in architecture they are primary. The starting point is only the distance from one wall to another, which can be subjected to addition or division. A liking for roundness is understandable, it's inborn in us, and we spend a long time clinging to the egg; but

the circle is a limited form. The organizational system is based on the square, and within it every circle is inscribed in a square.[132]

Bodo Rasch reports Mies in similar terms:

Scharoun and Häring looked for a form that would exactly match the function. Mies later gave this the name of efficient form. He was against it, for the following good reason: complicated forms are hard to build and cost a lot of money. So, if I now make the space rather bigger and leave plenty for room for the function, I attain my object very much more cheaply and have the additional advantage of being able to vary the function.[133]

Following the example of such famous architect brothers as the Tauts and the Luckhardts, the Rasch brothers opened a joint office in 1926 and worked together on a number of projects before they parted company in 1930. They wrote five books, in all, on the basics of architecture and of design in its wider sense: the first was the third Werkbund publication, *Wie bauen?*, in which the construction methods and materials of the Weissenhofsiedlung are set out in detail, together with some projects for suspended structures that were years ahead of their time. For this book

they assembled a system for building, made up of the constructional concepts, arch, beam, suspension, the concepts of masonry and component assembly, and of the use of plane surfaces—surfaces strengthened by ribs, and curved surfaces.

Then a systematic mechanical application of these factors led them to a wealth of previously unknown forms of construction. When the first sketches were made for a shell structure and a suspended structure, both Rasches were carried away—they felt like prospectors in Alaska who had just struck gold—and went on projecting the future until it became known and present fact.[134]

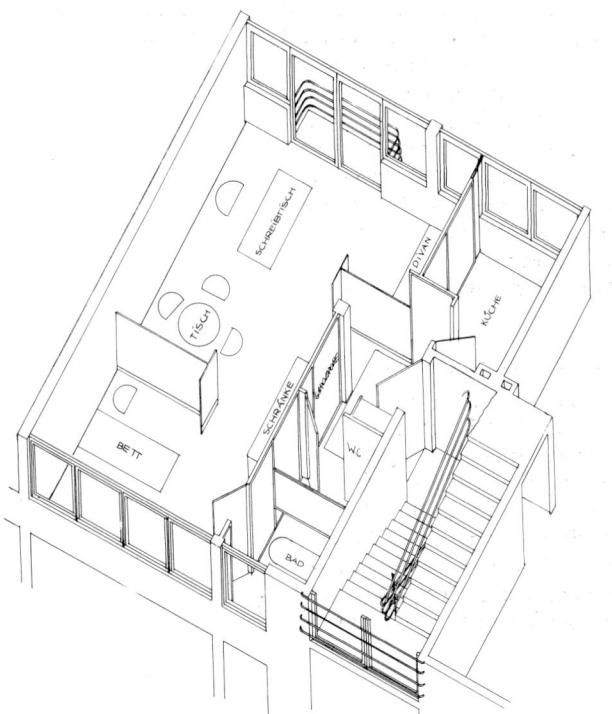

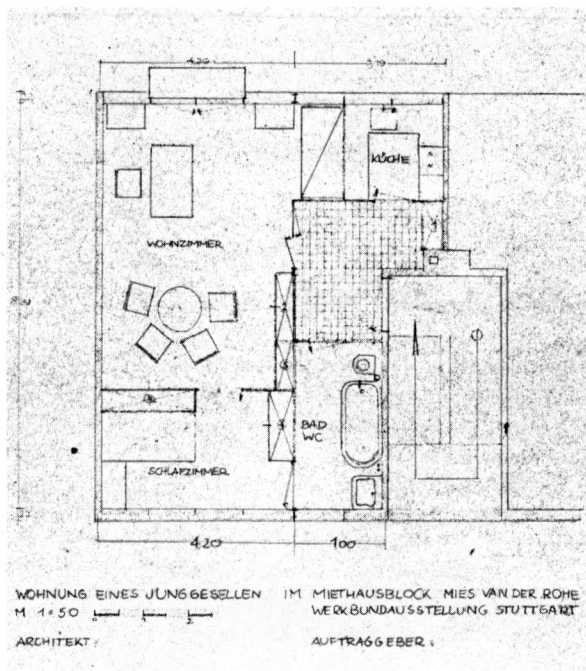

Apartment 18: Heinz and Bodo Rasch, isometric view and plan

Heinz Rasch has pointed out that it was—among other things—"especially the conversations with my brother Bodo in connection with the books that we edited . . . that clarified our ideas and enabled us to put them into words."[135] Their next publications were *Der Stuhl* and the second edition of *Wie bauen?*, both in 1928, and *Zu—Offen* and *Gefesselter Blick*, both in 1930.

The Rasch brothers' direct contribution to the Weissenhof project of 1927 consisted first in the interior design of an apartment "for a bachelor,"[136] as the letter of invitation has it, in Mies's apartment building; second, in the design of the apartment initially assigned to Else Oppler-Legband in Peter Behrens's building; and third, in the book *Wie bauen?* itself.

Wie bauen? partly owed its origin to the strained relations between Mies and Döcker. Döcker had the job of putting together jointly with the individual architects a book covering all the buildings in the Weissenhofsiedlung, setting his name to it as editor, finding a publisher, and if possible securing some payment for the architects. When the publishers concerned tried to finance all this by accepting advertisements from the contractors involved in the building, the Werkbund board banned the publication on ethical grounds, two weeks before publication. Döcker backed out, and negotiations began with the Rasch brothers, to whom Döcker handed over the photographs and process blocks.[137]

The interior design of Apartment 18 in Mies's building followed the principle of free, flowing space. Partitions in wood with incorporated insulating material, some of them rising to ceiling-height and some half-way, divided the floor space into areas set aside for different functions—with an eye to Mies's basic idea of a flexible floor plan. Mies was interested, according to Heinz Rasch, in "trying out multipurpose wallboards, previously known only in temporary structures, in that building of his, which seemed positively predestined for them."[138]

The designs for the furniture and light fittings shown in the apartment dated from previous years;[139] they were made by a number of firms in Stuttgart.[140] "The furnishing concept was simple," writes Heinz Rasch; "in both cases [Mies building and Behrens building] it was based on cantilever chairs and frameless tables, all of which worked perfectly, except one table in the Mies apartment, which developed a twist that had to be dealt with."[141]

In later years, Heinz Rasch tried to have his cantilever chairs put into mass production, and was unsuccessful because the patent had already been claimed by Mies. Rather than gloss over this side of Mies's character, it is worth giving Rasch's account of the episode:

So—I hoped [Mies] would give me a certificate—I showed him the photographs of the model I had developed in the meantime, and my description of the registered design, and promised to involve him; but then I had a disagreeable surprise. Mies said, with unusual vehemence, that it affected his patent and that I should keep out of it, because this time the whole thing was at stake! (From which it was apparent that I was not the first person he had had dealings with on this matter.) Then, quite calmly, with a sly smile, he explained where the patented principle lay. In one old American patent, which someone had tried to use against him, the tubing had been carried right round one and a half times, like the spring of a safety pin, whereas his new invention made do

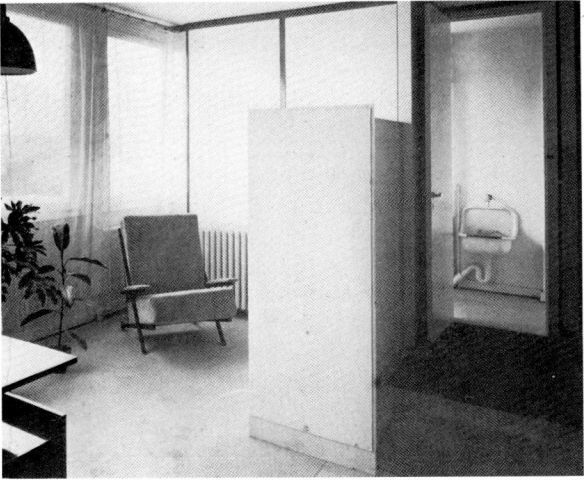

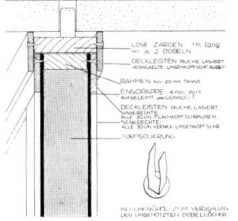

with a half turn, a semicircle: and that was all! But whether this semicircular curve came right up to the seat, or whether it remained small and close to the ground as in my version, did not affect the principle, in his view. I did not agree and mentioned Stam, whereupon Mies snapped back angrily: "But you know better than anybody that he made rigid corners with braces!"

So there I was, out on the street—and Stam too, Stam of all people, who had given him the idea . . . the three or four years in which I had worked so intensively on the idea seemed to have wasted—and people tried to comfort me by saying "You provided the stimulus!" Who cares. "There are always stimuli, from all sides; what matters is to recognize them and use them," said Mies as he showed me out. He may have meant to express sympathy, and even some recognition of my work. He grinned rather uncertainly, and yet with a barely suppressed glint of triumph in those bright, black eyes.[142]

After World War II, Heinz Rasch worked to have the Weissenhof houses classified as protected monuments,[143] and in 1977 Bodo Rasch set up a society of Friends of the Weissenhofsiedlung. Paragraph 2 of its articles of association reads as follows: "The Society is committed to the preservation and restoration of the Weissenhofsiedlung built in Stuttgart in 1927 and will work to this end through publicity. It aims to assemble a complete documentation and promotes the planning and financing of a restoration of the Weissenhofsiedlung."[144]

Apartment 18:
Clockwise:

Living room by Rasch brothers

Ceiling light by Rasch brothers

Detail of partition

Living room by Rasch brothers, with view into kitchen

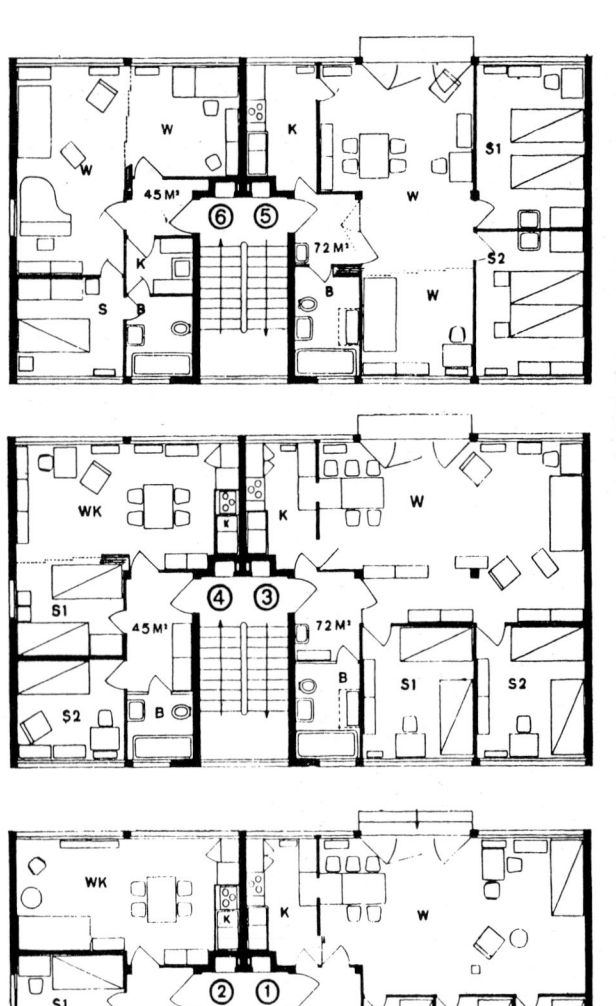

Apartments 19–24, by Schweizer Werkbund collective

Apartment 24 (6, third floor left): bachelor
Apartment 23 (5, third floor right): family with 2 children
Apartment 22 (4, second floor left): family with 1 child
Apartment 21 (3, second floor right): family with 2 children
Apartment 20 (2, first floor left): family with 1 child
Apartment 19 (1, first floor right): family with 4 children

Apartment 19:

Living room by Schweizer Werkbund collective

Twin bedroom by Schweizer Werkbund collective

HOUSE 4, MIES VAN DER ROHE BUILDING

The entire interior design of the apartments in this house, 19 through 24, both floor plans and furnishing, was carried out collectively, under the direction of Max Ernst Haefeli, Zürich, by the following architects, members of the Schweizer Werkbund: Ernst F. Burckhardt, Zürich; Karl Egender, Zürich; Alfred Gradmann, Zürich; Max Ernst Haefeli, Zürich; Hans Hofmann, Zürich; Wilhelm Kienzle, Zürich; Werner Moser, Zürich; Hans Weisse, Zürich; R. S. Rütschi, Zürich; Rud. Steiger, Zürich; Franz Scheibler, Winterthur; Pane Artaria & Hans Schmidt, Basel.

The division into rooms is as follows: in Apartment 19, kitchen, bathroom, living room, three sleeping cubicles; in Apartment 20, living room with kitchen alcove, cubicle, bathroom, bedroom; in Apartment 21, kitchen, bathroom, living room, three bedrooms; in Apartment 22, living room, with cooking alcove, cubicle, bathroom, bedroom; in Apartment 23, kitchen, bathroom, living room, two bedrooms; in Apartment 24, kitchen, bathroom, living room, bedroom.[145]

In December of 1926 it was still planned that three-quarters of the interiors in Mies's building should be designed by Werkbund groups from outside Germany: six by the Swiss, six by the Austrians, and six by the Dutch. The only group which actually participated as a body was the Schweizer Werkbund; there is nothing in the files to record any negotiations with the other two organizations.

The participation of the Neubühl-Gruppe, representing the Schweizer Werkbund, came about through the mediation of its secretary-general, Friedrich T. Gubler: "Gubler decided which members of our group would take part."[146] The group was founded, according to Rudolf Steiger, because he, Steiger, had the idea of forming a working group of friends for large commissions. I thought to myself, an undertaking like Neubühl . . . to plan and carry through a whole housing development is just too much responsibility for one person alone. You might fall under a streetcar, and the whole thing collapses. This was a new idea. In those days the normal thing was the great, autonomous, omnicompetent architect. Let's take the Weissenhofsiedlung as an example; Gropius, Oud, and the others, were all cast in a heroic mold. Individuals, not collectives.

72

I could already see that, for the tasks that lay ahead, this was not going to work any longer.[147]

The Neubühl-Gruppe formed the nucleus of the team, but not all the Swiss designers at Weissenhof were members of it. On March 28, 1927, the names of ten architects were published who had "volunteered and undertaken to take part." All were members of the Schweizer Werkbund. They were joined later by Werner Moser, son of Karl Moser (the professor of architecture who had selected the Swiss contributions to the *Internationale Plan- und Modellausstellung*); R. S. Rütschi, of Zürich; and Pane Artaria, who shared an office with Hans Schmidt.[148] Haefeli was chosen as the spokesman for the Schweizer Werkbund group.[149]

Before the individuals were chosen and their individual responsibilities allotted, discussions took place between the Werkbund exhibition directorate—as represented by Stotz and Hagstotz—and the Schweizer Werkbund, on the occasion of the exhibition *Das neue Heim*, at the Kunstgewerbemuseum in Zürich in December of 1926, which both men visited and described as small but "very well executed, entirely in the Werkbund spirit." It was on the strength of this that Stotz (hard to please, as ever) raised the prospect of assigning the interior design of one building of six apartments at Weissenhof to each of the three foreign Werkbünde, Swiss, Austrian, and Dutch.[150] In the end, the only contribution from any of these sources—aside from the work of the Austrians, Oskar Wlach and Walter Sobotka, in the Behrens building—was the work of the Swiss collective in House 4 of the Mies building.

When Hagstotz, the chief city hall representative on the exhibition directorate, saw the designs of the Swiss architects, he wrote Mies on 24 April 1927,

> Herr Haefeli, of Zürich, has just been here, and although I am no architect, I have the impression that these gentlemen have found solutions for your apartment building, both for the division of the interiors and for the decor, which may be among the best things the exhibition has to show. We have always had the impression that basically it is only in your building, and in Oud's houses, that the Werkbund's original exhibition idea has really been put into practice.[151]

Franz Krause, too, Döcker's assistant, who acted as an intermediary between Döcker and Mies when they were no longer on speaking terms,[152] was to recall in 1977: "The Swiss architects' apartments in the Mies building stood out by the quality of their furniture. The doors in those apartments—unlike the Mies apartments, where they went right up to the ceiling—were only 2 meters [6½ feet] high."[153]

Haefeli told Ludwig Glaeser, who interviewed him for the Mies van der Rohe Archive, in New York, that he had "simply done the practical management," and had been the one who went to Stuttgart to "sort the thing out," and in whose office the plans had been "done." Special characteristics of the apartments had been the variant forms of kitchen, including one built like a chemical laboratory with a vapor extraction hood; the narrow sleeping cubicles designed by Hans Schmidt; and the wide variety of furniture designs.

The simple chairs were assembled from aluminum members, "Elektron precision castings," with an L-shaped cross section, solid at the lower end and hollowed out at the top to save material.[154] These chairs never went into production. Haefeli replied to an enqui-

Apartment 21: Dining area with view into kitchen, by Schweizer Werkbund collective

Apartment 22: Kitchen alcove with vapor hood made for chemical laboratories, by Schweizer Werkbund collective

Apartment 23: Dining area with Elektron chairs, by Schweizer Werkbund collective

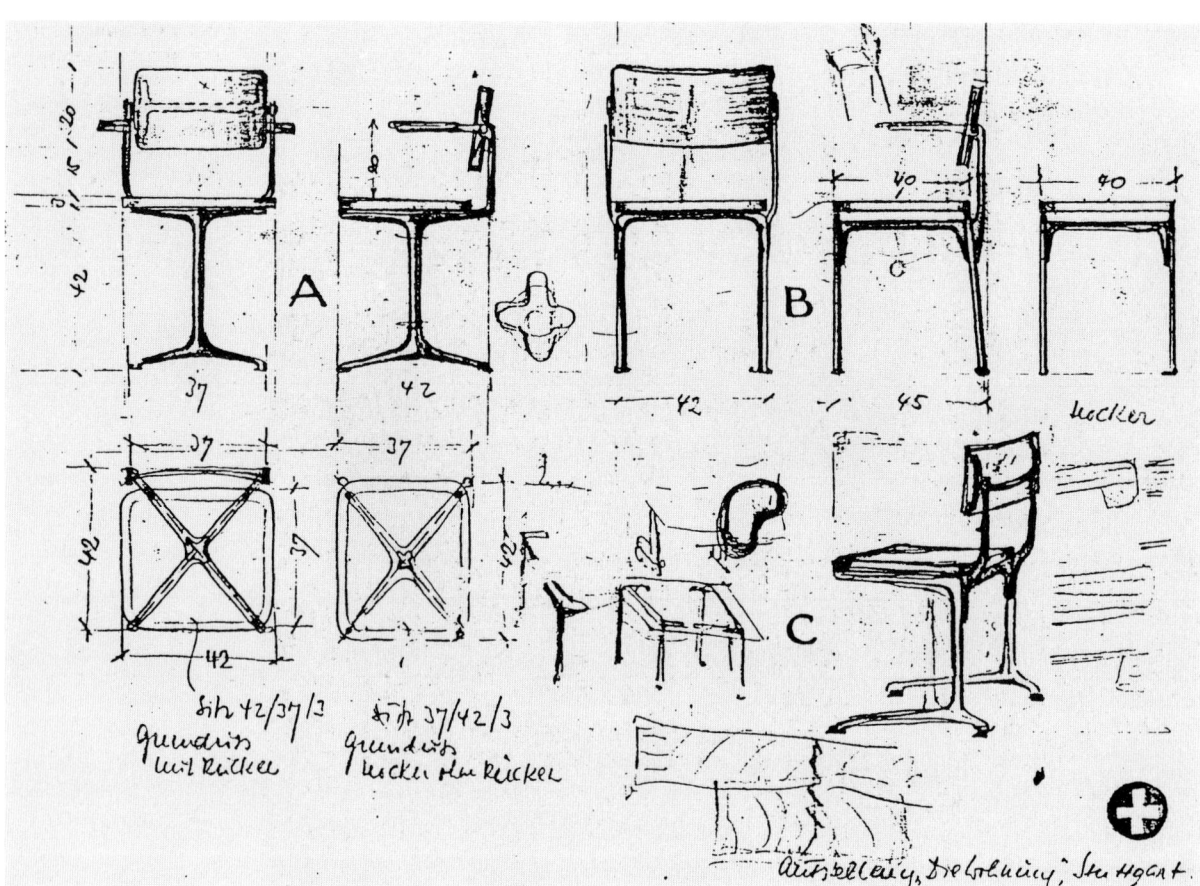

Schweizer Werkbund collective: Elektron chair in cast aluminum

Max Ernst Haefeli: tubular steel bed with red polished beech handrail at each end; metal parts ivory lacquer.

ry from Germany, "I am afraid I have to tell you that for the moment our lightweight metal chairs remain at the experimental stage."[155] Their designer's name is lost in the collective; but even today they look extraordinarily interesting. The use of small cast components and bent plywood meant easy and convenient assembly, space-saving storage, and most probably considerable comfort. The range was completed by a matching table and stool. Various sizes of tabletop afforded a versatile range of products for a wide variety of needs. The prices quoted were sixty Swiss francs for the chair, fifty for the stool.[156]

As well as this Elektron furniture, Haefeli's own add-on wooden seating was interesting: the legs were inserted in a kind of shoe glued to the underside of the curved seat, and the back was fastened to similar pieces on the upper side. In the version with arms, the legs were not tucked under the seat but brought to the side, and the back legs and chairback were in one piece. These chairs were made of bentwood in beech or walnut. The walnut version had a cane back and seat—rather an expensive-looking variant in which the principal load point was reinforced and the whole seat was constructed as a ring to take the tension off the caning. The only table to match was a low stool table; for a dining table the Elektron table was used. The solid-seated chairs were spray-lacquered. Max Ernst Haefeli was credited as sole designer: so much for collective responsibility!

Wilhelm Kienzle, who taught at the Kunstgewerbeschule in Zürich, also designed some chairs, which in this company look rather stiff. In function and also in character, Kienzle seems to have been a Swiss counterpart of Adolf Gustav Schneck, of the Kunstgewerbeschule in Stuttgart.[157]

By great good fortune, a drawing of the bed design used in House 4 has survived. This too was by Haefeli,

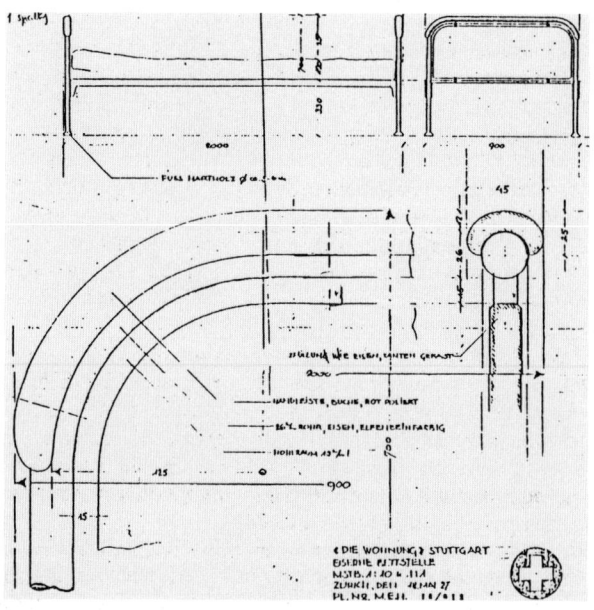

and its special feature was a red polished beechwood strip applied to the "ivory" lacquered steel tube of the bedrail. A highly interesting "wall clothes hanger," which unfortunately does not appear in any photograph, was found in the archive of the architectural partnership of Haefeli Moser Steiger.

The intense commitment with which the Swiss architects went about their work and their eagerness to pass on the knowledge that they acquired manifest themselves in a description written by one of the most important individuals involved. Hans Schmidt, who regarded the building of small dwellings as his specialty,[158] and who, according to Haefeli, did important work both in the partnership Artaria & Schmidt and in

the design of the periodical *ABC*,[159] not only designed most of the floor plans of the apartments but published a detailed account of the thinking that went into them.

> Above all, the apartment must have a large, communal living room . . . which allows the maximum freedom of movement and in any case can accommodate very different groups of furniture and so transcend the tedious explicitness of the usual dining room and salon in favor of a less formal arrangement. This living room absorbed the unlit central passage, which became unnecessary just as soon as we had gotten used to the idea, perfectly acceptable within a self-contained household, that the less-used bedrooms could be entered direct from the living room.[160]

The number of bedrooms, according to Schmidt, was determined by the normal composition of a family: one room for the parents and two for the children, one for each sex. To exemplify this form of floor-plan, governed by the number of bed places, the Swiss group showed examples of interiors for families with four children (19, first floor right), two children (21 and 23, second and third floors right), and one child (20 and 22, first and second floors left), and for a bachelor (24, third floor left). The apartments for families with more than one child had a separate kitchen (for which 6 square meters [65 square feet] was considered adequate), but in the small-family and bachelor apartments there were cooking alcoves ventilated like chemical laboratories by means of a closable vapor hood covering both cooker and sink.

The furniture for these apartments was envisaged as a set of mass-produced products, based on individual forms on which the designer lavished all the resources of his formal invention. In Schmidt's words,

The furniture currently in production, with its endless studies in fumed oak and bedrooms in polished mahogany, marked by utterly superficial variations of "style," ultimately conveys a much greater uniformity and lack of inspiration than the dissemination of standard types can ever do. . . . Very light and handy tables and chairs made out of Elektron metal and wood were assembled, a patented model of easy chair was improved, and the beds were developed as a single type in iron and wood.

The Schweizer Werkbund contingent, according to Schmidt, saw its role as that of a stimulus, setting out to prompt solutions to a variety of technical, formal, and sociopolitical problems and thus open the way to types which, after years of experiment and adaptation, would eventually become standard. Schmidt continued,

> The architect's task today is to gain an oversight over the whole, to organize the parts into a result that will work. If the Swiss contribution to the Stuttgart exhibition has achieved anything, this has nothing to do with the technical detail of the work as such: it resides in the conclusion that, in our day, it is collective work on the problems of the home and its interior design . . . that produces the liveliest results; and that there is no need to impose harmony on the home by formal means: harmony appears of its own accord where every object, seemingly oblivious of every other, fulfills its own essential nature and does its work in accordance with its allotted purpose.[161]

The last word, in this account of the Mies van der Rohe apartment building, might go to Kurt Schwitters, who wrote in *i 10*, the Amsterdam avant-garde magazine:

Mies van der Rohe combines Spirit of the Age and Format. What is Format? A new slogan for architects. Painters can have quality, but architects can have Format. Format stands for Quality of Perception. So quite a small thing may well have format. And, at the same time, Mies's building is big, the biggest in the whole development. Inside, it feels gigantic, because its doors reach up to the ceilings. I can't imagine just walking through these doors; you stride though them. Grand, noble figures stride through the doors, full of the new spirit. Hopefully, at least. It can of course also turn out as it did in the Frankfurt housing developments, where people moved in with their green plush sofas. The future occupants may well turn out to be less mature and free than their own doors. But let us hope that the building will ennoble them.[162]

Mies van der Rohe's building survived the war and the postwar period. When it was renovated in 1986, it was painted pink, the conclusion of the specialists who analyzed the wall surfaces. Mies himself fought hard to get his building painted; whether the color he had in mind was pink is another matter.[163]

Jacobus Johannes Pieter Oud

Houses 5, 6, 7, 8, 9

Design: J.J.P. Oud, city architect, Rotterdam, Avenue Concordia 28A.

Five single-family row houses: cellar, first floor, second floor. Construction: concrete, Kossel system. Load-bearing walls lightweight concrete—external walls lightweight concrete, cavity construction—interior partitions plaster on wired tile lath—roof covering Ruberoid. Iron windows, iron door frames, plywood doors.[1]

"We do not hesitate," wrote a Swiss critic in his account of the Weissenhofsiedlung, "to hand the palm to friend Oud: he has nowhere strayed from the program, and has found the most purposeful and pleasing form for all the necessary requirements: not a monument, a house."[2]
Even before the first short-list of prospective architects was drawn up, it was clear that Oud, like Le Corbusier, was indispensable.[3] Both Mies and Stotz were familiar with Oud's achievements in the planning of housing developments in Holland, with his work, and with his thinking. In 1925 he had proclaimed a program:

I bend the knee before the wonders of technology, but I do not think that a steamship can be compared with the Parthenon . . . I can feel enthusiastic about the beautiful lines of a car, but the airplane still looks rather clumsy to me. I can understand why American silos are shown as examples of contemporary art—but I wonder where in the building art has hidden itself? . . .
I loathe those railway bridges whose forms resemble those of Gothic cathedrals—but the purely "functional" architecture of many vaunted examples of engineering leaves me equally cold . . .
I long for a home which satisfies all the demands of my love of comfort; but a house is something more to me than a "machine for living in"![4]

It was in this spirit that Oud approached the task set him by Mies. Mies proposed that Oud should design a group of four two-story units and an adjacent single-family house. Each unit should contain three rooms plus kitchen, bathroom, and maid's room, and the single-family house six rooms plus the same subsidiary rooms. The cost was to be 35 marks per cubic meter of enclosed space, wrote Mies; and Oud, like every architect, would receive 2,000 marks as a fee, which Mies would endeavor to have raised to 3,000 marks.[5]
Illness and another commission prevented Oud from starting work straight away. This did not, however, prevent him from raising queries about German living habits: "What does three rooms mean? Three bedrooms and living room, or two bedrooms and living room? Or am I allowed to make three bedrooms if that is possible?"[6] In his reply, Mies enlarged upon the purpose of the exhibition:

In the individual buildings, the nature of the home is our central concern. We want to get right down to the function of a dwelling and the problem of economy . . . I would like to stress that even in the smallest dwelling we want to provide three bedrooms or cubicles. This seems to be the least demand we can make. And every dwelling must have a bath.[7]

Oud's design took its time in arriving. The official deadline of December 20, 1926, passed, and the drawings had not yet arrived. The building committee of Stuttgart city council took a look at the proposals received and remarked on the absence of small three- or four-bedroom houses affordable by workers or low-paid office workers.[8] Oud was behindhand with his drawings, and so, when Mies wrote Oud on January 3, 1927, he took the opportunity of spelling out City Hall's requirements: the units should be simple but good-looking, cost no more than 12,000–14,000 marks per unit, and form a continuous row with a width per unit of 5–6 meters (16–20 feet). It would probably be useful, wrote Mies, if the block were to consist not of apartments but of "four single-family houses," and if the adjacent single-family house were also to be of minimum capacity. "It would be desirable to keep this type, too, smaller than was originally intended."[9]
Oud's answer came back swiftly. He wrote that he must have been visited by the "Spirit of Prophecy," because his designs were exactly what Mies had asked him for: single-family row houses.[10] On January 17, 1927, Oud sent his design to Döcker, whose reaction is not known, and told him:

Instead of four, I have designed five houses according to a single type. For one thing, this makes the building cheaper, because a separate type takes a lot of time (more time than I can spare, after the delay caused by my illness), and it's better to have one good type than two bad ones. It also seems to me, as far as I can see, rather too much of a good thing to add one more new type to all the many that are already to be expected: a bungalow, what is more, a form that is not going to be used in your country any more than in ours, because the density is too high, the land too expensive, the footings too costly, etc. For these reasons I have not, for the moment, produced more than one type, and I hope that you will find this acceptable.[11]

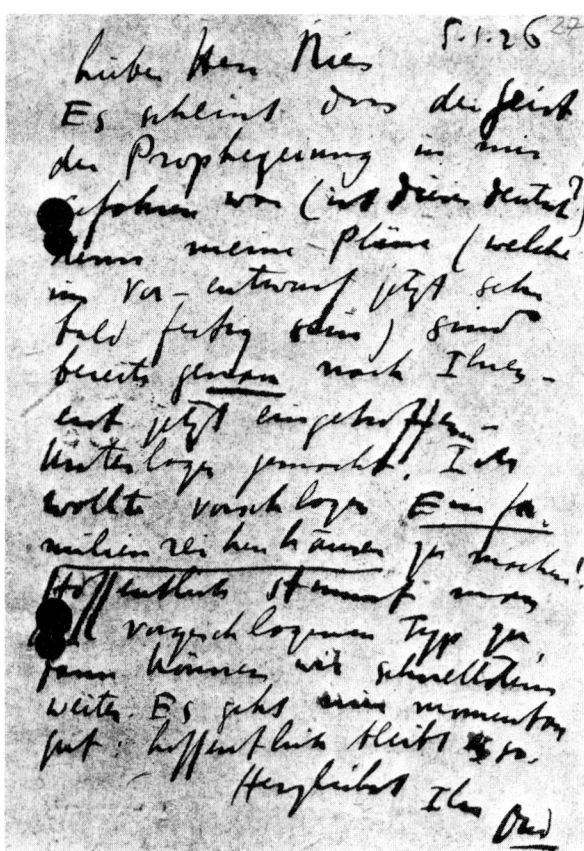

Postcard from Oud to Mies, January 5, 1927: "It seems that the Spirit of Prophecy had come on me (is this German?) because my plans (which will soon be ready in a preliminary form) are done exactly according to your instructions, only just received. I meant to propose single-family row houses! Hopefully the type proposed will be agreed to, then we can get ahead as quickly as possible. We are well at the moment; hopefully it will stay that way. Kind regards, Oud."

gestion, like those of Mies, came too late: Oud had already worked through the guidelines he had been given. He told Döcker:

> In designing the type I tried to follow the suggestions of the Stuttgart Housewives, Dr. Erna Meyer, and so on, as closely as possible (naturally as far as this is practicable within the specified framework of the program). This has led me to make the north yard as small as possible as a space and to design it not as a garden (no point!) but as a yard for the kitchen etc.[16]

Close study of the guidelines that Oud described as the basis of his little kitchen yard reveals only one sentence that might possibly have inspired his decision. Erna Meyer had recommended that, in apartments in blocks (not in single-family houses),

> each kitchen should be provided, not only with the food closet listed as 4(a), which in small households replaces the larder, but with a small housework balcony, on which shoes can be cleaned, and rugs etc. shaken. This should be protected from the rain and bounded not with a grille but with a solid masonry wall; its area should be not more than 3/4 square meter [8 square feet].[17]

The little utility yards of Oud's houses measure 3 × 3.1 meters, or in other words "not more than 3 × 4 meters [10 × 13 feet]"! There may have been a misreading of the notation; the conclusion is tempting. The yards, together with the adjacent rooms such as the laundry, the bicycle store, and the drying room above, give a rhythm and sculptural life to the row houses through the alternation of light and shadow, advancing and receding surfaces, and lend an impression of individuality to each house.

According to the description that Oud sent to Döcker, the yard had the function of accommodating daily deliveries of groceries, coal, and so on, together with bicycles, garbage, and a clothesline in summer. Some of the laundry work might also take place in the yard. In winter, clothes would be dried in the drying room above the laundry, to which it was connected by a dumbwaiter; ironing would be done in the drying room, on an ironing board hinged to the wall. Oud went on:

> Behind the dwelling, a little street is envisaged (just a footpath for the five dwellings) which would only be for visitors and residents. The back (south) yards are then as big as possible, flower gardens (completely free of the kitchen!) behind the living room; on the far side of the footpath, a communal garden for children to play in (sandbox, etc.)[18]

All later descriptions of the houses, including the brief one in the 1927 summer issue of the Werkbund periodical *Die Form*, and the highly detailed one in the Werkbund book *Bau und Wohnung*, are based on this initial letter from Oud to Döcker. Details are explained more fully, and the urban planning aspect of row houses of this type is spelled out:

> The layout presupposes that the house has access to two streets. Both should be equally presentable: not a street for show on one side and a utilitarian alleyway on the other. These should be distinguished simply by their character (in accor-

Thus a group of houses was added which, as Councilman Karl Beer—the committee member who was also an architect—had demanded, "should show new ways for the building and interior design of good and cheap dwellings suited to the needs of the broad masses of the population."[12] Oud's houses were intended and regarded as "workers' housing," although everyone was clear that "these decidedly working-class houses are not in a decidedly working-class area."[13] (If the Oud houses had been at the other end of the Weissenhofsiedlung, where Scharoun's House 33 stands, they would have been very close to some working-class housing, because the adjoining portion of the Gauchergelände is occupied by the Schönblick development which Karl Beer himself built for the Bau- und Heimstättenverein in 1927–29.)

Oud, like all the other architects concerned, received information on the position of his buildings within the development, plus guidelines for the design of the kitchen and utility area supplied by the Stuttgart housewives' organization and by Dr. Erna Meyer. Most of the Weissenhofsiedlung architects were rather cavalier in their treatment of these specifications and failed to draw much inspiration from them; Oud was an exception.

Oud had been in touch with Erna Meyer through Bruno Taut in 1925;[14] this was probably in connection with the preliminary work for her book *Der Neue Haushalt* (1926). In all its many editions she illustrated an exemplary design by Oud for doors in a hallway. Erna Meyer did not actually meet Oud until work started on the Weissenhofsiedlung, but she was a fervent admirer of him, as were many others connected with the Stuttgart exhibition, where he was affectionately known as "Bob."[15]

On January 10, 1927, Erna Meyer suggested to Oud that they work together on the design of his Weissenhof project; she had seen the drawings of other architects in Stuttgart, and had not liked what she saw. The sug-

dance with their functions). The combination of both streets into a single one would lead to a lively street scene, which would offer, in place of the formalistic tedium of identical facades, the variety of an organically based grouping. This is proposed here as a principle (the buildings themselves cannot demonstrate it, for the good reason that there is only one row). The situation outlined here has the additional advantage that the streets can be very narrow: they need only serve the needs of the traffic (which on streets of this kind is very light), while the back yards will take care of the need for daylight: this can be taken into consideration in setting the street widths. Other consequences would include a saving in road surfacing and in utilities of all kinds, as well as greater ease of policing.[19]

The reference to "ease of policing" seems a little odd: perhaps it has something to do with Oud's experience as a city architect. The account in *Bau und Wohnung* also tells us that the north (kitchen) yards were bounded on the street side by a thin wall of cement on wired tile lath, and that the yard gate was open at the top to enable the housewife to see visitors from the kitchen. The door could be opened electrically from the kitchen, and unnecessary trips to the door were eliminated by having deliveries—which were much more frequent in those days than they are now—passed in through the kitchen window.

The whole floor plan was worked out to give maximum economy in walling. By amalgamating allied functions, and by linking them together in rational sequences, Oud achieved mature form. He keeps practicalities very much in mind: Erna Meyer wanted as many kitchen chores as possible to be done in a seated position, and he provided for this, together with a rational arrangement of wall closets, walk-in closets (laundry), a serving hatch with a sliding glass door to enable the housewife to keep an eye on the children, a balcony on the upper floor to air the bedding, independent access to all bedrooms, two bedrooms with direct access to the bathroom, a separate toilet, and so on.

Oud's intellectual penetration and his ability to see beyond the stated requirements reveal him as a master. Erna Meyer, whose own reputation for good sense was well established,[20] recognized all these points in Oud's drawings and paid him an enthusiastic tribute: "Yesterday I went through your project, and I hope you will not take it as an empty compliment if I tell you that I like it enormously, by far the best of all I have seen thus far."[21]

She had no criticisms of Oud's kitchen design, which she found "quite extraordinary." The only snag she could see was the fact that the visitor came in through the backyard directly into the living room, and that the mailbox was also on this side. She ended her letter:

It is a sad sign of the times that one still has to waste so many words on basic practical matters that ought to be utterly taken for granted; I hope it will not be long, now, before every architect knows these things in his bones. Then no house will have such basic shortcomings, and it will be possible to assess the architect's achievement without having to worry about obvious basics: for architecture starts where they leave off. But where these things have not even started to be done, as I am afraid is the case even with our best architects today—then the most magnificent architecture is no use![22]

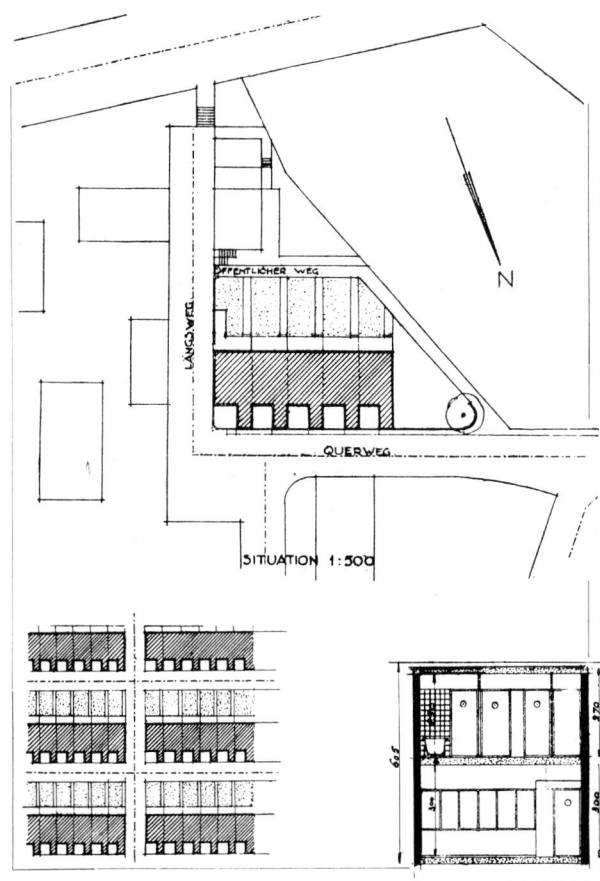

J.J.P. Oud: block plan of Houses 5–9, row arrangement, and section of one house

The works of the Weissenhof architects whom she thus criticized puzzled Erna Meyer—as she told Oud in another letter—"from a psychological point of view. Because you would expect mental indolence and complacency to be balanced out at least to some extent by fear of criticism, even if no higher motives are to be expected."[23] In her later lectures and publications, she described Oud's and Schneck's solutions as the only ones worth taking as a model.

The building of the Oud houses began with the placing of the building contract on March 25, 1927. The work was given to the Bossert company at a price of 13,400 marks per house, but Bossert backed out two weeks later, so that a new contract had to be placed on April 14, three months and ten days before the opening, with the Bremen firm of Kossel. The price of each house was now set at 13,500 marks, amounting to 76,500 marks in all. The final accounts of the superintendent, Döcker, show the total cost of the five houses as 74,518.67 marks.[24]

On May 2, 1927, when Deputy Mayor Sigloch conducted an on-site inspection with contractors, representatives of City Hall departments, superintendent, and exhibition directorate to examine progress, the Oud houses had not yet been started as negotiations with the Bremen firm were still in progress. Oud was to write in *Bau und Wohnung*:

The original idea was to build in lightweight precast blockwork, a cheap material that is highly suitable for residential building because of its porous composition (useful for insulation against damp, heat, cold, noise) but is far too little used. Incomprehensibly, building in this material turned out to be much more expensive than in concrete.

Houses 5, 6, 7, 8, 9
Architect: J.J.P. Oud
Plans and elevations
drawn from the archi-
tect's building code
submissions of May 5,
1927

Left, first floor; right,
second floor

Elevations from south
(back yard), north
(kitchen yard, Pan-
kokweg)

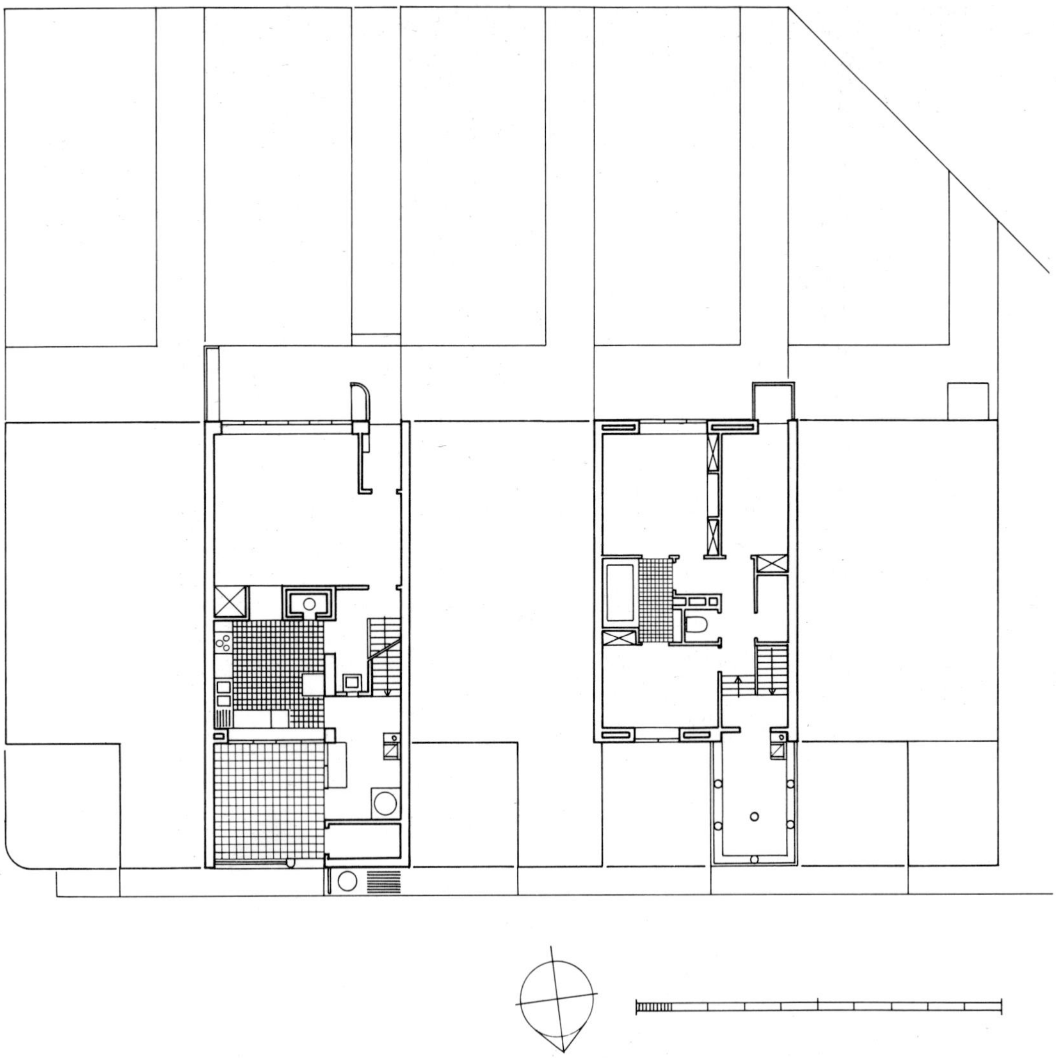

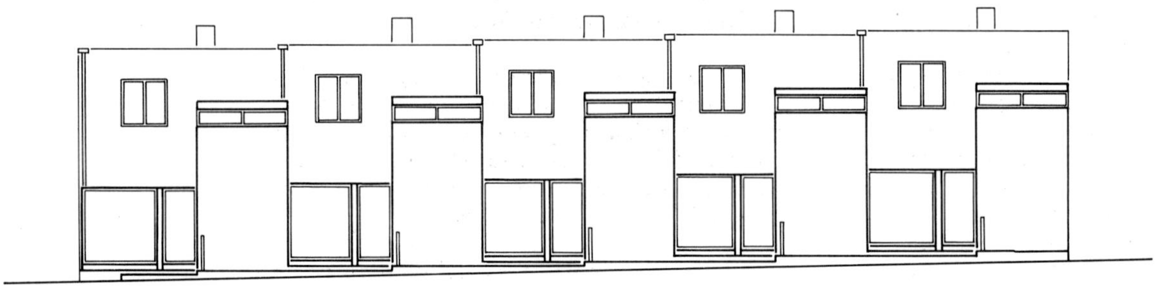

The concrete construction was assigned to the firm of Kossel, Bremen (Schnellbau Kossel system). This system has proved its worth in Holland in the building of many hundreds of dwellings. The basic principle of the process is the use of coal-saving aggregates (gravel, sand, pumice, blast-furnace slag, clinker from garbage incineration), bound by a comparatively small proportion of cement. The resulting material is highly porous, has good heat-insulation properties, and is nailable. It is consequently used in all walls serving as heat insulation (in the inhabited parts). The foundations and load-bearing members are made of a gravel-based concrete. The walls are cast in one piece within the formwork and—to improve heat insulation, promote drying, and save materials—they contain cavities which, to prevent circulation of air, are divided horizontally at intervals of 50 cm [20 inches]. This technique offers the advantage of easy heating and good heat retention; it holds the warmth in winter and the cool-

ness in summer . . . The drawback of the system is the primitive shuttering, which militates against precision of finish.[25]

This was not the only drawback, as will be seen. On the other hand, the Kossel system was not called Schnellbau, "Quick Build," for nothing:

The Oud houses sprang up as if by magic. In a short time the formwork was up, the concrete poured, the shuttering removed, and the houses finished. All the recesses for closets, pipes, etc., were incorporated in the formwork. There was nothing left for the mason to do.[26]

That was the Rasch brothers' enthusiastic account of the technique whereby the concrete was poured into the formwork by machine.[27] The Bremen firm did not actually do the on-site work: this was left to the Stephan company, of Stuttgart, "because the transportation of machines and equipment would have wasted much valuable time."[28]

Early in May Oud received Döcker's circular Number fifteen in which he was invited to send in a resident architect of his own.[29] He chose Paul (Pál) Meller, a young and enthusiastic Hungarian architect. Like Alfred Roth, acting for Le Corbusier and Jeanneret, and Ernst Walther, for Mies, Meller kept his principal posted on events at Weissenhof. But whereas Le Corbusier's and Mies's resident representatives treated their bosses with respect and veneration the relationship here seems to have been closer: in his letters to Rotterdam, Meller affectionately called Oud "Father" or "Daddy" (Väterchen). It is a pity that Oud's answers to these delightful, youthfully indiscreet letters have not survived. Oud probably wrote them by hand and kept no copy—in contrast to Le Corbusier, who kept a carbon of everything.

When Meller arrived in Stuttgart, he described the "status of building work" as very good and reported that the "two lowest houses are already out of their formwork" and that the dimensions were exactly right. From then on the correspondence covers every problem of detail and all the decisions that were requested and given. There is, in the Oud–Meller collaboration, no sense—as there is between Le Corbusier and Roth—that the resident architect has been left alone to cope with a task which is beyond him.

As well as events on the site, Meller reported on personal matters, with the charm of authenticity:

Rooms are almost unobtainable in Stuttgart, let alone up at Weissenhof. Of course, after arriving in Stuttgart at 8 A.M., I had a room by 12, obliquely opposite the Siedlung! Why am I giving Hugo Keuerleber two conducted tours of Rotterdam? It's his house . . . The food at the Keuerlebers' is good, and Schneck sends his regards . . . The hotel here has a bible next to the telephone instead of a directory.[30]

As opening day crept closer and closer Meller arranged for the making of the tubular steel furniture to Oud's design, and defied the building office by hiding specially thin electric cables in the plaster and quickly covering up the evidence. He told Oud:

I am fighting the Gods, Döcker, Schmid, and the World for the sake of our cause. God have mercy on the Siedlung! But I am still on top . . . Forgive all these scraps of paper. But here there is nothing left. No paper, no enthusiasm—just bitter despair. No one wants anything to do with the Siedlung anymore, they've had it right up to here.[31]

But not long after this, probably in response to an anxious letter from an ailing Oud, Meller took an optimistic line, wishing Oud "a return of the divine dadanature"—four days before opening day, when the finish woodwork had not even been contracted for, and many of the contractors were threatening to put down tools.[32]

On opening day Meller wrote, "One house was ready to be visited. The kitchen was fitted up temporarily—it didn't look at all good. The house was furnished with pieces by Kramer, with no linoleum. The furniture looked very clumsy." White terrazzo steps led up to the second floor, and Meller reported that "many hundreds of people" had visited the first house, and "one heard this and that. But generally the building was understood." Later: "The specialist critics are enthusiastic, especially when they hear the comparative figures; the housewife is content and feels at home; only the war profiteer and his like consider this too little and that too steep."[33]

On opening day Meller was in his element. There were three parties. A big supper at the Villa Berg, then "a wild party at the Clou, and (yesterday) a nighttime party thrown by Mies in the tower of the railroad station. Frau Giedion was there, and I spent the whole evening with that wonderful woman. My alcohol released all the inhibitions from her soul, and her confessions filled my soul. Papa, much when we meet."[34]

After the opening, when the well-nigh unbearable "gigantic tension" was released and "the city fathers largely lost interest," the situation was one described by Meller as "running around and rescuing." But he also said: "The white passage with the peepholes above is sensationally beautiful!" Meller was as enthusiastic about Oud's design as Roth was about Le Corbusier's. After the "opening day commotion," there seemed to be "no supervision," and everything was "left vague." But work on the houses went on. The outsides were painted,

and everything out of true, crooked, or imprecise is lost to view. What does it look like? . . . I think it is very beautiful, and I am tormented by the awareness that so much geknoei [botching] lies behind it. This is no Hook of Holland. In the backyards, 4 of the patios are finished and paved paths and posts for two houses. The grille separating the patios is very fine, separating and yet transparent; 2 of the benches are also in place. By the middle of next week the grass will be sown and flowers planted.[35]

Oud's tubular steel furniture was made under Meller's supervision by the Arnold company of Schorndorf (who also made furniture for Le Corbusier, Mies, Lilly Reich, Stam, and the Rasch brothers). Meller thought Oud's designs "marvelous," and told him with delight that the house with his interiors (House 8) would be complete on August 10. "When will it all be ready? I think, at the present speed, never. My whole energy is concentrated on your house!"[36]

This laudable concentration was no match for the intractable facts of construction work. Concrete is made with water, and it has to dry out before paint, floorings, or anything else can be applied to it. The Kossel method could speed up construction, but not this drying. Meller prescribed "artificial" drying—heaters were brought in and all the apertures left open. This worked, but even so the painters could not start work on painting "everything white except for the colored living room and colored banisters."[37] The terrazzo steps were white, and in the bedrooms "white opaque roller blinds, as in trains and streetcars. In the unfurnished house [House 5], splendid blue drapes."[38] Meller's taste for "roller blinds, as in trains and streetcars" was shared with his colleague Roth, Le Corbusier's resident architect, who, however, preferred them in brown.

The damp problem in the Oud houses was to persist. The first tenants complained that the basement rooms and the upstairs laundry room were unusable, and that the structures were damp throughout. Oud's reply was laconic:

On the dampness of the structure, I need say nothing. I warned of this all along. In Holland we say: in the first year give a new house to your enemy, in the second year to your friend, and in the third year live in it yourself. The house just needs time to shake off the defects of "newness."

And when a housewife complained that the drying room, ideal in itself, could only be used with the greatest caution, because such a room ought above all to be dry, Oud answered: "the moldy shoes must, it seems to me, have belonged to the occupier's 'enemy.' For the rest, better ventilation is called for."[39]

Like many of the other houses, those by Oud were declared to be "completed" only on September 6.[40]

A sharp-tongued and sharp-eyed observer of work in progress, Meller seems to have kept a particular watch on Oud's compatriots: he described the interior design by Sybold van Ravesteyn (Oud's House 7) as "arty-crafty preciosity." He did, however, admit that "you can sit down in tolerable comfort." He took a much harsher line with the work of Mart Stam:

> Then Stam! God have mercy. Like the village girl who arrived in town at ten after six and wanted to be chic by seven! His living room is revolting. Before it was furnished, the room astonished us all. It was beautiful. But in its beauty it showed me the corruption of my own aesthetic attitude. I think a giant garage is *beautiful*; I think factory workshops are *beautiful*. There are living rooms that are *beautiful*. The fallacy lies in the equation, beautiful = beautiful. No such math exists in real life. And so I overlooked the fact that Stam's living room is a *beautiful* garage or a beautiful bit of a factory. It tolerates no furniture, and furniture makes it neither one thing nor the other. A small automobile would really be at home in it.
>
> And furnished! Father, It would knock you flat. Frank's brothel is a nursery by comparison. Black plush and colored cushions en masse. Easy chair in the same vein. Fantastic lamps, pure Arts and Crafts.[41]

Meller does not mention Stam's cantilever chair, or any of the other positive details that were certainly there. He was young and irreverent; his contemporaries remembered him as a lovable, amusing character.[42] Ferdinand Kramer dedicated his own account of the Weissenhofsiedlung to the memory of Paul Meller;[43] for Meller was murdered by the Nazis in Brandenburg-Görden jail in 1943, classified as "politically dangerous."[44]

The interior design of Oud's five houses was undertaken by Oud himself, Rudolf Lutz, Sybold van Ravesteyn, and Ferdinand Kramer. One house was left unfurnished. No precise furnishing plans of the individual houses have been found, but photographs taken during the exhibition give some idea of how they looked then.

HOUSE 5

The accommodation is as follows.
Cellar: coal cellar, storage space.
First floor: entrance from back yard with cloakroom space, living room, kitchen, laundry (with dumbwaiter to drying area on upper story), bicycle store, and kitchen yard. Warm-air heating from kitchen for the whole house.
Second floor: one twin and two single bedrooms, bathroom, toilet. All rooms with built-in closets.[45]

As the description of all the row houses is identical, it is

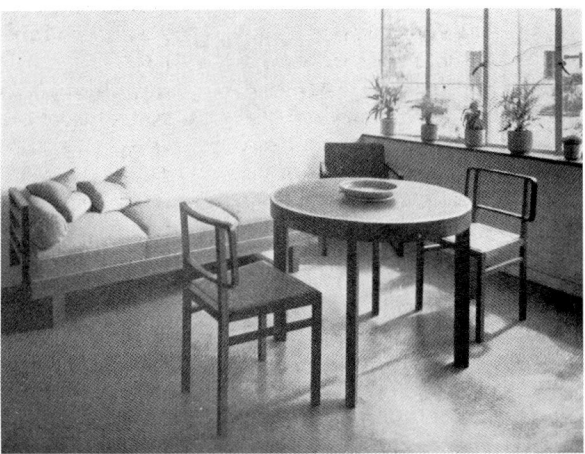

House 6:
Interior by Rudolf Lutz

not repeated below in the discussion of Houses 6–9.

House 5 was shown without furniture; Meller mentioned its "splendid blue drapes."

HOUSE 6

Interior design: Rudolf Lutz, architect, Stuttgart, Gerokstrasse 7.[46]

Rudolf Lutz, who had studied at the Kunstgewerbeschule in Stuttgart and also at the Bauhaus during its first, Weimar phase, was in private practice as an architect in Stuttgart. Like many others, he turned to interior design for want of building commissions. He had been a member of the Werkbund since 1925.

Lutz was commissioned to design the interior of this Oud house after Stotz had recommended that the designer initially chosen, Julius Metzke-Rovira, should be asked to work on one of Max Taut's houses instead and replaced by "Rudolf Lutz, who works in a plainer, more practical way."[47] The invitation came from Mies, who asked Lutz to consult with Oud over the color scheme and to avoid "any hint of the salon."[48] There is little to say about the interiors themselves; the omission of the padding in the chairbacks hardly amounts to an individual design concept.

HOUSE 7

Interior design: S. van Ravesteyn, Utrecht (Holland).[49]

Sybold van Ravesteyn was an architect by training but had made something of a name for himself in the course of the 1920s as a designer of applied art objects and furniture. Some of his furniture was awarded a prize at

House 7:
Interior by Sybold van Ravesteyn

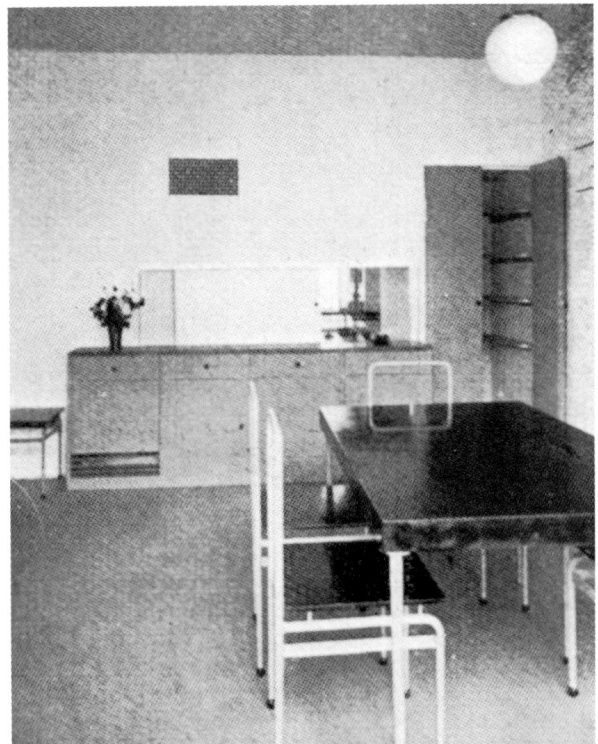

the Paris Exposition of 1925. His invitation was probably suggested by Oud.

Meller did not mince his words about Ravesteyn and his interior design ideas for Weissenhof, which were certainly not as uncompromising as that of Stam, Breuer, and Oud. (Oud's own opinions have not been preserved.) Meller dismissed Ravesteyn's "nickel furniture with black velvet and red *boai'*" as "arty-crafty preciosity." In his opinion, Ravesteyn "has grasped the spirit of your [Oud's] house just as well as he has . . . the whole tendency"—which is to say, not at all.[50]

Even so, Ravesteyn's designs do have a certain lightness and freshness by comparison with the worthy but often dull furniture contributed by German designers—about whom Meller was even more caustic.[51]

HOUSE 8

Interior design: J.J.P. Oud, city architect, Rotterdam.[52]

We know from Meller that this house was painted white throughout with the exception of the banisters and the living room. Unfortunately no color indications for the living room have survived. Drawings of color schemes from the Oud archive show only light yellow external and internal doors, red painted shelves, and a picture on Oud's picture rails in primary red, blue, and yellow on a white ground.

The tubular steel furniture, made by Arnold, is marked by extremes of asceticism: graphically clean in its lines almost to the point of immateriality, and dedicated to the proposition that the best form of seating is one that obliges the body to remain in constant motion.

According to the Oud–Meller correspondence, the wooden components of the walk-in closet in the corner and of the piece of furniture incorporating the serving hatch, as well as the side table and table-top, were to be in "natural wood"—whatever that may mean. The light fittings were designed by W. H. Gispen of Rotterdam: a "light-diffusing, opalized glass globe."[53]

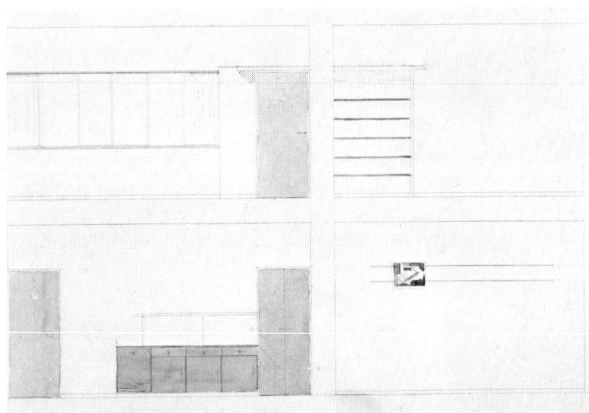

What of the kitchen, so much praised by Erna Meyer? What improvements did it offer for housekeeping? Erna Meyer began her description with a reference to a pet preoccupation:

Right against the wide, roughly north-facing kitchen window, we have the kitchen table, at which it is possible to work while seated. To the left is the pantry, with its outside ventilation, to the right the garbage pail, into which the waste can be thrown as it is produced in the course of the work. The draining board (which normally covers the sink) slides out to cover the garbage pail as soon as dishwashing begins. This work can also be . . . done in a seated position. The cooker has working surfaces to left and right; then comes a serving hatch to the dining room, and a folding table and folding chair which a servant, if any, can use for rest and meals. Another particularly gratifying feature of the kitchen is that the serving hatch has a glazed door, so that the mother can keep her children under supervision as she works, when they are in the living room or the yard, without allowing cooking odors to enter the living room.

Most of the available wall space in the kitchen

House 8:

Kitchen by Oud

Isometric view of kitchen

House 9:
Living room by Ferdinand Kramer

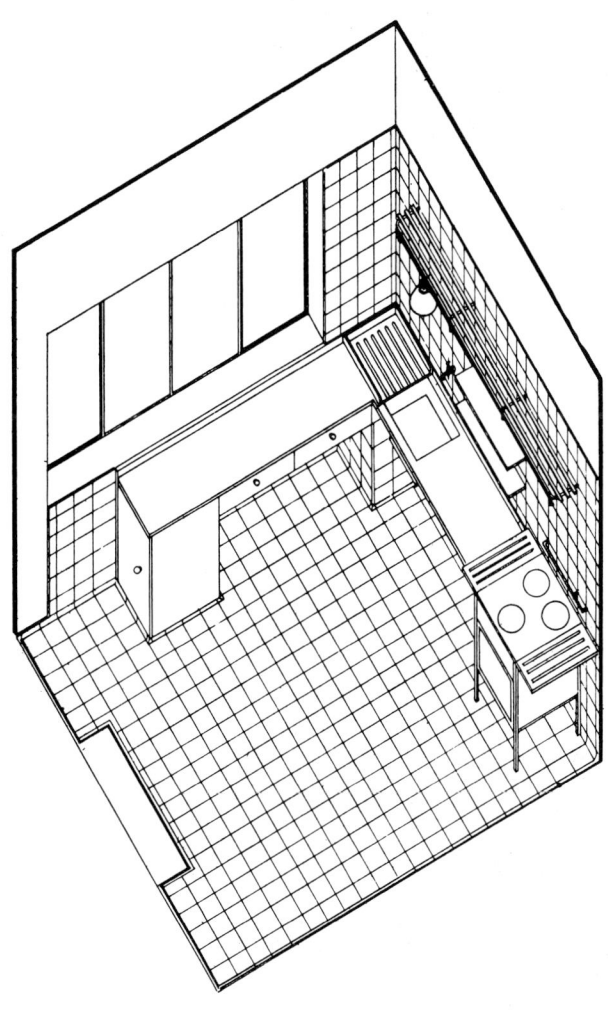

in the melancholy trivia of everyday existence! But this can only happen if she, for her part, is ready to respond to the architect's new spirit with a new spirit of her own, and to give the lie to what Oud—with some justification, I am afraid—has said of her: "The housewife seems at the moment to prefer a long span of physical work to a short span of mental work."[54]

HOUSE 9

Interior design: F. Kramer, architect and civil engineer, Frankfurt am Main, Oppenheimer Strasse 44.[55]

Ferdinand Kramer furnished his Oud house—as he did his apartment in the Mies block—with standard pieces from the range of the city-owned household goods organization, Frankfurter Hausrat. Of these Kramer wrote,

> Our age demands the utmost care in the elaboration of the design model which is to be entrusted to the machine, because once the machine is running it will maintain its standard and produce cheaply, cleanly, and precisely. The contact between the piece of work and the hand craftsman has been abolished one and for all by the machine. Social, economic, technical, and aesthetic arguments thus unite to greet the production of standard furniture.[56]

Meller's verdict that Kramer's furniture was "clumsy" seems unwarranted. It is straight and honest, and goes far beyond a merely simplifying approach to furniture.

The specialist press was generally complimentary about Oud's Stuttgart version of the row house. Edgar Wedepohl, who reported from the exhibition for the architectural journal *Wasmuth's Monatshefte*, was positively enthusiastic. His article, and the ensuing correspondence, deserve to be quoted at length:

> The most functional and best thought-out structure in the exhibition is the row of small houses by J.J.P. Oud, of Rotterdam. Here the Dutch master's rich experience has fulfilled our expectations of the exhibition itself: a type of humane, comfortable, and practical small dwelling which uses the available space well, and which is suitable for mass production. . . .

is occupied by closets, so that all the working utensils are within reach in the place where they are used, and can at the same time be stored in dust-free conditions.

After praising the perfect communication between laundry room and airing room, the built-in ironing board, and the cross-ventilation, Erna Meyer went on:

> Who could deny that in such a house the working woman can look forward to a new life? A life which no longer makes her into a martyr to the family, but liberates her from all unnecessary toil, *free for more important things* than burying herself

In this exhibition, at any event, the Oud formula towers above all others. By contrast with common German practice, and the corresponding building codes, it is noticeable that in the Dutch manner the bathroom and toilet are on the second floor in the center of the house. This position makes possible a narrower frontage than when the bathroom and the toilet have to have windows in an outside wall. It also necessitates a flat roof: otherwise it would be no easy matter to light and ventilate these two rooms directly from above. . . .

The exterior of this group is as clear as the interior: a rectilinear block with continuous window bands and wings built at regular intervals. Not only does this form seem to spring logically from the interior, the floor plan, the construction, and the material: here an ordering will has formed the whole into a unified form; mind has prevailed over matter and created not only something useful but something beautiful. The puritan austerity of which Oud is accused could easily be turned to charm and cheerfulness by the addition of a little color. [57]

In a subsequent letter to Oud, Wedepohl raised a number of questions, to which Oud replied,

I am happy to answer a number of some points raised in your letter. Of course I was delighted by your article in *Wasmuth's Monatshefte*, firstly because I value you as a critic, and secondly because I did not at all expect my block at the exhibition to arouse any great interest: it is no more than an attempt to build a proper dwelling house: a problem that hardly enters the province of architecture at all. Since nowadays, everything, even the smallest trifle, is expected to be architecture, I did not expect my un-architectural block to receive as much attention as it has.

Oud went on to discuss specific points such as color, windows, banisters, the flat roof—questions of doctrine, as in 1925:

I take your third point first: color.

Ten years ago I made repeated attempts, together with the Cubist painters, to make space into a colored "space picture." I regard this as the only logical conclusion from the painting that was being done then . . .

Today I still consider color to be in its proper place in a big city, where (in the center) life needs strong influences! In the greenery, among the trees, there is atmosphere; there one needs to be very careful with color, because of the changing light, and therefore the changing colors of trees, greenery, plants, etc. I like to see greenery and flowers around a dwelling, much more than I like colors; just because the dwelling, too, is an inconspicuous piece of nature: quite unlike the large building, which dominates, or at least can speak for itself. Inside, one can tolerate rather more color, because there one is more or less in control of the atmosphere: but not too much, even there, because then the objects in the space are too much tied down by the color that defines everything. The internal space must not become obtrusive in itself, and that is what color does. In exteriors (in interiors too, but less disruptively), the space of the house is very much altered by

color: the form is often actually destroyed, which is why, in my opinion, only "shapeless houses"— like the later houses of Le Corbusier—can tolerate color at all. I thought for a long time whether to use a little color or none: I decided for the best. Life itself can bring in any color it likes, outside and inside, without clashing. And so my house comes "alive" when it is in use. It seems to me to be "puritanical" only so long as it remains an exhibit, to be visited. Life has to have freedom to live, not to be crushed by a building: this, for me, is the difference between modernism and academicism.

On question 1 (windows), I would like to say that in my view a lot of light is indeed "modern." We, that is people, urgently want this at the moment. How far to go? I meant to run a survey— perhaps you will do it?—about where the limits come, where the increased heating costs and the discomfort of too much sunlight call a halt. I don't think these two factors have to be absolutely decisive: cheerful sunlight is such a good thing in itself. This is why we should accept some discomfort in return (we go to the theater, although the streetcar ride is no pleasure!) In my house the central heating finally had to be omitted because of cost; otherwise there would have been good heaters under the windows. You in Germany are a bit too sensitive in this respect: our windows are much bigger anyway, and there have always been long rows of windows in the English country house. And finally: for me, the rational is only a starting-point (a matter of conscience, but still only a starting-point). Function and form constantly interact, and so the building takes shape. Why should I deny that I find this particular window in this particular room beautiful? I don't give a damn for pure function without form; and the same goes for the machine for living in!

On 2 (the balustrade), I have this to say. I consider this sort of balustrade beautiful. I lived for seven years on an upper floor with a balcony 10 meters [33 feet] above the street. Balustrade: excellent, iron uprights and iron wire mesh in between. Even so, for five years my wife and I were always terrified when the little boy was alone on the balcony. I think children should always be watched, so that they never go on a balcony alone, because they always climb up on the balustrade.

On 3 (flat roof). I don't understand all the talk there is today about flat roofs: neither the pros nor the cons. Mostly, it seems to me, the flat roof is practical (here it has already lasted very well for twenty years, despite poor construction), so in that case use it: when it is not practical, as at Oud-Mathenesse, then I don't use it. To me "pro" is just as dogmatic as "con," and if I am now on the "pro" side this is primarily because virtually the whole world is "con," which means that we have to win equal rights for both.

"Aesthetically," I am entirely on the side of the flat roof. Our tight contemporary architecture does not suit the pitched roof, which is very "rough"; and I am disturbed by the useless triangular spaces within, which breed only dust and bad design. Generally speaking, therefore, I say Flat Roof. But when life (not the art professors) demands otherwise, then I say, if it's better, then a pitched roof. "Modernity" is an attitude, not a doctrine: it finds expression in any material. In a hilly district like Stuttgart, I find flat roofs decidedly better looking. The slope of a pitched roof does not relate well to the slope of a mountain. And so I can very well understand why the Weissenhofsiedlung is all flat.[58]

Wedepohl replied appreciatively: Oud's answers, he wrote, confirmed him in his belief that Oud would "one day be one of the classics of the new architecture . . . it is precisely your endeavor always to design something that is alive, and not to base yourself on hard and fast formulations, that distinguishes you from those modern formalists whose academy, in my view, is the Bauhaus."[59]

It is worth mentioning here that in January of 1928 the editor of *Wasmuth's Monatshefte*, Werner Hege-

mann, launched an attack on Mayor Lautenschlager of Stuttgart which nearly led to a libel action (only averted by an apology), and which included a reference to Oud's houses "as one of the most melancholy chapters in the story of the exhibition." Hegemann had read the correspondence between Oud and Wedepohl, but totally ignored Oud's answers to Wedepohl's questions.[60]

After Weissenhof Oud went through a very quiet period. In 1936 he wrote Döcker that he had designed a few houses but had not "got to the building stage" with anything since Stuttgart: "Thus far, it is all—except the furniture—just paper!"[61] His five row houses in Stuttgart survived the war and the postwar period comparatively well; since 1984 they have stood in all their renovated splendor, protected by law as historic monuments, much admired, and enjoyed by their occupants.

HOUSE 10

Design: Victor Bourgeois, architect
Brussels, Boulevard Léopold II, 271

Single-family house: cellar, first floor, second floor.
Construction: hollow pumice concrete blocks, plastered internally and externally, Feifel zigzag ceilings, Feifel partitions.
Interior design: Victor Bourgeois, architect, Brussels.[1]

The house built by Victor Bourgeois was built and shown in conjunction with the Weissenhofsiedlung; but it has a separate history—or rather two histories—of its own. It stands for itself, and it also stands for a building that ought to have been part of Weissenhof but never was: a house by Adolf Loos. It should really have a plaque saying "Here the great Austrian architect, Adolf Loos, was to have built a house." He was not allowed to do so because he had been rather too free with insults, polemics, and accusations of plagiarism.

In the summer of 1924 Loos broke a journey to Paris[2] to visit Stuttgart and look at the Werkbund exhibition *Die Form*. With a little enlightened guesswork, what happened next can be reconstructed.

Loos had certainly heard that this was a show exclusively devoted to objects that bore no ornament whatever, but relied entirely on their own elegance of form. The title of the book which was issued in the following year was *Form ohne Ornament*, "Form Without Ornament." However, neither in the exhibition nor in the book was there any mention of the campaign which Loos himself had waged against ornament, with great vigor and acerbity, in all his writings, especially in the provocative essay "Ornament and Crime" (*Ornament und Verbrechen*) of 1908. In this he declared that anyone with a tattoo is either a criminal or a future criminal—with the sole exception of those who die before their criminal proclivities come to light.

In the same year, 1908, in an essay whose title was a manifesto in itself, Loos had assailed the founders of the Deutscher Werkbund as "The Superfluous Men" (*Die überflüssigen*): men who aspired to set the world to rights and make the human environment into an honest, dignified one, while at the same time winnning Germany a place in world markets and improving the earning potential of the design industry. "Now they have gotten together and met in Munich. They have once more told our industry and our craftsmen how important they are.[3] He wrote elsewhere that "the members of this federation are people who are trying to replace our present-day culture with a different one. Why they are doing this, I do not know."[4]

The Werkbund's members had certainly not forgotten Loos's words. And so, in 1924, he came to Stuttgart to see an exhibition which he had good reason to re-gard as based on his own example, and—as he had probably expected—found no mention of his name. Eye-witnesses report—and here history takes over from speculation—that Loos threw a major scene. Voices were raised, things turned very unpleasant, and echoes of the quarrel reached the ears of the public; so we hear from Mia Seeger, the grand old lady of the Werkbund.[5]

In 1925 the success of *Die Form*, organized and selected by the administrator of the Werkbund's Württemberg section, Gustaf Stotz, gave rise to the idea of a larger exhibition, covering "The Home" in all its aspects—the germ of the Weissenhofsiedlung. In 1925, too, the carousel of possible participant architects started to turn. Loos's name appears, rather surprisingly, on Stotz's own initial list of September 24, 1925, then disappears. It reappears for four whole days from July 20 through July 24, 1926,[6] only to be struck out very forcefully by the pen of the Stuttgart Deputy Mayor for urban design, Dr. Daniel Sigloch.[7]

Loos himself wrote in 1929 of his nonparticipation in the 1927 exhibition:

When I sought to build a house in Stuttgart, I was turned down flat. The organizers of the exhibition themselves could not agree on a pretext for this refusal. In Stuttgart they said the mayor had something against me personally. Indignant denial from the mayor. Then they talked about lack of space. But at the last moment they had to bring in the architect Bourgeois, although the client would gladly have had a house by me. In Frankfurt am Main, the local representative on the national board of the Deutscher Werkbund opined that I was not a good enough German nationalist. This is probably true, in his sense of the word. In those circles, when I said "Why have the Papuans a culture and the Germans none?"[8] it was interpreted as anti-German, or as a mischievous joke. The fact that this was the heartfelt cry of a bleeding German soul is something that Germans of that kind are never going to understand.

I would have had something to exhibit, namely a way of dividing living rooms in space, not just in floor plan, as has previously been done story by story. Through this invention I might have saved humanity much labor and time in its evolution.

[Footnote: For this is the great revolution in architecture: the resolution of a floor plan in space! Before Immanuel Kant, humanity was incapable of thinking in spatial terms, and the architects were forced to make the toilet as tall as the drawing room. The only way they could get lower rooms was by dividing the height in half. And, just as humanity will one day learn to play chess in

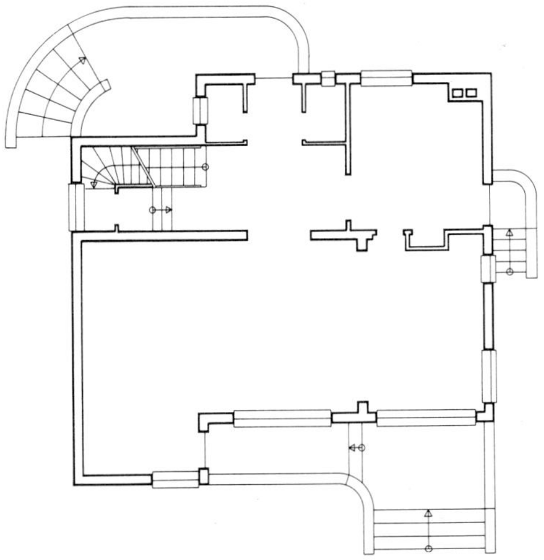

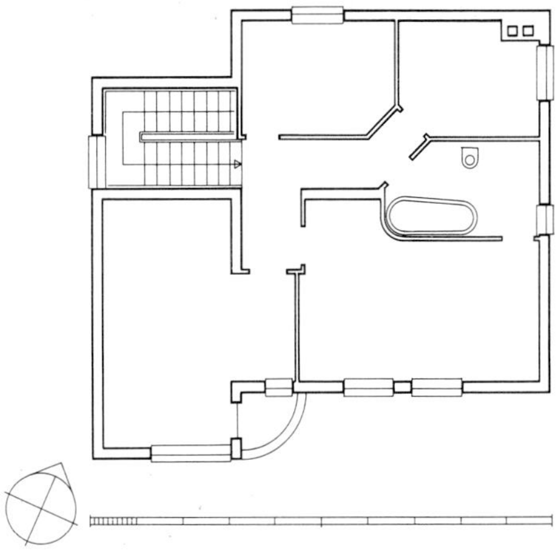

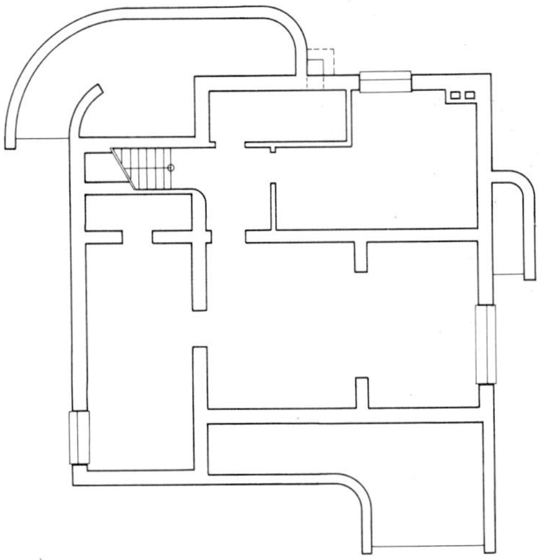

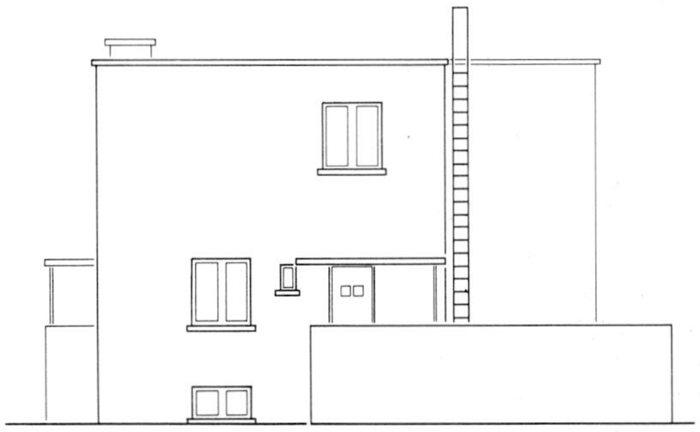

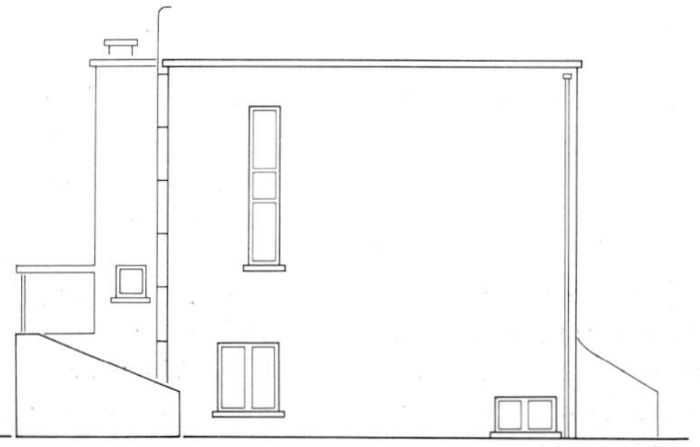

House 10
Architect: Victor Bourgeois
Plans and elevations drawn from the building code submissions of April 18, 1927, drawn up to the prescribed scale of 1 : 100 by the client, Dr. Boll, from Bourgeois' 1 : 50 drawings

First floor; second floor

Cellar

Elevations from north, west, south, east

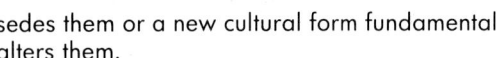

three dimensions, so other architects will one day resolve their floor plan in spatial terms.]

But once things have been resolved, further evolution is possible. They remain in the same form for centuries, until a new invention super-sedes them or a new cultural form fundamentally alters them.

[Footnote: For the uninitiated, who do not understand the aggressive tone of this essay: the difference between me and the others is as follows.

I maintain that use determines the cultural form and the form of objects. The others maintain that newly created form can influence the cultural form (sitting, living, eating, etc.)][9]

Loos's words "although the client would gladly have had a house by me" have this significance: when Loos gave a well-attended lecture in the Liederhalle in Stuttgart on November 12, 1926, on "The Modern Housing Project [*Siedlung*],"[10] he made the acquaintance of a young art historian, Dr. Walter Boll, of the Württembergisches Landesmuseum. "In a long conversation," they found that their ideas coincided to "a considerable degree."[11] Dr. Boll was to recall,

> The land at the top of Friedrich-Ebert-Strasse (which was not then built up) had been offered by the Württemberg finance ministry for an extension of the city exhibition ground [Weissenhof], to be made available on a hereditary leasehold basis to public servants who were interested in building houses for themselves. There were three lots which were assigned to Professor Schneck, to Dr. Christ, . . . and finally to myself, then an assistant at the Landesmuseum art collection.[12]

This was the lot that Boll wanted Loos to build on.

> However, the original intention was negated by a veto from the exhibition directorate, and at the behest of the architect Van de Velde his student, Victor Bourgeois, was recommended to me instead. And so this tall man with blond hair and blue eyes, who did not understand one word of German and was a great expert on the works of Immanuel Kant, came to see me in Stuttgart. It was a good collaboration. At the opening of the exhibition, he was there again, with a Belgian minister, and I invited him to my house. I heard later that he went to Russia with Ernst May, with whom as the creator of the Cité Moderne he felt a close affinity, and I heard no more of him . . .

The rejection [of Loos] by the exhibition directorate[13] sprang from Loos's well-known aggressive statements against the Werkbund, which had already found expression in 1924, on the occasion of the exhibition *Die Form ohne Ornament*.

It may also be of interest that at the invitation of Gustaf Stotz (whom I of course knew well, along with Schneck and all the others), I myself had been in joint charge of the press advertising [for *Die Form*].[14]

Boll also remembered that Loos said, "I'll do something for you that will make all the other Werkbund people stand on their heads. A connection between upstairs and downstairs." Boll liked this idea so much that he told Bourgeois, and in the latter's first design there remained a pathetic remnant of the Loos idea: the study on the second floor had a window looking out over the staircase, from which Boll would have been able to get an idea of what was going on downstairs."[15]

Bourgeois's second design disappointed Boll, because "there was too much tradition in it." But time was too short for any rethinking and he accepted it. However, the staircase was redesigned yet again, and the electric heating was abandoned on the advice of the power company. A wine cellar—in ashlar masonry, not cast concrete—was included.

Too much tradition may have been a drawback for

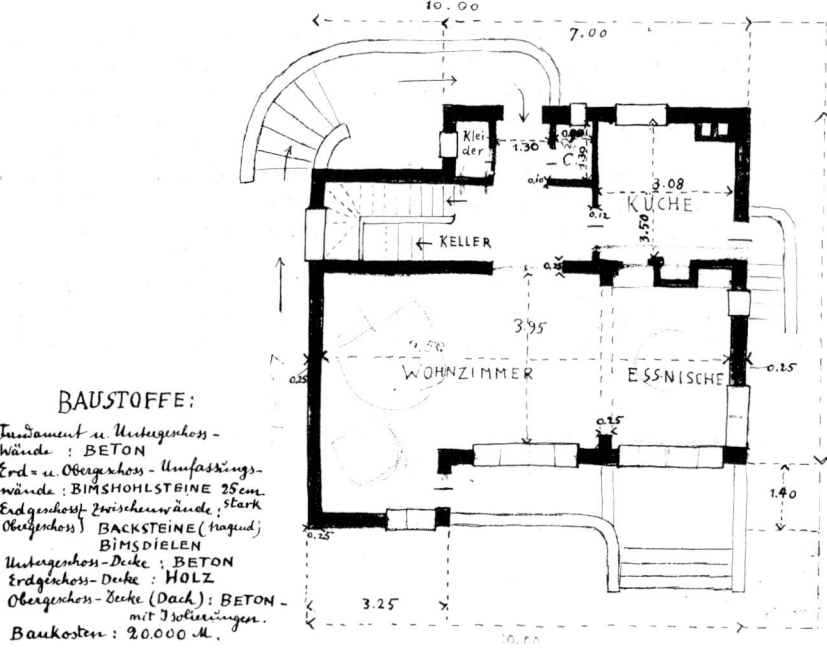

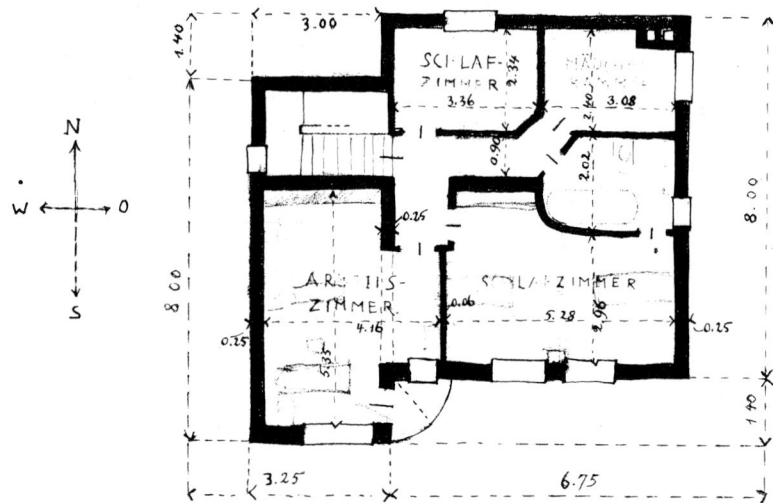

Stuttgart, den 18. April 1927.
Der Bauherr: Dr. phil. Walter Boll

Boll, but for others the design was a bold step forward. "You're a brave man, going along with a flat roof design," his professional colleagues—including Hans Hildebrandt—apparently told him; Boll replied, "Look, you write about it, and I believe it!"[16]

At a meeting of the main committee of the Werkbund exhibition on January 15, 1927, Stotz reported that the Belgian government had asked, through its consul, "whether there might not still be a possibility of giving leading Belgian architects an opportunity to build in the Weissenhofsiedlung itself."[17] City Hall representatives pointed out that there was no more city land on which "owner-occupied houses" could be built. By March, further negotiations with the Württemberg finance ministry had revealed that it was willing to assign a stretch of land originally intended for the Kunstgewerbeschule on a 75-year hereditary lease to three state officials, Schneck, Dr. Christ, and Dr. Boll:

> The Werkbund agreed to this development . . . because this provided an opportunity to give a building commission to the Belgian architect,

Dr. Boll's 1 : 100 drawings of House 10

Bourgeois. Herr Bourgeois demanded no fee, and would bear all the expenses himself, which he would presumably then recover from interested parties in Belgium.[18]

One month later, on April 14, the application for building consent was signed, not by Bourgeois but by Boll. Bourgeois had sent in the drawings at a scale of 1:50—as did Le Corbusier—and this in the eyes of German officialdom was inappropriate for the purpose. As redrawn by Boll, the application was reported on and certified to be "architecturally in keeping with the Christ and Schneck applications, already received." It was pointed out that the structure was immediately adjacent to "the Werkbund housing development now in course of building, and therefore the structure will not be without impact on this unified and unique development," for which reason the building committee of the city council involved itself with the project. "In accordance with the declaration of the urban expansion office, dated April 27, 1927, the Boll application is in keeping with the criteria for the development of the state-owned land specified by the building committee and agreed with the building section of the finance ministry."[19]

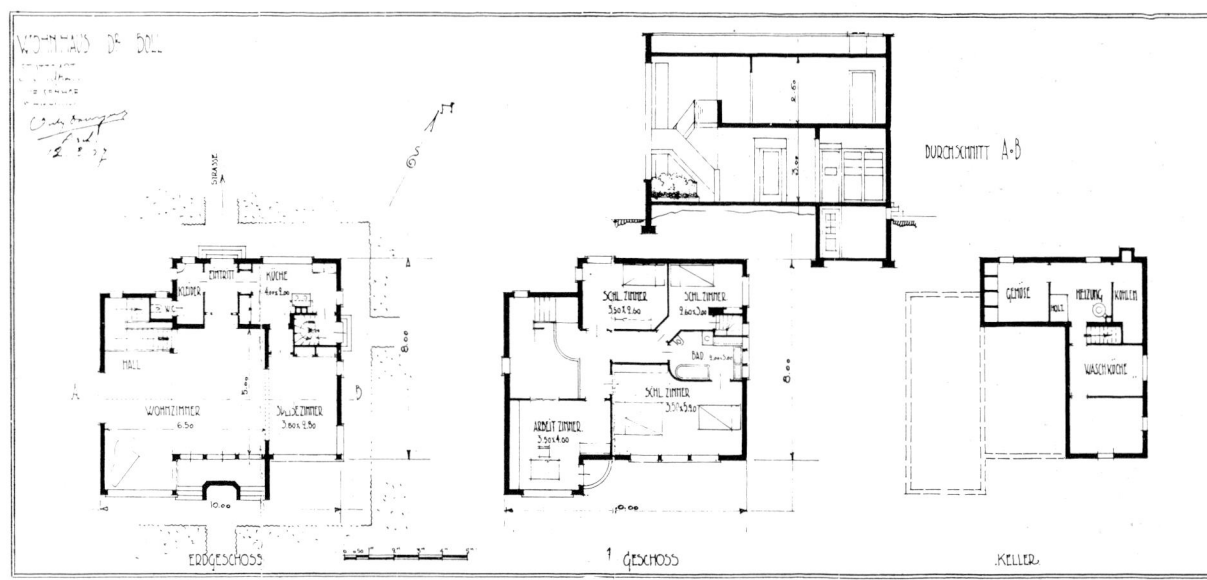

Victor Bourgeois: first version of House 10 with internal window overlooking staircase from study

House 10 from the southeast

The supervision and building work were undertaken by the Gustav Epple company, of Degerloch, Stuttgart. The cost of the house was initially intended to be 15,000 marks; but by the end of May the projected cost had risen to 20,000 marks, as the record of the exhibition subcommittee shows.[20] The client, Walter Boll, recalled that these figures were plucked out of thin air: in reality, the house had cost him far more than twice as much.[21] The interiors were done by "the exhibition directorate in consultation with Bourgeois,"[22] and by an architect from Würzburg, P. Feile,[23] who designed the study furniture and the lighting fitments. Boll remembered,

The architect Feile was a relative of mine (a brother-in-law). A student of Josef Hoffmann's in Vienna, he was then building a modern house in Würzburg. But we did not see eye to eye, because, although I respected [Josef] Frank, I agreed with Loos in rejecting Josef Hoffmann as "fancy-dress [Gschnas]."[24]

During the exhibition the house contained a number of items from Belgium: carpets designed by P. Haesaerts, paintings by P. Flouquet, and sculptures by Oscar Jespers of Brussels. But

those furnishings and fitments that came from Belgium went back there . . . After the exhibition I bought a number of pieces of furniture . . . three leather chairs with the brand name "Neuzeitsessel," one geometric seat and an upholstered bench, together with the famous Thonet chairs . . . The house had linoleum floors in light colors without patterns (white, gray, and blue), and I had the walls painted in a variety of tones in consultation with the painter [Willi] Baumeister (exterior walls [?] white, interior walls colored)."[25]

No interior views of the Bourgeois house are reproduced in any of the Werkbund publications. Bourgeois, who like Boll was only thirty years old at the time, wrote in an article on his house for the Werkbund book Bau und Wohnung of the pernicious influence of "Formal-

ism" on the young, "for they use it as an easy way of showing some originality." This was from a man who permitted himself quadrant forms in his external features, delightful square panes in the front door, a highly decorative roof ladder, and a balcony outside the study that looks like the most important thing in the house—its trade mark, as it were.

The house is hollow pumice-concrete block masonry with ceilings and partitions in the Feifel zigzag system.[26]

Concrete, iron, and glass offer undreamed-of opportunities for innovation in plastic form. In the presence of so much imperfectly understood wealth, overconfidence on the architect's part is positively foolhardy: he has the handicap of inadequate technical experience.

The conquest of materials may well mean that all is permitted; but let the architect reflect, in all the boldness of his inventive spirit, upon his own limitations![27]

The plan is neat and well-thought-out; the proportions of the elevations are well balanced; but the maid's room is the same size as the child's bedroom.

Bourgeois, who had built his Cité Moderne in Brussels in the early 1920s, was to become a founding member of CIAM in 1928. His great preoccupation was with the organization of minimal, subsistence housing. He has left no documents on his contribution to the Weissenhof project; in consequence, the archivist at the Archives d'architecture moderne in Brussels came to the conclusion that he "invited himself to the Werkbund exhibition,"[28] an unthinkable hypothesis. Others did try to tag themselves onto the Werkbund exhibition; but they were uninvited, and they were not admitted. Their houses, present on the Weissenhof site but ignored, include the house built for the Schwäbischer Siedlungsverein by Theo Klemm and Ernst Wagner,[29] and Wagner's house for Dr. Christ, which actually stands between those of Schneck and Dr. Boll.

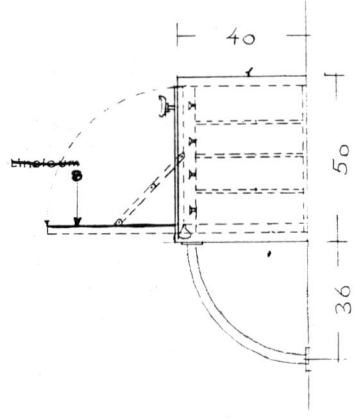

Wall cabinet on tubular steel quadrant brackets

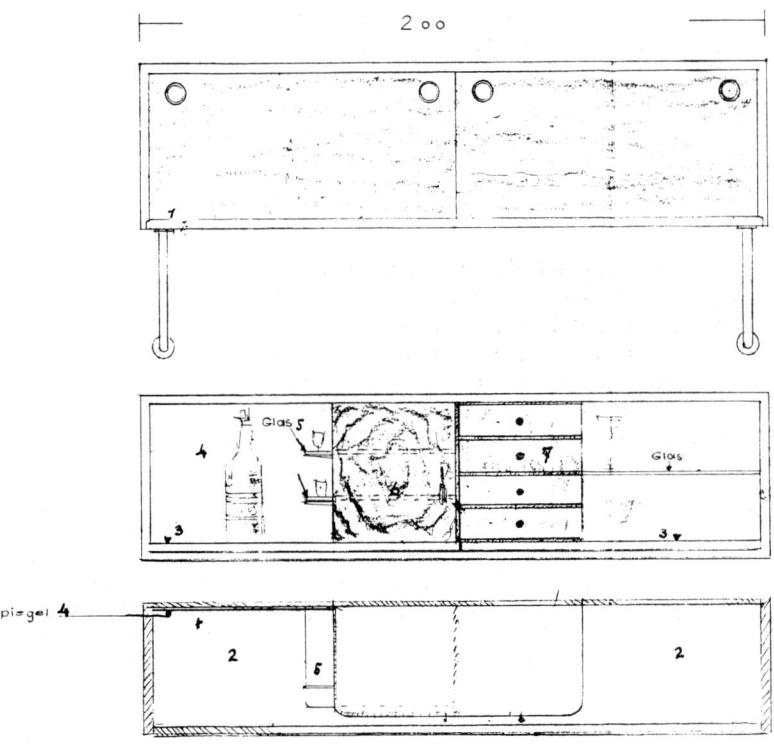

Adolf Gustav Schneck

HOUSES 11, 12

Design: Professor Ad.G. Schneck, architect Stuttgart, Viergiebelweg 16

HOUSE 11

Single-family residence for the architect, Professor Ad.G. Schneck, Stuttgart.
Construction: hollow pumice concrete blocks, plastered inside and out. Interior partly plywood wall panels, reinforced concrete ceilings.
The accommodation comprises:
Cellar: cellar, laundry, drying room, storeroom, furnace room and coal cellar, toilet.
First floor: patio, cloakroom, living room, dining room, terrace, study, kitchen, larder.
Second floor: two bedrooms, one small bedroom, guest room, maid's room, bathroom, toilet, terrace, sunbath.

HOUSE 12

Single family residence: cellar, first floor, second floor. Interior design: Professor Ad.G. Schneck, architect, Stuttgart.
Construction: Liasit blocks, plastered inside and out, ceilings by Rapid.
Cellar: drying room, furnace room and coal cellar, cellar and laundry, storeroom.
First floor: entrance lobby, living and dining room, small terrace room, kitchen, larder.
Second floor: parents' bedroom, two children's bedrooms, small storeroom, toilet, bathroom, terrace, light and air bath.[1]

Adolf Gustav Schneck was well represented in the Weissenhof project and in the Werkbund exhibition as a whole as an architect, interior designer, and furniture designer. Apart from his two single-family houses, one for his own family, he furnished an apartment in the Mies building and was instrumental in securing employment for several of his Kunstgewerbeschule students as interior designers for both Mies's and Behrens's buildings.

Was Schneck overrepresented? It is occasionally said that other architects would have better deserved a place on the project; but in most specific cases the reasons for their nonparticipation have become apparent. Schneck was one of the more important early Modernist architects, although he certainly was not one of the international "motive forces" in the movement. He had all the credentials for inclusion in the Werkbund's Weissenhof project—as any doubter might have learned from the *Internationale Plan- und Modellausstellung*—

as a designer of unpretentious furniture, unassuming houses, and moderately modern competition designs.

Schneck's Weissenhof houses (like those of Josef Frank) did not challenge the visitor to take up a passionate position for or against them. This clever man, a craftsman in International Style clothing, designed furniture technically exciting in its use of plywood which, in formal terms, matched the vaunted ideal of simplicity—sober to the point, at times, of tedium.

It is to be assumed that what has been called his overrepresentation at Weissenhof was not entirely intentional, even on Schneck's own part: it just happened that way. A letter from Mies in September of 1926[2] reveals that Mies knew of Schneck's involvement in planning "dwellings for civil servants" for the Württemberg government, and that only the choice of site was now in question. The acquaintanceship was evidently already a close one; Mies, who was scrupulous about correct forms of address, began his letter "Dear Schneck," and later used the informal "thou" pronoun, *Du*. The correspondence also reveals that Mies had Schneck in mind as a participant from the very beginning; all the lists include his name.

The idea of subsequently turning Schneck's contribution to the exhibition into a dwelling house for the Schneck family was probably already under consideration in the early fall of 1926: on November 10 Schneck was asking for the size of the budget and adding, "I can't yet commit myself on whether I shall be able to move into the house." A house large enough for his family would have to be a "seven-room house with the usual subsidiary rooms."[3]

The size of the budget for the Schneck house was 21,000 marks.[4] Schneck's application to the city council building committee to plan his house in accordance with his own needs and later purchase it from the city was rejected. The committee resolved that

> to maintain the original idea of the Weissenhof project, whereby there can be no question of building parts of the development, or individual houses, for predetermined purchasers: the buildings are to be regarded as impersonal specimens of work that could be carried out anywhere in exactly the same way . . . this decision of the build-

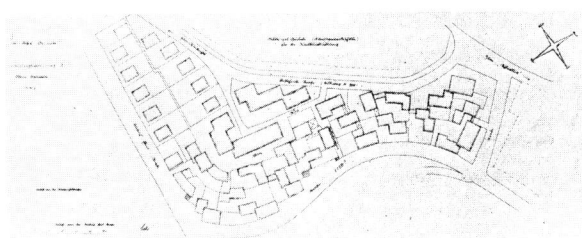

Adolf G. Schneck: block plan showing the Weissenhofsiedlung with Schneck's projected public service housing on adjacent state-owned land

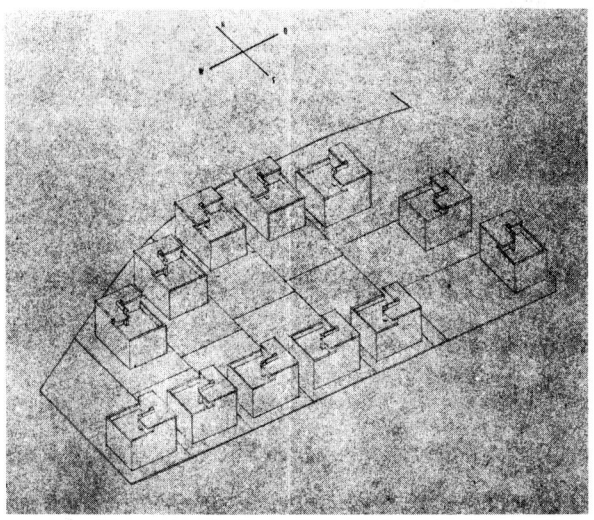

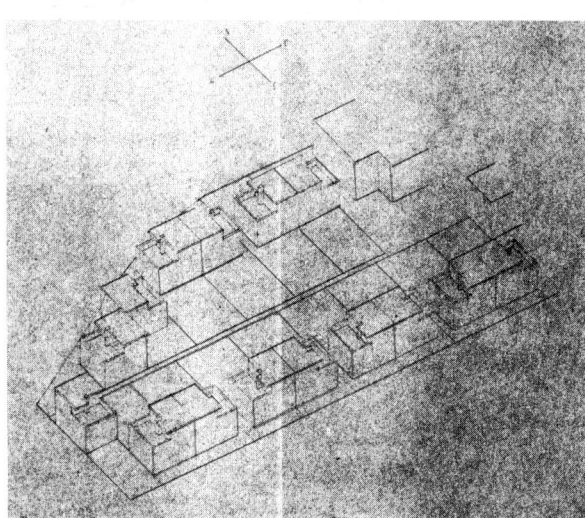

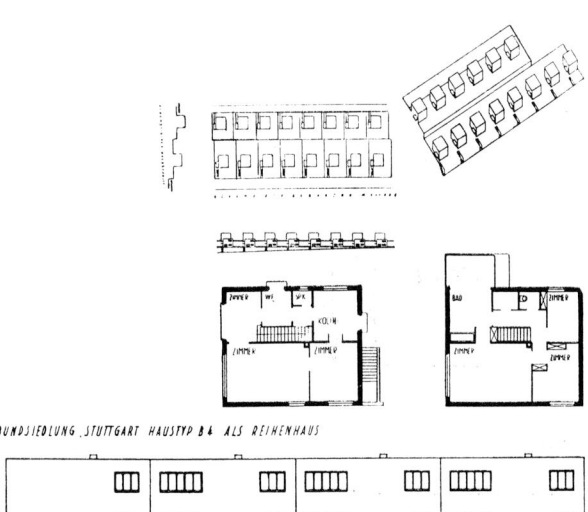

BUNDSIEDLUNG STUTTGART HAUSTYP B4 ALS REIHENHAUS

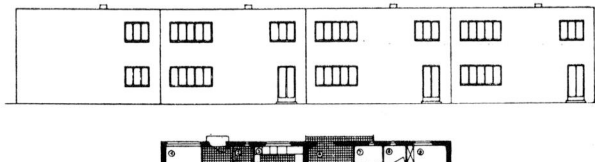

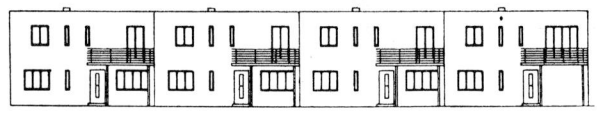

V. PL. 47-50

ing committee rests in this respect, as on others, on the idea of creating dwellings which will keep within reasonable cost limits and be suitable for mass construction anywhere in Germany.[5]

If Schneck wanted to build a house for himself and his family some other way had to be found. In the course of December 1926 or January 1927 the government-owned land adjacent to the Weissenhof development was made available as building lots for government employees. This may well have taken place on Schneck's initiative, as he had good connections with the relevant government departments through his work on civil servants' housing.

This planning work had been assigned to Schneck, along with a project for the extension of the Kunstgewerbeschule, by way of compensation for not accepting "numerous offers of posts . . . including that of the director of the Kunstgewerbeschule in Stettin, and of that in Cologne, and of the Akademie in Dresden."[6] The Kunstgewerbeschule extension was never built but the civil service housing began with the building of his own house and continued, after the Werkbund exhibition closed, with other buildings. Victor Bourgeois's house for Dr. Boll and Ernst Wagner's for Dr. Christ, both on government-owned land, probably also arose from Schneck's initiative.

Schneck's House 11, like the others built on state land, was not subject to the supervision of the building committee or that of the superintendent architect, Döcker. Like Bourgeois's House 10, however, it came under Mies's supervision and was included among the Weissenhof buildings for exhibition purposes, as Wagner's house was not.

Building costs for House 11 were the private responsibility of the client; in a financial statement found among Schneck's papers the total is given as 50,412.15 marks. The contract for House 12 was placed with the Stephan company on February 25, 1927, at a stipulated price of 20,464 marks, and the "net total building costs" were computed by Döcker's office on December 20, 1927, as 21,545.10 marks.[7]

Both of Schneck's houses are based on the same planning criteria, as combinable in rows and thus usable as prototypes for the civil servants' housing program. In three planning sketches which Schneck sent to Mies, he illustrated the possibilities of grouping: solid rows, duplex houses, and detached houses.[8] This at least was a response to City Hall's demand for type houses rather than individual designs! The type shown differs from both House 11 and House 12; the drawings probably date from 1925, or the summer of 1926 at the latest. By moving the side windows round to the front or back it was possible to achieve a tight arrangement of units, either in straight lines or staggered.

In his contribution to the Werkbund book *Bau und Wohnung* Schneck points out that, when it comes to standardization and rationalization, architects are ultimately powerless: any real saving in costs can be achieved only through the efforts of industry. All that falls within the province of the architect is "the creation of a plan in conformity with economy and with the forms of use"; his task—basing himself on English precedents—is to create standard basic types which allow for a maximum of variation:

In my proposal, which I worked out for the city of Stuttgart in the Werkbund *Die Wohnung* project, and in which I had the task of building a single house [House 12] which could be used in groups

Adolf G. Schneck: two isometric views of projected public service housing: detached houses; paired houses, combined and staggered

Adolf G. Schneck: Demonstration of the suitability of his Type B 4 units (House 12) as row housing

House 11
Architect: Adolf Gustav Schneck
The architect's own family residence
Plans and elevations drawn from the architect's building code submissions of May, 1927 (undated)

After objections from a neighbor, Schneck made changes for which no new submission was made; the penthouse, and also the roof balustrade, were omitted.

Second floor; roof level

First floor; cellar

Elevations from south, east, north, west

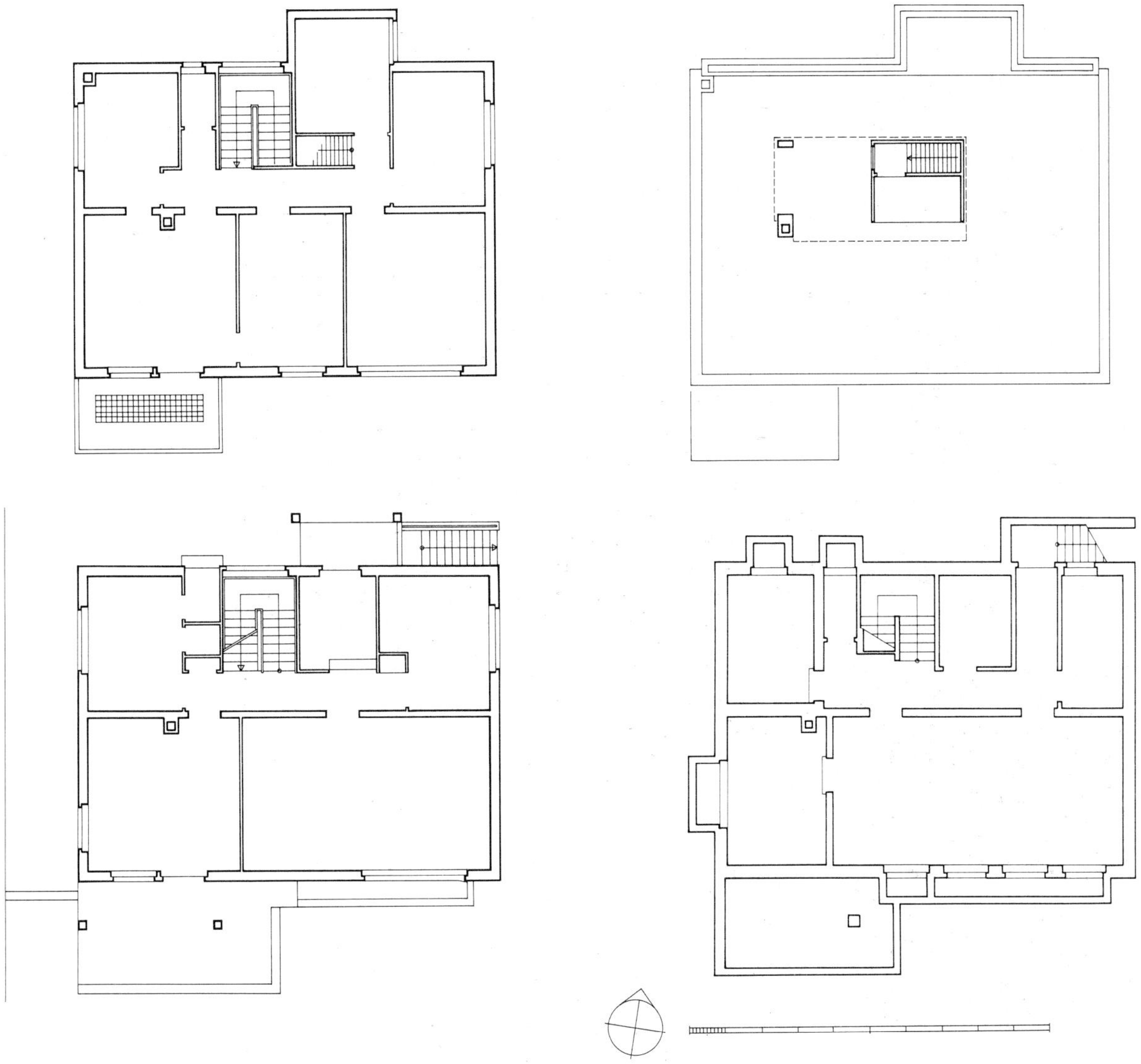

and mass produced as a row house, I endeavored to shape the plan in such a way that neither the position of the staircase nor that of the other spaces is fixed and predetermined. I was presented with the task of building a house for 20,000 marks, in which the interior space would cost 35 marks per cubic meter. My ground plan is divided into two spaces by a cross wall which is load-bearing. Within these two spaces, great freedom and mobility in the design of the living space is possible. The staircases are arranged in various ways, and the standard plan is established. This flexible plan emerged from my attempts to dispense with the roof space. The housewife has one flight of stairs the fewer to climb, and one story the fewer to maintain. When the rooms are properly laid out, this represents a considerable saving of labor.[9]

Schneck's justification of the flat roof as a labor-saving device comes as something of a surprise, as does his statement that "the flat roof is not a matter of form but a requirement based on economics."[10]

The plans now before us represent the final phase of planning; the files record several previous reworkings. In December of 1926 Döcker wrote to Mies as artistic director that the city building commissioner, Dr. Sigloch, did not accept the "designs of Herr Schneck."[11] Erna Meyer also wrote Mies that she had seen plans of the Schneck house in Stuttgart and would be able to tell what improvements were necessary if the designs were now submitted to her at an early stage.[12]

Schneck's houses were more or less ready on opening day, July 23. Edgar Wedepohl gave the readers of *Wasmuth's Monatshefte* a description of Schneck's House 12, which he unhesitatingly classified as a detached house for a middle-class family:

What stands here is really a small villa, more or less tastefully and practically worked out. . . .

The pleasantly unassuming Schneck house (House 12) comes closest to the enlightened average taste of the middle classes, and allies itself in this to the buildings by Frank (of Vienna), Poelzig, Döcker, and Hilberseimer. The Schneck house even has noticeably good-looking, simple closets. Dining and living rooms, combined into one long room, could equally well be divided by a light partition. The division and handling of space are adapted to solid middle-class requirements. The exterior is not designed with the same care as the interior, but the cubic simplicity of the structure is pleasant. The spacious bathroom upstairs is very fine, with its big sunbathing terrace.

The construction is solid, in Liasit blocks manufactured from an oil-bearing shale found in Württemberg.[13]

According to Schneck's former student—and the author's own teacher—Eberhard Krauss, Schneck involved his students directly in his Weissenhofsiedlung work. He himself designed all the interiors of his own residence, House 11; but he allowed the Kunstgewerbeschule workshops, in association with Hilde Zimmermann, to equip the kitchen (if not more) of House 12.[14] In its revised form this kitchen met with the approval of Erna Meyer, who held it up as a model of its kind, alongside those of the Oud houses.[15]

"In the two houses by A. G. Schneck of Stuttgart, the tasteful colors will be much appreciated," wrote a Swiss

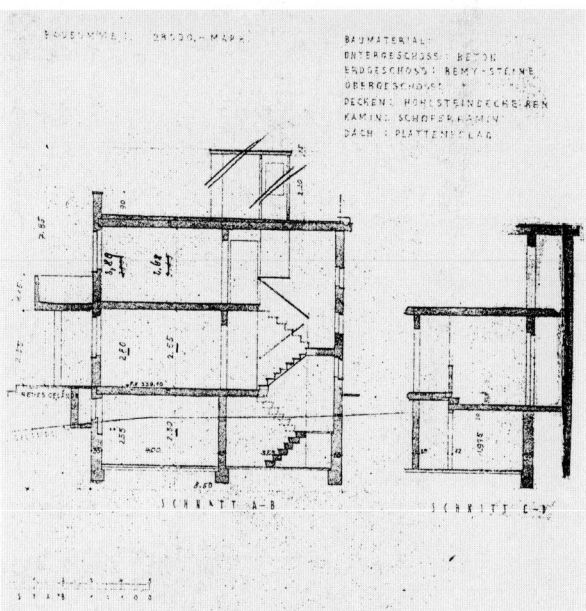

House 11 from the southwest

Adolf G. Schneck: House 11, sections and south elevation (from Friedrich-Ebert-Strasse)

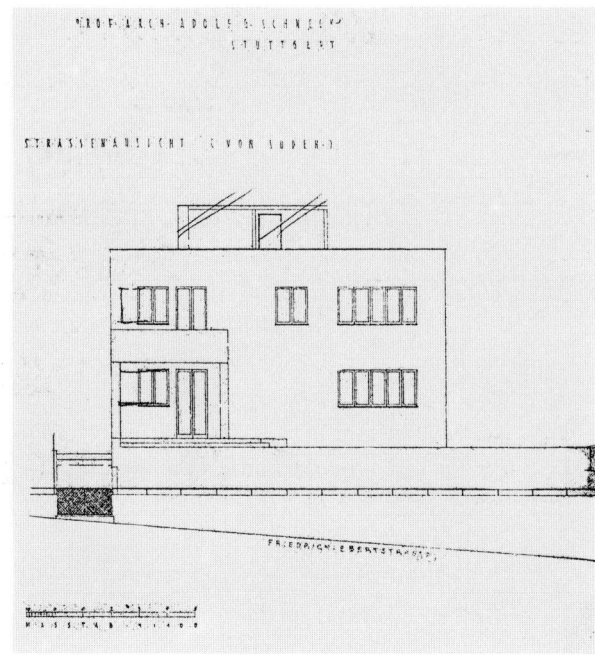

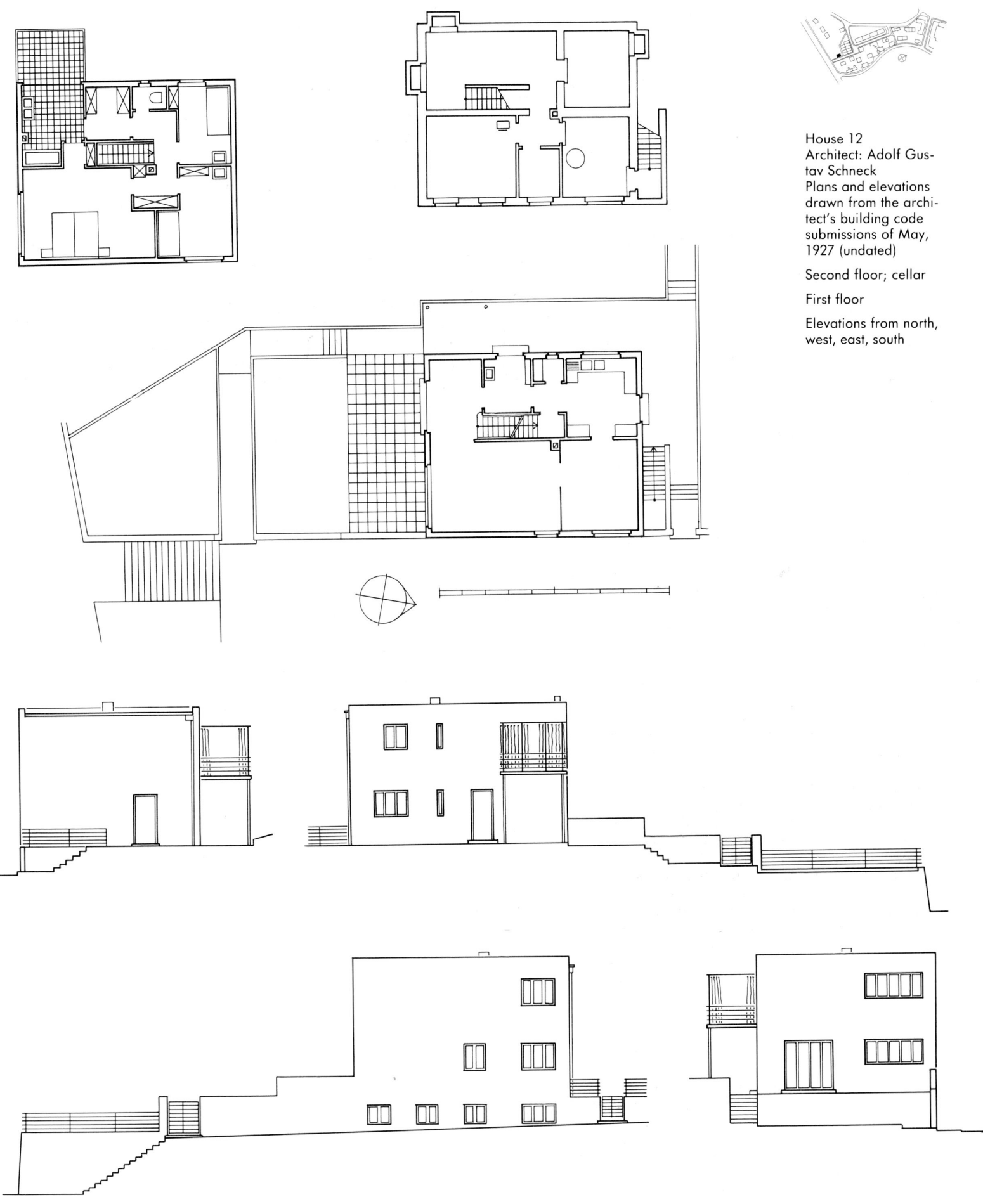

House 12
Architect: Adolf Gustav Schneck
Plans and elevations drawn from the architect's building code submissions of May, 1927 (undated)

Second floor; cellar

First floor

Elevations from north, west, east, south

House 12:
Clockwise:
View from the north-west, taken on the footpath adjoining Oud's House 9

Three views of living room by Schneck

Bedroom by Schneck

Outdoor seating by Schneck

Adolf G. Schneck: bathroom with open-air balcony

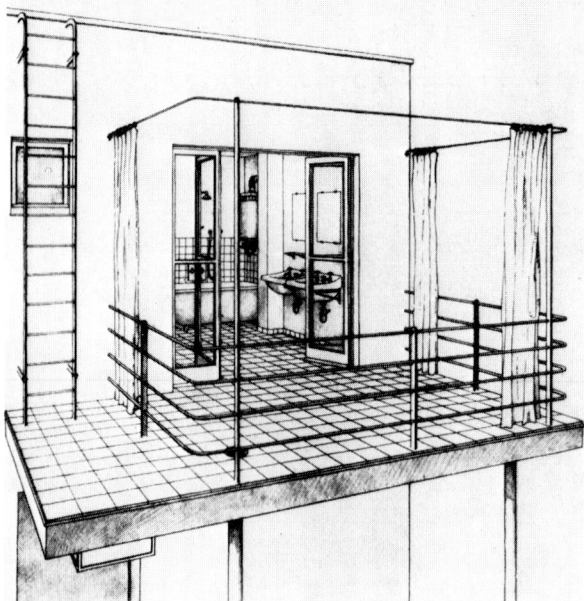

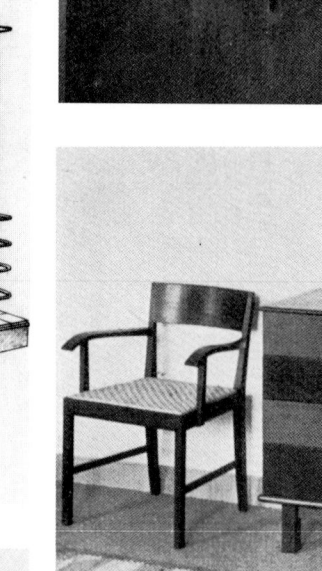

98

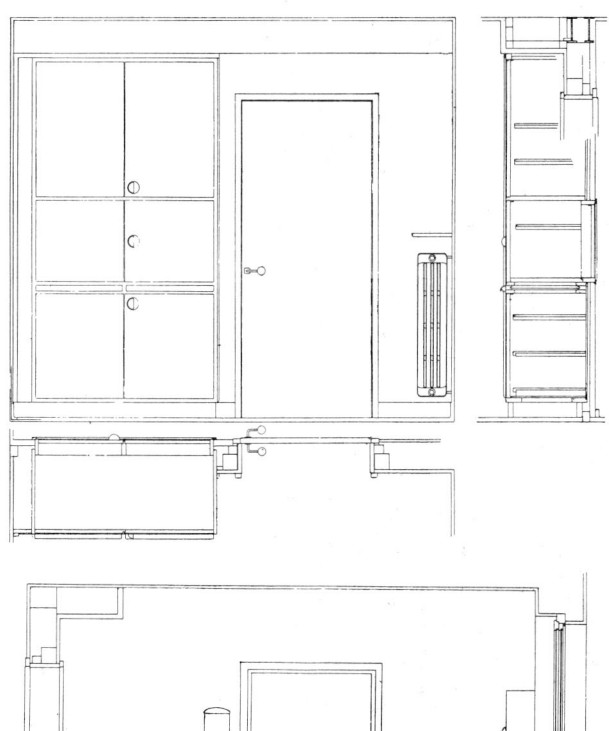

In between, for this architect as for so many others, lay the dark years of the Third Reich, in which he built a number of houses with the gable roofs which he had dismissed as uneconomic but which now, strangely enough, turned out to be quite possible after all. He is believed to have submitted an entry to the competition, launched in 1938, for a military headquarters intended for Stuttgart on the very site of the Weissenhofsiedlung. This was a

closed competition, to which only Paul Bonatz and Kurt Dübbers, Paul Schmitthenner, Alfred Kicherer, and the firms of Eisenlohr-Pfennig and Horsch-Hehl-Hettler, plus Adolf G. Schneck, were invited to submit designs. Schneck is assumed to have taken part, but the available records do not make this certain. Schneck himself never mentioned either the invitation or the competition.[16]

The fact of the invitation itself is remarkable enough. No relevant correspondence from the Weissenhof or Third Reich period is to be found among Schneck's papers.[17]

House 12:
Drawings of kitchen

Le Corbusier and
Jeanneret

observer in *Das Werk*, without going into any details as to the colors themselves. As in Victor Bourgeois's House 10, the color scheme may well have been devised by Baumeister.

In Mies's apartment building, Schneck exhibited furniture from the "Low-Cost Home" (Die Billige Wohnung) range of Deutsche Werkstätten. In his own houses, however, only the textiles were from that source. The lighting fitments were by Metallwerke Stuttgart.

Schneck's presence in the Werkbund exhibition can be ascribed, apart from his professional qualifications, to one weighty consideration: he had succeeded in gaining the friendship and professional respect of the implacable Stotz. After they had worked together on such enterprises as the *Die Form* exhibitions in Stuttgart in 1924 and in Monza in 1925, it was natural that the association would continue. Even so, Stotz was such a perfectionist that if he had not been convinced by Schneck—or even if he had become critical of him over the years—he would certainly not have asked him to work on the Weissenhofsiedlung.

Fate has preserved both of Schneck's houses from destruction through World War II and the postwar period, intact apart from changes due to interior remodeling. In 1928 and 1929 Schneck added two more houses for civil servants nearby with load-bearing cross walls like Houses 11 and 12. He went on to build the remarkable Haus auf der Alb, near Urach, in the Swabian Mountains (1928–30). After World War II he took up the same theme in the Friedrich-Hilda-Heim, near Bühl, in Baden (1953).

HOUSES 13, 14, 15

Design: Le Corbusier, architect, with Pierre Jeanneret, Geneva and Paris
Paris, Rue de Sèvres 35

House 13: single-family house
Houses 14 and 15: two-family house

HOUSE 13

Single-family house: basement story, living story, mezzanine, and terrace story.
Construction: reinforced concrete frame with pumice concrete hollow block infilling. Built-in closets.
Interior design: Le Corbusier, architect, with Pierre Jeanneret, Geneva and Paris.
The accommodation comprises:
Basement story: entrance lobby, cloakroom, toilet, furnace room and coal cellar, store cellar, laundry.
Living story: patio, large living room leading to dining area, kitchen, maid's room.
Mezzanine: parents' sleeping area, dressing room, bathroom and toilet, storeroom.
Terrace story: nursery, guest room, toilet, roof terrace.

HOUSES 14 and 15

Two-family house: basement, living story, terrace story.
Construction: concrete and iron skeleton. Infilling of pumice concrete hollow blocks.
Interior design: Le Corbusier, architect, with Pierre Jeanneret, Geneva and Paris.
Each dwelling comprises:
Basement story: entrance lobby with cloakroom, furnace room, coal cellar, laundry, provision store, maid's room, storage.
Living story: large living room which can be subdivided by sliding partitions into sleeping compartments (sliding beds); kitchen and breakfast room, bathroom and toilet.
Terrace story: study and library, sunbathing terrace and roof garden.[1]

Le Corbusier and his distant cousin, Pierre Jeanneret, were practically never at Weissenhof in person; but they may be described as leading performers in the story of the 1927 Werkbund exhibition. Mies, who avoided setting up "any guidelines whatever," preferring to chose individual architects "whose work gave cause to expect interesting contributions to the question of the new home,"[2] attached the utmost importance to making sure that Le Corbusier would be one of those individuals. Le Corbusier's book, *Vers une architecture*,[3] and the ideas published as early as 1920 in the periodical *L'Esprit Nouveau* by him and Amédée Ozenfant, together with his and Jeanneret's spectacular contribution to the Paris Exposition of 1925, had made him so famous that no exhibition of modern architecture without his participation could have achieved any international recognition and credibility.

The genesis of the houses by Le Corbusier and Jeanneret is reconstructible from first-hand testimony as with almost no other part of the Weissenhof project. The preliminary design stages and the instructions for building—right down to the authentic color schemes—were carefully preserved and documented, and indeed published in part as early as 1927.

It is thus possible to begin the account of House 13 with an incident in 1920, when Le Corbusier and Jeanneret were eating in a little "cabdrivers' diner" in Paris and suddenly became aware of its spatial characteristics. Le Corbusier describes the scene, with

a bar (of zinc), kitchen in the back, a gallery which divided the height of the room; the front opened out toward the street. One fine day they discovered this place and noticed that here all the elements were present that were necessary for the organization of a dwelling house. Simplification of light sources; only one window at each end; two transverse bearing walls, a flat roof above—a box which could really be used as a house.[4]

The idea of the Citrohan House was born. The design of House 13 on the Weissenhofsiedlung was based on this type, of which Le Corbusier said in 1921 that it was "a house like a motor-car, conceived and carried out like an omnibus or a ship's cabin." He called the house "Citrohan (not to say Citroën) . . . we must look upon the house as a machine for living in or as a tool. When a man starts any particular industry he buys the necessary equipment of tools; when he sets up house he rents, in actual fact, a ridiculous dwelling. Idiotic apartments."[5]

So the phrase "a machine for living in" had embarked on a career in which it was to be acclaimed as much as misunderstood: a reproach to some, an inspiration to others. Le Corbusier had also written that one might well take pride in having a house that was "as serviceable as a typewriter"; this formula failed to register on the startled minds of the public.

The provocation was made complete by a first-rate scandal: the directorate of the Paris Exposition of 1925 (*Exposition internationale des Arts décoratifs et industriels modernes*) concealed the Pavillon de l'Esprit Nouveau, by Le Corbusier and Jeanneret, from the public gaze behind a twenty-foot fence. The fence came down only after a personal intervention from the minister of fine arts, Anatole de Monzie, and the public could see for itself how grossly these Swiss architects were neglecting *les Arts décoratifs* in favor of *les Arts industriels modernes*. Le Corbusier and Jeanneret set out to show that industry, given a strict process of selection, can mass-produce articles of real quality. It would thus, they reasoned, be possible to standardize the home, and to produce practical, comfortable, and good-looking living capsules which, added together, would produce a major housing development. Their pavilion was furnished with items which did not really qualify as furniture at all. Le Corbusier told the world,

> A new term has replaced the word "furnishing." . . . The new word is the equipment of a house. . . . In replacing the innumerable furnishings of all shapes and sizes, standard cabinets are incorporated in the walls or set against the walls. . . . They are constructed not of wood, but of metal, in the shops where office furniture is fabricated. The cabinets constitute, in themselves, the sole furnishing for the house, thus leaving a maximum amount of available space within each room. Only the seats remain, and the tables. The study of the seats and tables leads to entirely new conceptions, not of a decorative but of a functional nature.[6]

In Stuttgart, however, the work that Le Corbusier here assigns to the manufacturers of office furniture was done by the masons already working on the lot; not until shortly after Stuttgart did his new forms of seating make their appearance.[7]

Mies wrote Le Corbusier on October 5, 1926, to tell him that he was in charge of the exhibition and that he intended "to give a platform to the leaders of modern architecture"; the city of Stuttgart had made an extremely fine site available and he asked Le Corbusier to undertake a "single-family-house group . . . Others who will be taking part: Oud, Stam, Gropius, Mendelsohn, Taut, Döcker, Hilberseimer, Scharoun, and myself."[8]

Mies's list corresponds broadly to List VII, approved by the city council building committee on October 1, 1926, which, however, also included the names of Frank, Häring, Rading, and Schneck. Mies's failure to name Häring, in particular, is interesting; the latter's name was still on the list, but the difficulties that were to lead to his and Mendelsohn's exclusion from the project were already quite evident. Mies concluded, "I would be glad to have a positive answer from you very soon. May I stress that I set particular store by your participation, and I would regard it as a serious deficiency in the whole enterprise if you were not to be present in it."[9]

The date of the invitation is significant; it was sent as soon as Mies had the consent of the building committee.[10] On July 20, 1926, Le Corbusier had been second, after Oud, on the list presented to the committee by the Werkbund, and his name had been struck out without official comment. In August Commissioner Sigloch made moves to have the name restored, and a debate ensued in which Le Corbusier was excluded on a majority vote "for national reasons"—that is, because he was from the western part of Switzerland.[11]

September 14, 1926, Mies and Stotz met City Hall representatives to make it clear to them how important Le Corbusier's participation was for the Werkbund project as a whole. They argued, notably, that "his name . . . will have a powerful effect, abroad in particular," and that his book, *Vers une architecture*, "which is attracting great attention everywhere . . . has furthermore been published by [Deutsche] Verlags-Anstalt in

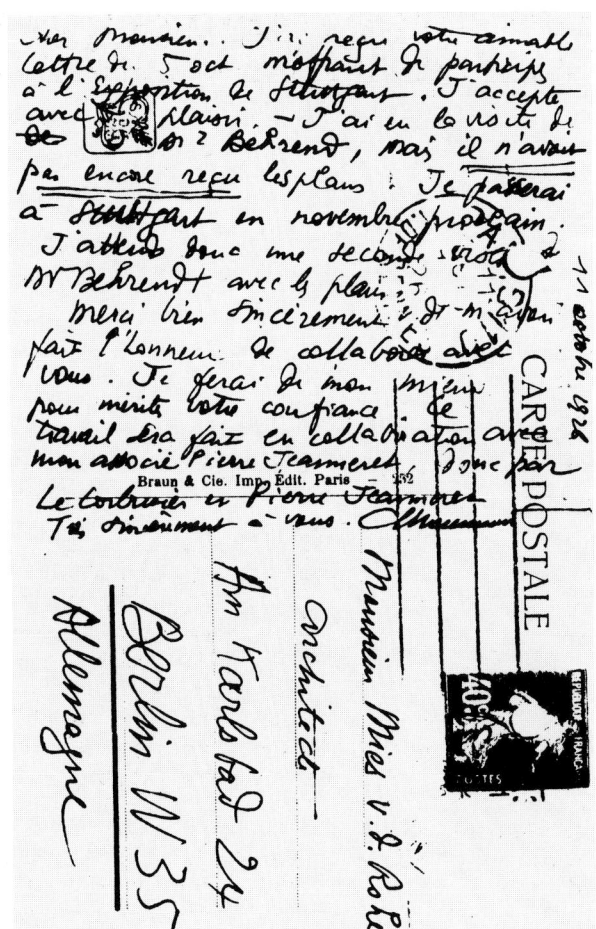

Postcard from Le Corbusier to Mies, October 11, 1926: "My Dear Sir, I have your kind letter of October 5, offering me an opportunity to take part in the Stuttgart exhibition. I accept with pleasure.—I have had a visit from Dr. Behrendt, but he had *not* yet had the plans. I shall go to Stuttgart in November next. So I shall expect a second visit from Dr. Behrendt with the plans. Thank you, most sincerely, for giving me the honor of working with you. I shall do my best to justify your trust. The work will be done in collaboration with my associate, Pierre Jeanneret, and thus by Le Corbusier and Pierre Jeanneret. Very sincerely yours, Le Corbusier."

Stuttgart."[12]

On September 21 the Werkbund asked for the inclusion of Le Corbusier and Mendelsohn, and the building committee agreed on October 1.[13] The list was reworked once more on November 12, but by then Le Corbusier's participation had been assured.

Mies did not rest content with his written invitation to Le Corbusier. He asked Dr. Walter Curt Behrendt, who was paying a visit to Paris, to deliver a plan of the Weissenhof project, and "to have an introductory talk with Herr Le Corbusier and obtain his agreement." Mies also left it to Behrendt to tell Le Corbusier the fee of 3,000 marks.[14]

"*J'accepte avec plaisir*," Le Corbusier replied on October 11, on a picture postcard of the Pavillon de l'Esprit Nouveau at the Paris Exposition of 1925. He added that the work was to be jointly credited to himself and to his associate, Pierre Jeanneret.[15] On a postcard of "*Les Quartiers modernes Frugès*" and in a subsequent letter he asked for information on the type and purpose of the houses, the kind of occupants envisaged, the program, the proposed energy source, the deadline for completion of plans, conditions of execution, and how the furnishing was to be dealt with.[16] Mies replied,

> The house Block 11 is a single-family house and is to contain 6 rooms, kitchen, bathroom, and maid's room. The building costs may rise to 25,000 marks. As a price of 35 marks per cubic meter is to be expected in Stuttgart, the available built volume is 720 cubic meters.
>
> Block 15, also a single-family house, with 5 rooms, kitchen, bathroom, and maid's room. Here the available sum is 23,000 marks. Which, at 35

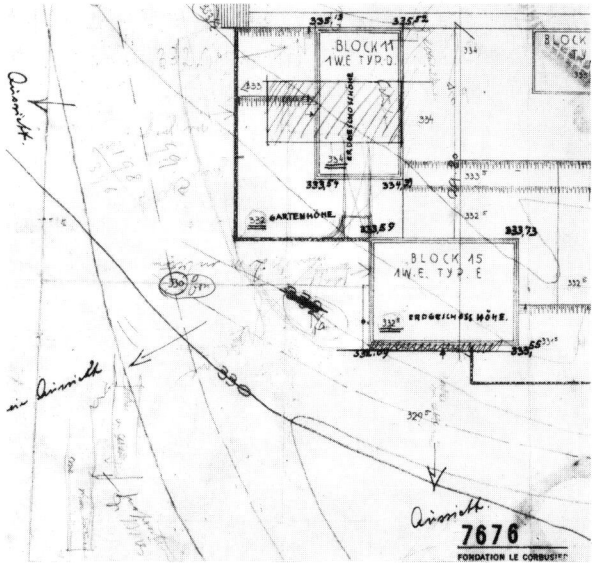

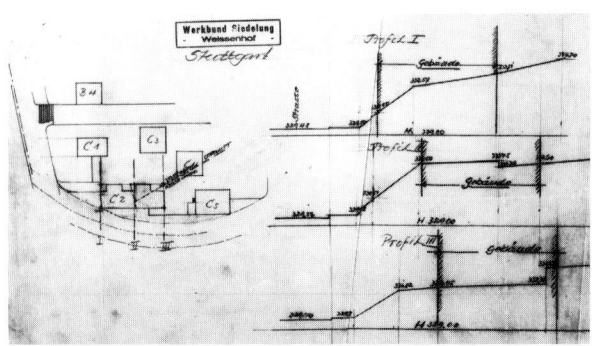

Section of contour plan with the outlook (*Aussicht*) indicated in Mies's hand

Ground profiles, sent by Mies to Le Corbusier

treated as a momentous occasion. A third architect, Mart Stam, was present, and his face would have been visible on the photograph which records the meeting had not the photographer, Heinz Rasch, touched him out, presumably because the likeness was not a particularly happy one.

In an article in the *Stuttgarter Neues Tagblatt* on November 29 Rasch neatly characterized all three architects, so different in origin and in their strongly held views on architecture. He described Le Corbusier as a person

> who is used to hard work. This shows in his appearance. A dogmatist, without necessarily being a system-builder. Endowed with all the puritanical rigor of his native country. He stems from the upper Rhône area, where the banished Albigensians settled hundreds of years ago. The great rationalists, Rabelais and Rousseau, are his compatriots. This is far from irrelevant.

Stam, on the other hand, Rasch described as an architect who rejected the word "architecture" from the very start: "For him, the only problems are technical, not formal or spatial."

And as for Mies:

> Mies van der Rohe, finally, is not the best known, but certainly one of the most mature and full-blooded of the German "Moderns." All inner weight and stability . . . Mies presents all his ideas and actions with startling simplicity, as if stating the obvious. That is his greatness.

Rasch has also preserved for us a statement of Le Corbusier's

> on the conflicts between the young and the old, which had been particularly exacerbated by the Werkbund exhibition . . . "Why turn disagreements of principle into value judgments? Conflicts of this kind are like a horse race: the greatest enemies are not the first and last runners but the first and the second." . . .

marks per cubic meter, represents 660 cubic meters of built volume. Both houses are intended for the educated middle class.[17]

In the rest of his letter Mies made it clear that these prescriptions were by no means to be followed to the letter: all that was necessary was that three bedrooms and a maid's room should be present. The form of the house, as indicated in the block plan, was not binding but only "schematic."

On his postcard of acceptance in October Le Corbusier had told Mies that he intended to come to Stuttgart in November. Mies wrote, "I shall be in Stuttgart on [November] 22, and shall be staying in the Hotel Marquar[d]t. There I hope to meet with you."[18]

The intentions of the Werkbund were made known to Le Corbusier through the handout written by Hilberseimer (Appendix A); the lie of the land through the layout plan of July, 1926, which served as a basis for the work of all the architects. Mies also enclosed a drawing showing the configuration of Le Corbusier's own lot in three profile sections, together with a plan marked with an arrow to show the direction of the best unobstructed view. The sections clearly show that on the site of "C 1" (House 13) the land rises sharply at first, then levels off considerably to rise gently toward the street (Bruckmannweg).

In Stuttgart, in November of 1926, Le Corbusier visited the land on which his houses were to be built. He did not join Mies at the Marquardt but stayed at the Schlossgartenhotel next to the station. There he met with Richard Herre, who was doing the graphic design for the German edition of *Vers une architecture moderne*.[19]

The encounter between Mies and Le Corbusier was

Mies and Le Corbusier in Stuttgart on November 22, 1926. Mart Stam's head (but not his coat) between them has been touched out

"Architecture is a suit which has to fit," said someone.

"No," retorted Le Corbusier. "Architecture is more than a suit. The value of architecture does not depend on material and body size. Of course, both are elements in it: the technique and the spatial program. But the essence of architecture is the expression that can be achieved through it, the design. *Architecture is a crystallization.*"[20]

The three architects did not, of course, restrict their discussions to theoretical basics, but also discussed such mundane matters as completion dates and the likelihood that these would not actually hold.

Le Corbusier, whose office was busy with his competition entry for the League of Nations building in Geneva, announced that he would probably not be able to embark on the design of the Stuttgart houses before the end of December. Nevertheless, like all the other participant architects in the Weissenhof project, he received in due course a circular setting out the deadline for delivery of final drawings (January 2, 1927) and recommendations as to materials, construction, and finish, all of which were settled at a meeting of Werkbund architects in Dessau on Friday, December 3, 1926, on the eve of the opening of the new building of the Dessau Bauhaus.[21]

On December 13 Mies urgently asked him, in spite of the understandable delay, to "send the items specified in the circular, and to undertake at this stage that your buildings will be completed by July 1, 1927."[22] The items required, Mies reminded him, were the following: drawings to scale 1:100 in quintuplicate, with ground plans, sections, and elevations at 1:50, specifications and costings. These were to be sent to Döcker, who would "undertake to act as superintendent architect only on condition that this is done." All of the architects received the same letter.

On December 15 Le Corbusier and Jeanneret sent off their first drawings from Paris.[23] In this initial design, both buildings were still conceived as single-family residences in accordance with Mies's instructions, and were related to each other by their *pilotis*; the partly open basement level of the house which faced the lower street (later Rathenaustrasse) was exactly level with that of the house on Bruckmannweg.

The drop in height from Bruckmannweg down to Rathenaustrasse was to be covered in two stages: a ground-level bridge was to lead from Bruckmannweg to the main living floor of the upper house; then there would be a external spiral stair to the basement, and more steps down to a garage on the Rathenaustrasse level. Access to the lower house was to be by a long, straight flight of steps which rose through its front garden to an elevated, airy ground-level which was level with the actual basement of the Bruckmannweg house. A flight of stairs with a landing would lead up to the main floor, which was thus on the level of Bruckmannweg.

This was beautiful and logical, in theory; but unfortunately, the actual lie of the land was different. It is interesting to follow the efforts that were made to salvage the basic idea and minimize the inevitable sacrifices.

The spatial plan—the *Raumplan*, as Loos would have called it—of the upper, Bruckmannweg house (referred to at this stage as "Block 11") is essentially that of the Citrohan House. The external stairs have been replaced by internal ones, thus eliminating the need for the spiral stair in the living room. The beds are differently arranged; the basement floor is adapted to the

given requirements but not yet—if we ignore the little spiral stair—treated visually. The living room, which rises through two stories like that in the Citrohan House, is similarly divided according to function; the gallery runs straight across. The boudoir (dressing room), bedroom, and bathroom form a spatial unit which can be shut off from the living room by movable partitions, as in the Pavillon de l'Esprit Nouveau of 1925; the plan of the roof terrace is taken over from that design almost literally.

This design remains fundamentally unaltered in the finished House 13, of which Le Corbusier wrote,

It was the application of a ten-year study of the "Citrohan" house type . . . The roof construction and fenestration were standardized, a large living room contrasted with the smaller rooms, the

Le Corbusier and Pierre Jeanneret: plans and isometric view of first version of Blocks 11 (C1) and 15 (C2) as two single-family houses with their pilotis on the same level, December 16, 1926

dimensions of which could have been reduced even further—had the municipal authorities given their approval.[24]

The spatial plan of the projected lower house (Block 13) on Rathenaustrasse shows a single-family house on pilotis with rooms opening off a centrally placed staircase core. Here Le Corbusier designed space in the free, geometric shapes that he was later to describe as characteristic of his work in Stuttgart: "cubic composition (pure prism)."[25]

The main living floor is reached by three flights of steps. A right turn leads into the living and dining area, from which a ramp leads to the garden. On the left a long, relatively narrow passageway leads past three bedrooms to the kitchen with maid's room. All the rooms are lit by a long ribbon window. All the single bedrooms—including the maid's room—have wash basins of their own, and the tiny bathroom is attached to the parents' bedroom. There are two toilets: one in the basement, next to the cloakroom, and one just before the kitchen section of the main floor. Up on the terrace level, reached by another three flights of stairs, there is a bedroom with wash basin for a guest. To the right and left of the stairhead and bedroom one steps out onto roof gardens, sheltered on the street side by a narrow strip of roof.

This design, Block 15, was not built. At the end of December 1926 Döcker sent out a circular[26] to say that the architects' drawings had been submitted to the city council building committee on December 23, and that, because of cost overruns, there would have to be a reduction in "built volume" of 15 percent. He also wrote all the architects, including Le Corbusier, that the committee was disappointed by the designs in general because most of them were more like "villas"—i.e. detached residences for the middle class—than had been intended. He asked that in future German should be used in letters and on drawings in order to avoid the inconvenience of having translations made.

On the designs themselves, Döcker told Le Corbusier that the volume of Block 11, now called Type C1, would have to be reduced, that the toilet on the third level would either have to be moved to an external wall or to be ventilated by way of the roof, and that according to the building code the proposed ceiling height of 2.20 meters [7 feet 3 inches] in the rear part of the main story and in the mezzanine must be raised to 2.40 meters [7 feet 10½ inches]. Döcker said that he had argued for the retention of Le Corbusier's intended heights, as he assumed that was what the architect would have wanted.

The budget for the lower house, Type C2, had been set at 25,000 marks, although Le Corbusier's project costed out at 32,000 marks. As the budget had now been cut by 10 percent, it followed that the size would have to be cut, as in the case of C1. Here, too, the toilet (on the ground floor) would have to be moved to an external wall.

Döcker made no comment of his own on the design, and wrote Mies only that the built volume would have to be reduced by 30 or 40 percent, and that the building code authorities were making difficulties about the room heights.[27] However, the designs from Paris had aroused great interest in Stuttgart, as is proved by a letter from Schneck to Mies in which he mentions that he is returning Le Corbusier's plans and that, according to his own calculations, the houses would cost twice the sum of money that was available; unless "his building method reduces the cost per cubic meter. I think it a very good thing to have this breath of fresh air blowing

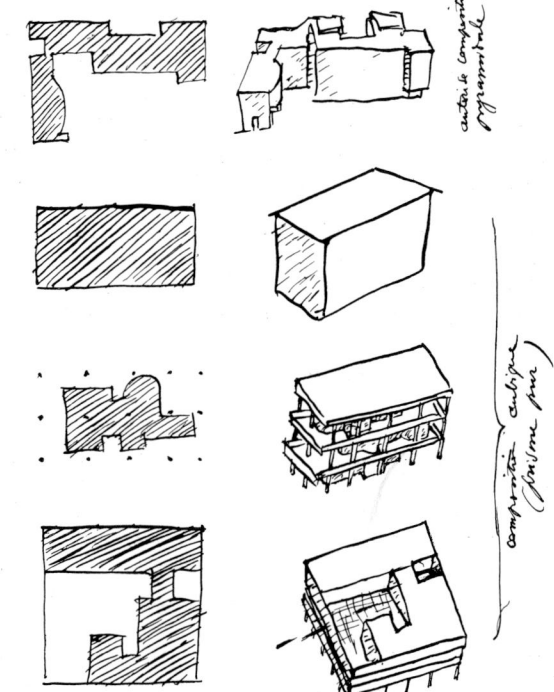

Le Corbusier: four compositions; no. 3, "Cubic composition," is "House in Stuttgart"

through the exhibition."[28]

Erna Meyer, who was consulted as an expert on home economics and kitchen design, told Mies, "One thing in confidence: I was disappointed by Corbusier most of all! What has happened to all the principles in his book? Is this what he means by engineer's architecture?"[29] Mies answered,

I shall not send Le Corbusier's designs to you again, because I know what you dislike about them, and I am quite clear in my own mind that these issues mean something different in France from what they mean here. I find Le Corbusier's designs exceptionally charming [scharmant] and fabulously French, and I don't know whether it would be so very perverse to make a point of displaying this specifically French quality.[30]

He added that criticizing Le Corbusier was a risky business, because of the danger that he might walk out. (The danger with German architects was less; they did not need quite such careful handling.)

On January 12 Le Corbusier told Döcker not to expect "final drawings before February 10."[31] Three days later he sent off highly detailed drawings for C1 (House 13): all plans, sections, and elevations 1:20, details of windows and important parts 1:10 and 1:1. Drawings for C2 were promised shortly.

The C2 drawings were dispatched from Paris on March 18, after renewed pressure from Döcker and repeated promises from Le Corbusier. Meanwhile, the 1:20 drawings for House 13 that Döcker did have were not of much use to him as in Germany the scale for submissions to the building office was immutably laid down as 1:100. Mies felt no urgent need to redraw them to a scale of 1:100, as the design was complete. (There were difficulties of the same kind with the house built by the Belgian, Bourgeois; his client, Dr. Boll, finally had to redraw them himself.)

Almost four months to the day before the opening of the Werkbund exhibition, the designs for Type C2 arrived in Stuttgart. In a letter, Le Corbusier pointed out that he and Jeanneret had ventured upon an alteration of a fundamental, and also a highly interesting, kind.

Instead of designing a house that met the same criteria of use as C1, they had decided to present a novel and transformable design. C2, previously thought of as a single-family house, had been made into a two-family house occupying the same space as the single house previously submitted. The only additions were the staircases.

One unit (House 14) was one bay wider than the other (House 15); during the exhibition, Le Corbusier suggested, one could be equipped for daytime use and the other for the night. Visitors would then be in a position to decide for themselves what could be done with this minimal type (type très réduit). The architects hoped, Le Corbusier wrote, that the change would not only be acceptable but would be welcomed. Designs for the new block, C2 and C2bis, were in the post, and the detail and structural drawings would be sent off on March 23.

In the building committee meeting of March 25, scheduled for the selection of contractors, no contracts were placed for the houses by Le Corbusier and Jeanneret or for those by Gropius. A debate ensued:

The execution of the designs by the architect, Le Corbusier, now to hand, would cost a total of 134,000 marks, so that there was a shortfall of around 70,000 marks if these designs were to be executed. The question now arose, whether in these circumstances the designs by Le Corbusier should not simply be abandoned—there seemed to be a legal justification for so doing—and instead of the Le Corbusier houses the city architectural department should be commissioned to build the remaining three houses for a sum of approximately 64,000 marks.[32]

In the course of some heated exchanges—one has only to remember the previous attempt to exclude Le Corbusier on "national" grounds—Building Commissioner Sigloch moved that the additional sum of 70,000 marks be made available. Councilman Beer, the Socialist architect, proposed that the single-family house be built together with just one of the paired houses—the city architectural department should investigate whether this half-house could be moved along "to allow for the absence of the other house." Beer's motion was passed by seven votes to four. The decision was passed on to the executive departments and to Döcker as superintendent architect.

On March 26, Le Corbusier wrote to press for an acknowledgment of receipt of his designs and for a response concerning their "usability."[33] Döcker wrote back on March 29 to break the news of the cost estimate of 130,000 marks for building the complete project, C1, C2, and C2bis, and of the building committee's idea of halving the C2 block.

Le Corbusier replied that he and his partner were amazed and appalled. They found it utterly inconceivable that a house like C2 could cost more than 92,000 francs, or about 15,000 marks. The size of the estimate showed, they said, that people in Germany and in France had very different ideas of what constituted low-cost housing, and that the building method chosen must have been a highly expensive and durable one to arrive at such a price. No one of limited means could ever pay such a sum:

Simple people prefer to buy a habitable, "decent" house rather than to dream of an immaculate, irreproachable show house that they could never possibly afford.

Our houses in Bordeaux cost 36,000, 40,000, 41,000, and 42,000 francs, and Gropius said of them, "It's just a pity they're so badly built."

The key to the problem of low-cost housing lies in the description "badly built." "Badly built," to Gropius, equals the sum total of the badly executed details. For us, "well built" means a healthy (clean) conception of the design and an irreproachable constructional principle, executed with good materials: reinforced concrete and masonry.[34]

Le Corbusier went on to say that he and his partner found it unthinkable to build only one of the paired houses. "Low-cost, lightweight" materials should be used: cement panels for flooring, limewash finish, pine for the finishing carpentry. The main part of the house began above the pilotis; so the garages, part of the basement, and the garden walls, should be omitted. The foundations should nevertheless be so constructed that they would allow the omitted portions to be added later. "Our program," wrote Le Corbusier, "had nothing to do with breaking records for cheap housing, but with presenting to you house types that reflect the technical and architectural advances that we have made in recent years." He offered to come to Stuttgart if that were considered useful.

At that point in time, work on the League of Nations competition project was completed. Alfred Roth and a French draftsman "who did nothing" were the only staff members remaining in Le Corbusier and Jeanneret's office at 35 Rue de Sèvres. Years afterward, Roth told researchers from the Werkbund-Archiv,

I made all the drawings, and then they were sent to the exhibition in Stuttgart. Then the answer came back from Stuttgart that they couldn't follow them, and Le Corbusier was to come to Stuttgart in person, and so on, and so forth. So then he did go to Stuttgart, and he got back pretty stunned and came over to my drawing board. We were bemoaning our fate, when on the spur of the moment I said, why shouldn't I go to Stuttgart and take over as resident architect. He wanted the initiative to come from me, so that he would no longer be involved.[35]

Le Corbusier's visit to Stuttgart took place between April 15 and 18. On April 19 he wrote Döcker that he had had the necessary new drawings made and that work could begin at once on the basis of these improved plans. Then he sent Roth off to Stuttgart. With City Hall's agreement to shoulder the additional cost and build all three units, C1, C2, and C2bis (Houses 13, 14 and 15), to Le Corbusier and Jeanneret the problem seemed to have been solved.

To assist you in the realization of Blocks C1 and C2 and C2bis, we are sending you an outstanding draftsman, M.Roth, an employee of ours. He drew the plans of C1 and C2. You need not pay him, but if you could manage to provide him with board and lodging, you would be doing us a great service. M.Roth will deal with the contractors, the supervision of the building work, and will endeavor to expedite the work.

He is a highly correct and intelligent boy. You will derive great pleasure from giving him the benefit of your own advice. I hope that you will take a favorable view of this decision, which we

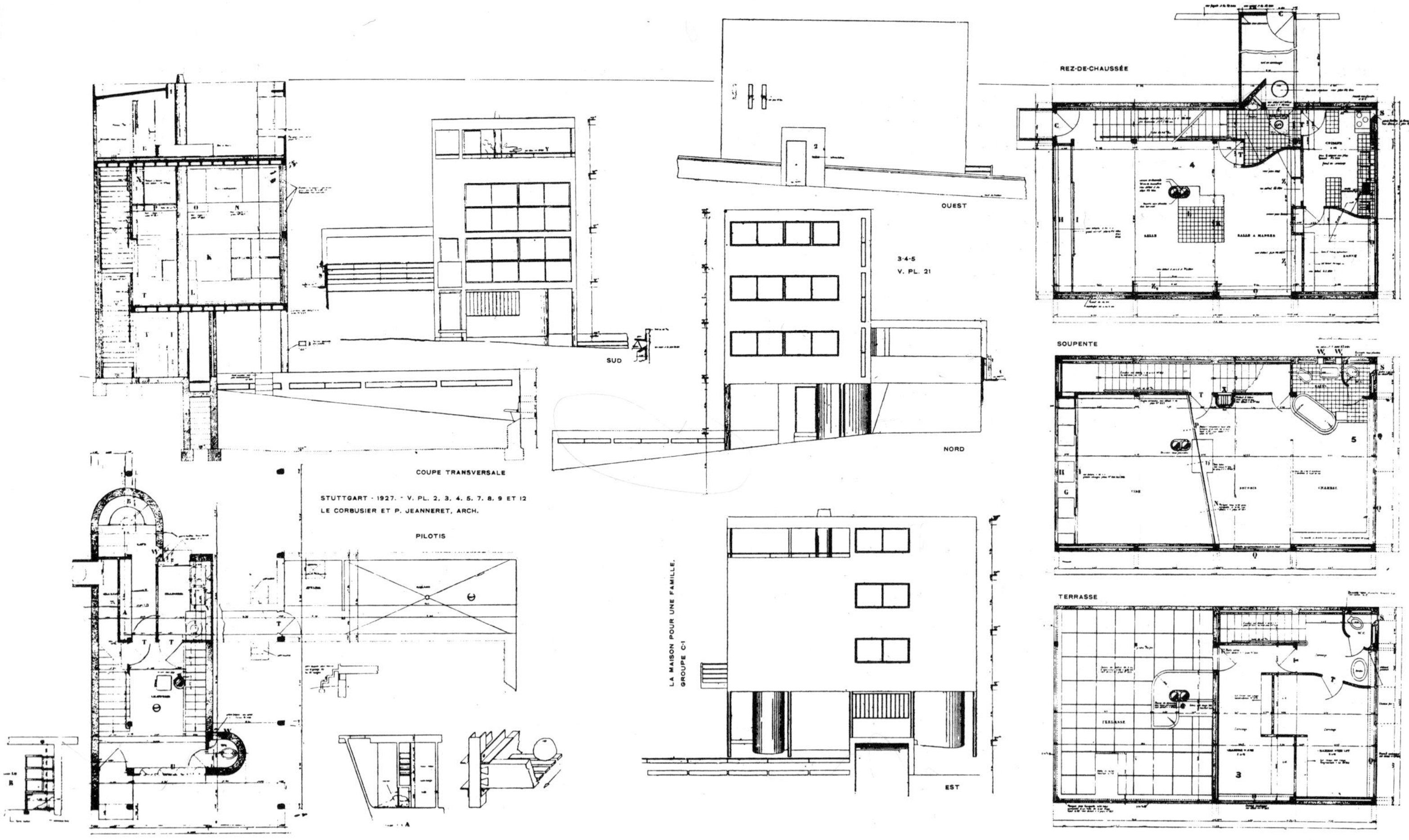

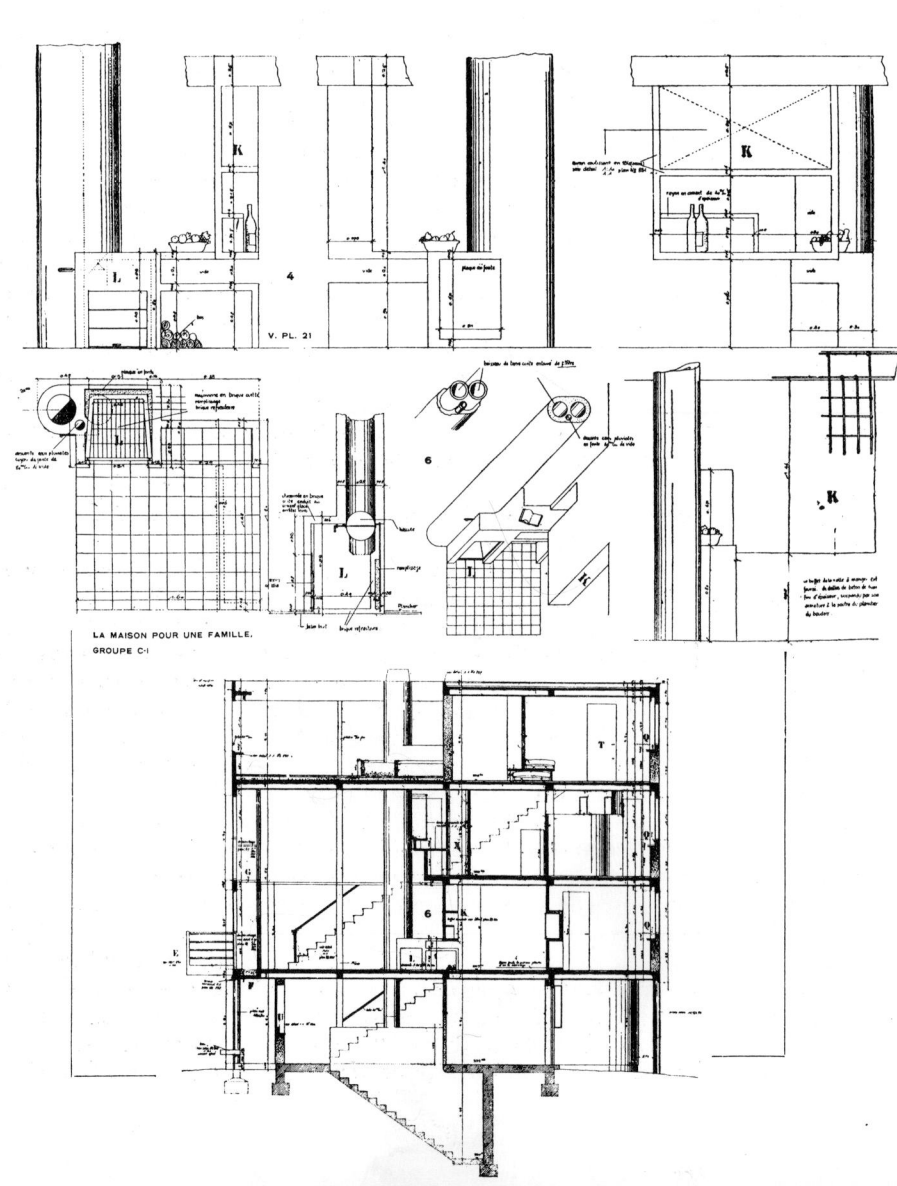

OUEST

SUD

NORD

COUPE TRANSVERSALE

STUTTGART - 1927. - V. PL. 2, 3, 4. 5. 7. 8. 9 ET 12
LE CORBUSIER ET P. JEANNERET, ARCH.

PILOTIS

EST

REZ-DE-CHAUSSÉE

SOUPENTE

TERRASSE

LA MAISON POUR UNE FAMILLE.
GROUPE C-1

LA MAISON POUR UNE FAMILLE.
GROUPE C-1

have taken in order to support you in your ardu-ous task.[36]

No notes of Le Corbusier's conversations in Stuttgart have survived. It must however have been clear by this time that extensive changes would have to be made as a result of the architects' misinterpretation of the lie of the land. The disappearance of the garages from the paired houses was a comparatively trivial matter by comparison with the necessity to rethink the main en-trance to the upper house, C1 (House 13). The sacrifices were painful: the access from Bruckmannweg—across a light, airy bridge with ingenious details which in-cluded an integrated coal chute—now had to be aban-doned because the street was not on the level of the main floor but of the basement. To execute the original design, the height of one story would have had to be excavated from the slope, which was infeasible on grounds of time and of money. Realizing this, Le Corbu-sier decided to put the main entrance in the basement and the coal chute almost at second-floor level, with a grotesque little flight of steps in the front garden so that the coal delivery man could tip the sacks down the chute from his shoulder. In Roth's drawings, this object is marked *Schemmel* [sic], "footstool."

In the circumstances it is understandable that in his book *L'Architecture vivante en Allemagne*, published in 1927, Le Corbusier chose to print the ideal plans: sin-gle-family house with entrance bridge and paired hous-es with garages. In 1960, however, when the survey of his works, *Le Corbusier 1910–1960*, was being pre-pared for publication, he opted for the version as built.

Alfred Roth arrived in Stuttgart on April 28, 1927, and set to work at once. In his first letter to Paris he wrote in glowing terms of the beauty of the Weissenhof site and the warm welcome he had received from Döck-er and from Baumeister. He then kept his employers posted on the entire course of building operations, the decisions that had to be made, the queries that arose, the disagreements with contractors, and the uncooperative attitude of the superintendent architect and his team. Roth worked out wiring and heating plans, suggested floor coverings, came up with new ideas for the design of numerous details, designed furniture, obtained brochures on various products, and clarified a succession of practical aspects of construction. He did his best to find a way through successive financial crises, to ensure that due weight was given to aesthetic concerns, and to direct the contractors and the tradesmen in accordance with the master's wishes. A tall order for a young architect with very little experience! Roth has recalled that it was not until after Weissenhof that he built his own very first building, in his native Switzerland—a pigpen.[37]

Through all the ensuing conflicts in Stuttgart Le Corbusier and Jeanneret left Roth very much to fend for himself. He was constantly kept waiting for drawings, and decisions were constantly being put off. The correspondence from that stressful time is full of requests from Roth for prompt return of plans; for specifications of exterior and interior paint finish; for sketches of furniture, which he offered to work up into finished drawings and pass on to makers in the Stuttgart area; and for designs for landscaping. He generally got his answers, but for the furniture, and in a number of other respects, he was driven by pressure of time to take matters into his own hands.

The way in which Roth approached these decisions reveals him as a highly responsible and scrupulous architect. He took as his models the furniture that Le Corbusier had designed for the Pavillon de l'Esprit Nouveau, using Thonet bentwood chairs which at the very last moment were painted dark gray and tables with tubular steel frames made by Arnold of Schorndorf. The design for the tubular steel beds which fitted in beneath the closets incorporated in the concrete walls was Roth's own, for which he never received official credit—a fact that irks him to this day.

On top of all this, Roth found himself with an additional job to do. On July 17, 1927, one week before the opening of the Werkbund exhibition, he wrote Le Corbusier that the firm of Akademischer Verlag had decided to publish a *cahier extra*, a special booklet, on the two Le Corbusier/Jeanneret buildings. "I have been asked to consult you over the text and the design," wrote Roth, and he asked his principals if they were interested or whether—as the publishers had suggested—he should take on the job himself.[38]

The answer came back that he should do it; that Hans Hildebrandt might advise him, and perhaps write a brief foreword; that Baumeister should look after the typography; and that the "Five Points of a New Architecture" should be printed at the beginning. He was reminded to credit the partnership correctly: "Le Corbusier and Pierre Jeanneret, Paris and not Geneva!"[39]

Unfortunately, Le Corbusier wrote, he would not be able to come to Stuttgart before August 15–20; he added further details on the readying of the houses for opening day. He went on to ask Roth what he intended to do next and gave him an unusually candid opinion of German architecture:

In Stuttgart you have had a unique opportunity to make a highly interesting study. Maybe you are excited about Germany at the moment. We cannot say the same for ourselves. The League of Na-

tions exhibition in Geneva has all too clearly revealed the superficiality of German architecture.[40]

On May 2, 1927, the earthwork began. Now that City Hall had made up its mind to absorb the additional costs and build all three houses, all efforts were concentrated on completing the work by opening day. The Le Corbusier houses were given top priority.

Initially Roth had nothing but good news about the progress of the work and the attitude of the contractors. As time wore on, however, he could not rid himself of the impression that they were cutting corners and trying—as they did not feel tied to the quoted prices—"to make as much money as possible."[41] In *L'Architecture vivante*, Le Corbusier attributed the difficulties encountered in Stuttgart and the high cost of the houses partly to the fact that

the contractors were taken aback to receive a sizeable heap of exact drawings, and so they imagined that these houses must be hard to build. They themselves admitted to me that they were not used to reinforced concrete; and this admission is enough in itself to excuse me from any further examination of their exorbitant prices, which bear no comparison with those in France.[42]

Alfred Roth, deep in the minutiae of construction work on the lot, driven by the desire to do everything right—and on time, too—would have liked "a little car, to go downtown. It's always a long walk."[43] But even without a car, half an hour's walk away from the city center, he succeeded in having more or less completed houses at the opening. Le Corbusier and Jeanneret, whom he constantly begged to come to Stuttgart for consultation, did not visit the houses once during construction. From Paris, they decided which windows to glaze with mirror

glass; to tile staircases and passages in black; to accept Roth's suggestion of flooring with linoleum instead of parquet, because it could be laid without a joint; that the linoleum should be white, "*marque DLW*"; and that the Thonet chairs should be painted gray. There can be no doubt that one visit from them would have eliminated many of the shortcomings for which the houses were subsequently criticized.

The salary of 400 marks per month which Roth, together with all the other young resident architects, received from City Hall ceased to be paid at the end of June, in the very heat of the struggle; the only concession was an offer of 100 marks to make it possible for him to stay until July 8. "If you wish to go on working here after that—and I would be only too glad if you were to do so—you would have to bear the costs yourself, or else have Herr Corbusier reimburse you," wrote Döcker to Roth, with a carbon copy to Le Corbusier.[44]

At the same stage, with opening day only weeks away, the city building office was making difficulties which touched on a crucial nerve. The officials approved of the constructional system used in the buildings but did not like the unplastered pilotis. At one point they decided that the whole Weissenhofsiedlung was unsafe and considered halting construction altogether; at another they were inclined to think that it would be dangerous "for the duration of the exhibition, to allow more than two persons per square meter in the rooms on show, or in passages, stairways, and terraces."[45]

This was too much even for Deputy Mayor Sigloch. It was entirely as a result of his intervention that the conscience of the "building police" was laid to rest for the duration of the Werkbund exhibition. There were no accidents. But after the exhibition was over the controversy over the low ceiling heights, the dwarf partition between bathroom and bedroom in the single-family house, the heights of the balustrades and handrails, and so forth, flared up again.

The opening ceremony on July 23, 1927, took place in the absence of the two architects. In the previous few days work had proceeded at full steam ahead. Roth wrote to Paris, "15 painters start work Monday on the interior."[46] A day later he wrote that the city of Stuttgart was extremely happy "to have built our blocks. The city is proud and glad; without them the exhibition would be *really poor.*"[47]

The last few hectic days before the opening had their effect on everyone on that huge exhibition ground, as Roth wrote to Paris two weeks after the opening:

> Dr. Döcker has really been of no help at all. He is not interested in our blocks (the same goes for the others). Mies van der Rohe, a man of some character and very likable, was too overburdened to have any time to advise us. And so one was quite alone, and I could tell you some tales that would more than anger you. The Germans have not shown much organizational talent this time!
>
> Even so, our blocks are very nearly finished. Block C2 [Houses 14 and 15] was handed over to the city last Monday [August 1, 1927]. Tomorrow it will be Block C1 [House 13], which means that the work is officially at an end.
>
> The inaugural day was a fateful one: after it, the pace of work was halved. I had to take vigorous steps to get any workers to finish the buildings. It's a shame we couldn't use oil-based paints for the interiors because the plaster was not completely dry. After the exhibition, the houses will

House 13 under construction, from the south

Entrance lobby to House 13, showing the boiler

Houses 13, 14, 15, from Friedrich-Ebert-Strasse

House 13
Architects: Le Corbusier and Pierre Jeanneret
Plans and elevations from the building code submissions of May, 1927 (undated), drawn up to the prescribed scale of 1 : 100 by Richard Döcker from the architects' 1 : 50 drawings

Left:
Roof terrace

Mezzanine (*soupente*)

First floor

Basement

Right: elevations from north, south, east, west

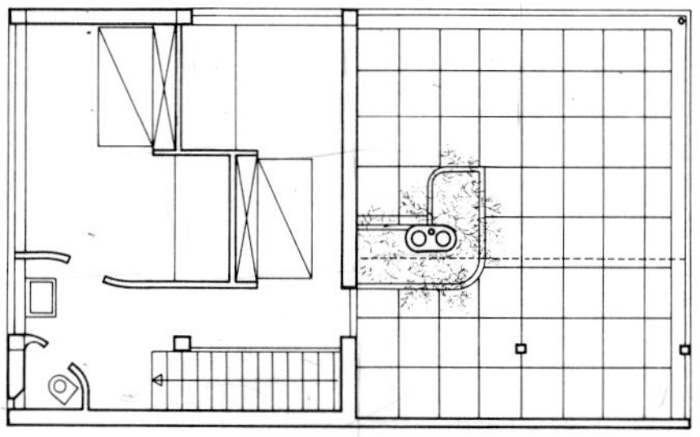

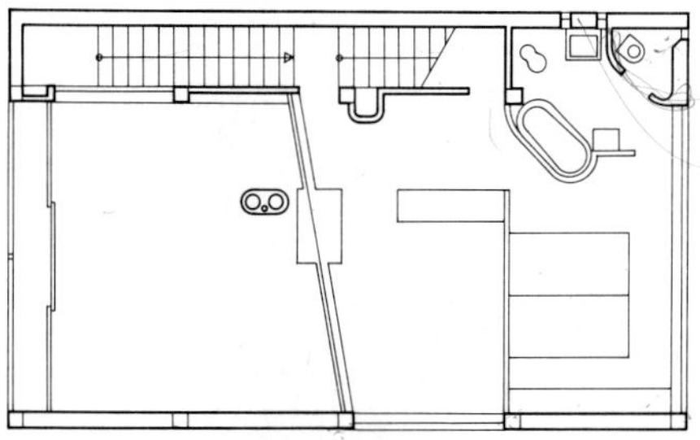

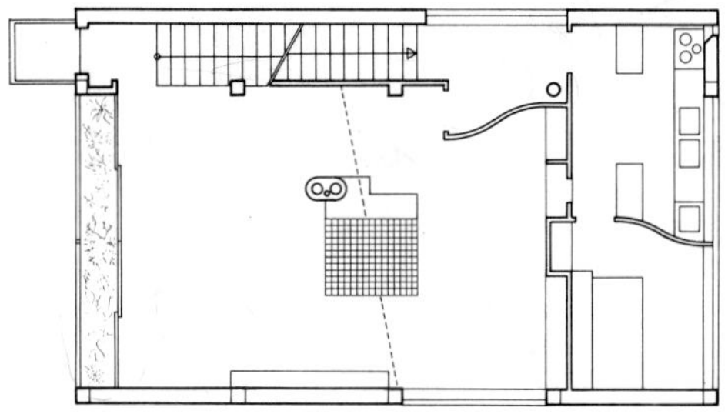

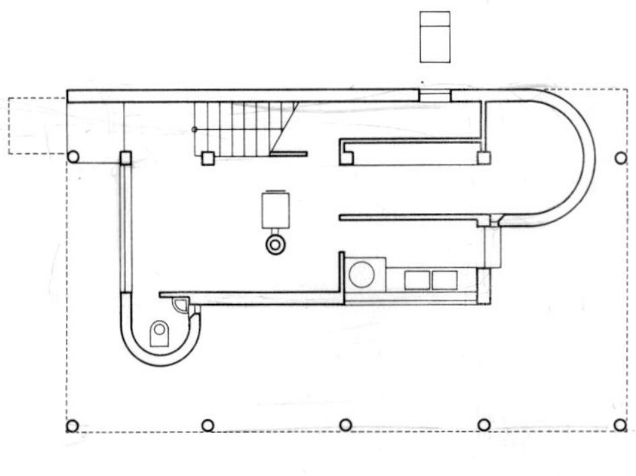

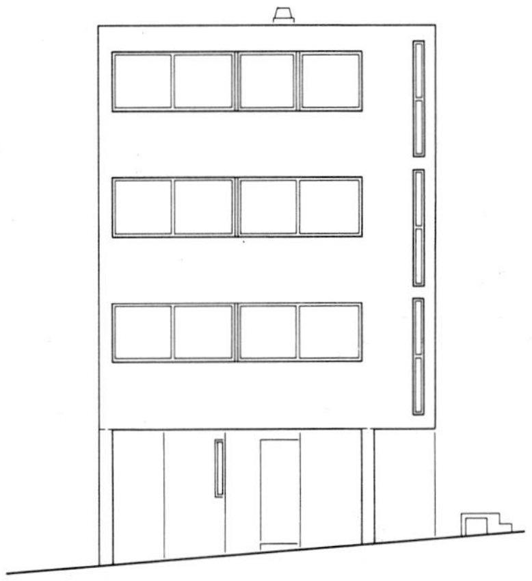

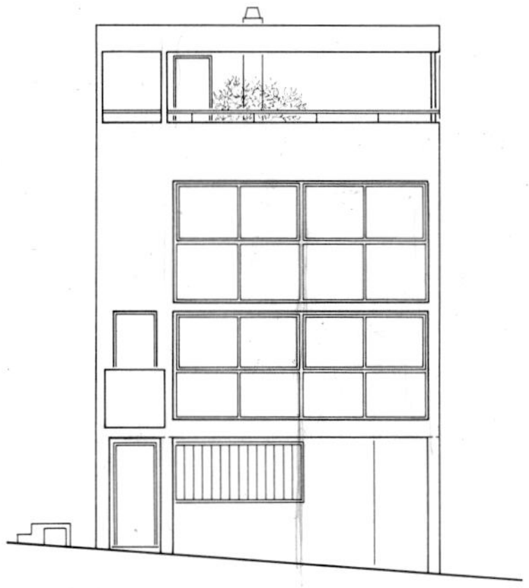

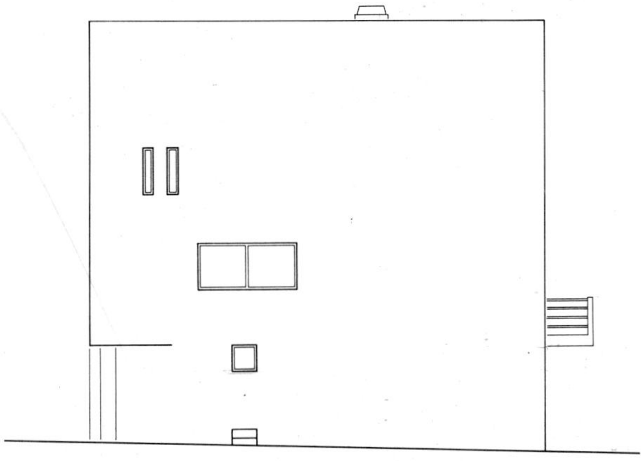

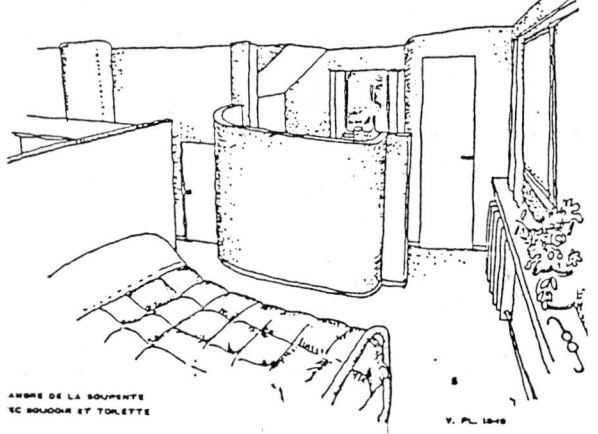

ANGRE DE LA SOUPENTE
EC BOUDOIR ET TOILETTE

V. PL. 18-19

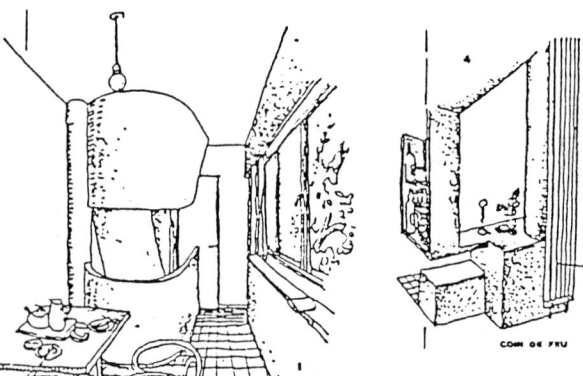

V. PL. 18

COIN DE FRU

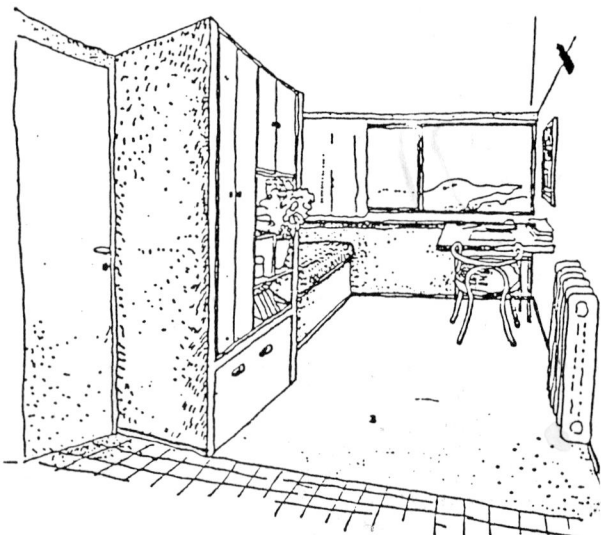

House 13:
Alfred Roth: three sketches of the interior

Boudoir on mezzanine
floor. The dwarf parti-
tion was intended to
be closable to ceiling
height by sliding pan-
els; these were omit-
ted, probably for
reasons of cost. The
three paintings are by
Willi Baumeister: *Fig-
ure on Green* (1921),
Head (1919–22), and
Archaic Figure (1921)

Two views of living
room by Le Corbusier
and Pierre Jeanneret,
with painting by
Baumeister

certainly have to be renovated. . . .

Our blocks inspire strong reactions. There are
widely divergent opinions among the members of
the public: on the way out, people are *amused*
and crack jokes.

The Thonet chairs will be coming in 14 days,
the tables next week. Yesterday Willi Baumeister
brought me some paintings, not all of which I
liked. . . . Today, Sunday, there is an enormous
crush of people.[48]

Four weeks later Roth wrote, "The exhibition is attracting large crowds. The tour of Block C2 has to be carefully organized because of the narrow passageway."[49]

Early in 1984 Roth revisited C2, Houses 14 and 15,
then in the course of restoration. He remarked that no

one would believe what a crush there had been "with all those beer bellies."[50] An amateur cartoonist was inspired to an inept effort which he captioned: "Narrow is the Way."[51]

In one of his last messages to Paris, Roth gave an exact inventory of the contents of the houses. We can therefore form an almost complete mental image of what was to be seen there:

Thonet chairs, painted dark gray.
Tables, as in the photographs of the [Pavillon de l']Esprit Nouveau.
A leather chair [ordered from Bühler in Stuttgart because things looked so empty without it].
A fine Persian carpet.[52]
A Radio.
A telephone on the desk.
Paintings by Willi Baumeister.
Vases of flowers.
Books: *Kommende Baukunst.*
White drapes everywhere.
The closets in C1, in the nursery and maid's room, have not been built (lack of money). After much toing and froing I have succeeded in having the closet in the boudoir made.
I am trying to add more final touches. Now our houses can show themselves.[53]

This was one month after opening day!

Roth's booklet *Zwei Wohnhäuser von Le Corbusier und Pierre Jeanneret* came out at the end of August 1927, long before the official Werkbund publication *Bau und Wohnung.* His efforts in Stuttgart had been an all-round success. He left on September 16, summing up as follows:

To organize an exhibition of this kind with success, the following would be necessary: more cooperation between the organizers, more time, more money, and, for the quality of the architecture on display, a different choice of architects.[54]

On September 28 Le Corbusier and Jeanneret visited Stuttgart for the exhibition. Over the following weekend, on September 30, the members of the Werkbund traveled to the exhibition from their convention in Mannheim. As Roth had given notice of this in one of his letters to Paris, it may well be that the architects of the exhibition's star attraction did after all make personal contact with their German colleagues.

The contracts for the houses were placed with a single contractor at an agreed price of 41,500 marks for the single-family house, 13, and 62,400 marks for the two-family house, 14 and 15. The "total net building cost," as eventually computed by Döcker, was 45,208.89 marks for House 13 and 63,085.72 for 14 and 15: together, instead of 135,000 marks, the houses cost 108,294.46 marks.

It was à propos of the Werkbund exhibition in Stuttgart that Le Corbusier formulated his "Five Points of a New Architecture." He also discussed them in two articles, one that dealt with the question "How does one live in my Stuttgart houses?" and one on the treatment of the interiors. Before reporting on the expressions of enthusiasm and revulsion which greeted Le Corbusier's and Jeanneret's houses—for they left no one cold—we first list the Five Points:

The Five Points of a New Architecture:

Willi Baumeister: postcard to Le Corbusier and Pierre Jeanneret, August 5, 1927, with pencil drawings: "(1) M. Roth explaining the architecture; "(2) Mme Baumeister watering the plants; "(3) M. Baumeister cleaning the big window: a number of weird figures. BUT THE CREATORS: PIERRE J., LE COR."

Assiduous and stubborn research has resulted in partial realizations which can be considered as having been acquired in a laboratory. These results open new prospects for architecture; they present themselves to an *urbanisme* which can find the means therein to arrive at the solution of the great sickness of our present-day cities.

1. The house on columns [*pilotis*]! The house used to be sunk in the ground: dark and often humid rooms. Reinforced concrete offers us the columns. The house is in the air, above the ground; the garden passes under the house, the garden is also on the house, on the roof.
2. The roof gardens. For centuries the traditional rooftop has usually supported the win-

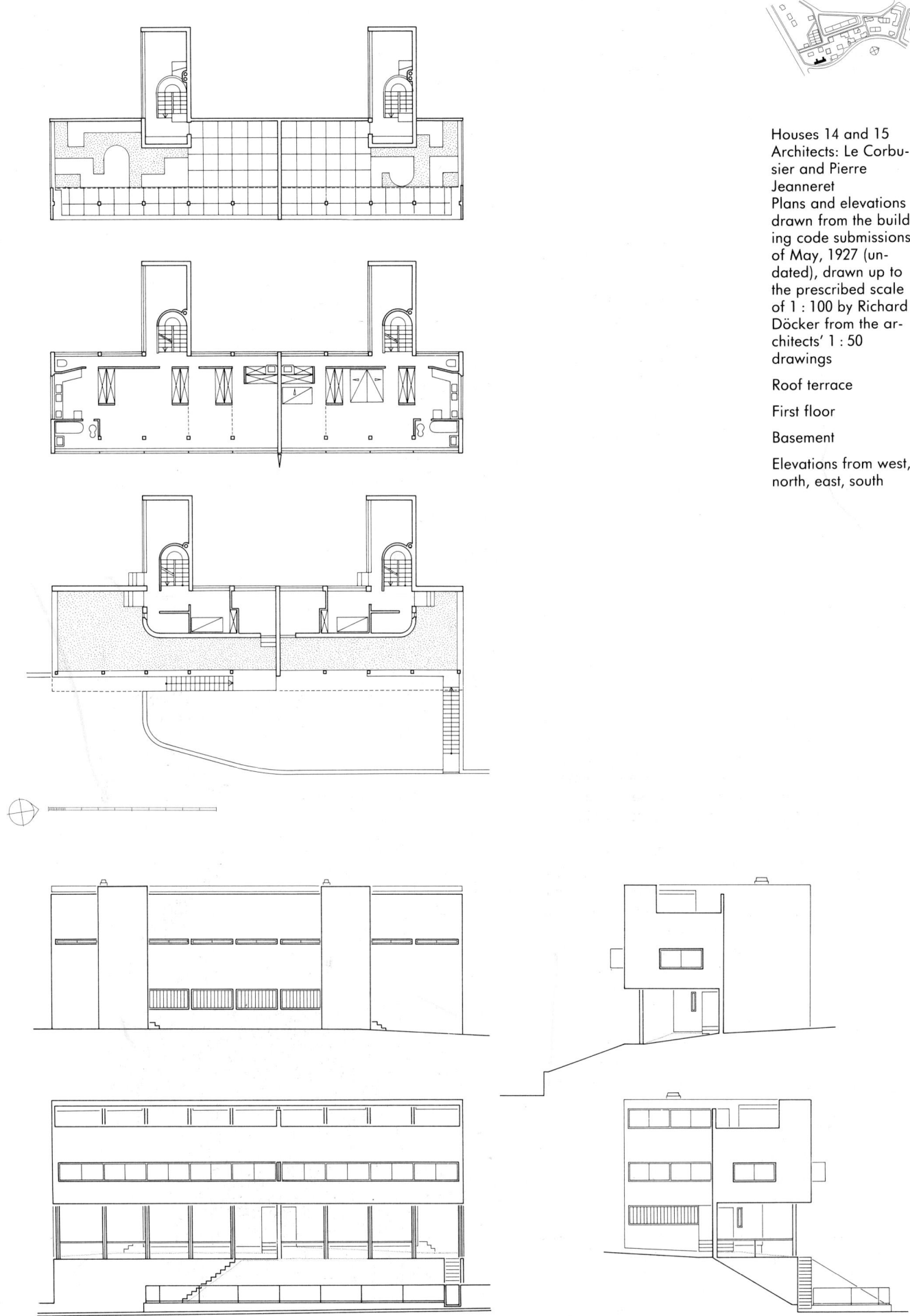

Houses 14 and 15
Architects: Le Corbusier and Pierre Jeanneret
Plans and elevations drawn from the building code submissions of May, 1927 (undated), drawn up to the prescribed scale of 1 : 100 by Richard Döcker from the architects' 1 : 50 drawings

Roof terrace

First floor

Basement

Elevations from west, north, east, south

ter with its layer of snow, while the house has been heated by stoves.

From the moment central heating is installed, the traditional rooftop is no longer convenient. The roof should no longer be convex, but should be concave. It must cause the rain-water to flow toward the interior and not to the exterior.

A truth allowing of no exceptions: cold climates demand the suppression of the sloping rooftop and require the construction of concave roof-terraces with water draining toward the interior of the house.

Reinforced concrete is the new means for realizing a homogeneous roof. Reinforced concrete experiences a great deal of expansion and contraction. An intense movement of this sort can cause cracks in the structure. Instead of trying to rapidly drain away the rain-water, one should maintain a constant humidity for the concrete of the roof-terrace and thereby assure a regulated temperature for the concrete. An especially good protection: sand covered by thick cement slabs laid with staggered joints; the joints being seeded with grass. The sand and roots permit a slow filtration of the water. The garden terraces become opulent: flowers, shrubbery and trees, grass.

Thus we are led to choose the roof-terrace for technical reasons, economic reasons, reasons of comfort, and sentimental reasons.

3. The free plan. Until now: load-bearing walls; rising up from the basement they are always superimposed, forming the ground and upper floors, right up to the roof. The plan is a slave of the bearing walls. Reinforced concrete in the house brings about the free plan! The floors no longer superimpose rooms of the same size. They are free. A great economy of constructed volume, a rigorous use of each centimeter. A great financial economy. The easy rationalism of the new plan!

4. The long window. The window is one of the essential goals of the house. Progress has brought about a liberation. Reinforced concrete has brought about a revolution in the history of the window. Windows can now run from one edge of the facade to the other. The window is the repetitive mechanical element of the house; for all our town-houses, all our villas, all our workers' housing, all our apartment houses.

5. The free facade. The columns are now set back from the facades, toward the interior of the house. The floor extends outward in a cantilever. The facades are now only light membranes composed of insulating or window elements.

The facade is free; the windows, without being interrupted, can run from one edge of the facade to the other.

These five points embody a fundamental aesthetic reaction. Nothing remains of the architecture of the past, or of the theories of the academies.[55]

Somewhat less like a manifesto, a gift to humanity in

Postcard from Willi Baumeister to Le Corbusier: "THE GHOST OF MR. LE C. Dear friend. The buildings are growing like the grass with the best desires of your friends. . . . A. Roth, Willi Baumeister, Margit Baumeister."

Houses 14 and 15, seen from House 13

Houses 14 and 15, seen from Rathenaustrasse

general and to architects in particular, is the tone of Le Corbusier's answer in *L'Architecture vivante* to the question "How does one live in my Stuttgart houses"?

A house like a car, all right: but now tell me whether you are buying a racing car or a town car, 5 horsepower or 40, etc., etc. Please define the *category*. We have defined the *type-elements* of a house, and we shall combine them to suit you.

In this way, using the same elements (floors, pillars, windows, stairs, etc.), we have designed village houses at Pessac, artists' houses in Paris, large or small villas for people of means, and the League of Nations building in Geneva.

In Stuttgart, vexed because what you found was not the house that you needed, you went away blaming us; you failed to perceive that the absolutely revolutionary freedom conferred by new technical resources had enabled us to construct two kinds of houses that differ totally in their uses: one was a combination of sleeper and parlor car, arranged for daytime or nighttime use; the other was a home that had derived from the *primitive* house a certain strength and a certain simple manner of life.

By day, the sleeper became a parlor car (Group C2 [14, 15]). One of the two houses in this group contained three entirely separate bedrooms, linked together by ordinary doors between the steel pillars and the windows, and linked to the remainder of the house (thus becoming entirely independent of each other) by that famous corridor, 70 cm [27½ in] wide, at which so many visitors took fright. This corridor, of the same width as the corridor in every railroad car in the world, along which thousands of passengers pass every day in trains hurtling along at 100 kilometers per hour, served to link the bedrooms with the toilet, the wash basin, the bathroom, the kitchen, the roof garden, the garden itself.

In practice, this "emergency corridor" was hardly ever used.

By the addition of standard elements 2.5 meters [8 feet] wide, this house type could be enlarged by one, two, or three extra bedrooms, etc. In each of the resulting cells or cabins, 2.5 × 4 meters [8 × 13 feet], there was a special, economical, reinforced concrete construction that allowed the bed to be stowed away and provided closets so designed as to offer the occupant of each cell hanging space for clothes, shelves for underwear and bed linen, hats, shoes, etc.: in short, a complete set of shelving, carefully designed to replace all the furniture that normally clutters bedrooms and forces architects to build them larger: too large.

In the morning, the occupants of the house find their breakfast served in the lobby, which is continuous with the stairwell. This lobby can also be used to receive the occasional unseasonably early caller. The maid has her bedroom down under the pilotis, and her access to the kitchen is direct and independent.

In the evening, when the children are asleep, Monsieur can work in peace and quiet in his study, which opens directly onto the roof garden, and I imagine that in fine weather he will have a very pleasant time up there. In the daytime, all these cabins can be transformed at will into a single large room, with direct access to the stairs—

or into two rooms, if desired. Our sliding partitions are so designed as to provide much better soundproofing than an ordinary door.

In order to make our intentions clear to visitors to the exhibition, we decided to build a two-family house, so that one half would be set up *for the daytime* and the other *for the night*. But when we got to Stuttgart on September 28, we found to our dismay that both houses were shown with their *daytime* setup, so that our intentions remained unintelligible.

The other house (Group C1 [13]) represents a style of living that, uncommon though it may be in Germany, presents great advantages for anyone living in Paris.

It is untrue that, as has been alleged, only a person of "bohemian" and well-nigh immoral habits could bear to spend ten days in such a house. The second floor, at roof-garden level, consists of two children's rooms with four beds, or else one child's bedroom with twin beds and one study.

The first floor is of double height, i.e. it contains a low mezzanine 2.2 meters [86½ inches] high.

The utilities—kitchen, toilet, and maid's room—are kept together and independent.

Once the children are in bed, therefore, Monsieur and Madame have at their disposal a huge space on the first floor and a large boudoir, bedrooms, bath, and toilet on the mezzanine. Large standard closets separate these mezzanine rooms and fulfill specific functions.

I have to confess that, in the course of construction, one important feature was simply left out: on the boudoir parapet, overlooking the living room, there were to be sliding screens to permit the entire sleeping area, bathroom, boudoir, etc., to be closed off. We introduced this form of separation in the Pavillon de l'Esprit Nouveau, 1925; and if our plans are looked at with this omitted feature in mind, it will not seem such a bad idea after all.

We have been much censured for the long window in the living room. I devised this type of win-

House 14, furnished for the daytime. Painting by Willi Baumeister: *Composition with Red Rectangle* (1925–26)

dow more than ten years ago, 1,000 meters [3,300 feet] above sea level, in a country where the snow lies 1.5 meters [5 feet] thick, and we proposed the very same system to solve the lighting and heating problems in the great assembly hall of the League of Nations. What is obtained is not, in fact, a *cooling* surface but a *neutral* surface. This is done by setting the inner and outer windows 60 cm [2 feet] apart and passing the heating pipes along between them. A *warm* space is thus created, and the window becomes a kind of greenhouse in which plants will grow in a bed of earth and at a constant temperature; these plants will form a charming curtain of greenery. Glazing of this kind also serves in our "Villa Blocks" to provide insulation, both thermal and visual.

I maintain that, in a house of this kind, families who are quite *normal*, but who love comfort, space, and light, will find a type of home that possesses a certain splendor, very different from the tiny identical bedrooms that are commonly found in villas of this size.[56]

In a second article—which became his contribution to Werner Graeff's Werkbund book, *Innenräume*—Le Corbusier went on to deal with questions of furnishing:

Let us just try to answer the straightforward question, "What is furnishing?"

Answer: in a house one sleeps, one wakes, one acts, one works, one rests, one talks, one eats, and one goes to sleep.

Where is the logical connection between these functions and traditional items of furniture? Where do they agree?

The bed remains, the table remains, the seats remain.

But the chests of all kinds (consoles, sideboards, bookcases, etc.) are ill suited to these functions, cost a lot of money, and take up a great deal of space; they force the architect to design large and expensive rooms, and those large rooms are made small by the furniture that is installed in them.

For precise functions other than those of sitting down, working, or eating at table, I have the following answer: a specific compartment corresponds to a specific function, and the function arises regularly in a specific place. *Specific places call for specific compartments.*

These specific compartments are standard items, because they contain only the objects for which they are intended. Our limbs are of standard dimensions, taking one with the other: underwear, bedlinen, clothes, shoes, hats, glasses, bottles, cups, plates, etc. These objects have long since been standardized by industry. They have common dimensions. Compartments of standard form can be designed and precisely located.

These functions involve handling; as the word itself implies, this is done with the hands, and so the most useful position for these compartments will be at hand-height.

A specific object is taken from its compartment and replaced in the same compartment. (Let us not try to pretend that we act differently because we are "free human beings": order is liberty; disorder is slavery.) . . .

Tables? Why so many kinds of table in my apartment? If, once a week, I entertain ten of my friends to dinner for three hours, am I going to be burdened, all my life, with a gigantic table that completely fills my dining room?

I have proposed the following sensible course of action: define, as a type, a table of minimum useful dimensions (for example, 80 × 120 cm [$31\frac{1}{2}$ × $47\frac{1}{4}$ inches]). Instead of five different sorts of table in my apartment, I have five identical ones; but they can be combined, and their legs (in welded bicycle tubing) are separate from the tabletop. The top has a stout frame, but it is made of plywood sheet and is consequently light in weight. I can move my tables around with ease, and I can dine anywhere I like in my apartment, as the mood takes me. I realize that this is pretty anarchistic!

And the chairs? I have this to say: the laws of traditional etiquette have succumbed to the advance of the machine (automobile, bicycle, subway, sport, office, etc.) The way women dress today is abundant proof of this. The chairs that we have inherited from our ancestors were sat upon only in certain circumstances and in "polite" poses governed by etiquette. Etiquette went hand in hand with fashion, and with social relations. We have left all that behind us long ago, and yet we continue to sit very uncomfortably and disagreeably in our own houses. At the office, and especially at the club, or on the decks of ocean liners, we have allowed ourselves *new habits of sitting*.

New habits of sitting: this can take us a long way, I promise you! There are different ways of sitting, according to whether one is working, reading, talking, resting, etc.

This is the direction in which we have been working for years: for, as things are at present, the market is served by the decorators and the cabinetmakers, who fail to provide us with useful kinds of seating—except, as we have said, in clubs.

And so our house becomes livable: perfectly and delightfully, in peace and in comfort. To satisfy reason is to make the lady of the house happy . . .

In Stuttgart we left our houses empty (apart from mock-ups of the storage compartments), and with no seats or tables (what was done was a gesture, and beyond our control). This was because—and let it be said once for all—we were prevented by overriding force of circumstance from going to Stuttgart before the end of September.

And all our excellent intentions appeared to us to have been very ill reflected by the execution, of which it might be said . . . but the less said the better.

In the summer of 1927, we were unable to organize the making of the seats in question, or of the tables, because the funds available were zero, and zero will come of zero!

Our houses therefore remained empty. Those who visited them will grant us, at least, that the bride was not overadorned!

In lieu of furniture, I offer these theories.

"Theories!" people will say. "More theories!" But consider that they are based on twenty years of practice. [57]

In these texts, Le Corbusier covers the essentials of his

The color scheme of Houses 14 and 15, by Le Corbusier and Pierre Jeanneret. The colors were determined in 1984 from original paint layers on and in House 15, which has been restored throughout. They are described in accordance with DIN 6164, as a ratio of hue : saturation : darkness.

Key to color indications on plans (right):
1 white – : 0 : 0.5
2 pale green 22 : 2 : 1
3 light blue 17 : 2 : 2
4 venetian red 5 : 4 : 3
5 dark brown 5 : 2 : 6
6 mid-gray – : 0 : 3.5
7 dark blue-gray 16 : 1 : 5
8 pale yellow 1 : 2 : 1

Plans:

Roof terrace floor with library in back addition

Main floor with study in back addition

Basement with laundry and maid's room

Color of exterior	white	– : 0 : 0.5
Staircase additions	pale green	22 : 2 : 1
Sight screen, second floor	mid gray	– : 0 : 3.5
Pilotis	dark blue-gray	16 : 2 : 6

Roof terrace floor

Soffit of canopy	pale green	22 : 2 : 1
Parapet inner side (east)	pale blue	17 : 2 : 2
Flooring	concrete slabs	
Sides of staircase	pale green	22 : 2 : 1
End of stair addition (west)	pale blue	17 : 2 : 2
West wall (all)	dark brown	5 : 2 : 6
North wall	pale yellow	1 : 2 : 1
Door to staircase	dark blue-gray	16 : 1 : 5

"Library" on roof terrace floor

West wall	venetian red	5 : 4 : 3
East wall	dark brown	5 : 2 : 6
North wall	pale yellow	1 : 2 : 1
Inside of window frame	dark brown	5 : 2 : 6
Radiators	blue	17 : 5 : 4
Ceiling and chimney breast	white	– : 0 : 0.5
Wall below windows	pale yellow	1 : 2 : 1
Baseboard	dark blue-gray	16 : 1 : 5
Iron parts of fireplace	black	
Stair tiles 15 × 15 cm [6 × 6 in.]	black	
String and balustrade of stairs	dark blue-gray	16 : 1 : 5
Curved staircase wall	pale yellow	1 : 2 : 1
Central handrail, metal	dark blue-gray	16 : 1 : 5

Main floor
Study as library, kitchen:

Ceiling and walls	pale gray	– : 0 : 2.5
Window and wall above window	white	– : 0 : 0.5

Bathroom:

North wall	pale gray	– : 0 : 2.5
Wall above window	pale yellow	1 : 2 : 1
Window frame	dark blue-gray	16 : 1 : 5
Flooring, plastic	white	– : 0 : 0.5

Living and sleeping area

Flooring, plastic	white	– : 0 : 0.5
Ceiling	white	– : 0 : 0.5
Baseboard	dark blue-gray	16 : 1 : 5
South and north walls	pale blue	17 : 2 : 2
Wall to lobby	dark brown	5 : 2 : 6
Doors, sliding door	mid-gray	– : 0 : 3.5
Closets, rolling shutters	mid-gray	– : 0 : 3.5
Front edges of closets	white	– : 0 : 0.5
Sliding door frame to kitchen/bath	dark blue-gray	16 : 1 : 5
Piers	mid-gray	– : 0 : 4
Wall above and below window	pale yellow	1 : 2 : 1
Radiators	blue	17 : 5 : 4
Front edge of window seat	dark brown	5 : 2 : 6
Window seat	white	– : 0 : 0.5
Window frame	white	– : 0 : 0.5
West wall of small lobby	pale yellow	1 : 2 : 1

Basement
Laundry, maid's room

Staircase wall inside, upward	pale yellow	1 : 2 : 1
Staircase wall to cellar	dark brown	5 : 2 : 6
Flooring, plastic	white	– : 0 : 0.5
Walls, ceiling, wall below window	mid-gray	– : 0 : 3.5
Radiators and pipes	blue	17 : 5 : 4

Entrance lobby

End wall	dark brown	5 : 2 : 6
Front door and door to yard	dark blue-gray	16 : 1 : 5
Wall to garden	pale yellow	1 : 2 : 1
Ceiling	white	– : 0 : 0.5
Curved staircase wall to cellar	dark brown	5 : 2 : 6

Curved staircase wall to cellar	dark brown	5 : 2 : 6

Maid's room

Flooring, plastic	white	– : 0 : 0.5
End wall, ceiling	white	– : 0 : 0.5
East wall	pale blue	17 : 2 : 2
North wall	pale green	22 : 2 : 1
Baseboard	dark blue-gray	16 : 1 : 5

Exterior

Balustrade on stairs	mid-gray	– : 0 : 5
Entrance window	dark brown	5 : 2 : 6
Cellar wall	mid-gray	– : 0 : 3.5
Wall of entrance steps	venetian red	6 : 3 : 4
Deck soffit	pale blue	17 : 2 : 2

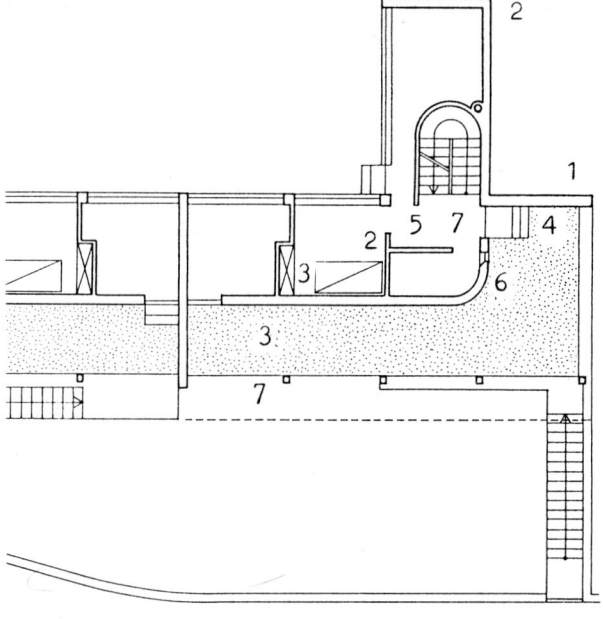

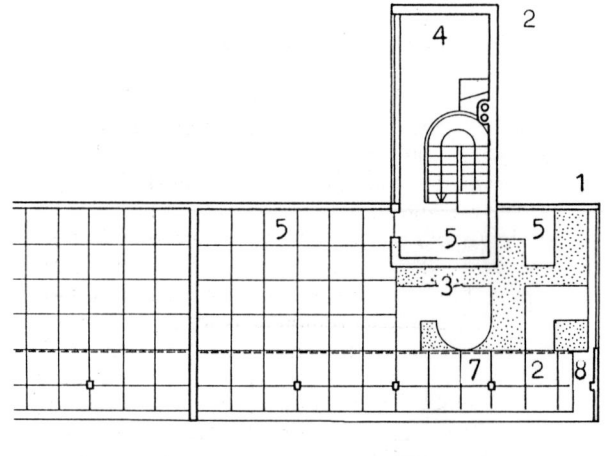

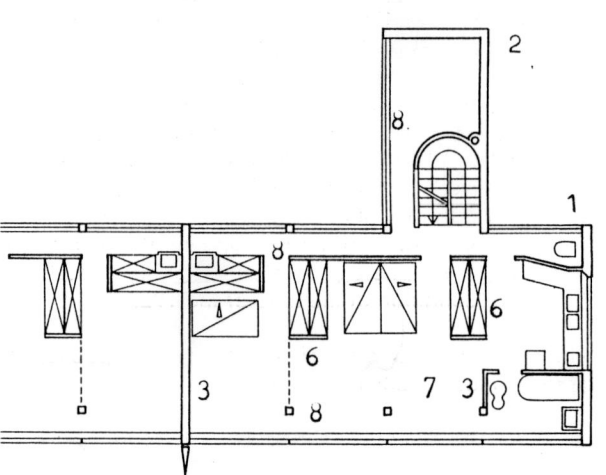

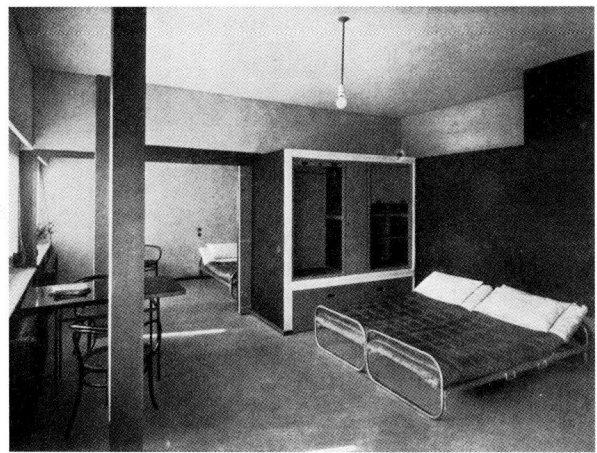

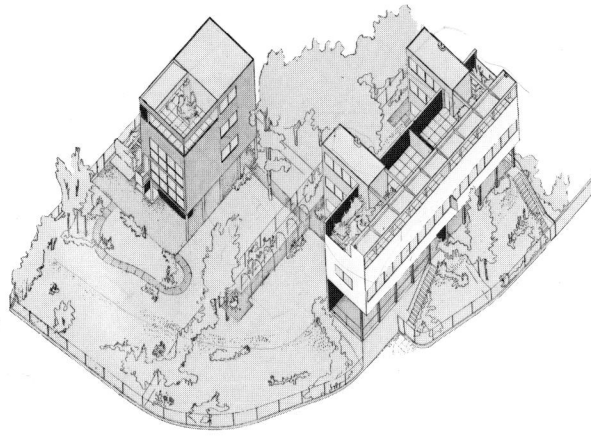

architectural approach. The coloring of his houses is dealt with in Roth's *Zwei Wohnhäuser von Le Corbusier und Pierre Jeanneret*. After first elucidating Le Corbusier's principles of material and color, Roth goes on:

> For the color scheme of both houses, Le Corbusier selected a basic color chord of umber, dark gray, red ocher, light gray, pink, and light blue. These, together with white, establish the mood of the color. The placing of white is predetermined: 1. The window wall, as the unlit and therefore darkest surface, in white. A blue accent, or a pronounced brilliant blue, has found a place in earlier buildings. Blue suggests remoteness, and, when used on the window wall, it can expand the space. 2. The ceilings: white is appropriate here because of its disembodied nature, in order to lend height, and of its capacity to reflect light. 3. Walls which are lit from one side by a raking light, in accordance with the reflective effect.[58]

In describing Le Corbusier's palette Roth omitted to mention *vert pâle*, the startling pale green on and in Houses 14 and 15. The original color scheme has been restored inside the right-hand, smaller house of the pair, and outside both houses more or less accurately (although still not in oil paint!), and so it is possible to visualize, from photographs and first-hand observation, their condition at the time of the 1927 exhibition.

How did the architectural world, and the public, respond to the Le Corbusier houses?

If the type of home reflects the type of man, then one can imagine as dwellers in the Le Corbusier houses only one specific class of intellectuals: those individualists who—untrammeled by "historical ballast," unsentimental, footloose, nowhere at home, free of all ties—might want to inhabit such a nomadic tent of concrete and glass, which in spite of the hardness of its materials is not firmly, heavily earthbound—indeed not ground-based at all—but seems to have settled momentarily on the earth like some brightly colored butterfly. That international type of intellectual, that extreme form of deracinated urban man, is to be found everywhere—but especially where there is a smell of newsprint and printer's ink. True, the intellectual is one form of today's humanity; but is he *the* type, whose needs and aspirations are to determine the form of home building that will go into mass production and cater for mass need? Not everyone wants to be permanently reduced to a bed space for the night, and to push his bed into a closet in the daytime, as in Le Corbusier's houses. There are many who would like an enclosed bedroom, in which they can not only rest and dream, but also make love, procreate, give birth, and die.[59]

This critic, Edgar Wedepohl, called the hypothetical occupants of Le Corbusier houses "the live-in machinists." Le Corbusier's famous phrase "a machine for living in," launched in *Vers une architecture moderne*, was intended to convey the idea that houses might be built with the same precision, seriousness, professionalism, and logic as automobiles, airplanes, and expensive technological inventions. However, it was open to misinterpretation as an attack on tradition and on comfort itself, as well as on all forms of inadequate mental response to the upheavals of the age.

Very few critics were as open about their own intimate fears as Wedepohl. Most attempted to attach their unease to tangible and visible details:

> First of all, I think I may say that these buildings do not really belong in Stuttgart. With elevations of this type, disproportionately large window areas, and flat roofs, I should be pleased if these houses had been designed for a more southerly climate.[60]

And again: "If we were to find this house at Ospedaletti, or at Castagnola, we would be delighted to rent it for a couple of months."[61]

Starting with the "suburb of Jerusalem" to which Bonatz had compared Weissenhof, the critics seemed to be anxious to put as much geographical and climatic distance as possible between their own homes and this architectural provocation—or to displace it into the equally alien and incomprehensible territory of art.[62]

There were, in fact, quite a number of details in the houses that were open to criticism: "It is not everyone's wish, on first walking into the house [House 13], to come upon the central heating furnace, blazing away in the cloakroom."[63] A Swiss critic described the effect:

> A detached house, in an area of lawn crossed by narrow paths in curves. The front door is somewhere, an arrow shows where, the owner presumably knows already. You walk in, and everything is black: floor, stairs, heating boiler. For there, in front of you, is the boiler. And a meager little wall sink; also a narrow toilet door. But no cloakroom.

Doors to the laundry, to the cellar. Somewhat daunted, you climb the black stairs, a straight flight, patched together out of floorboards with no particular care. A landing, just big enough to land on, for the kitchen and the big living room . . .

And then the living room, the centerpiece of the house, extending through two stories, with a gallery halfway up, all facing toward the great front window. . . .

From this large room, a straight stairway leads on—and opposite the foot of the stairs is a skimpy door to a tiny balcony. Halfway up, one reaches the gallery, a place designed as a work area or study; and behind, against the back wall of the house, divided from the study only by a screen— a solid one, 1.56 meters [5 feet] high—is a sleep station, with room for two beds: and further on, again divided off only by a dwarf partition, are a bathtub and a bidet, close up against the narrow door of a toilet. . . .

Are we, in the future, to disregard the smell and the noise for the sake of an interesting spatial creation—rather as we have to disregard all sorts of discomforts in buildings by Schinkel, or Semper, or Poelaert, for the sake of monumentality? Are these interpenetrating spaces a kind of program for living itself? Or is it all—as we suspect— a mere paraphrase and continuation of studio life, where an improvised dinner stands on a wobbly table next to the easel, where if necessary the clatter of dishes and the strumming of the piano can be reconciled with desk work, and where bed is always there for a model and girl friend, complemented by bath and bidet? Or are we taking the whole thing too seriously, too pedantically?[64]

Bed, bath, and bidet, with no solid wall to divide them from the rest of the family home, and in the two-family house the irritation of the daily and nightly need to convert the living rooms: these were the main points of detail that unleashed a few primal fears at the time—and often still do. In 1984 when the renovation of Le Corbusier's Houses 14 and 15 was almost complete and the concrete closets were in place (this time made of wood chipboard), the first potential tenants visited House 15. They were a middle-aged couple, both rather stout, who had earned the right to public housing by years in the public service. They looked around, looked at each other, and were struck mute. They said not one word. They did not take the house: an artist now lives there.

Many observers did see Le Corbusier's houses as the epitome of modernity and grasped their artistic value. Karl Konrad Düssel, arts editor of the *Stuttgarter Neues Tagblatt* and one of the few with an eye for the color of the Weissenhofsiedlung, "a picture with a beauty all its own," wrote:

The impression is even stronger if the development is seen from the main access road. There the eye is caught at once by the two blocks by Le Corbusier. The pink of one, with its facade dominated by one gigantic window. The pale green and white of the other, with wide, asymmetrically placed windows. It was a superb idea to place these two in such a dominant position in the foreground. They are like a signal. They emphasize that the Weissenhofsiedlung is a place dedicated to the New Home. One starts to realize what life in the New Home is all about. These two buildings seem wide open to light and air. No confinement

and seclusion. The lungs and the pores are to be wide open. The human being who lives here must love light and wide open spaces.

On coming closer, one is overcome with surprise and admiration at the beauty of these two buildings. They mark the discovery of a totally new, absolutely convincing form of dwelling. The strange way in which both structures rest on slender supports (even seeming to hang in mid-air) gives an entirely new feeling of the structural nature of a house. And all the proportions are wonderfully judged. These houses stand before us, quite without burdensome weight, and yet powerful and decisive. Looking at them, one gains an immediate impression of the type of human being who has his dwelling here.

Only a great and above all a totally consistent and logical artist can convey so much fullness of expression in the external form of a building. Of all those who have built at Weissenhof, Le Corbusier is the strongest artist, the one with the most sovereign mastery of formal ideas. His spatial design fascinates; his proportions seem to have been chosen with an ultimate intuitive sureness. One begins to understand how this architect, who in his radical book demands the rationalization of the dwelling house into a "machine for living in," can also speak of the "Platonic Idea" of architecture: he ultimately distinguishes the mere utilitarian technician from the true architect by saying "The art of architecture proclaims itself through an inner poetic gift."

Le Corbusier builds from an idea. To the point of utopia. This is not to say that he simply fantasizes into thin air: on the contrary, in designing a house he reckons with the relationships, needs, and potentialities of the human being whom he expects to emerge from our economic and sociological conditions. Le Corbusier does not set out to mediate, or to ease a transition. He wants a new form of house, because he believes in a new meaning for the home. He is entirely obsessed by his idea. And so he is the most decisive and the most consistent of all architects. It is no wonder that he is also the most controversial and the most fiercely resisted.[65]

The highest praise was reserved for the single-family house, House 13. Sergius Ruegenberg, who had worked in Mies's office, noted in 1984 that "on completion, Mies's response was: The most beautiful & best thing at Weissenhof is the Le Corbusier house (interior). Ruegenberg points to apartment building—Mies makes firmly dismissive gesture (at own achievement)."[66]

Recognition came to the two-family house later: the administration building of the Neue Staatsgalerie in Stuttgart, by James Stirling, completed and inaugurated in 1984, is a homage to Le Corbusier's Houses 14 and 15 at Weissenhof. With an element of Mannerist exaggeration, the basic, admittedly superficial, motifs—pilotis, ribbon windows, free facade design, and a hint of a roof garden—all reappear.

In February, 1981, Charles Moore began his contribution to a symposium organized by Jürgen Joedicke at the University of Stuttgart:

Imitation, we are told, is the sincerest form of flattery. There is also honesty in the desire to complement ideas and objects which have appeared in our time, to complete them or to react to them, just as in China the Yin completes the Yang and simultaneously counteracts it. What is certainly no flattery at all is to ignore what has been done before our own time. And so, if I enumerate Le Corbusier's "Five Points" and counter them with five of my own, this is not intended as a snub to him or to the other architects of the Weissenhofsiedlung, but springs from an attitude of respect for their work and from the attempt to be equally open to our own, very different time.[67]

There is no more unequivocal praise and honor than Düssel, Mies, Stirling, and Moore have paid to the work of Le Corbusier. And finally, Hans Hildebrandt anticipated later judgments when he wrote in 1927,

There are buildings in which the essence of an age, and of a people, are concentrated. . . . Le Corbusier's houses are such buildings; they are the symbols of a present which points to the future. They could only have been created in a century in which man has fulfilled an age-old wish and learned to fly. These buildings have lost their heaviness. The earth's force of attraction seems to be overcome, and they free themselves from its spell.[68]

HOUSES 16, 17
Design: Walter Gropius, Dessau

HOUSE 16

Single-family house: basement, first floor, upper floor. Construction: large pumice concrete hollow blocks, plastered externally, interior dry-lined. Partitions and ceilings, zigzag wood construction.
Interior design: Professor Walter Gropius, architect, Dessau, Bauhaus, Friedrichsallee.
The accommodation comprises:
First floor: entrance, lobby, toilet, parents' bedroom, bedroom, living and dining room, kitchen, pantry, utility room, terrace and children's play area.
Upper floor: lobby, laundry and ironing room, washroom with toilet, study, children's bedroom.

HOUSE 17

Construction: dry construction, using prefabricated constructional elements with no moisture. A prefabricated model house for industrial mass production. Concrete raft foundation, iron frame, cork panel infilling, exterior siding of asbestos cement sheets, interior Enso-Celotex-Lignat boards.
Interior design: Professor Walter Gropius, architect, Dessau, Bauhaus, Friedrichsallee.
The accommodation comprises:
First floor: entrance, lobby, living and dining room, kitchen with adjoining cool pantry, utility and store room.
Upper floor: lobby, three bedrooms, laundry serving as ironing and drying room, bathroom, toilet.[1]

"I am glad," said Mies in 1953, "that I had once the possibility in Stuttgart to give Gropius a hand so that he could demonstrate his ideas on industrialization and standardization and on prefabrication. He built two houses there, which were the most interesting houses in the exhibition."[2]

To Mies, Stotz, Bruckmann, and the members of the city council building committee, there was no question that Walter Gropius must somehow be induced to participate in the 1927 exhibition. Gropius, in his turn, was by no means disposed to refuse. In 1926 he duly signed the contract drawn up by City Hall, and he thereafter concentrated on ensuring the conditions which would enable him to make his ideas a reality. At the meeting of Der Ring in Berlin in the following year, which led to Mies's resignation (his good work as organizer of the Werkbund exhibition was acknowledged, but he was sharply criticized for failing to give Weissenhof suffi-

cient publicity as the centerpiece of the exhibition), it was Gropius who attempted to mediate.[3]

In 1926 Gropius's primary concern was to familiarize himself with the Weissenhof project, and to make his ideas tell in the best way possible. He wrote Mies in September,

> In the meantime I have been delving into the Stuttgart layout plans, and the more I look at them the more questions and difficulties naturally come to light. Today I came upon one doubtful point that I would like to pass on right away:
> With both of the blocks that you have assigned to me—as on other blocks on the north side—the house directly adjoins the next lot. It follows that there has to be a blank wall on this side, and also that this house can never become a standard type, because a type house must have a laterally invertible plan that can be oriented in any direction. We want to present the houses, as costed, in mass-produced form, and for this they must fulfill the prime requirement of versatility in use.
> Here you really must find us an answer, otherwise we shall be designing unrepeatable, one-shot floor plans, which cannot possibly be in keeping with the overall objective. So: either shift the building back to clear a space, or extend the boundary.[4]

Ignoring the continuing internal disputes within Der Ring, Gropius once more chased Mies for an answer on the question of the boundary of the lot: "this issue is basic for my further work on the project."[5] No answer has been preserved.

Distracted by the demands on his time made by the opening of the new Bauhaus in Dessau on December 4 and 5, 1926, Gropius was unable to attend the meeting of the Weissenhofsiedlung architects who were in Dessau for the celebrations, at which the recommended materials and constructional principles were settled. His absence had two consequences: planning work on his houses ground to a halt, and he found himself in disagreement with the technical restrictions that had been agreed. He also considered it unnecessary to have finished drawings ready by the stipulated deadline of January 2, 1927, on the grounds that

> with building methods such as I for example shall be using . . . the preparation is what really counts, the building work then progresses very quickly. As the technical problems involved are new, it is unthinkable to complete the working drawings in eight to ten days from the date for submission to the building office.
> To have the plans drawn up in Stuttgart is quite

impossible in my case. I shall endeavor to make sure from here that everything works. My experience here has shown that this is possible.[6]

By "experience here," Gropius meant the housing development in the Törten neighborhood in Dessau, initially consisting of sixty housing units, assigned to him by the Dessau city council on June 25, 1926, by a majority of twenty-six votes to seven.[7] The second and third stages of the project, built in 1927 and 1928, were to bring the Törten development to around 316 units. As both projects, Törten and Weissenhof, were in hand more or less concurrently, whatever Gropius says about one or the other may be taken as an indication of his preoccupations and intentions in general.

In a lead article for the magazine bauhaus on "systematic preliminary work for rational housing" Gropius pointed out that the construction industry was in a state of upheaval and that the time for New Architecture manifestos was past. The next stage was to be one of "sober calculation and careful utilization of practical experience." Gropius maintained that "the dwelling house is an industrial organism," and that identical needs might be satisfied in consistent and identical ways:

There is thus no reason why every house should have a different plan, a different exterior, different building materials, and a different "style." This means waste and a mistaken emphasis on the individual. Our clothes, our shoes, our valises, our automobiles have a strong, consistent presence, and even so the individual can still preserve the personal nuance. Every individual retains freedom of choice among the types which concurrently appear. The most highly evolved type—representing a simple solution which is nevertheless versatile enough to satisfy the majority of demands and desires—is the only one that is ready to be elevated to the status of a norm. To create such a thing is not the work of any individual. Its evolution is the work of an age as a whole.[8]

With this in mind, and in pursuit of his own ideas on the transformation of the construction industry, Gropius formulated twenty-one points, beginning with the demand for a comprehensive long-term construction program for the whole of Germany "which will place industry in a position to carry out planned preparatory work over a period of years." He also called for research into the legal, planning, social, and practical aspects of rationalization in housing, leading to a reduction in cost for all affected classes of the population.

Gropius's houses in the Weissenhofsiedlung are not models intended for standardized production in the narrow sense; they are—as Gropius tried to make clear—individual examples of what could be done with the components of a standard "construction set." In this he agreed with Le Corbusier, who also wanted to conjure multiplicity out of carefully devised standard components. (Josef Frank's comment nevertheless comes close to the mark: "Everyone standardizes, and everyone does it differently.")[9]

Gropius gave a combative and eloquent lecture at a meeting of the Schweizer Werkbund on September 10, 1927, at which he spoke immediately after the Frankfurt planner, Ernst May. A contributor to Das Werk credited only as B." defined the difference between the two:

How different was Gropius, who followed May to the rostrum: a rather frail-looking figure, of medium height, with a scholar's head. His speech much more hesitant, reflective: searching for the best, most telling expression. The face and body in constant tension. The features of a man at odds with his surroundings, workworn, tense. His speech wide-ranging, a clear framework: well thought out and grand, but not really assured or even confident. Rather seeking, probing, elucidating. In constant mental effort.

Radical was his word: to solve the new problems from the root upward, from their innermost essence; all the work that has carried us forward has been work that has started from basics. A fine conviction that the progress of technology requires clearer and clearer heads; the more inventive the people, the richer the nation. But no rhetoric, heaven forbid; and no unsubstantiated assertions, either. All is positive, constructive. It was a unique pleasure, and a noteworthy experience, to see and hear these two very different representatives of the new architecture in close succession. As a result, the human element may now explain, support, excuse, what the mute structure itself could never convey: the idea that, encountered piecemeal, could never convey its innermost essence.[10]

With the same apparently axiomatic clarity and logic that Gropius applied to the design of floor plans, he challenged Mies over the attempt to restrict his choice of building materials:

either mass production, using every means of reducing costs, or a wide range of available options, affording a maximum of choice, so that experience can be gained. I would therefore prefer not to restrict myself to these lists for my units.[11]

The change in lot boundaries was achieved, and access to Gropius's houses was obtained from the upper street level (Bruckmannweg) instead of from the lower (Rathenaustrasse).[12]

When the city authorities demanded a cost reduction of 10–15 percent for all the houses Gropius was one of those who had to alter his plans, entailing a further delay in the placing of the building contract.[13]

It was not until April 14, 1927, almost two months after the first contracts had been signed, that the Epple company contracted to build Gropius's houses. The agreed all-in price of 49,000 marks for both houses was a compromise: the first estimates had come out at 60,000 marks, and attempts were made to maneuver the price down to 45,000 because of the very high costs of Le Corbusier's two buildings.[14] This indefensible attempt to link the two contracts was not, however, the reason for the change of constructional system which now took place.

Gropius had intended to use the construction system marketed by the Dessau firm of Junkers under the name of "Urbanbauweise"; but Döcker traveled to Dessau and found out that the company could not deliver, whereupon Gropius agreed to a change and Döcker took charge of the redesign work in Stuttgart.[15] (The same happened with Hilberseimer's House 18.)

Gropius's Houses 16 and 17 were contracted at a price of 25,546 + 23,932 = 49,478 marks. The "total net building cost" computed by Döcker after the exhibi-

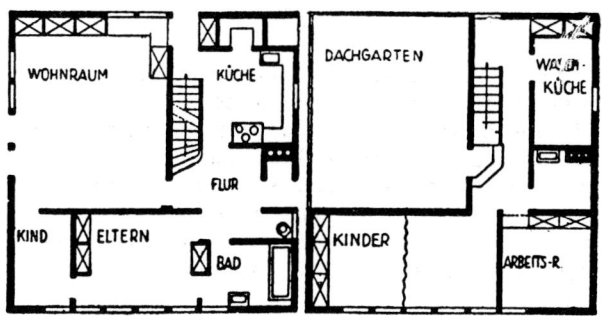

House 16:
View eastward across Bruckmannweg from the Oud houses

Plans of first and second floors

tion closed was 26,146 + 24,574.32 = 50,720.32 marks.[16]

Construction work was completed in just a hundred days, or three months and ten days, from contract to opening day. When representatives of City Hall, the contractor, the superintendent architect, and the building committee visited the lot in May, it was placed on record that the scaffolding was in place and "excavations" had begun. Progress was certainly not much helped when the contractor, Epple, told the steel supplier, Schneider—without reference to the architects concerned—that the Gropius houses should be given lower priority than the Mies apartment building.[17] Even so it became apparent that the houses would be ready, and even furnished, for opening day.[18]

When Mies inquired about the color for the exteriors Gropius answered,

in reply to yours of 4th inst. I agree that the outside paint finish of the houses should be basically off-white . . .

Altogether I have great difficulties, because the division of responsibility is so ill-defined that no one knows who takes the decisions. The contractor takes matters into his own hands, the superintendent does not support the architects, etc. I have just fired off another pistol in the direction of Stuttgart, because it simply cannot go on like this.[19]

What had happened? Gropius told Mies only that he had had "great difficulties"; it was Commissioner Sigloch who heard the rest. Together with the other architects from outside Stuttgart Gropius had been invited to send a resident representative of his own to Weissenhof to expedite the work. He sent a Bauhaus student, Hans Volger, who had helped with the project previously. Volger had been at the Bauhaus since 1923 (and remained there until 1932!) as a student of mural painting; he worked in Gropius's studio, liked to travel, and at the time of his appointment as a resident architect at Weissenhof he was all of twenty-three years old.[20] Gropius asked Sigloch to make a telephone call to clarify the "issue of authority":

the firm of Epple has claimed the right to go against my and my resident architect's instructions in completing the work "according to local practice." This would of course be an untenable position, as the whole point of the buildings we are constructing there is not to build "according to local practice" but to experiment with *new methods*. After meticulous preliminary work I have now organized everything in such a way that I can definitely finish, and I have two able, handpicked resident representatives[21] who are working hard to complete the work. They are, however, constantly obstructed in their efforts . . . by the atti-

tude of the contractor. The responsibility for this seems to lie less with the director of the firm of Epple than with an employee. . . . the preparatory work has been so carefully done by me and my representatives that everything is prepared for the contractor down to the smallest detail. It seems, to me, however, that he exploits the situation to make more money and intends to incorporate in the structure whatever building components he may happen to have on hand. He has, for example, without asking me, replaced the intended gas-fired heating with coal-fired heating.[22]

Gropius went on to decline all responsibility if the contractor were to continue disregarding his instructions. As a postscript he referred to a registered letter just received from Epple and quoted from it the statement that the contractor would "follow the instructions of commissioner Sigloch to complete the new buildings in the quickest way and entirely as we think fit."[23] Gropius asked Sigloch to set matters to rights: "on my buildings I am in charge and not Herr Epple and Herr Epple must be unequivocally told that he is to follow my directions."

On the same day Epple wrote Döcker, with a copy to Sigloch, complaining bitterly about Gropius's representatives:

I shall very soon have had quite enough of working with Herr Volger. Herr Volger is working with new constructional ideas that bear no relation to any possible future building practices. . . . If building in the future is going to have to be done in the way in which Herr Volger means to have it done at the Werkbund exhibition, then we builders might as well have ourselves buried right away, because in my opinion all this is the precise opposite of how any practical building person in the future can ever operate.[24]

The further course of the dispute is now a matter of conjecture. Disagreements of much the same kind occurred over practically all of the houses at Weissenhof. Mies was supportive and told Gropius, "With regard to your houses, please be firm and if necessary threaten to halt the work: this seems to be the only tactic that works in Stuttgart."[25] Gropius, who had seen war service as an officer, gave a soldierly answer:

I have discharged a heavy field piece in the direction of Stuttgart, because I was simply getting nowhere with the site management there. The contractor is given more rights than we architects. I have voiced quite specific demands and made my continued participation conditional on them.[26]

In all probability Gropius's "heavy field piece" was discharged in the direction of Döcker, whose files as superintendent have not survived.

What sort of houses did Gropius present to visitors to the exhibition as types for the future?

House 16 was not of any particular interest from the constructional point of view. The avoidance of the need for internal plastering by using wall boards suited to the needs of the rooms concerned may well have simplified the interior finish considerably, and will at least have mitigated the damp problems that occurred in other houses.

The entirely dry construction of House 17 precluded problems of this kind. Edgar Wedepohl, architect and critic, commented on the design:

The floor plans are economically and methodically worked out, but nothing out of the ordinary. One noteworthy feature is the upstairs room for laundry, ironing, and drying, which has several advantages. It is doubtful whether the majority of occupants will be able to afford the machine installations. A number of constructional details are not entirely convincing, such as the flimsy balustrade on the iron stairway, through which children might easily fall. It is also clear that plywood external doors are not adequate for exposed positions. The doctrinaire Constructivism of the Bauhaus gives the houses a curiously dry, pedantic look, and at the same time a temporary, hutlike quality that robs them of any cheerfulness or charm. This also shows up in the furnishings, with [Marcel] Breuer's metal chairs: without actually being uncomfortable, they give the impression of being not so much chairs as machines for sitting on. There is something unnervingly mechanical about them.[27]

Other critics were far from enthusiastic about Gropius's contributions to the New Architecture: "In the Gropius house, interest will be primarily directed to the treatment of the kitchen and the closets, the light fitments, and the furnishings; and how it all tends—perforce, as it were—toward a new conception of house building."[28]

Apart from the kitchens and the furniture, another feature that fascinated visitors was a cavernous serving hatch, no less than 1.41 meters [55½ in] deep, passing through two layers of wall (House 17): "Woe betide the serviceable soul who has to pass a pile of plates through there."[29] Another critic said of the emphatically functional interiors, with their tubular steel furniture by Breuer and their glass-topped tables, that they had "a strangely sober, clear face. . . . It is easy to imagine that a person might want this Constructivist objectivity [Sachlichkeit] in a room; but then he must not shudder at recollections of dentists and operating rooms."[30]

We—who are no longer unnerved by Sachlichkeit, or by the cool clarity of these interiors, who are used to the look of the Wassily chair, to couches with tubular steel runners, not to mention built-in closets and room dividers—can still admire in the photographs of the Gropius interiors, their boldness and their Utopian remoteness. What we see here is the polar opposite of the furniture by Schneck and his students or by the other designer-architects who showed their work in Mies's and Behrens's apartment buildings. When one thinks of Weissenhof one remembers the furniture of Breuer, Stam, and Mies: all the rest seems merely quaint, and serves only to point the contrast.

Almost exactly identical in area, the two Gropius houses were pleasantly varied, and at the same time simple and logical in their internal division.

The first occupants of House 16 were a couple with three offspring, two of them adults. Apart from minor complaints and flaws in materials, attributable to lack of time, the occupants' response to the house was highly positive. House 17 could not really be judged fairly by its first tenants, because it was hopelessly overcrowded:

Occupants: twelve persons. Woman . . . , six small children, three adolescent children, maid, helper. Enquiries revealed that eight children belong to the housewife, who is professionally active (craftswoman). The pantry is furnished as a bedroom. Four children sleep in the (upstairs) laundry.[31]

When asked about House 17 in this state, Gropius was quoted as saying, "The house has irresponsibly been filled with twice the intended number of people, so that even I am quite unable to form any judgment of its performance in terms of home economics."[32]

This situation cannot have lasted for long, as the Stuttgart street directory for 1930 records that a doctor and his wife lived in the house.

The gas-fired central heating in all the rooms turned out to be very expensive to run: "In two months, heating and hot water alone cost more than 170 marks."[33] In this matter it was not the contractor but the architect who had his way—rather at the occupants' expense. Frank's House 27 was thus not the only "Gas House" on the Weissenhof development: Gropius's prefabricated House 17 was another. In the pursuit of new methods and new energy sources, the heating of whole houses with gas was a bold gesture, but belonged strictly within an exhibition context.

Mies's favorable verdict on Gropius's houses (not echoed by many critics) was based on the strict modular grid which governed the organization of the floor plans and the interrelated dimensions of walls, floors, and ceilings. The solids and voids in the walls are consistently determined by the grid, and the steel skeleton initially intended for use in both houses[34] was designed to fit what were then unusually close structural tolerances. The conversion of House 16 to load-bearing masonry construction, using large-size blockwork, was done in such a way that the prefabricated board used in the interiors could be installed to fit. The grid for both houses is 1.06 by 1.06 meters [41¾ × 41¾ in].

Lay observers, and even those with a professional interest, may well have failed to notice the strict modular nature of the design as even the floor plans published by the Werkbund did not include the grid. However, in the fourth issue of bauhaus for 1927, along with photographs of house 17 under construction and a section drawing, there are plans which do show the grid. House 16 was submitted to the building office as a modular grid construction and its design remained the same when the constructional system was changed.

Gropius's Weissenhof houses deserved Mies's praise. They were among those that were destroyed in World War II; it would be highly desirable to rebuild them, particularly as they represent an early instance of the use of prefabricated construction—a method which offered the architects of the 1920s the advantage of year-round working to high technical standards. Gropius wrote:

dry construction ensures the advantage of removing the dependence on season and weather, and

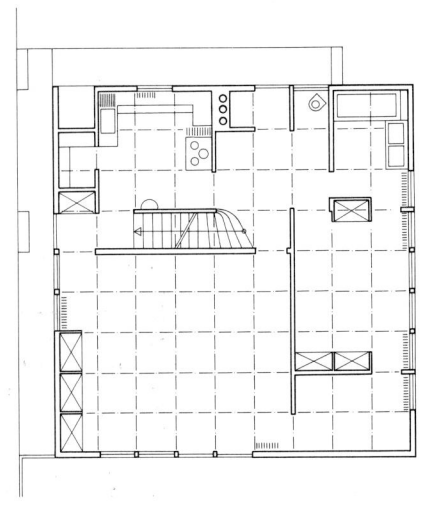

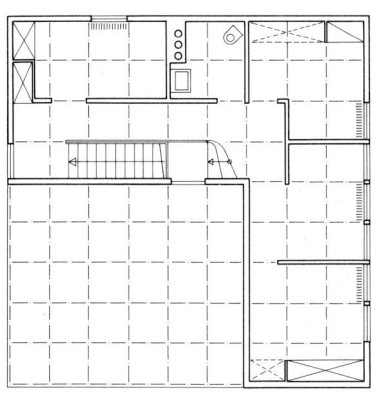

House 16:
Architect: Walter
Gropius
Plans and elevations
drawn from the archi-
tect's building code
submissions of March
22, 1927

First floor; second
floor

Cellar

Elevations from west,
north, south

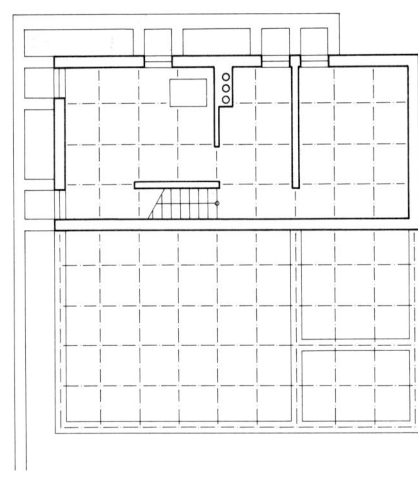

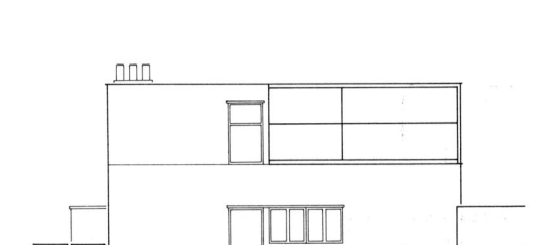

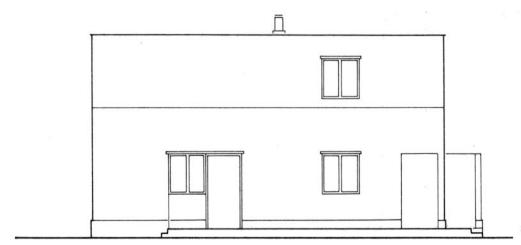

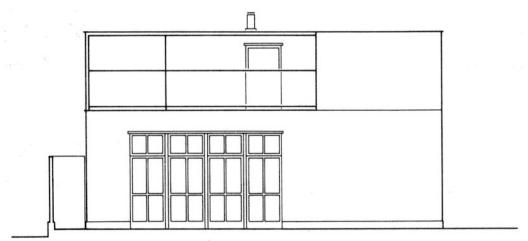

House 17
Architect: Walter
Gropius
Plans and elevations
drawn from the archi-
tect's building code
submissions of March
22, 1927

First floor

Second floor. Ade-
quate headroom on
the stairs is obtained
by placing the child's
bed on a platform

Elevations from west,
north, east, south

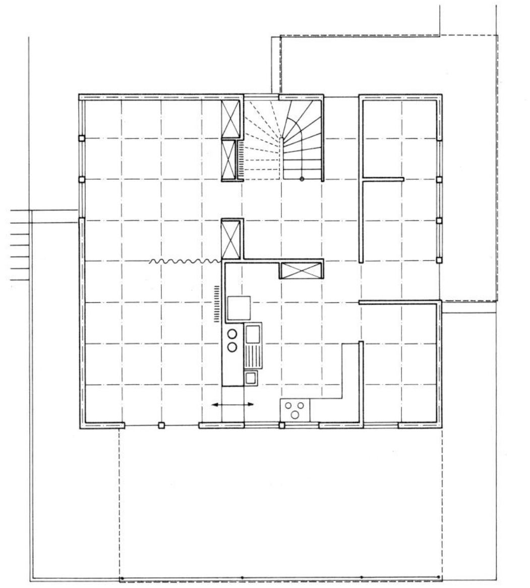

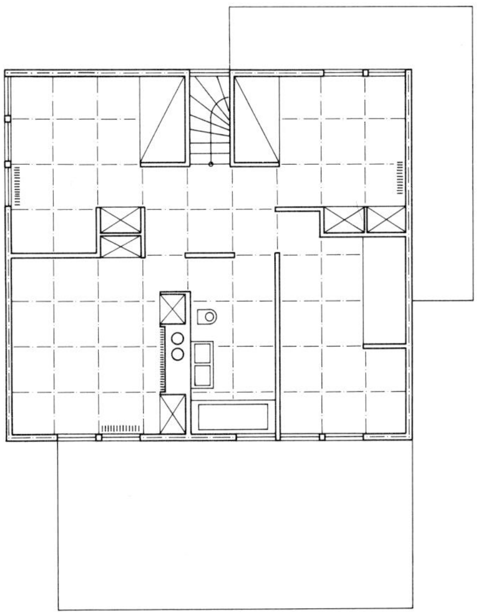

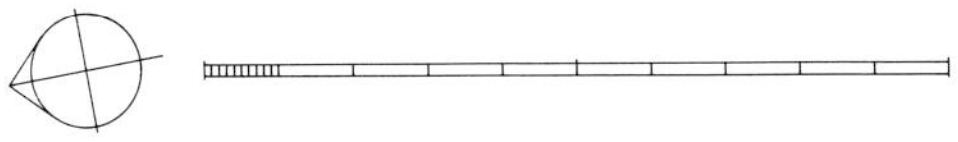

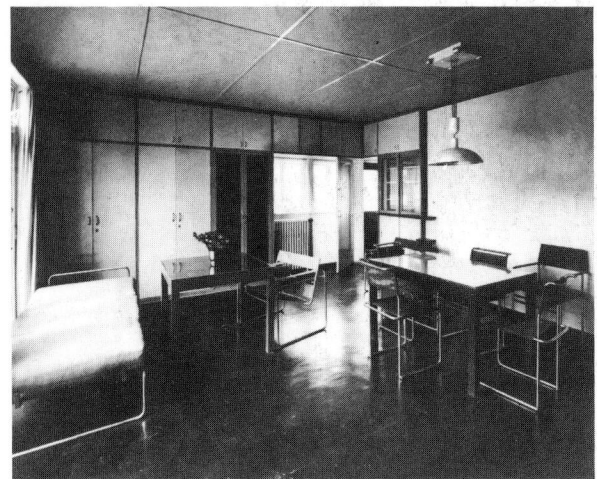

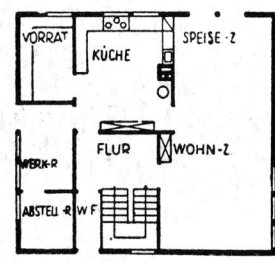
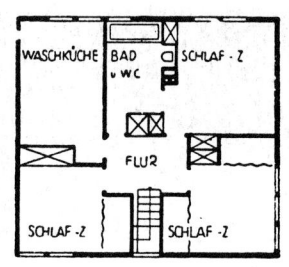

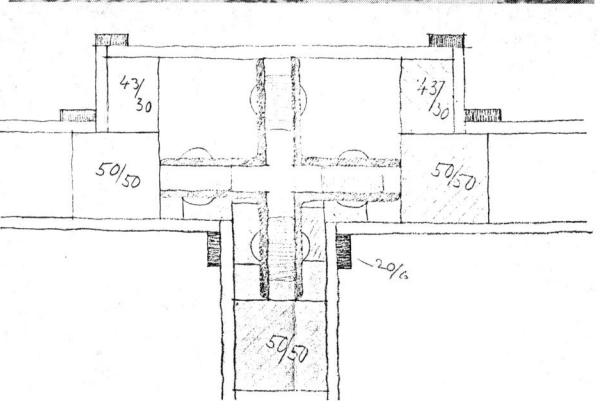

thus the stabilization of construction into a constant operation in contrast to the hitherto prevailing system of seasonal work; the elimination of damp during construction; an accurate fit between machine-made building components; firm prices; and a short, precisely determined, guaranteed construction time.[35]

The Gropius houses were characterized by clarity of conception, logical construction, and uncompromising interior finish: "All closets are within the walls, some in wood, some in sheet steel like the stairs, and are regarded as part of the structure itself." On the second floor of House 17 was a bed which must also be regarded as an immutable part of the structure: it was only by incorporating a raised platform beneath it that enough headroom was afforded for the stairs. The rest of the furnishings were mobile in every sense of the word, designed by Marcel Breuer and grouped by Gropius for "a middle-class family of 4–6 people with one maid."

Breuer gave the following account of his furniture, and of his aims in designing "modern spaces," in the magazine *Das Neue Frankfurt*:

metal furnishings are parts of a modern room. They are "styleless," because—aside from their function and from the structural features which that entails—they express no deliberate forming process. The new room is not there to present a self-portrait of the architect, or any preconceived notion of the psyches of its users.

Today, as a result of the intensive and varied impressions we receive from the external world, we change our lives more rapidly than in the past. It is natural that our environment must undergo corresponding changes. This leads us to installations, rooms, buildings, all or most of whose components can be converted, moved, and recombined. The furnishings, and even the walls of the room, are no longer massive, monumental, apparently rooted to the spot, or literally bricked in. Rather, they are airily perforated and, as it were, outlined in space; they obstruct neither movement nor the view across the room.

The room is no longer a composition, a rounded whole—since its dimensions and elements may radically change. One comes to the conclusion that any right and useful object "fits in" with any room in which one may happen to need it, just as a living entity might: a person or a flower. The illustrations show metal furniture of the same, structurally determined, formal character in the most varied spaces: in a theater, an auditorium, a studio, a dining room, and a living room. I have chosen metal, in particular, for this furniture, in order to endow it with the properties of modern spatial elements, as defined above. The heavy, portentous padding of an easy chair is replaced by a taut textile surface and a number of lightweight, elastic, curved tubular elements. The materials used, steel and particularly aluminum, are startlingly light for the considerable stresses they

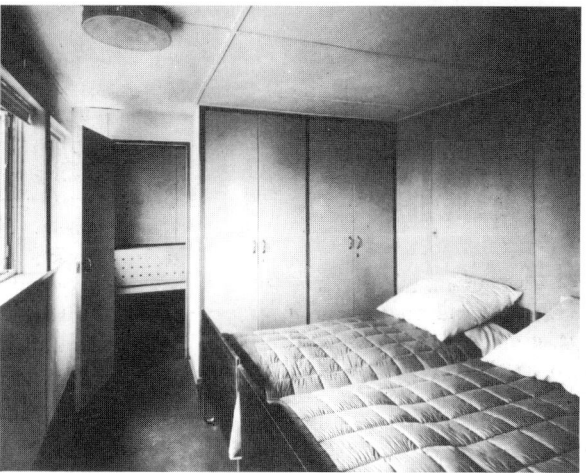

designed for building lots of limited size (outer suburbs, etc.) as dwellings on two levels; incorporating the possibility of letting off the upper story separately after slight modifications. As a matter of principle, great emphasis has been laid on sanitation, and also on the provision of separate bedrooms for growing children.[37]

bear (the stretching of the fabric). The runner form enhances mobility. All types are made of the same standardized, simple, instantly demountable and replaceable components.

These metal furnishings are intended simply as necessary equipment for present-day life.[36]

Gropius's building specifications record that the houses were

In his explanatory statements, Gropius constantly emphasized practical and functional qualities. But this was not his sole preoccupation. As he said in 1928, "It is quite wrong to suppose that the modern movement is guided only by function and not by beauty. The contrary is the case."[38]

Ludwig Hilberseimer

HOUSE 18

Design: Ludwig Hilberseimer, architect Berlin-Wilmersdorf, Emserstrasse 14

Single-family house: lower floor, upper floor.
Construction: external walls Feifel blocks, partitions and ceilings zigzag wood construction, plastered.
Interior design: Ludwig Hilberseimer, architect, Berlin. Spatial divisions within the house:
Lower floor: entrance, lobby, toilet, bedroom, maid's room, furnace with coal store, laundry and drying room, provision cellar.
Main floor: living room with dining area, two bedrooms, [kitchen,] bathroom, toilet, small study, terrace.[1]

When Ludwig Hilberseimer died in Chicago in 1967, Gropius wrote a letter of condolence to Mies.[2] Mies had lost someone who had been his friend for fifty years: they had worked together since the November-gruppe, the magazine G (for *Gestaltung*), and the Bauhaus in Dessau.

In 1923 Mies wrote in G, "We know no problems of form, but only of building. The form is not the goal, but the result, of our work. There is no form, as such."[3] In an article in the same issue on "building craft and building industry," Hilberseimer went further:

Far sooner no architects than bad ones! Formerly, architecture determined the forms of utensils, even tools; but now technology fertilizes architecture. . . .

It will be for the new generation to make its work fruitful by facing the present with courage and the future with determination. Not ignorance, but acceptance and mastery of the facts of life and of production, leads to the goal: makes it possible to achieve the ultimate synthesis.[4]

Werner Graeff, the press officer of the 1927 Werkbund exhibition, was certainly right when as the youngest person involved (at twenty-one), he spontaneously answered the question "What really unites us?" by saying: "Very simple! We are united by the ability to think and to design in elementary terms!"[5] Nearly forty years later, Graeff declared that the sentence could still stand—with the one reservation, that it should not be the "ability," but the "effort," to think, to design, and to speak, in elementary terms.

This effort to achieve elementary form through elementary thinking is vital to any consideration of Hilberseimer; his Stuttgart house is to be seen in this context.

Hilberseimer, like Mies, left Nazi Germany in 1938 to live and teach in Chicago. In 1963, asked on a visit to his native country "what he had really achieved," he answered that he had achieved nothing.[6] And yet, for better or for worse, Hilberseimer's principles of urban design had played a major conscious or unconscious role in the planning work of numerous former students and intellectual successors—even though in many cases what was put into practice was not the coherent overall conception but those parts of it that seemed to make economic sense at the time.

In his contribution to the Werkbund book *Bau und Wohnung*, Hilberseimer gave a very precise account of his ideas:

The best form of dwelling will be that which has become a perfect utilitarian product and has thus reduced the friction of everyday life to a minimum. This will be attained when the home—formerly a showplace, now rather confined—comes to be so organized that the individual rooms and their contents are shaped throughout in accordance with purpose and function.

On a wider scale Hilberseimer visualized the redesign of the city in accordance with people's needs:

If the inhabitants of large cities are seen in terms of their housing demand they fall into two groups: those who want to live in town, and those who prefer to live out of town. Both desires are entirely legitimate, and must be fully met.

The position of the child in city life will change entirely. The threat posed by city life to the physical and psychic development of the child has already become an insoluble problem. It will therefore be a basic assumption, in future, that children, and all instructional and educational establishments, will be accommodated outside the cities.

One possibility of realizing this idea of giving city-dwellers homes in accordance with their needs consisted, for Hilberseimer, in the construction of hotel-like buildings to house single people and childless couples:

The apartment house will more and more set itself free from its false model, the private house, and come more and more to resemble the hotel, which is the most comfortable form of home today.

Individual houses for families with children should be built on the edges of cities:

These individual homes will also be equipped with every imaginable comfort and will combine to form great park and garden suburbs [*Siedlungen*], connected to the city by a rapid transit rail system which can cover great distances.

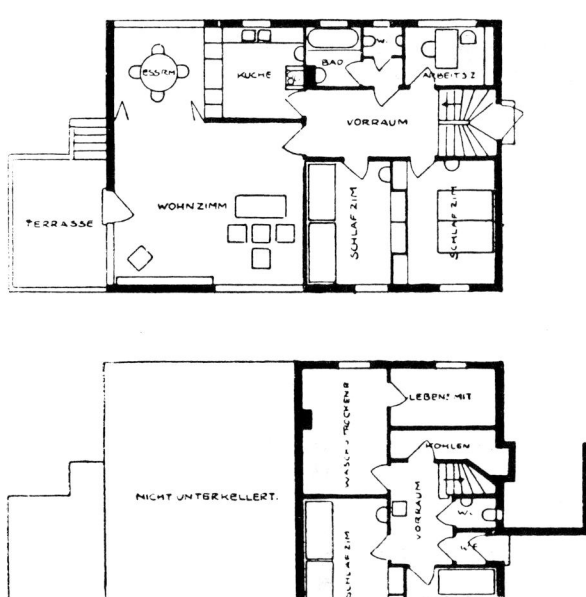

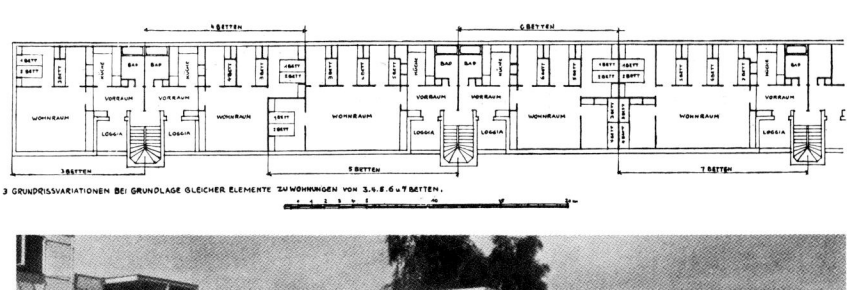

The house built by me [at Weissenhof] is an experiment in designing an individual house of this sort, intended for a metropolitan park and garden suburb. In spite of the restrictions imposed by the given setting, the effort was made to create a specific type—principally through the fitness for purpose of the individual rooms and their spatial relationship to each other.[7]

And so, logically enough, Hilberseimer also designed "boarding houses [sic]," for the childless, which were shown in the *Internationale Plan- und Modellausstellung* alongside the separate suburbs designed for families to live in. High-rise in the city, and high-density low-rise in the residential areas; a room with a view for childless adults, and closeness to the earth for families with children. That was Hilberseimer's idea of his city. He devised his floor plans according to the number of occupants, and consequently of bed spaces, and in his house formula the bedrooms were added together to give the size of the living room. The living room for a family with two children was smaller than for a family with four children:

The variations of plan for dwellings for three, four, five, six, and seven occupants are all based on the same spatial elements and thus serve to satisfy the various spatial needs. The basics are: lobby, kitchen, bathroom, bedroom, bed cubicle, and loggia, all of which recur in dwellings of all sizes. Only the largest room, the living and dining room, changes its size as the number of occupants increases. Through the building-in of all closets and kitchen equipment, the maximum use is made of the available space . . .[8]

In Stuttgart "the attempt was made so to organize the spatial demands of a family of six that, taking the given situation into account, the most frictionless pattern of use is made possible."[9]

Hilberseimer thus provided a sleeping cubicle with a wash basin for each occupant, another cubicle as a study for the householder, and a living room tailored to the size of the family. This single-family house has to be imagined as part of a neighborhood of similar houses,

packed closely together, so that the density would be similar to that of a high-rise development, where, for adequate sunlight, the buildings need to be further apart:

To this is added the factor that low-rise homes are considerably cheaper to build than high-rise. High and low rise can thus be regarded as of equivalent value as far as the utilization of urban space is concerned. The most practical course in future will be to combine them in mixed developments, in which the low-rise house with a garden would be best suited to families with children, while for childless households and single people the most appropriate form of housing is the high-rise building with its extensive views.

The basic problem of house and housing forms is a social one. They will differ in every case according to whether the society tends toward preserving the family, dispersing it, or leaving the choice of life style to individuals.[10]

Today, a general respect for the founding fathers of Modernism has given way to a reaction against the rigor of their approach, and also against profit-motivated travesties of their architectural impulses. The result has been a return to "motif building"[11] or "motif salad."[12] Even so, satellite cities are now inconceivable without their light, air, and sun. The building patterns typical of every capital city in Europe in the early part of this century have now been thinned out, their airless courtyards opened into green spaces.

In his ideology, as in his architecture, Hilberseimer was rigorous. His proposals were meant humanely and yet this rigor made them almost inhuman; there was no room in his logical mind for minor transgressions against the code of objectivity. The design of Hilberseimer's house in the Weissenhofsiedlung embodies this ideology: the plan of both floors is clean and clear, devoid of any surprising corner or view.

The building contract was placed with the Feifel company on the first scheduled contract date, February 25, 1927; the agreed price was 25,623 marks. The total net cost was recorded by Döcker on December 30 as

Ludwig Hilberseimer: upper and lower floor plans of House 18

Ludwig Hilberseimer: variations based on identical elements, giving dwellings with 3, 4, 5, 6, and 7 beds

House 18: View from Rathenaustrasse

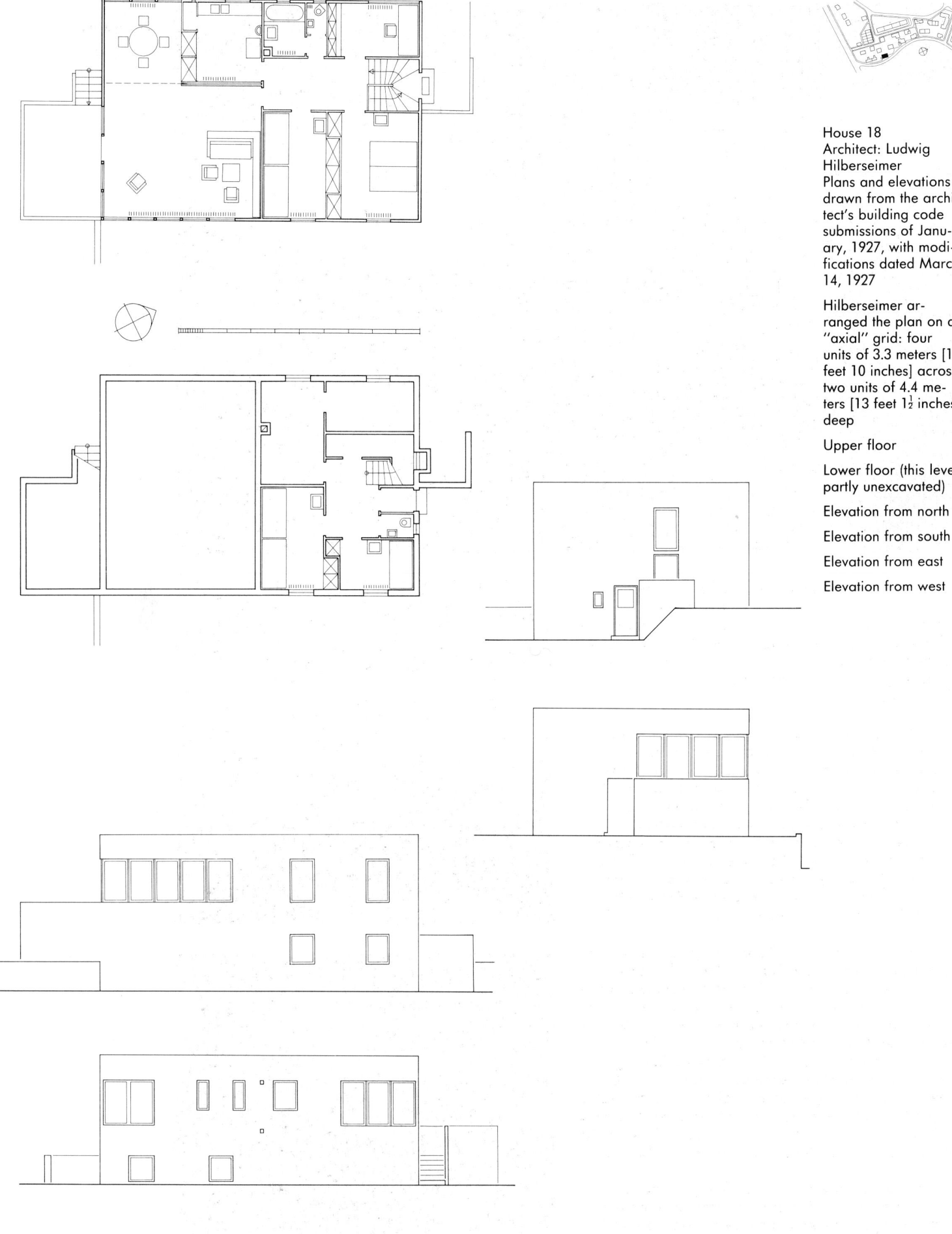

House 18
Architect: Ludwig Hilberseimer
Plans and elevations drawn from the architect's building code submissions of January, 1927, with modifications dated March 14, 1927

Hilberseimer arranged the plan on an "axial" grid: four units of 3.3 meters [10 feet 10 inches] across, two units of 4.4 meters [13 feet 1½ inches] deep

Upper floor

Lower floor (this level partly unexcavated)

Elevation from north

Elevation from south

Elevation from east

Elevation from west

26,905.18 marks. From signature of contract to opening day was 148 days. Junkers's Urban skeleton construction system, which figures in the original building office submission, was abandoned in April in favor of the Feifel zigzag system because of supply problems with Junkers. (Gropius was affected in the same way.)[13] Hilberseimer said,

> In the course of construction, the Urban system originally intended was abandoned, because Urban could not deliver, and the main contractor stepped in. As you probably know, there are always difficulties when contracts are varied in this way, and the execution of the work suffers.
>
> There is a question of principle here: most of the architects on the Werkbund project had little or no influence on the construction and were given a free hand only in the design. Even in this, freedom was by no means total.[14]

Hilberseimer's dismay, at the lack of progress in building his own house and others at Weissenhof prompted Mies to fire off his lengthy telegram of April 24, 1927—to the discomfiture of City Hall and superintendent architect alike—and to announce that he was sending along a resident architect of his own.

In his annoyance at Mies's criticisms, Döcker gave a misleading account of the matter in his Circular No. 14, in which he blamed the change of construction system for the fact that, in the four days Hilberseimer had spent in Stuttgart, virtually no work had been done on his house.[15] On May 3 Hilberseimer wrote Döcker,

> The slow progress in the building of my house during my stay in Stuttgart has nothing to do with the change in construction system. This mainly affects the upper story, for which I brought the necessary drawings with me, and which I discussed

House 18:
Kitchen

Wooden partitions
and flooring (Feifel
zigzag system)

in detail with Herr Feifel. The work in hand at that time was on the foundations, which are totally un-affected by the change, and here there was indeed no sign of progress. I discussed this with yourself, during our last telephone conversation, and also with Herr Feifel.[16]

Construction work at Weissenhof had more surprises in store for Hilberseimer. Graeff recalled one:

One day, I remember, Ludwig Hilberseimer arrived in Stuttgart after a long absence. The buildings were almost complete. I took him up to Weissenhof in a little open two-seater (an Opel Laubfrosch), drove along the lower boundary road, past Le Corbusier's houses, and braked in front of Hilberseimer's house.
"There," I said. "there is your house."
Hilbs shook his head, smiling. "No, that's not my house."
What? I was stupefied. Had I managed to confuse his building with someone else's, in the catalogue and throughout the entire printed literature? Then he suddenly went white as a sheet and said, "Oh no! It is!"
It emerged that, without asking him, they had installed an entirely ordinary (and cheaper) type of window construction instead of the new sliding sash system designed and specified by him. Apart from this, the street frontage of his house, marred already by the unsuitable windows, was utterly ruined by the insertion, next to a bedroom window on the slope, of an additional window of arbitrary and inappropriate dimensions. This was done to comply with some provision of the building code, but it was a gross insult to the architect that he had neither been asked nor told. The curious con-

sequence of this act of sabotage was that Hilberseimer did not at first sight recognize his own building. The critics later said that in his house you had to climb into the bathtub to open the bathroom window—and the way it was built meant that this was unfortunately true.[17]

Hilberseimer himself put it this way:

The windows, as executed, are indeed a very weak point. I must add, however, that I had intended sliding sashes, and casements in the kitchen and bathroom. These were not made in accordance with my drawings. Hence the highly unsatisfactory result.[18]

On opening day Hilberseimer's house was ready. The furnishings were not specially designed but already on the market: Thonet bentwood chairs, upholstered furniture by Knoll (then of Feuerbach, near Stuttgart, and now of Herrenberg), and bedsteads by Lämmle, the firm which, with Arnold of Schorndorf, supplied most of the iron beds for the Weissenhof houses.
The house, painted light gray, was a clear, austere structure whose excellent floor plan was generally praised. The presence of "2 water closets" was generally welcomed, but the all-too-accessible room for the maid was not unanimously acclaimed:

In Hilberseimer's house, social solidarity is carried to an extreme, as the maid's room is on the lower floor, facing onto the street, unsupervised and unbarred . . . . The front door, with its large, unprotected glass pane, testifies to a powerful faith in humanity and a denial of the existence of burglars and thieves.[19]

How fatefully these words match the insight expressed by Ernst Bloch in *Das Prinzip Hoffnung*:

The wide window, full of the outside world, requires an outside world that is full of attractive strangers, not full of Nazis. A glass door, stretching down to floor level, really does presuppose that, if there is going to be anything peeping in, or pouring in, it will be the sunshine and not the Gestapo.[20]

The Hilberseimer house failed to survive World War II and the postwar urge to reconstruct: its place is now taken by a regrettably roofed replacement.

In speaking of Ludwig Hilberseimer, it should not go unmentioned that the Werkbund statement issued in December, 1926—the one in which the Weissenhofsiedlung was announced—was written by him, on Mies's recommendation, and after a briefing from Stotz.[21]

Bruno Taut

HOUSE 19

Design: Bruno Taut, former city architect, Berlin,
Berlin W 9, Linkstrasse 20.

Single-family house: cellar, first floor, upper floor.
Construction: iron frame with Thermos panels, interior
finish plasterboard, exterior plastered.
Interior design: Bruno Taut, architect, former city archi-
tect, Berlin.
The accommodation comprises:
Cellar: furnace, laundry, coal store, cellar space.
First floor: lobby, large divisible living room, dining
room with built-in closets incorporating serving hatch to
scullery, kitchen with built-in furniture, two bedrooms,
bathroom.
Second floor: lobby, two small bedrooms, large roof
terrace.[1]

"This house, by virtue of its program, is the proletarian
among the single-family houses in the exhibition."[2] That
was how Bruno Taut presented his own Weissenhof
house. His social commitment to the poorer sections of
the population led him to elaborate an architecture with
a prime emphasis on economy, intended to make a real
contribution to the alleviation of the housing crisis.

However, Bruno Taut's house on Bruckmannweg attracted most attention not as a prototype of detached
housing for the proletariat but through its powerful coloring in a neighborhood of otherwise—with few exceptions—off-white or light-colored houses.

Bruno Taut had been a late addition to the list of
Weissenhof architects: the Taut whom Stotz and Mies
wanted all along was Max, the younger brother, and
not—contrary to the general assumption—Bruno, who
was actually better known through his writings and
planning work. A telephone conversation between Max
and Mies first brought Bruno's name into consideration,
and Mies had to devote some thought to finding a lot
for him.[3] Bruno was merely informed of the result by
Mies, on October 22, 1926:

> I have discussed the lot question with your broth-
> er, and we both feel that this position best meets
> your intentions. The size of building that has been
> sketched in is of course not binding on you. Your
> brother felt the lack of a precise definition from
> me of the meaning and purpose of the exhibition,
> and so I would like to emphasize that its themes
> are both the problem of the home and the techni-
> cal construction of the house. Neither must be ne-
> glected in favor of the other.[4]

On November 12 the city council building committee
agreed on the new list of architects (List IX), which replaced Häring, Mendelsohn, and Tessenow with Bruno

Taut, Poelzig, Scharoun, and Behrens.

On the very day of his official nomination Bruno Taut
drew out the design of his house, and he sent it off to
Mies three days later with the specifications:

> I have kept very closely to the program for Type
> C, and would like to add once more that the
> house, small though it is, is intended to carry on
> the movement of your large group on the street
> that runs across the development, as shown in the
> little perspective sketch above right.
>
> I should be grateful for your comments, so that
> I can finalize the necessary details right away.[5]

When most of the houses were reduced in size to lower
costs, Bruno Taut's house was not affected: he was told,
again through his brother, that his design met "the criteria for the minimum built volume for the type," and thus
need not be redesigned.[6]

In his official explanatory text Bruno Taut mentioned
that his house could be "mass produced . . . fully
equipped for around 10,000 to 12,000 marks"; the price
specified in the building contract with the firm of Hangleiter was 24,000 marks.[7] Döcker, in his final accounts
as superintendent submitted to the building committee
on December 30, 1927, gave a final figure of 23,767.88
marks in an account containing, as well as some almost
imperceptible variation costs (75 marks), a number of
deductions for supplies not charged for (398.12 marks).[8] However, the final cost as computed by City Hall
was much higher—no less than 33,700 marks.[9]

The program for Type C comprised a living room
with dining alcove; two bedrooms, one of which it
would be possible to subdivide for children; a small
workroom or rest room (special provision for children
in kitchen or living-dining room).[10] So Type C was intended to have four rooms and accommodate one
maid. Bruno Taut's specifications clarify his approach:

> Specifications for design of a single-family house
> of Type I C for the Stuttgart Werkbund develop-
> ment 1927. . . .
>
> The main rooms are all on the first floor, partly
> in order to provide an example of the principle of
> the single-story house, but also because the pub-
> lic markedly prefers to have both living and
> sleeping accommodation at ground level.
>
> The rooms are so oriented that the kitchen and
> scullery are on the northwest corner; the west
> side, facing the prevailing wind, is taken up by the
> entrance, toilet, and bathroom. The living room
> with its covered terrace has a view down the slope
> to the east, and the bedrooms to the south.
>
> A special feature of the plan is that the large
> living room may be subdivided in accordance

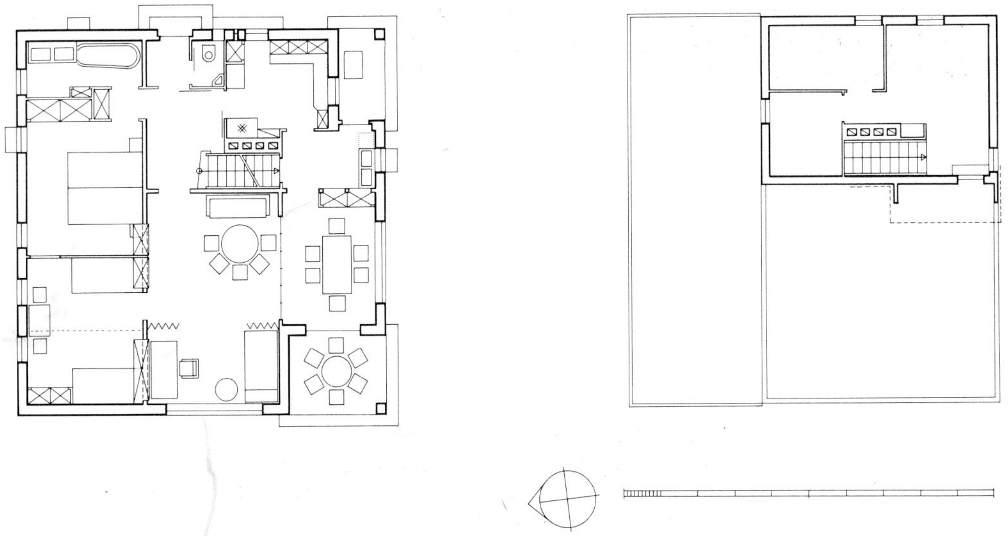

House 19
Architect: Bruno Taut
Plans and elevations
drawn from the archi-
tect's building code
submissions of No-
vember 12, 1926, with
modifications dated
March 10, 1927

First floor; second
floor

Cellar

Elevations from south,
east, north, west

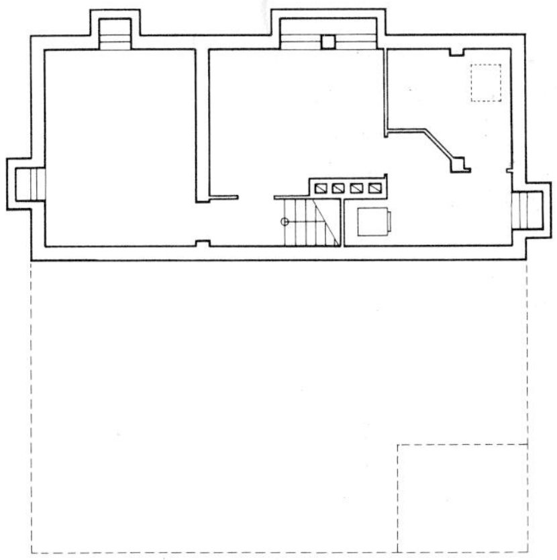

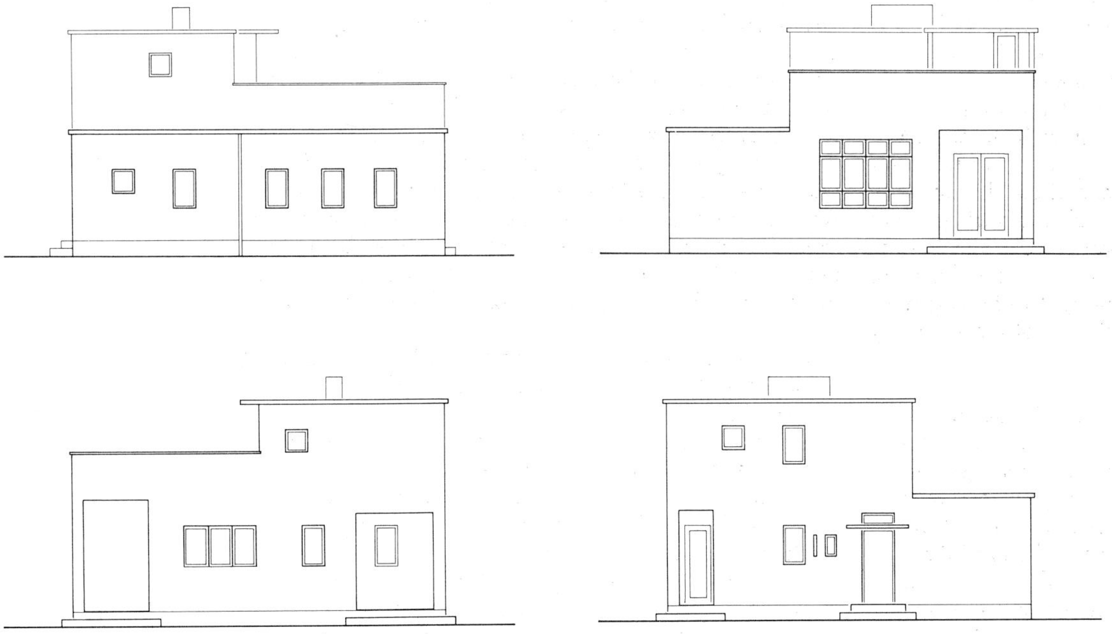

House 19:
View from living room
into "study" alcove

Straight, built-in, therefore cheapest stairs. Upper lobby for drying laundry with closet for moth-proof storage etc., then small room for maid and sewing room with guest bed (folding back).

For the first-floor rooms a height of 2.50 meters [98½ in] clear, except for the living room and its alcoves, which rise to 2.95 meters [116 in] clear. Above, a terrace for air and sunbathing; therefore protected by a solid parapet. Also, ideally, a shower bath under the roof overhang, which can be used to hang sun blinds. The pillar at the corner of the veranda serves the same purpose, and is also a structural support.[11]

As Bruno Taut in his specifications had left the constructional system open, Döcker opted for the Thermos system, a lightweight method with layered wall panels giving good thermal insulation.[12] The floors were in Sanitas flooring, a kind of magnesite or woodwool slab combined with an iron skeleton frame, which gave grounds for complaint, probably because of faulty workmanship.[13] The record of the May 2 inspection of building works at Weissenhof includes the following note: "Here a reinforced concrete upper floor had been intended, and the formwork was already in place. But now this floor is to be in wood. The reasons for this are not apparent."[14]

Criticized features included the lack of headroom on the stairs and in the toilet and bathroom, and the bedroom windows, which were small and opened directly onto the public footpath so that anyone could reach in. After the exhibition closed bars were installed. To keep bedroom windows small was one of Bruno Taut's principles; he himself deplored the absence of a strip of grass, but this would have reduced the size of the little square at the junction of Bruckmannweg and Pankokweg, between the Mies and Oud buildings.

The toilet door alongside the front door was considered inconvenient because it opened inward into too small a space. Aware of this, Bruno Taut had suggested a sliding door to Döcker, but this had not been acted on.

This was the only house in the Weissenhofsiedlung to be equipped with both gas and coal-fired cookers. Bruno Taut justified this by saying that the house was not going to be occupied by the "upper classes," and that a coal stove would "definitely have a point."

There was much in Bruno Taut's house—as in most of the others—that was not done in accordance with the architect's wishes. Bruno Taut nevertheless had no complaint to make about Döcker's work as superintendent: "Because the city of Stuttgart made up its mind too late, everything was done in too much of a rush." On the unexpectedly high building costs, Taut had this to say:

I estimate that, according to the interest calculations in force in Berlin in 1926 for houses erected with the proceeds of property tax, the house would have attracted a monthly rent of 150 marks at most.[15] To this must be added the fact that, because the city authorities insisted on the use of local contractors, not only has the execution turned out to be very inferior, but the cost of building this house has turned out approximately 4,500 marks higher than necessary.[16]

Another feature of the house that came in for much criticism was the color scheme. The tenants, when they moved in, repainted the interiors, "irritated by the original tones."[17] In 1919 Bruno Taut had concluded his

with a number of different functions. The dining alcove is separated from the room as a whole by a folding glass partition in six sections, so that it can be used either alone or together with the rest of the room. The study alcove can be partitioned off by a sliding concertina partition, or else used in the same way as part of the total space. This living room can thus be used in four ways: with both alcoves partitioned off (to give three separate rooms); with both movable partitions opened; and finally with either alcove open without the other.

The dimensions of the rooms are reduced to the minimum necessary for living without inconvenience. Remarks on these:

The dining table is in close proximity to the serving hatch-cum-sideboard, on the far side of which is the scullery table. (The housewife's place at table is next to the sideboard, so that she need not stand up during meals). The veranda as a direct continuation of the dining alcove. The scullery providing a seal against kitchen smells, as well as supplementary access to kitchen and access to cellar. Kitchen in minimum dimensions. Equipment: closet for food on west side by window, table to left folds down flat against wall. From here continuous working surface with substructure and typical kitchen cabinet on west wall. At other corner, toward scullery, next to cooker, small cabinet for cooking utensils (spoons, etc.). Door from kitchen to hallway, and inner porch door, to be simple sliding doors.

All static furniture in the house to be built in. Closets in living room toward bedrooms above height of 1.20 meters [4 feet], as book shelving in the study and as glass-cabinets elsewhere. In children's room a closet for clothes; beds possibly fold back; above each, a closet for schoolbooks and toys. In parents' bedroom two closets, backing onto broom closet in lobby and linen closet in bathroom, all ventilated. Twin wash basins in bathroom. Toilet with wash basin separate from bathroom. Drainage run from scullery through kitchen, toilet, and bath in one line. In kitchen a ventilator on water pipe.

"Call for Colorful Building," signed among others by Behrens, Gropius, the Luckhardts, Poelzig, and Schmitthenner, with the words:

> We utterly reject the avoidance of color in houses that stand in a natural setting. Not only the green landscape of summer but, especially, the snowy landscape of winter, cries out for color. In place of the dirty gray house let there be, at last, the blue, red, yellow, green, black, white house, in pure, glowing tones.[18]

In 1927 Wedepohl told the readers of *Wasmuth's Monatshefte* that

> Bruno Taut's crass color scheme . . . screams uninhibitedly out across the landscape and makes apparent, especially alongside the subtle coloration of Le Corbusier's buildings, that the weaker the color sense the more intense the color values and contrasts. The interiors are colored on the same principle. The only people who could live in such rooms would be those with blunted visual nerves, who need the strongest possible visual stimuli: the equivalent in chromatic terms of the hard-of-hearing.[19]

Bonatz, who had known Bruno Taut since they worked together in the office of Theodor Fischer, was to write in his memoirs,

> In the Weissenhofsiedlung in 1927, [Bruno Taut] had built two [sic] fairly undistinguished houses, which were utterly bourgeois in layout; but the rooms were in brutal lake colors, straight out of the paint box, in six different tones. The ceiling bright yellow, one wall bright blue, the other bright red, the third bright green . . . and the floor pitch-black—*pour épater le bourgeois* [to shock the bourgeois].[20]

Incomprehension was general. Anecdotes proliferated, and were preserved by eye-witnesses and other contemporaries: Max Berling, who was working as resident architect for Poelzig, and a number of his colleagues—who no doubt would have done anything for a laugh—are said to have turned up at Mies's building with pails to put out a fire which turned out to be nothing but the reflection of the evening sun from the red wall of Bruno Taut's house.[21] Graeff recalled

> I remember one Stuttgart furniture designer showing me the apartment in Mies's building which he had partitioned and furnished. I walked in and stopped short in amazement; the furniture seemed quite good in its proportions and craftsmanship, but I could not help asking, "Why use nothing but red materials and then paint the walls red?"
>
> With despair on his face, the man said, "It never occurred to me, but the sun's shining today, and straight on Taut's house!" I stepped forward: so it was! The whole apartment, which was full of light colors, had turned blood-red from the reflection. Bruno Taut had painted his house, which was fairly cubic in form, bright red on the [Bruckmannweg] street side, with one side wall deep blue and a third wall yellow from top to bottom. One day, when I was walking through the Weissenhofsiedlung with Le Corbusier, he started back at the sight of the house and said: "My God, Taut is color-blind!"
>
> On the other hand, Mies—who was extremely restrained in his own use of color—had some sympathy for Taut. He said once, "I can see why Taut, when he was city architect in Magdeburg, wanted to have everything dipped in color—it's such a gray, dismal place."[22]

A third testimony comes from Le Corbusier's resident architect, Alfred Roth. According to him, the young, committed architects who were there as residents to represent their mentors had been horrified by Bruno Taut's positively gaudy color scheme. Taut agreed to discuss the matter—in the dining room of his house, with its intensely colored walls, each a different color. According to Roth, Taut concluded the discussion by saying, "My dear young architects, the human eye is degenerate, and it is part of the task of architecture to regenerate the human eye."[23]

Bruno Taut himself made a number of statements about his Stuttgart color scheme and about the principles governing the use of color in this architectural context, although all remained general. No more precise information now exists on the color scheme of his house than the statements quoted above; nor is it possible to analyze old paint layers, for the good reason that the house has been destroyed. What follows, therefore, is an attempt to elucidate Taut's principles and understand his intentions on the basis of his other statements.

In his 1927 book *Ein Wohnhaus*—a description of his own house near Berlin, from which he quoted in the Werkbund book *Bau und Wohnung*—Bruno Taut said,

> The house must fit its occupant like a good suit; it must clothe him. The main aesthetic principle is this: the look of the rooms without people in them is irrelevant; what counts is how the people look in them . . .
>
> Almost all human beings, except those who themselves work with color, react to it subjectively: nearly everyone has his own favorite colors, his antipathies and sympathies, and there is no reason not to follow these personal inclinations and base the color scheme on them.[24]

Accordingly, when Taut heard that the first tenants had changed the colors he wrote, "The colors painted for the exhibition cannot possibly be right for every tenant; nor was that the intention."[25]

What Bruno Taut did at Weissenhof was not simply an experiment, provocative because it was short-lived. He was profoundly concerned both with color and with architecture at that time, and had been so for more than twenty years. It was his objective to create a synthesis of the two. His own inner conflict as to which direction his personal development would take—painting or architecture—is evident in his journals of the early 1900s:

> Now I am constantly preoccupied with the thought of painting. It seems to me that I shall express my own nature in my life better through this than in architecture. How far does my talent extend? Am I capable of giving people great and profound thoughts in an unique and powerful form? I always want to say Yes . . .
>
> I am still preoccupied with the thought that I have been carrying around with me for two years now: to unite my talent for color with my architectural ability. Colored spatial compositions, colored architecture—these are areas in which I may be able to make personal statements. It is just because painting always brings me back to architecture, and vice versa, that I probably have no need to fear the fragmentation that has destroyed many an artist before he reached the point of creating anything.[26]

At Chorin, a village in the depths of the Brandenburg forests, among a circle of friends who included the painter Max Beckmann, Bruno Taut absorbed the color of forests and lakes. Much later, when living in Japan, he wrote in his journal: "I would like to stay here for a few weeks, quietly listening to everything, now in Japan, as I did, thirty years ago, at Chorin, when with Japan inside me I . . . listened and drew, by the water, in the ice, in the grass. From 1903/04 through 1933/34, a closed curve."[27]

In Kaunas, Lithuania in 1919 Bruno Taut was delighted to learn that *taut* in Lithuanian means "folk" or "peo-

ple."[28] He was struck by the "orgies of color" in the Lithuanian villages, and apostrophized his fellow West Europeans:

> Gray wooden houses, gray roofs, interspersed with buildings plastered and painted in bright pink, yellow, and white, and with white church towers, or red ones from the age of the Teutonic Knights. . . . Now look at the colorful, glowing ultramarine, red, brown, green, yellow painted shutters on windows and doors. . . . Learn, at long last, that a gray wall in dirty tones is really dirt! The fable that bright colors are justified only in the sunny south must finally be abandoned . . . and there is nothing more delicious than glowing, colored houses in the snow.[29]

From that moment on he made use of color—deliberately, consideredly, meaningfully in his own eyes, if not always in those of other people. In Stuttgart he had his little house painted in bright colors as a counterpoint, a contrast, to Mies's prescribed off-white; perhaps he was thinking of "glowing, colored houses in the snow"—even if others thought of fires and fire buckets. The coloring of Taut's house did not arise from a lack of consideration of the means he was using but from conscious reflection on its position within the Weissenhofsiedlung, its relation to the street, and above all its orientation to the points of the compass:

> The distances between the houses, across the intervening gardens, were intended to look as great as possible. Consequence: deep, saturated colors; for white, say, or light yellow, would have reduced the distance to the eye. Glass-roofed loggias necessarily darken the living rooms beyond; if the house walls are dark in color, and these loggias are painted white, this creates the illusion that the loggias, reflecting light into the living rooms, are especially light. Furthermore: if I reduce the length of a block of houses, i.e. of the garden strip in front of them, by painting the side walls facing onto the lateral street in a glowing yellow, I maximize the effect of the width of the front garden strip: the elongated rectangle of garden is shortened and widened. The narrowness of the street, and thus of the gap between the houses, makes it necessary to make them seem less tall than they are. Here this is done through the horizontal articulation in the roof line. Then it is necessary to make use of the relationship between color and sunlight, the light of the various times of day. Morning light is cool; afternoon light is warm. Therefore: the east sides are painted green, the west sides dark red, both tonally more or less equal . . . for the paint finish on windows and doors, the structure is the most natural guide.[30]

This supplies the following putative color scheme for the Stuttgart house: west wall, with entrance door and kitchen and toilet windows, red (this was the side that faced the Mies building); second-floor facade above the bedrooms, probably also red; kitchen veranda, white; south side with inset bedroom windows, yellow; east side facing garden, green; dining room veranda, white again; north side—perhaps—blue.

If it is possible to extrapolate from other projects, the window frames at Weissenhof may well have heightened the overall effect by a color scheme of "white, red, and yellow against red plaster; yellow, red, and white against green plaster."[31]

For the internal color scheme, we have no evidence beyond the accounts of eye-witnesses and the information in Bruno Taut's building specifications. An inventory of the furnishings—not recorded in any photograph—reveals that Bruno Taut's house was equipped with "ready-made" furniture,[32] which means that no designs by the architect were included. The furnishings consisted of metal beds (some of which had to have a foot rail at each end, as the normal head rails were too tall to fit into the recesses under the built-in closets with access from the living room; see the specifications);[33] a desk and chair; seating in the living room; a divan and table in the dining room with Thonet chairs. The light fittings were made to Bruno Taut's own design, but no picture exists.[34]

The room divisions in the living-room area were effected with sliding doors and a leather-covered concertina partition.[35] The spatial design of the first floor can be described as clear and economical—too economical in places. The floor plan is incompletely worked out. The furnishings seem to correspond to a household of six people. The size of the maid's room upstairs seems demeaning to us today and it is surprising to find a socially committed architect like Bruno Taut proposing to accommodate a human being in a space 4.3 square meters [46¼ square feet] in area. The maid was apparently expected to wash herself in the laundry in the cellar—quite normal at that time, but, again, not what one might have expected from Bruno Taut.

Mies's reaction to Bruno Taut's "orgy of color" is interesting. In the specifications acompanying his design Taut had stipulated only that the chimney stack was to be painted black; a further, detailed color scheme (since lost) was to follow. When Mies came to lay down the overall coloring of the Weissenhof project, he excluded the houses of the Taut brothers from his scheme and allowed them to be treated separately.[36] However, on July 22, 1927, one day before the opening, Mies sent a wire to Bruno Taut whose content can be deduced only from Taut's reaction to it:

At this distance I can do nothing about your cable of today's date about the color of my house, because I do not know whether the people there have followed my color indications exactly, how the material looks, etc. If my instructions have been followed, it is perfectly possible that in the present unfinished state of the whole project my house might stand out from its surroundings as the only finished one. I made careful enquiries as to the colors of the neighboring houses, and heard that, beside white, Le Corbusier is using a pink; on looking at the site, and from the photographs I had taken, I came to the conclusion that in relation to the large expanses of white in the neighborhood this small building in the specified color scheme would be exactly right. If it seems out of place in the present state of the project, this may well mean, not that the colors have been wrongly used, but that the surrounding buildings are unfinished. I would ask you, therefore, to make the following enquiry: ask Krause, of the superintendent architect's staff, whether the colors used were exactly as specified by me; if not, the contractor must change them. Otherwise, however, please wait for the whole project to be completed. At that stage, if the colors still jar, you can be certain that I shall be the first to press for a change.[37]

Nothing was changed. Perhaps the delightful effect of a colorful house in the snow was really achieved. But Ilya Ehrenburg is said to have said of Taut's colored houses in Magdeburg "we have become too sober for that kind of visual affront."[38]

In 1924 in a book entitled "The New Home—Woman as Creator" Bruno Taut had written,

The Japanese home is built, as is well known, without masonry walls, i.e. on posts, between which the walls slide into position in grooves above and below. This applies not only to the internal walls but also to the external walls . . . the house can be divided into many rooms, just as it can be transformed, in summer, into a completely open portico . . .

The delicacy and restraint of the color, and the way the delicate colors blend into the large but gentle light-reflecting surfaces, is entirely in keeping with the costume of the individual Japanese. Just as he lays cushions in glowing colors on the floor, he himself wears garments of colored silk. This individual in his own room is supremely himself, and he underlines this through the plainness of the forms and colors of the room, and through the prominence afforded to his own costume. . . .

It might be asked, in this connection, whether we can make the same use of color for ourselves. The first requirement would be the colorful costume; but, as this cannot be introduced overnight, and would therefore look like fancy dress, we should conclude, by analogy from the Japanese model, that our largely colorless clothing should go with colorful walls. And it is a fact that a person dressed in gray or black has more physical presence in front of a red background than in front of a gray one—all the more so because we use glass instead of paper. In color terms, what will suit us is, so to speak, the converse of the Japanese situation. The clarity of the juxtaposition of the colored planes of ceiling, wall, and floor corresponds to the planar quality of our buildings, which are not built as frameworks, as Japanese houses are. The harmony set up by this combination of the person and the room will create the desired psychological balance.[39]

In the 1930s, when Bruno Taut was himself living in Japan, his color sense underwent a change:

More and more, I see the debilitating power of . . . aniline dye. It is strong and loud, but without any power. This color-loving land has been conquered and anilinized by I.G. Farben. . . . This Japan almost drives one to the point of seeing natural pink flowers as paper ones, and I now understand Herr Hirai's remark last year: "Isn't cherry blossom like flat beer?" In Tokyo it is just that. This subtle, delicate bloom . . . is impossible in a context of asphalt roads and automobiles . . . really empty and flat.

To fight against aniline dyes is to be in favor of vegetable dyes. The Japanese blue! It comes from the ai plant; the color extracted from this, also called ai, is stronger than that of the plant itself; hence the proverb, ai is stronger than ai, that is to say the student is stronger than his teacher, etc.[40]

Toward the end of his account of the Stuttgart exhibition

Kurt Schwitters advised future visitors to travel home "in some friendly private car" by way of the Black Forest, and on the way there to visit, among other places, the Baroque palace of Bruchsal:

Bruchsal was painted to designs by Taut, who also has the most colorful house in the Weissenhofsiedlung. But Mies van der Rohe has rightly calculated that this colorful house is just in the right place in the overall picture. Otherwise Bruchsal is more rococo than Taut.[41]

He who shuns color,
Sees no universe.[42]

Hans Poelzig

HOUSE 20
Design: Professor Hans Poelzig, architect, Berlin
Potsdam-Wildpark, Neues Palais, Commun 1

Single-family house
Construction: external and load-bearing internal walls in timber framing (woodwool). Inner and outer skins of 1 square meter [10¾ square feet] Fonitram woodwool slabs. Non-load-bearing walls in light timber frame construction with wallboard infilling. Exterior wall surfaces plastered. Interior wall surfaces plastered or finished with plywood or laminated wallboard. Floors in Fonitram floor slabs. Ceilings with woodwool panels between joists.
Interior design: Professor Hans Poelzig, architect, Berlin. Basement: furnace room, provision cellar, laundry, maid's room.
First floor: hallway, lobby, living room, dining room leading to large terrace, lobby with kitchen and toilet. Upper floor: parents' bedroom, children's room, bathroom. Large open sunbathing terrace.[1]

Hans Poelzig and Peter Behrens, the oldest of the Weissenhof architects, had been teachers and role models to many of the younger men. Even some perhaps for that very reason—there was some resistence to the idea of including them in the project. Poelzig's name was on Lists I-III (and Behrens's on I-IV); but they then disappeared (in Poelzig's case, from October 1925 down to November 1926). Along with Bruno Taut and Scharoun, they were late substitutes for Häring, Tessenow, and Mendelsohn.[2]

On November 12, 1926, Poelzig was adopted without objection (for Scharoun there had to be a special vote) to build one Type C house at Weissenhof.[3] The Type C formula meant that the presence of one maid was to be assumed and that the house was to contain four bedrooms, one of them "divisible for children" (of different sexes). Others whose houses were of Type C were Le Corbusier, Gropius, Hilberseimer, Bruno Taut, Döcker, and Max Taut, though comparisons are difficult because Mies gave so much latitude to the architects in interpreting his specifications.

The information about the identity of possible tenants which Mies gave to the architects was probably given verbally in Poelzig's case. Mies's files, generally very complete, contain no record of an instruction such as Le Corbusier received to build "for the educated middle class"; but there does seem to have been some such message, because Poelzig himself wrote that his house was intended "to serve the needs of the brain worker, without expecting him to switch to entirely new habits of living."[4]

Like virtually all the other architects involved, Poelzig was affected by the order handed down by City Hall to reduce the built volume of the house. He wrote Mies, "The upshot is that I cannot reduce the Stuttgart house by another 25 percent, or else it's going to look like a hovel."[5] If it did later come to look like a hovel for a time this was not Poelzig's fault or that of his resident representative, Max Berliner (later Berling), but that of the chosen building material; this is a topic to which we shall return.

The building contract was placed on the third contract day, March 11, 1927, with the Stuttgart firm of Baresel (which still exists), for an all-in price of 26,000 marks.[6] (However, Döcker's final accounts, of December 30, 1927, specify a contract price of 19,000 marks; it is not clear whether this is meant to refer to the contract with Baresel or to the later ones with Hangleiter and/or with Fonitram.)[7] Döcker's total net building cost came out as 25,391 marks.

Costs were not the primary problem. Baresel withdrew from the contract[8] and a new contractor had to be found. On Poelzig's recommendation Döcker proposed the Rostock firm of Fonitram, in conjunction with Hangleiter of Stuttgart, the builder of House 25 for Rading, House 19 for Bruno Taut, and House 23 for Max Taut.

The Rasch brothers described the construction of Poelzig's house as follows:

> Timber framing with woodwool slabs, approximately 5 cm [2 inches] thick, known as Fonitram slabs, lathed and plastered. The interior has been lined with boards of polished, colored hard plaster, known as "marble cement panels." These panels are also hung between the ceiling joists and held by strips nailed in place beneath them. The joists are thus visible throughout. The floors are laid with square tiles of woodwool. The wood-framed vertical sash windows slide down into the sills, like those in a railroad car. They are balanced by counterweights.[9]

Further details, recorded in the Rasch brothers' book, *Wie Bauen?*, reveal that test certificates were produced to show the Fonitram slabs to be "totally dry-rot-proof and decay-proof," "fireproof," "an outstanding insulating material against variations in temperature," and "frostproof."[10] The Fonitram company was selected, according to Berling, in the following way:

> Poelzig had no dealings with the Fonitram company either before or after Stuttgart. On my own first visit to Stuttgart (in February, 1927), several construction systems had been commended to me as those which Stuttgart firms could undertake to operate. Before we came to make a choice, Poelzig was visited by someone from Fonitram—I think it was Herr Monich, who later became its

House 20
Hans Poelzig: Early
versions of design

Hans Poelzig: ground
plan with landscaping

Max Berling:
Perspective drawing,
April 24, 1927

director. Poelzig called me in and told me that he considered this system suitable for the Stuttgart house. So I revised the design to specify Fonitram construction—this was when the enclosed perspective drawings were done—and met . . . with Herr Butzek of Fonitram in Stuttgart, after he had worked out a costing.[11]

The Fonitram slab, and the firm that made it, are said to have taken their name from that of the inventor of the product, one Martinof, read backwards.[12]

In the official catalogue and the Rasch brothers' account of the construction system the outside of the house is described as plastered, not sided with Fonitram slabs. Max Berling wrote,

> Originally the slabs intended for the exterior were to have had a weatherproof external finish, so that there would have been a pattern of joins, as in the perspective drawing. But Rostock sent along slabs without the finish, which apparently had not stood up to wear; and so a plaster coat became necessary, applied to galvanized wire lath nailed to the slabs.
>
> To determine the dimensions of the interior wall boards, all the walls had to be drawn at a scale of 1:20. These boards were made not of Fonitram but of gypsum plasterboard with a finish in the colors specified, and with a slight marbling effect. In the living room, these were replaced by gabon plywood panels with wood moldings to cover the joins. These wall surfaces, which were then given a very dark stain, made an effective setting for the red and blue lacquered furniture; but they led Alfred Roth, in a speech he made in French on the evening of opening day, to describe *une certaine obscurité* [a certain darkness] as a characteristic of this house.[13]

The house that Poelzig built for the Werkbund exhibition was a very simple, well-thought-out design which won the unanimous approval of the contemporary critics. It, alongside Frank's two-family house (Houses 26 and 27), alone was regarded as worthy of "a lady of breeding" by the sharp-tongued Werner Hegemann of *Wasmuth's Monatshefte*, in his momentous and libelous article of January 1928 (see Appendix D).

The first floor, entered by way of two flights of steps and a large terrace, was emphatically set aside as a living and dining area. The front door led directly into the living room, with a large south-facing drop window

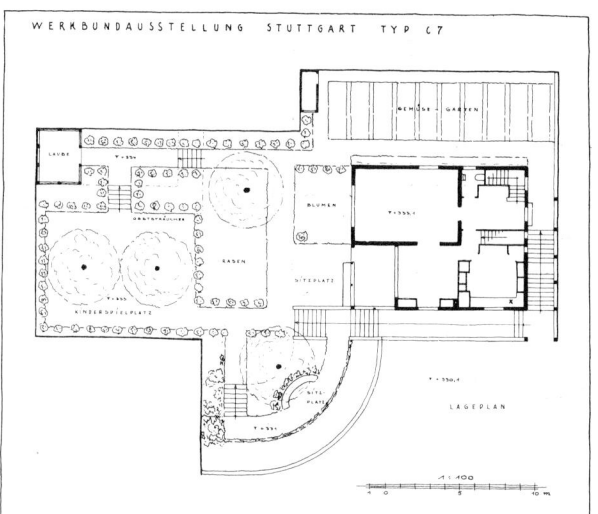

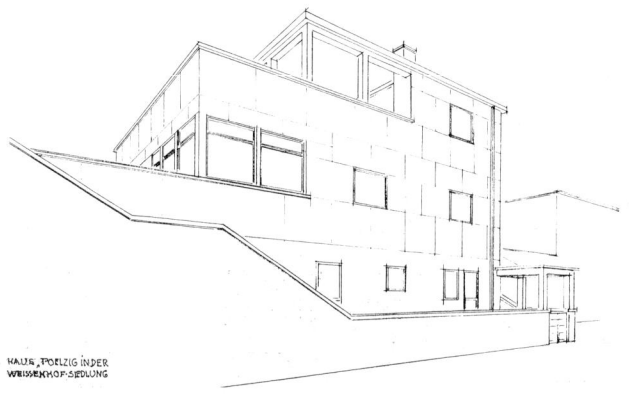

which slid down into the floor. An opening in direct alignment with two windows on opposite sides of the house led from the living room into the dining room, and this in turn led both to the spacious kitchen and, through double glass doors and an enclosed veranda, to the garden. A winter garden with direct access to the garden was also on the main floor; on the upper level was a large terrace for light, air, and sun, easily reached by way of the generous stairs with two half-landings, or directly from the adjoining bedroom. In strict compliance with Mies's Type C specifications, Poelzig planned only one children's bedroom, a spacious one with two beds, for possible division—although access to one of the divided rooms would have had to be through the other.

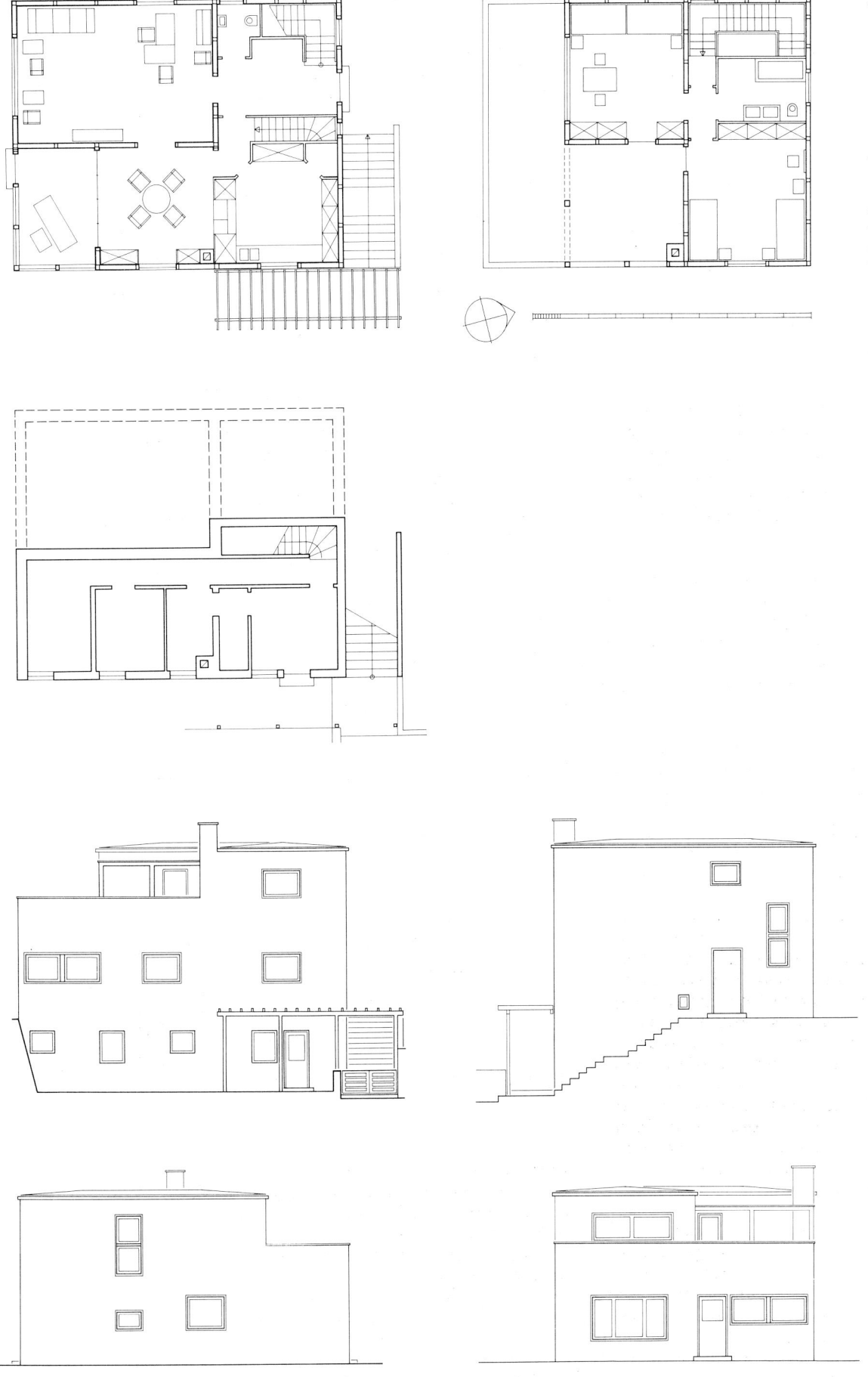

House 20
Architect: Hans Poelzig
Plans and elevations drawn from the architect's building code submissions of July 21, 1927 (version with external plaster, internal Fonitram panels)

First floor; second floor

Cellar

Elevations from east, north, west, south

The occupants of the house from 1928 through 1939—its only occupants, before it was first requisitioned and later destroyed—were the architect Hans Herkommer and his family. They moved in with four children and increased in number until the house was full to overflowing. The terrace—on which, in the early years, the whole family slept under the stars on summer nights—eventually had to be built over and turned into bedrooms for the children.[14]

Immediately after the exhibition closed Herkommer applied to City Hall for permission to excavate the area beneath the living room. After much toing and froing the work was done at Herkommer's expense and risk and under the supervision of the city architectural office.[15] Later, when serious shortcomings became evident in the Fonitram slabs, the makers attempted to shield themselves from legal responsibility on the grounds of Herkommer's excavation work and subsidence in the timber frame. Eventually a settlement was reached with City Hall under which Fonitram was to pay half of the repair costs of around 1,200 marks—at that stage the firm ceased trading and went into liquidation.[16] The miracle wall slabs had crumbled at the edges and had failed to live up to their promise. Poelzig was not affected by the collapse of the firm.[17]

The interior and furniture design were attributed by all contemporary observers to Poelzig's wife, Marlene,[18] but her name does not appear in any of the official literature. It should be mentioned, however, that Poelzig was the only Weissenhof architect who, in the book Bau und Wohnung, gave credit to his associate and resident architect, Max Berling (then Berliner). This scrupulous care in mentioning the names of his associates and coworkers is characteristic of Poelzig—and it in no way detracts from his own fame. Poelzig's former associate Karl-Heinrich Schwennick revealingly wrote to Julius Posener in 1969, "In the big exhibition of Poelzig's work organized for his sixtieth birthday [in 1929]

by the Akademie der Künste . . . he had the names of his associates, in due order according to the size of their contributions, marked beneath every one of his projects and buildings, an unheard-of thing in those days."[19]

In his explanatory note on his house Poelzig wrote, "The house is so arranged that it is closed to north and west, but open—for the sun and for the beautiful view—to the south and east."[20] The subsidiary rooms faced north or northwest. The maid's room was in the basement, along with the furnace, the store room, and the laundry. Edgar Wedepohl commented, "In an otherwise well-equipped house, which steers clear of all excess, to relegate the maid to a fusty little hole in the basement strikes one as socially undesirable."[21]

The same critic went on, however, to describe the house as furnished "with . . . elegance, even a certain lavishness," and it was praised for its palpable sense of being well thought-out: "the plan is free of contrived idiosyncrasies and is distinguished by a practical arrangement of spaces. As far as is possible, the house is one that can be run without effort."[22]

A Swiss observer wrote, "The house by Poelzig of Berlin stands out by virtue of its very strong color, and in particular through the skillful use of drop windows."[23] Another commentator compared Poelzig with Oud:

> Poelzig builds very much more lavishly, and presents one of the most comfortable houses in the development. The whole layout of the rooms; the dining room in conjunction with the large terrace; a second terrace with a sunbathing area upstairs, where the bedrooms also are; ample space in the ground-floor rooms: all this provides a beautiful, pleasantly inhabitable house. In the interior design, Poelzig further emphasizes the comfort of his rooms.[24]

Wedepohl records the impression that "the furniture has a hint of East Asia."[25] Strong colors, comfort, a hint of the East: these words recur in the descriptions. As the Poelzig house—unlike Bruno Taut's—was very restrained in its external coloring, the strong color inside must have had a powerful effect.

The furniture, which survived the house and is still preserved in Stuttgart, is indeed very brightly colored. It is lacquered furniture with a baked finish,[26] which means that an advanced form of lacquer coating is baked into the surface in large ovens. The firm which did this has a special credit in the official catalogue. Alongside Hans (or Marlene) Poelzig, other designers who showed lacquered furniture were Oskar Wlach and Paul Thiersch, both in the Behrens apartment house. In his later years Schneck, too, was to acquire a reputation as a specialist in lacquered furniture.[27]

Max Berling remembered the furniture in the living room: "Seating: arms, runners, feet, old rose to colcothar or thereabouts. Covers: steel-blue, corduroy. Closets: steel-blue." The surviving pieces have been relacquered, but according to the present owners the colors were renewed in accordance with the unfaded colors on portions which had not been exposed to the light. The color scheme is as follows: frames in a matt greenish blue, with a dull tomato red, for the closets and cabinets; the frames of the seating and footstools tomato red throughout, with gray-green-blue corduroy covers.

The hint of "Southeast Asia" is found in certain tiny details of the closets and cabinets: flat surfaces terminate in an upturned lip, and the carcass is vertically divided and placed on a stand which projects beyond it. One little drawered cabinet is more reminiscent of Art Deco than of Asia: the slight slope of the carcass, the downward taper, the long, tapering legs, and the knobs pointing in opposite directions are now immediately apparent, although contemporary observers may not have been aware of it.

All observers agree that the furnishings of the parents' bedroom were lime-green. Those in the children's room might have been red, according to Berling: "The beds were so constructed that the sides did not run, as is usual, between the head and foot: their upturned ends were slung alongside the head and foot."[28]

That the color scheme might have been tomato red and gray-blue, with elements of green, gains support from a remark made by one of the earliest occupants of the house. He remembered that the wall closets dividing the dining room from the kitchen and running along the outer wall of the dining room had tomato red

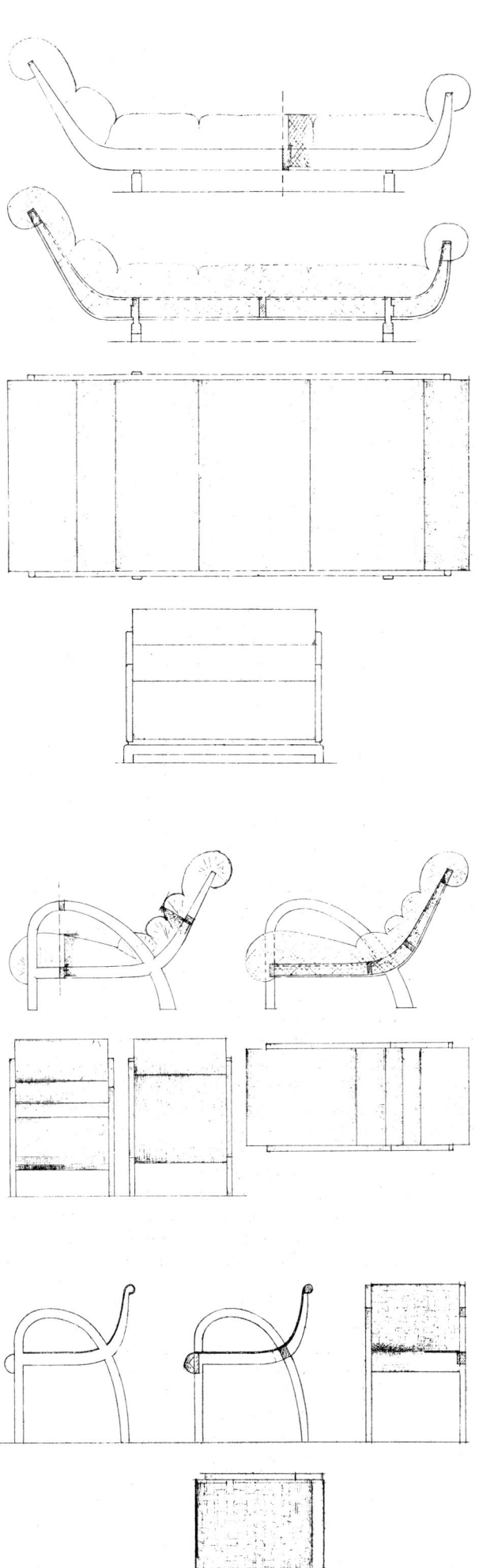

Hans Poelzig: furniture designs for House 20

wood trim. It would be easy to imagine matching chairs. The seating in the veranda, as remembered by Berling, was "Naples yellow with gray corduroy." Another color mentioned by him, colcothar (*caput mortuum*, a dark pink with a touch of blue), would also have looked well combined with steel-blue corduroy.

Hans Poelzig's biographer, Theodor Heuss—who became the first President of the Federal Republic of Germany—wrote that the Weissenhofsiedlung in Stuttgart, and similarly the Zagfah-Siedlung in Berlin, were intended to help to find "a form of house for the upper to average middle-class family." According to Heuss, Poelzig did not care in the least whether the roof was pitched or flat. He dismissed the whole question as misconceived:

> When he found that the feuds which arose over Stuttgart had turned the flat roof into a kind of dogma, he astonished a good number of his friends, the next chance he had to exhibit his work in Berlin, with a good, steep, old-fashioned pitched roof. The Weissenhof house, like the few houses he built in Fischtalgrund [Berlin], was intended by him to be seen in purely practical terms: How do I lay out the rooms in order to achieve a saving in time spent walking around, plus comfort, plus plenty of light? In both, he paid special attention to making it possible to sunbathe in comfort; the handling of the external walls is completely unconstrained, entirely determined by the articulation of interior space. The interior in Stuttgart . . . shows an unaffected elegance.[29]

"Unaffected"—the adjective seems entirely appropriate in the context of Poelzig. Julius Posener was another who used it:

> His attitude to home building might be described as affectionately unaffected. His own concern with the subject remained a sporadic one. His dwelling houses were far removed from what his contemporaries were doing; mostly they were better. Even so, let us admit: the dwelling house was not central to his work: the great theater surely interested him more than the little house.[30]

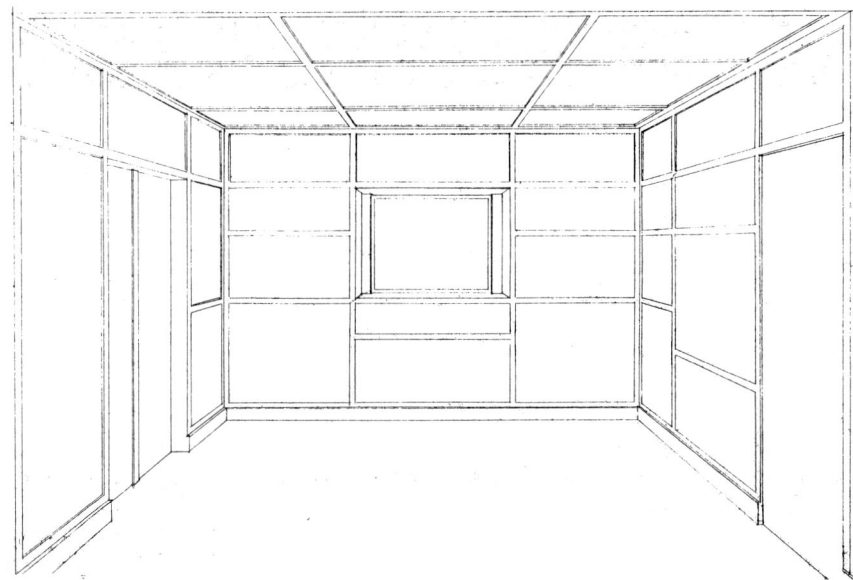

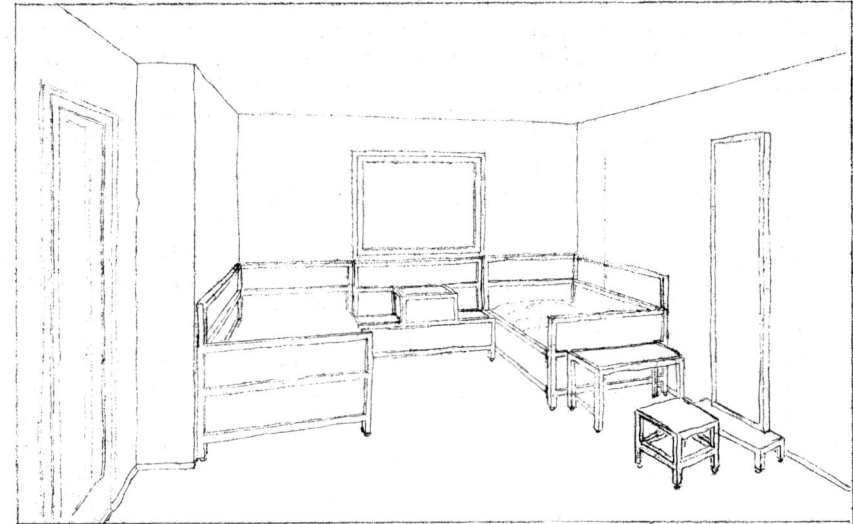

Hans Poelzig: interior designs for House 20 (living room and children's room)

Richard Döcker

HOUSES 21, 22
Design: Dr.-Ing. Richard Döcker, architect, Stuttgart
Stuttgart, Nussklinge 7

HOUSE 21

Single-family house: one-story type, extension possible.
Construction: external and internal walls, floors in Feifel
zigzag construction (wood), interior pumice concrete in-
filling behind plasterboard and plaster, exterior building
paper, wired tile lath, and plaster. Special construction
of window reveals in sheet metal profiles.
Interior design: Dr.-Ing. Richard Döcker, Stuttgart. Spa-
tial divisions of the house:
Basement floor: furnace room, coal store, laundry, cel-
lar, and large drying room.
Main floor: so-called sleeping wing with parents' bed-
room, bathroom, and divisible bedroom for children;
living room, with raised dining area leading to kitchen,
and serving hatch; toilet, maid's room, kitchen, kitchen
balcony, and pantry.
Sunbathing terrace.

HOUSE 22

Single family house: so-called story-and-a-half type on
slope. Construction: load-bearing frame in wood, sid-
ing and internal walling in 4–6 cm [1½–2½ in] Tekton pan-
els (sawdust and cement), external rendering in cement
with Ceresit additive, interior normal plaster. Interior de-
sign: Dr.-Ing. Richard Döcker, Stuttgart. Spatial division:
Lower floor: two bedrooms for twin beds, drying room,
garage with workshop space, cellar, laundry, furnace
room.
Upper floor: large living and dining room; partly roofed
terrace; large bathroom as gymnasium; parents' bed-
room; study, garderobe, toilet, maid's room, sewing and
mending room, kitchen with serving hatch.[1]

Richard Döcker, who built two single-family houses at
Weissenhof and acted as resident superintendent in
overall charge of building work, was also the frustrated
star of the show. "All that is new comes only *through
Struggle!*" he was to write in an essay for *Bauwelt* in
1928, which bore the title "Fulfilled and Unfulfilled."[2]

Weissenhof, for Döcker, was above all a struggle: a
struggle for the cause, a struggle to complete the work,
a struggle against the slapdash practices of his fellow
architects, a struggle against the greed of the contractors, and a struggle against the exhibition's sometimes
dilatory and indecisive artistic director, Mies van der
Rohe. The evidence in all those dry files—his twenty circulars to the participant architects, the minutes of meet-

ings at City Hall—also shows that too often Döcker's
struggle was against himself.

The struggle went on all his life. Mentioned in one of
the Weissenhof files as a member of "the left wing of
the Stuttgart School," Döcker was and remained at
odds with the right wing of that school, as most promi-
nently represented by Paul Schmitthenner. It was, we
gather, Schmitthenner who in 1926–27 frustrated Döcker's desire to obtain a teaching post at the Technische
Hochschule in Stuttgart: Keuerleber was appointed instead. Just so long as Schmitthenner's influence counted
for anything in Stuttgart, Döcker's counted for nothing;
and after World War II, when the boot was on the other
foot, Döcker succeeded in preventing Schmitthenner's
return to office.[3] He told Gropius that Schmitthenner
would never return to the Technische Hochschule so
long as he, Döcker, was there.[4]

This conflict first came to a head in the planning
stage of the Weissenhof project, and it intensified in the
second phase of the planning of the neighboring project, the Kochenhofsiedlung: in 1933 the drawings and
other planning materials for this project, planned as a
showpiece for local Stuttgart architects, were actually
confiscated from Döcker—by order of the Nazi state
commissioner, Strölin—and handed over to Schmitthenner, who then directed the final phases of the project.
The Kochenhof houses were built as part of a timber
construction exhibition, *Deutsches Holz für Hausbau
und Wohnung Stuttgart 1933.*

To return to the Weissenhofsiedlung: Döcker has every claim to be regarded as the most important representative of Stuttgart among those architects who were
committed to the New Architecture. After studying, and
working as an assistant, under Bonatz, he attracted professional notice through a number of highly interesting
and original projects, the most noteworthy of which was
his large hospital at Waiblingen. He gathered around
him a circle which included Willi Baumeister, painter
and graphic designer; Karl Konrad Düssel, of the *Stuttgarter Neues Tagblatt*; and many fellow architects,
among them Hugo Keuerleber, Ernst Wagner, Richard
Herre, Gustav Schleicher, Franz Krause, and the Rasch
brothers. In 1926 Döcker wrote,

> The longing for the conquest of something new;
> the impetus toward the unprejudiced honesty and
> absolute truth of a pure objectivity free of all that
> is sentimental or transient; the will to spurn the
> blinkered vision which sees only its own preor-
> dained limits, in order to think things out for one-
> self and to achieve a wider range of awareness:
> all these are unbourgeois phenomena, in contrast
> to the bourgeois replication of a preordained
> conventional norm that is already thought out,
> lived out, and consequently worn out.

Active energy, youth, and the life-affirming powers of creativity unite to enact the will of the age and of its spirit.[5]

Döcker and his group were influential in Stuttgart, but in no way as powerful as he himself was to claim in his old age. The rumor, constantly cited as a fact, that at the inception of the Weissenhof project the Werkbund, through Bruckmann, had asked Bonatz to prepare a "layout plan with model," that this plan had been for a development of "gable houses," and that "Bonatz, Döcker, Keuerleber, Schneck, Scharoun, and Rading" were to have been the architects—whereupon the "younger element" of the "progressive group" had exerted "massive pressure" to thwart Bonatz in his desire both to keep his gable design concept and to involve Schmitthenner—is not supported by the documentary evidence.[6]

In planning his own houses Döcker kept scrupulously to the principles laid down by Mies. (The friction between Mies and Döcker is dealt with in detail in the section above on Mies van der Rohe's Houses 1–4.) Together with the other architects, he received a layout plan on September 9, 1926, showing the two adjoining lots on which he was to build his two houses. On the revised plan the land stretched from Rathenaustrasse, the lower boundary of the Weissenhofsiedlung, up to Bruckmannweg. He described his approach to the design of his houses in a contribution to *Die Form* in 1926:

> The individual structure is an element which subordinates and integrates itself, shaping space within the framework and the overall rhythm of the existing buildings—a part of the whole. It is not left to the whim and the ambition, the playful impulses and random actions, of one creator. The planning consequently becomes natural, self-evident, inevitable—in contradistinction to the forced, the absolute, and the arbitrary.[7]

Döcker planned his houses to reflect the overall context of the Weissenhofsiedlung and to present themselves as a whole, built into or onto each other, in accordance to the principle of urban architecture which he himself formulated: "Just as the individual space, the room, the piece of furniture, the aperture, the material, the construction system, etc., are interdependent members of a specific whole, the building itself is only one stone in the manifold structure of an urban organism."

By linking his two houses together Döcker became the only one of the participating architects who adhered to the original underlying idea of Mies's layout proposal. In January of 1927, after seeing his fellow architects' designs, Döcker wrote Mies:

> Should I now maintain the linking of my two types, C 8 and C 9, as shown in my preliminary design, based on your layout plan? My types are the only instance in which two structures are joined together. All the others have not made the linkages implied in your plan. Have you taken another look at your model, or at the layout plan, in the light of this . . .?[8]

Mies no doubt gave his answer verbally, in the course of one of his visits; it does not appear in the correspondence. The rooms composing the connecting wing, which are missing from the plan as submitted to the building office in January 1927, were still present in the preliminary drawings of November 1926: House 21 had

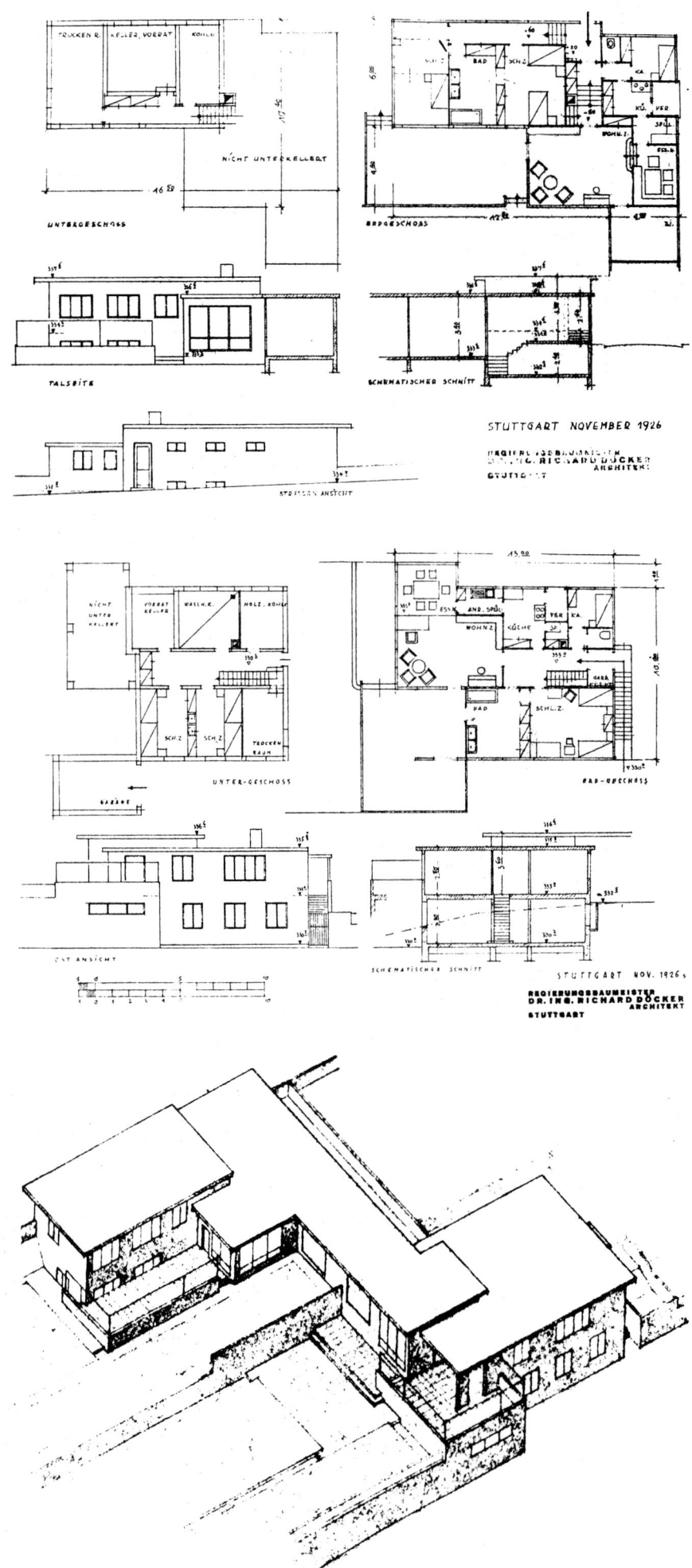

Richard Döcker: first version of House 21, November, 1926. The connection with House 22 was to be made by the room appended to the living room (*ERDGE-SCHOSS*, lower right)

Richard Döcker: first version of House 22, November, 1926. The connection with House 21 was to be made by the dining area (*ERDGESCHOSS*, top)

Richard Döcker: isometric view of Houses 21 and 22, showing connection

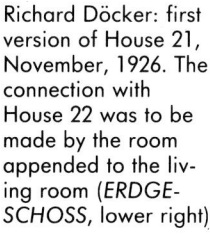

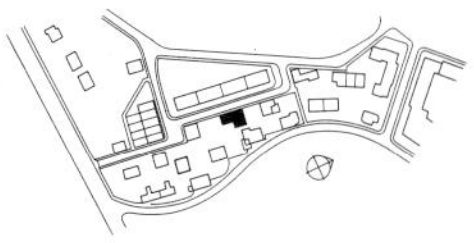

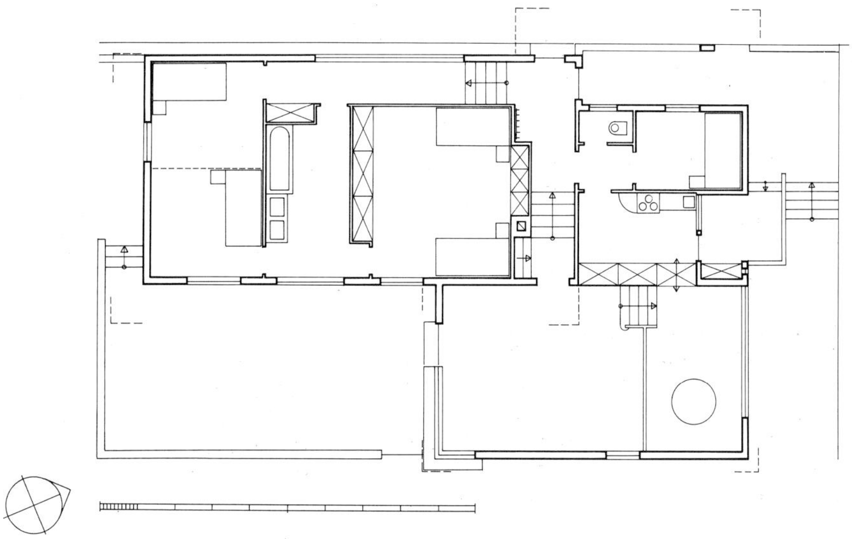

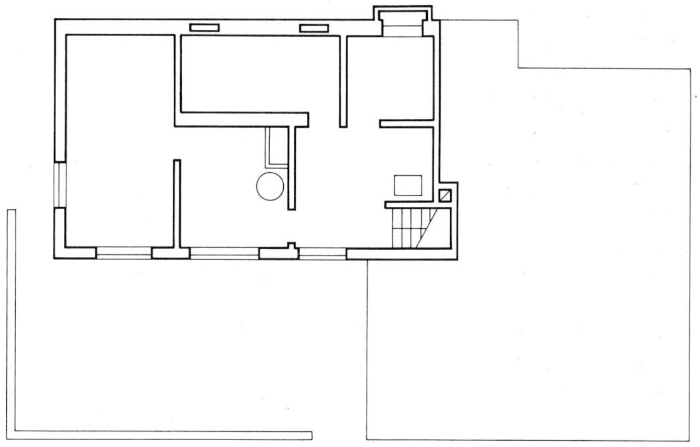

House 21
Architect: Richard Döcker
Plans and elevations drawn from the architect's building code submissions of January, 1927 (undated)

Main floor ("single-story type")

Cellar

Elevations from south, north, west, east

149

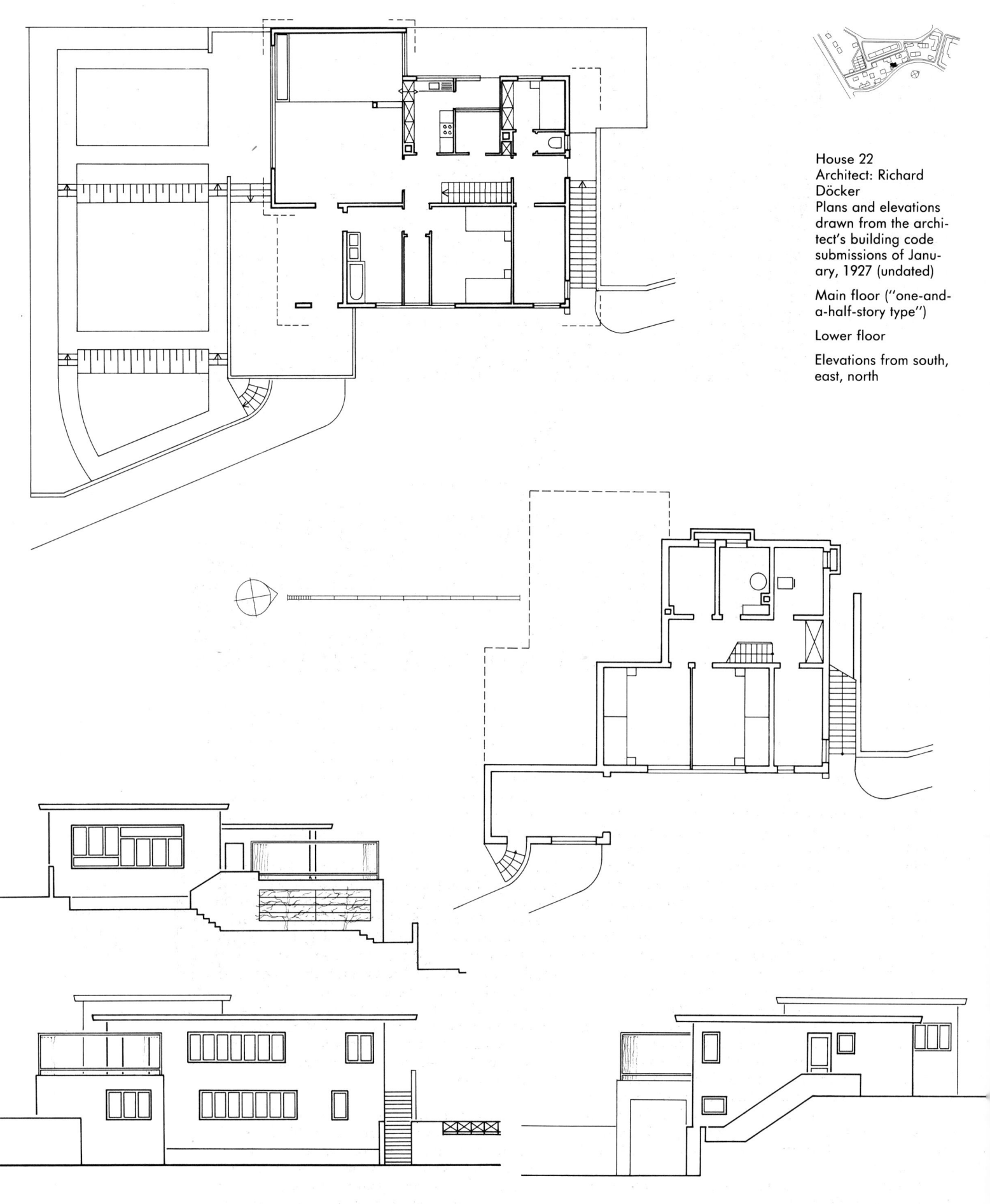

House 22
Architect: Richard Döcker
Plans and elevations drawn from the architect's building code submissions of January, 1927 (undated)

Main floor ("one-and-a-half-story type")

Lower floor

Elevations from south, east, north

Houses 21 and 22:
View from Bruckman-
nweg (House 21 in
foreground)

View from Rathenaus-
trasse (House 22 in
foreground)

View from south
(House 21 in fore-
ground)

an added study which abutted an extension of the dining room of House 22. This connection produced an S-
shaped complex in which, to keep the main floors of
both houses on the same level, the floor level of the upper house had to be lowered and that of the lower
house raised. This would certainly not have been done
if Döcker had not initially intended to keep to Mies's
idea. Without the connecting wing the relationship between the plans is not particularly evident, whereas in
combination they seem to complement each other. To
the visitor the connection would not have been clear as
the houses were reached from two different streets, not
seen as a whole from a linking footpath with steps.

There exists, in Mies's archive, a drawing by Döcker
in which he shows his allotted space occupied by three
terraced blocks, shown with schematic, and rather conservative, plans. Mies's reaction is not known.[9]

Döcker's houses, of Type C (for a family with one
maid),[10] were assigned on the third contract date,
March 5, 1927, to two different contractors. The contract for House 21 went to Feifel for 21,000 marks, and
for House 22 to Stuttgarter Baugeschäft for 26,000 marks.[11] Döcker's final account showed a total net cost of
19,982.70 marks for House 21 and 26,482.87 marks for
House 22.[12] The furnishing was done by Döcker himself.[13] The completion schedule was not in question at
any stage.[14]

The Rasch brothers gave the following account of the
construction of House 21:

The house by the architect Richard Döcker has
been built in the zigzag construction system in-

vented by the architect Feifel. The zigzag walls
are lined internally with plasterboard and plastered, and externally plastered on wood or wired
tile lath. In the large living room the zigzag structure of the floor above has been left visible. The
roof is covered with tar-free roofing paper. Gut-
ters are formed by the high, parapet-like fascia
boards, onto which the paper is drawn.[15]

The zigzag (Zickzack) construction system was the invention of the ingenious and prolific Albert Feifel,[16] of
Schwäbisch-Gmund, who used it in his own buildings
mainly for internal partitions. Its external use with plastering in House 21, and the need to offer additional
weather protection, led to roof overhangs that were exceptionally wide by Weissenhof standards and en-
dowed Döcker's houses, in formal terms, with
something of the look of country houses by Frank Lloyd
Wright. According to Heinz Rasch Mies agreed to the
overhangs only because of the wood construction.[17]

The Rasch brothers described the construction of
House 22, with

Wood braced frame construction. The lintel over
the wide window is made as a binder of the
frame. There are wide roof overhangs to protect
the external skin. The frame is sheathed inside
and out with Tekton lightweight wallboards and
then plastered. Foundation and cellar are concreted and have a solid floor of reinforced concrete beams above them (Pelikandecke)."[18]

The lintel that also served as a binder or plate was the object of a malicious comment by Mies's resident architect, Ernst Walther, in a letter to his principal: "N.B. Dr. Döcker has built a wooden binder across his house that is so wrong that even Commissioner S[igloch] noticed it. All the diagonals are under tension instead of compression."[19]

The building records of the city of Stuttgart contain a drawing and an exchange of letters on this beam. The fault was remedied by inserting additional supports; after an inspection in 1930 it was decided that "there will be no further objection to the window lintels, which are at the limits of their loading capacity, in view of the fact that the building is under the constant supervision and care of the city architect's department."[20] In the report of the building office inspection of May 31, 1927, the construction of the window is described as "not ideal" but acceptable after "improvements."[21]

It may be assumed that these difficulties arose though the change in building materials: Döcker's plans as originally submitted to the building office specify "walls and floors solid (iron or concrete frame with infilling)," which was later changed to "Feifel zigzag wood construction."[22]

On the color scheme Döcker wrote Mies, who had proposed "off-white" for all the houses: "As for the color scheme for my own house, I will have the various wings painted differently in light tones."[23] No details of the colors were recorded.

It is not really possible to speak of "truth to materials" in the case of these houses: a solid masonry house would have looked just the same. This may have been the consideration that led Döcker to leave the living room of House 21 unceiled, thus revealing the zigzag construction of the floor above.

In House 21, which was approached from the upper street, Bruckmannweg, the three functional divisions of the house were separated. The lobby led to the kitchen, the maid's room, the kitchen veranda, and the dining area. Five steps led up to the bedroom wing, which contained two bedrooms separated by a bathroom: the second bedroom, at the end, was intended to be divisible for use by children, but one of the resulting single rooms would have been accessible only through the other, or through the bathroom.

The bedrooms make up what is virtually a separate wing, consisting of a hallway with rooms on the sunny side. The wing can be extended at any time by lengthening the hallway. From the entrance lobby or porch, six or so steps lead down to the living room and the raised dining area. From the living room, a three-leafed glazed door leads to the terrace, which can be curtained off all around, and on which there is a shower with hot and cold water.[24]

Next to the entrance to the living room three more steps led down to the lower floor, with boiler, coal store, store cellar, laundry with hot and cold water, and a large drying room.[25]

The living room of House 21 inspired a Swiss critic to observe that this was probably the most beautiful room in the entire exhibition: "a small, raised eating area with a balustrade and six steps down to the living room, and beyond the wide glass doors the paved, sunken terrace."[26] A less friendly voice (Edgar Wedepohl again, in *Wasmuth's Monatshefte*), opined that "the new experiments do not possess the same power to convince, the same peaceful self-evidence and sureness, as do perfect gabled houses,[27] which are neither formless nor overformed, but in the best sense of the word authentic and genuine, because they do not set out to be original."[28]

Richard Döcker: undated block plan for the Weissenhofsiedlung

Feifel zigzag method: "Wall construction. The walls are constructed out of boards in the same way as the floors. Nailed in both directions, the boards with their continuous string boards at either end form a rigid structure."

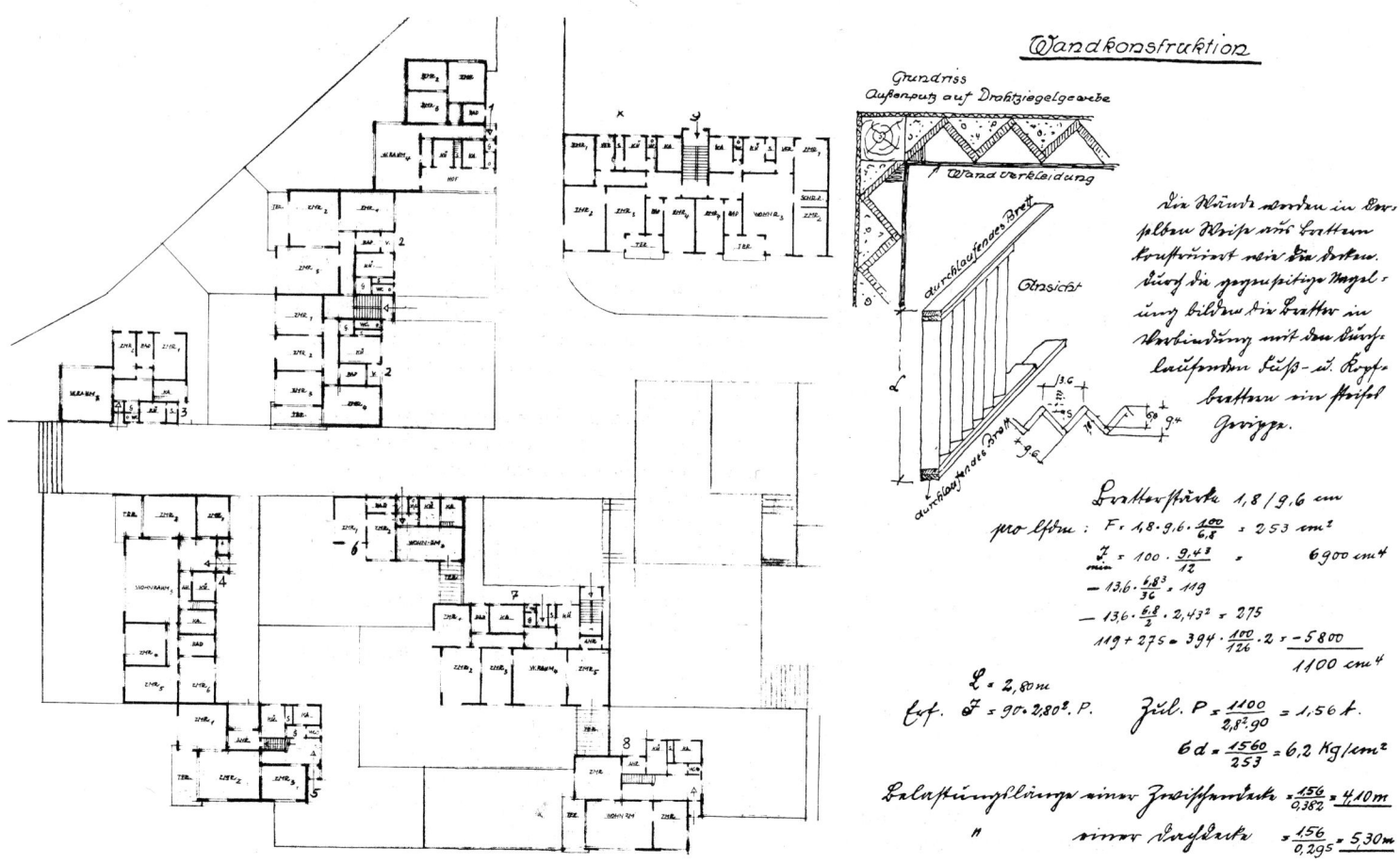

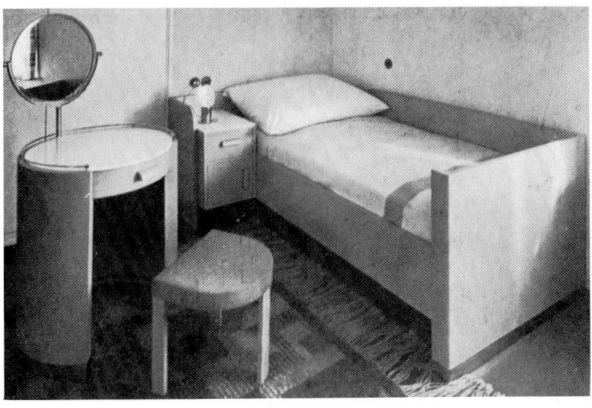

House 22 was reached from Rathenaustrasse by way of a flight of nineteen steps. As one entered through the lobby, the cloakroom and study were on the left, and a guest toilet and maid's room on the right. A straight hallway led to the living room and the partitionable dining area, and also gave access to the kitchen and to the sleeping section with bedroom, bathroom, and closet room. The terrace, part of which was roofed, could be reached from the living room and from the bathroom. Its closeness to bath and bed was perceived as particularly pleasant: "On the terrace there are wall-bars for gymnastics, together with a shower-bath. The terrace affords direct access to the bathroom, which is large and spacious and can also serve as a gymnasium."[29]

As it also had to serve for the occupants of the two bedrooms on the lower floor, the size of the bathroom was by no means excessive. (The maid, as was then customary, would not have used the family bathroom but the guest toilet and the laundry.)

From . . . the main floor there are stairs downward, a drying and store room on the right, a coal store with a chute, a store cellar, boiler. Toward the front are two more bedrooms with two beds in each.

From the street one can drive straight into a spacious garage with an adjoining room and direct access to the garden.[30]

This was the one and only Weissenhof house (apart from the one built by Klemm and Wagner for the Schwäbischer Siedlungsverein, outside the exhibition proper) that had a garage of its own. And all this for a "total net building cost" of 26,482 marks! Döcker succeeded in keeping the overrun on the contract price to less than 500 marks; on House 21 he managed to come in below the agreed building price of 21,000 marks. The only other architects to keep even slightly below the "all-in contract price" were Oud and Bruno Taut.[31]

The interiors, as said, were by Döcker himself. Most of the furniture, too, was by him—a fact which he seems to have taken for granted, as it is not even mentioned in the official catalogue. Whether the furniture in both houses was the same is uncertain, but probable, as the same manufacturers are listed.[32] (There are no photographs of the interiors of House 21.) Worth mentioning are the armchair with hinged flaps to stand small items on, and the classically beautiful floor lamp. The painting on the wall was by Willi Baumeister.

Whether the "magnificent toning of the [internal] walls"[33] of Houses 21 and 22 was devised by Baumeister is not possible to establish with certainty, but we may assume so. The same goes for the houses by Bourgeois, Schneck, probably even Oud, and others. This would explain why Graeff's Werkbund book, Innenräume, includes a chapter on "Colors in Space" by Baumeister:

Architecture today is the "creation of spaces." It nevertheless dissolves the individual cells in favor of a continuing spatial feeling. The color scheme is deduced from this guiding idea. Bedrooms, bathrooms, kitchen, and stairs are to be left white, to create their own chiaroscuro effects. If a room is given a single color, there appears a tonal contrast which is relatively strong even if that color is pure white.

Accordingly, in opting for color in the other rooms, the following factors have to be taken into account. Considerations of economy of light induce us to paint the darkest surface, the window wall, white, with the second color on the other surfaces. The tonal value of the window wall is thus rectified, it has the feel of an external wall, and in artificial light it becomes a subsidiary light source. . . .

With rich color, there is a danger of an undesirably garish effect. Nevertheless there are color harmonies which, in spite of contrasts, create activity and tranquility. The pure harmony of tensions, to which we respond, is found in the best examples of abstract painting. All surfaces of detached or engaged piers, lintels, and dwarf partitions, must be of the same color. This leads to an interpenetration of the architectural members which makes constructional principles visible and palpable.[34]

There are no authentic descriptions of the color as it was. We know, "for reasons of cheapness," the colors were mixed with distemper.[35] Both of Döcker's houses were destroyed in World War II. Consideration is being given to rebuilding one or both.

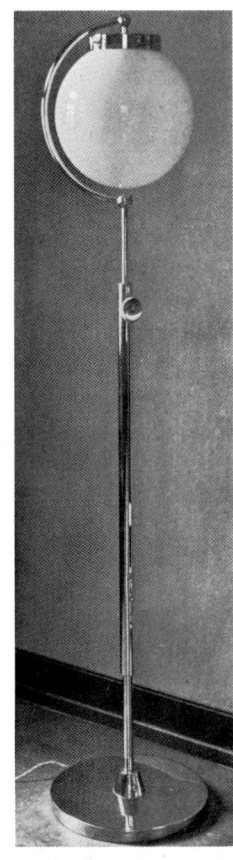

House 21:
Floor lamp by Richard Döcker

Living room by Richard Döcker

Parents' bedroom by Richard Döcker

Living room by Richard Döcker, with painting by Willi Baumeister

Max Taut

HOUSES 23, 24

Design: Max Taut, architect, Berlin
Berlin, W 9, Linkstrasse 20

Construction: iron frame with Thermos panels. Lined with plasterboard and plastered. Siding of Laponized cement panels.

HOUSE 23

Single-family house.
Cellar: laundry, store cellar.
First floor: entrance, lobby, main living room communicating with dining area, kitchen, pantry, terrace.
Second floor: two bedrooms, maid's room, bathroom, toilet, terrace.

HOUSE 24

Single-family house.
Interior design: Richard Herre, architect, Stuttgart, Nekarstrasse 63.
Spatial divisions of the house:
Cellar: laundry, store cellar.
First floor: entrance, cloakroom, toilet, living room, kitchen with scullery and pantry, two bedrooms, bathroom, terrace.
Second floor: study, two bedrooms.[1]

Neither of Max Taut's houses was acclaimed as an outstanding example of modern house construction. The comments of contemporaries occasionally sound positively aggrieved, and Max Taut's own written explanation is laconic. His arguments are all practical ones:

> The planning of the houses was determined by the simplest of principles: the points of the compass determine the orientation of the house and of its rooms. . . .
> For the relative positions of the various spaces, the determining factor was simplicity of use. The bedrooms, living room, and dining room are arranged in a logical sequence.
> Technique is governed by the demands of economy. Rapid construction methods are imperative in order to minimize loss of rental income.
> So: soon built and soon occupied![2]

One might think that these were indeed decisive arguments in a time when there were great shortages of housing, of materials, and of capital, and a prevalent cultural ethos of New Objectivity (Neue Sachlichkeit). And yet these houses provide a clear demonstration—

as does that built by Max Taut's elder brother, Bruno—that architecture is and must be something more than the sum total of purely economic considerations and objective planning.

It was Bruno Taut who put into words the fear that is now proving all too justified:

> It was right to reduce architecture to a matter of efficiency, and thus emancipate it from its misidentification and confusion with painting and sculpture; this removed, at last, its character as decoration. But now that we . . . have finally shaken off those fetters, we have a new enemy to contend with: an enemy born of the concentration on function and objectivity as the highest laws of architecture. To see function in terms of shallow utilitarianism, and—worse—of cost effectiveness, would be the death of architecture. The current debasement of the achievements of the pioneers clearly illustrates the disastrous consequences of such a doctrine.[3]

Max Taut was a successful architect in Berlin, where he worked a great deal with the city architect, Martin Wagner.[4] Mies had a high regard for him, as the surviving correspondence shows, and as far as Mies was concerned Max, not Bruno, was "the" Taut—as the late addition of Bruno's name to the Weissenhof shortlist indicates. Far from taking an emotional or idealistic line, Max Taut was matter-of-fact, practical, and objective enough to protest against the inadequacy of the fee specified in the contract offered by the city of Stuttgart, almost to the point of bringing the whole enterprise to a halt at the end of September of 1926.[5] Max Taut—and in his wake his brother, Bruno—participated in the Werkbund project, but repeatedly made it clear that they had no intention of taking responsibility for the fulfillment of instructions imposed by the city of Stuttgart which conflicted with the rules of the BDA.[6]

Max Taut sent in the plans for his houses on time and pointed out in February of 1927 that delaying tactics on the part of City Hall threatened to lead to a "fiasco" for which he and his brother would be in no way responsible, as they had been early in completing their design work.[7]

The building contracts were placed on the first contract date, February 25, and there was never any doubt that Houses 23 and 24 would be completed on schedule. The cost overruns were around average, and Döcker's team praised the comprehensiveness of the drawings.

Houses 23 and 24 were built in an iron skeleton construction system, with Thermos panels as "infilling."[8] This was in accord with Max Taut's preference for dry construction: "The use of water during construction

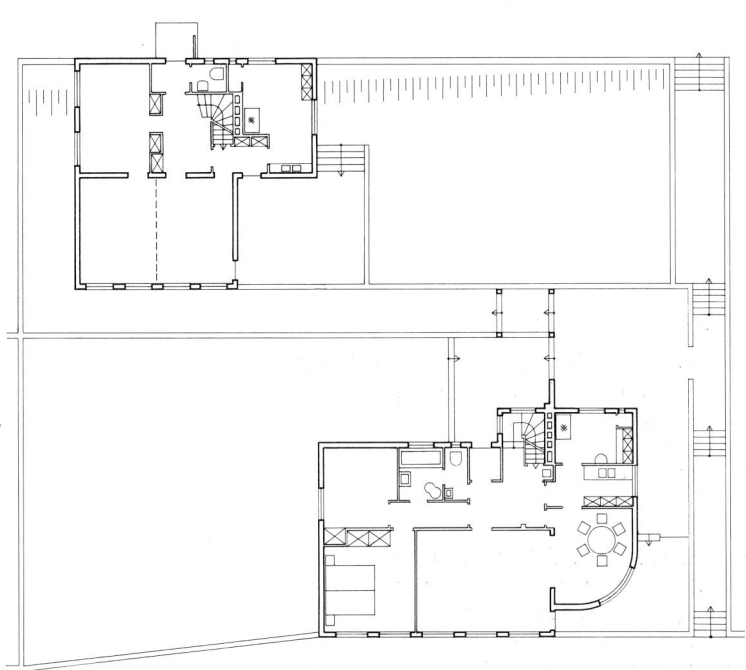

Houses 23 and 24
Architect: Max Taut
Plans and elevations drawn from the architect's building code submissions of March 10, 1927

First floor of Houses 23 and 24

Second floor of Houses 23 and 24

Elevation from south (House 23 on left)

Elevation from north (House 24 on left)

Elevation from east (House 23 on left)

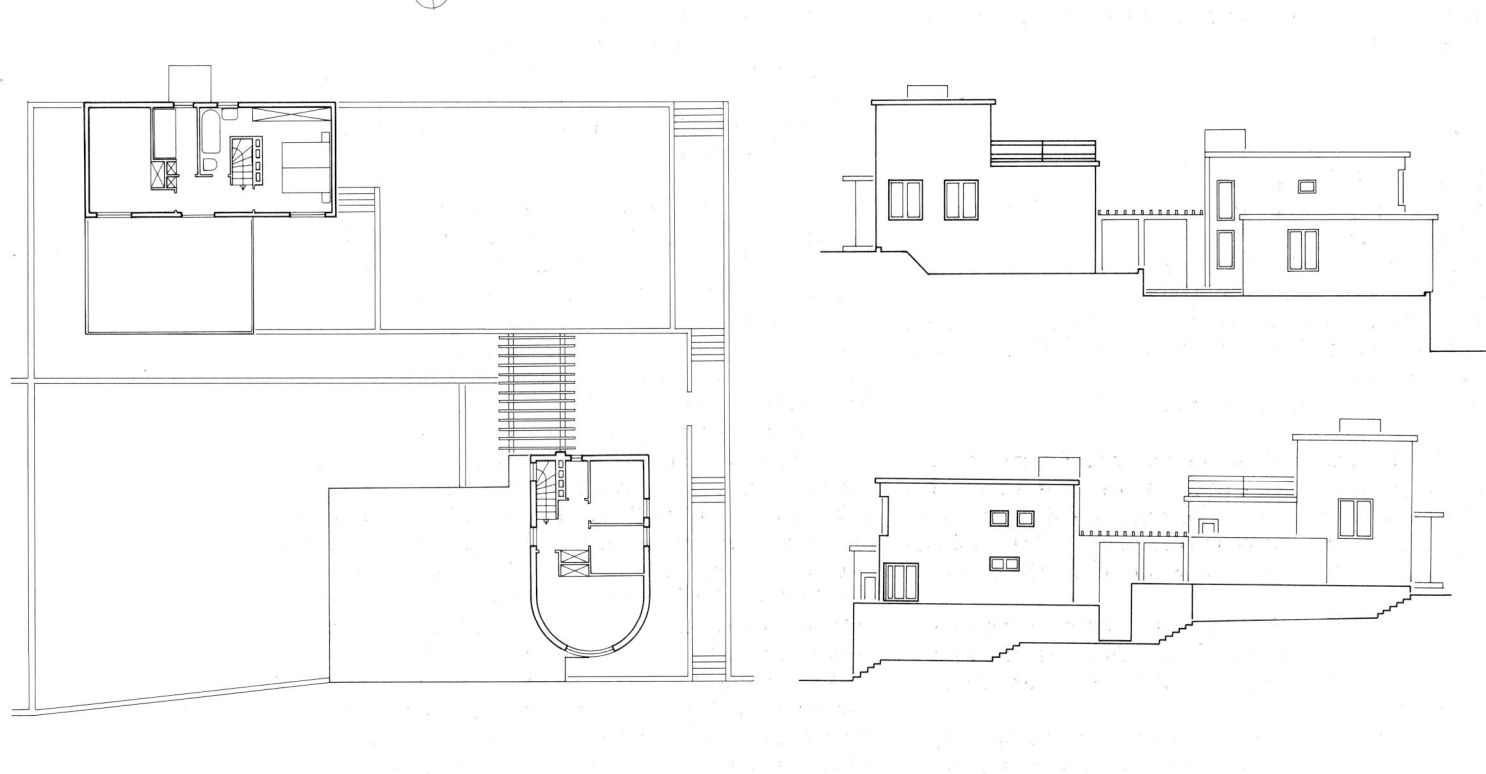

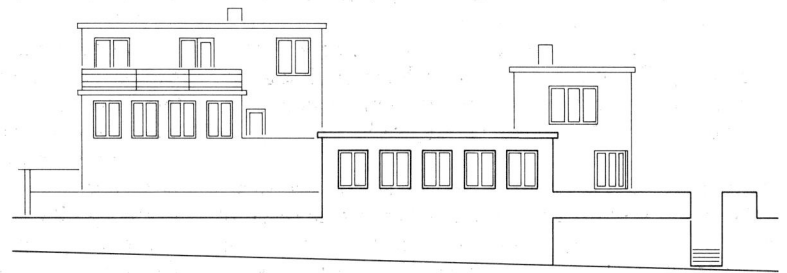

should be avoided as far as possible," he wrote in *Bau und Wohnung*.[9]

Extra costs arose from the granting of Taut's request for an additional siding of cement panels, with which he was not ultimately very happy. After the installation of the cement panels, which were "Laponized,"[10] i.e. given a colored glaze ("known as cold-glazed panels"),[11] it became apparent that the colors of the panels were "nothing out of the ordinary," such as would be worthy for the eyes of a critical public. "I of course consider," wrote Max Taut to Mies shortly before opening day, "that if the colors have not come out right they must definitely be changed. I would ask you to give some thought to how we should change the color; I think white or gray."[12]

This change (which cost another 600 marks) led a contemporary critic to the reflection that the Modernist cult of truth to materials could not really count for so very much, if the original surface had to be covered with a layer of light gray paint.

Max Taut had no interest in furnishing the houses, and House 23 was shown empty. When the Württemberg Werkbund, through Mies, enlisted a number of local Stuttgart interior designers, House 23 was one of the houses set aside for them. Mies asked Julius Metzke-Rovira to "take on the interiors of the upper Taut house," stressing as always that the interiors should be planned "avoiding any hint of the salon, and all superfluity," and that Metzke-Rovira should contact the architect direct to discuss "finish and treatment of color."[13]

Metzke-Rovira agreed at first, and was quite happy for Taut to reserve the kitchen for himself.[14] Then, without warning or explanation, he backed out: "I hereby beg to notify you that I withdraw from the furnishing of the house by Max Taut. Please forgive this late notification, but I have arrived at this decision only in the last few days."[15] Metzke-Rovira's contribution to the Werkbund exhibition was thereafter restricted to his membership in Döcker's technical bureau.[16]

When it became clear that Max Taut's House 23, on Bruckmannweg, was not going to be furnished, the subcommittee of the main exhibition committee had the idea of putting in a "wine restaurant" for visitors to the

House 24:
Two views of living
room by Richard
Herre

exhibition. Taut would have been quite happy for this to be done, as the record shows;[17] but the restaurant never opened. The only sources of refreshment in the Weissenhofsiedlung were the "exhibition restaurant" in the adjoining Schönblick tower and the delicatessen in the basement at the north end of the Mies apartment house.[18]

As no specifications, either by Mies or by the architect, have survived for Max Taut's houses—it may be that Mies did everything by word of mouth—it can only be assumed, as the Döcker block plan shows, that these were intended as houses of Type C, i.e. with four rooms and one maid.[19]

Max Taut himself described House 23 as a "small dwelling house" (which is to say one in which the pitch of the stair, according to him, was normally 20:21). He countered criticism of the difficulty of access to the bathroom and toilet windows by saying that if the window hardware specified by him had been used there would have been no problem. The kitchen, which the eventual tenant housewife did not seem to get along with, was explained by him as conceived in two parts:

a kitchen proper, and a scullery for dishwashing.[20]

The interior design of House 24 was by Richard Herre, a Stuttgart architect whose name had been shortlisted in the early stages of the selection process for the Weissenhofsiedlung as a building architect. It appears in an apparently secure sixth position on the Werkbund's List IV of April 1926, sinks to a hopeless twentieth place as a "reserve" in List V, on July 20, and does not reappear. What had happened? On July 8, 1926, Herre had sent Stotz, at the Württemberg Werkbund, the following letter:

From a number of reliable sources I learn that the selection of those who are to form the Stuttgart contingent of architects in the Werkbund exhibition of 1927 has already been made. I gather that of these 50 percent are purely interior designers.

If this hearsay is correct, I beg the Württemberg Section once again, and at this late hour, to included me in such a way that I receive the same commissions for architectural and interior work as the interior designers already adopted. . . .

Since I set up in independent practice some years ago, I have been active in virtually all departments of interior design and decorative art in a consistently modern spirit. I cannot escape the painful question how it can be possible—when the majority of those taking the decisions must surely know my work—for me to remain ignored in the context of an exhibition which sets out to sail under a radical flag, and does so, in part, with those who have previously catered to a good, but moderate and conservative taste.[21]

Herre went on to give details of his training, his projects, his work in textile design, advertising graphics, and product design: all of high quality. But his attack, which was mainly aimed at Schneck, had been too explicit. It was not until April of 1927, after Herre (with

Graeser and Metzke-Rovira) had made repeated applications to Mies for interior design work,[22] that he was entrusted with the interiors of House 24.[23]

In a letter written in November of 1926 to Le Corbusier, who was staying at the Schlossgartenhotel in Stuttgart and intended to meet with Mies to visit the Weissenhof site, Herre wrote: "New and specific circumstances—in consequence of my rejection as a participant in the Werkbund exhibition—prevent me from seeing you in the same company as last year: M. and Mme Hildebrandt, M. Döcker."[24] What really happened to exclude Herre from the shortlist will probably never be known.

These painful experiences apart, Herre designed the interiors of Max Taut's house with great distinction. The official catalogue mentions light fitments, drapes, and carpets as having been designed by Herre himself; but in fact most of the furniture was his as well. All showed him to be a highly individual and imaginative designer; it is high time that he was given his due as the best of all the Stuttgart furniture designers represented at Weissenhof. His designs do not suffer from the stiffness of Döcker's, or the pedestrian quality of Schneck's. Herre's Weissenhof furniture is resourceful, elegant, with never a "hint of the salon." Herre might have occupied a leading place in the Modern Movement; it looks as if he was his own worst enemy.

Herre seems to have approached the coloring of his interiors rather in the same way as Bruno Taut. One critic spoke of "the aniline madness that rages on the walls . . . combined with black-painted ceilings."[25] Herre's predilection for extremes of color is confirmed by his contemporaries, Oscar Heinitz and Heinz Rasch.

Max Taut's Houses 23 and 24 are among those that are no longer standing.

Adolf Rading

HOUSE 25

Design: Professor Adolf Rading, architect, Breslau, Kaiserin-Augusten-Platz 3

Single-family residence: cellar, first floor, second floor. Construction: iron frame construction with Thermos infilling. Outer skin pumice cement panels, inside plasterboard. Plastered inside and out. Partitions plasterboard. All closets built in. The accommodation comprises: Cellar: lobby with stairs and exit to kitchen yard, provision cellar, furnace room with coal store. First floor: living room divisible with folding doors into dining, study, and sitting areas, terrace; on lower level bedrooms, hallway and bathroom, cooking space. Second floor: maid's bedroom, laundry and ironing room, sunbathing terrace and play area.[1]

At first, when Mies showed me my lot on the Weissenhof development, I had no idea what to do.

I myself inclined to the view that the project was there to show a series of type houses that would combine a design suited to the life style of our time with maximum economy. And now here was this lot, irregular in every respect, and these surrounding buildings that could not simply be ignored.

Of course it all happened as it usually does. Reality turned out to be much more complicated than thought and imagination. When we fifteen architects sat down together, we soon saw that— if we adopted the approach that I, and probably most of the others, had in mind—we were never going to get anywhere. Economy was quite right; but we had omitted to reckon with time and evolution. It soon became clear to us that what we had to produce had to be something organically coherent, which would be economical, but in which economy could not have the last word. Even so, we endeavored as best we could to maintain the principle of economy, and to manage with the sums laid down for us. Many of us drew our own conclusions when we were told one day that the city of Stuttgart had decided to employ only Stuttgart contractors to execute our designs. At that point, if economy had still been the critical factor for us—as it initially had been—then we would have stopped work there and then, because of course from that moment on there could be no free price negotiation.[2]

These words were part of Adolf Rading's response to a request for an explanation of his work for *Die Form*, the organ of the Deutscher Werkbund. It is true that the location assigned to him was of a curious shape: an acute-angled corner lot on the eastern boundary street, Am Weissenhof, caught between Mies's dominant apartment house on one side and the three row houses by Mart Stam on the other, and crowded from behind by Josef Frank's Houses 26 and 27 and Max Taut's Houses 23 and 24. On the other hand, the lot is large enough to place a type house intended for a more regular space. The compulsion to depart from the type house idea was, objectively speaking, not at all so great as Rading would have had his readers believe.

On this lot, he decided to create

something that would represent a deliverance from the stuffiness and the timorous, inhibited, petit-bourgeois atmosphere of our ordinary housing developments, on which, year after year, thousands and thousands of homes are built that are manifestly out of tune with the way we think and feel today. . . .

If I plan my house entirely at ground level, to avoid pointless journeys up and down stairs, this may perhaps seem reasonable as a general principle. But if I give the laundry and ironing room— the room set aside for domestic chores—a fine view out across the terrace, instead of relegating this "necessary evil" to its usual place in the cellar, then a large proportion of my fellow human beings will take it very much amiss. They fail to reflect that such a room is among the most used in the whole house, and that the housewife or the maid will be grateful to have her often monotonous work cheered by doing it in beautiful surroundings.

I wanted to build a house that would pay heed to people and their natural characteristics; and so all customary measurements have been reassessed and adapted to fit the human individual. Accordingly, the living rooms are so arranged that they can be divided off at will, with wide folding partitions, and convertible from three rooms to one. I cannot help it if one person finds a room too narrow or too wide, another wants the staircase wider. Of course, such things are justified, from the individual point of view; but I have had to keep to the prescribed budget and to postulate average, normal living requirements.

Psychologically, the attitude is that the living rooms are outward-looking. Life faces outward: the occupant does not find himself retreating, in the usual way, into his cave. The bedrooms, on the other hand, are accessible only by walking through the entire house. Here one has the feeling of being protected by the whole fabric of the house (by the distance one has walked); and yet the link with "outside" has not entirely been lost, because from the main bedroom there is direct access to the garden.

The long landing at the top of the stairs serves in conjunction with the sun terrace as a play space for the children. The children remain within earshot of the kitchen, and the space unfolds lengthwise, to give the children somewhere to run. The house is characterized by this same longitudinal emphasis throughout, so that one no longer feels shut in within one's own "four walls," but has a feeling of wide open spaces, as on the promenade deck of a ship. Thus, the living rooms open out through folding doors directly onto the terrace and the garden.

The position of the kitchen is another thing that will be disliked from an old, entrenched standpoint. When the folding doors are opened, so that the whole downstairs space is used as one, the maid can no longer reach the street without passing through the living room. Conversely, no one can go upstairs except by stepping inside the kitchen. Both remain possible, however—as a glance at the plan will show—without disturbance either to home life or to housework. This arrangement might have been avoided by a few minor modifications, but in contemporary circumstances, and in view of the way of life implied by the size and layout of the house, such a sharp division seemed to me unthinkable and incongruous. The routines and the needs of some great household with a position to maintain, or those of a hotel, have no application to middle-class circumstances—whatever people in this country may do for the sake of feeling grand and important.

All in all, the essential thing for me was to loosen up the house and bring it into relation with the garden, and I believe that this was an essential feature of all the houses. Let us hope that our efforts are successful.[3]

Although Rading's design may thus seem to have emerged from the given facts of the situation, its most important aspect—the pursuit of the greatest flexibility and freedom in the use of the space—had been and remained a constant preoccupation of his. This is borne out by statements such as "We must therefore make a plan that leaves every option open,"[4] or

The type, the home . . . must not be something that confines but something that liberates. For mass housing, this would mean arriving at a solution whereby confinement would as far as possible be avoided and a perfect elasticity of plan achieved, so as to adapt to every need. . . . This means . . . the home as liberation, not as confinement; material as a stimulus to evolution, not as oppression![5]

Thus it comes as no surprise to find Rading, along with Mies, using skeleton construction to realize his housing ideas. In 1926 he worked out plans with fixed entrances and "paired" bath and kitchen units, but with partitions that could be omitted or moved in accordance with family size or individual needs to provide a variety of possible plans. Rading said of these proposals, "From the occupier's point of view, totally standardized mass construction does not mean regimentation but the fulfillment of individual housing needs."[6]

It was not out of incompetence that Rading left the floor plan to develop freely; nor was it any lack of feel-

ing for the practical requirements of housekeeping that led him to put the laundry upstairs. He wanted to embark on new, and liberating, paths; to create the best possible working conditions for the maid, or for a housewife with children, running a house on her own. His design was an invitation to the occupants to try out new forms of living and household economy, to break free of old paths and ways of thinking, to rethink the idea of the home in itself. To this end, the traditional order of things seemed to have been stood on its head. The maid's room, "painted lemon yellow,"[7] the laundry, and the children's playroom, all faced directly onto a terrace with a distant view—as if to say: Look at that, and why not?

Rading took a skeptical view of ingrained habits and well-established patterns. He wrote in *Die Form* in 1927,

I have the impression that we have now, fortunately, reached the stage where there is no longer any point in asking the occupants anything. They no longer know what their needs are. Over the generations, they have become fatalists. They no longer have an opinion; they no longer trouble to think about what their needs might be. There would be no point. When they rent a home, their minds are monopolized by just one thought: How shall we fit our furniture in? (The Home as Furniture Depository.)[8]

Whether the visitors to the 1927 exhibition, or the critics, appreciated Rading's endeavors to free the home from the accumulated ballast of centuries remains a question. Wedepohl told the readers of *Wasmuth's Monatshefte*,

The Rading house is interesting by virtue of its un-

House 25:
Views from the east and from the west (along Am Weissenhof, with Oud's houses, Behrens's apartments, and Karl Beer's Schönblick tower restaurant)

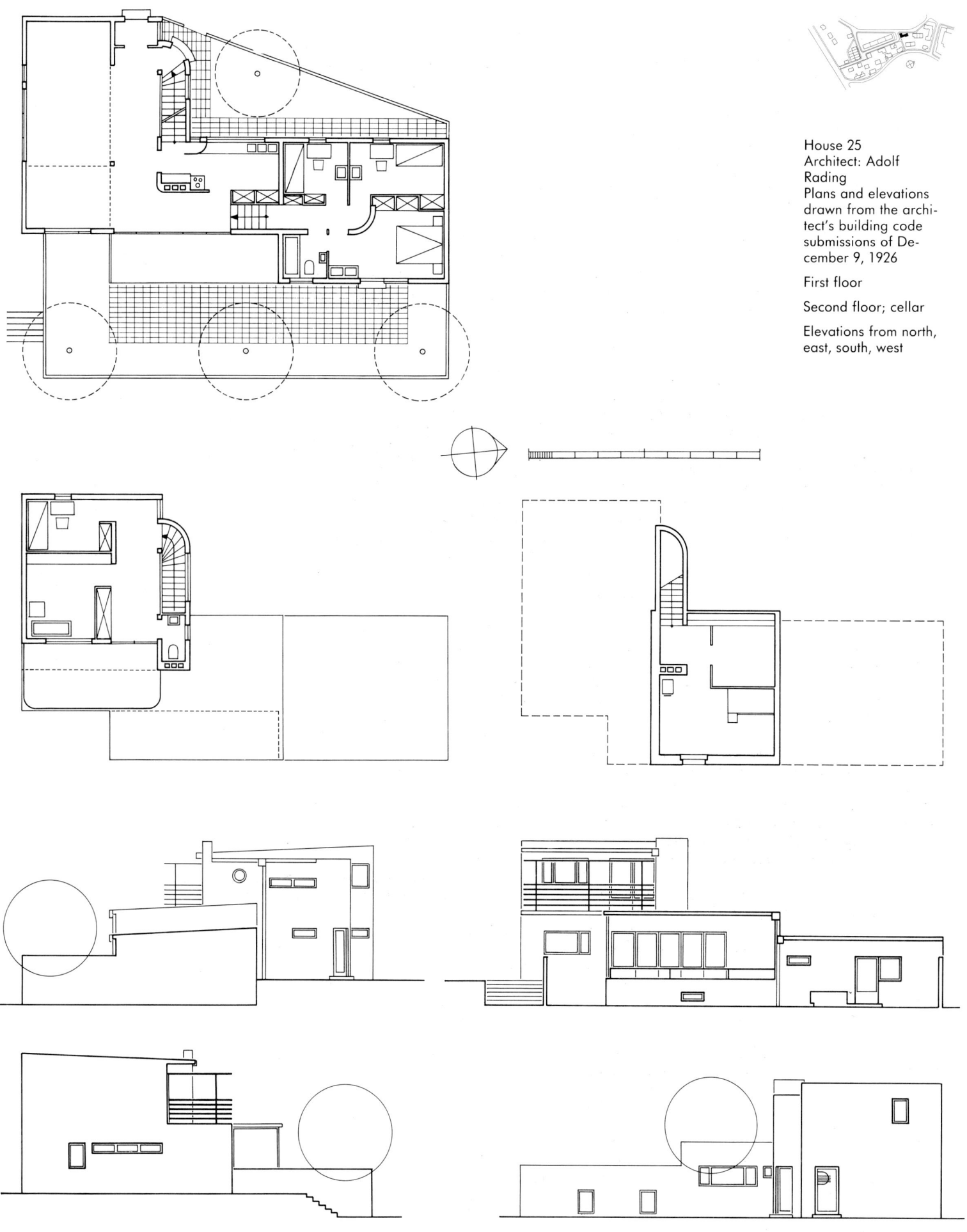

House 25
Architect: Adolf
Rading
Plans and elevations
drawn from the archi-
tect's building code
submissions of De-
cember 9, 1926

First floor

Second floor; cellar

Elevations from north,
east, south, west

usual relationship between living and transit areas. It almost seems as though the whole house has been designed for the sake of the hall which is produced by sliding back the doors of the living rooms. The direct approach to the kitchen is not the shortest, but even an unathletic person can step from the street into the bedroom through the window.[9]

But the editor of *Der Baumeister*, Rudolf Pfister, considered Rading's design "inept" and "amateurish."[10]

The folding doors allowed the use of the living area to vary according to the season: in summer the house opened out toward the garden and in winter it shut itself off. At any season one could retreat into the bedrooms or keep house, undisturbed, in the housekeeping area.

Apart from the built-in closets the house was furnished with "ready-made" furniture. Only the light fitments were designed by Rading. The sliding and folding screens were described as working well, and the access to the garden was praised as more successfully managed than in any other house on the Weissenhofsiedlung.[11]

One particularly eye-catching feature must have been the plumbing pipes, which were on the surface, above the plaster. This was not necessarily part of Rading's intention, but may be traced back to a building code requirement that no utilities were to be incorporated in walls less than 38 cm [15 inches] thick. Rading made a virtue out of necessity, as Wedepohl described it:

The utilities, in almost all the houses, are on the surface of the walls. But the electric wiring, in Rading's case, is carried through the rooms in a positively ornamental fashion on wooden brackets about 4 cm [1½in] clear of the wall. Wiring that stands out in this way, rather like varicose veins, certainly does not make the house any simpler to keep clean; and the question is whether the obtrusive coloring of the gas, water, and heating pipes actually does anything to make the house more like a home.[12]

Schwitters, inimitably, poked fun:

Interestingly, Rading has built his entire house for the sake of the electrical wiring. But then the wiring really does look terrific. It is mounted throughout on tiny pieces of wood which stand 5 cm or so clear of the ceilings and walls. This looks impeccable. I hope the idea will catch on; then we shall soon have in our own houses those beautiful overhead wires that so pleasantly adorn the urban scene.[13]

The building of Rading's house was not attended by any particular difficulties: the contract was placed on March 5, 1927, and there was a slight delay at one stage because of a shortage of Thermos wall panels, which affected other houses as well. The house was easily ready for opening day, and Rading's only cause for complaint was the delay in paying his fee.[14] Döcker's final account shows a total net cost of 24,557.60 marks, only 557.60 marks above the contract price.

Adolf Rading, one of the forgotten architects of Weissenhof, left Germany in 1933, in protest at the advent of the Nazis.[15] He never lived there again, and his house no longer stands. A member of the Novembergruppe, of Der Ring, and of the Deutscher Werkbund,

Rading wrote articles for *Die Form* and other magazines, was an associate of Peter Behrens and of August Endell, and taught at the Akademie für Kunst und Kunstgewerbe in Breslau. He invited Hans Scharoun to Breslau, and shared an office with him in Berlin from 1927 through 1933.[16] Scharoun was to write, in the catalogue of an exhibition of Rading's work:

Adolf Rading's intuition and intelligence always had an animating and clarifying effect on the practice and theory of building. His concern was with the relation between function and design: with translating into spatial and technical terms the insights that life had given him. Rading's design was marked by the intensity with which he could absorb and make use of ambient conditions and relationships, and by his openness to things, to people, and to decisive change. He, and his works, were by nature receptive.[17]

What emerges from Rading's Stuttgart contribution, above all, is its human scale, and its love of humanity—not excluding the maid of all work.

In *Bau und Wohnung* the description of his house was printed under the heading "Slow Motion" in tiny type, so that it was almost lost to view. What mattered much more to him was this:

If you put no trust in life, then life will put no trust

House 25:
Two views of living room by Adolf Rading

in you. That is why you hate to live in your cities; that is why no subtle refinement of housing law is going to give you any joy in your homes. Let us toss this whole mess of stupid inhibitions right overboard; let us have no fear of hardness and ugliness, if they can give us, in place of dismal compromises, life in all its fullness and color.

Human beings are neither villains nor children.

Only irredeemable stupidity and arrogance could seek to keep them in a state of tutelage. In all modesty, let us recognize that the attempt to play Providence has failed. A sin against humanity: mere impotent goodwill and the wish to help.

Let us recognize that we must give humanity its due, treat responsibility as a birthright, and let it grow.[18]

Josef Frank

HOUSES 26, 27

Design: Professor Dr. Josef Frank, architect
Vienna IV, Wiedener Hauptstrasse 64

Two-family house: cellar, first floor, second floor.
Construction: solid masonry, without timbers. Feifel
building blocks, plastered inside and out. Stephan
floors, doors, and iron doorframes. Sliding sash windows.

HOUSE 26: ELECTRIC HOUSE

Paired unit: first floor, second floor.
Interior design: Professor Dr. Josef Frank, architect, Vienna.
The accommodation comprises:
Cellar: furnace, laundry, store room.
First floor: large living room leading to open-air seating
area, kitchen, maid's room, pantry, hallway to stairs,
toilet.
Second floor: two large bedrooms and one small bedroom with large closets, balcony outside bedrooms,
bathroom. Built-in closets.

HOUSE 27: GAS HOUSE

Paired unit: first floor, second floor.
Interior design: Professor Dr. Josef Frank, architect, Vienna.
The accommodation comprises:
Cellar: furnace, laundry, store room.
First floor: large living room leading to open-air seating
area, kitchen, maid's room, pantry, hallway to stairs,
toilet.
Second floor: two large bedrooms and one small bedroom with large closets, balcony outside bedrooms,
bathroom. Built-in closets.[1]

Josef Frank had been chosen by Mies to devise an example of a two-family house for families with children
and—as was customary, and as expected—each with
a housemaid. In the context of building operations at
Weissenhof, Frank turned out to be something of a paragon, a bright spot on the often troubled horizon of
Döcker and his staff. Without difficulty and without
complaint, his plans were ready, complete, and right on
time. The contractors did not complain about unorthodox building methods, and completion by opening day
was never in any doubt.
    On February 25, 1927, the contracts were placed for
his two units of Type D: each a two-story single-family
dwelling with five rooms (actually six), kitchen, servant's
room, and three bedrooms, for an all-in price of 19,340

1 Amtlicher Katalog,
S. 64.

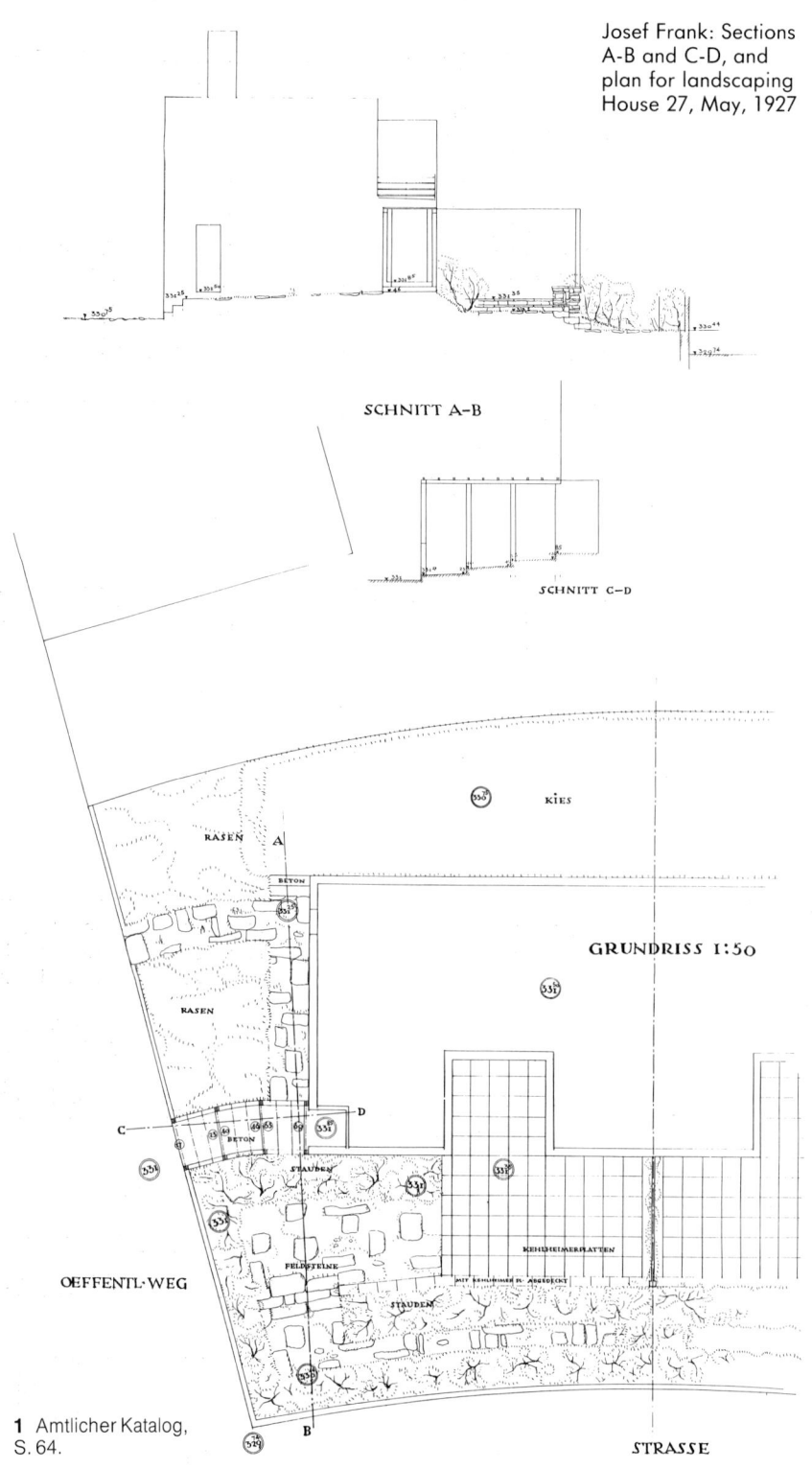

Josef Frank: Sections
A-B and C-D, and
plan for landscaping
House 27, May, 1927

SCHNITT A–B

SCHNITT C–D

GRUNDRISS 1:50

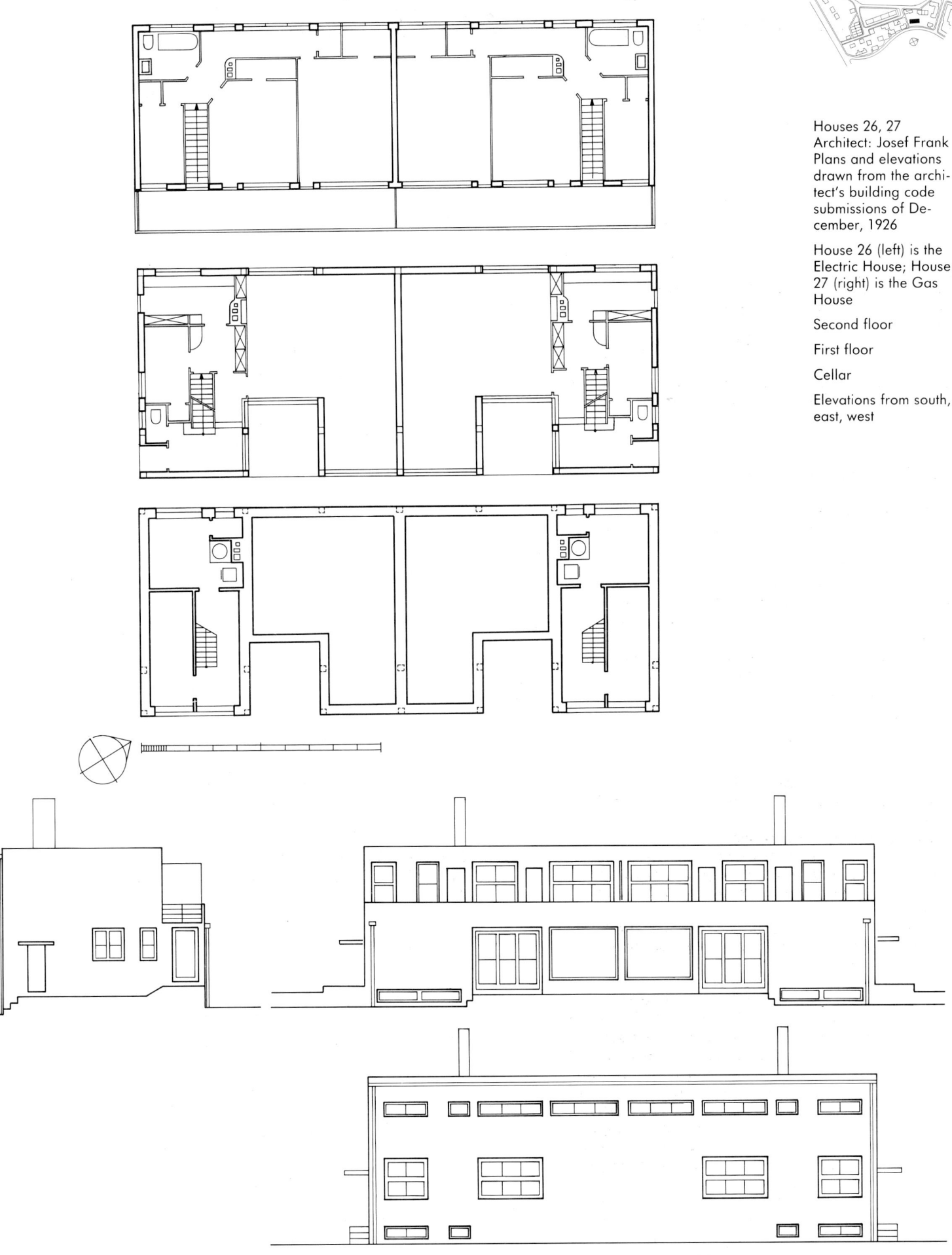

Houses 26, 27
Architect: Josef Frank
Plans and elevations
drawn from the archi-
tect's building code
submissions of De-
cember, 1926

House 26 (left) is the
Electric House; House
27 (right) is the Gas
House

Second floor

First floor

Cellar

Elevations from south,
east, west

marks. They were initially scheduled to be built in an iron frame construction system with masonry panel walls, but in the course of January and February of 1927 this was changed to a solid masonry construction with Feifel blocks, plastered inside and out. From the issue of the contract to the opening of the exhibition on July 23, 1927, five months elapsed. The building cost rose to 19,611 marks per house.[2]

On opening day, one of the pair, the Electric House, was fully furnished with furniture by the Vienna firm of Haus und Garten, run by Oskar Wlach since 1925. Visitors were not able to see the Gas House in a furnished state until August 19 when a loan from the Württemberg craft office, the Landesgewerbeamt, paid for more furnishings from local makers.[3]

Frank's units were regarded—by comparison with the other houses—as moderate and acceptable. Werner Hegemann even said that he had "placed an almost exclusive emphasis on . . . so designing his rooms that they might be thought of as suitable environment for a lady of breeding." Such a phrase would have been resented as a deadly insult by what Hegemann called

the so-called Red Press Agency, the mouthpiece of the architectural clique which had its say in Stuttgart to the exclusion of all others. . . . And indeed, most of what we see in Modernist architectural creations does not seem to be created for women of sensibility and education but for the figures in a Dr. Caligari fantasy film, or for the female inmates of a literary coffeehouse.[4]

Where Le Corbusier shocked the world, Frank imparted a touch of well-bred elegance and subtle irony. Where Gropius defiantly came out with furnishings by Marcel Breuer, Frank wooed the eye with subtle colors and deployed a Viennese charm with a hint of a sting in the tail. Off-white outside was relieved within by vast quantities of many colored, subtly patterned cushions[5] and textiles to create an atmosphere of urbane comfort, even elegance. Graeff remembered the Frank dwellings as furnished in an "almost provocatively old-fashioned way,"[6] partly with furnishings designed by Frank himself and partly with "ready-made" pieces. All were in wood, with an aura of Liberty, Windsor, Tutankhamen, and Scandinavian restraint. Oud's Weissenhof resident, the sharp-tongued Paul Meller, even referred in one letter to "Frank's brothel."[7]

The interiors may have been "provocatively conservative," but that made the energy concept all the more spectacular. It was not without reason that the completion and furnishing of the Electric House was given priority: a fully electric house was an absolutely new idea in Stuttgart, which had been electrified only since 1924.

In the Electric House, all the equipment and heating were powered by electricity, just as in the Gas House everything ran on gas. The installation was done by, and at the expense of, the city's electric power utility. The running cost of the electric storage heaters was 24 to 40 pfennigs an hour at the night rate; the gas consumption was so high that the costs amounted to twice those entailed in using solid fuels. The areas of glass in the terrace and living room area tended to promote heat loss.[8]

In Frank's Stuttgart design he was able to realize—although partly in hints—his conception of an ideal house. The floor plans are an expression of his idea of the "House as Way and as Place." The occupants are able to make their way to the bedrooms, the kitchen, the cellar, or the yard without disturbing any of the activities taking place in the home. The servant has a part to play in the public and official life of the household at ground level, but not in the private sphere of the upper

House 26 or 27, second floor under construction

Houses 26 and 27 from Rathenaustrasse, 1927

Houses 26 and 27 from public footpath, 1927

floor. A bathroom with access from the landing also serves to minimize disturbance to the members of the family.

Frank attached great importance to clarity, so that the layout of a house would be evident, as it were, from the front door; this is apparent in the clear demarcation between rest zones and transit zones within the living area, in the clarity of interior and exterior layout, and in the easy transition to the natural environment. His landscaping design, not executed in 1927, clearly shows the practical application of his principle of shaping the transitions between house and nature unobtrusively but unmistakably: "The paving and the planting will be regular, and the door lies in a recess which prepares for entry while one is still standing outside."[9]

Nothing in this method of planning seems to be left to arbitrary decisions. To Frank, horizontal windows are natural "because we live in a horizontal world, and our eyes are alongside each other and not one above the other."[10] The light admitted is intended to be directional rather than evenly diffused.

It would not be difficult to find a justification in Frank's voluminous writings for every single design decision. But most importantly, while everything is well thought out and carefully considered, "it must all be taken for granted and not shown off, so that the intention is not made too obvious; otherwise the house easily becomes theatrical."[11]

This is a Soft Modernism, marked by lucidity and a deliberate choice of the "objective" path. A slight penthouse roof masked by side parapets, when the flat roof seems problematic; no steel furniture to alarm the bourgeoisie; but a critical awareness of "Fancy Dress [Loos's *Gschnas*] for the Feelings, and Fancy Dress as a Problem," the title of Frank's chapter in *Bau und Wohnung*. Frank furnished his houses in wood, while musing that "the God who planted iron intended no wooden furniture."[12] Looking at steel furniture by Breuer, he reflected that "steel is not a material but a world-view." His verdict on all the efforts to rationalize and standardize—including his own—was this: "Everyone standardizes, and everyone does it differently."[13]

Frank's experiences in Stuttgart and his provocative assertion that "every human being has his own specific quota of sentimentality, which he must gratify"[14] led him into some brisk controversy. The question "What is modern?" which he posed at the Werkbund convention in Vienna in 1930 revived an old Werkbund quarrel.[15] Frank proclaimed:

Anything that can be used, can be used. Anything that becomes unusable eliminates itself. You cannot ride in Achilles' chariot today, any more than you can in Napoleon's carriage; but you can sit on their decorated armchairs. And who is more modern in his thinking: he who accepts these things as they are, or he who perpetuates what is transient in them, by modernizing it?[16]

Josef Frank's two-family house has survived the destruction of World War II and the far worse havoc of the postwar period, and has been restored externally to its 1927 condition. The people who live in Houses 26 and 27 feel good in them.

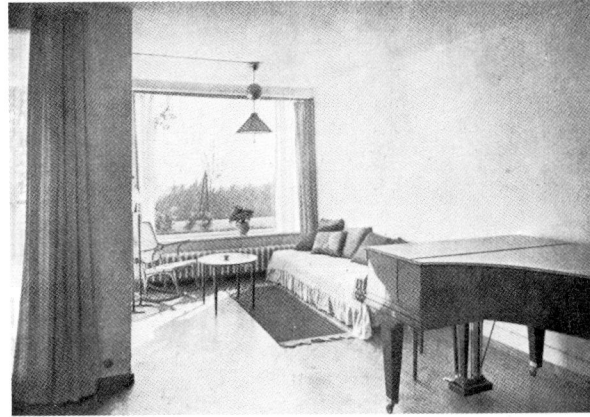

Two views of the living room of House 26 (the Electric House), with furniture by Josef Frank and Oskar Wlach for Haus und Garten, Vienna

Bedroom of House 26 (the Electric House), with furniture by Haus und Garten, Vienna

Living room of House 27 (the Gas House), with off-the-peg furniture

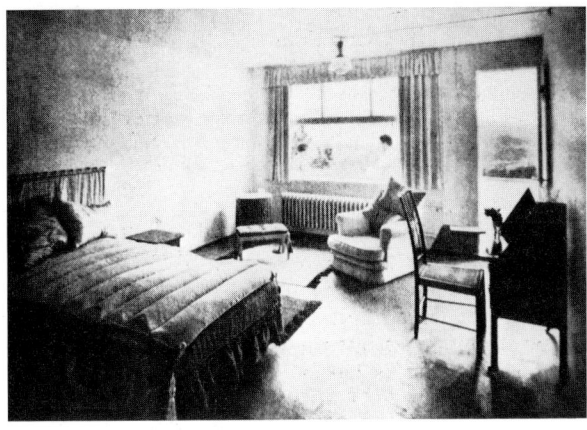

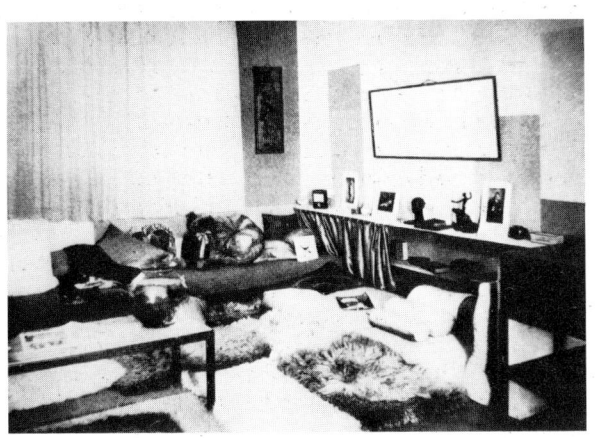

Mart Stam

HOUSES 28, 29, 30
Design: Mart Stam, architect, Rotterdam
Rotterdam, Maarland 17 Vreewijk

3 single-family houses: cellar, first floor, second floor.
Construction: steel-reinforced frame with hollow concrete blocks, reinforced concrete upper floors, plastered inside and out, built-in closets, iron window frames.

HOUSE 28

Interior design: Mart Stam, architect, Rotterdam.
The accommodation comprises:
Cellar: warm air heating plant, cellar, coal store, laundry, store room.
First floor: two interconnecting living rooms, kitchen, toilet, terrace.
Second floor: two bedrooms with terrace, maid's room, toilet, bathroom, spiral stair to yard.

HOUSE 29

Interior design: Mart Stam, architect, Rotterdam.
The accommodation comprises:
Cellar: warm air heating plant, cellar, coal store, store room, laundry.
First floor: large living room leading down to basement study. Small living room, kitchen, toilet.
Second floor: two bedrooms with terrace, maid's room, bathroom, toilet.

HOUSE 30

Interior design: Marcel Breuer, Dessau.
The accommodation comprises:
Cellar: warm air heating plant, coal store, store room, laundry.
First floor: large living room leading down to basement study. Small living room, kitchen, toilet.
Second floor: two bedrooms with terrace, maid's room, bathroom, toilet.[1]

"The goal for a new generation is to achieve in every field, through its own thought, a more independent and artistically wide-reaching view."[2] This programmatic statement forms part of the introduction to *ABC—Beiträge zum Bauen,* a periodical published by a group of young architects at Thalwil, near Zürich, from 1924 onward. One of these young architects was Mart Stam; others included Hans Schmidt, Paul Artaria, and Hans Wittwer (four members of the Schweizer Werkbund collective which designed the interiors of Mies's House 4); El Lissitzky, who had previously worked on *G—Zeitschrift für elementares Gestalten;* and Hannes Meyer,

who was to be Gropius's successor as director of the Dessau Bauhaus. They proclaimed that

ABC demands the dictatorship of the machine . . .

Why	Why
Austrian	French
French	Dutch
German	Hungarian
Swiss	English
express train cars? . . .	houses?[3]

With this magazine—the problems it raised, the solutions it offered, and the examples it presented—the group soon made a place for itself in the international debate concerning new paths for architecture. They showed themselves to be pioneers and soulmates of those in modern architecture who sought to replace

(1) the handcrafted by the mechanical,
(2) the capricious, the individual, by the collective, the standardized,
(3) the fortuitous by the precise.[4]

In 1924 and 1925 *ABC* printed pictures of "the steel skeleton of a skyscraper in Baltimore"; Le Corbusier's Dom-Ino system; examples of Russia's new architecture; Mies van der Rohe's glass skyscraper and his reinforced concrete office building (with detail drawings by Mart Stam); and designs by Stam for a "business and residential building, [and] a counter-proposal to the competition for the railroad station in Geneva—the latter with a recommendation addressed to art critics that they should follow the example of putting forward constructive counter-proposals."[5]

All these projects remained on paper. But, even unexecuted, they were a vital contribution to the debate on the New Architecture. Stam published works of his own and worked as an assistant in others' offices. During the period which led up to the 1927 Werkbund exhibition he was working for J. A. Brinkman and L. C. van der Vlugt in Rotterdam; he had previously worked for Max Taut and Hans Poelzig in Berlin and for Karl Moser in Zürich. He was in touch with Gropius and the Bauhaus, with the Novembergruppe, with De Stijl, and with the periodical *i 10,* produced in Amsterdam, to which Oud contributed.

So it comes as no surprise to find Mies, with exquisite courtesy, writing to his younger colleague on November 5, 1926, to invite him to work on the Weissenhof project: "In this exhibition, modern architects must show what they mean by building and by homes. Above all things, the function of the home is central to the work. Of course, we also want to apply new building techniques, as far as possible."[6]

Mies went on to say that he had it in mind that Stam might be responsible for a group of three single-family houses. He stressed the point by listing the architects

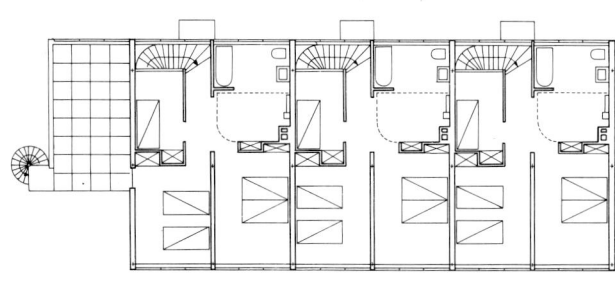

Houses 28, 29, 30
Architect: Mart Stam
Plans and elevations drawn from the architect's building code submissions (undated)

The panel joints visible on the elevations suggest that the house was originally intended to be built from prefabricated wall panels

Second floor

First floor

Basement (with exit to back yard)

Elevations from north, east, south, west

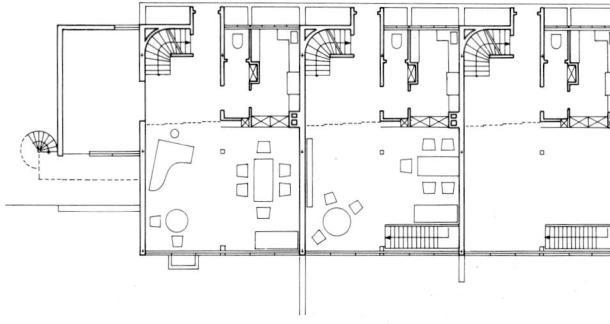

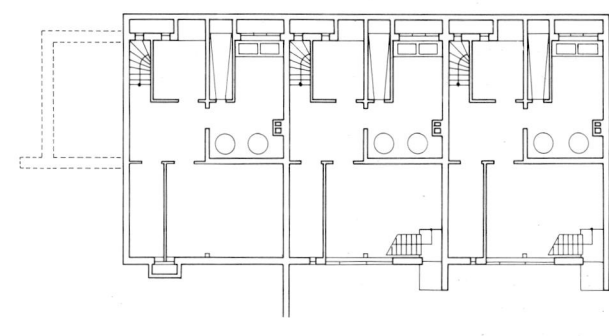

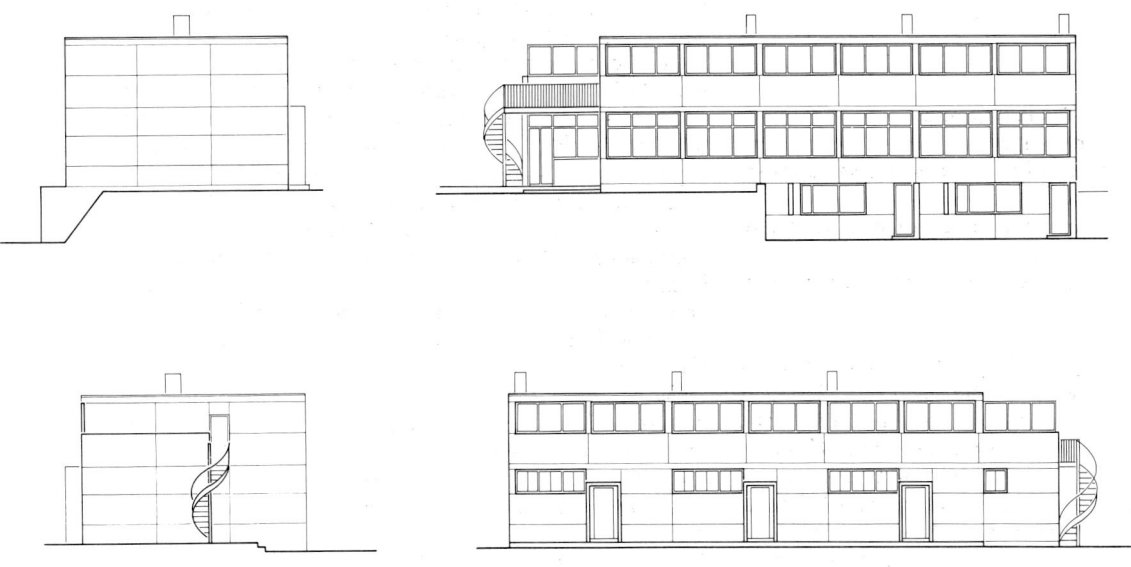

who had already agreed to take part, omitting only Schneck (and Bourgeois, who had not yet been invited).

Rightly, Stam regarded the invitation as a great honor, and in his letter of acceptance he wrote, "I particularly value both the manner of the invitation and the way in which different talents have been brought together."[7] His question concerning the purpose for which the houses were to be built—"Is the intention to build housing for workers or houses for the middle class?"—received no answer in writing from Mies. An article of Stam's in *i 10* reveals, however, that he understood his houses to be for middle-class occupation, but to be run without a maid; the housewife would be able to run them with the equipment provided, and with the help of a daily cleaner. Mies sent to Stam—as he did to all the other Weissenhof architects—the guidelines prepared by Erna Meyer and the Stuttgart housewives' organization for the design of the kitchen and domestic area, with a note saying "to be followed as you think fit."[8]

Having mentioned that the unified appearance of the district should be underlined by the use of flat roofs, Mies found it necessary to draw Stam's attention once more to the overriding purpose of the exhibition:

> In yesterday's letter I omitted to tell you that the main concern, in the Stuttgart project, is to explore the problem of the home. The function of the home as a place to live in, and its economic management,[9] are central to all our efforts. In addition, new building techniques are to be used; this does not mean that we are to engage in pure experimentation, which the city of Stuttgart does not want. We do, however, consider that new techniques should be applied where possible—although only where we are convinced that they are practicable. Pure experiment should be avoided as far as possible, as these houses are regarded as permanent buildings.[10]

Soon after this, on November 21 and 22, Mies and Stam met in Stuttgart in that memorable encounter at the Hotel Marquardt and at Weissenhof which drew much of its luster from the presence of Le Corbusier.

Heinz Rasch, who wrote the meeting up for the *Stuttgarter Neues Tagblatt*, told how he had been present when Stam, "on the back of Willi Baumeister's wedding announcement" (Baumeister had been married on November 20[11]), drew the profile of his cantilever chair ("chair with no back legs") and it was decided to include a number of the chairs in the exhibition.[12]

Stam's place in Weissenhof's demonstration of the New Architecture had been assured throughout the selection process, apart from a short period in the summer of 1926. It is not known when he sent in his drawings; but early in 1927 there was strong criticism of his work, mainly directed at the design of the staircase and at the fact that there was an upstairs room with no natural light. Döcker wrote to Mies in February,

> On the basis of the discussion with Dr. Erna Meyer, I have written to Herr Stam that there is a likelihood that his design will not be accepted because of the small bedroom with no direct light, and that he should now send me proposals for changes. In his letter of January 15, he positively refuses to make any change. I take note of his letter and shall let matters take their course. Perhaps you as exhibition director would like to intervene, if you consider it necessary . . .
>
> For the rest, I take it that the designs have your

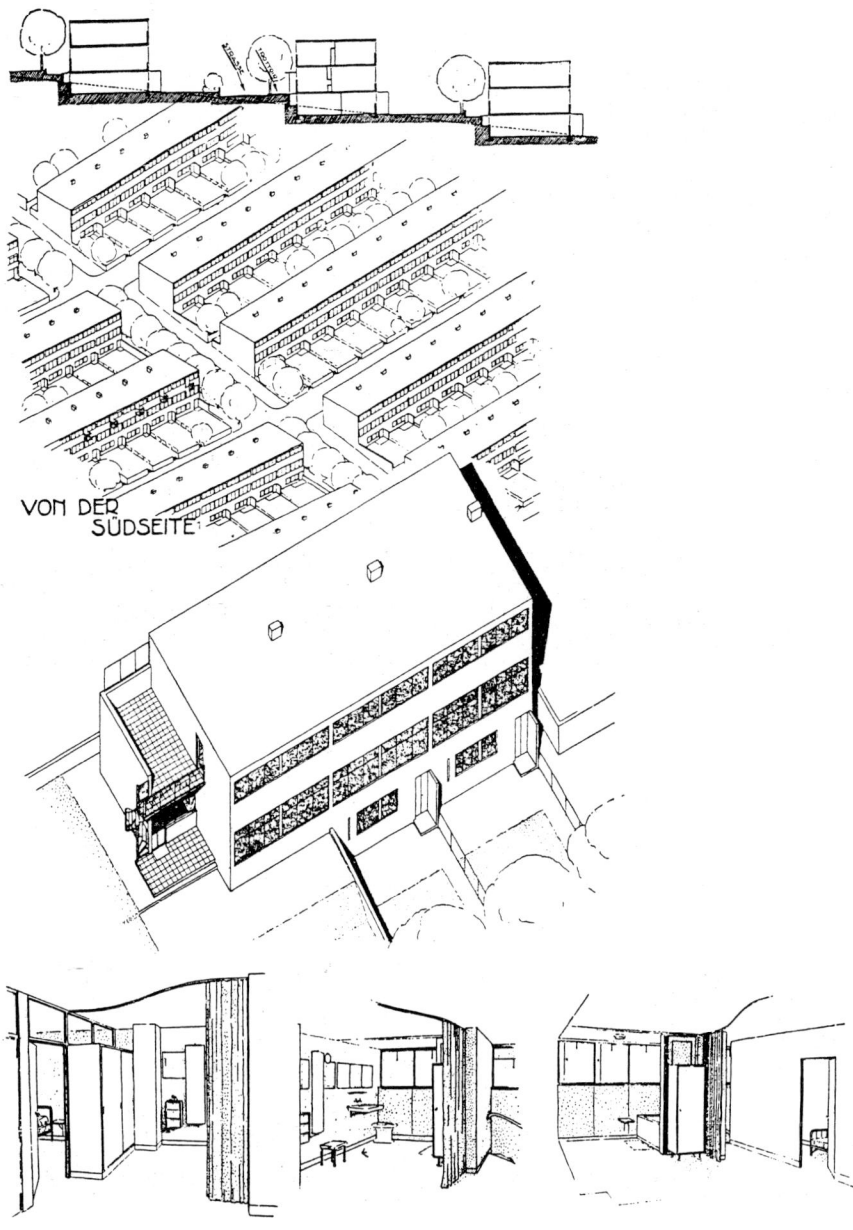

VON DER SÜDSEITE

approval as exhibition director. I should like to avoid future recriminations on the topic, which is why I am putting this in writing. Every architect of course bears, together with yourself, the responsibility for whatever he causes to be built.[13]

Mies, who is described by those who knew him as rather lethargic by nature—he avoided public criticism and disregarded his fellow architects' errors, however blatant—does not seem to have written to call Stam to order.

In an article for *i 10* Stam set out his ideas with express reference to the dubious value of any types that were not the product of a process of modification and correction:

> In the Weissenhofsiedlung in Stuttgart, dwellings have been built which, although they were originally intended to be types, have only partly turned out to be so. The three houses built by me were done . . . in full awareness, on the one hand, that the German way of life should be taken into account—the custom of doing laundry inside the house, that of making preserves, and that of lay-

Mart Stam: section and isometric view of row housing; isometric view and interiors of Houses 28, 29, 30

Houses 28, 29, 30 under construction; this picture is captioned in *Bau und Wohnung* as if Stam's intention, "an iron skeleton system with breeze block infilling," had been carried out. It also refers to the "warm-air heating on an American system."

Houses 28, 29, 30 from the south

House 28: Spiral stair

Right to left: Houses 28, 29, 30 from Am Weissenhof

ing by a store of provisions for the winter—but also in the full knowledge that this is the kind of chore that cannot be done economically except by large commercial undertakings. The Weissenhofsiedlung represents the beginning of a process whereby an ultimate perfect type—like the bicycle, for instance—is worked out through the interaction of design with daily use.

I deliberately set out from the start to use a series of evenly spaced supports, and a skeleton assembled in the simplest possible way from profiles on a single, unbroken underfloor (or foundation) constructed from prefabricated pumice-concrete beams.

The external walls are designed as solid masonry walls of pumice concrete blocks covered with a thin outer skin. This principle would—given good planning—make possible a very rapid and economical construction process for the building of a large number of identical housing units. Such a simple constructional system, with regularly spaced supports, can also make it simpler to add to the structure. For reasons of economy, the structures were designed as compact rather than articulated masses, because the latter would in

every case require more external walls which would entail much extra cost. . . .

On the first floor, along with the necessary cloakroom and toilet, there is a small, manageable kitchen and a large living room. This room is unmistakably the largest in the house and leads directly to the stairs (a sliding partition makes it possible to introduce a separation). In two of the three houses it also leads to a study and garden room located at a lower level.

On the upper floor there are three bedrooms and a bathroom which also serves as a dressing room.[14]

It was a particular concern of Stam's to simplify housekeeping and to abolish the outdated, laborious working habits of women:

The family will have to give up doing its own laundry, because this is an exhausting task and prevents the housewife from giving her attention to her husband and children and from taking an interest in any but day-to-day concerns. . . . The housework must be reduced, which means that the number of dust-traps, rooms, and items of fur-

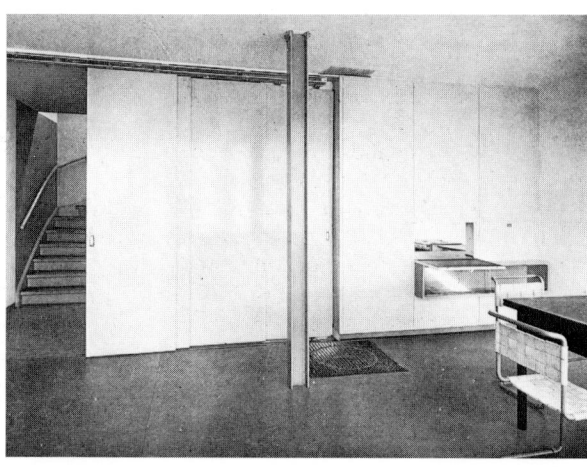

niture must be reduced. The home is designed to be as simple as possible, and to make help unnecessary. All those jobs that need not be done separately in every household, but can be done collectively in an establishment shared by several families, must disappear from the home. Nowadays, we do not all bake our own bread. In fifty years' time we shall no longer wash clothes, bake apple pies, make noodles, or bottle vegetables and fruit for the winter. We shall no longer do it, for the simple reason that it will be highly uneconomic. . . . [15]

In his essay "Away with Furniture Artists" published in the Werkbund book of Weissenhof interiors, *Innenräume*, Stam was even more unequivocal:

The more simply and rapidly [the modern, creative human being] can dispatch the work necessary to support life, the better he likes it. He wants no store cellar in the house (a relic of the medieval castle), because the circulation of goods permits central warehousing; no laundry, because machines can take over the washing and drying and do more work in less time. What if it does ruin the clothes! Sooner ruin the clothes than the housewife. [16]

Stam saw the vital task of the age as that of devising a type of minimal housing which took account of "modern ways of life" and not of "existing habits." He asserted that "the creation of the minimal home is an undertaking that would have been of great value for the Werkbund exhibition in Stuttgart,"[17] while remaining well aware—as he told the readers of *i 10*—that those responsible had had no intention of creating anything of the sort.

The translation of Stam's constructional ideas into reality seems to have been no easy matter. Mies wrote him in April,

On a visit to Zürich, I met with your friend Meier, from Basel, to whom I explained the difficulties that have emerged in Stuttgart in executing the building system chosen by you. Herr Meier undertook to report to you, and to put to you suggestions for changes. I fail to understand why this has not happened. I am sorry that you, too, have had occasion to note that in Stuttgart there is a lack of the necessary commitment to the intentions of the individual architects. [18]

There seem to have been further contacts between Mies and Stam, because Mies wrote to Döcker "that Stam is forcefully complaining that constructional changes have been made without his knowledge and without reference to him."[19]

What had happened? Döcker remarked in his Circular No. 14 that "building according to the specifications of Herr Stam would cost approximately 70,000 marks," and that he, Döcker, had contrived, "without prejudice to the fittings, or the appearance, and without altering the idea of the design, simply by using another working method, to reduce the building cost to 57,000 marks, because I should never have obtained consent to spend 70,000 marks. What is more," added the by now thoroughly exasperated architect in charge, "in the present situation I have to have a free hand to make changes of this kind."[20]

In a costing drawn up by City Hall on December 22, 1926, in which the construction systems used in almost all the houses are detailed, none is specified for Stam's houses. There is only a projected cost per house of 16,500 marks, totaling 49,500 marks, and the indication that the houses are to be of Type D.

The Rasch brothers' Weissenhof book, *Wie bauen?*,[21] affords more detail:

Building by the architect Mart Stam, Rotterdam. The building was planned as an iron frame construction . . . but for local reasons was built as a masonry construction in hollow pumice concrete blocks. . . . The result testifies to the compressive strength of the porous block. Four thin cross walls carry the upper floor. And these cross walls provide perfect insulation against noise from the next-door house. [22]

Even though, as Döcker emphasized, nothing of the basic conception was lost, to switch from skeleton construction to masonry construction represents an entirely inadmissable interference with the architect's design. Absurdly, the *Bau und Wohnung* book shows the houses under construction as an unmistakable masonry structure with an explanatory caption which tells us that "the construction takes the form of an iron skeleton system with breeze block infilling. This makes construction extremely rapid."[23]

The official catalogue refers to "iron mesh reinforcement with hollow concrete blocks," and the plan submitted to the building office over Stam's signature on March 22, 1927 has "reinforced concrete supports [not a steel skeleton], with breeze blocks between." According to these plans the floors were to have been cast in reinforced concrete, but in fact "flooring in reinforced concrete hollow members by the Spörle Company" was used.

The only publication, therefore, in which the construction of the houses is accurately described is the Rasch brothers' book *Wie bauen?* It may be that the exhibition authorities were trying to make amends by doctoring their texts to reflect Stam's original intentions.

Not only was the construction system changed, but also the planning context of the houses. In Oud's houses the idea of row housing is at least suggested by the path which runs along the garden side of the houses; in the case of Stam's houses this is completely missing. As Stam's drawing of a neighborhood of the houses shows, they ought to have been accessible, like Oud's, from two sides, which would of course have entailed a change in the status of the combined study and garden room into a true garden room.

Inside, the room with no external walls, described by Stam in *i 10* as a child's bedroom, remained a problem. Incomprehensibly, he did not eliminate this design fault by moving the staircase to the center of the house: perhaps he felt he was getting too close to Oud. As this room was universally regarded as the maid's room, the general condemnation of it involved—and involves to this day—an element of social criticism.

The interior design of Houses 28 and 29 was by Stam himself; that of House 30 was by Marcel Breuer. Stam's interiors exuded cool clarity. Paul Meller, Oud's resident architect, opined that only a compact car would feel comfortable in them.[24] Stam furnished House 28 with items of his own design and House 29 with "ready-made." And so House 28 contained those exciting chairs with no back legs, while House 29 had bentwood chairs by Thonet. In both Stam used chairs and sofas covered with black plush and a startling profusion of cushions—almost as many as in Josef Frank's houses. The upholstered chairs are interesting: a extremely simple mechanism increases the angle between seat and back for a more relaxed posture. The bedrooms were equipped with Dutch hospital beds, not very different from German ones, and simple chairs by Thonet of Berlin.

The real sensation in Stam's houses was largely ignored by the press: his chairs, which—as chairs go—are the invention of the century. When Stam made his first sketch in the Hotel Marquardt in 1926 and thus inspired Mies to his "further development" of the idea, he had been thinking about a reduction in the number of legs on a chair since 1921 or 1922. It irritated him that the chair, by virtue of its quadrupedal form, formed an unwanted cube within the space of the room without supporting anything but a surface to sit on. Stam was increasingly perturbed by the way in which the mass of this particular form of furniture competed with the lines of the ambient walls, subtracted from the external shape, and interfered with "the transparency of the unbounded horizontals and verticals: the universal, uninterrupted flow." This was a central theme within Stam's architectural and artistic work: the longing to eliminate, as far as possible, "gravity, volume, matter, and opacity."

Stam made his first chair out of the scrap tubing that people used to beg from the gas company to use on their private vegetable plots. One of the vegetable growers helped him to solder the bends. The chairs shown in Stuttgart in 1927 were made by the Arnold company of Schorndorf, specialists in metal furniture. According to Stam, the people at Arnold regarded his new design as a joke and felt confirmed in their view when the first model collapsed under the firm's boss,

Armchair by Mart Stam with adjustable seat and back. Modern replica by Tecta, Lauenförde

Study of House 28, with cantilever chairs by Mart Stam

Study of House 29, with steel stairs leading up to first floor

173

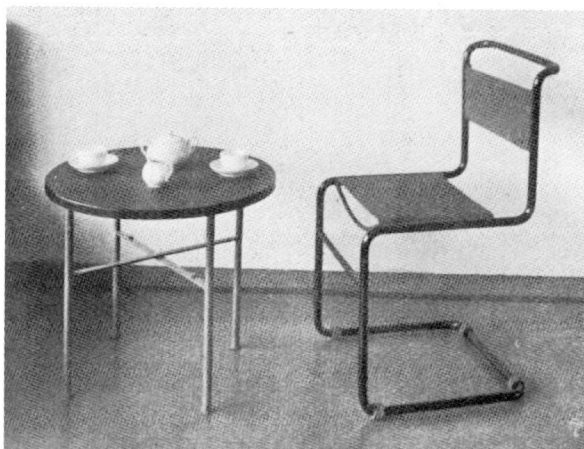

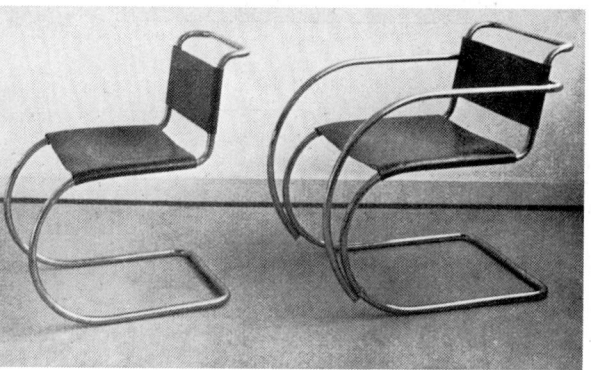

Cantilever armchair
by Mart Stam

Table and cantilever
chair by Mart Stam

Cantilever chairs by
Mies van der Rohe:
the *Freischwinger*

who, unsurprisingly, made a show of dropping with all his considerable weight onto the "controversial little chair."

The foreman at Arnold's later said that Stam had wanted a "rigid chair" and had been concerned to obtain "the thinnest tube with the smallest radius."[25] The chairs for Weissenhof were actually made from steel rod; later production runs were made from tubing.

In their absolutely minimal form Stam's cantilever chairs illustrate better than anything else the altruistic, socially conscious attitude of Stam; objects—like architecture—in the human environment should be as restrained, simple, transparent, and serviceable as possible: disciplined, deliberate, controlled, but not—as some interpret it—rigid.[26] Heinz Rasch commented that

> the Viennese [Thonet] chair, which belonged to the age of bicycles and electric lamps, was followed in the age of radio and airplanes by the cantilever chair, which is now known as the *Freischwinger*. And so Stam, the inventor, and Mies, one of those who perfected the idea, deserved credit for having enriched the world by a new dimension; and both of them knew it: Stam, who had made a great discovery, and also Mies, who had expressed the spring effect of the chair through the sled form.[27]

A legal action to determine priority confirmed Stam in the "artistic" nature of his chair idea, which means that it enjoys permanent protection. The manufacture of the chairs was transferred from Arnold to the Thonet company.[28]

The seating shown by Stam at Stuttgart was lacquered black, and the seats were strips of rubber.[29] "You know Mart Stam's chair, the one with only two legs?" asked Schwitters. "Why have four legs, when two will do?"[30]

That the leaves of the sliding partitions in the Stam houses were made of obscured glass was considered by visitors and critics alike to be entirely inappropriate, especially in the sleeping and bathroom areas. The individual panels, 80 cm [31½ in] wide and 2.5 meters [98½ in] high, were disliked on grounds of expense and because they collected dirt.[31] The warm-air heating was widely criticized because small children could drop all kinds of things into the openings in the floor. A Swiss critic remarked on the fact that even the bathroom could be included in the open-plan complex of living room, study, and stairs: these were houses where you could not even write a postcard in peace.[32] But there was praise for the use of asbestos cement panels with a polished finish in the bathroom, on the market only since 1926.[33]

House 30, with interiors by Marcel Breuer, was as austere and uncompromising as its neighbors. The seating here was not cantilevered but the chairs were tubular steel, with runners. The nesting tables were tubular steel too, nickel plated, and the closets were sheet steel. The low "tea tables" cost from 16 to 24 marks, according to size; the horsehair-seated chair, which weighed 3.5 kilograms [7¾ pounds], cost 32 marks, and the glass-topped dining table 120 marks.[34]

In his chapter on "metal furniture" in *Innenräume* Breuer wrote,

> two years ago, when I saw my first steel club chair complete, I thought to myself that of all my work this one piece would be most criticized. It is the most extreme, in its appearance as in the expressive quality of its material; it is the least artistic, the most logical, the least "homelike," the most machinelike . . . .
>
> the strict standardization of the elements—the use of the same elements in different types of fur-

174

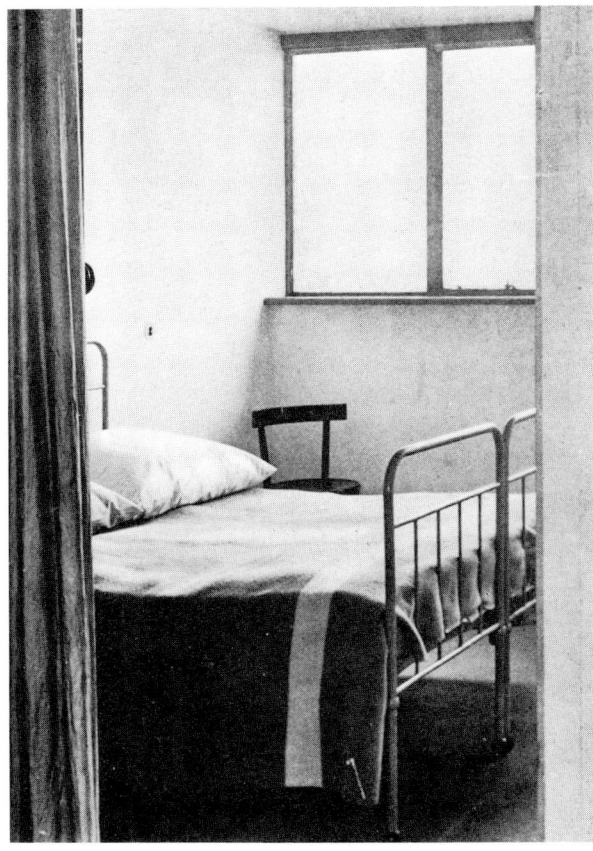

```
M.Stam                          Rotterdam 9.6.27
Architect                       Maarland 15 Vreewyk

Herrn Mies van der Rohe
B e r l i n   W.35

Gehrter Herr Mies van der Rohe,
                              In Beantwortung des Schrei
bens Ihres Vertreters teile ich Ihnen mit,dass meine
Häuser weiss werden;nur die kleinen XXX Eingangsvorbauten
möchte ich hell-grau streichen;die Fenster Stahlblau.
Die Beleuchtungskörper der Firma Zeiss kommen für meine
Häuser nicht in Frage.
                              Mit besten Gruss,
```

niture—the possibility of packing them flat (over 50 club chairs in a cubic meter [10¾ cubic feet]): economy in transportation and complete respect for production requirements enabled me to meet the social criterion—a price affordable by the masses at large—without which the whole undertaking would not have been particularly satisfying to me.[35]

Nowadays Stam's cantilever chairs, Mies's *Freischwinger*, and Breuer's tubular steel chairs on runners are among the classics of Modernism, and are certainly not cheap. However, low-cost imitations are on offer from furniture warehouses and they, at least, have found their way into the homes of "the masses at large."

Back in 1927 Karl Konrad Düssel, the same Stuttgart critic who wrote of Breuer's furnishings in Gropius's houses—"The well-known chairs in nickel-plated tubing with horsehair belts . . . , the tables with glass tops throughout"—that they evoked "memories of dentists and operating rooms," went on to say, "The Dutchman, Stam, too, uses these Breuer furnishings in his three lavender-blue row houses, and they fit in very well with the sober, clear, firm way in which he has designed his rooms."[36]

Düssel was the only contemporary observer who mentioned "lavender-blue"; the color analysis of old paint layers undertaken for the modern restoration of the houses produced a blue defined as 17:2:2 (DIN 6164), close to the color remembered after sixty years by Mia Seeger. These lavender facades were set off by a porch for each house (light-colored, not dark as in the restoration) reached by climbing five steps and crossing a little bridge. The three bridges, gradated in length (House 30 had the longest), were not part of the design submitted by Stam but were the work of an architect on Döcker's resident staff, Franz Krause.

Interestingly, Stam's contemporaries were divided in their recollection of the color scheme, and his closest associates were those who shook their heads at the very mention of the lavender-blue finish now on the restored houses, which they regarded as a travesty, a "violation."[37] The file seems to bear them out. On May 30, 1927, Mies broached the topic of the color scheme for the project as a whole. He wrote to Le Corbusier and to Stam to ascertain their wishes and to ask for "as light a tone as possible for the paint finish of your house . . . as a uniformly light tone would serve to maintain the unity of the project."[38]

Stam's answer was unequivocal—the postcard is reproduced here—, and Mies passed his instructions on to Döcker almost verbatim: "Herr Stam has told me that his houses are to be painted white: only the little porches should be a light gray, and the windows steel-blue."[39]

How the fronts of the houses then came to be painted lavender-blue, with yellow on the side and rear elevations, has yet to become apparent. However, as the analysis shows, lavender-blue and yellow it was.

As for the color inside the house, neither the files nor the contemporary publications give any indication. Here, too, the paint layers were examined and various colors emerged. From today's viewpoint Stam's houses would have embodied his ideas more purely in the clarity of white, which would eliminate the anomaly of an apparently unmotivated color scheme.

Stam's houses were costed in December, 1926, at just 50,000 marks and contracted on March 11, 1927, for an all-in price of 59,000 marks; they were built for a total net building cost, as computed by Döcker in December of 1927, of 61,881.94 marks.[40]

The houses have survived World War II and the postwar period. With blue front elevation, light yellow rear elevation, and dark porches, they stand in their renovated state between Behrens's terraced citadel in light ocher and Mies's apartment house in pink.

Peter Behrens

HOUSES 31, 32

Design: Professor Peter Behrens, architect,
Berlin-Babelsberg

Apartment house: cellar, first floor, second, third, and
fourth floors.
Construction: external walls hollow pumice concrete
blocks, reinforced concrete floors, stairs in artificial
stone, walls plastered inside and out.[1]

"The old team from the studio in Neubabelsberg was
back together again. The New Architecture had found
its conclusive realization on the Killesberg in Stuttgart."
That is how Franz Schulze, in his book on Mies, describes the meeting of minds and buildings on the Weissenhof project.[2] And indeed the number of participants
who had been students or associates of Peter Behrens
is surprisingly high. Among those who built houses there
were Mies, Gropius, Le Corbusier, and Rading, who
had all worked in his office for varying periods of time;
the architects who worked on interior design included
Adolf Meyer (a student of Behrens's in his early Düsseldorf period and his earliest associate in Berlin from
1907 on), Paul Thiersch (an assistant in Düsseldorf,
1906–7), Wilhelm Kienzle (a member of the Schweizer
Werkbund collective who had worked under Behrens
in the summer of 1914), and Hans Zimmermann from
Stuttgart (with Behrens from August 1910 through
March 1911).

Walter Gropius gave the following account of his old
chief:

> He was an impressive personality, always very
> well dressed, with the rather cool air of a conser-
> vative Hamburg patrician. Strong-willed and
> highly intelligent, he was more of a rational than
> an emotional type, but he took a fresh and prej-
> udiced approach to every new design problem.
>
> I owe him a great deal: above all, the habit of
> thinking in principles.[3]

For many of those who later became his rivals Peter Behrens's office, and his personality, represented a land-
mark both in professional education and in self-
discovery. Behrens was a role model in personal as well
as in professional terms—a model from whom it was
necessary to break free in order to find one's own way.

As a result, Behrens's name did not feature on every
shortlist of architects for the Weissenhofsiedlung. He
appears on Stotz's List I in first place and in Mies's and
Häring's List II in second place after Berlage. In List III
he is back on top, before sinking to tenth place on List
IV and disappearing entirely from subsequent lists; he
reappears only on List IX, in the fall of 1926.

In 1912, according to Franz Schulze, Mies had trans-

Behrens's office in
Neubabelsberg, Ber-
lin, before March
1910. Left to right:
Walter Gropius, Adolf
Meyer, Jean Krämer
(?), Ludwig Mies van
der Rohe, Peter Gross-
mann (?)

ferred his admiration from Behrens to Berlage.[4] Behrens was invited to participate only after Tessenow,
Häring, and Mendelsohn had dropped out; the idea
seems not to have come spontaneously from Mies but
as a result of a timely letter from Behrens himself:

> One hears so much of the Werkbund exhibition
> in Stuttgart. I understand that the execution and
> organization are in your hands. I would like to en-
> quire whether it might not be possible to put my
> idea of a Terraced Block into practice there. As I
> have described the Terraced Block in the last is-
> sue of *Blätter des Deutschen Roten Kreuzes*, I shall
> take the liberty of sending you a copy. Please con-
> sider, after looking through the plans, whether
> there is a chance of carrying out my suggestion. I
> also enclose a large charcoal sketch which will
> give a clearer idea.
>
> Here in Vienna, it almost reached the point of
> being put into practice. Then the city building of-
> fice here made every conceivable objection, and
> certain standard forms apply, so I have had to fol-
> low the compulsory building pattern in my build-
> ings for the city. If ever this type of Terraced Block
> is translated into reality, I believe that it can do a
> great deal for the health of the people.[5]

On November 12, 1926, when the Stuttgart city building
committee was informed by the Württemberg Werkbund that Häring, Mendelsohn, and Tesserow were not
going to build on the Weissenhof project, Behrens's
name went forward as a substitute together with those
of Poelzig, Bruno Taut, and Scharoun. A list of celebri-
ties, which was starting to look full of gaps, had been
replenished with equally resonant names; at the same
time honor was paid to two respected teachers, Behrens

and Poelzig, and to two stimulating innovators, Taut and Scharoun.

Mies sent to Behrens, as to all the other architects, along with the necessary planning information, a warning that the fee would be more or less nominal. When Behrens asked how the fees were divided, Mies replied,

Of the total fee of 50,000 marks, Herr Döcker receives 5,000 for acting as site architect. From the remaining 45,000 marks, each of the 15 participating architects receives 3,000 marks irrespective of the size of his project. In addition to these 3,000 marks, each architect is at present to receive traveling expenses of 600 marks. As work progresses, I will endeavor to obtain from the city an improvement in the sum for expenses.[6]

Behrens's office took its time delivering the drawings. After a reminder from Mies[7] the contract was finally placed on March 11, 1927, for an all-in price of 117,000 marks. Building work at Weissenhof had been in progress since the beginning of March. Before the contract was finally placed with the Wolfer & Goebel company, the building committee debated whether in view of the general increase in costs the Behrens block could be built one story lower.[8] Presumably when the model was viewed on Saturday, March 12, 1927, the committee decided to refrain from this act of mutilation—an example of restraint not followed after World War II, when the building was garnished with a gable roof (removed in the course of restoration work in 1984).

In spite of the conventional masonry construction employed, with hollow pumice concrete blocks, there were cost overruns and delays. On April 22, 1927, Döcker informed the building committee that "the working drawings do not agree with the drawings in the building application"; the preliminary work had been wasted, and work would proceed on the basis of the 1:50 working drawings.[9]

The building was not ready for opening day. Along with several others, it was not declared ready for viewing until September 6, 1927.[10] The total net building cost as computed by Döcker's office at the end of 1927 was 120,698.02 marks.[11]

The Rasch brothers wrote in *Wie bauen?* that

The apartment house by Peter Behrens can stand as a model of perfect masonry construction. The living units are stacked in cubic shapes. The windows are cut out as holes in the masonry. The parapets are high and massive, like those of a castle. The floors and staircases are similarly massive. The half-light of the stairwells, with their high, cage-like balustrades, draws one into the still interior. The internal spaces are strictly demarcated from the outside world. The building leaves one with an impression of settled seclusion.

The building's four stories contain 12 apartments with a total of 62 rooms. Each apartment is set back from the one beneath and so has a large terrace. The terraces all face south and afford a view down into the valley.[12]

Other observers and critics took a much less benign view of Behrens and his building. Ernst Völter, for instance, wrote in *Die Baugilde* that "the castle-like external form with its numerous terraces arouses great expectations for the interior" which were in many cases disappointed by the individual apartments.[13] And what

the Rasch brothers called "cage-like balustrades" reminded another critic of

the balustrades we find on the stairways of prisons. . . . The handrail of a balustrade has hitherto always run straight along the line of the stair, to give the advantages of comfort in use and ease of cleaning. In this exhibition building, the handrails have been made stepped and horizontal, like the steps themselves, thus making both use and cleaning more difficult.[14]

The iron balustrades were painted with "red lead" and the unorthodox handrail was "light oak," according to Rudolf Pfister in his critical account of Weissenhof for *Der Baumeister*.[15] Another observer remarked, "the placing of the cooker in these apartments has a touch of Swabian folly. It is so positioned that the cook has his back to the only window in the kitchen and is standing in his own light."[16]

It is curious that very few critics perceived and mentioned Behrens's principal concern, the promotion of health: the healing of so great a social evil as tuberculosis through building reform. It was even said that "it seems as if the architect, in pursuit of his programmatic intentions, has sacrificed many advantages in the positioning of his building and of his apartments" and that the "terrace for every apartment" had yet to stand the test of experience.[17]

This is all the more surprising if we reflect on the scale of mortality from tuberculosis, especially in the greater European cities. A survey published in a specialist housing journal in 1926 had shown that in Budapest between 1911 and 1922 71.5 percent of girls

Heinrich Zille: "The welfare doctor prescribed high-altitude air."

Der Kassenarzt hat nur Höhenluft verordnet—
— — .Zille

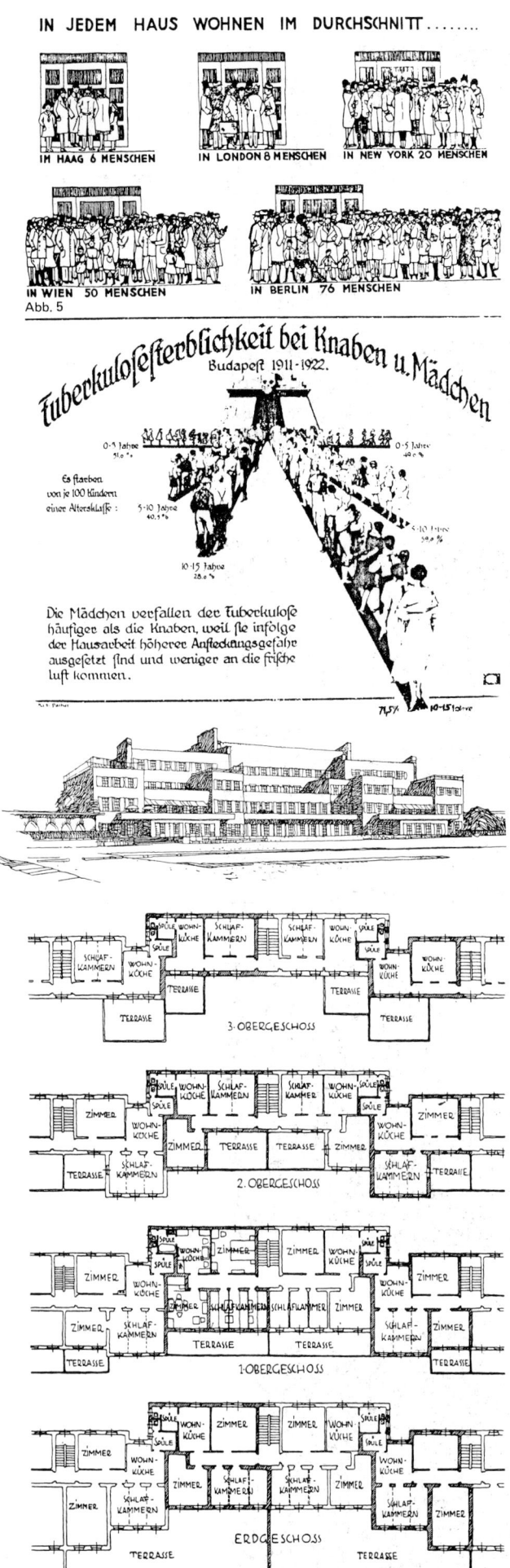

IM HAAG 6 MENSCHEN

IM LONDON 8 MENSCHEN

IN NEW YORK 20 MENSCHEN

IN WIEN 50 MENSCHEN
Abb. 5

IN BERLIN 76 MENSCHEN

Tuberkulosesterblichkeit bei Knaben u. Mädchen
Budapest 1911-1922.

3·OBERGESCHOSS

2. OBERGESCHOSS

1·OBERGESCHOSS

ERDGESCHOSS

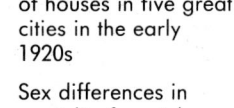

between ten and fifteen died of the disease, and 28 percent of boys in the same age range. The discrepancy was attributed to the fact that girls, "because of domestic work, are exposed to greater risk of infection, and that they have less access to fresh air." Infant mortality was around 50 percent for both sexes, and between five and ten years old it was 59 percent for girls and 40.5 percent for boys.[18]

In 1927 the periodical *Die Wohnung* took up the idea that "the occupants of unhealthy dwellings exhibit all kinds of ill-health which can be regarded as a consequence of the housing. Mostly the cause is a combination of forms of housing deprivation which operate concurrently and produce bodily effects which are hard to define."[19]

In 1924 Thomas Mann's novel *Der Zauberberg* (*The Magic Mountain*) began, "A simple young man traveled in high summer from Hamburg, his ancestral home, to Davos-Platz in the Grisons. He went to stay for three weeks."[20] It was exactly this, a kind of "Davos-Platz" or home sanitarium, that Behrens intended for the tenants of his apartment house: access to fresh air from every apartment and the possibility of moving sickbeds outside on cold, sunny days; both prevention and therapy. True, almost all of the Weissenhof architects had done as much for the occupants of their houses; but it must be remembered that Behrens wanted his idea put into practice for the great mass of those in need of homes. What he had been unable to do in Vienna, he wanted to show in Stuttgart—to wage war against "the vast misery . . . in the existing mass tenements of the great cities," and against apartments as "focuses of infection" for those who had no chance of ever living in a detached single-family residence with its own back yard:

> In order to make some impact on tuberculosis, it is apparent that every dwelling, even in a multistory building, needs to have a sizable space open to the sky. It is no less necessary to ensure that all dwellings have thorough ventilation. The spaces, which will represent roof gardens, must have enough depth to allow beds and other reclining furniture to be moved into the open and back into the apartment. . . .
>
> The "Terraced Block" which I have projected is a conglomeration of houses of one, two and three stories which are combined in such a way that the flat roof of the lower house forms the terrace for the house immediately above it.[21]

That was Behrens's own description of his intention, and he accompanied it with a perspective sketch and four plans of the block he had proposed for Vienna. He saw

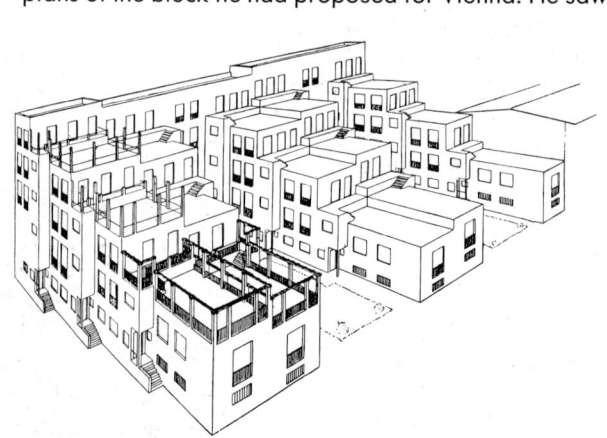

Average occupancy of houses in five great cities in the early 1920s

Sex differences in mortality from tuberculosis in Budapest, 1911–22

Peter Behrens: design for a terraced block, September, 1926

Adolf Loos: terraced apartment block, 1924

it as the advantage of his design that, by contrast with all other terraced block designs, it avoided an excessive front-to-back depth in the ground-floor apartments. His remark in *Bau und Wohnung* that "previous designs often created apartments more than 13 meters [$43\frac{1}{2}$ feet] deep" refers to some proposals by Adolf Loos and Oskar Strnad, roughly contemporaneous with his own designs for the city of Vienna and "probably for the same building lot."[22]

Whereas Loos, in a kind of ideal plan, stacked small two-story suburban houses "with a large kitchen/living room and auxiliary workrooms on the lower floor and bedrooms on the upper floor, with staggered landings,"[23] Behrens aggregated three- and four-room apartments on a single level and simply replaced living rooms in a lower story with terraces or balconies in the story above. So the basic plans of the apartments remain the same from the ground upward. The walls become thinner toward the top but the projections remain the same, so that in some of the apartments, although the number of rooms is the same as that of the apartment beneath, the area taken for the balcony or terrace is subtracted from the kitchen and living area. This is presumably what the critics meant when they said that Behrens had sacrificed a great deal of comfort in pursuit of his idea.

Kitchens and bathrooms are the Cinderellas of the building, an echo of its bathless Viennese forerunner. At best, the apartments for Vienna had a bath jammed into the scullery next to the kitchen/living room; the scullery also gave access to a family toilet. In most of the Stuttgart apartments, by contrast, Behrens made the main access through the centrally placed living room, from which doors led to the separate, partitionable bedrooms. This prompted one critic to write that "the former 'hallway' is now called the living room."[24] Behrens's defenders felt constrained to argue that this form of layout might well be a sufficient antidote to the evil of subletting.[25] Behrens himself wrote,

> I have had to limit myself in many respects, in my apartment house at Weissenhof, but at least I have been able to put into practice the central principle of a hygienic, modern apartment house, which is the addition of spacious terraces to all the dwellings. It has also proved possible to protect the walls against extremes of heat and cold through the use of hollow, porous building blocks.

179

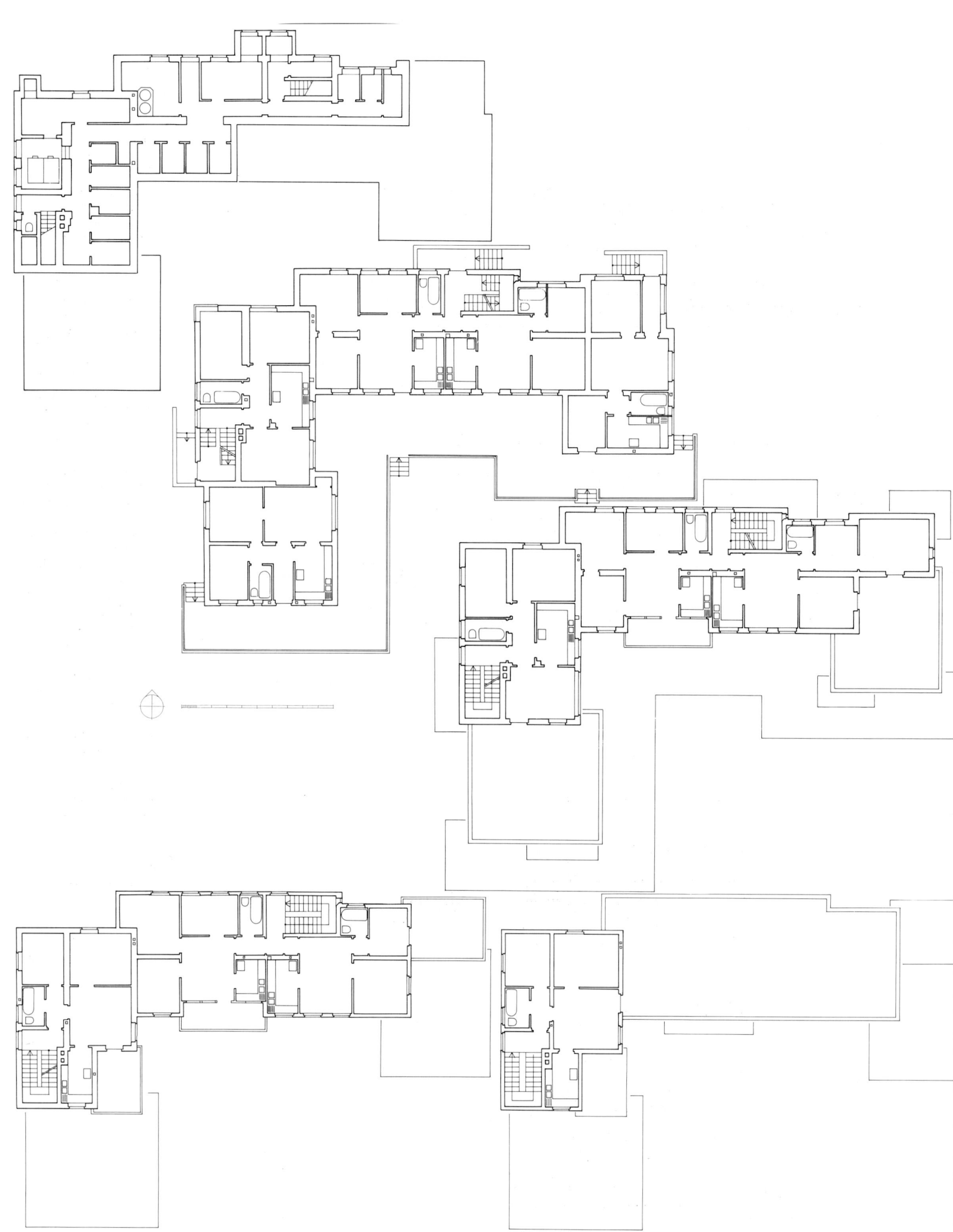

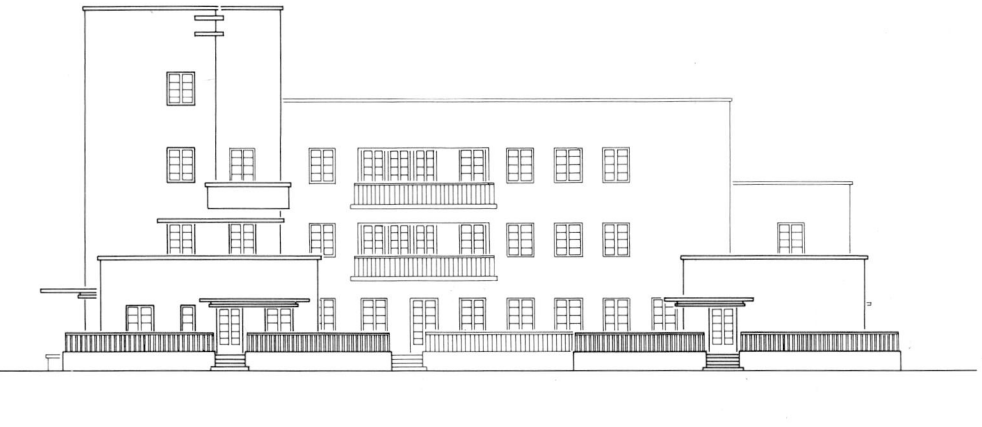

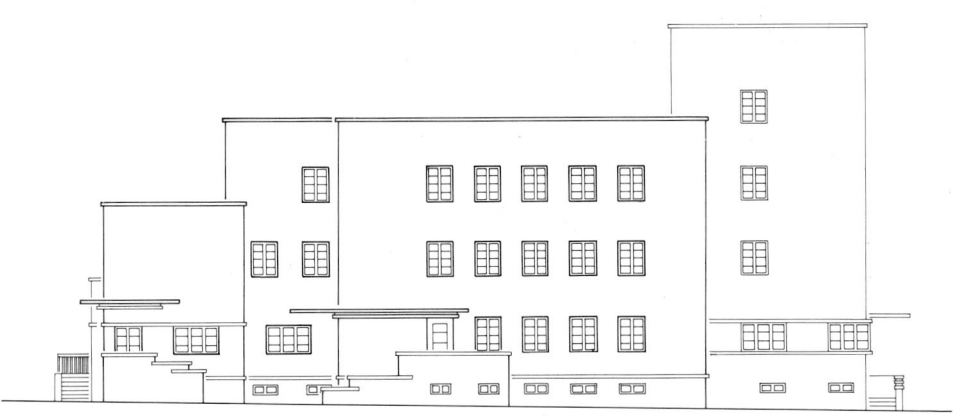

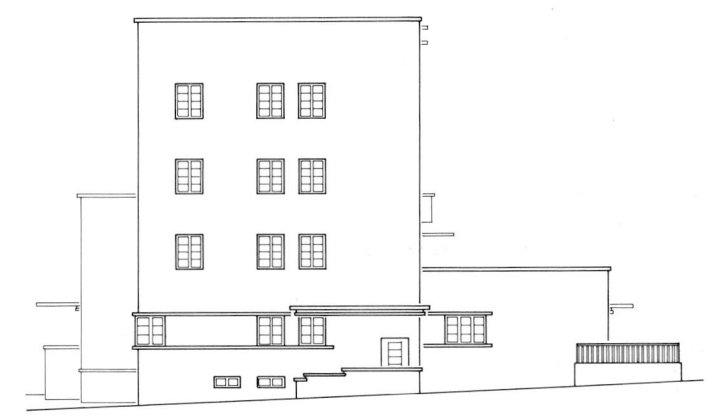

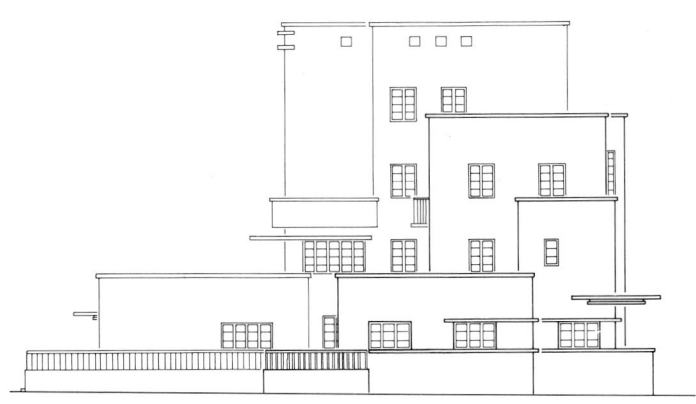

House 31/32
Architect: Peter Behrens
Plans and elevations drawn from the architect's building code submissions (undated)

Opposite:
Cellar

First floor: 3-room apartment, interior by Hermann Gretsch; 3-room apartment, interior by Heinz and Bodo Rasch (intended for Else Oppler-Legband); 4-room apartment, empty (intended for Peter Behrens); 3-room apartment, interior by Reinhold Stotz; 3-room apartment, interior by Oscar Heiniz

Second floor: 3-room apartment, colored furniture by M. Kohler company, Stuttgart (intended for Oswald Haerdtl); two 3-room apartments, interiors by Paul Griesser

Third floor: two 4-room apartments, interiors by Paul Thiersch; 3-room apartment, interior by Oskar Wlach

Fourth floor: 3-room apartment, interior by Walter Sobotka

Elevations from south, north, west, east

Unfortunately, I did not succeed in enlisting the aid of gardeners to plant the terraces in order to give them the look of small gardens. I regret this, because it is surely well enough known how deeply the inhabitants of great cities long for open-air activities and closeness to nature, as the profusion of flowers on their tiny balconies often so touchingly shows.

I also regret that, because of my own remoteness from the lot, and the difficulty of finding craftspeople ready to execute the work, it proved impossible to furnish two of the apartments, as I had hoped, to designs by Frau Else Oppler-Legband and by myself. It is especially unfortunate that the apartment by Frau Else Oppler-Legband never came to fruition, because it was designed entirely in the spirit of the modern housewife.[26]

The apartment originally assigned to Behrens's close friend and associate, Else Oppler-Legband—who had been one of Lilly Reich's teachers [27]—was designed by the Rasch brothers, and the one intended for Behrens himself remained empty. Indications to the contrary in the official catalogue (printed before the exhibition opened) are incorrect.

It had been intended that some of the apartments in the Behrens block should have interiors designed by members of the Österreichischer Werkbund; in the end the only Austrians to contribute were Oskar Wlach and Walter Sobotka. The Staatliche Hochschule für Handwerk und Baukunst, Weimar, directed by Otto Bartning (the successor to the Bauhaus in its first home), was considered, but ultimately did no work in Stuttgart. The Kunstgewerbeschule, Halle an der Saale (Burg Giebichenstein), worked on one apartment.

Behrens suggested to one designer, Gerta Schroedter, of Thalheim near Stuttgart, that she should offer her services to the exhibition directorate, or rather to Mies. Along with a number of other applicants she was turned down, probably by Stotz.[28] In March, 1927, the exhibition directorate asked Behrens whether he agreed to having a number of Stuttgart interior designers work on interiors in his apartment house (plus Werkstätten Stadler of Paderborn, for which Paul Griesser, a former student of Schneck's, now worked).[29] Behrens seems to have agreed to the selection and three Stuttgarters, Hermann Gretsch, Reinhold Stotz, and Oscar Heinitz, displayed their wares in his buildings. Camille Graeser was slated to take part but asked Mies for a more interesting assignment in Mies's own building.

Three-room apartment on first floor

Interior design: Diplomingenieur Gretsch, architect, Stuttgart-Feuerbach, Haldenstrasse 14.[30]

Hermann Gretsch had studied architecture at the Kunstgewerbeschule, Stuttgart, under Bonatz, Schmitthenner, and later Pankok and had been a member of the Werkbund since 1925. He showed designs of great simplicity, unit furniture and seating which differed only in details from that of Schneck, Griesser, and other Kunstgewerbeschule designers.[31]

Three-room apartment on first floor

Interior design: Frau Else Oppler-Legband, Berlin-Schöneberg, Babelsberger Strasse.[32]

As Behrens explained, this apartment had been re-

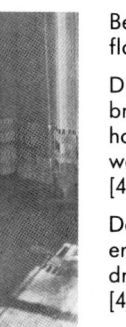

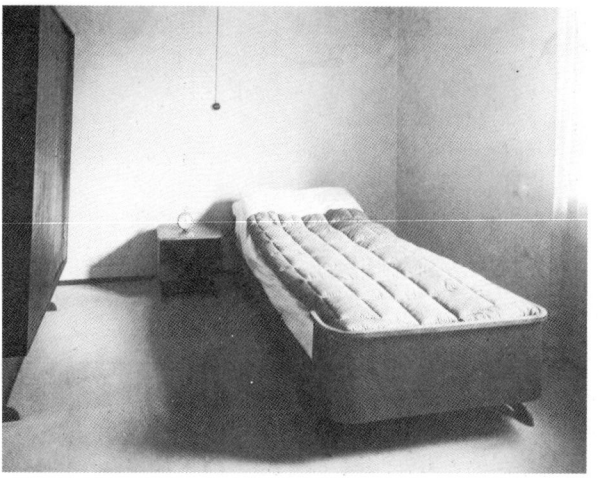

Behrens building, first floor:

Dining area by Rasch brothers, showing silk hangings; the chair weighs 2 kilograms [4½ pounds]

Desk by Rasch brothers; weight including drawers, 20 kilograms [44 pounds]

Bedroom by Rasch brothers

served for Else Oppler-Legband; in her stead[33] the Rasch brothers equipped it with furniture of great lightness—their favorite material was 3 mm [⅛ in] plywood. One chair weighed 2 kilograms [4½ pounds]; the desk "with all the drawers" weighed 20 kilograms [44 pounds].[34]

Heinz Rasch said that they tried to relieve the baldness of the rooms and the general impression of "office furniture" by hanging the walls with "raw silk drapes," as in Mies's own apartment, Am Karlsbad, in Berlin. This, he said, gave the living room, at least, a more welcoming look.

Four-room apartment on first floor

Interior design: Professor P. Behrens, architect, Berlin-Babelsberg.[35]

Originally intended to have an interior by Behrens him-

self, this apartment was left unfurnished.

Three-room apartment on first floor

Interior design: Reinhold Stotz, architect, Kirchheim-Teck.[36]

Stotz, who—with his wife, Margarete—also designed the bedroom in Apartment 1 of Mies's building, was a former student of Schneck's. His furnishings in the Behrens building show his teacher's influence very clearly: simple, restrained, and devoid of superfluous ornament, they are also uninspiring.

Three-room apartment on first floor

Interior design: Heiniz, Stuttgart.[37]

Oscar Heiniz, later Heinitz,[38] was one of the young

Stuttgart architects associated with the "Uecht-Gruppe" led by Schlemmer and Baumeister. A founder member of the group, Albert Mueller, was a lifelong friend of Heinitz's. These architects and painters in Stuttgart all knew each other; almost all belonged to the Werkbund and they were united in the endeavor to promote new work and to take a stand against the ideas and personalities of the establishment.

However, none of this entitled them by right to participate, in the ambitious exhibition planned by the Deutscher Werkbund. Far from it: outside a very restricted circle (Bruckmann, Stotz, and probably Schneck), the Stuttgart members of the Werkbund were kept largely in the dark and heard of the Werkbund project only at a late stage.

In the summer of 1926 Heiniz, Herre, Graeser, and Metzke-Rovira wrote a letter to Mies asking to be allowed to take part, and Heiniz went so far as to formulate "decision aids" for the exhibition directorate in order to promote the participation of experienced working architects. Stotz's reply is an interesting example of his approach to applications of this kind:

> In all its undertakings, the Werkbund has always based itself on the recognition that success is possible only if decisions are not taken by committees and majority votes, but if an exhibition is the responsibility of one individual, with very definite purposes in view. You can rest assured, in this case as in others, that the person entrusted by the Werkbund with that responsibility, who is himself an architect, will bear every relevant consideration in mind in deciding on those who are to be involved in the planned development. Your suggestion that the architect members of our [Württemberg] section put forward names from their own midst would undoubtedly lead to a result which would neither satisfy the membership nor further the project itself. Experience shows that such proposals tend to produce erratic results which would undermine the unity that we desire to see in the project as a whole.[39]

Heiniz did not hear from Mies until April 17, 1927, although his name had appeared on the list of interior designers, attached to the Behrens building, on April 11.[40] On April 17, two letters crossed. One was from Heiniz to Mies: "I hereby declare that I am and have been prepared to participate under the same conditions as the others included in the allotment of work. There

Behrens building, first floor:

Two views of living room by Reinhold Stotz

Bedroom by Reinhold Stotz

Living room by Oscar Heiniz

has been no formal withdrawal on my part, nor has any other person been authorized to withdraw on my behalf."[41] The other, from Mies to Heiniz, was calculated to mollify:

> May I inform you that the assignment of the furnishing of individual dwellings has now begun. We would like to ask you to undertake the interior design of an apartment in the Behrens building. . . .
> I would not like to miss this opportunity of stressing once more the character that is aimed at in the exhibition, which sets out to show simple, well-thought-out dwellings, avoiding any hint of the salon, and all superfluity. With regard to the furnishing and color scheme, I would recommend that you establish direct contact with Professor Peter Behrens.[42]

Heiniz was not by any means the last to be invited to participate; but he was certainly not one of the first, either. He carried out his instructions. The furniture was not sold at the end of the exhibition, but remained in the designer's possession. In 1985 Oscar Heiniz, now Heinitz, and his wife presented the original Weissenhof furniture to the Landesmuseum. The apartment originally furnished and decorated by Heiniz is now occupied by an exhibition space, the Architektur-Galerie, run by the BDA.

Three-room apartment on second floor

Interior design: Oswald Haerdtl, architect, Vienna I, Stubenring 3.

"Interior furnishings supplied by the following companies: furniture, M. Kohler, Stuttgart; paint finish on furniture, Mezger & Sohn, paint workshop, Stuttgart."[43] That is the account of the apartment that appears in the official catalogue. As no photograph of the apartment, or other information, was to be found, a long search ultimately led the author to Oswald Haerdtl's widow, still living in Vienna. Her answer was unexpected:

> It come as a surprise to me to find Oswald Haerdtl described as having designed the interior of a three-room apartment at the Weissenhofsiedlung in 1927, in Professor Behrens's house. . . . I married Oswald Haerdtl in 1927; we visited Stuttgart once, in 1937, and went to see the Weissenhofsiedlung. He never said a word about having had any part in it. Is there a prospectus of the exhibition in which Oswald Haerdtl is named as an interior designer? In 1927, Oswald Haerdtl was appointed to manage Josef Hoffmann's office; it could be that this was why the work for Professor Behrens was never done.[44]

Presumably, the exhibition directorate found furniture for the apartment somehow, rather than leave it bare.

2 three-room apartments on second floor

Interior design: Professor Paul Griesser, architect, Bielefeld, Oststrasse 101.[45]

Paul Griesser had studied under Schneck, but also under Wilhelm Kreis,[46] and was thus both an architect and an interior designer (*Innenarchitekt*). From 1925 through 1960, he was head of the department of interior design

at the Werkkunstschule, Bielefeld.[47]

Griesser furnished his two apartments in Behrens's building with furniture he had designed for Werkstätten Stadler in Paderborn, a firm with which he also furnished the first-class smoking room of the Hapag steamer *New York*.[48] It was this collaboration that drew the exhibition directorate's attention to his name: in a letter to Behrens, Stotz and Hagstotz mentioned "Werkstätten Paderborn (designs by Prof. Paul Griesser, Kunstgewerbeschule Bielefeld, a student of Schneck's)."[49]

Griesser was invited and wrote a delighted letter of thanks.[50] His furniture, in lacquer and walnut, was in keeping with Schneck's doctrines of standardization and combinability. Griesser later worked for W. K. Verband for which he developed furniture which made it, "for the first time since its foundation, into a factor with a positive influence on the market. . . . Inspired by the Schneck rooms of Deutsche Werkstätten [for Weissenhof]." W. K. Verband was commended for "securing for its new, low-cost furniture a modern artist of repute."[51]

2 four-room apartments on the third floor

Interior design: Professor Thiersch, architect, Halle.[52]

In 1928 Walter Riezler wrote in his obituary of Paul Thiersch:

> Thiersch was one of the younger leaders of the arts and crafts movement, almost part of the second generation: when, after early successes as an architect, he entered the movement, it had already consolidated itself, and thus he was the first to be able to put into practice what the older leaders had always demanded in theory. He placed the workshop in the center of the educational process of which he was in charge: not as a kind of "teaching workshop," which could only serve as a practice-ground for the students, but as a fully effective work-place that had to make things to be sold, and which soon created a steady market for itself. At every exhibition and fair, the work of Werkstätten der Burg Giebichenstein attracted attention.[53]

Born into an architectural family in Munich whose most celebrated and effective member was his uncle, Friedrich von Thiersch,[54] Paul Thiersch studied at the Technische Hochschule, Munich, was an assistant under Behrens in Düsseldorf, and worked as office manager for Bruno Paul and as his assistant at the Kunstgewerbeschule, Halle, of which he became director in 1916.

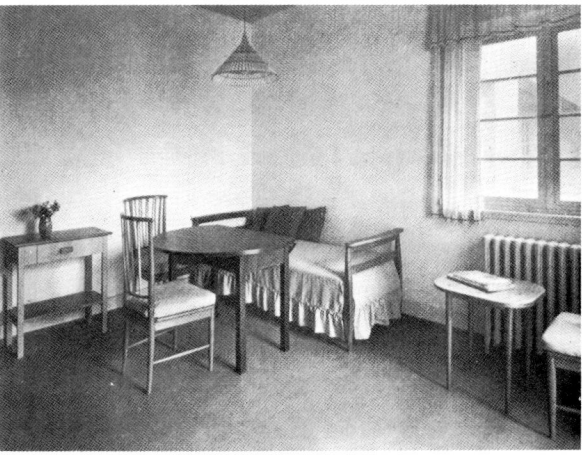

Behrens building, third and fourth floors:

Living room by Paul Thiersch

Living room with sofa-bed by Oskar Wlach

Thiersch had been a member of the Werkbund since 1910 and was well acquainted with its plans. At a very early stage, on September 4, 1926, he reminded Mies of a conversation in Berlin at which the idea of his participation in a Werkbund exhibition had been raised:

I am particularly keen that our teaching workshops [at Giebichenstein Castle] should be represented at the exhibition, especially because the Dessau Bauhaus and Bartning [Staatliche Hochschule, Weimar] are also exhibiting there. I should regard it as a great setback relative to these two institutions, if we were not to be admitted on the same footing and on the same scale ... and I therefore ask you once again to admit us to participate and, as far as possible, to give us a clearly defined assignment which will represent an artistic unity, in terms both of architecture and of interior design.[55]

Ten days after the date of this letter, Mies was discussing the choice of architects with the representatives of the city architectural and urban expansion departments. He asked them "to replace the architect Bartning, who was nominated for the sake of the Weimar Hochschule, by Mendelsohn of Berlin. What concerns us here is rather a consortium of individuals than representatives of the various schools."[56]

It may be pure speculation to suppose that Bartning was struck off the list to obviate further pressure from Thiersch; the idea becomes more plausible, however, if we reflect that earlier, when Mies was working in Paul's office, it was Thiersch who recommended him to Behrens. Neither Mies nor Thiersch could have forgotten the fact.[57]

Thiersch wrote once more at the beginning of October 1926 to ask if he might take part;[58] after that his name does not reappear until the end of the following March, when the exhibition directorate included his name (with those of Griesser and two or three Stuttgart interior designers) among those submitted to Behrens for his approval as designers for his building.

When Behrens answered in the affirmative, Mies wrote Thiersch on April 12, 1927, to ask him and his school to participate: "and we would like to ask you to take charge of a pair of apartments in the apartment house by Professor Peter Behrens." As with all the other invitations, Mies made his usual reference to "the character that is aimed at in the exhibition" and the avoidance of "any hint of the salon." At what point it became known that Thiersch's Kunstgewerbeschule was going to become financially involved is uncertain; what is

clear is that Stotz triumphantly told City Hall, in the context of the raw material loans from the Landesgewerbeamt and the provision of furniture free of charge by exhibitors, that "the city of Halle has made available to Professor Thiersch in Halle, i.e. to the workshop under his direction, to facilitate participation, i.e. for the execution of their designs for two apartments in the Behrens building, the sum of 8,000 marks."[59]

Writing on Weissenhofsiedlung furniture for a commemorative issue of the *Württembergische Zeitung*, Oscar Heinitz commented, "Thiersch's furnishings smack of the exhibition hall, although in many ways they are highly usable. Where they are made quite simply out of plain plywood, they are convincing, unequivocal, with simple, appropriate covers." [60]

Three-room apartment on third floor

Interior design: Wlach, architect, Vienna VII, Museumstrasse 5A.[61]

Oskar Wlach and Walter Sobotka were the only members of the Österreichischer Werkbund—apart from Josef Frank—to take part in the Weissenhof project.

Wlach trained as an architect, took his doctorate in Vienna, and spent some time abroad before returning to work alongside Hoffmann, Frank, and Strnad on city housing programs. In 1925, with Frank, he founded a design and furnishing business, Haus und Garten. Frank furnished one of his Weissenhof houses with Haus und Garten pieces, but the furnishings designed by Wlach for the Behrens building were made by a firm nominated by the exhibition directorate.

Some of the furniture was painted with colored lacquer; the sofa opened up into a bed, with the bedclothes stored in its lower part.[62]

Living room by Walter Sobotka

Wlach built two houses in the Werkbundsiedlung in Vienna in 1932, and in 1938 he emigrated via Switzerland to America. He worked as an architect in New York and died there in poverty.[63]

Three-room apartment on the fourth floor

Interior design: Sobotka, architect, Vienna IV, Wiedener Hauptstrasse 60B.[64]

Walter Sobotka, like Wlach, worked as an architect in Vienna. Apart from the seating, by Thonet, the furniture for this apartment was made in the Stuttgart area.

In 1937 Sobotka went to America, and in 1938–39 he worked as a designer for Thonet furniture in New York. Later he held professorial appointments at the University of Pittsburgh and the Carnegie Institute.[65]

Hans Scharoun

HOUSE 33
Design: Professor Hans Scharoun, architect, Breslau, Akademie

Single-family house: cellar, first floor, second floor.
Construction: iron frame with Thermos panel infilling. Pumice concrete panels outside, plasterboard inside, plastered inside and out.
Interior design: Professor Hans Scharoun, architect, Breslau.
Room divisions of house:
Cellar: furnace room and coal store, laundry, store cellar.
First floor: entrance, cloakroom, toilet, living room with study and covered terrace, kitchen, maid's workroom, and maid's bedroom.
Second floor: three bedrooms, bathroom, terrace.[1]

"The members of the family," said Hans Scharoun, "must be given the kind of living space that really makes life possible, both as a family and with friends."[2]

Just as Bruno Taut's house shattered the much-discussed "unity of effect" of the Weissenhofsiedlung by its use of primary color, Scharoun did the same in formal terms by creating a shape that retains little of the strict cube, or of form reduced to basics. The author of the first article on Weissenhof to appear in *Die Form*, Walter Riezler, expressed astonishment and satisfaction at the thought that "it has already become possible to collect a dozen architects from all over Europe for a common task and to give them a completely free hand on all external features with the exception of the roof form, without impairing the unity of the overall effect in any way" while specifically excepting Scharoun's house with its "curious curvilinear romanticism, which is certainly not without originality."[3]

Scharoun, previously known in his profession largely through competition entries, had attracted attention through the highly individual nature of his formal invention, and through his unorthodox approach to every kind of program. Some observers were captivated by his creativity; some were revolted.

Accordingly, his presence at the 1927 Stuttgart exhibition was certainly no foregone conclusion. His name always appeared as a reserve, and he dropped out of the lists altogether between July 24 and November 12 of 1926. It was only Mies's dispute with Hugo Häring, and the disappearance of Häring, Tessenow, and Mendelsohn from the list that made some new names necessary and resulted in his promotion to the ranks of the "building" architects along with Bruno Taut, Poelzig, and Behrens. Scharoun was the only one of the four whose name went to a separate vote of the building committee, on the grounds of his "particularly idiosyncratic" artistic attitude.[4] He was voted in by six to one,

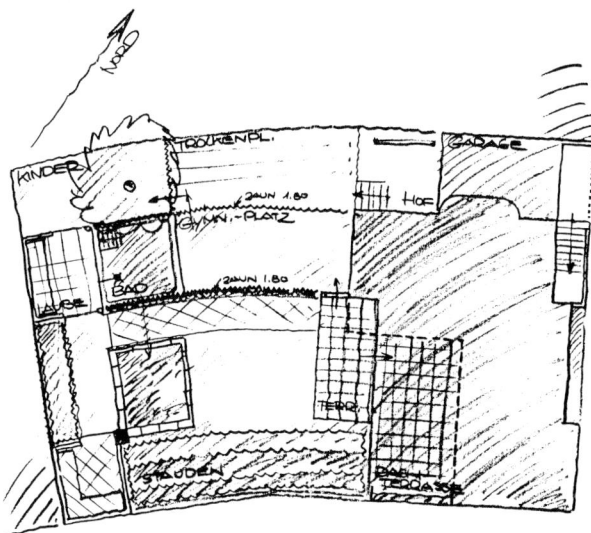

Hans Scharoun: sketch for landscaping

with three abstentions, and assigned a house of Type D. Single-family houses of Type D were specified as containing a parents' bedroom, a children's bedroom (partitionable), a living and dining room, and a kitchen and small rest room (with space set aside for children in kitchen or living and dining room). Type D was designed to be run without a servant.[5]

The house was thus meant as a single-family house with three rooms. As in the Type D houses by Stam, Rading, Behrens, and Frank, the room which emerged as the maid's room was specified in Mies's instructions as a "rest room" and not as a place for the help to live in. This has the advantage of serving as a pretext for its diminutive size as well as for the absence of any storage space for clothes.

Scharoun lost no time in embarking on his design or in making sure of Mies's agreement.[6] He altered the design several times; this evolutionary process is highly interesting. As the final plan retains only hints of the original multiple outdoor areas, the functions crowded together in Scharoun's sketch deserve some attention here. On an available area of 405 square meters [4,359 square feet], about average for the Weissenhof building lots (Bruno Taut's was the smallest, at 317 square meters [3,412 square feet], and Poelzig's the largest, at 586 square meters [6,308 square feet]), Scharoun initially set out to accommodate the following features: a children's play area with a shade tree; a laundry drying area adjoining the small kitchen yard; an arbor with a bench overlooking the swimming pool, which—together with the gymnastics area—was to be surrounded by a wall 1.80 meters [6 feet] high to shield it from being overlooked; a lawn; a herbaceous border; a seating corner; and a separate planting area, directly accessi-

187

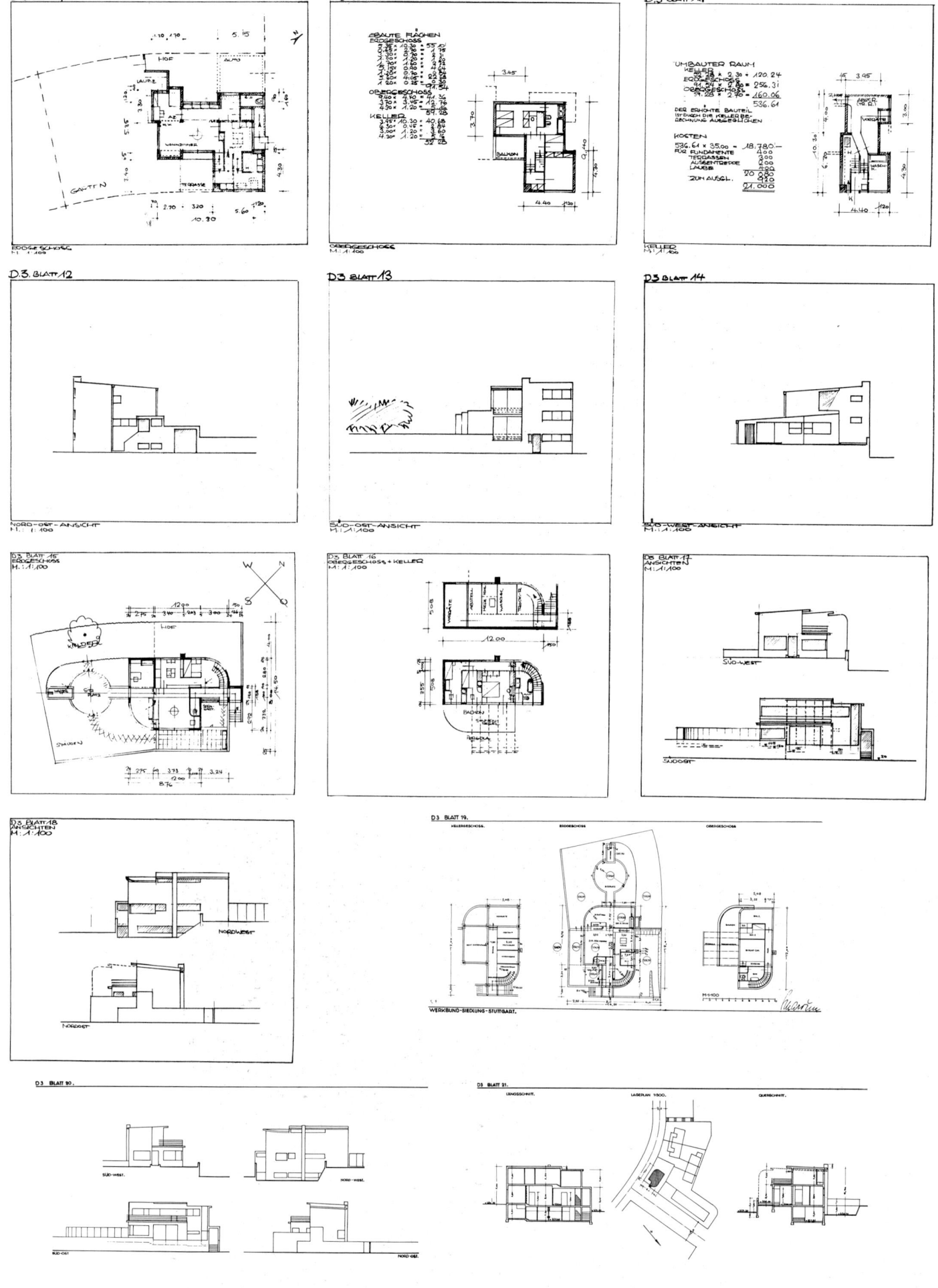

ble from the terrace of the living room.

Another early design is equally elaborate. In subsequent phases of planning it is possible to follow the process by which Scharoun came progressively closer to his definitive solution. His objective idea was to unify the indoor and outdoor areas and to contrive a ground plan which would make the movement through the house to the open-air seating area clear. The curved staircase makes its appearance together with its formal complement, the curved window facing out over the front yard and the view.

The form of the staircase is externally visible in the plan—but not yet in the elevation—from an early stage. It is not inconceivable, though impossible to prove, that Scharoun's decision to make the roof over the staircase follow the line of the stairs themselves was taken as a result of pressure from city hall to reduce costs through reductions in volume. Estimates based on "cubing" are always highly approximate, and it is open to doubt whether the reduction of the air space above the stairs really resulted in any reduction in costs. The making of the complicated, eccentrically shaped roof certainly did not represent any saving.

The contract for the Scharoun house was placed on the second contract date, March 5, 1927, with a local Stuttgart firm for a price of 26,000 marks. Döcker's final accounts show the cost to have been 30,121.81 marks.[7]

In *Wie bauen?*, the Rasch brothers gave the following account of the construction of the house:

The single-family house by the architect Hans Scharoun was conceived as a pure masonry construction. One is constantly aware of the clay model. This small group does not really fit the strict discipline of frame construction. Nobody is going to believe that the porch additions are not solid masonry. The construction is interesting: an iron skeleton frame with insulating panels as in-

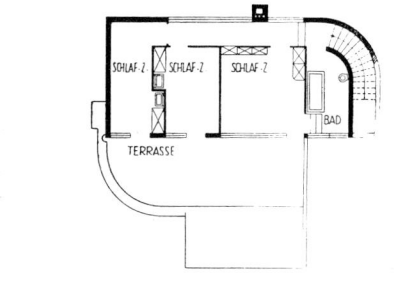

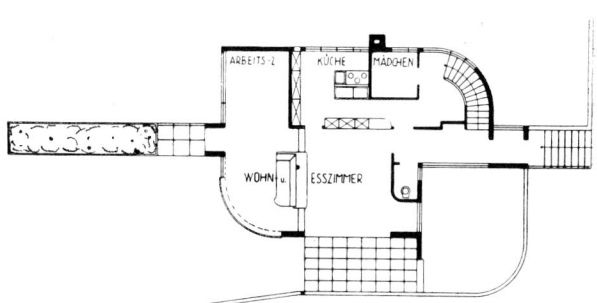

Opposite page:
Hans Scharoun: preliminary sketches, undated

Hans Scharoun: floor plans of House 33

House 33 from the east (Rathenaustrasse)

House 33 from the north (Hölzelweg)

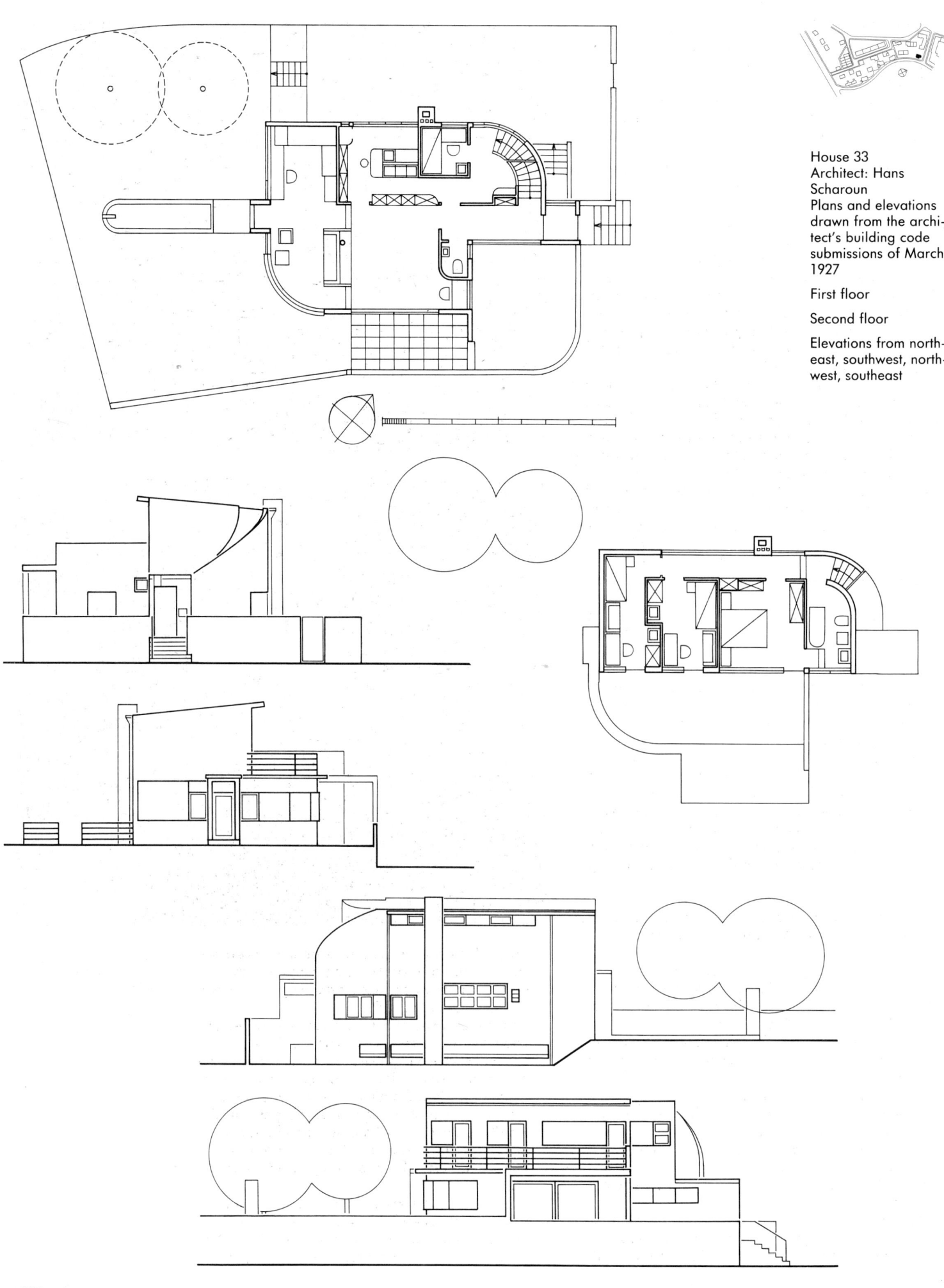

House 33
Architect: Hans Scharoun
Plans and elevations drawn from the architect's building code submissions of March, 1927

First floor

Second floor

Elevations from northeast, southwest, northwest, southeast

filling. The siding consists of breeze blockwork, with a plaster coating. The insulating panels (Thermos boards) consist of a wooden frame containing several layers of paper stretched with small gaps between them. This creates three separate air-filled spaces, which have a powerful insulating effect.[8]

Döcker seems to have exercised his functions as superintendent in an idiosyncratic, if not downright arbitrary, fashion. Stam had planned his houses as steel skeleton frame constructions and he was given masonry; Scharoun wanted masonry and his house was laboriously converted to steel frame construction.

There were delays in construction of House 33 because the Thermos insulating panels needed in large quantities for the Weissenhof houses were unobtainable for a time. The assembly of the steel frame also caused problems; at one time there was a proposal to convert to wood framing.[9]

As for the color scheme, Mies asked Scharoun whether he would agree, "like Schneck, Oud, Corbusier, Mies, Rading, Stam, and Dr. Frank," to a basic off-white: "It is of course open to anyone to emphasize particular details through color. Please let me know by return whether you wish to follow this example."[10] Scharoun did so wish.[11] Individual sections of ceiling and roofing inside and out, and probably sections of wall, were given a colored treatment, with a preference for rust red, in conjunction with some highly idiosyncratic ceiling lights made by the lighting company owned by Gustaf Stotz's brother.[12]

In his chapter of the book *Bau und Wohnung*, Scharoun wrote,

House 33 is a spatial expression of the joy in a new material and new demands. The organizational aspect of a wing set aside for household work; the ship's cabin quality of the functional sleeping space; the link between room inside and room outside; the choice between togetherness and separateness in the living room: these are the starting points of the design. The observer will not find too much that is standardized. Diversity in the home becomes standard only when it is mass produced. The whole is not intended to represent the fulfillment of anything, only one step among many.[13]

In an article for the Werkbund periodical, *Die Form*, Scharoun set out his intentions in more detail:

This house belongs to the smallest category of single-family houses on the development. It was intended to be clear in its layout and to appear absolutely and relatively large.

To leave visitors with an unequivocal impression, not simply that of having "toured some rooms."

I sought to achieve this:
through a clear demarcation between living, sleeping, and utility areas;
through marked contrasts of size between living rooms and bedrooms;
through combining different functions in a single space;
through playing off line against space in the axis which runs through the entire house (the axis was intended to terminate outdoors in a longitudinal

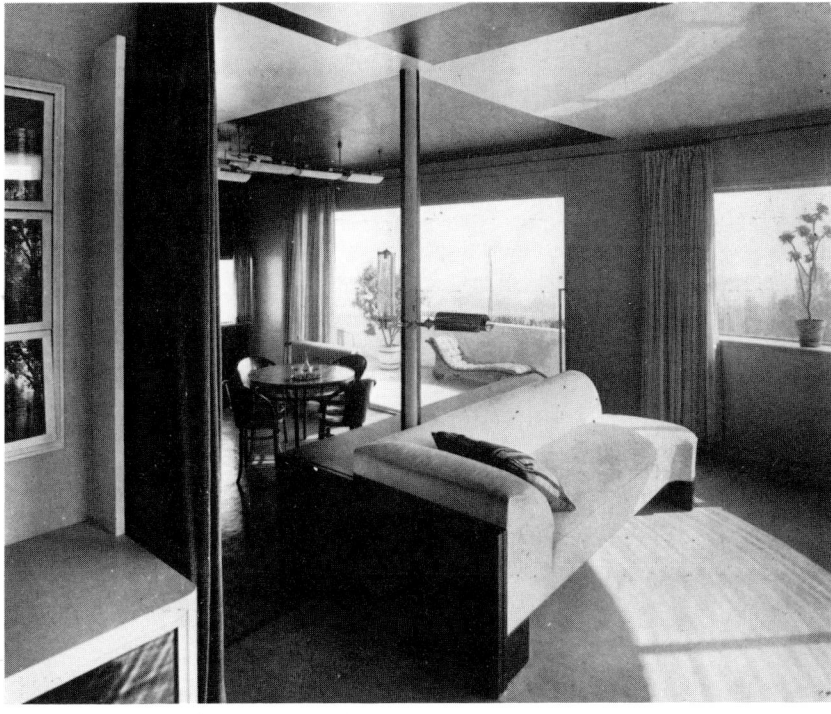

pool, which was omitted for economic reasons); through the form of the living room, which conveys a sensation of space extending far beyond the confines of the walls;
through bringing the landscape—an especially beautiful one, in this case—into the house.

Similar reasoning—along with utilitarian considerations—underlies the design of the utility area. Here, too, the attempt is made to preserve the impression of a single overriding space. The maid's cabin thus functions as a small space within a larger one. The actual kitchen area itself is as much a piece of spatial design as of functional design.

In all this, naturally, the question of standardization imposes itself. The application of a unitary measure constitutes the last stage, not the first, in a standardization process. In window construc-

Two views of living room by Hans Scharoun

tion, for instance, standardization has in my opinion led to a rigid and unnecessary restrictiveness which is economically unjustifiable and psychologically depressing. An ideal formula for standardization would presumably be found at the exact point where the wishes of the designer, the technician, and the occupant coincide. For the moment, all we can do is to whet the appetite by showing an abundance of desirable things. Eventually, the response from the public and from the technicians will lead to a limited scale of standardized individual forms.

Our immediate task is to show possible spatial combinations for various needs, along with individual objects, such as different methods of window construction—designed for a view, for ventilation, or for light; opening or fixed—and to bring these windows, in accordance with their type and size, into the right relationship with the spaces we want. Ultimately, a range of windows—corresponding to a range of requirements on the user's part—will emerge as standard designs. The same applies to all the other elements of the building and of the dwelling, such as built-in furniture, doors, the corridor, and so on.[14]

Scharoun designed no movable furniture for his house. The kitchen and closet fittings were all built in, as was a couch in the living room. All the other furniture was ready-made. The kitchen was something special in its conception. Along with a number of built-in cabinets, it showed a unit with free access on three sides, with a work surface at the end and a rack above for pots, pans, and lids; the sink and draining board were along one side, the cooker and another sink on the other. The faucet swiveled to serve either sink. The provision of water next to the cooker, the slit in the work surface for waste, the ironing board in the staircase area which folds up away against the wall next to the housemaid's "rest room," and the expressed desire for "20 electric power receptacles in the living room"[15] show Scharoun to be an architect fifty years ahead of his time. He was denied the receptacles on the grounds that "expenditure on experiments could not be authorized."[16] The kitchen, the maid's room, the ironing room, and the landing at the top of the cellar stairs form a self-contained spatial unit: a notable achievement in view of the smallness of the house.

The floor coverings were linoleum, and magnesite for the kitchen area. The first occupants described the linoleum as "too delicate" and the magnesite as "of

very inferior quality."[17]

Aside from the sensation caused by the rounded staircase ("Scharoun is one of the few who dare to use curves"[18]) and the annoyance of the delayed delivery of Thermos panels, the building of House 33 went comparatively smoothly. Its exposed position, visible from far down the hill, meant that this house absolutely had to be ready for opening day. The position of the house thus had one great advantage, from Scharoun's point of view; but it also had one massive disadvantage. From Stuttgart, on August 17, 1927, he wired Mies in Berlin: "Please wire instructions for removal flagpoles fronting my house. Appearance infuriating. Photography impossible. Scharoun."[19]

Scharoun's efforts during his stay in Stuttgart to have the flags removed, were thwarted.[20] When all else failed Scharoun wrote to Commissioner Sigloch himself with the request "that the poles be taken down, far enough in advance of the Werkbund convention to enable photographs to be available at that time if not before, and to afford an unobstructed view, during the convention, of my house *as of all the others.*"[21]

Sigloch passed on the complaint to Hagstotz, as administrator of the exhibition, who told him in reply that Mies van der Rohe had ordered the flagstaffs to be placed there, and that they were very difficult to remove because they had been concreted in 1.5 meters [5 feet] deep in order to support the weight of the outsize flags. Hagstotz claimed to be at a loss to understand why Scharoun was getting so excited; the skeleton frame for the Bau-und Heimstättenverein housing block (on the adjoining Schönblick site) was going to be visible in the background anyway. He went on to complain that by his insistence Scharoun was holding up the publication of *Bau und Wohnung*, with highly unfortunate consequences.[22]

Whether Scharoun succeeded in getting rid of the flags before the exhibition closed is doubtful: Hagstotz considered—as did others, no doubt—that if Scharoun did not like the photographs that were taken during the exhibition he could have his house photographed afterward.[23] The shots of the house printed in *Bau und Wohnung* show no flags,[24] but this might have been achieved by a wide-angle lens and a skillful choice of camera angles.

Press comment on Scharoun's house tended to stress the curved staircase, which from outside reminded one observer of a "fairground slide."[25] But another wrote,

Scharoun's work grasps life passionately from its elemental, natural aspect, far from all the simple-

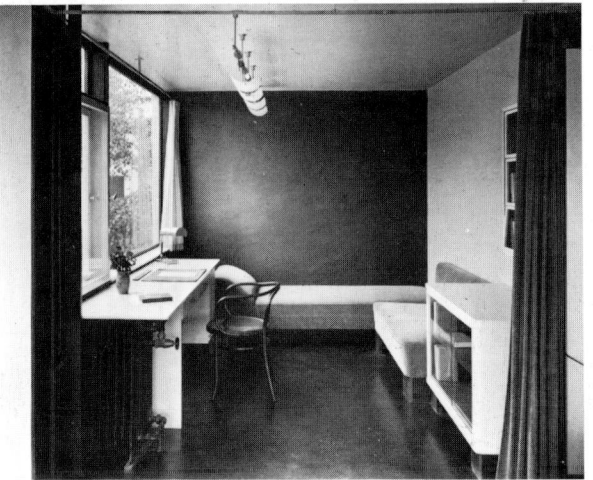

Study and kitchen by Hans Scharoun

minded geometry of the straight line and the right angle. His buildings, and his designs even more so, recall natural formations, and the copiousness of his creative imagination reminds one of Balzac, of whose features Lamartine said "He had the countenance of an elemental force."[26]

In a memoir written a quarter-century after the event, one eye-witness recalled,

The tower restaurant [by the architect and city councilman, Karl Beer] was the meeting place for all the architects involved with the Weissenhofsiedlung. There was a lot of shoptalk up there. The house by the Breslau architect, Scharoun, right across the street from the restaurant, was the

butt of most of the jokes. Scharoun parried every wisecrack with one of his own. The roof of the addition to his house bore a fatal likeness to a fairground slide. He was restrained, with considerable difficulty, from using it as just that, as an instance of "rational utilization," pleasurable to himself and to others.[27]

As well as this comparison, another was made with a "certain mechanical form."[28]

Almost sixty years later, after the Scharoun house had been renovated, its occupant paid the architect a great compliment: "Scharoun did not just plan the house; he dreamed it; he built it into the sun. We are always very much aware of the house we are living in. It is not par-

The Weissenhofsiedlung floodlit, with Hans Scharoun's House 33 in the foreground

ticularly large, but it is used functionally with great skill."[29] Such praise from the user of Scharoun's house exactly captures the deeper meaning of his work as an architect.

Heinrich Lauterbach, Scharoun's friend for many years, wrote of him,

Scharoun's work is not primarily or exclusively directed toward the artistic, aesthetic, formal conception of his buildings. His primary conception is that they must become organs for the human beings whom they serve. Organ, *organon* in Greek, means something "working," something that makes an achievement possible. "Every new object, rightly seen, opens up a new organ in us." (Goethe.)[30]

THE DEUTSCHER WERKBUND ANNOUNCES THE 1927 STUTTGART EXHIBITION, DECEMBER 1926

THE HOME: WERKBUND EXHIBITION STUTTGART 1927

We live in an age of reorientation. In politics and in economics, new paths must be sought if we are to answer the challenges of the present day. The forces which must create this new beginning are still beset by disunity and even by conflict; it is for us to find our way to a harmony which will transform conflict into cooperation and allow a full deployment of forces that have hitherto gone to waste.

As it is in general, so it is in the specialized field of home building. People still feel constrained to cater to the past rather than to allow the New to develop freely. As a result, the New has found practical expression only in rare and isolated instances. It has been reduced, all too often, to theoretical debate, and has had too little opportunity to try its strength in real work.

One might expect that those who are working to end the present housing crisis would be prompted to study the latest ideas in the field of housing. But they show comparatively little interest. Large industrial concerns are compelled to remodel their operations in line with new discoveries, in order to remain competitive. Those responsible for solving the housing crisis, however, still fail to respond to present-day needs and opportunities, and society as a whole suffers.

In the construction of dwellings, the floor plan presents a problem of essential, basic importance; it must arise from an exhaustive study of the living requirements of human beings today. On this the usability and usefulness of a dwelling depends.

With the least expenditure of space, a dwelling must permit a comfortable, practical style of life, in which all needs are met. The size and choice of rooms depends on the needs that indispensably must be satisfied. There is a need for rooms in which to live, eat, sleep, wash, and cook, divided according to purpose but fitted together through the floor plan, and so organized as to satisfy every need within a minimum space. Small dwellings, in particular, need to be designed with great care, because here the resources available are most limited.

No portion of space, however small, must remain unused. Logical design can make it possible to install oneself in comfort and satisfy the most exacting demands, according to need. If the home is to be made economic, all closets for linen, boxes, dishes, etc., must be built in, and the kitchen fully equipped.

Simplified, functional internal construction, with everything unnecessary eliminated, will simplify and ease the work of housekeeping.

Equally important for the reorganization of housing is the transformation of the technical basis of building through the use of new constructional systems and new materials.

The construction industry has too long stood aloof from industrialization and standardization and the benefits which these bring. In every field of work the strict division of labor has led to a production process in keeping with new demands. In many ways, however, the construction industry has yet to adapt to new circumstances. It has remained basically unchanged, and so have its working methods. Instead of presenting the engineer, the chemist, the industrialist, with demands for new building systems and materials that will lead to newer possibilities of building, it has simply used new building systems and materials, without regard to their true nature, as replacements for the old.

The need today is for the new materials provided by industry and the new building systems proposed by the engineers to be tested in practice, developed, and modified as necessary. Great attention must be paid, in particular, to prefabricated, dry construction. This transfers work from the building lot to the factory, in which the individual building components are manufactured, ready for assembly, so that they can be assembled on the lot in the shortest possible time, according to a carefully devised assembly schedule. As no drying time is necessary, the building can be occupied at once.

The industrialization of building naturally presupposes a strict standardization of structural elements and detailing. The design of housing, and that of the apartment house in particular, needs not an individual but a collective design process. The whole industry presses irresistibly toward standardization. Lately even hand craftsmanship has been moving in a related direction. And—just as in the automobile industry, for instance— the industrialized building of homes will progress through standardization and the lessons of standardization toward purer types and ever more perfect designs. Given proper organization and adaptation, hand craftsmanship, too, will face important challenges and find valuable work to do.

A systematic approach to the New Home, and all the associated organizational, spatial, constructional, technical and hygienic problems, is the basis of the planned Werkbund exhibition, THE HOME, which is to be organized by the Deutscher Werkbund at the suggestion of its Württemberg section. It will take place in Stuttgart in 1927. Early in 1926, the city of Stuttgart decided to assign aproximately 60 rental units of its 1926–27 building program to be built from designs supplied by the Werkbund. The chosen site is a piece of land at Weissenhof which not only allows the individual buildings to be organically grouped but, thanks to its elevated position, offers a magnificent view over the city. The layout plan has been devised by the architect Mies van der Rohe, deputy chairman of the Deutscher Werkbund, and finalized in conjunction with the urban expansion office of the city of Stuttgart. For the design of the individual houses the following architects from Germany and elsewhere have been selected, as proposed by the Deutscher Werkbund:

 1 Dr. Frank, Vienna
 2 J.J.P. Oud, city architect, Rotterdam
 3 Mart Stam, Rotterdam
 4 Le Corbusier, Geneva
 5 Professor Dr. Peter Behrens, Berlin and Vienna
 6 Dr. Richard Döcker, Stuttgart
 7 Walter Gropius, Director of the Bauhaus, Dessau
 8 Ludwig Hilberseimer, Berlin
 9 Mies van der Rohe, Berlin
10 Professor Hans Poelzig, Berlin
11 Professor Rading, Breslau
12 Professor Scharoun, Breslau
13 Professor Adolf G. Schneck, Stuttgart
14 Bruno Taut, Berlin
15 Max Taut, Berlin

The artistic direction of the whole exhibition has also been entrusted to the architect Mies van der Rohe.

The layout of the development is based on the intention of demonstrating that the new production methods can be readily applied to home building. This development is thus a testing ground to establish the principles of modern mass construction. The underlying principle is the definition of the new functions of the home through the use of old and new materials. In consequence, the development cannot present the methods of modern mass construction, but only a preliminary model.

At the same time, it will serve to refute the widespread view that the industrialization of house building must necessarily lead to uniformity. The existing apartment houses in large cities are indeed uniform, a fact that the department-store romanticism of their facades cannot conceal. But it is the purpose of this exhibition to show that the building of homes can be industrialized without doing violence to the individual. The objective is not the industrial production of whole apartments and buildings but the mass production of standardized building components and details. With the aid of these components and details, any variation may be achieved, with the greatest possible respect for individuality.

With clearly defined and predetermined elements, different house types can be combined in accordance with the needs of their occupants; a multitude of variations is possible.

A test lot adjoining the development will display details of the building systems, methods, and materials employed, along with other noteworthy new departures.

As it is impossible to give a comprehensive picture of all the latest technical, hygienic, and artistic achievements through buildings alone, separate exhibition halls will give a complementary survey of areas associated with the exhibition program. The equipment shown will be primarily that which is suited to simpler households, for which its purchase will actually save on housekeeping costs. All the constantly improving devices and installations which so ease the housewife's task will be shown: technical aids for the kitchen, the laundry, the bathroom, household cleaning, etc., as well as the products necessary to furnish the home, such as furniture, textiles, wallpapers, floorings, etc. But all these groups will be shown not in the manner of a trade fair but on a strictly selective basis, in keeping with the policy of the Deutscher Werkbund.

In connection with this, there will be an International Plan and Model Exhibition of New Architecture which will cover not only housing but also high-rise blocks, hydroelectric power plants, large garages, aircraft hangars, and factory and office buildings.

This exhibition will provide no definitive answers. It cannot do so, nor is it intended to: things today are still too fluid for that. But in its own restricted field it will set out to summarize the valuable experience and the plans that exist to date, and to suggest what may be best suited to improve housing conditions in the spirit of our age. In its overall arrangement, in its presentation, and in its results, it will address itself to the broad masses of our people. It is probably the first building and housing exhibition to be based on a productive principle: it wastes no money on useless exhibition buildings but makes its own contribution, through the building of the Weissenhofsiedlung, to the amelioration of the housing crisis and thus serves the public interest.
Stuttgart, December, 1926.

Deutscher Werkbund		Württemberg section of Deutscher Werkbund
Peter Bruckmann Chairman	Mies v. d. Rohe Deputy Chairman	Gustaf Stotz The Administrator

MIES VAN DER ROHE'S UNDATED LIST OF TYPES (*Siedlungstypen*)

Housing Types
I = single-family house
II = apartment house (only 3 or 4 rooms)
A = 6 rooms (2 servants)
B = 5 rooms (1–2 servants)
C = 4 rooms (1 servant)
D = 3 rooms (0 servant)

Types A–C include a maid's room. All types have bathrooms. Type I, A–D, has its own laundry, possibly combined with bath. II, central laundry. The room described as "study" can also be furnished as a bed sitting room for a temporary guest or for another resident family member (mother, aunt, etc.) It should always be designed in such a way that a person can sleep there.

I-A 6 rooms
2 servants, one a nursemaid, so nursery has alcove for her (closed off by a door)
Kitchen (1) work alcove small, eating and rest room large
(2) workroom large, eating alcove small
(3) workroom separated from rest room
Laundry with linen and ironing space
Rooms: *Parents' bedroom, two children's bedrooms* (either sleeping and living area separate, in which case the bedroom can be divided once more, or two bed-sitting rooms which can be divided according to the number of children. Possibly a large living room with a number of bedrooms arranged round it, with or without doors). *Living and dining room, living room, study/guestroom.*

I-B 5 rooms
As I-A, without the second separate living room.

I-C 4 rooms
Kitchen. Workroom smaller than rest room (space set aside for children in kitchen or living/dining room)
Living room with dining alcove
Small *study/guestroom*
2 bedrooms, one of them divisible for children (possibly study over kitchen)

I-D 3 rooms
(a) *with children:*
1 parents' bedroom
1 children's bedroom (divisible)
1 living/dining room (space set aside for children in kitchen or living/dining room)
kitchen, workroom smaller than rest room

(b) *childless:*
1 parents' bedroom
1 living/dining room
1 study/guestroom
kitchen, workroom smaller than rest room

II-C 4 rooms
living/dining room
parents' bedroom
children's bedroom (divisible)
study/guestroom
maid's room
kitchen, workroom smaller than rest room
space set aside for children

II-D 3 rooms
(a) *with children:*
living/dining room
parents' bedroom
children's bedroom (divisible)
study/guestroom
maid's room
kitchen, workroom smaller than rest room

(b) *childless:*
children's bedroom replaced by study/guestroom

II-D *alternative formula* (division of the 3-room type into one 2-room apartment and one 1-room apartment for professional people)
(a) 2 rooms, kitchen, bathroom
bedroom
living room
kitchen with alcove

(b) 1 room with small utility room (bath)

House with collective kitchen

1 room with small utility room (bath)
2 rooms with small utility room (bath)

MIES VAN DER ROHE SUMS UP, 1927

In the summer of 1925, at the convention of the Deutscher Werkbund [DWB] in Bremen, the proposal from the Württemberg section of the DWB to deal with the problem of the home in an exhibition in Stuttgart was accepted, and the execution of the task was entrusted to me.

On July 29, 1926, the proposal was accepted by the city council of Stuttgart, and the layout development plan prepared by us was agreed to. In mid-November of 1926 the *Verein Werkbund-Ausstellung "Die Wohnung"* was incorporated, and on March 1, 1927, the first sod was cut on the land set aside for the project at Weissenhof.

In taking on this work, it was clear to me that we would have to execute it in a way contrary to ideas generally current, because everyone who has concerned himself seriously with the problem of home-building has become aware of its complex character. The slogan, "Rationalization and Standardization," and also the call for an economic home building industry, touch only on partial problems, which are highly important in themselves but take on a real importance only when seen in proportion. Alongside or rather above these requirements there is the spatial problem, *the creation of a New Home.* This is a problem of the mind, one that can be solved only through creative power, not by mathematical or organizational means. I have therefore refrained from setting up any guidelines; I have simply sought out those individuals whose work leads me to expect interesting contributions to the question of the New Home. From the outset, the exhibition was conceived as an experiment, and as such it has a value quite distinct from the results achieved.

Each of the participating architects has investigated the new materials now on the market, and each has made his choice for his own building on his own responsibility. Our endeavors in this direction have, however, been restricted by the present state of building technology.

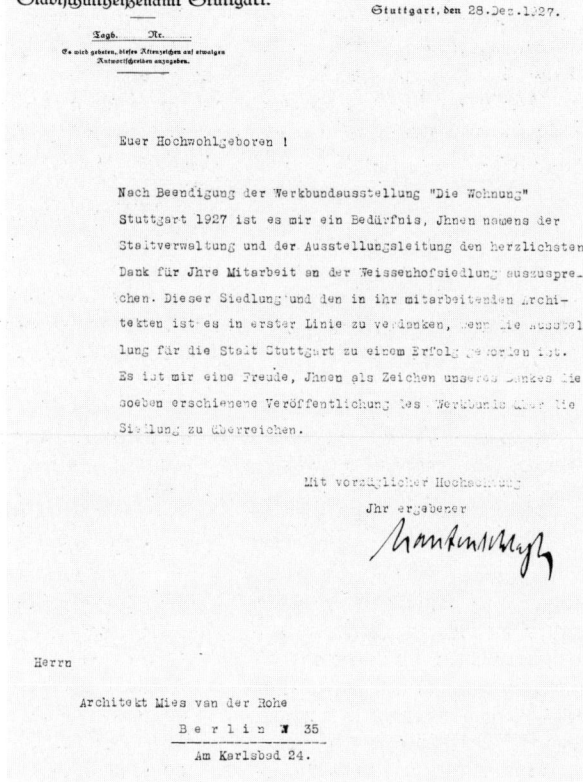

Letter from Mayor Karl Lautenschlager to Mies, December 28, 1927: "Dear Sir, Now that the Werkbund exhibition *Die Wohnung*, Stuttgart 1927, has come to an end, I feel impelled to express to you, on behalf of the city administration and the exhibition directorate, our heartfelt gratitude for your work on the Weissenhofsiedlung. It is primarily to this project, and to the architects who have worked on it, that the city of Stuttgart owes the success of the exhibition. I take great pleasure in presenting to you, as a token of our gratitude, the volume recently published on the *Siedlung* by the Werkbund. Yours faithfully, Lautenschlager."

The organizational problem cannot be solved without the collaboration of the construction industry. This was denied to us in Stuttgart, as we had no say whatsoever in the placing of the contracts. We were thus precluded from any influence on the quality of the execution. We were entirely free only in dealing with the spatial problem: the truly architectural issue.

Die Form (1927), page 257

APPENDIX D

SOME CONTEMPORARY REACTIONS

"An assemblage of flat cubes swarms up the slope in a succession of horizontal terracing, looking more like a suburb of Jerusalem than dwellings in Stuttgart."[1] Paul Bonatz's criticism refers to Mies's first layout plan, before the houses were built. By the summer of 1927, after a close study of the development, the same Bonatz wrote,

> The articulated cubes create picturesque overlapping, and the light colors create an agreeable overall impression. In cubic forms assembled in this way, it is literally impossible to create an ugly overall impression; everything combines into a certain unity.
>
> If one imagines the whole of Stuttgart transformed in this way overnight; in place of distorted and ugly roofs, in place of pointless ornaments and dull bricks, only articulated cubes in clean colors; that would be a fantastic and beautiful townscape.[2]

Bonatz's criticism was taken up in January of 1928 by the editor of the architectural journal *Wasmuth's Monatshefte*, Werner Hegemann, who added some caustic and offensive comments of his own. Bonatz had dealt with the whole Weissenhof project comprehensively and objectively; Hegemann cut out the appreciative passages from the text and replaced them with polemics:

> When the mayor of Stuttgart (or whoever it is who has him on a string) decided to support the plan for the Stuttgart Werkbund exhibition, he lost sight of the realization (if he ever had it) that in the course of the past decade Stuttgart has become the seat of the leading architectural school in Germany, if not in Europe.[3]

City Hall was furious. Deeply offended, Mayor Lautenschlager turned to his legal advisers, had opinions drawn up, made enquiries as to Hegemann's reputation, and checked over the remarks of Bonatz (who had been quoted anonymously). Bonatz made a formal apology and sent in the original text of his paper, "A Postscript to the Werkbund Project at Weissenhof," to City Hall.

The opinions obtained from attorneys were based on the assumption that the place of jurisdiction for any libel action would be Berlin, and that the cosmopolitan Berliners were likely to assume an attitude of scornful superiority to the provincials of Stuttgart. So Lautenschlager decided not to sue and contented himself with letters of apology.[4] A public retraction appeared in the *Stuttgarter Neues Tagblatt* on March 21, 1928, under the title "Das Ende eines Pamphlets [The End of a Lampoon]."

Bonatz, in his original paper, referred to the question of giving practical, objective justifications for architectural decisions: "There is not one line in the Werkbund project that can be justified on grounds of objective necessity. Such arguments are superfluous, where the designer stakes a claim, from the outset, to total artistic freedom."[5]

In 1927, shortly before his death, Hermann Muthesius, who had been a member of the Werkbund from its foundation until the split which took place in 1914, wrote a review of the Stuttgart exhibition published in the *Berliner Tagblatt* under the headline "The Last Words of a Master." He too took the question of justifiability as his starting point:

> Does the progress of the age really demand a new form of architecture? . . . Apart from the two objectives which the exhibition pursues [the struggle against "utter barbarism" in building and "propaganda for a bettering of living conditions"], there are references here and there to something called the *New Will to Form*. And, indeed, the nub of the whole movement is here. Anyone who takes the trouble to look into the matter closely will realize that what really interests the members of that circle is really New Form. *New Form* is so important to them that all other considerations are relegated to the background. This New Form has so powerful an influence on its proponents that the two other dominant themes—and especially that of rationalization, on which such stress is laid—are suppressed, even crushed. It is the New Form that ordains the *flat roof* and causes acceptance of all the manifold, still-to-be-foreseen disadvantages which that brings in its train. It is the New Form that leads to the inordinate *overlighting* of rooms, because it dictates to its exponents that, at all costs, uninterrupted strips of window must run all around the house. It is the New Form that leaves the external walls defenceless against the weather by avoiding the roof overhangs which have hitherto been customary in our climate. All these things have absolutely nothing to do with rationalization, or with economy, or with constructional necessity. These are purely formal issues. The ideal is the building of *cubic masses*. The individual cubes are interlocked and combined into a more or less well-constructed group, in which masses other than cubic ones are virtually excluded from consideration.[6]

In an article for *Wasmuth's Monatshefte* which reads like a critical testament, Muthesius wrote of the new architecture,

> Agreed, the contemporary sensibility, which tends toward smooth, clear, unadorned form, has been better served [by it] than by warmed-over styles from the past. But why all this argument from constructional rightness, function, and economy? Why, in particular, the defense of the flat roof, which is considered an essential feature of the new architecture, on grounds of a saving in cost? *The essence of the cubic constructional style has nothing to do with practicalities.*[7]

Alongside the formal criticism, criticism of the justifications offered for the form, and the criticism of the flat roof as such, there was criticism of the political tendency which was thought to underlie Modernist architecture—a criticism which concealed itself behind such apparently objective considerations as adaptation to climate, protection of local character (*Heimatschutz*), and human comfort. A holder of the rank of government architect wrote in the Berlin trade journal *Deutsche Bauzeitung*,

> The brutality of the tall, completely blank, block-like structures standing on thin iron stalks is like the cry of an artist embittered by the ugliness of the world, who rips the delusive upholstery from a basically cruel civilization and *builds a civilized stall for the beast in man*, as it is or as he sees it. . . . Our evolution has room for many, and can afford to be wide in its sympathies. Only in one thing must it be inexorable: *in distinguishing the charlatan from the prophet, the hypocrite from the individualist, the bungler from the master!*[8]

In the 1930s critical abuse of the Weissenhofsiedlung rose to new heights. "The good-natured Swabian people," according to another trade paper, *Die Deutsche Bauhütte*, in 1932, soon rejected the Weissenhof buildings as "Oriental imitations," "broken-down living-machines," "single-family houses on the Squash System," "collective anthills of vicious Central African termites," or just because they looked like "Little Jerusalem." The Werkbund had provided the world at large with "examples of typical German extravagance."[9]

After the Nazi "assumption of power" on January 30, 1933, and the "Enabling Act" of the following March, the Weissenhofsiedlung was officially regarded as "a shameful blot on the face of Stuttgart," the product of "theater architects" and "shrewd masters of extravagance" who had put up "fantasy foul-ups" in the hope of coming by bigger commissions in other cities. Mies was accused of having built the largest building himself in order to pocket the largest fee—which might have been true if the fees had been calculated in the customary manner. Even the subsidy from the governmental building research body, the Reichsforschungsgesellschaft, was alleged to have been arbitrarily raised by 200,000 marks to 350,000 marks.

The photomontage reproduced here was printed in a local *Heimatschutz* yearbook for 1941 with the caption:

> In 1927, the Werkbund development adjoining Weissenhof in Stuttgart was opened, and the victory of the New Architecture was proclaimed to an astonished world (see *Schwäbisches Heimatbuch*, 1928). At the evening reception before the opening of the exhibition, which was expressly directed against the native style of building advo-

Abb. 14. Araberdorf (Weißenhofsiedlung Stuttgart - Schwäb. Kunstverlag, H. Boettcher, Stuttg.)
(Vgl. Schw. H.=B. 1934, Abb. 132)

Im Jahr 1927 wurde mit Fahnen und Fanfaren die Werkbundsiedlung beim Weißenhof in Stuttgart eröffnet und der staunenden Welt jubelnd der Sieg des Neuen Bauens verkündet (vgl. Schw. H.=B. 1928). Auf dem Begrüßungsabend vor der Eröffnung dieser Bauausstellung, die mit Betonung gegen die vom Heimatschutz vertretene heimische Bauweise gerichtet war, machte sich auch der damalige Geschäftsführer des württembergischen Werkbundes über das traditionsverbundene Bauen des Heimatschutzes lustig. Aber die Herrlichkeit der Sieger dauerte nicht lange. Es hieß nur zu schnell: „Ach wie bald schwindet Schönheit und Gestalt! Gestern noch auf stolzen Rossen, heute durch die Brust geschossen." - Jetzt macht man sich über die Erzeugnisse der Weißenhofsiedlung lustig (Abb. 14).

Wer zuletzt lacht, lacht am besten!

cated by the *Heimatschutz* movement, the then administrator of the Württemberg Werkbund made fun of traditional *Heimatschutz* building. But the glory of the victors was not to last long. All too soon, it was "Ah, how beauty and figure fade! Yesterday riding high, now shot and bound to die." Now it is the productions of the Weissenhofsiedlung that are a laughing-stock.
He who laughs last, laughs longest![10]

If verbal abuse had been all, the lives of the Weissenhof architects would have taken very different courses. Some, indeed, were able to compromise, conform, and continue a tolerably regular life. But many of the most committed were forced to emigrate or to submit to humiliations beyond their strength to bear. Gustaf Stotz, the former administrator of the Württemberg section of the Werkbund, died in 1940, one day before the thirteenth anniversary of the 1927 opening. He had been systematically frozen out, deprived of work and of income.[11] Paul Meller, Oud's resident architect, was murdered in a Nazi prison. The biographical notes at the end of this volume record the departure from Germany of Marcel Breuer, Josef Frank, Werner Graeff, Camille Graeser, Walter Gropius, Ludwig Hilberseimer, Arthur Korn, Ferdinand Kramer, Ernst May, Erna Meyer, Ludwig Mies van der Rohe, Adolf Rading, Walter Sobotka, Bruno Taut, Oskar Wlach, and Hilde Zimmermann. Richard Döcker became a student of biology, because he—along with Hugo Häring, Max Taut, Hans Zimmermann, and others—received no commissions to build. Their personal fate was closely tied to their attitude to building: their work was treated as a political statement.

After the end of World War II and of the Reich that was intended to last a thousand years attitudes to the

Published before World War II as a postcard, this photomontage shows the Weissenhofsiedlung as it was seen by the *Heimatschutz*, and by the Nazis. The caption (which dates from 1941) is translated in the text of Appendix D

architecture of the interwar period changed very slowly, where they changed at all. Pitched roofs were stuck onto the houses and unsuitably roofed houses were built in the gaps left by the war. In 1956, more than ten years after the end of the "Nazi idiocy" [Naziotie],[12] a proposal to declare Le Corbusier's House 13 a historical monument was described as a "bad joke," a disgrace to the historic buildings department, and a sign of the "curious approach and attitudes of certain circles."[13]

In 1987, the year of the sixtieth anniversary of the Weissenhof project, the debate was revived—but this time in terms of the exemplary character of the architecture built then, as an attempt to lead young architects along the true path of Modernism, away from Postmodernism and the revival of the same "motif building" against which the younger architects of the 1920s directed their rebellion. And yet—all design reflects the spirit of its own time, whether by using stylistic features from past centuries or by pursuing honesty and simplicity, social commitment, or luxury and prestige. All designers respond to such impulses in their work, and all their responses express something of their own political and human attitudes. And so—quite rightly—the younger architects of the present are not going to do as they are told, any more than the young architects of the 1920s did.

CHRONOLOGY

1907
October 6 Deutscher Werkbund founded in Munich.

1920
February 6 Württemberg section (Württembergische Arbeitsgemeinschaft) of Deutscher Werkbund founded in Stuttgart. Chairman: Peter Bruckmann. Deputy Chairman: Paul Schmitthenner.

1924
City of Stuttgart sets aside 400,000 marks for public housing program.
Stuttgarter Kunstsommer art festival, with *Bauausstellung* (building exhibition) and *Die Form* (Werkbund exhibition of "form without ornament"). The idea of a Werkbund exhibition entitled *Die Wohnung* is first mooted.

1925
Stuttgart public housing budget raised to 1,500,000 marks.
March 30 Werkbund national board meeting in Berlin. Bruckmann puts forward idea of housing exhibition. Ludwig Mies van der Rohe and Walter C. Behrendt named as consultants.
April 16 First mention of Werkbund exhibition in Stuttgart city files.
June 27 First memorandum of intent, signed by Bruckmann and Mayor Karl Lautenschlager.
July 10 Building committee of city council agrees to 40 units of housing for Werkbund exhibition as part of 1926 building program.
September 24 First shortlist (List I) of architects drawn up by Gustaf Stotz.
September 26 List II drawn up by Mies and Hugo Häring.
October 8 Exhibition postponed to 1927.
Werkbund officially informs the city of Stuttgart that Mies is appointed artistic director. First official Werkbund list of architects (List III).
October 14 Layout sketch (block plan) by Mies.
November 2 Werkbund board meeting in Hanover confirms Mies's appointment.

1926
January Memorandum, "Wohnung der Neuzeit."
March 5 Werkbund proposal presented to newly elected city council.
March 29 City council assigns 60 units of housing (out of 1,600) to the Werkbund project.
April 16 Bruckmann addresses building committee.
April Württemberg Werkbund submits List IV of architects, classified as "Stuttgarters," "outsiders," and "foreigners."
May 5 Paul Bonatz and Paul Schmitthenner publish articles condemning Mies's block plan. Bruckmann and Mies abandon their intention of visiting Bonatz to ask for his collaboration. Bonatz sends warning letter to City Hall.
May 8 Building committee decides to maintain Mies in office.
May 14 Committee of Württemberg Werkbund meets to discuss Mies's quarrel with Bonatz and Schmitthenner.
June 12 Württemberg Werkbund elects a new committee.
July 1 Mies presents a new layout plan.
July 20 Werkbund, Berlin, draws up List V of architects.
July 24 Building committee draws up List VI.
July 29 City council votes by a clear majority to accept the Werkbund project.
July 30 Building committee entrusts city architectural department with the management of the project.
August 24 List VI sent by city building commissioner, Bürgermeister Dr. Daniel Sigloch, to Bruckmann.
August 27 Committee rejects Le Corbusier "on national grounds." Draft agreement for signature by City Hall, Mies as artistic director and representative of the architects, and Döcker as superintendent architect.
September 14 After discussion with city representatives, Le Corbusier's name is restored to the list, along with that of Mendelsohn. Further discussion of appointment of superintendent. Mies suggests Councilman Karl Beer.
September 18 Lots assigned to individual architects.
September 24 Representatives of architects and of City Hall meet to discuss fees.

September 29 Disagreements among architects, especially involving Hugo Häring.
September 30 First contracts with architects signed, but selection and contracting process continues until November. Letter from Häring to Mies leads to Häring's exclusion from the project.
October 1 Building committee agrees on List VII.
October 2 Mies tells Häring that the Stuttgart exhibit is a Werkbund matter and no business of Der Ring. "Setting out" begins at Weissenhof.
October 6 Peter Behrens asks to build his "Terraced Block" at Weissenhof.
October 7 Der Ring meets to discuss Häring-Mies conflict. Agreement reached, but Häring withdraws, followed shortly by Mendelsohn.
October 16 Stotz draws up List VIII.
November 5 Werkbund statement (Appendix A) drafted by Ludwig Hilberseimer for issue in December.
November 12 List IX, as revised by building committee to take account of the events of September and October. Scharoun's name goes to a separate vote.
November 15 Bruno Taut submits the design for his house.
Mid-November Corporate body inaugurated to run the exhibition, Verein "Werkbund-Ausstellung Die Wohnung."
November 22 Mies meets with Le Corbusier, Mart Stam, and other architects in Stuttgart. Stam sketches his cantilever chair on the reverse of Baumeister's wedding announcement (dated November 20).
December 3 Weissenhofsiedlung architects meet in Dessau for the Bauhaus opening on December 4.
December 13–14 Contacts with Schweizer Werkbund.
December 21 Building Commissioner Sigloch signs contracts with Mies and Döcker.
December 28 Mies informs his colleagues of the size of the fee: each of the fifteen (not counting Pierre Jeanneret or Victor Bourgeois) receives 3,000 marks, irrespective of the size of his building, and Döcker as superintendent architect an additional 5,000 marks.
December 30 Döcker sends circular announcing that, to achieve a cost saving of 15–20 percent, all buildings will have to be scaled down.

1927
January 9 The city is asked to provide monies for "technical experiments in construction and for an experimental housing development aimed at low-cost small dwellings" (the Kochenhofsiedlung). Building committee decides to place building contracts for Weissenhofsiedlung only with local contractors.
January 29 Reich labor ministry is asked to provide 200,000 marks for Weissenhofsiedlung.
January 31 Döcker asks Mies to confirm in writing that he approves the projects submitted by the architects, and declines to guarantee completion by July 1, 1927.
February 25 Building contracts signed for the houses by Bruno and Max Taut, Hilberseimer, Schneck, Frank, and others, but not for those by Oud, Gropius, or Le Corbusier.
March 1 The first sod is cut at Weissenhof.
March 25 Le Corbusier's involvement is once more called in question, this time on grounds of cost.
April 11 Assignment of houses and apartments to interior designers.
April 14 Further building contracts issued. First forecasts of completion: most of the single-family houses will be ready for opening day, but the apartment houses will not, because of incomplete structural calculations and drawings.
April 22 Schmitthenner submits detailed proposal and cost estimates for Kochenhofsiedlung.
April 24 Mies wires exhibition directorate to protest lack of progress.
April 25 Lilly Reich appointed to design exhibits in Gewerbehalle and in subsidiary halls on Stadtgartenumgang.
April 26 Ernst Walther arrives to act as resident architect for Mies.
April 28 Alfred Roth arrives to act as resident architect for Le Corbusier.
May 2–3 Decision to invite other architects to send their own resident representatives. City Hall agrees to fees. Visit of inspection by city architectural department to record progress. There is some consideration of canceling the Oud and Poelzig houses, as they have not yet been begun. Management of Weissenhofsiedlung vested in Döcker. Opening day set for July 23.
May 4 Mies informs mirror manufacturers, Vereinigte Spiegelglasfabriken, that they may participate in the indoor hall exhibition. The Mies-Döcker conflict grows more acute and lasts until May 27. After that they

avoid each other. Döcker declines any responsibility for Mies's apartment building.
May Mies and architects agree on color scheme for the project.
June 9 Mies tells the city that all the houses—except those of the Taut brothers—are to be painted off-white.
June 30 Assessment of cost overruns.
July 1 City agrees to pay an additional 145,000 marks in anticipation of subsidies from the Reichsforschungsgesellschaft.
July 4 Discussion of individual houses with a view to completion by opening day. Commissioner Sigloch stresses the importance of completing the Le Corbusier houses, which he considers to be among the most interesting in the whole project.
July 13 On behalf of the Werkbund, Mies declares invalid a contract signed by Döcker with Akademischer Verlag for a Werkbund book.
July 21 Street names on and around the Weissenhofsiedlung chosen by city council.
July 22 Mies wires Bruno Taut on the color scheme for his houses.
July 23 The Werkbund exhibition *Die Wohnung*, Stuttgart 1927, opens its doors.
The Kochenhofsiedlung project is announced.
August Complaints over the unfinished state of the development.
August 16–17 Reichsforschungsgesellschaft committee of experts meets in Stuttgart; Schmitthenner, a committee member, presents program and plans for Kochenhofsiedlung.
August 19 The city denies Mies permission to scaffold his building for painting.
August 26 Der Ring meets in Berlin. Mies is accused of failing to promote the Weissenhofsiedlung adequately, and resigns from Der Ring.
September 6 Exhibition directorate announces that the exhibition can now be regarded as complete and ready for showing.
September 19–23 Week of lectures: Cornelis van Eesteren on "Urban Planning"; Henry Van de Velde on "Artistic Design Questions in the Modern Construction Industry"; Walter Gropius on "Technical Questions"; Karl Moser on "Higher Education and Modern Architecture."
September 28 Le Corbusier and Pierre Jeanneret see their houses for the first time.
September 30 and October 1 Werkbund convention in Mannheim, including visit to the Stuttgart exhibition.
October 9 The indoor exhibition in the Gewerbehalle closes.
October 15 The city council decides not to sell off the Weissenhofsiedlung houses.
October 19 "Provisional Program for the Experimental Housing Project 'Am Kochenhof,' Stuttgart."
October 31 The Werkbund exhibition *Die Wohnung*, Stuttgart 1927, closes.
November Recriminations over cost overruns, variations, attribution of blame, building code stipulations. The attempt to sell the furnishings is successful only in a few cases.
November 9 Final account drawn up by city architectural department.
November 17 City council resolves to build a new experimental housing development on the hilly terrain above Kochenhof.
December Publication of the Werkbund book *Bau und Wohnung*, a record of the Weissenhof project.
Applications for structural alterations to a number of the Weissenhof houses, some of which are granted and carried out.
December 30 Döcker submits his final accounts as resident superintendent.

1928
January–December Differences with City Hall and the Reichsforschungsgesellschaft lead to the cancellation of Schmitthenner's Kochenhof project, and he is commissioned to build at Hallschlag, Bad Cannstatt, instead.
February 17 The corporate body inaugurated to run the exhibition, Verein "Werkbund-Ausstellung Die Wohnung," is wound up.

1931
Bodo Rasch suggests the building of a model housing project using timber construction. Discussions with Deputy Mayor Sigloch; the city makes the Kochenhof land available, and the Werkbund takes on the project.

1932

October Döcker placed in charge of Kochenhof project.
November 16 First layout plan for Kochenhofsiedlung.
December 19 Building committee agrees to transfer of Kochenhof land.

1933

January 30 Adolf Hitler is appointed Reich Chancellor. "Assumption of Power" by the Nazi Party. Döcker works out a provisional layout plan, scheduled to be replaced by a final model on March 22. Bonatz is invited to participate.
February 24 Model to building committee, with provisional forms of buildings.
March 8 Schmitthenner gives expert opinion on Döcker's "Provisional layout model." His criticisms are published in the *Stuttgarter Neues Tagblatt*, and Döcker publishes a reply.
March 16 Bonatz declines to take part on the grounds of the "formal aesthetic nature" of the design.
May 11 Döcker defends his plan against the criticisms of his old teacher, Bonatz.
March 30 Press statement by Deutscher Werkbund.
April 4 The state commissioner appointed by the Nazis to run the city, Dr. Karl Strölin, issues a decree which is published in the city gazette, *Amtsblatt der Stadt Stuttgart*. The Werkbund is virtually excluded from further participation in its own project at Kochenhof, with the remark (in boldface) that "the Weissenhofsiedlung, for which the Deutscher Werkbund bears the responsibility, is the clearest proof of the decline of German architectural ideas during the postwar period. It is the public duty of all those whose attitude is truly German to prevent all such cosmopolitan experiments. Our beautiful city of Stuttgart must be protected against any further desecration." The plans are removed from Döcker's office, and it is announced that the exhibition *Deutsches Holz* (German Wood) will be under the direction of Schmitthenner.
September 23 The timber-built housing project, Holzsiedlung am Kochenhof, is opened.

1933

Street names at Weissenhof changed: Friedrich-Ebert-Strasse becomes "Steinstrasse, Freiherr vom," and Rathenaustrasse becomes "Scharnhorststrasse."

1938

March Supreme Army Command in Berlin decides on the construction of a vast new complex for General Command V, to occupy the Weissenhof site. Construction is scheduled to start on April 1, 1939. A restricted competition is held: those invited to enter are Paul Bonatz with Karl Dübber, Eisenlohr & Pfennig, Herbert Hettler, Ernst Horsch with Walter Hehl, Alfred Kicherer, Paul Schmitthenner, and Adolf G. Schneck. The land is bought by the military for 1,300,000 marks, although building work never starts.

1939

April 1 Expiry of notice to quit for all tenants. Some houses used as offices for a garden exhibition in 1939, and troops of an anti-aircraft unit later quartered in some others. The Mies building used as a hospital for children with scarlet fever and diphtheria. (Source for events of 1938–39: Joedicke and Plath, 1968, 54.)

1942–1944

Stuttgart heavily damaged by bombing; city center destroyed; damage to neighboring Kunstgewerbeschule. The following houses on the Weissenhofsiedlung are wholly or partly destroyed: 16 and 17 (Gropius), 18 (Hilberseimer), 19 (Bruno Taut), 20 (Poelzig), 21 and 22 (Döcker), Max Taut (23 and 24), Rading (25).

1945

Steinstrasse and Scharnhorststrasse revert to the names of Friedrich-Ebert-Strasse and Rathenaustrasse, respectively.

1956

As a result of a proposal made by Heinz Rasch in 1953, those Weissenhofsiedlung houses that have survived the war and the postwar period are listed as historical monuments (*Landesverzeichnis der Baudenkmale*).

1968

On the occasion of the exhibition *20 Jahre Bauhaus*, in Stuttgart, the surviving houses are repainted and provided with identifying plaques.

1977

The society of "Freunde der Weissenhofsiedlung" is founded at Oberaichen, near Stuttgart, on the initiative of Bodo Rasch.

1981–1986

Rehabilitation and reconstruction by city architectural department.

1987

July 23 Sixtieth anniversary of the Weissenhofsiedlung.

BIOGRAPHIES

ARTARIA, PAUL[1]
1892 Born in Basel, August 6.
1906–1908 Apprenticeship as architectural draftsman.
1909–1911 Studies at Gewerbeschule, Basel; partly self-taught.
1911–1913 Works in various architectural offices in Basel and Lausanne.
1913–1920 Assistant to Hans Bernoulli.
1920 Own architectural practice in Basel.
1922–1924 Partnership with Karl Zaeslin.
1925–1930 Partnership with Hans Schmidt.
1927 Works as member of Schweizer Werkbund collective on interior design for House 4 in Mies apartment building at Weissenhofsiedlung.
1929 Dies at Heiden.

BEER, KARL[2]
1886 Born in Ulm, May 16.
Studies at Stadtbauschule, Stuttgart, and travels.
1912 Own architectural practice in Stuttgart.
1924 Foundation of Bau- und Heimstättenverein, for working-class housing, with Beer as first administrator.
1926–1933 Member of SPD group on city council, member of building committee.
1927 After initial doubts, lends decisive support to the Werkbund exhibition *Die Wohnung* and the Weissenhofsiedlung. For Bau- und Heimstättenverein, builds the adjoining Friedrich-Ebert-Bau as housing and Schönblick tower restaurant as a welfare building (intended to feed unemployed workers).
1933 Deprived of office and taken into "protective custody". The Nazis forbid him to practice.
1935 Emigrates to Switzerland.
post–1945 Active in postwar reconstruction.
1965 Dies in Zürich, November 17.

BEHRENS, PETER[3]
1868 Born in Hamburg, April 14.
1886–1889 Studies painting in Karlsruhe and Düsseldorf.
1890 Painter in Munich.
1893 Founder member of Munich Secession.
1896 Long study trips to Italy.
1897 Founder member of Vereinigte Werkstätten für Kunst und Handwerk, Munich.
1900 Invited to join artists' colony in Darmstadt, where he does his first work as architect (Behrens house).
1902–1903 Holds master courses at Bayerisches Gewerbemuseum, Nuremberg.
1907 Moves to Berlin; artistic consultant to electrical combine, AEG (industrial architecture, industrial design, graphics).
1922–1936 Professor and director of Meisterschule für Architektur at Akademie, Vienna.
1926–27 Design and construction of an apartment house at Weissenhofsiedlung, Stuttgart.
1936 Director of architecture section, Preussische Akademie der Künste, Berlin.
1940 Dies in Berlin, February 27.

BERLING, MAX[4]
1904 Born Max Berliner in Moscow, May 29.
1922–1926 Studies architecture at Technische Hochschule, Berlin, under Hans Poelzig; master student at Preussische Akademie der Künste, to which admitted by Max Liebermann.
1926–1933 Works as master student and project manager in Hans Poelzig's office.
1927 Resident architect for Poelzig at Weissenhofsied-

lung, Stuttgart.
1932–1933 and 1945 to present: Member of Deutscher Werkbund and BDA.
1934 Forbidden to practice by Reichskammer der bildenden Künste, works in estate management.
1936–1943 Works in craft business run by his wife, Asta Berling.
1940 Drafted by mistake into Luftwaffe construction battalion in Gütersloh; discharged.
1944 Drafted into civilian construction corps, Organisation Todt.
1945–1980 In private practice as architect in Osnabrück.
1967 Official architectural consultant to Chamber of Commerce and Industry, Osnabrück. Lives in Osnabrück.

BOURGEOIS, VICTOR[5]
1897 Born in Charleroi, Belgium, August 29.
1914–1919 Studies at Académie royale des beaux-arts, Brussels.
1920 Architect in Brussels. Professor at Ecole nationale supérieure d'architecture, Brussels, and Université du travail Paul Pasteur, Charleroi.
1922–1925 Housing development, Cité moderne, at Berchem-Saint-Agathe near Brussels (designs shown in *Internationale Plan- und Modellausstellung*, Stuttgart 1927).
1927 Design and construction (perhaps from December, 1926) of a single-family house for a private client, accepted by Mies van der Rohe as part of the Weissenhofsiedlung; his name recommended by Henry Van de Velde.
1928–1940 Founder member and vice-president of CIAM, founded at La Sarraz 1928.
1962 Dies in Brussels.

BREUER, MARCEL[6]
1902 Born in Pécs, Hungary, May 21.
1920–1928 Studies at Bauhaus in Weimar and Dessau, mainly furniture making; director of furniture making from 1926. Develops the first tubular steel chairs.
1927 Interior design of one of Mart Stam's row houses at Weissenhofsiedlung. Furniture for both of Walter Gropius's houses.
1928–1935 Lives in Berlin. Travels to Spain, North Africa, Greece, Switzerland.
1935 Emigrates to London, where he works as an architect. Association with F.R.S. Yorke.
1937–1946 Professor of architecture at Harvard University; until 1941, association with Gropius.
1946 Moves his office to New York.
1956 Sets up Marcel Breuer & Associates and a Paris branch, Marcel Breuer Architecte.
1981 Dies.

BRUCKMANN, PETER[7]
1865 Born in Heilbronn, January 13.
1883–1886 Studies at Kunstgewerbeschule and Technische Hochschule, Munich.
1887 Enters family firm of Silberwarenfabrik P. Bruckmann & Söhne, Heilbronn.
1897 Deputy chairman of exhibit in Heilbronn: *Industrie-, Gewerbe- und Kunstausstellung*.
1900 and 1904: shows at expositions, Paris and Saint Louis.
1905 Awarded the title of Hofrat (councillor); centennial celebrations of Bruckmann company.
1907 Founder member of Deutscher Werkbund; gives inaugural speech.
1908–1932 Continuous service as chairman and sometimes as vice-chairman of Werkbund; honorary chairman thereafter.
1914 Deputy chairman of historic Werkbund exhibition in Cologne.
1915 Elected to Württemberg parliament (Landtag) as member of Progressive People's Party. Begins work on Neckar Canal.
1916 Awarded title of privy councillor (Geheimer Hofrat). Chairs working committee of Südwestdeuscher Kanalverein, Maulbronn.
1920 Württemberg section (Arbeitsgemeinschaft) of Werkbund founded; Bruckmann in chair (deputy chairman, Paul Schmitthenner).
1921 Neckar-AG founded. Chairman of German Democratic Party, Württemberg.
1924 Chairman of Werkbund exhibition *Die Form*.
1925 Honorary doctorate of engineering from Technische Hochschule, Stuttgart, "for services to the improvement of German craftsmanship." Negotiations for Weissenhofsiedlung begin.
1926 Accepts chairmanship of Deutscher Werkbund at

the request of Mies van der Rohe (who becomes deputy chairman).
1927 A street in the Weissenhofsiedlung, Bruckmann-weg, is named after him.
1937 Dies in Heilbronn; obituary by Theodor Heuss.

BURCKHARDT, ERNST F.[8]
1900 Born.
1927 Works as member of Schweizer Werkbund collective on interior design for House 4 in Mies apartment building at Weissenhofsiedlung.
1958 Dies.

DIECKMANN, ERICH[9]
1886 Born Kauernik, West Prussia.
1914 War service; after severe wounds to left hand and forearm, seven semesters studying architecture in Danzig, one year studying painting and drawing in Dresden.
1921–1925 Studies at Bauhaus in Weimar (recommended by Gerhard Marcks).
1925–1930 Apprenticeship in furniture making at Staatliche Hochschule für Handwerk und Baukunst, the successor of the Bauhaus in Weimar.
1931 Starts work at Kunstgewerbeschule, Halle, housed in the castle of Giebichenstein. Works with a variety of cabinetmakers and furniture manufacturers.
1944 Dies in Berlin.

DÖCKER, RICHARD[10]
1894 Born at Weilheim an der Teck, Württemberg, June 13.
1912–1914 Studies architecture at Technische Hochschule, Stuttgart.
1914–1917 War service.
1917–1918 Resumes his studies and takes examination.
1921 Government architect, then in private practice. Works for Paul Bonatz.
1922–1925 Assistant to Bonatz at Technische Hochschule, Stuttgart.
1924 Doctorate of engineering; member of Werkbund by 1925. Private practice, frequent visits to Berlin.
1926 Member of Der Ring.
1926–1927 Appointed to act as resident superintendent architect of Weissenhofsiedlung, where he also designs and builds two single-family houses of his own.
1932–33 Exhibition project for proposed Werkbund exhibition at Kochenhofsiedlung.
1933 After Nazi takeover, forced to hand Kochenhof project over to Schmitthenner.
1933–1945 Virtually unemployed. Drafted to work in Wiederaufbauamt (reconstruction bureau) of Saarland, Saarbrücken.
1939–1941 Studies biology at Technische Hochschule, Stuttgart.
1945 Chairman of BDA.
1946 Becomes Stuttgart's first Director of Building (Generalbaudirektor).
1947 Founder member of the building and housing research institute, Forschungsgemeinschaft Bauen und Wohnen.
1947–1958 Professor of urban planning and design at Technische Hochschule, Stuttgart.
1958–1968 In private practice.
1968 Dies in Stuttgart, November 9.

EGENDER, KARL[11]
1897 Born at Mühlhausen, Switzerland, September 25.
1912–1915 Trainee in an architectural office.
1920–1921 Studies architecture at Technische Hochschule, Stuttgart, under Paul Bonatz; otherwise self-taught. Travels in Germany, France, Africa, India.
1922–1929 Partnership with Adolf Seeger.
1927 Works as member of Schweizer Werkbund collective on interior design for House 4 in Mies apartment building at Weissenhofsiedlung.
1930–1939 Partnership with Wilhelm Müller.
1969 Dies in Zürich (or at nearby Meilen).

FRANK, JOSEF[12]
1885 Born at Baden bei Wien, July 15.
to 1910 Studies at Technische Hochschule, Vienna; doctoral dissertation on "The Original Form of the Church Buildings of Leone Battista Alberti."
1910 Own architectural practice in Vienna, often working with Oskar Wlach and Oskar Strnad.
1919–1925 Professor of building construction at Kunstgewerbeschule, Vienna.
1925 Founds interior design business, Haus und Garten, with Wlach.
1926–1927 Design and building of paired houses at Weissenhofsiedlung.

1928 Founder member of CIAM.
1930 Directs International Werkbund Exhibition, Vienna.
1932–1936 Constantly employed by Svenskt Tenn.
1934 Emigrates to Sweden, returning periodically to Vienna until 1938.
1939 Swedish nationality.
1967 Dies in Stockholm, January 8.

FRANK, RUDOLF[13]
1898 Born in Untertürkheim, Stuttgart, September 8.
1923 Studies interior design at Kunstgewerbeschule, Stuttgart, under Adolf G. Schneck.
1924–1933 Assistant and instructor at same school.
1927 Interior design of one apartment in Mies apartment building at Weissenhofsiedlung.
1933–1939 Freelance interior designer.
1939–1945 War service.
1945–1974 Freelance interior and furniture designer.
1974 Dies at Döffingen, near Stuttgart.

GRADMANN, ALFRED ARNOLD[14]
1893 Born in Augsburg, January 17, a citizen of Aarau, Switzerland.
1912–1914 Office and on-site work in Zürich.
1914–1918 Studies architecture at Eidgenössische Technische Hochschule, Zürich, under Karl Moser.
1919–1924 With one interruption, works for Vogelsänger & Moser, architects, Rüschlikon.
1921–1922 Studies under Paul Bonatz, Stuttgart.
1924 Own architectural practice in Zürich.
1927 Works as member of Schweizer Werkbund collective on interior design for House 4 in Mies apartment building at Weissenhofsiedlung.

GRAEFF, WERNER[15]
1901 Born in Wuppertal, August 24.
1921–1922 Studies at Bauhaus, Weimar. Friendship with Theo van Doesburg.
1923 Member of De Stijl group.
1924 Joint editor of periodical G, with Hans Richter, El Lissitzky, and Ludwig Mies van der Rohe.
1926–1927 From December 1926 through November 1927, chief press officer of Werkbund exhibition Die Wohnung, Stuttgart; works with Mia Seeger.
1927 Edits Werkbund books Bau und Wohnung, Innenräume.
1930–1937 Directs photographic courses in a number of schools.
1937 Emigrates to Spain and then to Switzerland.
1950 Returns to Germany.
1951–1959 Instructor at Folkwang-Schule, Essen.
1957–1958 Secretary General of International Design Congress.
1959–1978 Painter and sculptor at Mülheim/Ruhr.
1978 Dies in Blacksburg, Virginia, August 29.

GRAESER, CAMILLE[16]
1892 Born in Carouge, Geneva, February 27.
1898 Moves to Stuttgart.
1908–1911 Apprenticeship as cabinetmaker.
1911–1913 Draftsman in various furniture-making workshops.
1913–1915 Kunstgewerbeschule, Stuttgart, master student under Bernhard Pankok, studies graphics with J. V. Cissarz.
1915 Private student of Adolf Hölzel.
1915–1916 Works in Berlin; member of Der Sturm.
1919 Own studio for interior design, graphics, and product design in Stuttgart; member of Deutscher Werkbund.
1927 Interior design of one apartment in Mies apartment building at Weissenhofsiedlung.
1933 Destroys his work and flees from Germany. Opens new studio in Zürich.
1953 Member of Südwest group, Stuttgart. Working as artist in Switzerland.
1980 Dies in Zürich, February 21.

GRETSCH, HERMANN[17]
1895 Born in Augsburg, November 17.
1914–1918 War service.
1918–1922 Studies architecture at Technische Hochschule, Stuttgart, under Paul Bonatz and Paul Schmitthenner.
1922–1923 Kunstgewerbeschule, Stuttgart, qualifies as potter under Bernhard Pankok.
1923 Assistant craft teacher for Württemberg education ministry.
1927 Interior design of one apartment of Behrens building at Weissenhofsiedlung.
1928 Doctorate of engineering.

1929 Craft education official with title of Gewerbeschulrat, Stuttgart.
1930 Official of Landesgewerbeamt with title of Baurat, Stuttgart.
1931 Artistic consultant and associate, Arzberg porcelain company.
1932 Board member of Landesgewerbemuseum, Stuttgart.
1936 and 1939: Designs whole German section of VIth and VIIth Triennale, Milan.
1940 State commissioner in charge of Kunstgewerbeschule, Stuttgart.
1941 State commissioner in charge of building consultancy, building conservation department, Landesgewerbeamt, Stuttgart.
1945 Freelance architect in Stuttgart.
1950 Dies in Stuttgart, May 29.

GRIESSER, PAUL[18]
1894 Born at Wasseralfingen, Württemberg, September 6.
Studies architecture under Wilhelm Kreis. Studies under Schneck. Member of Werkbund before 1925.
1925 Teaching appointment at Meisterschule für das gestaltende Handwerk (later Werkkunstschule), Bielefeld.
1927 Interior design of one apartment of Behrens building at Weissenhofsiedlung.
1960 Retires from Werkkunstschule, Bielefeld, after 35 years.
1964 Dies in Bielefeld, June 6.

GROPIUS, WALTER[19]
1883 Born in Berlin, May 18.
1903 Studies architecture in Munich.
1905–1907 Studies architecture in Berlin.
1907–1910 Assistant in the office of Peter Behrens, Berlin. Meets Mies van der Rohe.
1910–1914 Own office in Berlin, with Adolf Meyer. Member of Werkbund before 1912.
1914–1918 War service.
1918 The grand-ducal government of Weimar appoints him director of two institutions, Kunstgewerbeschule and Hochschule für bildende Kunst, on the recommendation of Van de Velde.
1919–1928 Director of the amalgamated body, the State Bauhaus (and of its successor from 1924, the Hochschule für Gestaltung, Dessau), also in charge of furniture making, some teaching of architecture.
1928–1934 Own office in Berlin: architecture and exhibition design.
1934–1937 Emigrates to England. Works with Maxwell Fry.
1937–1952 Professor of architecture at Graduate School of Design, Harvard University.
1938–1942 Collaboration with Marcel Breuer.
1946 Sets up The Architects' Collaborative.
1969 Dies in Boston, Massachusetts, July 5.

HAEFELI, MAX ERNST[20]
1901 Born in Zürich.
1919–1923 Studies architecture at Eidgenössische Technische Hochschule, Zürich, under Karl Moser.
1923–1924 Works in office of Otto Bartning, Berlin.
1925 Architectural partnership, Burkhard & Haefeli, Zürich.
1927 Own architectural office in Zürich.
1927 In charge of Schweizer Werkbund collective working on interior design for House 4 in Mies apartment building at Weissenhofsiedlung.
1937 Partnership with Werner M. Moser and Rudolf Steiger.
1976 Dies at Herrliberg, Switzerland.

HAGSTOTZ, CARL[21]
1886 Born at Göppingen, Württemberg, May 12.
1900–1911 Office career in Stuttgart from 1906.
1911–1912 Works manager in craft industry.
1912–1940 With some interruptions, board member, chief executive, and director of city exhibition, convention, and tourist offices in Stuttgart (Städtisches Ausstellungsamt, Handelshof A.G., Ausstellungs- und Tagungsstelle, Ausstellungs- und Fremdenverkehrsamt).
1924 Organizer and administrator of building exhibition, Bauausstellung, Stuttgart 1924.
1925–1928 With Gustaf Stotz, organizer and administrator of Werkbund-Ausstellung "Die Wohnung," Stuttgart 1927.
1933 Organizer and administrator of timber building exhibition, Ausstellung Deutsches Holz für Hausbau und Wohnung, Stuttgart 1933.

1935–1939 Organizer and administrator of garden exhibition, *Reichsgartenschau, Stuttgart 1939.*
1940 Dies in Stuttgart, December 4.

HEINIZ (LATER HEINITZ), OSCAR[22]
1890 Born in Stuttgart, June 15.
1910–1914 Studies architecture at Technische Hochschule, Stuttgart, under Paul Bonatz and Martin Elsässer.
1914–1918 War service.
1916 Examination at Technische Hochschule, Stuttgart.
1918–1924 Lacking commissions, works on graphic design, trade journalism, and crafts. Member of Werkbund before 1925.
1925–1936 Works with Hermann Peter Eckart, government architect.
1936–1939 City architect (Baurat) at Lehrte.
1939–1948 City architect (Baurat) at Herne.
1948–1955 Government architect (Regierungsbaurat) at Staatliches Hochbauamt, Schwäbisch Hall.
1955 Own practice at Neuhausen/Filder, near Stuttgart.

HERRE, RICHARD[23]
1885 Born in Stuttgart, August 2.
Studies architecture and art history at Technische Hochschule, Stuttgart, and follows his teacher, Theodor Fischer, to Munich and to Zürich.
1914–1918 War service.
1919 Back in Stuttgart, works on graphics and interior design. Attaches himself to the circle around Adolf Hölzel. Takes part in the work of the Uecht-Gruppe. Member of Werkbund before 1925.
1925 Contact with Le Corbusier in Paris.
Participates in a number of Werkbund exhibitions, in some cases working closely with Döcker.
1926 Graphic design of *Kommende Baukunst*, German edition of Le Corbusier's *Vers une architecture.*
1927 Interior design of House 24, by Max Taut, at Weissenhofsiedlung.
Works mainly as interior and furniture designer in Stuttgart until 1944.
1944 Studio destroyed in bombing.
1945–1959 Governmental commissions, book design.
1955 Translates Le Corbusier's *Le Modulor* (1954, 1957) into German, also works by Jean Giono.
1959 Dies in Stuttgart, December 26.

HILBERSEIMER, LUDWIG[24]
1885 Born in Karlsruhe, September 14.
Studies at Technische Hochschule, Karlsruhe.
1910–1928 Own practice as architect in Berlin.
1919 Member of Arbeitsrat für Kunst and Novembergruppe; first urban planning work. Member of Werkbund before 1925.
1926 Member of Der Ring.
1926–1927 Design and construction of one single-family house at Weissenhofsiedlung. Design of associated exhibition, *Internationale Plan- und Modellausstellung.*
1928–1932 Instructor at Dessau Bauhaus, first in charge of building theory and teaching constructional design, then director of the housing and urban planning seminar.
1928 Emigrates to U.S.
1931 Board member of Werkbund.
1938–1955 Professor of city and regional planning, Illinois Institute of Technology, Chicago.
from 1955 Director of new Department of City and Regional Planning at IIT.
1967 Dies in Chicago, May 6.

HOENE, MAX[25]
1884 Born in Rudolstadt, Thuringia.
Attends school at Ernestinum, Gotha. Studies sculpture under Wilhelm von Rümann and Balthasar Schmidt at Akademie der bildenden Künste, Munich. Study trips to Rome.
from 1907 Works as sculptor, ranging from medals to monumental figures, including portraits and memorials. Member of Werkbund before 1925.
1926 Chairman of Reichsverband bildender Künstler.
1927 Interior design of one apartment in Mies building at Weissenhofsiedlung, for Bayerische Hausratshilfe GmbH, Munich.
1947 Member of Munich Werkbund.
1965 Dies, probably in Munich.

HOFMANN, HANS[26]
1897 Born in Zürich, April 8.
1917–1918 Studies medicine for one semester and transfers to Kunstgewerbeschule to study craft for one semester.
1918–1922 Studies architecture at Eidgenössische Technische Hochschule, Zürich, under Karl Moser.
1922 Studies for one semester under Paul Bonatz in Stuttgart.
1922–1925 Works in architectural offices of Paul Mebes and Paul Emmerich, Berlin.
1925 Own architectural practice in Zürich.
1927 Works as member of Schweizer Werkbund collective on interior design for House 4 in Mies apartment building at Weissenhofsiedlung.
1928 Partnership with Adolf Kellermüller.
1937–1939 Chief architect to Swiss national show, *Schweizerische Landesausstellung.*
1940 Honorary doctorate of philosophy, Zürich University.
1942 Professor at Eidgenössische Technische Hochschule, Zürich.
1957 Dies in Zürich, December 25.

JEANNERET, PIERRE[27]
1896 Born in Geneva.
1913–1915 Studies architecture at Ecole des beaux-arts, Geneva.
1918–1921 Continues and terminates his studies.
1921–1923 Works in office of Perret brothers.
1923–1940 Works in Paris with his cousin, Charles-Edouard Jeanneret, known as Le Corbusier.
1926–1927 With him, builds single-family house and pair of houses at Weissenhofsiedlung.
1940 Studies of prefabricated building in association with Jean Prouvé (Nancy), Charlotte Perriand, G. Blanchon, and A. Masson.
1941 Moves to Grenoble; partnership with Blanchon until 1949.
1944 Returns to Paris.
1951–1965 Own projects, and director of school of architecture, Chandigarh, India. Execution of designs by Le Corbusier; director of urban planning. Appointed chief architect and planner for the Punjab.
1965 Returns to Switzerland.
1967 Dies in Geneva.

KIENZLE, WILHELM[28]
1886 Born in Basel, March 23.
1901–1903 Apprenticeship as cabinetmaker.
1903–1909 Draftsman and furniture designer in a number of firms.
1909–1911 Own workshop in Munich.
1912–1914 Works in various architectural offices, including that of Peter Behrens in Berlin.
1914–1916 Works as interior designer in a furniture factory in Munich.
1918–1951 Chief instructor in interior design classes at Kunstgewerbeschule, Zürich.
1927 Works as member of Schweizer Werkbund collective on interior design for House 4 in Mies apartment building at Weissenhofsiedlung.
1958 Dies in Zürich, August 3.

KORN, ARTHUR[29]
1891 Born in Breslau.
1909–1911 Studies at Königliche Kunst- und Gewerbeschule, Berlin.
1914 Works in city planning office, Greater Berlin.
1919 Partnership with Erich Mendelsohn.
1922–1934 Own architectural practice with Siegfried Weitzmann.
1923–1924 Secretary of Novembergruppe.
1926 Member of Der Ring.
1927 Interior design of one apartment in Mies building at Weissenhofsiedlung.
1934 Delegate at CIAM, London.
1935–1937 Emigrates to Yugoslavia.
1937 Moves to London.
1978 Dies in Vienna, November 14.

KRAMER, CARL AUGUST FRIEDRICH FERDINAND[30]
1898 Born in Frankfurt am Main, January 22.
1916 At Oberrealschule, Frankfurt.
1916–1918 War service.
1919 Studies at Technische Hochschule, Munich, under Theodor Fischer.
1920 Member of Werkbund.
1923–1924 Own architectural practice in Frankfurt.
1924 Shows pots and stoves at *Die Form* exhibition, Stuttgart.
1925–1930 Works for Ernst May at city architectural office, standardization and planning department, Frankfurt. Designs furniture, covers. Develops standard furniture designs for Hausrat GmbH.
1927 Interior design of one row house by Oud and two apartments in Mies building at Weissenhofsiedlung.

1930–1937 Own architectural practice in Frankfurt.
1933 Resigns from Werkbund.
1937 Forbidden to practice; his work exhibited as "Degenerate Art."
1938–1952 Emigrates to U.S.; own architectural practice.
1952–1964 Returns to Germany; director of planning and building bureau, Goethe University, Frankfurt.
1965–1985 Own architectural and design practice in Frankfurt.
1983 Honorary doctorates from Technische Hochschulen, Stuttgart and Munich.
1984 Honorary member of Deutscher Werkbund.
1985 Dies in Frankfurt.

KRAUSE, FRANZ[31]
1897 Born at Hemmoor, Lower Saxony, May 21.
Attends high school (Realgymnasium); studies architecture in Darmstadt and Stuttgart.
1924 Designs café and beer tent for *Bauausstellung Stuttgart.*
1927 Deputy to resident superintendent, Richard Döcker, at Weissenhofsiedlung, with special responsibility for outdoor works, paths, and garden walls.
to 1937 Architect in Berlin.
1937–1979 Architect in Wuppertal.
1937–1944 Partnership with Oskar Schlemmer and Willi Baumeister.
1950–1952 Preapprenticeship, Werkkunstschule, Wuppertal.
Painting (regular exhibitions) and sculpture in Styropor (exhibited 1971); also working as a photographer, inventor, and writer.
1979 Dies in Wuppertal, October 29.

LAUTENSCHLAGER, KARL[32]
1868 Born in Stuttgart, May 15.
Studies law in Tübingen and Leipzig.
1894 Administrative trainee in local government in Stuttgart, Ludwigsburg, and Untertürkheim.
1897–1911 Official in city government, promoted to rank of Regierungsrat.
1911 Elected mayor (Oberbürgermeister) of Stuttgart with support of National Liberal party, Center, and Conservatives; remains in office until 1933.
1913 City architectural department reorganized to include an urban expansion department.
Weissenhof area purchased by the city of Stuttgart.
1914 New local building code, which comes into force in 1919. Large scale projects: water supply, filtration plant, preliminary work for Neckar Canal.
1911–1916 Filtration plant built.
1917 Water provision for Stuttgart ensured by supply from Niederstotzingen.
1914 First contract signed for Neckar canal.
1916 Südwestdeutscher Kanalverein set up at Maulbronn.
1918 Lautenschlager refrains from ordering the use of force in connection with revolutionary activities in Stuttgart.
1921 Police brought under state control. Stuttgart joins in Neckar-Aktiengesellschaft. Honorary doctorate from Technische Hochschule, Stuttgart.
1925 Inauguration of city's first public housing program.
1925–1928 Plays major role in planning, execution, and supervision of Weissenhof project along with other building programs.
1926–1928 Planning of alternative project, Kochenhofsiedlung.
1928–1930 Expansion of city gas utility.
1931 Reelection as mayor.
1933 Ejected from office by Nazis and replaced by state commissioner, Dr. Karl Strölin.
1944 Moves to Aglishardt, near Urach, south of Stuttgart.
1945 Honorary citizen of Stuttgart.
1952 Dies, December 6.

LE CORBUSIER[33]
1887 Born in La Chaux-de-Fonds, Switzerland.
1901 Attends art school in La Chaux-de-Fonds; trains as engraver, principally under Charles L'Eplattenier.
1905 Builds first single-family house. Study trips to Italy, Greece, Turkey.
1908 Meets Josef Hoffmann (Vienna) and Henri Sauvage (Paris).
1908–1909 Works for Auguste Perret in Paris.
1910–1911 Works for Peter Behrens, Berlin; study trip to Germany on behalf of La Chaux-de-Fonds art school. Encounters Hermann Muthesius, Karl Ernst Osthaus, and Heinrich Tessenow, in whose office he works unpaid for a short time.

1914–1915 Development of the Dom-Ino house building system.
1917 Moves to Paris.
1920 First number of periodical, *L'Esprit nouveau*, October 15. Design for "Maison Citrohan."
1922 Partnership with his cousin, Pierre Jeanneret.
1923 Publishes the book *Vers une architecture*. Adopts the pseudonym of Le Corbusier.
1925 *L'Esprit nouveau* pavilion at *Exposition internationale des arts décoratifs et industriels modernes*, Paris.
1926–1927 Competition for the League of Nations building, Geneva. Design and construction of three houses at Weissenhofsiedlung. Designs and models included in accompanying *Internationale Plan- und Modellausstellung*.
1928 Inauguration of CIAM at La Sarraz.
1930 French citizenship.
1940–1944 Theoretical studies and painting, away from Paris.
1945–1965 Own architectural practice in Paris.
1965 Dies at Roquebrune, Cap-Martin, August 27.

LISKER, RICHARD[34]
1884 Born at Gräfenhainichen, near Bitterfeld, July 27. Studies painting in Munich, Berlin, and Düsseldorf.
1909–1911 Assistant to director, Staatliche Zeichenlehrerseminar, Düsseldorf.
1911–1912 Study trips to Italy, Holland, Egypt, France.
1912–1914 Painter in Berlin.
1912 Member of Werkbund (on recommendation of Walter Gropius).
1914–1918 War service as volunteer.
1918–1924 Studio and workshops for textile printing.
1924–1928 Professor, and after 1933 director, at Städelschule, Frankfurt am Main.
1925 Frankfurt consultant of Werkbund, board member.
1927 Interior design of one apartment in Mies building at Weissenhofsiedlung (introduced by Lilly Reich).
1939–1945 War service.
1945–1955 Painter and freelance textile designer.
1955 Dies at Jungingen/Hohenzollern, December 5.

LUTZ, RUDOLF[35]
1895 Born in Heilbronn, November 11.
1914 Enrolls at Kunstgewerbeschule, Stuttgart.
1916–1918 War service.
1919–1921 Studies at Bauhaus, Weimar, under Gropius and Johannes Itten.
1921–1922 Works in architectural offices in Prague and Stuttgart.
1924–1926 Own architectural practice in Stuttgart; also painter.
1925 Member of Werkbund, involved in Werkbund exhibitions.
1927 Interior design of one row house by Oud at Weissenhofsiedlung.
1966 Dies in Stuttgart, March 1.

MAY, ERNST[36]
1886 Born in Frankfurt am Main, July 27. Studies at University College, London, at Technische Hochschule, Darmstadt, and Technische Hochschule, Munich, under Friedrich von Thiersch and Theodor Fischer.
1910–1912 Works in the urban planning office of Raymond Unwin in London.
1918–1925 Technical director of a housing association (Heimstättengesellschaft) in Breslau.
1925–1930 Head of architecture and housing development for the city of Frankfurt am Main; the city's outstanding suburban neighborhood developments sprang from his initiative.
1925 Member of SDP—after taking office as city architect (Stadtbaurat)—and of Werkbund.
1927 Represented at the 1927 Werkbund exhibition in Stuttgart by a prefabricated *Plattenhaus* on the test lot and by a "Frankfurt Kitchen" in the indoor exhibition.
1930–1933 Large-scale city plans in USSR, including general plan for Moscow region (in association with Mart Stam).
1934–1954 Lives as farmer and architect in Nairobi, and later in Dar-es-Salaam; interned during World War II.
1954–1961 Heads planning section of nonprofit housing corporation, Neue Heimat, Hamburg, and plays a prominent role in replanning Germany's shattered cities.
1957 Professor at Technische Hochschule, Darmstadt.
1961 Head planner for city of Wiesbaden. General plan for Bremerhaven.
1970 Dies in Hanover, September 11.

MELLER, PAUL (PÁL)[37]
1902 Born in Ödenburg (Sopron), a Hungarian city from

1922.
1920 Graduates from high school in Sopron.
1920–1923 Studies architecture in Vienna.
1923–1925 Studies architecture in Karlsruhe.
1925–1929 Works for J.J.P. Oud, Amsterdam.
1927 Oud's resident representative during construction of his five row houses at Weissenhofsiedlung.
1929–1930 Works for Erich Mendelsohn, Berlin.
1930 Own architectural practice with Ludwig Fütterer, Berlin.
1931–1942 Works in Otto Bartning's architectural office, Berlin; from 1936 sole associate.
1942 Denounced to police, imprisoned in Plötzensee jail, Berlin, then in various concentration and labor camps in the vicinity of Berlin.
1943 Poisoned in Brandenburg-Görden prison.

MEYER, ADOLF[38]
1881 Born at Mechernich, Eifel, June 17.
1895–1897 Apprenticeship as furniture-maker, taking in technical drawing.
1897–1901 Employed in furniture workshops.
1904–1907 Studies at Kunstgewerbeschule, Düsseldorf, under Peter Behrens and Mathieu Lauweriks.
1907–1908 Works in Behrens's office in Berlin, where he encounters Gropius.
1909 Works in office of Bruno Paul in Berlin.
1910–1914 Architectural partnership with Gropius in Berlin. Member of Werkbund.
1915–1918 War service.
1919 Member of Novembergruppe and of Arbeitsrat für Kunst.
1919–1924 Partnership with Gropius in Weimar; instructor at Bauhaus.
1925–1926 Own architectural practice in Weimar, from April 1, 1926, city architect in Frankfurt am Main (recommended by Gropius).
1927–1929 Director of architecture class at Technische Hochschule, Frankfurt.
1927 Layout and interior design of two apartments in Mies building at Weissenhofsiedlung.
1929 Drowned in North Sea off the island of Baltrum.

MEYER, ERNA, NÉE POLLACK[39]
1890 Born in Berlin, February 13.
University education; Ph.D.
1926 Publishes book, *Der Neue Haushalt*, which runs into 29 considerably augmented editions by 1928; illustration section includes work by Oud and Schneck.
1926–1927 Consultant to architects at Weissenhofsiedlung on domestic economy; with Hilde Zimmermann, designs kitchens in Gewerbehalle indoor exhibition.
1934 Leaves for Palestine, May 15.

MIES VAN DER ROHE, LUDWIG[40]
1886 Born in Aachen, March 27.
1902 Draftsman in architectural offices in Aachen.
1905–1907 Works in office of Bruno Paul, Berlin.
1907 First independent commission (Riehl house).
1908–1911 On Paul Thiersch's recommendation, works as architectural draftsman in Peter Behrens's office in Berlin, where he encounters Gropius.
1912–1914 Own architectural practice in Berlin.
1914–1918 War service.
1919–1938 Own architectural practice in Berlin.
1922–1925 Member of Novembergruppe; chairman from 1923.
1923 Der Zehnerring emerges from regular meetings at Mies's home.
1924 Member of Werkbund.
1925 March 30: Werkbund board resolves to hold Stuttgart exhibition, *Die Wohnung*, and names Mies and Walter C. Behrendt as consultants. June 20: Werkbund annual convention in Essen; Mies elected to board and named artistic director of *Die Wohnung* exhibition.
1925–1927 Planning and building of Weissenhofsiedlung. Overall direction.
1926 Werkbund annual convention in Essen; Mies elected deputy chairman under Bruckmann.
Der Zehnerring enlarged to become Der Ring.
1926–1932 Deputy chairman of Werkbund.
1927 Resigns from Der Ring.
1929 Building of German Pavilion at Barcelona exhibition.
1930–1933 Director of Bauhaus in Dessau.
1931 Exhibition of German domestic architecture in Berlin: *Die Wohnung unserer Zeit*.
1933 Design of several exhibitions and single-family houses.
Bauhaus moves to Berlin and is closed by police.
1938 Emigrates to U.S.
1938–1958 Director of department of architecture, Illi-

nois Institute of Technology, Chicago. Own architectural practice, Chicago.
1969 Dies in Chicago, August 17.

MOSER, WERNER M.[41]
1896 Born in Karlsruhe.
1921 Diploma from Eidgenössische Technische Hochschule, Zürich. Studies at Technische Hochschule, Stuttgart, under Paul Bonatz and others.
1922–1923 Works in Grandpré-Molière architectural office, Rotterdam.
1923–1926 In U.S., works with Frank Lloyd Wright in Chicago and Los Angeles.
1927–1928 Works in the office of his father, Karl Moser, in Zürich.
1927 Works as member of Schweizer Werkbund collective on interior design for House 4 in Mies apartment building at Weissenhofsiedlung.
1928 Own architectural practice in Zürich.
1930 Works with Mart Stam and Ferdinand Kramer in Frankfurt am Main (old people's home for Henry and Emmy Budge Foundation).
1934 Sets up partnership with Max Haefeli and Rudolf Steiger.
1955–1956 Visiting professor at Harvard University.
1958–1963 Professor at Eidgenössische Technische Hochschule, Zürich.
1970 Dies in Zürich, August 19.

OUD, JACOBUS JOHANNES PIETER[42]
1890 Born at Purmerend, Holland, February 9. Trains at Quellinus craft school and at Rijksnormaalschool voor Tekenonderwijs, Amsterdam. Studies at Technische Hogeschool, Delft. Works in offices of P.J.H. Cuypers and Jan Stuyt in Amsterdam and of Theodor Fischer in Munich. Lives in Stuttgart for a while and subsequently works for W.M. Dudok in Leiden. Own architectural practice at Purmerend.
1916 First meeting with Theo van Doesburg.
1917 Active member of De Stijl.
1918–1933 City architect in Rotterdam; builds outstanding neighborhood housing projects.
1926–1927 Designs and builds five row houses at Weissenhofsiedlung; one house with own interiors and furniture.
Foreign member of Novembergruppe.
1933–1963 Own architectural practice.
1963 Dies in Wassenaar, April 5.

POELZIG, HANS[43]
1869 Born in Berlin, April 30.
1889–1894 Studies at Technische Hochschule, Berlin.
1899 Government architect in ministry of public works.
1900–1916 Instructor and from 1903 director at Königliche Kunst- und Gewerbeschule, Breslau (from 1911 Königliche Akademie für Kunst und Kunstgewerbe).
1916–1920 City architect (Stadtbaurat), Dresden.
1919 Chairman of Werkbund.
1920 Moves to Berlin.
Member of Novembergruppe.
1923–1933 Professor at Technische Hochschule, Berlin.
1924 Member of Der Zehnerring.
1926 Member of Der Ring, board member of BDA, board member of Werkbund.
1926–1927 Design and construction of a single-family house at Weissenhofsiedlung; numerous designs in *Internationale Plan- und Modellausstellung*.
1933 Director of United Art and Crafts Schools (Vereinigte Staatsschulen für freie und angewandte Kunst), Berlin; dismissed in the same year.
1936 Invited to work in Turkey; dies in Berlin, June 14.

RADING, ADOLF[44]
1888 Born in Berlin.
1911 Works with August Endell.
1919 Works with Behrens and Gessner.
1919–1923 Instructor at Akademie für Kunst und Kunstgewerbe, Breslau; works with August Endell.
1923–1932 Professor of architecture in Breslau.
1926 Member of Der Ring.
1926–1933 Partnership with Hans Scharoun in Berlin.
1926–1927 Design and construction of a single-family house at Weissenhofsiedlung.
1933 Emigrates to France.
1936–1943 Moves to Haifa.
1943–1950 City architect of Haifa.
1950 Moves to London; own architectural practice.
1957 Dies in London.

RASCH, BODO[45]
1903 Born in Elberfeld, February 17.
1919 Traineeship in agriculture.

1922–1926 Studies agriculture in Hohenheim, Stuttgart, concurrently completing an apprenticeship and working as a cabinetmaker.
1923–1924 Works as maker of craft objects and chairs.
1926–1930 Partnership with his brother Heinz.
1927 Interior design of one apartment in each of the buildings designed by Mies and Behrens at Weissenhofsiedlung; represented in *Internationale Plan- und Modellausstellung*. Joint author of book on Weissenhof project, *Wie bauen?* Design of suspended constructions.
1927–1930 *Wie bauen? 1 + 2, Der Stuhl, Zu—offen, Gefesselter Blick.*
from 1930 Own practice as architect and designer.
1977 Initiator and founder member of Verein der Freunde der Weissenhofsiedlung, and tireless work for preservation and restoration. Now lives at Oberaichen, near Stuttgart.

RASCH, HEINZ[46]
1902 Born in Charlottenburg, Berlin, February 15.
1916 Attends Kunstgewerbeschule, Bromberg.
1920–1923 Studies architecture at Technische Hochschule, Hanover, and Technische Hochschule, Stuttgart (Bonatz).
1923–1924 Manufactures wooden lighting fitments and chairs.
1924 In charge of exhibition press office, Bauaustellung, Stuttgart.
1925 Editor of periodical *Die Baugilde*.
1926–1930 Own architectural practice in Stuttgart; partnership with his brother Bodo.
1927 Interior design of one apartment in each of the buildings designed by Mies and Behrens at Weissenhofsiedlung; represented in *Internationale Plan- und Modellausstellung*. Joint author of book on Weissenhof project, *Wie bauen?*
Design of suspended constructions.
1927–1930 Books: *Wie bauen? 1 + 2, Der Stuhl, Zu—offen, Gefesselter Blick.*
1930 Member of Werkbund; own architectural practice in Berlin.
1933 Working in Wuppertal.
1956 Raises proposal to make the Weissenhofsiedlung a protected monument. Now resides in Wuppertal.

RAVESTEYN, SYBOLD VAN[47]
1889 Born in Rotterdam, February 18.
1906–1912 Studies at Technische Hogeschool, Delft.
1921–1957 Civil engineer for Nederlandse Spoorwegen, Netherlands State Railroad.
1919–1927 Designs furniture and craft objects.
1925 Prize for furniture at *Arts Déco* exhibition, Paris.
1927 Interior design of one row house by Oud at Weissenhofsiedlung. Design for a signal tower in *Internationale Plan- und Modellausstellung*. Latterly lived in Utrecht.

REICH, LILLY[48]
1885 Born in Berlin, June 16.
Studies at Akademie der Bildenden Künste, Vienna, under Josef Hoffmann.
1908 Works at Wiener Werkstätte in collaboration with Else Oppler.
1912 Member of Werkbund; board member in the 1920s.
1914 Contributes to Cologne Werkbund exhibition, and later works in Messeamt (fairs administration), Cologne.
1923 Own tailoring workshop in Berlin.
1924–1926 Runs annual Werkbund display, known as *Haus Werkbund*, for Messeamt, Frankfurt am Main.
1926 Moves back to Berlin and opens own studio.
from 1926 Occasional collaboration with Mies van der Rohe, including Wolff house, Guben.
1927 Appointed to design indoor exhibitions in Gewerbehalleplatz for Werkbund exhibition *Die Wohnung*, Stuttgart.
1929 Design of silk exhibit, *Seda alemana*, in German Pavilion of International Exposition, Barcelona.
1930 Takes part in German section of Paris Exposition.
1931 Designs and (jointly with Mies) directs Bauaustellung Berlin; also interiors for small low-rise dwelling and gallery exhibit of various materials in Hall 2.
1932–1933 Instructor at Bauhaus, in charge of weaving and interior design department until closure.
1934 Designs section "Gebrannte Erde" (ceramics) at exhibition *Deutsches, Deutsche Arbeit*.
1936 Textile section of exhibition *Gebt mir 4 Jahre Zeit* (directed by Mies).
1937 Textile stand at Paris World Exhibition.
1939 Assigned to work in office of Ernst Neufert. Travels to U.S.
1945 Own tailoring workshop in Berlin.

1946 Designs for neon fittings (Siemens company).
1947 Dies in Berlin, December 11.

ROTH, ALFRED[49]
1903 Born at Wangen im Allgäu, May 21.
to 1926 Studies at Eidgenössische Technische Hochschule, Zürich, under Karl Moser.
1927–1928 Works in architectural office of Le Corbusier and Pierre Jeanneret, Paris.
1927 Works on projects for two buildings by Le Corbusier and Jeanneret at Weissenhofsiedlung, acts as resident architect for both. Publishes an account of the houses, *Zwei Häuser von Le Corbusier und Pierre Jeanneret*, Stuttgart 1927; new edition, Stuttgart 1977.
1928–1930 Own architectural practice in Göteborg, Sweden.
from 1931 Own architectural practice in Zürich, partnership with Emil Roth.
from 1939 Own architectural practice in Zürich.
1949–1952 Visiting professor at Harvard University.
1957–1971 Full professor of architecture at Eidgenössische Technische Hochschule, Zürich. Numerous publications, honors from Switzerland and abroad; honorary doctorates from Technische Universität, Munich, and Istituto Universitario d'Architettura, Venice. Lives in Zürich.

SCHAROUN, HANS[50]
1893 Born in Bremen, September 20.
1912–1914 Studies at Technische Hochschule, Berlin.
1914–1918 Works for building consultancies in East Prussia.
1919–1925 Own architectural practice at Insterburg, East Prussia; competition entries.
1925–1932 Professor at Staatliche Akademie für Kunst und Kunstgewerbe, Breslau (appointed on the recommendation of Adolf Rading).
1926 Partnership with Rading and H. Kruchen in Berlin; member of Der Ring.
1926–1927 Design and construction of one single-family house at Weissenhofsiedlung.
1929 Builds a hostel at Werkbundsiedlung, Breslau, as part of Werkbund exhibition *Wohnung und Werkraum*.
1932–1943 Own architectural practice in Berlin; no public commissions.
1945–1946 Councilman and director of building and housing department, municipality of Greater Berlin.
1946–1958 Professor at Technische Universität, Berlin.
1947–1950 Director of institute of building at Deutsche Akademie der Wissenschaften, Berlin.
1955–1968 President of Akademie der Künste, Berlin.
1972 Dies in Berlin, November 25.

SCHEIBLER, FRANZ[51]
1898 Born.
1927 Based in Winterthur; works as member of Schweizer Werkbund collective on interior design for House 4 in Mies apartment building at Weissenhofsiedlung.
1960 Dies.

SCHMIDT, HANS[52]
1893 Born in Basel.
Studies at Technische Hochschulen, Munich and Zürich; through 1918; trips to Holland and U.S.S.R.
1922–1923 Working in Holland.
1924–1928 Coeditor with Mart Stam and Emil Roth of periodical *ABC—Beiträge zum Bauen*, published from Thalwil, near Zürich.
1926–1929 Own architectural practice in Basel. Member of Schweizer Werkbund.
1927 Works as member of Schweizer Werkbund collective on interior design for House 4 in Mies apartment building at Weissenhofsiedlung.
1928 Founder member of CIAM.
1929–1930 Works as architect on Werkbundsiedlung, housing project at Neubühl, Zürich.
1930–1937 Goes to Moscow as member of Ernst May's team; works on planning of Magnitogorsk and Orsk.
1937 Back in Switzerland; own architectural practice.
1956 Moves to German Democratic Republic, initially as chief architect of Institut für Typung (Standardization Institute) of ministry of construction.
1958 Director of Institute of Theory and History of Architecture, Deutsche Bauakademie.
1963 Professor at Deutsche Bauakademie.
1969 Returns to Basel.
1972 Dies at Bergell, Switzerland.

SCHNECK, ADOLF GUSTAV FRIEDRICH[53]
1883 Born at Esslingen, Württemberg, June 7.
1897–1900 Apprenticeship as saddler and upholsterer in family business.

1900–1907 Journeyman in a number of workshops; attends Gewerbeschule, Basel.
1907–1917 Takes over family business; studies at Kunstgewerbeschule and Königliche Technische Hochschule, Stuttgart, under Bonatz.
1917–1918 Teacher of drawing at Realschule, Geislingen an der Steige.
1919–1921 Own practice as architect and furniture designer.
1921–1949 Instructor at Kunstgewerbeschule, Stuttgart, initially as assistant to Bernhard Pankok, then instructor, professor and full professor; school latterly amalgamated with Staatliche Akademie der bildenden Künste.
1924 Artistic director of Werkbund exhibition *Die Form*.
1925 Directs German section of repeat exhibit in Monza; member of Werkbund.
1926–1927 Design and construction of two single-family houses at Weissenhofsiedlung. Design of one apartment in Mies building, furnished with pieces from the low-priced range, "Die Billige Wohnung," made by Deutsche Werkstätten at Hellerau, near Dresden. Competition entries and projects included in *Internationale Plan- und Modellausstellung*.
1928 Standard works on furniture design published. Designs exhibition *Der Stuhl* at Landesgewerbemuseum, Stuttgart, in collaboration with Hugo Keuerleber.
1933–1945 No buildings, but continues teaching.
1938 Recorded as shortlisted for competition to design new military headquarters on the Weissenhof site.
1945 Acting rector of Staatliche Akademie der bildenden Künste (incorporating Kunstgewerbeschule).
1948 Founder member of new Werkbund Baden-Württemberg. Numerous honors.
1949 Honorary doctorate from Technische Hochschule, Stuttgart.
1971 Dies at Schmiden, near Stuttgart, March 27.

SCHNEIDER, WALTER[54]
1902 Born in Reutlingen, Württemberg.
Apprenticeship as cabinetmaker at Schramberg in the Black Forest.
1922–1924 Studies at Kunstgewerbeschule, Stuttgart, under Schneck.
1925–1941 Works as designer for the Walter Knoll furniture company in Feuerbach (Stuttgart) and later at Herrenberg.
1927 Interior design for living room of Apartment 1 in House 1 of Mies building at Weissenhofsiedlung.
1941–1947 War service.
1949–1969 Works as architect and later as chief architect for interior design firm of Schildknecht, Stuttgart.
1983 Dies at Calw, Black Forest, March 16.

SCHUSTER, FRANZ[55]
1892 Born in Vienna, December 26.
Studies at Kunstgewerbeschule, Stuttgart, under Heinrich Tessenow.
1919 Moves with Tessenow to Handwerkerschule, Hellerau, near Dresden.
1923–1925 Chief architect to Österreichischer Verband für Siedlungs- und Kleingartenwesen.
1926–1927 Instructor at Kunstgewerbeschule, Vienna.
1927 Director of architecture class at Kunstgewerbeschule, Frankfurt am Main.
1927 Interior design of one apartment in Mies building at Weissenhofsiedlung.
from 1927 Publishes several books.
from 1937 Director of architecture class at Akademie für angewandte Kunst, Vienna.
1949 Awarded title of (supernumerary) professor.
1950–1967 Full professor.
1952–1957 Director of housing and building research unit, city of Vienna.
1972 Dies in Vienna, July 24.

SCHÜTTE-LIHOTZKY, MARGARETE[56]
1897 Born in Vienna.
Studies at Akademie für angewandte Kunst, Vienna, under Oskar Strnad and Heinrich Tessenow.
First traineeship in an architectural office in Holland.
1921 Works with Adolf Loos on housing project for disabled war veterans in Vienna.
1921–1925 Works at Österreichischer Verband für Siedlungs- und Kleingartenwesen for Vienna city housing development agency, under the direction of Adolf Loos.
1926–1930 Works in Frankfurt am Main city architect's department under Ernst May. Involved in all housing work, including the *Plattenhaus*, the first industrially prefabricated housing; design of "Frankfurt Kitchen."
1927 Frankfurt Kitchen and *Plattenhaus* exhibited at Werkbund exhibition, *Die Wohnung*, Stuttgart (indoor exhibition and test lot).
1929 Two specimen houses at international Werkbund

exhibition, Vienna. Works for clients in France, Luxembourg, Poland.
1930–1937 In Moscow with Ernst May group, as a specialist in building for children. Seven years' work on construction of new cities in U.S.S.R.
1933–1940 Spends time in U.S., China, France, Turkey.
1941–1945 Imprisoned for her membership in Austrian resistance movement against the Nazi regime.
1946–1947 Founds and directs an agency for building for children in Sofia, Bulgaria.
from 1947 Own architectural practice in Vienna.

SEEGER, MIA[57]
1903 Born in Bad Cannstatt, Stuttgart, May 9.
1921–1922 Studies at Kunstgewerbeschule, Stuttgart, in Ernst Schneidler's graphics class. Private tuition with Albert Mueller, a student of Hölzel and founder member of the Uecht-Gruppe.
1923 Works in "Haus moderner Kunst" and Kunsthaus Wanner, in the building occupied by the Württemberg section of the Werkbund and by the Südwestdeuscher Kanalverein.
1924 Works on Werkbund exhibition Die Form.
1924–1932 Works for Württemberg section of Werkbund and, from 1928, for central Werkbund in Berlin. Involved with all major Werkbund exhibitions inside and outside Germany.
1926–1927 Participates in preparation and realization of the Werkbund exhibition Die Wohnung, Stuttgart. Runs press office with Werner Graeff.
1933 Unemployed after Nazis stop the work of the Werkbund.
1934–1936 Works in state craft agency, Landesgewerbeamt, Stuttgart, under Hermann Gretsch.
1937–1953 Editor for book publisher, Verlag Julius Hoffmann, Stuttgart.
1949 Board member of Deutscher Werkbund Baden-Württemberg and of Deutscher Werkbund, Düsseldorf.
1952 Appointed to presidium of national design council, Rat für Formgebung, Darmstadt.
1952–1967 Commissioner for numerous exhibitions, member of important committees. Numerous honors and honorary memberships.
from 1967 Consultant to companies and designers; jury work; authoritative historical witness and informant to scholars and students. Lives in Stuttgart.

SIGLOCH, DANIEL[58]
1873 Born in Ulm, Württemberg, December 4.
Studies constructional engineering at Technische Hochschule, Stuttgart.
Trains as government architect.
Member of town council, Hamborn, Westphalia.
1910 Elected as first professionally qualified, paid member of Stuttgart city council, December 9.
1911 Enters office, March 1. Lautenschlager elected mayor of Stuttgart (Oberbürgermeister), May 12.
1916 Awarded the rank of mayor (Baubürgermeister) in his capacity as deputy mayor for urban design for the city.
1923 Honorary doctorate of engineering, Technische Hochschule, Stuttgart, for "his outstanding services in connection with the establishment of the X-ray laboratory at the Technische Hochschule, Stuttgart, and for his efforts to relieve the hardships suffered by students."
1925–1927 Carries overall responsibility for the building of the Weissenhofsiedlung.
1937 After friction with the new holders of power, finds work in industry.
1948 Appointed principal rapporteur on building and housing for Stuttgart; board member of research body, Forschungsgemeinschaft Bauen und Wohnen.
1953 Awarded Grand Cross of Merit of the Order of Merit by Theodor Heuss, President of the Federal Republic.
1961 Dies in Stuttgart, September 2.

SOBOTKA, WALTER[59]
1888 Born in Vienna, July 1.
1907–1912 Studies at Technische Hochschule, Vienna, under Carl König.
1919–1923 Architect in the office of Karl Korn.
1924–1927 Own practice as architect in Vienna.
1927 Interior design of one apartment in Behrens building at Weissenhofsiedlung.
1929 Member of Österreichischer Werkbund.
1932 Builds one house at Werkbundsiedlung, international Werkbund exhibition, Vienna.
1932–1938 Vice president of Österreichischer Werkbund.
1937 Emigrates to U.S.
1938–1939 Furniture designer for Thonet Inc., New York.

1939–1942 With Russell Wright (?).
1941–1958 Professor at Pittsburgh University, and until 1948 also at the Carnegie Institute.
1974 Dies, probably in New York, May.

STAM, MART (MARTIN ADRIAAN)[60]
1899 Born at Purmerend, Holland, August 5.
1911–1916 Traineeship in the office of J.M. van der Mey.
1917–1919 Studies at Rijksnormaalschool voor Tekenonderwijs, Amsterdam.
1919–1922 Works for a succession of Rotterdam architects: Grandpré-Molière, Verhagen, Kok.
1922 Works for Max Taut and Hans Poelzig in Berlin; encounters Bruno Taut and El Lissitzky.
1923–1924 Works in the office of Karl Moser, Zürich.
1924–1925 Works for Johannes Itten at Thun, Switzerland.
1924–1928 Coeditor with Hans Schmidt and Emil Roth of periodical ABC—Beiträge zum Bauen, published from Thalwil, near Zürich. External member of Novembergruppe.
1925 Returns to Paris by way of Holland; works in the office of J.A. Brinkman and L.C. van der Vlugt.
1925–1928 Member and for a time chairman of the group De 8, later De 8en Opbouw, Rotterdam.
1926 Model of a cantilever chair.
1926–1927 Design and construction of a group of three row houses at Weissenhofsiedlung. Projects on show in Internationale Plan- und Modellausstellung, Stuttgart. Interior design for one of the houses, incorporating the cantilever chair and a tubular-steel armchair version.
1928 With Werner M. Moser and Ferdinand Kramer, wins competition to design old people's home, Frankfurt am Main, for Henry and Emma Budge Foundation. Founder member of CIAM.
1928–1930 Construction of the old people's home in Frankfurt. Visiting instructor at the Bauhaus, Dessau; lectures on elements of architectural theory and planning.
1930–1934 Works in U.S.S.R with Ernst May team; city plans for Magnitogorsk, Makeyevka, Orsk.
1934 Returns to Holland.
1935–1948 Own architectural practice in Amsterdam.
1939–1948 Director of arts and crafts school, Amsterdam.
1946 Editor of visual design periodical, Open Oog, with Brusse, Jaffé, Kloos, Rietveld, Sandberg.
1948 Director of Akademie der Bildenden Künste and Hochschule fur Werkkunst, Dresden.
1949–1953 Director of Kunsthochschule, Weissensee, East Berlin.
1953 Returns to Amsterdam; partnership with Benjamin Merkelbach and P. Elling.
1966 Moves to Switzerland.
1986 Dies in Switzerland, February 23.

STEIGER, RUDOLF[61]
1900 Born in Zürich, October 4.
1918–1923 Studies at Eidgenössische Technische Hochschule, Zürich, under Karl Moser. Works in Brussels and in the practice of Arthur Korn, Berlin.
1924 Own architectural practice in Basel; builds Sandreuter house, Riehen, the first example of architectural modernism (New Architecture) in Switzerland.
1925 Collaboration with his wife, Flora Crawford-Steiger; joint projects published in ABC—Beiträge zum Bauen. Member of Schweizer Werkbund.
1927 Works as member of Schweizer Werkbund collective on interior design for House 4 in Mies apartment building at Weissenhofsiedlung.
1928 Founder member of CIAM. Takes part in exhibition das neue heim, Zürich: shows houses on Wasserwerkstrasse under overall direction of Haefeli.
1930–1932 Werkbundsiedlung at Neubühl, near Zürich.
1929–1937 Partnership with Carlo Hubacher, Zürich.
from 1937 Partnership with Haefeli and Werner M. Moser, Zürich.
1982 Dies in Zürich.

STOTZ, GUSTAF[62]
1884 Born in Stuttgart, December 6, the son of Paul Stotz, owner of a craft workshop business.
Attends Kunstgewerbeschule. Instructor in workshops of Peter Bruckmann & Söhne, Heilbronn, Württemberg.
Friendship with Theodor Heuss, the future president of the Federal Republic.
Lives in Berlin for a time.
Manager of Kunsthaus Schaller, Stuttgart.
1919 Member of Werkbund.
1922 Administrator of Württemberg section of Werkbund and of Südwestdeutscher Kanalverein, Stuttgart.
Organizes exhibitions including Werkbund exhibition of Württemberg products, with Richard Döcker as artistic

director.
1924 Initiator and co-organizer of the Stuttgarter Kunstsommer festival. Werkbund exhibition Die Form, with Adolf Schneck as artistic director. Preparations begin for the Werkbund exhibition Die Wohnung, planned jointly with the city administration.
1925–1927 Planning and organization of the Werkbund exhibition Die Wohnung, including the building of the Weissenhofsiedlung.
1929 Initiates and organizes international Werkbund exhibition Film und Foto, Stuttgart.
1930 Works on Werkbund exhibition, Paris, May–July. Housing exhibition at city housing development (Siedlung), Wangen-Untertürkheim.
1933–1940 Suffers under Nazi rule.
1940 Dies in Tirol, July 22. Theodor Heuss speaks at his funeral in Stuttgart.

STOTZ, REINHOLD[63]
1898 Born at Rosenheim, Württemberg, September 23. Craft training.
1918–1922 Studies at Kunstgewerbeschule, Stuttgart, under Schneck, and together with his future wife, Margarete.
1924–1926 Employed as a furniture designer by Möbelwerkstätten Schäufele, Kirchheim unter Teck, Württemberg.
1925 Member of Werkbund.
1927 Interior design of bedroom in Apartment 1, House 1, of Mies building (together with his wife, Margarete), and interior design of one apartment in Behrens building, at Weissenhofsiedlung.
1927 Appointed to Kunst- und Gewerbeschule, Barmen.
1931 Promoted to professorship.
1973 Dies in Wuppertal, July 20.

TAUT, BRUNO[64]
1880 Born in Königsberg, East Prussia, May 4.
1901 Graduates from Baugewerkschule, Königsberg.
1903 Works in the office of Bruno Möhring, Berlin.
1906–1908 Works in the office of Theodor Fischer, Stuttgart.
1909 Partnership with Franz Hoffmann, joined in 1914 by Taut's brother, Max.
1910 Member of Werkbund.
1918 Founder member of Arbeitsrat für Kunst, member of Novembergruppe.
1919 Originates Die Gläserne Kette, an exchange of letters between young architects.
1920–1922 Editor of the periodical Frühlicht.
1921–1924 City architect in Magdeburg.
1924 Own architectural practice in Berlin; member of Der Zehnerring.
1926 Member of Der Ring.
1926–1927 Design and construction of one single-family house at Weissenhofsiedlung.
1930–1932 Professor at Technische Hochschule, Berlin.
1933–1936 Emigration to Japan.
1936 Professor in department of architecture, Academy of Art, Istanbul; head of architectural bureau of Turkish ministry of education.
1938 Dies in Istanbul (or in Ankara), December 24.

TAUT, MAX[65]
1884 Born in Königsberg, East Prussia, May 15.
Attends Baugewerkschule, Königsberg.
1906–1911 Works in office of Hermann Billing, Karlsruhe.
1911 Own architectural practice in Berlin.
1914 Partnership with Bruno Taut and Franz Hoffmann; member of Werkbund.
1918 Founder member of Arbeitsrat für Kunst and of Novembergruppe; member of Die Gläserne Kette.
1923–1924 Founder member of Der Zehnerring.
1926 Member of Der Ring.
1926–1927 Design and construction of two single-family houses at Weissenhofsiedlung.
1933–1945 No public commissions.
1945–1953 Professor at Akademie der Bildenden Künste, Berlin, head of department of architecture.
1967 Dies in Berlin, February 26.

THIERSCH, PAUL[66]
1879 Born in Munich, son of August Thiersch and great-nephew of Friedrich von Thiersch.
1897–1898 Studies at Technikum, Winterthur.
1898–1899 Attends Gewerbeschule, Basel.
1900–1905 Studies at Technische Hochschule, Munich.
1906–1907 Assistant to Behrens in Düsseldorf, then in Berlin.
1907–1909 Office manager for Bruno Paul in Berlin; advises his subordinate, Mies, to work for Behrens.

1909 Own architectural practice in Berlin.
1915–1928 Director of Handwerker- und Kunstgewerbe-schule, Halle, which moves in 1922 to the castle of Giebichenstein, converted for the purpose by Thiersch.
1927 Interior design of two apartments in Behrens building at Weissenhofsiedlung.
1928 Professor at Technische Hochschule, Hanover.
1928 Dies in an accident in Hanover, November 15.

VOLGER, HANS[67]
1904 Born in Strasbourg.
Apprenticeship as mural painter; travels; spends one year with Heinrich Vogeler at Worpswede.
1923–1932 Student at Bauhaus (Weimar and Dessau): architecture and mural painting.
1925 Resident architect for building of Bauhaus faculty housing, Dessau.
1926–1927 Works on planning and acts as resident architect for single-family houses by Gropius at Weissenhofsiedlung.
1932–1937 Own practice in Würzburg. Studies architecture in Karlsruhe, as Bauhaus examinations not recognized as valid.
1937 Working in rural and neighborhood housing construction.
1938 In charge of building office, Krefeld, responsible for air-raid protection; member of Nazi party.
1939–1945 Thanks to his efforts, Krefeld has the lowest mortality of any German city in relation to explosive tonnage dropped.
1946 Head of city architectural department, Krefeld; own practice.
1961 Early retirement. Consultant on building damage.
1973 Dies at Bad Krozingen.

WLACH, OSKAR[68]
1881 Born in Vienna, April 18.
1898–1903 Studies at Technische Hochschule and Akademie, Vienna. Specialties: interior design and office building, under König and Ohmann.
1905 Major commission in Trieste.
1906 Returns to Vienna; doctorate.
1907 Visits Italy. Collaboration with Josef Frank and Oskar Strnad.
1917–1919 Works in Istanbul.
City projects in Vienna with Hoffmann, Frank, and Strnad; member of Österreichischer Werkbund.
1925 Starts furnishing business, Haus und Garten, with Josef Frank.
1927 Interior design of one apartment in Behrens building at Weissenhofsiedlung.
1932 Two houses at Werkbund exhibition, Vienna.
1938 Emigration via Switzerland to U.S.
Own architectural practice in New York.
1963 Dies in poverty in New York.

ZIMMERMANN, HANS[69]
1886 Born in Stuttgart (?), September 14, brother of Hilde Zimmermann.
1904–1905 Apprenticeship as cabinetmaker with M. Kohler, Stuttgart (whose firm was to make furniture for the Weissenhofsiedlung).
1907–1909 Attends training school at Königliches Kunstgewerbemuseum, Berlin; architecture and interior design classes with Professor Rieth and Bruno Paul.
1908–1909 Works in the office of Bruno Paul.
1909–1910 Design exercises at Technische Hochschule, Stuttgart, under Bonatz.
1910–1911 Works in the office of Peter Behrens.
1911–1912 Works in the office of Taut and Hoffmann.
1915 Own architectural practice (probable date). Member of Werkbund by 1925.
1926 Recommended by Le Corbusier to a prospective client in Stuttgart who has asked for a house by Le Corbusier himself.
1927 Interior design of kitchen in Apartment 1, House 1, in Mies building at Weissenhofsiedlung. Builds school at Kräherwald, Stuttgart.
1954 Dies in Stuttgart (?), May 15.

ZIMMERMANN, HILDE[70]
1890 Born in Stuttgart, August 20.
1916 Qualifies as domestic science teacher.
1924 Publishes Haus und Hausrat, a handbook for domestic science students and housewives; twenty-eight editions down to 1929.
1924–1927 Head of publicity and advice center for household use of gas, municipal utility, Städtisches Gaswerk, Stuttgart.
1927 Leading position in Stadtwerke, Essen.
1933 Emigrates to London.
1981 Dies in Stuttgart (?).

Notes

PREFACE
1   Ludwig Mies van der Rohe, address to members of the Deutscher Werkbund, Stuttgart, September 30, 1927.

I THE CLIMATE AFTER WORLD WAR I
1   *Verfassung des deutschen Reiches*, 3–4.
2   Willett, *Art and Politics*, 95.
3   Kurt Junghanns, "Bruno Taut in seiner Zeit," as cited in *Bruno Taut*, 9–10.
4   Theodor Heuss, in *Ansprachen und Vorträge*, 16.
5   Margold, "Form und Rationalisierung," 788.
6   Le Corbusier, *Vers une architecture*, 8.
7   Ibid., 10.
8   Heuss, *Vorspiele des Lebens*, 303.
9   Mia Seeger in conversation with the author.
10 Street directories, City of Stuttgart, 1919–27.
11 Bruckmann, ed., *Erinnerung an den 60*. In this festschrift, the landmarks in Bruckmann's life down to 1925 are listed and dated, the speeches made on the occasion are printed, and collages by his artist friends are reproduced. The choice was made by Bruckmann himself. The quotations here are from Fritz Elsass, ibid., 37.
12 *Stuttgarter Kunstführer* 3. no. 13 (April 1, 1922), Werkbund issue.
13 Württembergische Arbeitsgemeinschaft des deutschen Werkbundes, undated, Bundesarchiv Koblenz, Nachlass Redslob. The duration of the show is given as "mid-June through early August, 1924."
14 Exhibition catalogue *Die Form ohne Ornament, Werkbund-Ausstellung 1924* (Stuttgart, 1924), 22. Alongside "articles of use and ornament in noble and base metals, wood, glass, leather, textiles, and paper," items on show included furniture and—in the courtyard—"a group of gravestones." See *Süddeutsche Zeitung*, no. 271 (June 30, 1924).
15 Mia Seeger in conversation with the author, April 13, 1984.
16 Mannheim, Frankfurt/Main, Kaiserslautern, Ulm. See *Zehn Jahre Werkbundarbeit*, 7.
17 Ausstellungsbedingungen, exhibition catalogue *Bauausstellung Stuttgart 1924*, Stuttgart 1924, 5–7, Stadtarchiv Stuttgart.
18 Heinz Rasch and Felicitas Karg-Baumeister, in conversation with the author, May 17, 1986; another version in Joedicke and Plath, *Die Weissenhofsiedlung*, 9.
19 *Zehn Jahre Werkbundarbeit*, 6.
20 *Die Bauzeitung*, no. 44 (November 1, 1930), 522–23.
21 *Zehn Jahre Werkbundarbeit*, 4.
22 Maur, "Stuttgarts Beitrag," 1.
23 Ibid., 38, n. 16 (Willi Baumeister, unpublished journal, January 15, 1933).
24 Julius Posener, "Weissenhof und Danach," in Joedicke and Schirmbeck, eds., *Architektur der Zukunft*, 20.
25 Peter Bruckmann, "Die Gründung des Deutschen Werkbundes 6. Oktober 1907," *Die Form* (1932), 297–99.
25 Ibid.
27 Ibid.
28 Wilhelm Lotz, ed., "Aus der Werkbund-Entwicklung. Arbeiten und Gedanken aus den ersten zwanzig Jahren," *Die Form* (1932), 300ff.
29 Ibid., 329. Artists: Peter Behrens; Theodor Fischer; Josef Hoffmann; Wilhelm Kreis; Max Läuger; Adelbert Niemeyer; Joseph Olbrich; Bruno Paul; Richard Riemerschmid; J. J.Scharvogel; Paul Schultze-Naumburg; Fritz Schumacher. Companies: P. Bruckmann & Söhne; Deutsche Werkstätten für Handwerkskunst, Dresden; Eugen Diederichs Verlag; Gebrüder Klingspor; Kunstdruckerei Künstlerbund Karlsruhe; Poeschel & Trepte; Saalecker Werkstätten; Vereinigte Werkstätten für deutschen Hausrat; Theophil Müller, Dresden; Wiener Werkstätte; Wilhelm & Co.; Gottlob Wunderlich.
30 Heuss, *Hans Poelzig*, 42.

31 In his memoirs, Van de Velde gives a vivid account of this conflict of principle: Van de Velde, *Geschichte meines Lebens*, 354–55.
32 Campbell, *German Werkbund*, 163.
33 See *Arbeitsrat für Kunst 1918–1921*, and Kliemann, *Novembergruppe*.
34 Werkbund minutes: Vorstandssitzung, Bremen, June 20, 1925. Bundesarchiv Koblenz.
35 Werkbund minutes, Vorstansdsitzung, Essen, 10:15 A.M., June 23, 1926, Bundesarchiv Koblenz.
36 Ibid., 6:30 P.M.
37 Ibid.
38 Franz Pfemfert, 1879–1954, German writer, editor of the revolutionary Socialist periodicals *Die Aktion* (1911–32) and *Der rote Hahn* (The Red Rooster). Source: *Meyers Taschenlexikon* (Mannheim, 1981).
39 Karl Jakob Hirsch, "Novembergedanken," *Kunst der Zeit* 3, nos. 1–3 (1928), special issue to commemorate ten years of the Novembergruppe, 18–19.
40 Conrads, ed., *Programme und Manifeste*, 36.
41 *Arbeitsrat für Kunst 1918–1921*, 86.
42 Bruno Taut, *Das Architektur-Programm*, 1st ed. December 1918, 2d ed. early 1919, reprinted in *Arbeitsrat für Kunst 1918–1921*, 86.
43 "Architects involved" in this case is taken to include not only those who actually worked on the project but those whose names had come under consideration for it.
44 "Ein neues künstlerisches Programm," flyer, two pages, dated December 18, 1918, in *Arbeitsrat für Kunst 1918–1921*, 87.
45 "Erste Sitzung der Novembergruppe," *Kunst der Zeit* (see note 39), 10.
46 "Novembergruppe," in Lampugnani, ed., *Hatje-Lexikon der Architektur*.
47 Heinz Rasch, *Die Baugilde*, vol. 7, no. 12 (July 27, 1925), 801.
48 "Kehraus einer Kunstausstellung," *Volk und Zeit* (September 28, 1919), in *Kunst der Zeit* (see note 39), 58.
49 "Die Ausstellung der Novembergruppe," *Berliner Börsenzeitung*, no. 283 (July 1, 1920), in *Kunst der Zeit* (see note 39), 58.
50 Will Grohmann, in *Kunst der Zeit* (see note 39), 3.
51 See Kliemann, *Novembergruppe*, 9–16.
52 Ibid.
53 In 1922, Mies exhibited his glass skyscraper at the *Grosse Berliner Kunstausstellung* and was shortly afterward appointed to direct the architecture sections of all Novembergruppe exhibitions. Schulze, *Mies van der Rohe*, 109; Kliemann, *Novembergruppe*, 91–136.
54 According to Franz Schulze, Der Zehnerring was founded on April 14, 1924, two weeks *after* Ludwig Hoffmann (see text) was pensioned off. Its members came from the Bund Deutscher Architekten (BDA), which Mies had joined in 1923. Schulze, *Mies van der Rohe*, 123; Lauterbach and Joedicke, eds., *Hugo Häring*, 10.
55 Luckhardt brothers to Scharoun, April 25, 1926. See Pfankuch, *Hans Scharoun*, 59ff.
56 Gropius to Döcker, May 5, 1955, cited in Isaacs, *Walter Gropius*, vol. 2, 1026.
57 Luckhardt brothers to Scharoun, April 8 and 27, 1926; minutes of Der Ring secretariat, June 5, 1926; in Pfankuch, *Hans Scharoun*, 59ff.
58 "Architekten-Vereinigung 'Der Ring,' " notice in *Die Form* (1926), 225. The other six were Otto Haesler, Karl Krayl, Bernhard Pankok, Hans Soeder (whose work was included in the show of models and drawings, *Internationale Plan- und Modellausstellung*, which accompanied the Weissenhof exhibition of 1927), Walter Schilbach, and Karl Schneider.
59 "Der Block," *Baukunst* 4, no. 5 (May, 1928): 128–29.
60 *Die Baugilde* 10, no. 10 (May 25, 1928).
61 *Die Baukunst* 4, no. 5 (May 1928), 129. For the evolution of the Kochenhofsiedlung, see the Chronology at the end of this volume.

II THE WERKBUND EXHIBITION
1   Provisional plan for the execution of the Werkbund exhibition, Stuttgart 1926. Copy sent to Mies by the Württemberg section of the Werkbund, June 27, 1925. Mies van der Rohe Archive, New York.

2 Policy statement, Württemberg Werkbund, 1926.
3 Policy document, November 5, 1926. Mies van der Rohe Archive, New York.
4 Amtsblatt der Stadt Stuttgart (August 12, 1926), 463.
5 Ibid.
6 Die rote Fahne (May 1, 1927), cited in Ferdinand Kramer.
7 Württembergische Zeitung, no. 170 (July 25, 1927).
8 Ibid., 1, 2. The words are those of Mayor Lautenschlager, in his opening address.
9 Final drawings lodged with City Council, March 1925, Stadtarchiv Stuttgart.
10 Württembergische Zeitung (see note 7).
11 Ibid.
12 "I feel it my duty to thank my companions, the architects involved in the [Weissenhof] housing development, and, very briefly, to speak in justification of their work . . ." Stein, Holz, Eisen, special issue no. 3 (August 11, 1927).
13 Werkbund-Ausstellung 1927, 5.
14 Württembergische Zeitung (see note 7).
15 Hauptausschuss der Werkbund-Ausstellung "Die Wohnung," March 14, 1927, Stadtarchiv Stuttgart.
16 Stahl, "Die Wohnung." Cited in Schwäbisches Heimatbuch, no. 14 (Esslingen, 1928), 88.
17 Ibid., 91.
18 Ibid.
19 Werkbund-Ausstellung 1927; Werkbund exhibition directorate, Mitteilungen der Ausstellungsleitung (3), May 1927, Mies van der Rohe Archive, New York.
20 Unterkommission des Hauptausschusses der Werkbund-Ausstellung, paragraph 94, July 18, 1927, Mies van der Rohe Archive, New York.
21 Werkbund-Ausstellung 1927, 5 (speech at opening).
22 Werkbund-Ausstellung 1927, 6, 7.
23 Mitteilungen der Ausstellungsleitung (see note 19).
24 Postage stamp design, Baumeister-Archiv, Stuttgart.
25 Die Form, no. 2 (1927), 24.
26 Willi-Baumeister-Archiv, Stuttgart.
27 Paul Schmitthenner, "Zur Frage der Versuchssiedlungen" (April 22, 1927), Stadtarchiv Stuttgart.
28 Amtsblatt der Stadt Stuttgart 27, no. 24 (July 26, 1927).
29 Kurt Schwitters, i 10 (1927); Bauwelt, no. 27 (1977). [The Heimatschutz was a conservative, antimodernist pressure group; but a Schutzmann is a police patrolman: two ideas which the Tübingen representative had contrived to confuse.—Tr.]
30 Special exhibition supplement no. 12, "Die Wohnung," Württembergische Zeitung, no. 208 (September 7, 1927).
31 See Otto Völter, in Die Baugilde (1927), 836; Stuttgarter Neues Tageblatt, July 17, 1927; Die Form, no. 2 (1927), 251.
32 Werkbund-Ausstellung 1927, 102–12.
33 Ibid., 102.
34 Unterkommission des Hauptausschusses der Werkbund-Ausstellung, paragraph 13, May 31, 1927, Stadtarchiv Stuttgart.
35 Le Corbusier to Graeff, undated, Fondation Le Corbusier, Paris.
36 Werkbund-Ausstellung 1927, 113, 114.
37 Ibid., Nos. 200, 201, 347.
38 Ibid. No. 309.
39 Hauptausschuss der Werkbund-Ausstellung, paragraph 89, May 2, 1927; at the same time, it was decided not to invite other cities to participate, because there was to be no separate section for urban planning in general.
40 Die Form, no. 2 (1927), 58.
41 Werkbund-Ausstellung, 1927, Nos. 22–24, 430.
42 Werkbund-Ausstellung, 1927, No. 425.
43 Das Werk, no. 9 (1927), 259–60.
44 Stuttgarter Neues Tageblatt, July 27, 1927, Stadtarchiv Stuttgart.
45 Wilhelm Lotz, Die Form, no. 2 (1927), 251.
46 Stotz to Mies, November 23, 1927, Mies van der Rohe Archive, New York.
47 Zehn Jahre Werkbundarbeit, 1930, 7.
48 Built in 1926 by Hugo Keuerleber; destroyed in World War II. It was in this hall that Adolf Hitler made a speech that was broadcast countrywide, and a group of brave young antifascists suc-

ceeded in cutting him off by distracting the guards and slicing through the transmission cable two meters above the ground. Hitler is said never to have forgiven Stuttgart for this act of sabotage.
49 Mies to Stotz, March 13, 1927, Mies van der Rohe Archive, New York.
50 Joint committee minutes, Hauptausschuss der Werkbund-Ausstellung, paragraph 64, March 14, 1927, Stadtarchiv Stuttgart.
51 "Ausstellungsbedingungen," paragraph 2, Stein, Holz, Eisen (January 6, 1927).
52 Stotz to Mies, March 31, 1927, Mies van der Rohe Archive, New York.
53 Hauptausschuss der Werkbund-Ausstellung, paragraph 73, April 25, 1927, Stadtarchiv Stuttgart.
54 "Ausstellungsbedingungen . . .," paragraph 8, Willi-Baumeister-Archiv, Stuttgart.
55 Die Form (1927), 213.
56 City council building committee minutes, Bauabteilung des Gemeinderats, October 21, 1927, Stadtarchiv Stuttgart.
57 Hauptausschuss der Werkbund-Ausstellung, paragraph 82, May 2, 1927, Stadtarchiv Stuttgart.
58 Carl Hagstotz, Hauptausschuss der Werkbundausstellung, paragraph 117, June 26, 1927, Stadtarchiv Stuttgart.
59 Kramer, "Soziale Nützlichkeit," 25ff.
60 See Kramer, "Zur sozialgeschichtlichen Entwicklung," 106–07.
61 Grete Schütte-Lihotzky, "Die Frankfurter Küche," Stein, Holz, Eisen, February 24, 1927, 157.
62 Grete Schütte-Lihotzky, "Arbeitsersparnis im Haushalt durch neuen Wohnungsbau," Wohnungswirtschaft, no. 10 (12 May 1927), 87.
63 Huse, Le Corbusier, 88.
64 Report by Stotz, Hauptausschuss der Werkbundausstellung, paragraph 73, April 25, 1927.
65 Mies to the Walter Knoll company, Feuerbach, near Stuttgart, August 12, 1927, Mies van der Rohe Archive, New York.
66 DLW to Mies, June 8, 1927, Mies van der Rohe Archive, New York.
67 Tegethoff, Mies van der Rohe, 68, n. 10. The sculpture is now in the Staatsgalerie, Stuttgart.
68 Mies to Knoll (see note 65).
69 Deutsche Bauzeitung, no. 10 (1983), 4.
70 See Tegethoff, Mies van der Rohe, 68.
71 Die Baugilde 8, no. 21 (November 10, 1926), 1186.
72 "Die Wohnung," supplement to Stuttgarter Neues Tagblatt, no. 2, July 30, 1927.
73 DLW to Mies, Hotel Marquardt, Stuttgart, July 26, 1927, Mies van der Rohe Archive, New York.
74 DLW (Berlin office), to Mies, August 9, 1927, Mies van der Rohe Archive, New York.
75 Supplement no. 9, Württembergische Zeitung, no. 187 (August 13, 1927).
76 Stuttgarter Neues Tageblatt (see note 72).
77 Das Werk, no. 9 (1927), 260.
78 Stuttgarter Neues Tageblatt (see note 76).
79 Supplement no. 11, Württembergische Zeitung (August 27, 1927).
80 Stuttgarter Neues Tageblatt (see note 76).
81 Heinz and Bodo Rasch, Wie bauen?, 169.
82 Albert Feifel was the author of a book on industrial building methods, Marksteine für technisches Bauen, Stuttgart [c. 1928].
83 Werkbund-Ausstellung 1927, 78–80.
84 "Technische Mitteilungen," Stein, Holz, Eisen, September 22, 1927.
85 Werkbund-Ausstellung 1927, 78.
86 Werkbund-Ausstellung 1927, advertising supplement, 53.
87 Unterkommission des Hauptausschusses der Werkbund-Ausstellung, paragraph 32, June 15, 1927, Stadtarchiv Stuttgart. May undertook to erect the house free of charge and to make it over to the City of Stuttgart at the end of the exhibition without payment. Assembly work started on opening day and was scheduled, at Mies's request, to avoid coinciding with the opening speeches.
88 Ernst May, "Die Frankfurter Hausfabrik," Stein, Holz, Eisen, October 21, 1926; Dr. Fritz Rupp, Die Baugilde 8, no. 21 (November 10, 1926), 1166.
89 Das Werk, no. 9 (1927), 268.
90 Ferdinand Kramer, April 3, 1984, and Grete Schütte-Lihotzky, August 23, 1984, to the author.

91 Heinz and Bodo Rasch, Wie bauen?, 5; see also Christoph Mohr and Michael Müller, Funktionalität und Moderne (Frankfurt, 1984), 42.

III THE WEISSENHOFSIEDLUNG

1 Joedicke and Schirmbeck, eds., Architektur der Zukunft, 16.
2 "Sezessions- und Werkbundabend," Süddeutsche Zeitung, no. 269 (June 14, 1926).
3 Meeting in mayoral office, Stadtschultheissenamt, May 7, 1925, Stadtarchiv Stuttgart. Those present were representatives of the Bau- und Heimstättenverein and of the relevant city departments, and Gustaf Stotz in his capacity as chief executive of the Württemberg section of the Werkbund.
4 Bauabteilung des Gemeinderats, July 24, 1925, Stadtarchiv Stuttgart.
5 Mies to Stotz, September 11, 1925, Mies van der Rohe Archive, New York.
6 Häring (at Mies's behest) to Stotz, September 26, 1925, Mies van der Rohe Archive, New York.
7 Häring to Stadterweiterungsamt, October 14, 1925, Mies van der Rohe Archive, New York.
8 Sergius Ruegenberg to the author, June 5, 1984.
9 Städtisches Hochbauamt, October 16, 1925, Stadtarchiv Stuttgart.
10 Meeting of city council, Gemeinderat, January 12, 1928, Amtsblatt der Stadt Stuttgart (January 24, 1928).
11 Württemberg Werkbund (Württembergische Arbeitsgemeinschaft) to Mayor Lautenschlager, October 8, 1925, Stadtarchiv Stuttgart.
12 Daybook of Stadterweiterungsamt. October 15, 1925, Stadtarchiv Stuttgart.
13 Bauabteilung des Gemeinderats, paragraph 2812, October 16, 1925, Stadtarchiv Stuttgart.
14 Häring to retired Ministerialrat Karl Neuhaus, December 24, 1951, Box 42, Nachlass Hugo Häring, Akademie der Künste, Berlin. I owe the reference to Matthias Schirren, who is writing a dissertation on Häring.
15 Bauabteilung des Gemeinderats, November 12, 1925, Stadtarchiv Stuttgart.
16 Ibid.
17 Press conference, January 22, 1926 (misdated 1925), Mies van der Rohe Archive, New York.
18 Bauabteilung des Gemeinderats, April 16 and 24, 1926, Stadtarchiv Stuttgart.
19 Schwäbischer Merkur, May 5, 1926.
20 Ibid.
21 Süddeutsche Zeitung 13, no. 205 (May 5, 1926, evening edition).
22 Vorstandessitzung, Württemberg Werkbund, May 14, 1926, Mies van der Rohe Archive, New York. The quotations that follow are drawn from this document.
23 Undated. The attribution to Stotz is based on the handwriting. Mies van der Rohe Archive, New York.
24 This contradicts the statement made by Richard Döcker and recorded by Jürgen Joedicke and Christian Plath on January 18, 1968. This is by no means the only inaccuracy that emerges from that record. Joedicke and Plath, Die Weissenhofsiedlung, 10.
25 Bauabteilung des Gemeinderats, paragraph 1285, May 8, 1926, Stadtarchiv Stuttgart.
26 Deutscher Werkbund, Berlin, to Stadtschultheissenamt, Stuttgart, June 5, 1926, Stadtarchiv Stuttgart.
27 "DWB-Mitteilungen," Die Form 1, no. 8 (1926).
28 Stotz to Mies, June 14, 1926, Mies van der Rohe Archive, New York.
29 Die Form (see note 27).
30 Döcker to Mies, May 18, 1926, Mies van der Rohe Archive, New York.
31 Ibid.
32 Mies to Döcker, May 27, 1926, Mies van der Rohe Archive, New York.
33 Bruckmann to Mies, June 12, 1926, Mies van der Rohe Archive, New York.
34 Meeting, July 1, 1926, Mies van der Rohe Archive, New York.
35 Stadterweiterungsamt, July 7, 1927, Stadtarchiv Stuttgart.
36 Meeting, July 1 (see note 34).
37 Bauabteilung des Gemeinderats, July 24, 1926, Stadtarchiv Stuttgart.
38 Gemeinderat, July 28–29, 1926, Amtsblatt der Stadt Stuttgart, nos. 91 and 92 (August 10 11, 1926). The Communist spokesman was Council-

39 man Müllerschön.
Mies to Oud, September 9, 1926, Oud-Archief, Rotterdam.

40 Vorstandssitzung, Deutscher Werkbund, Berlin, March 30, 1925, Bundesarchiv, Koblenz.

41 Mies to Stotz, September 11, 1925, Mies van der Rohe Archive, New York.

42 Häring to Stotz, September 26, 1925, Mies van der Rohe Archive, New York.

43 "Vorläufiger Plan zur Durchführung der Werkbund-Ausstellung 'Die Wohnung', Stuttgart 1927," Württemberg Werkbund to Mayor Lautenschlager, June 27, 1925, Stadtarchiv Stuttgart.

44 Häring to Stotz, September 26, 1925, Mies van der Rohe Archive, New York.

45 Stotz to Mies, September 24, 1925, Mies van der Rohe Archive, New York.

46 Häring to Stotz, September 26, 1925, Mies van der Rohe Archive, New York.

47 Württemberg Werkbund to Stadtschultheissenamt, 10 August, 1925, Stadtarchiv Stuttgart.

48 Württemberg Werkbund to Stadtschultheissenamt, April 1926, Stadtarchiv Stuttgart.

49 See Silvia Ress, "Hugo Keuerleber," Seminararbericht, Fachhochschule für Technik, Stuttgart; Baukultur, no. 2 (1985), 46.

50 Bauabteilung des Gemeinderats, April 16, 1926, Stadtarchiv Stuttgart.

51 Stotz to Mies, April 26, 1926, Mies van der Rohe Archive, New York.

52 Taut and Hoffmann to Stotz, September 25, 1926, with carbon copy to Mies, Mies van der Rohe Archive, New York.

53 Schwäbischer Merkur, no. 206 (May 5, 1926); Süddeutsche Zeitung, no. 205 (May 5, 1926). See the section on the choice of site.

54 Meeting between Bruckmann and Bonatz, May 7, 1926, Stadtarchiv Stuttgart.

55 See Chronology; papers in Stadtarchiv Stuttgart.

56 Baur to Stadtschultheissenamt, July 20, 1926, and unsigned draft kept by Mies, Mies van der Rohe Archive, New York.

57 To Württemberg Werkbund, June 17, 1926, Stadtarchiv Stuttgart.

58 Formerly Königlich Württembergische Baugewerkschule, and now Fachhochschule für Technik. See Von der Winterschule zur Fachhochschule (Stuttgart, 1982), 11.

59 Sigmund to Stadtschultheissenamt, June 5, 1926, and to Councilman Professor W. Weitbrecht, July 8, 1926, Stadtarchiv Stuttgart. Schneck to Mies, July 18, 1926, Mies van der Rohe Archive, New York. Herre to Württemberg Werkbund, Stadtarchiv Stuttgart. Oscar Heiniz to Württemberg Werkbund, July 20, 1926, carbon copy to Mies, Mies van der Rohe Archive, New York.

60 Bauabteilung des Gemeinderats, paragraph 2215, July 24, 1926, Stadtarchiv Stuttgart.

61 Bauabteilung des Gemeinderats, paragraph 2444, August 27, 1926, Stadtarchiv Stuttgart.

62 Mies to Stotz, September 3, 1926, Mies van der Rohe Archive, New York.

63 Stotz to Mies, September 8, 1929, Mies van der Rohe Archive, New York.

64 Mies to Tessenow, September 9, 1926, Mies van der Rohe Archive, New York.

65 Minutes of meeting, September 14, 1926, handwritten in cursive German script, Stadtarchiv Stuttgart.

66 Tessenow to Mies, September 16, 1926, Mies van der Rohe Archive, New York.

67 Mies to Rading, September 28, 1926, Mies van der Rohe Archive, New York.

68 Ibid.

69 Mies to Gropius, September 22, 1926, Mies van der Rohe Archive, New York.

70 Mies to Stotz, September 30, 1926, Mies van der Rohe Archive, New York.

71 Mies to Häring, October 2, 1926, Mies van der Rohe Archive, New York.

72 Mies to Rading (see note 67).

73 Stotz, for Württemberg Werkbund, to Max Taut, September 19, 1926, Mies van der Rohe Archive, New York.

74 Lauterbach and Joedicke, 1965.

75 Bauabteilung des Gemeinderats, October 1, 1926, Stadtarchiv Stuttgart.

76 Ibid.

77 Stotz to Mies, October 4, 1926, Mies van der Rohe Archive, New York.

78 Ibid.

79 Mies to Stotz, September 30, 1926, Mies van der

80 Rohe Archive, New York.
Schneck to Mies, October 8, 1926, Mies van der Rohe Archive, New York.

81 Stotz to Mies, October 8, 1926, and Mies to Mendelsohn, October 9, 1926, Mies van der Rohe Archive, New York.

82 Mendelsohn to Mies, October 13, 1926, Mies van der Rohe Archive, New York.

83 Vorstands- und Ausschuszsitzung, Deutscher Werkbund, at Flugverbandshaus, Berlin, October 16, 1926, Werkbund-Archiv, Berlin.

84 Ibid.

85 Behrens to Mies, October 6, 1926, Mies van der Rohe Archive, New York.

86 Bauabteilung des Gemeinderats, November 12, 1926, Stadtarchiv Stuttgart.

87 Ibid.

88 Stotz to Mies, October 8, 1926, Mies van der Rohe Archive, New York.

89 Mies to Döcker, November 13, 1926, Mies van der Rohe Archive, New York.

MIES VAN DER ROHE

1 Werkbund-Ausstellung 1927, 25.

2 Ludwig Mies van der Rohe, in Bau und Wohnung, 77.

3 Schneck to Mies, November 25, 1926, Mies van der Rohe Archive, New York.

4 Döcker to Mies and others, December 22, 1926, Mies van der Rohe Archive, New York.

5 Döcker to Mies, December 14, 1926, Mies van der Rohe Archive, New York.

6 Ludwig Mies van der Rohe, Frühlicht, no. 3 (1921); Frühlicht (1963), 214.

7 Mies to Erna Meyer, January 6, 1927, Mies van der Rohe Archive, New York.

8 Mies to Döcker, February 5, 1927, Mies van der Rohe Archive, New York.

9 Revised specifications, February 19, 1927, Mies van der Rohe Archive, New York.

10 Reichsforschungsgesellschaft, 1929, 144.

11 Stadterweiterungsamt to Mies, June 14, 1927, Stadtarchiv Stuttgart.

12 Ernst Walther to Mies, May 2, 1927, Mies to Döcker, April 16, 1927, Mies van der Rohe Archive, New York.

13 Cable from Mies to Ausstellungsleitung, April 24, 1926. Stadtarchiv Stuttgart.

14 Walther to Mies, April 28, 1927, Mies van der Rohe Archive, New York.

15 Walther to Mies, May 2, 1927, Mies van der Rohe Archive, New York.

16 Stephan to Hochbauamt Stuttgart, April 26, 1927, Mies van der Rohe Archive, New York.

17 Mies to Döcker, April 16, 1927, Mies van der Rohe Archive, New York.

18 Walther to Mies, April 28, 1927, Mies van der Rohe Archive, New York.

19 Werner Graeff, "Hinter den Kulissen der Weissenhofsiedlung," undated ms., Werner-Graeff-Archiv, Mülheim.

20 Max Berling in telephone conversation with the author, July 24, 1984.

21 Walther to Mies, May 4, 1927, Mies van der Rohe Archive, New York.

22 Döcker to Walther, June 27, 1927, Mies van der Rohe Archive, New York. In this letter, Döcker confirmed that Walther would be paid by the city for the period from April 28 through July 27. A handwritten note gives Walther's projected departure date as September 29 or October 1.

23 Heinz Rasch to the author, July 9, 1984.

24 Döcker to all participant architects, circular no. 14, probably May 1, 1927, Mies van der Rohe Archive, New York.

25 Stadtschultheissenamt to Mies, April 30, 1927, Stadtarchiv Stuttgart.

26 Ibid., and added note to Waldmüller: "Please discuss—revocation of contract."

27 Gemeinderat, paragraph 91, May 2, 1927, Stadtarchiv Stuttgart.

28 Ibid.

29 Ibid.

30 Döcker to all participant architects, circular No. 15, May 3, 1927, Mies van der Rohe Archive, New York.

31 Bruckmann to Le Corbusier (and all participating architects), May 13, 1927, Fondation Le Corbusier, Paris.

32 Record of meeting on May 28, 1927, Stadtarchiv Stuttgart, and circular of same date, Fondation Le Corbusier, Paris.

33 Note dated June 13, 1927, on letter from Mies dated June 9, 1927, Stadtarchiv Stuttgart.

34 Mies to Stadtschultheissenamt, June 9, 1927, Stadtarchiv Stuttgart and Mies van der Rohe Archive, New York.

35 Rechtsrat Dr. Waldmüller, Stadtschultheissenamt, to Ausstellungsleitung, August 19, 1927, Stadtarchiv Stuttgart.

36 Stadtschultheissenamt to Mies, August 15, 1927, and Mies to Stadtschultheissenamt, August 19, 1927, Stadtarchiv Stuttgart.

37 The word was "Anstreichverbot." Bauabteilung des Gemeinderats, August 26, 1927, Stadtschultheissenamt to Mies, September 3, 1927, Stadtarchiv Stuttgart.

38 Ausstellungsleitung to Stadtschultheissenamt, September 7, 1927, Stadtarchiv Stuttgart.

39 Walther to Mies, September 9, 1927, Mies van der Rohe Archive, New York.

40 Mies to Stadtschultheissenamt, August 25, 1927, Stadtarchiv Stuttgart.

41 Werkbund-Ausstellung 1927, 26.

42 Heinz Rasch in conversation with the author.

43 It was Häring who accused Mies of leaving everything to the other architects; letter, 1951.

44 Mies to Ausstellungs- und Tagungsstelle, April 11, 1927, Mies van der Rohe Archive, New York.

45 Luckhardt brothers to Mies, May 9, 1927, Mies van der Rohe Archive, New York.

46 Luckhardt brothers to Mies, May 30, 1927, Mies van der Rohe Archive, New York.

47 Wagner to Mies, June 17, 1927, Mies van der Rohe Archive, New York.

48 Lüdicke, Rähnitz-Hellerau, to Mies, June 6, 1927, Mies van der Rohe Archive, New York.

49 Werkbund-Ausstellung 1927, 26.

50 Testimonials in Hans Zimmermann Estate.

51 Le Corbusier to Burkhardt, December 16, 1926, Fondation Le Corbusier, Paris.

52 Statements by Julie Schneider, March 5, 1984, and Donatus Stotz, son of Reinhold, April 12, 1985.

53 Reichsforschungsgesellschaft, 1929, 54.

54 Werkbund-Ausstellung 1927, 54.

55 Lilly Reich to Frau Lisker, January 29, 1927, Lisker-Archiv, Stuttgart.

56 Erna Stotz to Lisker, November 28, 1927, Lisker-Archiv, Stuttgart.

57 Philipp Lehmann, "Menschliche Wohnung oder Maschinenraum?" Frankfurter Zeitung 72, no. 837 (November 11, 1927), Lisker-Archiv, Stuttgart.

58 Graeff to Lisker, October 28, 1927, Lisker-Archiv, Stuttgart.

59 Graeff, ed., Innenräume, 140.

60 Werkbund-Ausstellung 1927, 27, 28.

61 Mies to Meyer, June 11, 1927, Mies van der Rohe Archive, New York.

62 Meyer to Mies, June 10, 1927, Mies van der Rohe Archive, New York.

63 Mies to Meyer, June 11, 1927, Mies van der Rohe Archive, New York.

64 Werkbund-Ausstellung 1927, 28.

65 Werkbund-Ausstellung 1927, 28, 29.

66 Kramer, "Zur Werkund-Ausstellung 'Die Wohnung,'" 105. This text was written in March of 1984 for the present book.

67 Paul Renner, Die Form (October, 1927), 320–22.

68 Kramer to Mies, May 4, 1927, Mies van der Rohe Archive, New York.

69 "Ferdinand Kramer: Neue Möbel," Die Baugilde, no. 4 (1928).

70 Deutscher Werkbund Berlin (Baur) to Kramer, October 11, 1933, Werkbund-Archiv, Berlin. [The "German salute" was the Nazi salute.—Tr.]

71 Ausstellungsleitung to Lautenschlager, November 7, 1927, Stadtarchiv Stuttgart.

72 Werkbund-Ausstellung 1927, 29.

73 Information from Frank's daughter.

74 Schneck to Mies, November 25, 1926, Mies van der Rohe Archive, New York.

75 Werkbund-Ausstellung 1927, 29.

76 Ferdinand Kramer, interviewed by Michael Andritzky and Wolfgang Jean Stock, November 20, 1978, Werkbund-Archiv, Berlin.

77 Stotz to Mies, June 1, 1926, Mies van der Rohe Archive, New York.

78 Reich to Erna Stotz, August 20, 1927, Mies van

79 "War's Lilly?" *Der Spiegel*, no. 14 (1977).
80 Professor Herbert Hirche, in conversation with the author, 1980.
81 Siegfried Kracauer, *Frankfurter Zeitung*, July 31, 1927, Kramer-Archiv, Frankfurt.
82 Lilly Reich, "Modeformen," *Die Form* 1, no. 5 (1922), 7ff.
83 *Werkbund-Ausstellung 1927*, 30.
84 Mies to Dieckmann, June 11, 1927, Mies van der Rohe Archive, New York.
85 Dieckmann to Mies, July 13, 1927, Mies van der Rohe Archive, New York.
86 Dieckmann to Mies, July 2, 1927, Mies van der Rohe Archive, New York.
87 *Werkbund-Ausstellung 1927*, 30.
88 Dieckmann to Mies, July 2, 1927, Mies van der Rohe Archive, New York.
89 *Stein, Holz, Eisen*, November 24, 1927, 1069.
90 "Arbeiten von Dieckmann," ibid., 1071–72.
91 *Werkbund-Ausstellung 1927*, pp. 30, 31.
92 Heinz and Bodo Rasch, *Wie bauen?* 124–25.
93 Ludwig Mies van der Rohe, "Zu meinem Block," *Bau und Wohnung*, 1927, 77.
94 Ludwig Mies van der Rohe, *Die Form*, special issue no. 1 (1927), 257. See Appendix C.
95 Heinz Rasch, "Woran ich mich erinnere," *Werk und Zeit* 9, no. 11 (1960), 3.
96 Graeff, ed., *Innenräume*, 158 (mention of material).
97 *Werkbund-Ausstellung 1927*, 16.
98 Kramer to Mies, May 4, 1927, Mies van der Rohe Archive, New York.
99 *Werkbund-Ausstellung 1927*, 32.
100 See Vollmer, *Künstlerlexikon des XX. Jahrhunderts*; Thieme-Becker, *Allgemeines Lexikon der bildenden Künstler* (Leipzig, 1907–50). Also *München und seine Bauten* (Munich, 1984), 275 (thanks are due to Professor Peter C. von Seidlein for drawing this reference to my attention).
101 "Ein Serienmöbel mit Varianten, Entwurf von Max Hoene," *Stein, Holz, Eisen*, July 15, 1926, 134.
102 Ibid., 135.
103 Bayerische Hausrathilfe to Mies, April 9, 1927, Mies van der Rohe Archive, New York.
104 Bayerische Hausrathilfe to Mies, April 9 and May 21 and 24, 1927, Mies van der Rohe Archive, New York.
105 Bayerische Hausrathilfe to Städtisches Liegenschaftsamt, October 21, 1927, and note on file, October 26, 1927, Stadtarchiv Stuttgart.
106 *Werkbund-Ausstellung 1927*, 32.
107 Mies to Metzke-Rovira, Graeser, and Herre (care of Metzke-Rovira), Mies van der Rohe Archive, New York.
108 Camille Graeser, "Rationelles Wohnen," *Stuttgarter Neues Tagblatt*, March 13, 1926, supplement, "Haus und Wohnung."
109 Mies to Ausstellungsleitung, April 11, 1927, Mies van der Rohe Archive, New York.
110 Graeser to Mies, April 25, 1927, Mies van der Rohe Archive, New York.
111 Mies to Graeser, May 4, 1927, Mies van der Rohe Archive, New York.
112 Graeser to Mies, May 6, 1927, Mies van der Rohe Archive, New York.
113 Graeff, ed., *Innenräume*, 156.
114 *Werkbund-Ausstellung 1927*, 32.
115 Ibid., 33.
116 Schneck to Oud, February 12, 1926, Mies van der Rohe Archive, New York.
117 Kathinka Schreiber, "Adolf G. Schneck und seine Zeit," in *Adolf G. Schneck*, 15.
118 The letter dates from June 4, 1927, although the apartment had been allotted to Schneck on April 11.
119 Schneck to Ausstellungsleitung, April 11, 1927, Mies van der Rohe Archive, New York.
120 Adolf Gustav Schneck, *Deutsche Kunst und Dekoration* 60 (1927): 420, cited in Wichmann, *Aufbruch zum neuen Wohnen*, 63.
121 *Werkbund-Ausstellung 1927*, 33.
122 Stotz to Mies, September 29, 1926, Mies van der Rohe Archive, New York. Stotz referred to illustrations of Schuster's work in *Uhu* 3, no. 1.
123 Schuster to Mies, April 23, 1927, Schuster to Mies, April 27, 1927, Schuster to Mies, May 4 and 5, 1927, Mies van der Rohe Archive, New York.
124 See inscription on drawings, Mies van der Rohe Archive, New York.
125 Handwritten letter, Schuster to Mies, April 23,

126 Mies to Schuster, April 27, 1927, Mies van der Rohe Archive, New York.
127 Franz Schuster, "Möbelchaos," *Das Neue Frankfurt* 2, no. 1 (1928), 18–19.
128 *Werkbund-Ausstellung 1927*, 33.
129 Biography in Kliemann, *Novembergruppe*.
130 *Werkbund-Ausstellung 1927*, 33; Arnold catalogue, no. 31, in Geest and Máčel, *Stühle aus Stahl*, 122.
131 *Werkbund-Ausstellung 1927*, 34.
132 *Baukultur*, no. 1 (1981), 21–22, and transcript by Heinz Rasch, March 1986.
133 Sybille Maus, "bodo rasch zum achzigsten," in *Bodo Rasch, ideen projekte bauten*.
134 Bodo Rasch, "heinz und bodo rasch 1926–1930," in ibid., p. 4.
135 Heinz Rasch, "Zu meiner Person und zu dieser Schrift," n.d., 1.
136 Mies to Rasch, April 19, 1927, Mies van der Rohe Archive, New York.
137 Döcker to all participant architects, circular, July, 1927, Fondation Le Corbusier, Paris; telegram from Bruckmann to Döcker, July 9, 1927, Mies van der Rohe Archive, New York.
138 Heinz Rasch to the author, January 6, 1986.
139 Heinz and Bodo Rasch in conversation with the author.
140 *Werkbund-Ausstellung 1927*, 34.
141 Heinz Rasch, letter to the author, March 1986.
142 Heinz Rasch to the author, April 7, 1986: the Tecta-Möbel company wanted to "revive chairs with transverse struts."
143 *Der Baumeister* 50 (1953): 248.
144 Verein der Freunde der Weissenhofsiedlung, articles of association, incorporated November 17, 1979. The author thanks Heinz and Bodo Rasch for their invaluable support.
145 *Werkbund-Ausstellung 1927*, 35.
146 Rudolf Steiger and Flora Steiger-Crawford, interview, Zürich, January 4, 1979; Werkbund-Archiv, Berlin.
147 Ibid.
148 Hauptausschuss der Werkbundausstellung, paragraph 37, December 17, 1926, Stadtarchiv Stuttgart. Dealings with Schweizer Werkbund.
149 "Aus den Verbänden," *Das Werk*, no. 9 (1927), xxix.
150 Stotz to Mies, December 16, 1926, Mies van der Rohe Archive, New York.
151 Hagstotz to Mies, April 26, 1927, Mies van der Rohe Archive, New York.
152 Heinz Rasch in conversation with the author, July 9, 1984.
153 Krause to Heinz Rasch, November 1, 1977, Werkbund-Archiv, Berlin.
154 Haefeli to Dr. Ludwig Glaeser, taped interview, The Museum of Modern Art, New York, July 2, 1973.
155 Haefeli to Esch & Anke, architects, of Mannheim, March 4, 1929, GTA, Eidgenössische Technische Hochschule.
156 List of furniture in House 4 of Mies block, prices excluding customs duty, GTA, Eidgenössische Technische Hochschule, Zürich.
157 Haefeli to Glaeser (see note 154).
158 Steiger (see note 146), 8.
159 Haefeli to Glaeser (see note 154).
160 *Das Werk*, no. 9 (1927), 273.
161 Ibid., 275.
162 *i 10*, (1927), 345–46.
163 Sergius Ruegenberg, who was then working for Mies, clearly remembers that the Mies building was only plastered, not painted at all. Letter to the author, March 18, 1986.

OUD

1 *Werkbund-Ausstellung 1927*, 36.
2 *Das Werk*, no. 9 (1927), 265.
3 Stotz to Mies, July 13, 1925, Mies van der Rohe Archive, New York. Stotz's report on a visit to Holland.
4 J.J.P. Oud, "Von Technik und Baukunst," *Innendekoration* (August 1925), 292.
5 Mies to Oud, September 9, 1926, Mies van der Rohe Archive, New York.
6 Oud to Mies, September 14, 1927, Mies van der Rohe Archive, New York.
7 Mies to Oud, November 15, 1926, Mies van der Rohe Archive, New York.
8 Bauabteilung des Gemeinderats, December 23, 1926, paragraph 3881, Stadtarchiv Stuttgart.

9 Mies to Oud, January 3, 1927, Mies van der Rohe Archive, New York.
10 Handwritten postcard from Oud to Mies, January 5, 1927, Mies van der Rohe Archive, New York.
11 Oud to Döcker, January 17, 1927 (wrongly dated 1926), Oud-Archief, Rotterdam.
12 Bauabteilung des Gemeinderats (see note 8).
13 "Das Haus Oud," in Reichsforschungsgesellschaft, 1929, 64.
14 See Hans Oud, *J.J.P. Oud* (The Hague, 1984).
15 Postcards from Stotz to Oud with greetings from friends, Oud-Archief, Rotterdam.
16 Oud to Döcker (see note 11).
17 Guidelines from Dr. Erna Meyer, November, 1926, Oud-Archief, Rotterdam.
18 Oud to Döcker (see note 11).
19 *Bau und Wohnung 1927*, 87.
20 Mia Seeger, November 16, 1926.
21 Meyer to Oud, January 24, 1927, Oud-Archief, Rotterdam.
22 Ibid.
23 Meyer to Oud, February 2, 1927, Oud-Archief, Rotterdam.
24 Reichsforschungsgesellschaft, *Bericht über die Siedlung*, 144.
25 *Bau und Wohnung 1927*, 94.
26 Heinz and Bodo Rasch, *Wie bauen?* 63.
27 Ibid., 61.
28 Kossel to Oud, May 23, 1927, Oud-Archief, Rotterdam.
29 Döcker to all participant architects, circular no. 15, May 3, 1927, Mies van der Rohe Archive, New York, Fondation Le Corbusier, Paris, and Stadtarchiv Stuttgart.
30 Meller to Oud, undated, Oud-Archief, Rotterdam.
31 Meller to Oud, undated, Oud-Archief, Rotterdam.
32 Meller to Oud, July 19, 1927, Oud-Archief, Rotterdam.
33 Meller to Oud, undated, Oud-Archief, Rotterdam.
34 Meller to Oud, July 25, 1927, Oud-Archief, Rotterdam.
35 Meller to Oud, undated, c. August 1, 1927, Oud-Archief, Rotterdam.
36 Ibid.
37 Meller to Oud, July 21, 1927, Oud-Archief, Rotterdam. Unfortunately, the colors are not specified.
38 Meller to Oud, July 19, 1927, Oud-Archief, Rotterdam.
39 Reichsforschungsgesellschaft, *Bericht über die Siedlung*, 63.
40 Stotz to Stadtschultheissenamt, September 6, 1927, Stadtarchiv Stuttgart.
41 Meller to Oud, August 31, 1927, Oud-Archief, Rotterdam.
42 Ferdinand Kramer, April 9, 1984.
43 Kramer, "Zur Werkbund-Ausstellung 'Die Wohnung,'" Information on Paul Meller's death was received from his son, Pali Meller Marcovicz.
44 Hans Oud (see note 14), 105, n. 138.
45 *Werkbund-Ausstellung 1927*, 37–39.
46 *Werkbund-Ausstellung 1927*, 37.
47 Stotz to Mies, March 31, 1927, Mies van der Rohe Archive, New York.
48 Mies to Lutz, April 12, 1927, Mies van der Rohe Archive, New York.
49 *Werkbund-Ausstellung 1927*, 38.
50 Meller to Oud, undated, around August 1, 1927, Oud-Archief, Rotterdam.
51 Meller to Oud, August 31, 1927, Oud-Archief, Rotterdam.
52 *Werkbund-Ausstellung 1927*, 38.
53 Graeff, ed., *Innenräume*, 15, note to fig. 5.
54 Erna Meyer, "Wohnungsbau und Hausführung," *Der Baumeister* (June 1927), 92, 93.
55 *Werkbund-Ausstellung 1927*, 39.
56 Ferdinand Kramer, "Individuelle oder typisierte Möbel?" *Das Neue Frankfurt* 2 (January 1928): 10.
57 Edgar Wedepohl, *Wasmuth's Monatshefte für Baukunst* (1927), 394–95.
58 Oud to Wedepohl, undated, September–October 1927, Oud-Archief, Rotterdam.
59 Wedepohl to Oud, November 30, 1927, Oud-Archief, Rotterdam.
60 Wedepohl to Hegemann, carbon copy and covering letter to Oud, January 19, 1928, Oud-Archief, Rotterdam.

61 Oud to Döcker, January 22, 1936, Oud-Archief, Rotterdam.

BOURGEOIS
1 *Werkbund-Ausstellung 1927*, 40.
2 Information from Dr. Ing. habil. Dietrich Worbs, 1984.
3 "Die Überflüssigen" (1908), Loos, *Sämtliche Schriften*, 267.
4 "Kulturentartung" (1908), ibid., 271.
5 Mia Seeger in conversation with the author.
6 Deutscher Werkbund to Stadtschultheissenamt, July 20, 1926, Stadtarchiv Stuttgart.
7 Bauabteilung des Gemeinderats, July 24, 1926. Notes on margin of letter from Werkbund dated July 20.
8 "Ornament und Verbrechen" (1908), in Loos, *Sämtliche Schriften*.
9 "Trotzdem" (1931), ibid.
10 Stotz had told Mies of it a week previously: Stotz to Mies, November 5, 1926, Mies van der Rohe Archive, New York.
11 Dr. Boll to the author, July 3, 1985.
12 Ibid.
13 "That has been rejected," were Stotz's words. Walter Boll, telephone conversation with the author, September 1985. Dr. Boll died in November of 1985.
14 Boll to the author (see note 11).
15 Boll to the author (see note 13).
16 Ibid.
17 Hauptausschuss der Werkbund-Ausstellung, paragraph 45, January 15, 1927, Stadtarchiv Stuttgart.
18 Hauptausschuss der Werkbund-Ausstellung, March 14, 1927, Stadtarchiv Stuttgart.
19 Baugesuch Dr. Boll, April 18, 1927, and Gutachten, signed Burkhardt, May 6, 1927.
20 Unterkommission des Hauptausssschusses der Werkbund-Ausstellung, paragraph 3, May 24, 1927, Stadtarchiv Stuttgart.
21 Boll to the author (see note 13).
22 Boll to the author (see note 11).
23 *Werkbund-Ausstellung 1927*, 41.
24 Boll to the author (see note 11).
25 Ibid.
26 *Bau und Wohnung*, 149.
27 Ibid., 147.
28 Archives d'architecture moderne to the author, March 3, 1985.
29 See Schwäbischer Siedelungsverein, 1927.

SCHNECK
1 *Werkbund-Ausstellung 1927*, 42–44.
2 Mies to Schneck, September 9, 1926, Mies van der Rohe Archive, New York.
3 Schneck to Mies, November 10, 1926, Mies van der Rohe Archive, New York.
4 Mies to Schneck, November 13, 1926, Mies van der Rohe Archive, New York.
5 Sigloch to Döcker and Mies, December 3, 1926, Mies van der Rohe Archive, New York.
6 Frank Werner, "Annäherungsversuche an den Architekten Adolf G. Schneck," in *Adolf G. Schneck*, 101.
7 Reichsforschungsgesellschaft, *Bericht über die Siedlung*, 144.
8 Plans and isometric views, undated, Mies van der Rohe Archive, New York.
9 *Bau und Wohnung*, 118–120.
10 *Die Form* (August 1927), 267.
11 Döcker to Mies, December 14, 1927, Mies van der Rohe Archive, New York.
12 Erna Meyer to Mies, January 4, 1927, Mies van der Rohe Archive, New York.
13 Edgar Wedepohl, *Wasmuth's Monatshefte für Baukunst* (1927), 397.
14 *Werkbund-Ausstellung 1927*, 44.
15 *Stein, Holz, Eisen*, November 3, 1927.
16 Frank Werner (see note 6), 119.
17 Germanisches Nationalmuseum, Nuremberg: architectural collections, Munich.

LE CORBUSIER AND PIERRE JEANNERET
1 *Werkbund-Ausstellung 1927*, 45–47.
2 Mies van der Rohe, *Die Form*, no. 1 (1927), 257.
3 Le Corbusier, *Vers une architecture*; first translated into German by Hans Hildebrandt, and published by Deutsche Verlags-Anstalt as *Kommende Baukunst* (Stuttgart, 1926).
4 *Le Corbusier 1910–1965*, 25.
5 Le Corbusier, *Towards a New Architecture*, 222.

6 *Le Corbusier 1910–1965*, 28.
7 In the work of Charlotte Perriand.
8 Mies to Le Corbusier, October 5, 1926, Mies van der Rohe Archive, New York.
9 Ibid.
10 Bauabteilung des Gemeinderats, October 1, 1926, Stadtarchiv Stuttgart.
11 Western Switzerland here is French-speaking Switzerland; France is Arch-Enemy.
12 Handwritten minutes in cursive German script of a meeting concerning the Weissenhofsiedlung, September 9, 1926, Stadtarchiv Stuttgart.
13 See above, "The Selection Process."
14 Mies to Behrendt, Hôtel Voltaire, Paris, October 4, 1926, Mies van der Rohe Archive, New York.
15 Pierre Jeanneret and Charles-Edouard Jeanneret (Le Corbusier) were cousins.
16 Le Corbusier to Mies, postcard, October 26, 1926, and letter, November 3, 1926, Mies van der Rohe Archive, New York.
17 Mies to Le Corbusier, November 10, 1926, on letterhead of the exhibition directorate, overprinted with Mies's Berlin address for reply, Mies van der Rohe Archive, New York.
18 Ibid.
19 Herre to Le Corbusier, November 21, 1926, Fondation Le Corbusier, Paris.
20 Heinz Rasch, "Wege der neuen Architektur," *Stuttgarter Neues Tagblatt*, November 26, 1926, cited from *Stein, Holz, Eisen*, December 23, 1926. For the house as a "suit," see the chapter on Bruno Taut, House 19.
21 Döcker to Le Corbusier, December 6, 1926, Fondation Le Corbusier, Paris.
22 Mies to Le Corbusier, December 13, 1926, Fondation Le Corbusier, Paris.
23 Le Corbusier to Döcker, December 15, 1926, Fondation Le Corbusier, Paris.
24 *Le Corbusier, 1910–1965*, 60.
25 Ibid.
26 Döcker to all participating architects, circular no. 5, December 27, 1926.
27 Döcker to Mies, January 3, 1927, Mies van der Rohe Archive, New York.
28 Schneck to Mies, December 22, 1926, Mies van der Rohe Archive, New York.
29 Erna Meyer to Mies, January 10, 1927, Mies van der Rohe Archive, New York.
30 Mies to Erna Meyer, January 11, 1927, Mies van der Rohe Archive, New York.
31 Le Corbusier to Döcker, January 12, 1927, Fondation Le Corbusier, Paris. Le Corbusier's Paris office was still overburdened with work on the League of Nations project: Alfred Roth to the author, October 3, 1985.
32 Bauabteilung des Gemeinderats, March 25, 1927, Stadtarchiv Stuttgart.
33 Le Corbusier to Döcker, March 26, 1927, Fondation Le Corbusier, Paris.
34 Le Corbusier to Döcker, April 14, 1927. Handwritten; a German translation was made, but it is inaccurate in a number of essential points (undated handwritten draft). The author has used a German translation by Eugen Helmlé.
35 Alfred Roth, interview, Zürich, January 4, 1979, Werkbund-Archiv, Berlin.
36 Le Corbusier to Döcker, April 25, 1927, Fondation Le Corbusier, Paris.
37 Roth, interview, 1979 (see note 35).
38 Roth to Le Corbusier, May 29, 1927, Fondation Le Corbusier, Paris.
39 Roth's book came out the same year: Roth, 1927.
40 Le Corbusier to Roth, July 21, 1927, Fondation Le Corbusier, Paris.
41 Roth to Le Corbusier, May 29, 1927, Fondation Le Corbusier, Paris.
42 Le Corbusier, "Wie wohnt man," 10.
43 Roth to Le Corbusier, May 29, 1927, Fondation Le Corbusier, Paris.
44 Döcker to Roth, June 27, 1927, Fondation Le Corbusier, Paris.
45 Baupolizei-Abteilung des Gemeinderats, July 5, 1927, Stadtarchiv Stuttgart.
46 Roth to Le Corbusier, July 17, 1927, Fondation Le Corbusier, Paris.
47 Roth to Le Corbusier, July 18, 1927. The emphasis is Roth's: "vraiment pauvre."
48 Roth to Le Corbusier, August 7, 1927, Fondation Le Corbusier, Paris. (Roth's emphasis.)
49 Roth to Le Corbusier, August 23, 1927, Fondation Le Corbusier, Paris.
50 Roth, in conversation with the author, March 8, 1984.

51 Weissenhof-Karikaturen, Stadtarchiv Stuttgart.
52 Hassan: Roth in conversation with the author, March 8, 1984.
53 Roth to Le Corbusier (see note 49).
54 Ibid.
55 Published in Roth, 1927, in *Bau und Wohnung*, in *Die Form*, and in many other architectural journals. The version given here is from *Le Corbusier 1910–1965*, 44, where the last paragraph is in the German version only.
56 Le Corbusier, "La Signification de la cité-jardin," 13–15; a shortened German version, "Wie wohnt man in meinen Stuttgarter Häusern?" was published in *Das Neue Frankfurt* 2 (January 1928).
57 Le Corbusier, "L'Aménagement intérieur," 33–36; a German version by Alfred Roth, "Die Innenausstattung unserer Häuser auf dem Weissenhof," was published in Graeff, ed., *Innenräume*, 122–25.
58 Roth, *Zwei Wohnhäuser*, 36–37.
59 Edgar Wedepohl, *Wasmuth's Monatshefte für Baukunst*, no. 8 (1927), 396–97.
60 R. Blank, "Die Stuttgarter Wohnbauausstellung," *Das Wohnen* 3 (1928): 49.
61 *Das Werk*, no. 19 (1927), 263.
62 Wedepohl (see note 59), 396.
63 Wedepohl (see note 59), 397.
64 *Das Werk* (see note 61).
65 Karl Konrad Düssel, "Die Stuttgarter Weissenhofsiedlung," *Deutsche Kunst und Dekoration*, October 1927, 94.
66 Ruegenberg to the author, June 5, 1984.
67 Charles Moore, "Ort, Erinnerung und Architektur" (translated into German by Norbert Moest), in Joedicke and Schirmbeck, eds., *Architekur der Zukunft*, 54.
68 Hans Hildebrandt, foreword, in Roth, *Zwei Wohnhäuser*, 4.

GROPIUS
1 *Werkbund-Ausstellung 1927*, 48–50.
2 Mies, speaking at the Blackstone Hotel in Chicago on May 18, 1953, in honor of Gropius's seventieth birthday. Giedion, *Walter Gropius*, 21.
3 Isaacs, *Walter Gropius*, vol. 1, 388.
4 Gropius to Mies, September 21, 1926, Mies van der Rohe Archive, New York.
5 Gropius to Mies, October 2, 1926, Mies van der Rohe Archive, New York.
6 Gropius to Mies, December 15, 1926. Mies van der Rohe Archive, New York.
7 Isaacs, *Walter Gropius*, vol. 1, 384.
8 Walter Gropius, "systematische vorarbeit für rationalen wohnungsbau," *bauhaus*, no. 2 (1927), 1.
9 Frank, *Architektur und Symbol*.
10 *Das Werk*, no. 9 (1927), 270–71.
11 Gropius to Mies, December 21, 1926, Mies van der Rohe Archive, New York.
12 Döcker to Mies, December 31, 1926, Mies van der Rohe Archive, New York.
13 Gropius to Mies, December 31, 1926, Mies to Gropius, January 8, 1927, Stotz to Mies, February 23, 1927, all Mies van der Rohe Archive, New York. Bauabteilung des Gemeinderats, March 25, 1927, Stadtarchiv Stuttgart.
14 Bauabteilung des Gemeinderats (see note 13).
15 Döcker to Mies, April 9, 1927, Mies van der Rohe Archive, New York.
16 Reichsforschungsgesellschaft, *Berichtüber die Siedlung*, 144.
17 Record of site inspection, May 2, 1927, Stadtarchiv Stuttgart.
18 List of individual houses, May 2, 1927, Stadtarchiv Stuttgart.
19 Gropius to Mies, June 6, 1927, Mies van der Rohe Archive, New York.
20 *Fünfzig Jahre Bauhaus*, 363. In his résumé for this catalogue, Volger mentioned his work as resident architect and "the planning of the experimental Gropius house in the Weissenhofsiedlung in Stuttgart."
21 The identity of the second representative, if any, is not known. The only name mentioned in the files is that of Volger.
22 Gropius to Sigloch, June 2, 1927, Stadtarchiv Stuttgart.
23 Ibid.
24 Epple to Döcker, June 2, 1927, copy addressed to Sigloch, Stadtarchiv Stuttgart.

25 Mies to Gropius, June 9, 1927, Mies van der Rohe Archive, New York.
26 Gropius to Mies, June 11, 1927, Mies van der Rohe Archive, New York.
27 *Wasmuth's Monatshefte für Baukunst* (August 1927), 399.
28 *Das Werk*, no. 9 (1927), 269.
29 Ibid., 267.
30 Karl Konrad Düssel, "Die Stuttgarter Weissenhofsiedlung," *Deutsche Kunst und Dekoration* 21, no. 1 (October 1927), 96.
31 Reichsforschungsgesellschaft, *Bericht über die Siedlung*, 88.
32 Ibid.
33 Ibid.
34 Building office submission (*Baueingabe*), March 22, 1927, with changes marked, Bauaktei, Stadtarchiv Stuttgart.
35 Walter Gropius, "wege zur fabrikatorischen hausherstellung," in *Bau und Wohnung*, 59.
36 Marcel Breuer, "metallmöbel und moderne räumlichkeit," *Das Neue Frankfurt* 2 (January 1928): 11.
37 Building office submission (see note 34).
38 *Wasmuth's Monatshefte für Baukunst* (1928), 100.

HILBERSEIMER

1 *Werkbund-Ausstellung 1927*, 51.
2 Gropius to Mies, May 16, 1967, Bauhaus-Archiv, Berlin.
3 *G—Material zur elementaren Gestaltung*, no. 2 (September 1923), 2.
4 Ludwig Hilberseimer, "Bauhandwerk und Bauindustrie," ibid., 1.
5 Werner Graeff, "über die sogenannte 'G-Gruppe,'" *Werk und Zeit* (November 1962), Werner-Graeff-Archiv, Mülheim.
6 Hans Maria Wingler, "Nachruf auf Ludwig Hilberseimer," *Werk und Zeit*, no. 6 (1967), 6.
7 *Bau und Wohnung*, 69ff.
8 Hilberseimer, *Groszstadtarchitektur*, 31, 32.
9 *Bau und Wohnung*, 70.
10 Ludwig Hilberseimer, "Die Wohnung unserer Zeit," *Die Form* 6, no. 7 (1931): 249–70.
11 *Motivchen-Bauerei*: the phrase is Karl Gruber's.
12 *Motivchen-Salat*: the phrase is Bruno Taut's.
13 Döcker to Mies, undated; Mies to Döcker, April 16, 1927, Mies van der Rohe Archive, New York.
14 Reichsforschungsgesellschaft, *Bericht über die Siedlung*, 90, notes by Hilberseimer.
15 Döcker to all participant architects, circular no. 14, probably May 1, 1927, Mies van der Rohe Archive, New York.
16 Hilberseimer to Döcker, May 3, 1927, Mies van der Rohe Archive, New York.
17 Werner Graeff, "Hinter den Kulissen der Weissenhofsiedlung," Werner-Graeff-Archiv, Mülheim.
18 Reichsforschungsgesellschaft, *Bericht über die Siedlung*, 90.
19 Both quotations from Edgar Wedepohl, *Wasmuth's Monatshefte für Baukunst* (August 1927), 399.
20 Ernst Bloch, *Das Prinzip Hoffnung* (Frankfurt/Main, 1973), vol. 2, 859.
21 See Appendix A. Stotz to Mies, November 4 and 5, 1926, Mies van der Rohe Archive, New York.

BRUNO TAUT

1 *Werkbund-Ausstellung 1927*, 53.
2 *Bau und Wohnung*, 133.
3 Mies to Stotz, September 30, 1927, Mies van der Rohe Archive, New York.
4 Mies to Bruno Taut, October 22, 1926, Mies van der Rohe Archive, New York.
5 Bruno Taut to Mies, November 15, 1926, Mies van der Rohe Archive, New York.
6 Bruno Taut to Mies, December 9, 1926, Mies van der Rohe Archive, New York.
7 Building contract (*Vergabe*), February 25, 1927, Stadtarchiv Stuttgart.
8 Transaction of November 9, 1927: Bauabteilung des Generalrats, December 30, 1927, Stadtarchiv Stuttgart.
9 Final accounts of Werkbund exhibition, Finanzkommission des Generalrats, January 19, 1928, Stadtarchiv Stuttgart.
10 "Siedlungstypen," undated, Mies van der Rohe Archive, New York. See Appendix B.
11 Bruno Taut, "Baubeschreibung," November 12, 1926, Mies van der Rohe Archive, New York.
12 This system is described in detail in Heinz and Bodo Rasch, *Wie bauen?*
13 Reichsforschungsgesellschaft, *Bericht über die Siedlung*, 96.
14 Inspection on May 2, 1927, Stadtarchiv Stuttgart.
15 The equivalent figure for Stuttgart was about 240 marks (2,900 marks annually). Reichsforschungsgesellschaft, *Bericht über die Siedlung*, 148.
16 Ibid., 96–97.
17 Ibid.
18 Bruno Taut, "Der Regenbogen," *Frühlicht* (1919), in *Frühlicht 1920–1922* (1963), 97–98.
19 *Wasmuth's Monatshefte für Baukunst* (1927), 400.
20 Bonatz, *Leben und Bauen*, 146–47.
21 Max Berling, telephone conversation with the author, July 24, 1984.
22 Werner Graeff, "Hinter den Kulissen der Weissenhofsiedlung," Werner-Graeff-Archiv, Mülheim.
23 Alfred Roth, in a platform discussion on the occasion of the award of the second Farb-Design-Preis, at the Landesgewerbeamt, Stuttgart, March 8, 1984. Roth was a member of the jury.
24 *Bau und Wohnung*, 135.
25 Reichsforschungsgesellschaft, *Bericht über die Siedlung*, 97.
26 Bruno Taut, journal, March 17, 1905, cited in *Bruno Taut*, 65.
27 Journal, January 1, 1934, ibid., 129.
28 Bruno Taut, "Mein Weltbild," 1920, ibid., 65.
29 Bruno Taut, "Eindrücke aus Kowno," *Sozialistische Monatshefte* 24, no. 21/22, 899.
30 Bruno Taut, "Die Farbe," *Gehag-Nachrichten*, no. 16 (1930), cited in *Bruno Taut*.
31 Ibid., 68. This passage refers to the woodland housing (*Waldsiedlung*) at Zehlendorf and to the Onkel Toms Hütte subway station; "Im Fischtal," color scheme for fifth phase.
32 Mies to Ausstellunsleitung, April 11, 1927, Mies van der Rohe Archive, New York.
33 Reichsforschungsgesellschaft, *Bericht über die Siedlung*, 45.
34 Furniture was supplied by the following companies: Steiner + Co., Paradiesbettenfabrik; A. Beyerlein & Co., Büroeinrichtungen; Möbelfabrik May; Thonet, Berlin; Deutsche Luxfer-GmbH, Berlin.
35 Völckers, special issue, *Stein, Holz, Eisen*, no. 5 (1927).
36 Mies to Stadtschultheissenamt, June 9, 1927, Mies van der Rohe Archive, New York, and Stadtarchiv Stuttgart.
37 Bruno Taut to Mies, July 22, 1927, Mies van der Rohe Archive, New York.
38 Cited in Willett, *Art and Politics*, 92.
39 Bruno Taut, *Neue Wohnung*, 28–31.
40 Bruno Taut, journal, March 28, 1935, cited in *Bruno Taut*, 134.
41 Kurt Schwitters, *i 10*, (1927), 348.
42 Paul Scheerbart, cited by Bruno Taut (see note 18), 102.

POELZIG

1 *Werkbund-Ausstellung 1927*, 55, 56.
2 See above, "The Selection Process."
3 Bauabteilung des Gemeinderats, paragraph 4312, November 12, 1926, Stadtarchiv Stuttgart. For classification of types, see Appendix B.
4 Hans Poelzig, "Erläuterungen," in *Bau und Wohnung*, 97.
5 Poelzig to Mies, January 4, 1927, Mies van der Rohe Archive, New York.
6 Bauabteilung des Gemeinderats, March 11, 1927, Stadtarchiv Stuttgart.
7 Reichsforschungsgesellschaft, *Bericht über die Siedlung*, 144.
8 Bauabteilung des Gemeinderats, March 25, 1927, Stadtarchiv Stuttgart.
9 Heinz and Bodo Rasch, *Wie bauen?* 114–15.
10 Ibid., 115.
11 Max Berling to the author, July 24, 1984.
12 Max Berling to Freunde der Weissenhofsiedlung, February 6, 1981.
13 Ibid.
14 Jörg Herkommer in conversation with the author, June 12, 1985.
15 Bauabteilung des Gemeinderats, December 9, 17, and 30, 1927, Stadtarchiv Stuttgart.
16 Correspondence in Sammelakte 335, 1–45, Stadtarchiv Stuttgart.
17 Berling in telephone conversation with the author, January 18, 1985.
18 Although similar furniture designs by Poelzig himself exist, signed and dated April, 1927.
19 Cited in Poelzig, "Werkbundrede Stuttgart 1919," 258.
20 *Bau und Wohnung*, 97.
21 Edgar Wedepohl, *Wasmuth's Monatshefte für Baukunst* (August 1927), 398.
22 Ernst Völter, *Die Baugilde* 9 (August 12, 1927): 844.
23 *Das Werk*, no. 9 (1927), 264.
24 *Deutsche Kunst und Dekoration* (October 1927), 96.
25 Wedepohl (see note 21).
26 R. Sackur, "Das Schleiflack- oder Ofenlackmöbel," *Die Form* (1926), 218–221.
27 Erna Faerber, in undated clipping, *Stuttgarter Zeitung*, 1953.
28 Max Berling to the author, July 24, 1984.
29 Heuss, *Hans Poelzig*, 55.
30 Julius Posener, "Poelzig und das Einfamilienhaus," in *Hans Poelzig*.

DÖCKER

1 *Werkbund-Ausstellung 1927*, 57–59.
2 Richard Döcker, "Erfülltes und Unerfülltes," *Die Bauwelt*, no. 11 (1928), 269–76. Döcker to Dr. Sigloch, March 19, 1928, Stadtarchiv Stuttgart.
3 See G. K. Ringel, "Der Fall Schmitthenner," *Baukultur*, no. 2 (1985), 43–46.
4 Döcker to Gropius, March 30, 1949, Bauhaus-Archiv, Berlin.
5 Richard Döcker, "Zum Bauproblem der Zeit," *Die Form* (1926), 61. Formulated 1923–25.
6 See above, "The Selection Process."
7 Döcker (see note 5), 62.
8 Döcker to Mies, January 28, 1927, Mies van der Rohe Archive, New York.
9 Undated layout sketch by Döcker, Mies van der Rohe Archive, New York.
10 "Siedlungstypen," undated, Mies van der Rohe Archive, New York. See Appendix B.
11 Bauabteilung des Gemeinderats, March 5, 1927, Stadtarchiv Stuttgart.
12 Reichsforschungsgesellschaft, *Bericht über die Siedlung*, 144.
13 Mies to Ausstellungsleitung, April 11, 1927, Mies van der Rohe Archive, New York.
14 Site inspection, May 2, 1927, Hochbauamt record dated May 4, 1927, Stadtarchiv Stuttgart.
15 Heinz and Bodo Rasch, *Wie bauen?* 82.
16 Albert Feifel, *Marksteine für technisches Bauen* (Stuttgart 1927), 134.
17 Heinz Rasch in conversation with the author, July 9, 1984.
18 Heinz and Bodo Rasch, *Wie bauen?* 82.
19 Ernst Walther, unpublished manuscript diary, May 3, 1927, Mies van der Rohe Archive, New York.
20 Döcker, January 23, 1930, Bauaktei, Stadtarchiv, Stuttgart.
21 Döcker, May 31, 1927, Bauaktei, Stadtarchiv Stuttgart.
22 Döcker, March, 1927, Bauaktei, Stadtarchiv Stuttgart.
23 Döcker to Mies, June 10, 1927, Mies van der Rohe Archive, New York.
24 *Bau und Wohnung*, 43.
25 Ibid.
26 *Das Werk*, no. 9 (1927), 264.
27 The reference is to those that Döcker, in conjunction with Keuerleber, had built at Weissenhof in 1924.
28 Edgar Wedepohl, *Wasmuth's Monatshefte für Baukunst* (1927), 398.
29 *Bau und Wohnung*, 47.
30 Ibid.
31 Reichsforschungsgesellschaft, *Bericht über die Siedlung*, 144.
32 *Werkbund-Ausstellung 1927*, 58–59.
33 Reichsforschungsgesellschaft, *Bericht über die Siedlung*, 85.
34 Willi Baumeister, "Farben im Raum," in Graeff, ed., *Innenräume*, 135.
35 Reichsforschungsgesellschaft, *Bericht über die Siedlung*, 85.

MAX TAUT

1 *Werkbund-Ausstellung 1927*, 60, 61.
2 *Bau und Wohnung*, 139.
3 Bruno Taut, "Russlands architektonische Situation," in *El Lissitzky, Russland—Architektur für*

    eine Weltrevolution (Berlin 1965), 165.
4 Max Taut.
5 Stotz to Max Taut, September 29, 1926, Mies van der Rohe Archive, New York.
6 Max Taut to Mies, December 8, 1926, Mies van der Rohe Archive, New York.
7 Bruno and Max Taut to Döcker, February 9, 1927, carbon copy to Mies, Mies van der Rohe Archive, New York.
8 Bau und Wohnung, 139.
9 Ibid.
10 Laponisiert, Werkbund-Ausstellung 1927, 60.
11 Heinz and Bodo Rasch, Wie bauen? 132.
12 Max Taut to Mies, July 5, 1927, Mies van der Rohe Archive, New York.
13 Mies to Metzke-Rovira, April 12, 1927, Mies van der Rohe Archive, New York.
14 Metzke-Rovira to Mies, April 29, 1927, Mies van der Rohe Archive, New York.
15 Metzke-Rovira to Mies, June 3, 1927, Mies van der Rohe Archive, New York.
16 Werkbund-Ausstellung 1927, 15.
17 Unterkommission des Hauptausschusses der Werkbund-Ausstellung, paragraph 89, July 12, 1927, Stadtarchiv Stuttgart.
18 Werkbund-Ausstellung 1927, 15.
19 See the definition of Type C given in "Siedlungstypen" (Appendix B). Although this document frequently does not tally with the more detailed instructions given to individual architects, it seems in most cases to have been taken as a basis for the design.
20 Reichsforschungsgesellschaft, Bericht über die Siedlung, 98.
21 Herre to Stotz, July 8, 1926, Werkbund-Archiv, Berlin. The reference to participant architects who are "purely interior designers" is presumably aimed at Schneck.
22 Metzke-Rovira, Graeser, and Herre to Mies, February 23, 1927, Mies van der Rohe Archive, New York.
23 Mies to various interior designers, April 12, 1927, Mies van der Rohe Archive, New York.
24 Herre to Le Corbusier, November 21, 1926, Fondation Le Corbusier, Paris.
25 Rudolf Pfister, "Stuttgarter Werkbund-Ausstellung," Der Baumeister 26, no. 2 (1928), 68.

RADING
1 Werkbund-Ausstellung 1927, 62.
2 Adolf Rading, Die Form 2, no. 9 (1927), 287.
3 Ibid.
4 Spoken in connection with the town plan for Breslau, 1922. Pfankuch, ed., Adolf Rading.
5 Adolf Rading, "Neues Wohnen," Die Baugilde 8, no. 24 (December 29, 1926), 1315.
6 Adolf Rading, "Wohngewohnheiten," Die Form 2, no. 9 (1927), 42.
7 Reichsforschungsgesellschaft, Bericht über die Siedlung, 42.
8 Rading (see note 6).
9 Edgar Wedepohl, Wasmuth's Monatshefte für Baukunst (August 1927), 399; abridged also in Reichsforschungsgesellschaft, Bericht über die Siedlung, 78.
10 Rudolf Pfister, "Stuttgarter Werkbund-Ausstellung," Der Baumeister 26, no. 2 (1928), 68.
11 Das Werk, no. 9 (1927), 264.
12 Wedepohl (see note 9).
13 Kurt Schwitters, "Stuttgart. Die Wohnung," i 10 (1927), 347.
14 Rading to Sigloch, January 1928, and reply, January 27, 1928, Stadtarchiv Stuttgart.
15 Peter Pfanuch, "Einleitung," in Pfankuch, ed., Adolf Rading.
16 Ibid.
17 Hans Scharoun, in Pfankuch, ed., Adolf Rading.
18 Adolf Rading, "Zeitlupe," in Bau und Wohnung, 103–4.

FRANK
1 Werkbund-Ausstellung 1927, 64.
2 Reichsforschungsgesellschaft, Bericht über die Siedlung, 144.
3 Ausstellungsleitung to Stadtschultheissenamt, undated, Stadtarchiv Stuttgart.
4 Werner Hegemann, "Stuttgarter Schildbürgerstreiche und die Berliner Bauausstellung 1930," Wasmuth's Monatshefte für Baukunst, no. 1 (1928), 11.
5 Unterkommission des Hauptausschusses der Werkbund-Ausstellung, November 3, 1927, Stadtarchiv Stuttgart. "Under further questioning, Herr . . . admitted that he had also been the thief of the kitchen scales from the Mies block and a cushion in the Frank house."
6 Werner Graeff, "Hinter den Kulissen der Weissenhofsiedlung," Werner-Graeff-Archiv, Mülheim.
7 Meller to Oud, August 31, 1927, Oud-Archief, Rotterdam.
8 "Wie sind die Häuser der Werkbundsiedlung zu heizen?" Württembergische Zeitung, no. 7 (January 10, 1928).
9 Josef Frank, "How to Plan a House," 1939–45, in Geräte & Theoretisches (Vienna 1981), 165.
10 Ibid., 166.
11 Josef Frank, "Der G'schnas fürs Gemüt und der G'schnas als Problem," in Bau und Wohnung, 49–55.
12 "The God who planted iron meant to see no slaves," as an old German national song has it. [Tr.]
13 Frank, Architektur und Symbol, Vienna, 1931.
14 Ibid.
15 Christoph Mohr and Michael Müller, Funktionalität und Moderne (Frankfurt, 1984), 52.
16 Frank, Architektur und Symbol.

STAM
1 Werkbund-Ausstellung 1927, 67–70.
2 ABC—Beiträge zum Bauen, no. 1 (1924).
3 ABC—Beiträge zum Bauen, no. 4 (1927–28).
4 ABC—Beiträge zum Bauen, no. 2 (1924).
5 ABC—Beiträge zum Bauen, no. 6 (1925). Some of these designs by Stam were to be seen in the Internationale Plan- und Modellausstellung in Stuttgart in 1927.
6 Mies to Stam, November 5, 1926, Mies van der Rohe Archive, New York.
7 Stam to Mies, November 7, 1926, Mies van der Rohe Archive, New York.
8 Mies to Stam, November 15, 1926, Mies van der Rohe Archive, New York.
9 The phrase he used, wirtschaftliche Betriebsführung, stems from the German translation of Christine Frederick's handbook, Scientific Management in the Home (London, 1920), a work based on F. W. Taylor's time and motion methods.
10 Mies to Stam, November 16, 1926, Mies van der Rohe Archive, New York.
11 Information from Frau Karg-Baumeister.
12 Heinz Rasch in conversation with the author, July 9, 1984. See also Geest and Maček, Stühle aus Stahl, 26.
13 Döcker to Mies (at Hotel Marquardt, Stuttgart), February 19, 1927, Mies van der Rohe Archive, New York.
14 i 10 (1927), 342–43.
15 Mart Stam, "Wie bauen?" in Bau und Wohnung, 126.
16 Mart Stam, "Fort mit den Möbelkünstlern," in Graeff, ed., Innenräume, 129.
17 Ibid., 128.
18 Mies to Stam, April 16, 1927, Mies van der Rohe Archive, New York.
19 Mies to Döcker, April 4, 1927, Mies van der Rohe Archive, New York.
20 Döcker to all participant architects, circular no. 14, probably May 1, 1927, Fondation Le Corbusier, Paris.
21 This book, which concerns the materials and constructional methods used on the Weissenhofsiedlung project, has the same title—"How [Are We] to Build?"—as Mart Stam's chapter in one of the other Werkbund books, Bau und Wohnung.
22 Heinz and Bodo Rasch, Wie bauen? 41.
23 Bau und Wohnung, 129.
24 Meller to Oud, August 31, 1927, Oud-Archief, Rotterdam.
25 See Otakar Maček, Wonen TABK, no. 8 (1983).
26 Including the Arnold foreman; ibid.
26 Heinz Rasch, undated.
27 Heinz Rasch, undated.
28 For a highly detailed account see Geest and Maček, Stühle aus Stahl, 90, 123.
29 Graeff, ed., Innenräume, 27.
30 Kurt Schwitters, "Stuttgart. Die Wohnung," i 10 (1927), 347.
31 Reichsforschungsgesellschaft, Bericht über die Siedlung, 42.

32 Das Werk, no. 9 (1927), 267.
33 Die Baugilde, no. 14 (July 26, 1926).
34 Graeff, ed., Innenräume, 155, 157, 158.
35 Marcel Breuer, "metallmöbel," in Graeff, ed., Innenräume, 133–34.
36 Karl Konrad Düssel, "Die Stuttgarter Weissenhofsiedlung," Deutsche Kunst und Dekoration (October 1927), 96. See the section on the houses by Gropius, 16 and 17.
37 This goes for Ferdinand Kramer, Heinz Rasch, and other members of Stam's personal circle. On the other hand, Alfred Roth and Mia Seeger did remember a lavender blue; Frau Seeger thought it a shade darker (17:2:3) than the color presently on the houses.
38 Mies to Stam and Le Corbusier, May 30, 1927, Mies van der Rohe Archive, New York.
39 Mies to Döcker, June 11, 1927, Mies van der Rohe Archive, New York.
40 Reichsforschungsgesellschaft, Bericht über die Siedlung, 144.

BEHRENS
1 Werkbund-Ausstellung 1927, 71.
2 Schulze, Mies van der Rohe, 143.
3 Speech by Mies transcribed by von Horst Eitler and Ulrich Conrads and published by Bauwelt, Bauwelt Archiv 1, Berlin 1966.
4 Schulze, Mies van der Rohe, 67.
5 Behrens to Mies, October 6, 1926, Mies van der Rohe Archive, New York.
6 Mies to Behrens, December 28, 1926, Mies van der Rohe Archive, New York.
7 Mies to Behrens, February 23, 1927, Mies van der Rohe Archive, New York.
8 Contracts for Behrens, Stam, and Poelzig houses placed March 11, 1927: Bauabteilung des Gemeinderats, Stadtarchiv Stuttgart.
9 Report by Döcker, Bauabteilung des Gemeinderats, April 22, 1924, Stadtarchiv Stuttgart.
10 Stotz to Stadtschulteissenamt, September 6, 1927, Stadtarchiv Stuttgart.
11 Reichsforschungsgesellschaft, Bericht über die Siedlung, 144.
12 Heinz and Bodo Rasch, Wie bauen? 44–45.
13 Ernst Völter, Die Baugilde 9, no. 14 (August 12, 1927), 840.
14 Reichsforschungsgesellschaft, Bericht über die Siedlung, 43.
15 Rudolf Pfister, "Stuttgarter Werkbund-Ausstellung," Der Baumeister 26, no. 2 (1928), 70.
16 F. Hoffmann-Johannesthal, "Kritisches über die Stuttgarter Werkbundsiedlung," Bauwelt, no. 41 (1927).
17 Reichsforschungsgesellschaft, Bericht über die Siedlung, 52.
18 Die Wohnungswirtschaft (1926), cited in Kunst und Alltag um 1900 (Berlin, 1978).
19 Dr. Bräuning, "Wohnung und Tuberkulose," Die Wohnung, no. 6 (October 1927), 194.
20 Thomas Mann, Der Zauberberg (Frankfurt, 1963), 5.
21 Peter Behrens, in Bau und Wohnung, 17.
22 Burkhard Rukschcio and Roland Schachel, Adolf Loos (Vienna, 1982), 571–73; Worbs, "Raumplan," 74–75.
23 Ibid.
24 Rudolf Pfister (see note 15).
25 Edgar Wedepohl, Wasmuth's Monatshefte für Baukunst (1927), 392–93.
26 Peter Behrens, in Bau und Wohnung, 23–24.
27 Information from Heinz Rasch.
28 Correspondence between Schroedter and Stotz, April 16 through June 9, 1927, Mies van der Rohe Archive, New York.
29 Ausstellungsleitung to Behrens, March 30, 1927, Mies van der Rohe Archive, New York.
30 Werkbund-Ausstellung 1927, 72.
31 See Möbeldesignerporträts Baden-Württemberg.
32 Werkbund-Ausstellung 1927, 72.
33 Heinz Rasch had first met Else Oppler in Berlin in 1925.
34 Heinz and Bodo Rasch, Material, Konstruktion, Form.
35 Werkbund-Ausstellung 1927, 72.
36 Ibid.
37 Werkbund-Ausstellung 1927, 73.
38 Oscar Heinitz told the author that he had restored the lost "t" to the name by buying it back.
39 Stotz to Heiniz, carbon copy to Mies, July 22, 1927, Mies van der Rohe Archive, New York.

40 Stotz to Behrens (see note 19), and Mies to Stotz, April 11, 1927, Mies van der Rohe Archive, New York.
41 Heiniz to Mies, April 17, 1927, Mies van der Rohe Archive, New York.
42 Mies to Heiniz, April 17, 1927, Mies van der Rohe Archive, New York.
43 *Werkbund-Ausstellung 1927*, 74.
44 Carmela Haerdtl to the author, March 26, 1985.
45 *Werkbund-Ausstellung 1927*, 74.
46 Vollmer, *Künstlerlexicon des XX. Jahrhunderts*.
47 Obituary notice, issued by faculty of the Werkkunstschule, Bielefeld, 1964, Archiv der Stadt Bielefeld.
48 *Die Form* (1928), 398–99.
49 Stotz and Hagstotz to Behrens, March 30, 1927, Mies van der Rohe Archive, New York.
50 Griesser to Mies (German cursive script), April 26, 1927, Mies van der Rohe Archive, New York.
51 Wichmann, *Aufbruch zum neuen Wohnen*, 290.
52 *Werkbund-Ausstellung 1927*, 74.
53 *Die Form* (1928), 432.
54 See Fahrner, ed., *Paul Thiersch*.
55 Thiersch to Mies, September 4, 1927, Mies van der Rohe Archive, New York.
56 Record of a conversation, September 14, 1926.
57 See Schulze, *Mies van der Rohe*, 38.
58 Thiersch to Mies, October 8, 1926, Mies van der Rohe Archive, New York.
59 Ausstellungsleitung to Stadtschultheissenamt, June 22, 1927, Stadtarchiv Stuttgart.
60 Supplement no. 12, "Die Wohnung," *Württembergische Zeitung*, no. 208 (September 7, 1927).
61 *Werkbund-Ausstellung 1927*, 74.
62 Graeff, ed., *Innenräume* 156, note on fig. 82.
63 See exhibition catalogue *Die Vertreibung des Geistigen aus Österreich* (Vienna, 1985), 232. Information on Wlach and Sobotka has been hard to come by.
64 *Werkbund-Ausstellung 1927*, 74.
65 *Die Vertreibung* (see note 63), 228.

SCHAROUN

1 *Werkbund-Ausstellung 1927*, 75, 76.
2 Cited by Lauterbach, 1967, 15.
3 Walter Riezler, *Die Form* (1927), 260.
4 See above, "The Selection Process."
5 "Siedlungstypen," undated, Mies van der Rohe Archive, New York. See Appendix B.
6 Scharoun to Mies, December 28, 1926, Mies van der Rohe Archive, New York.
7 Reichsforschungsgesellschaft, *Bericht über die Siedlung*, 144.
8 Heinz and Bodo Rasch, *Wie bauen?* 129–30.
9 Inspection and record, April 25 and May 2 and 5, 1927, Stadtarchiv Stuttgart.
10 Mies to Scharoun, June 3, 1927, Mies van der Rohe Archive, New York.
11 Scharoun to Mies, June 9, 1927, Mies van der Rohe Archive, New York.
12 *Werkbund-Ausstellung 1927*, 76.
13 Hans Scharoun, "Zur Situation," in Graeff, ed., *Innenräume*, 111.
14 Hans Scharoun, *Die Form* (1927), 293–94.
15 Bauabteilung des Gemeinderates, July 1, 1927, Stadtarchiv Stuttgart.
16 Ibid.
17 Reichsforschungsgesellschaft, *Bericht über die Siedlung*, 91.
18 Edgar Wedepohl, *Wasmuth's Monatshefte für Baukunst* (August 1927), 400.
19 Scharoun to Mies, August 17, 1927, Mies van der Rohe Archive, New York.
20 Scharoun to Mies, August 19, 1927, and Lilly Reich to Erna Stotz, August 20, 1927, Mies van der Rohe Archive, New York.
21 Scharoun to Stadtschultheissenamt, September 17, 1927 (Scharoun's emphasis), Stadtarchiv Stuttgart.
22 Hagstotz (Ausstellungsleitung) to Sigloch (Stadtschultheissenamt), September 27, 1927, Stadtarchiv Stuttgart.
23 Ibid.
24 *Bau und Wohnung*, 114–15.
25 Edgar Wedepohl (as note 18).
26 *Stein, Holz, Eisen*, special issue, no. 1 (1927), 3.
27 The witness here was the wife of a city building official, Oberbaurat Faerber: Erna Faerber, "Hinter den Kulissen der berühmten Weissenhofsiedlung," *Stuttgarter Zeitung*, June 6, 1953.
28 *Deutsche Kunst und Dekoration* (October 1927), 97.

29 Eleonore Krümmel, *iwz*, no. 38 (1985), 11.
30 Lauterbach, *Hans Scharoun*, 14.

APPENDIX C

1 Paul Bonatz, *Schwäbischer Merkur* (May 5, 1926).
2 Paul Bonatz, "Ein Nachwort zur Werkbundsiedelung am Weissenhof," manuscript, summer 1927, Stadtarchiv Stuttgart.
3 Hegemann, "Stuttgarter Schildbürgerstreiche."
4 The last legal opinion was prepared by the public attorney's office at the Württemberg high court on March 31, 1928, after the legal advisers had carried out their researches. Letters of apology: Schmitthenner to Lautenschlager, January 20, 1928, Bonatz to Lautenschlager, February 13, 1928, Stadtarchiv Stuttgart.
5 Bonatz (see note 2).
6 Hermann Muthesius, "Die letzten Worte eines Meisters," *Berliner Tagblatt*, no. 522 (1927), cited in Felix Schuster, ed., *Schwäbisches Heimatbuch*, 95–97.
7 Hermann Muthesius, "Kunst- und Modeströmungen," *Wasmuth's Monatshefte für Baukunst*, no. 12 (1927), 496.
8 Gustav Langen, "Neues Bauen," *Deutsche Bauzeitung*, cited in Felix Schuster, ed., *Schwäbisches Heimatbuch*, 98–100.
9 *Die deutsche Bauhütte: Zeitschrift der deutschen Architektenschaft* (April 27, 1932), cited in *NS-Kurier* (July 22, 1932).
10 Felix Schuster, ed., *Schwäbisches Heimatbuch*.
11 Stotz died on July 22, 1940; biographical information supplied by Mia Seeger.
12 Dr. Friedrich Wolf to Döcker, March 17, 1946, Döcker-Archiv. Exhibited at Architekturgalerie, Weissenhofsiedlung, Stuttgart, 1982.
13 Schwäbischer Albverein to Staatliches Amt für Denkmalpflege, 1956. Cited in *info bau*, no. 2 (1983), 51.

BIOGRAPHIES

1 *Tendenzen der zwanziger Jahre*; GTA (department of history and theory of architecture), Eidgenössische Technische Hochschule, Zürich.
2 Stadtarchiv Stuttgart; Bau- und Heimstättenverein.
3 *Tendenzen der zwanziger Jahre*.
4 Information from Max Berling.
5 Lampugnani, ed., *Hatje-Lexikon*.
6 *Fünfzig Jahre Bauhaus*.
7 Bruckmann, ed., *Erinnerung an den 60*; Werkbund-Archiv.
8 GTA, Eidgenössische Technische Hochschule, Zürich.
9 *Tendenzen der zwanziger Jahre*; Wilhelm Neuhaus, *Burg Giebichenstein* (Leipzig, 1981).
10 Richard Döcker, 1894–1976.
11 Flüss and Tavel, *Künstlerlexikon der Schweiz*; GTA, Eidgenössische Technische Hochschule, Zürich.
12 Josef Frank.
13 *Möbeldesigner-Portraits Baden-Württemberg*.
14 Flüss and Tavel, *Künstlerlexikon der Schweiz*.
15 *Fünfzig Jahre Bauhaus*; W. G., obituary notice, *Tagesspiegel*, September 9, 1978; Heinz Rasch, obituary notice, *Bauwelt*, no. 38 (1978), 1419.
16 Flüss and Tavel, *Künstlerlexikon der Schweiz*; Camille-Graeser-Archiv.
17 *Möbeldesigner-Portraits Baden-Württemberg*.
18 Vollmer, *Künstlerlexikon des XX Jahrhunderts*; information from Stadtarchiv Bielefeld.
19 *Fünfzig Jahre Bauhaus*.
20 *Tendenzen der zwanziger Jahre*; archive at GTA, Eidgenössische Technische Hochschule, Zürich
21 Information from Magda Hagstotz.
22 Information from Oscar Heinitz.
23 Information from the family.
24 *Fünfzig Jahre Bauhaus*.
25 Vollmer, *Künstlerlexikon des XX. Jahrhunderts*; personal archive in Germanisches Nationalmuseum, Nuremberg.
26 Flüss and Tavel, *Künstlerlexikon der Schweiz*; GTA, Eidgenössische Technische Hochschule, Zürich.
27 *Tendenzen der zwanziger Jahre*.
28 Flüss and Tavel, *Künstlerlexikon der Schweiz*.
29 Kliemann, *Novembergruppe*.
30 *Ferdinand Kramer*.
31 *Franz Krause 1897–1979* (Düsseldorf: Edition Marzona, n.d.).

32 Stadtarchiv Stuttgart.
33 *Le Corbusier 1910–1965*.
34 Information from the family.
35 Information from the family.
36 J. Buekschmitt, *Ernst May* (Stuttgart, 1962); *Lexikon der Weltarchitektur* (Darmstadt, 1971); Lampugnani, ed., *Hatje-Lexikon*; C. Mohr and M. Müller, *Funktionalität und Moderne* (Frankfurt/Main, 1984).
37 Information from Meller's son, Pali Meller-Marcovicz, March 24, 1988.
38 *Fünfzig Jahre Bauhaus*, and other sources.
39 Standesamt, Tutzing; correspondence between Meyer and Mies, Mies van der Rohe Archive, New York.
40 *Fünfzig Jahre Bauhaus*, and other sources.
41 *Tendenzen der zwanziger Jahre*.
42 Lampugnani, ed., *Hatje-Lexikon*.
43 Heuss, *Hans Poelzig*; *Tendenzen der zwanziger Jahre*.
44 *Tendenzen der zwanziger Jahre*.
45 Bodo Rasch, *ideen projekte bauten*; Heinz and Bodo Rasch, *Material, Konstruktion, Form*.
46 Heinz Rasch, *Zu meiner Person*, privately printed (Stuttgart, 1971); Heinz and Bodo Rasch, ibid.
47 Vollmer, *Künstlerlexikon des XX. Jahrhunderts*; Geest and Máčel, *Stühle aus Stahl*.
48 U. Zickler, seminar paper, Fachhochschule für Technik, Stuttgart, 1983–84; *Fünfzig Jahre Bauhaus*; exhibition catalogue *Architektinnenhistorie* (Berlin, 1984).
49 Alfred Roth, *Architect of Continuity /Architekt der Kontinuität* (Zürich, 1985).
50 Pfankuch, *Hans Scharoun*; Peter Blundell Jones, *Hans Scharoun* (London, 1978).
51 GTA, Eidgenössische Technische Hochschule, Zürich.
52 *Tendenzen der zwanziger Jahre*; Schmidt, *Beiträge zur Architektur*.
53 *Adolf G. Schneck*.
54 Information from Frau Julie Schneider.
55 Vollmer, *Künstlerlexikon des XX. Jahrhunderts*; *Möbeldesigner-Portraits Baden-Württemberg*.
56 Andritzky and Selle, *Lehrbereich Wohnen 2* (Reinbek, 1979); Erika Strauss, seminar report, Fachhochschule für Technik, Stuttgart, 1983; exhibition catalogue *Architektinnenhistorie* (Berlin, 1984).
57 Information from Mia Seeger.
58 Personal file, Stadtarchiv Stuttgart.
59 Exhibition catalogue *Die Vertreibung des Geistigen aus Österreich* (Vienna, 1985).
60 *Fünfzig Jahre Bauhaus*; *Tendenzen der zwanziger Jahre*. Obituaries: Alfred Roth, *Tagesanzeiger*, Zürich; H. Rahms, *Frankfurter Allgemeine Zeitung*; *Stuttgarter Zeitung*. Corrections supplied by Mrs. Olga Stam.
61 *Tendenzen der zwanziger Jahre*; Lampugnani, ed., *Hatje-Lexikon*; Flüss and Tavel, *Künstlerlexikon der Schweiz*.
62 Theodor Heuss, obituary, *Schwäbischer Merkur*, no. 174 (July 27, 1940); Heuss, *Vorspiele des Lebens*, 303–04; information from Mia Seeger.
63 Wichmann, *Aufbruch zum neuem Wohnen*, 396.
64 Kurt Junghanns, *Bruno Taut* (Berlin, 1970); *Bruno Taut*.
65 *Max Taut*.
66 Fahrner, ed., *Paul Thiersch*; Thieme-Becker, *Künstlerlexikon* (Leipzig, 1956).
67 *Fünfzig Jahre Bauhaus*; information from the family.
68 Exhibition catalogue *Zur Vertreibung des Geistigen aus Österreich* (Vienna, 1985); Vollmer, *Künstlerlexikon des XX. Jahrhunderts*; Thieme-Becker, *Künstlerlexikon* (Leipzig, 1956).
69 Information from the family; letter from Le Corbusier to P. Burkhardt, Stuttgart, Fondation Le Corbusier, Paris.
70 Information from the family.

Bibliography

Adolf G. Schneck, 1883–1971. Exhibition catalogue. Stuttgart: Staatliche Akademie der bildenden Künste, 1983.

Adriani, Götz. Willi Baumeister 1889–1955: Peintures dessins: Gemälde Zeichnungen. Stuttgart: Institut für Auslandsbeziehungen, 1983.

Ansprachen und Vorträge 14: Jahresversammlung des Deutschen Werkbunds Bremen 1925. Oldenburg, 1925.

Arbeitsrat für Kunst 1918–1921. Berlin: Schriftenreihe der Akademie der Künste, 1980.

Argan, Giulio Carlo. Walter Gropius und das Bauhaus. Reinbek, 1962.

Bau- und Heimstättenverein e.G. 1924–1984: 60 Jahre Bauen in Stuttgart. Stuttgart, n.d.

Bauausstellung Stuttgart 1924. Exhibition catalogue. Stuttgart, 1924.

Bau und Wohnung: Die Bauten der Weissenhof-Siedlung in Stuttgart, errichtet 1927 nach Vorschlägen des Deutschen Werkbundes im Auftrag der Stadt Stuttgart und im Rahmen der Werkbundausstellung "Die Wohnung." Stuttgart: Deutscher Werkbund, 1927.

"Die Bayerische Hausratshilfe." In special issue, Hausrat: Eine Monatsschrift: Die Kunst im Heim für Jedermann (1921).

Behne, Adolf. Der moderne Zweckbau. Munich, 1926 (repr. Berlin 1964).

Behrendt, Walter Curt. Der Sieg des neuen Baustils. Stuttgart, 1927.

Behrens, Peter. "Städtebauliches." Jahrbuch des Deutschen Werkbundes 3 (1914).

Benevolo, Leonardo. Geschichte der Architektur des 19. und 20. Jahrhunderts. 2 vols. Munich, 1964.

Bischoff, Cordula, ed. Küche, Frauen, Kunst, Geschichte: Zur Korrektur des herrschenden Blicks. Giessen, 1984.

Blake, Peter. Three Master Architects: Le Corbusier, Mies van der Rohe, Frank Lloyd Wright. New York, 1960.

Blaser, Werner. Mies van der Rohe: Die Kunst der Struktur. Zürich and Stuttgart, 1965.

———. Mies van der Rohe: Möbel und Interieurs. Stuttgart, 1981.

———. Mies van der Rohe: Less Is More. Zürich, 1986.

Bloch, Ernst. Das Prinzip Hoffnung. Frankfurt, 1973.

Bonatz, Paul. Leben und Bauen. Stuttgart, 1950.

Borst, Bernhard, ed. Baukunst. Munich, 1928.

Bräuning, Dr. "Wohnung und Tuberkulose." Die Wohnung, no. 6 (October 1927).

Briggs, Ella. "Elektrizität im Haushalt." Wohnungswirtschaft, no. 10 (May 12, 1927).

Bruchhäuser, Axel. Der Kragstuhl / The Cantilever Chair, Schloss Beverungen: Stuhlmuseum, 1986.

Bruckmann, Peter, ed. Erinnerung an den 60: Geburtstag Peter Bruckmanns in Heilbronn 13. 1 1925. Heilbronn, 1925.

Bruno Taut. Exhibition catalogue. Berlin: Akademie der Künste, 1980.

Buddensieg, Tilmann. Die ästhetische Ausstattung des Lebens. Weinheim and Basel: Funkkolleg Kunst (Studienbegleitbrief 5), 1985.

Burckhardt, Lucius, ed. Der Werkbund in Deutschland, Österreich und der Schweiz: Form ohne Ornament. Stuttgart, 1978.

Busching, Paul. "Was können wir von Stuttgart lernen?" Zeitschrift fur Wohnungswesen in Bayern 25, no. 9/10 (1927).

Campbell, Joan. The German Werkbund: The Politics of Reform in the Applied Arts. Princeton, 1978.

Charlotte Perriand: Un Art de vivre. Exhibition catalogue. Paris: Musée des arts décoratifs, 1985.

Chase, Stuart. Tragödie der Verschwendung: Gemeinwirtschaftliche Gedanken in Amerika. Munich and Berlin, 1927. (Taylor and time and motion study.)

Choay, Françoise. Le Corbusier. New York, 1960.

Conrads, Ulrich, ed. Programme und Manifeste zur Architektur des 20. Jahrhunderts. Berlin, Frankfurt, and Vienna: Bauwelt Fundamente (1), 1964.

"La Conversione del moderno." Domus, no. 639 (1984). (Critical commentary on the renovation of the Weissenhofsiedlung.)

Cramer, J. and N. Gutschow. Bauausstellungen. Stuttgart, 1984.

Deutsches Warenbuch. Hellerau bei Dresden: Dürerbund (Werkbund Genossenschaft), 1916.

Dexel, Walter. Das Wohnhaus von Heute. Leipzig, 1928.

Dieckmann, Erich. Typenmöbel der staatlichen Hochschule für Handwerk und Baukunst. N.d.

Döcker, Richard. "Zum Bauproblem der Zeit." Die Form (1926).

———. Terrassentyp. Stuttgart, 1929.

———. "Ein neuzeitliches Wohnhaus." Die Bauzeitung 25, no. 40 (1928).

Doesburg, Theo van. "Der Wille zum Stil: Neugestaltung von Leben, Kunst und Technik." De Stijl, February–March, 1922, 25–41.

Drexler, Arthur. Ludwig Mies van der Rohe. Ravensburg, 1961.

Eckert, Hermann Peter. "Die Bauausstellung Stuttgart 1924." Die Baugilde 6 (1924).

——— (as H. P. Eckart). "Ergebnis? Ein Rückblick auf die Werkbundausstellung 'Die Wohnung' Stuttgart 1927." Die Bauzeitung, October 1, 1927.

Eckstein, Hans, ed. Fünfzig Jahre Deutscher Werkbund. Frankfurt, 1958.

———. Formgebung des Nützlichen: Marginalien zur Geschichte und Theorie des Design. Düsseldorf, 1985.

Fader, E. Auf dem Wege zum neuen Baustil. Berlin, 1927.

Fahrner, Rudolph, ed. Paul Thiersch, Leben und Werk. Berlin, 1970.

Fandray, Carla. Vom Raumkünstler zum Möbeldesigner: Zur Entwicklung des Möbeldesign in Baden-Württemberg." In Möbeldesign—Made in Germany. Stuttgart, 1985.

Fanelli, Giovanni. Stijl-Architektur. Stuttgart, 1985.

Fecker, H. "Zum Thema." info bau, no. 2 (1983).

Ferdinand Kramer: Architektur und Design. Exhibition catalogue. Berlin: Bauhaus-Archiv, 1982–83.

Feuchtwanger, Lion. Erfolg. Munich, 1930.

Film und Foto: Internationale Ausstellung. Exhibition catalogue. Stuttgart: Deutscher Werkbund, 1929.

Fitch, James Marston. Walter Gropius. New York, 1960.

———. American Building. Boston, 1966.

Fleischmann, Julius. "Die Wohnungsfinanzierung in Wien und deren Lehren für Deutschland." Wohnungswirtschaft (1927).

Flüss, Eduard, and Hans Christoph von Tavel. Künstlerlexikon der Schweiz des XX. Jahrhunderts. Frauenfeld, 1958–67.

Frank, Josef. "Handwerks- und Maschinen-Erzeugnis: Die Abgrenzung beider Gebiete." Die Innnendekoration 8, no. 3 (1923).

———. "Siedlungshäuser." Deutsche Kunst und Dekoration, 1924, 100–103.

———. "Formprobleme." Der Aufbau, no. 4 (1926).

———. "Der Volkswohnungspalast: Eine Rede anlässlich der Grundsteinlegung, die nicht gehalten wurde." Der Aufbau, no. 7 (1926).

———. "Das Wohnhaus unserer Zeit." Innendekoration (1927), 33.

———. "Vom neuen Stil." Baukunst 3 (1927): 234–49.

———. "Der Gschnas fürs G'müt und der Gschnas als Problem." In Bau und Wohnung, 1927, 48–57.

———. "Drei Behauptungen und ihre Folgen." Die Form, no. 4 (1927), 289–91.

———. "Was ist modern? Vortrag am 25. Juni anlässlich der Tagung des deutschen und österreichischen Werkbunds in Wien." Die Form 5, no. 15 (August 1930)

———. "Das moderne Haus und seine Einrichtung." Speech, Salzburg, October 1930.

———. "Das Haus als Weg und Platz." Der Baumeister (1931), 316.

———. Architektur und Symbol. Vienna, 1931.

———. Die internationale Werkbundsiedlung Wien 1932. Neues Bauen in der Welt, 6. Vienna, 1932.

———. "Die Werkbundsiedlung: Internationale Ausstellung Wien 1932." Deutsche Kunst und Dekoration, 1932, 227–28.

Frederick, Christine. Scientific Management in the Home. London, 1920.

Frieg, Wolfgang. Ludwig Mies van der Rohe: Das europäische Werk (1907–1937)." Dissertation. Bonn, 1976.

Fünfzig [50] Jahre Bauhaus. Exhibition catalogue. Stuttgart: Würtembergischer Kunstverein, 1968. Translated as Fifty Years Bauhaus (Chicago: IIT, 1969).

Geest, Jan van, and Otakar Máčel. Stühle aus Stahl: Metallmöbel 1925–1940. Cologne, 1980.

Genzmer, Walter. "Die deutsche Reichspavillon auf der internationalen Ausstellung Barcelona." Die Baugilde 11 (1929): 1654–57.

Geyer, Dietrich. Oktoberrevolution 1917. Funkkolleg Geschichte Studienbegleitbrief 9. Weinheim and Basel, 1980.

Giedion, Sigfried. "L'Exposition du Werkbund à Stuttgart 1927: la Cité du Weissenhof." In L'Architecture vivante. Paris, 1928.

———. "Architektur?" Die Baugilde 10 (1928).

———. Befreites Wohnen. Zürich, 1929.

———. "Die internationalen Kongresse für neues Bauen." In Die Wohnung für das Existenzminimum. Stuttgart, 1933.

———. Walter Gropius: Work and Teamwork. London and New York, 1954.

———. Raum, Zeit, Architektur: Die Enstehung einer neuen Tradition. Ravensburg, 1965.

———. "Die Chronologie der 1. Periode." In CIAM Dokumente 1928–1939. Basel and Stuttgart, 1979.

Glaeser, Ludwig. Ludwig Mies van der Rohe: Furniture and Furniture Drawings from the Design Collection and the Mies van der Rohe Archive. New York: The Museum of Modern Art, 1977.

Die Gläserne Kette: Visionäre Architekturen aus dem Kreis um Bruno Taut 1919–1920. Bergisch-Gladbach, 1963.

Graeff, Werner. "Für die neue Wohnung: Gedanken zur kommenden Werkbund-Ausstellung." Moderne Bauformen, no. 26 (1927).

———, ed. Innenräume: Räume und Inneneinrichtungsgegenstände aus der Werkbundausstellung "Die Wohnung," insbesondere aus den Bauten der städtischen Weissenhof-Siedlung in Stuttgart. Stuttgart: Deutscher Werkbund, 1928.

Graubner, Gerhard. Paul Bonatz und seine Schüler. Stuttgart-Gerlingen, [1955?].

Griesser, Paul. Das neue Möbel: Neuzeitliche Wohn-, Schlaf- und Arbeitsräume. Stuttgart, 1929.

———. Die neue Wohnung und ihre Möbel. Stuttgart, 1930.

Grohmann, Will. "Zehn Jahre Novembergruppe." Kunst der Zeit 3, nos. 1–3 (1928).

———. Bildende Kunst und Architektur: Zwischen den beiden Kriegen. Vol. 3. Berlin, 1953.

Gropius, Walter. "Die Entwicklung moderner Industriebaukunst." Jahrbuch des Deutschen Werkbunds 3 (1914): 29–32.

———. Adolf Meyer, Bauten. Berlin, 1923.

———. Internationale Architektur. Bauhausbücher, 1. Munich, 1925.

———. "Neue Baugesinnung." *Innendekoration* 36 (1925): 134.

———. "Systematische Vorarbeit für rationellen Wohnungsbau." *Bauhaus: Zeitschrift für Gestaltung* 1, no. 2 (1926–27), 1–2.

———, ed. *Das flache Dach: Internationale Umfrage über die technische Durchführbarkeit horizontal abgedeckter Dächer und Balkone.* Berlin, 1926. (Gropius's opinion survey on the flat roof, offprint from *Die Bauwelt*.)

———. "Moderne Bauprobleme." *Die Bauzeitung* 24 (1927): 141–43.

———. "Geistige und technische Grundlagen des Wohnhauses." *Stein Holz Eisen* 41 (1927): 315–19.

———. "Trockenbauweise." *Die Baugilde* 9 (1927): 1362.

———. "Wege zur fabrikatorischen Hausherstellung." In *Bau und Wohnung.* Stuttgart, 1927. (On Houses 16 and 17.)

———. "Wohnung und Wohnungsnot." *Die Bauzeitung* 24 (1927): 151ff.

———. "Der grosse Baukasten." *Das Neue Frankfurt* 1/2 (1927–28): 25–30.

Gruber, Karl. *Die Gestalt der deutschen Stadt.* 1937. Reprint. Munich, 1983.

Grünbaum-Sachs, Hilde. "Der Anteil der Hausfrau an der Gestaltung des Bauwesens." *Wohnungswirtschaft* 8/9 (1931–32).

Grunsky, E. *Siedlungen der 20er Jahre—heute.* Berlin, 1984.

Häring, Hugo. *Über das Geheimnis der Gestalt.* Berlin, 1954.

———. *Vom neuen Bauen: Über das Geheimnis der Gestalt.* Berlin, 1957.

Hartmann, G.B. von, and Wend Fischer, eds. *Zwischen Kunst und Industrie: Der Deutsche Werkbund.* Exhibition catalogue. Munich and Stuttgart: Die Neue Sammlung, 1987.

Hartmann, Julius. *Chronik der Stadt Stuttgart: Sechshundert Jahre nach der ersten denkwürdigen Nennung der Stadt (1286).* Stuttgart, 1886.

Hegemann, Werner. "Stuttgarter Schildbürgerstreiche und Berliner Bauausstellung 1930." *Wasmuth's Monatshefte für Baukunst und Städtebau* (1928).

Heiniz, Oscar. "Die Innenausstattung der Wohnungen in der Werkbundsiedlung." *Die Bauzeitung* 24, no. 39 (1927).

Hellwag, Fritz. "Lässt sich Schönheit mit Billigkeit vereinen? Zu den Arbeiten der Bayerischen Hausrathilfe." *Die Kunst* (1926).

Heuss, Theodor. *Hans Poelzig: Bauten und Entwürfe: Das Lebensbild eines deutschen Baumeisters.* Berlin, 1939; Tübingen, 1955; Stuttgart, 1985.

———. *Vorspiele des Lebens.* Tübingen, 1953.

———. *Erinnerungen 1905–1933.* Tübingen, 1963.

Hilberseimer, Ludwig, ed. *Internationale neue Baukunst.* Stuttgart: Deutscher Werkbund, 1927.

———. *Groszstadtarchitektur.* 1927. Reprint. Stuttgart, 1978.

———. "Handwerk und Industrie." *Bauhaus: Zeitschrift für Gestaltung* 3 (1929).

———. *Mies van der Rohe.* Chicago, 1956.

Hildebrandt, Hans. "Neues Bauen." *Die Bauzeitung,* July 23, 1927.

———. *Kunst des 19., 20. Jahrhunderts: Handbuch der Kunstwissenschaft.* Potsdam, 1927.

Hitchcock, Henry-Russell, and Philip Johnson. *The International Style.* 1932. Reprint. New York, 1966.

Hoffmann, Herbert. *Neue Villen: 124 grosse und kleine Einfamilienhäuser.* Stuttgart, 1929.

Hölzel und sein Kreis. Exhibition catalogue. Stuttgart: Württembergischer Kunstverein, 1961.

Howard, Ebenezer. *Garden Cities of Tomorrow.* London, 1902. Published in German as *Gartenstädte von morgen,* ed. Julius Posener (Berlin, Frankfurt, and Vienna, 1968).

Hübner, Herbert. "Die soziale Utopie des Bauhauses: Ein Beitrag zur Wissenssoziologie in der bildenden Kunst." Dissertation, Münster University, 1963.

Huse, Norbert. *Neues Bauen 1918–1933.* Munich, 1975.

———. *Le Corbusier in Selbstzeugnissen und Bilddokumenten.* Reinbek, 1976.

Hüter, Karl-Heinz. *Das Bauhaus in Weimar.* Berlin, 1976.

Isaacs, Reginald. *Walter Gropius.* Berlin, 1983–84.

Jaffé, H.L.C. *De Stijl 1917–1931.* Berlin, Frankfurt, and Vienna, 1965.

Jakob, H. "Der Freischwinger und seine Geschichte." *md,* no. 12 (1979).

Joedicke, Jürgen. *Geschichte der modernen Architektur.* Stuttgart, 1958.

———. "Geschichte der modernen Architektur." Present author's lecture notes, 1965–66.

———, and Christian Plath. *Die Weissenhofsiedlung.* Stuttgarter Beiträge, 4. Stuttgart, 1968.

———, and Egon Schirmbeck, eds. *Architektur der Zukunft der Architektur.* Stuttgart, 1982.

Johnson, Philip. *Mies van der Rohe.* 1947. Reprint. New York, 1978.

Josef Frank. Exhibition catalogue. Vienna, 1983.

Junghanns, Kurt. *Der Deutsche Werkbund und sein 1. Jahrzehnt.* Berlin, n.d.

Kliemann, Helga. *Die Novembergruppe.* Berlin, 1969.

Kohlhaas, Wilhelm, ed. *Chronik der Stadt Stuttgart 1918-1933.* Veröffentlichungen des Archivs der Stadt Stuttgart, 17. Stuttgart, 1964.

Kopetzny, Helmut. *Die andere Front: Europäische Frauen in Krieg und Widerstand 1939–1945.* Cologne, 1983.

Korn, Arthur. *Glas.* Berlin, 1928.

Kramer, Ferdinand and Lore Kramer. "Soziale Nützlichkeit, Sachlichkeit war unser wesentlichstes Anliegen." *Neue Heimat Monatshefte,* no. 8 (1981). (A text originally written for this book.)

———. "Zur Werkbund-Ausstellung 'Die Wohnung,' Stuttgart 1927: Betrachtungen eines Beteiligten." *Wissenschaftliche Zeitschrift der Hochschule für Architektur und Bauwesen, Weimar* (1985).

Kramer, Lore. "Zur sozialgeschichtlichen Entwicklung des Arbeitsplatzes Küche.'" In *Bundespreis Gute Form '79: Arbeitsplatz Haushalt—Design fur Küche und Hausarbeitsraum.* Darmstadt, 1979.

Krause, Franz. "Sonnenwinkel." *Die Baugilde* 7, no. 22 (1925).

Krischanitz, Adolf, and Otto Kapfinger. *Die Wiener Werkbundsiedlung.* Stuttgart, 1985

Kulka, Heinrich, ed. *Adolf Loos: Das Werk des Architekten.* Neues Bauen in der Welt, 4. Vienna, 1931.

Kultermann, Udo. *Die Architektur im 20. Jahrhundert.* Cologne, 1977.

Lampmann, Gustav. "Stuttgart 1927 'Die Wohnung,'" *Zentralblatt der Bauverwaltung,* October 26, 1927.

Lampugnani, Vittorio Magnago, ed. *Hatje-Lexikon der Architektur des 20. Jahrhunderts.* Stuttgart, 1983. Translated as *Encyclopedia of Twentieth-Century Architecture* (New York, 1986).

———. "Weder rein noch reaktionär: Die merkwürdigen Abenteuer der Architektur unter Hitler und Mussolini." *Die Zeit,* no. 5 (January 27, 1984).

Lang, Hugo. "Die neuzeitliche Küche." *Innendekoration* (December 1927).

Lauterbach, Heinrich, ed. *Poelzig, Endell, Moll, und die Breslauer Kunstakademie 1911–1932.* Exhibition catalogue. Berlin: Akademie der Künste, 1965.

———, and Jürgen Joedicke, eds. *Hugo Häring: Schriften, Entwürfe, Bauten.* Dokumente der modernen Architektur, 4. Stuttgart, 1965.

———. *Hans Scharoun.* Exhibition catalogue. Berlin: Akademie der Künste, 1967.

Le Corbusier. *Vers une architecture.* Paris, 1923. Translated as *Towards a New Architecture* (London, 1927).

———. "La signification de la cité-jardin du Weissenhof à Stuttgart" and "L'Aménagement intérieur de mos maisons du Weissenhof." *L'Architecture vivante,* spring/summer 1928, 10–15, 33–36.

———. "Wie wohnt man in meinen Stuttgarter Häusern?" *Das Neue Frankfurt* 2 (January 1928).

———. *Städtebau.* 1929. Reprint. Stuttgart, 1979.

Le Corbusier 1910–1960. Zürich, 1960. Revised as *Le Corbusier 1910–1965* (Zürich, London, and New York, 1967).

Le Corbusier, 1929: Feststellungen zu Architektur und Städtebau. Berlin, Frankfurt, and Vienna, 1964.

Le Corbusier: Synthèse des arts—Aspekte des Spätwerks 1945–1965. Exhibition catalogue. Berlin: Badischer Kunstverein, 1986.

Leitner, Bernhard. *Die Architektur von Ludwig Wittgenstein.* London, 1973.

Loos, Adolf. *Sämtliche Schriften in zwei Bänden.* Vienna, 1962.

Lotz, Wilhelm. "Die kulturelle Bedeutung des Deutschen Werkbunds." *Stein Holz Eisen,* September 16, 1926.

———. "Wohnen und Wohnung." *Die Form* (1927).

———. "Möbeleinrichtung und Typenmöbel." *Die Form* (1928).

———. "Der Werkbundgedanke in seiner Bedeutung für Industrie und Handwerk." In Dr. Erasmus (Gotthilf Schenkel), ed., *Geist der Gegenwart: Formen, Kräfte und Werte einer neuen deutschen Kultur.* Stuttgart, 1928.

Lüders, Marie-Elisabeth. "Baukörper ohne Wohnungen: Kritik der Weissenhofsiedlung." *Die Form* (1927), 316

Máčel, Otakar. "Stams eerste buisstoel had geen verend effect." *Wonen TABK,* no. 8 (1983).

Mang, Karl. *Geschichte des modernen Möbels.* Stuttgart, 1978.

Mann, Thomas. "Unordnung und frühes Leid." In *Erzählungen,* vol. 2. Frankfurt and Hamburg, 1967.

Margold, Emanuel Josef. "Form und Rationalisierung im neuen Bauen: Das Problem der Wohnmaschine." *Die Baugilde* 9, no. 14 (July 25, 1927)

Marzona, Egidio. *Franz Krause 1897–1979.* Düsseldorf, n.d.

Maur, Karin von. "Stuttgarts Beitrag zur klassischen Moderne." In *Stuttgarter Kunst im 20. Jahrhundert.* Stuttgart, 1979.

———, and Gudrun Inboden. *Malerei und Plastik des 20. Jahrhunderts.* Stuttgart, 1982.

Maus, Sybille. "Baracken der Zukunft auf milden Hügeln: Die Weissenhof-Siedlung in Stuttgart." *Frankfurter Allgemeine Magazin,* no. 262 (March, 1985).

Max Taut. Exhibition catalogue. Berlin: Akademie der Künste, 1964.

May, Ernst. "5 Jahre Wohnungsbautätigkeit in Frankfurt a.M." *Das Neue Frankfurt* 4, nos. 2–3 (February–March 1930).

Mehmke-Canivé, Jeanne. "Die Technik auf der Werkbundausstellung." *Stuttgarter Kunstführer,* April 1, 1922.

Meier-Oberist, I. "Kultur und Farbe." In *Die farbige Stadt.* 1933.

Meller, Paul. "Eine Wohnung mit Stahlmöbeln." *Innendekoration* (1932).

Menrad, Andreas. "Die Weissenhof-Siedlung—farbig: Quellen, Befunde und die Revision eines Klischees." *Deutsche Kunst und Denkmalpflege* (1986).

Meyer, Erna. *Der neue Haushalt.* Stuttgart, 1926.

———. "Richtlinien über die Küchenmöbel: Ausgearbeitet für das Reichskuratorium." *Frankfurter Zeitung* (November 3, 1926).

———. "Das Küchenproblem auf der Werkbundausstellung." *Die Form* (1927).

———. "Zweckmässige Küchenmöbel." *Bauwelt,* no. 9 (1927).

———. "Wohnung und Entlastung der Frau." *Wohnungswirtschaft* 10, no. 12 (May 1927).

⸻. "Über Wohnungseinrichtung." *Werkbund-Gedanken*, supplement to *Stuttgarter Neues Tagblatt*, no. 7 (July 15, 1927).

⸻. "Kritik der Werkbundausstellung: Anregungen zur Küchengestaltung auf der Werkbundausstellung." *Stein Holz Eisen*, November 3, 1927.

⸻. Küchengrundrisse und Küchenarten," *Die Baugilde*, 10 (1928).

⸻. "Grundsätzliches zur Einbauküche." *Die Baugilde* 10 (1928).

Meyer, Hannes. "Die neue Welt." *Das Werk*, no. 7 (1926).

Meyer, Peter. *Moderne Schweizer Wohnhäuser*. Zürich, 1927–28.

⸻. *Moderne Architektur und Tradition*. Zürich, 1928.

Michel, Wilhelm, et al. "Die Weissenhof-Siedlung: Erwägungen zur Werkbund-Ausstellung 1927." *Innendekoration* (December 1927).

Mies van der Rohe, Ludwig. *Mies in Berlin*. Autobiographical interview with Hors Eifler and Ulrich Conrads. Produced by RIAS, Berlin. Issued as phonograph record by the periodical *Bauwelt* as *Bauwelt-Archiv*, no. 1 (1966).

Mies van der Rohe. Exhibition catalogue. Berlin: Akademie der Künste, 1968.

Mies [van der Rohe] Reconsidered: His Career, Legacy, and Disciples. Exhibition catalogue. Chicago, 1986.

"Mies van der Rohe 27. März 1886." *Bauwelt*, no. 11 (1986).

Möbeldesigner-Portraits Baden-Württemberg. Stuttgart: Vereinigung von Freunden der Akademie der bildenden Künste e.V., 1985.

Moos, Stanislaus von. *Le Corbusier: Elemente einer Synthese*. Frauenfeld and Stuttgart, 1968.

Moser, Hans Joachim. "Die deutsche Musik in der Gegenwart." In *Geist der Gegenwart*. Stuttgart, 1928

Müller-Wulkow, Walter. *Die deutsche Wohnung der Gegenwart*. Königstein and Leipzig, 1930.

Münz, Ludwig, and Gustav Künstler. *Der Architekt Adolf Loos: Darstellung seines Schaffens nach Werkgruppen*. Vienna and Munich, 1964.

Muthesius, Hermann. "Kunst- und Modeströmungen." *Wasmuth's Monatshefte für Baukunst* (1927), 496

Nägele, Hermann. "Werkstattbericht." *info bau*, no. 2 (1983).

Naumann, Friedrich. *Der deutsche Stil*. Hellerau, Berlin, Munich, and Hanover, n.d.

"Neues vom Werkbund-Häuserbau in Stuttgart." *Deutsche Bauhütte* (1932).

Neumayer, Fritz. *Mies van der Rohe: Das kunstlose Wort*. Berlin, 1986.

Neundörfer, Ludwig. *Wie wohnen?* Frankfurt, n.d.

⸻. *So wollen wir wohnen*. Stuttgart, 1930.

Niedhart, Gottfried. *Weltpolitik nach 1917: Zwischenkriegszeit und Zweiter Weltkrieg*. Funkkolleg Geschichte Studienbegleitbrief 9. Weinheim and Basel, 1980.

Nierhaus, Bi. "Die Fabrik des Hauses: Die Küche für den Arbeiterhaushalt." In Cordula Bischoff, ed., *Frauen, Kunst, Geschichte: zur Korrektur der herrschenden Blicks*. Giessen, 1984.

Oud, Hans. *J.J.P. Oud*. The Hague, 1984.

Paul Bonatz zum Gedenken, Stuttgart, Technische Hochschule, 1957.

Paul Schmitthenner: Kolloquium zum 100. Geburtstag, Stuttgart: Fakultät fur Architektur und Stadtplanung und Historisches Institut, Universität Stuttgart, 1985.

Pehnt, Wolfgang. *Expressionist Architecture*. London and New York, 1973.

Peters, Paulhans. "Paul Schmitthenner: Zur 100. Wiederkehr seines Geburtstages." *Der Baumeister*, no. 12 (1984).

Pevsner, Nikolaus. *The Pioneers of Modern Architecture and Design*. London, 1957.

Pfaff, Karl. *Geschichte der Stadt Stuttgart nach Archival-Urkunden und anderen bewährten Quellen: Zweiter Theil, Geschichte der Stadt vom Jahre 1651 bis zum Jahre 1845*. Stuttgart, 1846.

Pfankuch, Peter, ed. *Adolf Rading: Bauten, Entwürfe und Erläuterungen*. Schriftenreihe der Akademie der Künste, 3. Berlin, 1964.

⸻. *Adolf Rading*. Berlin, 1970.

⸻. *Hans Scharoun*. Berlin, 1974.

Pfister, Rudolf. "Stuttgart, eine aufsteigende Stadt—und München? Der Block." *Baukunst* (May 1928).

⸻. "Der Fall Schmitthenner." *Der Baumeister* (1948). Reprinted Munich, 1968.

Pfleiderer, Wolfgang, ed. *Die Form ohne Ornament: Werkbund-Ausstellung 1924*. Stuttgart, 1924.

⸻. "Paul Bonatz." *Baukunst* (May 1928).

Platz, Gustav Adolf. *Die Baukunst der neuesten Zeit*. Berlin, 1927.

⸻. *Wohnräume der Gegenwart*. Berlin, 1930.

⸻. *Wohnräume der Gegenwart*. Berlin, 1933.

Poelzig, Hans. "Werkbundrede Stuttgart 1919." In *Gesammelte Schriften und Werke*, ed. Julius Posener. Berlin, 1972.

⸻. *Ein grosses Theater und ein kleines Haus*. Berlin, 1986.

Popp, Jos. "Die neue Wohnung: Aus Anlass der Stuttgarter Ausstellung." *Kunstwart* (November 1927).

Posener, Julius. *Anfänge des Funktionalismus: Von Arts and Crafts zum deutschen Werkbund*. Berlin, 1964.

⸻. "Vorlesungen zur Geschichte der Neuen Architektur." *arch +*, nos. 48, 53, 59, 63/64 (1979, 1980, 1981, 1982). (Special issues to commemorate Julius Posener's 75th birthday).

⸻. "Weissenhof und danach." In Joedicke and Schirmbeck, eds., *Architektur der Zukunft der Architektur*. Stuttgart, 1982.

⸻. "Walter Gropius, Ludwig Mies van der Rohe, Le Corbusier: Drei Meisterarchitekten des 20. Jahrhunderts." In *Die Grossen der Weltgeschichte 10*.

Rasch, Bodo. "50 Jahre Werkbundsiedlung Stuttgart-Weissenhof." *Deutsche Bauzeitung*, no. 11 (1977).

⸻. *ideen projekte bauten: werkbericht 1924–1984*. Stuttgart, 1984.

⸻, Frei Otto, and Berthold Burkhardt. *Fünfzig Jahre Weissenhofsiedlung: Eine neue Bauaustellung zum Thema "Wohnen."* Exhibition catalogue. Stuttgart, March 13, 1977.

Rasch, Heinz and Bodo. *Wie bauen?* Stuttgart, 1927.

⸻. *Material, Konstruktion, Form, 1928–1930*. Düsseldorf, 1981.

Rasch, Heinz [under the pseudomym of - b]. "Material, Konstruktion, Form." *Die Baugilde*, no. 9 (May 15, 1925)

⸻. "aus den frühen zwanziger jahren." *werk und zeit*, nos. 11–12 (1961).

Redslob, Edwin. "Steht Stuttgart vor einer neuen künstlerischen Entfaltung?" *Schwäbische Flugschriften*, no. 1 (Stuttgart), 1920).

⸻. *Gestalt und Zeit: Begegnungen eines Lebens*. Munich, 1966.

Reichsforschungsgesellschaft für Wirtschaftlichkeit im Bau-und Wohnungswesen. *Bericht über die Siedlung in Stuttgart am Weissenhof*. Berlin: Reichsforschungsgesellschaft (Sonderheft 6, Gruppe IV, no. 3, vol. 2), 1929.

Reinhardt, Brigitte. *Reinhold Nägele*. Stuttgart, 1984.

Richard Döcker, 1894–1968. Exhibition catalogue. Stuttgart, Bund Deutscher Architekten, Landesverband Baden-Württemberg. 1982.

Riemerschmid, Richard. "Ansprache des Vorsitzenden." In *Ansprachen und Vorträge: 14. Jahresversammlung des deutschen Werkbunds Bremen 1925*. Oldenburg, 1925.

Riezler, Walter, ed. *Das deutsche Kunstgewerbe im Jahr der grossen Pariser Ausstellung*. Berlin, 1926.

Roessler, Rudolf. "Siedlung, Wohnung und neue Baukunst: Die Werkbundausstellung 'Die Wohnung' in Stuttgart." Supplement, *Düsseldorfer Nachrichten*, no. 377 (July 28, 1927).

Rohde, Georg, ed. *Edwin Redslob zum 70. Geburtstag: Eine Festgabe*. Berlin, 1955.

Rohe, Georgia van der. *Mies van der Rohe*. Television film produced by ZDF, 1980, 1986.

Roth, Alfred. *Zwei Wohnhäuser von Le Corbusier*. 1927. Reprint. Stuttgart, 1977.

⸻. *Begegnung mit den Pionieren*. Basel and Stuttgart, 1973.

Roth, Michael. "Modellbaukasten—Wohnen im Denkmal Weissenhof: Trotz ihrer architektonischen Bedeutung sind die berühmten Häuser dieser Siedlung 'normalen' Mietern vorbehalten." *Illustrierte Wochenzeitung* (1985).

Ruegenberg, Sergius. "Skelettbau ist keine Teigware . . . Mies van der Rohes Berliner Zeit." *Bauwelt*, no. 11 (1986).

Sackur, R. "Das Schleiflack-oder Ofenlackmöbel: Bedeutung und Anwendung." *Die Form* (1926).

Scheffler, Karl. *Sittliche Diktatur: Ein Aufruf an alle Deutschen*. Stuttgart and Berlin, 1920.

Schmidt, Diether, ed. *Manifeste Manifeste 1905–1933: Schriften deutscher Künstler des zwanzigsten Jahrhunderts*. Vol. 1. Dresden, 1967.

Schmidt, Hans. *Beiträge zur Architektur 1924–1964*. Berlin, 1965.

Schmidt, Paul Ferdinand. "Europas kommende Baukunst." *Sozialistische Monatshefte*, no. 9 (1927).

Schmitthenner, Paul. "Der Weg zur deutschen Baukunst." *Kulturpolitik und Unterricht*. Daily supplement, *Völkischer Beobachter*, no. 3 (1936).

Schneck, Adolf Gustav. Moderne Innenarchitektur." Supplement, *Stuttgarter Neues Tagblatt*, no. 2 (July 30, 1927).

⸻. "Möbelbau und Innenausbau an der Württ. Staatl. Kunstgewerbeschule in Stuttgart." *Moderne Bauformen*, October, 1937.

Schneider, Fritz, and Julius Frank. *Kunst und Kultur in Schwaben: Stuttgarter Kunstsommmer 1924*. Stuttgart, 1924.

Schneider, Wolfgang Christian. "Hitlers wunderschöne Hauptstadt des Schwabenlandes: Nationalsozialistische Stadtplanung, Bauten und Bauvorhaben in Stuttgart." *Demokratie und Arbeitergeschichte*, Jahrbuch 2 (1982).

Schulz, Richard L. F. "Beleuchtungskörper." *Jahrbuch des Deutschen Werkbunds* 1 (1912).

Schulze, Franz. *Mies van der Rohe: Leben und Werk*. Berlin, 1986.

Schumacher, Fritz. *Stufen des Lebens: Erinnerungen eines Baumeisters*. Stuttgart, 1935.

Schuster, Felix. "Die Versuchssiedlung beim Schönblick." *Schwäbischer Merkur*, nos. 410, 434, 470, 482, 507 (September 3–October 29, 1927).

⸻. "Rückblick auf die Wohnausstellung." *Schwäbischer Merkur*, no. 518 (November 5, 1927).

⸻, ed. *Schwäbisches Heimatbuch*. Stuttgart: Bund für Heimatschutz in Württemberg und Hohenzollern, 1928; 1934; 1941.

Schuster, Franz. *Eine eingerichtete Kleinstwohnung*. Frankfurt, 1927.

Schütte-Lihotzky, Margarete (Grete). "Rationalisierung im Haushalt." *Das Neue Frankfurt*, no. 5 (1927).

⸻. "Die 'Frankfurter Küche': Typisierte Küche des Hochbauamts Frankfurt a.M." *Stein Holz Eisen*, (February 24, 1927).

⸻. "Arbeitsersparnis im Haushalt durch neuen Wohnungsbau." *Wohnungswirtschaft*, nos. 10–12 (May 1927).

⸻. "Rationalisierung im Haushalt und neuzeitliche Kücheneinrichtungen." *Die Wohnung*. Supplement no. 9 to *Württembergische Zeitung*, no. 187 (August 13, 1927).

⸻. "Wie kann durch richtigen Wohnungsbau die Hausfrauenarbeit erleichtert werden?" Supplement to *Moderne Bauformen* (1928).

Schwäbischer Siedelungsverein. *Das Typenhaus E.T. 27 des Schwäbischen Siedelungsvereins e.V. Stuttgart: Ausser Programm auf der Werkbund-Ausstellung "Die Wohnung" Stuttgart*. Stuttgart, 1927.

Slapeta, Vadimir. "Adolf Loos und die tschechische Architektur." In *Adolf Loos 1870–1933 Raumplan—Wohnungsbau*. Exhibition catalogue. Berlin, 1983–84.

Spaeth, David. *Mies van der Rohe*. New York, 1985.

Sperlich, Hans Günther. "Grau ist heller als Schwarz: Zur Geschichte einer Gesinnungsgemeinschaft." In *Baukunst und Werkform* (Nuremberg, 1956), 577–603. (On the Deutscher Werkbund.)

Stahl, Fritz. "Die Wohnung: Werkbund-Ausstellung in Stuttgart." *Berliner Tageblatt*. no. 426 (1927).

Stein, Werner. *Kulturfahrplan: Die wichtigsten Daten der Kulturgeschichte von Anbeginn bis heute*. Berlin, Darmstadt, and Vienna, 1946.

Stotz, Gustaf. "Über Wohnungseinrichtung." *Werkbund-Gedanken*. Supplement to *Stuttgarter Neues Tagblatt*, 1926.

————. "Die Krise des Deutschen Werkbunds." Supplement to *Schwäbischer Merkur*, no. 266 (November 12, 1932).

"Stuttgart: Werkbundausstellung 'Die Wohnung.'" *Rote Fahne*, May 1, 1927.

Taut, Bruno. *Die Stadtkrone*. Jena, 1919.

————. *Die neue Wohnung: Die Frau als Schöpferin*. Leipzig, 1924.

————. *Ein Wohnhaus*. Stuttgart, 1927.

————. *Bauen: Der neue Wohnbau*. Leipzig: Architektenvereinigung "Der Ring," 1927.

————. "Der gedeckte Tisch." *Wohnungswirtschaft*, no. 10/12 (May, 1927)

————. *Die neue Baukunst in Europa und Amerika*. Stuttgart, 1929.

————. "Russlands architektonische Situation." In exhibition catalogue *El Lissitzky*. Berlin, 1965.

Die Technische Hochschule Stuttgart: Bericht zum 125jährigen Bestehen. Stuttgart, 1954.

Tegethoff, Wolf. *Mies van der Rohe: The Villas and Country Houses*. New York, 1985.

Tendenzen der zwanziger Jahre. 15th Council of Europe exhibition catalogue. Berlin, 1977.

Teut, Anna. *Architektur im Dritten Reich, 1933–1945*. Berlin, Frankfurt, and Vienna, 1967.

————. "Wohnungs- und Siedlungsbauten der 20er Jahre." *Daidalos*, no. 2 (1981).

Ungers, Liselotte. *Die Suche nach einer neuen Wohnform: Siedlungen der zwanziger Jahre damals und heute*. Stuttgart, 1983.

Van de Velde, Henry. *Geschichte meines Lebens*. Munich, 1962.

Venturi, Robert. *Complexity and Contradiction in Architecture*. New York and Boston, 1977.

Verein Deutsches Holz. *Die 25 Einfamilienhäuser der Holzsiedlung am Kochenhof: Errichtet in zeitgemässen Holzbauweisen als "Ausstellung deutsches Holz für Hausbau und Wohnung Stuttgart 1933."* Stuttgart, n.d.

Die Verfassung des deutschen Reiches vom 11. August 1919: Den Schülern und Schülerinnen zur Schulentlassung. Schwarzburg, 1919.

Volkart, Hans. "Was nützt uns die Werkbundausstellung?" *Die Bauzeitung*, no. 39 (October 1, 1927).

Vollmer, Hans. *Künstlerlexikon des XX. Jahrhunderts*. Leipzig, 1955.

Völter, Ernst. "Die Wohnung: Bemerkungen zur Werkbundausstellung." *Die Baugilde* 9, no. 17 (1927).

Wedepohl, Edgar. "Die Weissenhofsiedlung der Werkbundausstellung." *Wasmuth's Monatshefte für Baukunst und Städtebau*, 1927.

Wendschuh, Achim. *Max Taut 1884–1967. Zeichnungen, Bauten*. Berlin, 1984.

Werkbund, Deutscher. "Der Deutsche Werkbund in Stuttgart." *Stuttgarter Neues Tagblatt*, no. 457 (October 1, 1927).

————. "Zur Gründungsgeschichte des Deutschen Werkbunds." *Die Form* 7 (1932): 329–31.

Werkbund Exhibition Directorate. *Kleiner Führer durch die Werkbund-Siedlung Weissenhof*. Stuttgart, 1927.

————. *Mitteilungen der Ausstellungsleitung, (1), 1. Febr. 1927; (2) [not for publication]. 15. März 1927*. Stuttgart, 1927.

————. *In- und Ausländische Pressestimmen zur Werkbundausstellung "Die Wohnung" Stuttgart 1927*. Stuttgart, 1927. (Extracts from press commentary to September 1, 1927.)

Werkbund-Ausstellung "Die Wohnung" 23. Juli–9. Okt. Stuttgart 1927. Exhibition catalogue. Stuttgart, 1927.

Werkbund-Ausstellung "Wohnbedarf" Stuttgart 1932. Exhibition catalogue. Stuttgart, 1932.

Werner, Frank. *Alte Stadt mit neuem Leben*. Stuttgart, 1976.

Der westdeutsche Impuls 1900–1914: Kunst und Umweltgestaltung im Industriegebiet. Exhibition catalogue for *Deutsche Werkbund-Ausstellung, Coeln 1914*. Cologne: Kölnischer Kunstverein, 1984.

Wichmann, Hans. *Aufbruch zum neuen Wohnen: Deutscher Werkbund und WK-Verband 1898–1970*. Stuttgart, 1978.

Wilk, Christopher. *Marcel Breuer: Furniture and Interiors*. New York, 1981.

Willett, John. *Art and Politics in the Weimar Period*. New York, 1978.

Windsor, Alan. *Peter Behrens, Architect and Designer*. London, 1981.

Wingler, Hans Maria. *The Bauhaus*. Cambridge, Mass., and London, 1969.

"Die Wohnungsausstellung Stuttgart 1927. *Das Werk*, no. 9 (1927).

Wolf, Paul. *Wohnung und Siedlung*. Berlin, 1926.

Wolfe, Tom. *From Bauhaus to Our House*. New York, 1981.

Wolfer, Oskar. "Die Werkbundausstellung 'Die Form' in Stuttgart." *Dekorative Kunst* 32 (1925): 20

————. "Die Werkbundausstellung 'Die Wohnung' in Stuttgart." *Die Kunst* 58 (1928): 33–36, 57–68.

Worbs, Dietrich. "Der Raumplan in der Architektur von Adolf Loos." Dissertation. Stuttgart, 1981.

————. "Der Raumplan im Werk von Adolf Loos." In Dietrich Worbs, ed., *Adolf Loos 1870–1933: Raumplan Wohnungsbau*. Exhibition catalogue. Berlin, 1983.

————, and Karin Carmen Jung. "Josef Frank, ein undogmatischer Funktionalist." *Bauwelt*, no. 26 (1985).

Zehn [10] Jahre Werkbundarbeit in Württemberg. Stuttgart. Württembergische Arbeitsgemeinschaft des Deutschen Werkbundes, 1930.

Zelzer, Maria. *Stuttgart unterm Hakenkreuz*. Stuttgart, 1983.

Zimmermann, Hilde. "Lehrküchen." *Württembergische Zeitung*, no. 229, supplement 15 (October 1, 1927).

————. "Bedeutung und Verwendung des Gases im Haushalt," *Die Form* (Berlin 1927)

————. *Haus und Hausrat: Ihre Entstehung, Bewertung und Erhaltung*. 28th ed. Stuttgart, 1929.

Die Zwanziger Jahre des deutschen Werkbundes. Darmstadt and Berlin: Deutscher Werkbund und Werkbund-Archiv, no. 12 1982.

Glossary of German Terms

The drawings have been left in the original German. The following glossary gives the terms as they appear on the plans; i.e. abbreviations in the plans are here given in their abbreviated form. When *z* and *r* appear at the end of a word, most times they are abbreviated forms of *z = zimmer* and *r = raum*.

abfalleinwurf = garbage disposal
abstellplatte = sideboard
abstellr = storage room
abtroffbrett = drying board
arbeitsr = den

bad = bathroom
beton = concrete
bett = bed
blumen = flowers
bücherregal = bookshelves

dachgarten = roof garden
divan = sofa; couch
drehstuhl = swivel chair

eisschrank = refrigerator
eltern = master bedroom
erdgeschoss = ground floor
essnische = eating nook
essraum = dining room

feldsteine = rocks
flur = entrance hall

gemüsegarten = vegetable garden
grundriss = cross-section

heizkörper = radiator
heizung = heating unit
herausziehbare abstellplatten = pull-out sideboards
herd = stove

keller = cellar
kies = gravel
kinderschlaf = children's bedroom
kinderspiel = children's playroom
kinderspielplatz = children's playground
kleider = wardrobe
kleiderschrank = closet
küche = kitchen

lageplan = layout
laube = loggia
liegesofa = sofa

massstab = scale
mädchen = girl's room
müll- und besenschrank = trash and broom closet

nord = north

obergeschoss = floor
obststräucher = fruit shrubs
oeffentl-(icher) weg = public path
ofen = oven
ost = east

rasen = lawn

schlafkammern = bed chambers
schlafz = bedroom
schnitt = section
schrank = closet
schreibtisch = desk
sitzplatz = sitting area
sonnenbad = sunroom
speiseschrank = food cupboard
speizez = dining room
spülbecken = sink
spüle = washroom
stauden = shrubbery
strasse = street
süd = south

tellergestell = dish-drying rack
terasse = terrace
tisch = table
topfschrank = cupboard for pots and pans

verglaster geschirrschrank = china cabinet
vorrat = supplies
vorratschrank = supplies cupboard
vorratschubladen = supplies drawer
vorraum = foyer

W.C. = toilet
waschküche = bath house
werkr = tool room
wohnraum = living room

Index

Photo Credits

10   Bruckmann, ed., 1926
11   Landesbildstelle Baden-Württemberg, Stuttgart; Kohlhaas, 1964
11   Zehn Jahre Werkbundarbeit in Württemberg, 1930
12   Richard-Herre-Archiv, Stuttgart
18   Stadtarchiv Stuttgart
19   Union Deutsche Verlagsgesellschaft, Stuttgart; Staatsgalerie, Stuttgart
20   The Museum of Modern Art, New York; Willi-Baumeister-Archiv, Stuttgart
21   Illustrirte Zeitung, no. 36 (1927)
22   Hans Hildebrandt Estate, Malibu, California
22,23 Spaeth, 1986
     Hans Hildebrandt Estate, Malibu, California; Hilberseimer, 1927; Moderne Bauformen (July, 1927); Innendekoration (August, 1925) Stadtarchiv Stuttgart
24   The Museum of Modern Art, New York
25   Bundespreis Gute Form, Darmstadt 1979
25   Berufsarbeit und Wissen für Bauplatz und Werkstatt, no. 8 (1927), supplement; Frederick, 1922; The Museum of Modern Art, New York
26   Erna Meyer, 1926
26   Stein, Holz, Eisen (February 24, 1927); Die Form (1927)
27   The Museum of Modern Art, New York
28   The Museum of Modern Art, New York; Tegethoff, 1981; Die Form (1928)
28   deutsche bauzeitung, no. 10 (1983)
29   Willi-Baumeister-Archiv, Stuttgart
29   The Museum of Modern Art, New York

30   Akademie der Künste, Berlin, Sammlung Baukunst; Heinz and Bodo Rasch, 1981; Die Form (1928); Willi-Baumeister-Archiv, Stuttgart; Christoph Mohr and Michael Müller, Funktionalität und Moderne, Frankfurt 1984
31   Archiv Margarete Schütte-Lihotzky, Vienna
32   Stadtarchiv Stuttgart
34   Stadtarchiv Stuttgart; Spaeth, 1986
35   Spaeth, 1986
36   Stuttgarter Neues Tagblatt (March 19, 1926)
37   The Museum of Modern Art, New York
38   The Museum of Modern Art, New York
39   Stadtarchiv Stuttgart
40   The Museum of Modern Art, New York; Stadtarchiv Stuttgart
42,43 Stadtarchiv Stuttgart
48   The Museum of Modern Art, New York
49   The Museum of Modern Art, New York; Stadtarchiv Stuttgart
54   Spaeth, 1986
55   Spaeth, 1986
57   The Museum of Modern Art, New York; Graeff, ed., 1928
58   Ferdinand-Kramer-Archiv, Frankfurt
60   Graeff, ed., 1928
61   The Museum of Modern Art, New York
63   Bauhaus-Archiv, Berlin; Erich Dieckmann, Möbelbau in Holz, Rohr und Stahl, Stuttgart 1931
64   Bau und Wohnung, 1927; Hilberseimer, 1927
65   The Museum of Modern Art, New York
66   Graeff, ed., 1928
66   Camille-Graeser-Stiftung, Zürich
67   Schneck, 1983
68   The Museum of Modern Art, New York; Graeff, ed., 1928
69   Eisenmöbelfabrik Arnold, Schöndorf, catalogue
70   Heinz and Bodo Rasch, 1981; The Museum of Modern Art, New York
71   Heinz and Bodo Rasch, 1981
72   Das Werk, no. 9 (1927)
73   Meyer, 1927/28
74   Institut für Geschichte und Theorie der Architektur, Eidgenössische Technische Hochschule, Zürich
75   Daimler-Benz-Archiv, Stuttgart
78   The Museum of Modern Art, New York
79   Le Corbusier, 1927
81   Hans Hildebrandt Estate, Malibu, California; Foto Marburg; Archiv Alfred Roth, Zürich
83   Graeff, ed., 1928; Oud, 1984
84   Jacobus-J.-P.-Oud-Archief, Rotterdam; Le Corbusier, 1927
90   Stadtarchiv Stuttgart
91   Archiv Walter Boll, Regensburg; Hans Hildebrandt Estate, Malibu, California
92   Archiv Walter Boll, Regensburg
93   The Museum of Modern Art, New York
94   The Museum of Modern Art, New York; Le Corbusier, 1927
96   Stadtarchiv Stuttgart; Hans Hildebrandt Estate, Malibu, California
98   Hans Hildebrandt Estate, Malibu, California; Technische Universität München, Architektursammlung
102 Fondation Le Corbusier, Paris; Bodo-Rasch-Archiv, Leinfelden
103 Fondation Le Corbusier, Paris
104 Le Corbusier, 1960
106 Le Corbusier, 1927
107 Fondation Le Corbusier, Paris
108 Hans Hildebrandt Estate, Malibu, California; Le Corbusier, 1927
110 Le Corbusier, 1927; Willi-Baumeister-Archiv, Stuttgart; Hans Hildebrandt Estate, Malibu, California
112 Fondation Le Corbusier, Paris; Bodo-Rasch-Archiv, Leinfelden
113 Willi-Baumeister-Archiv, Stuttgart Hans Hildebrandt Estate, Malibu, California; Le Corbusier, 1927
117 Staatliches Hochbauamt, Stuttgart
122 Le Corbusier, 1927
126 Bauhaus-Archiv, Berlin; Le Corbusier, 1927; Stadtarchiv Stuttgart
127 Hans Hildebrandt Estate, Malibu, California
127 Tecta, Lauenförrde; Bauhaus-Archiv, Berlin
129 Le Corbusier, 1927; Hilberseimer, 1927; Die Form (1927)
131 Stein, Holz, Eisen, no. 37 (1927); Le Corbu-

sier, 1927
132 Le Corbusier, 1927
136 Le Corbusier, 1927
137 Foto Marburg
142 Technische Universität Berlin, Nachlass Poelzig; Max-Berling-Archiv, Osnabrück
144 Hans Hildebrandt Estate, Malibu, California
145 Technische Universität Berlin, Nachlass Poelzig
146 Technische Universität Berlin, Nachlass Poelzig
151 Willi-Baumeister-Archiv, Stuttgart; Akademie der Kunst Berlin, Sammlung Baukunst
152 Graeff, ed., 1928
153 Akademie der Kunst Berlin, Sammlung Baukunst; Le Corbusier, 1927
156 *Die Form* (1927)
157 Richard-Herre-Archiv, Stuttgart
158 Richard-Herre-Archiv, Stuttgart
160 Stadtarchiv Stuttgart
161 Stadtarchiv Stuttgart; Archiv Walter Knoll, Herrenberg
164 Hochschule für angewandte Kunst, Vienna, Nachlass Josef Frank
166 Hans Hildebrandt Estate, Malibu, California; Stadtarchiv Stuttgart
167 Hans Hildebrandt Estate, Malibu, California; Institut für Geschichte und Theorie der Architektur, Eidgenössische Technische Hochschule, Zürich; Le Corbusier, 1927
170 *Zwischen Kunst und Industrie*, Stuttgart 1987; *i 10* (1927)
171 Le Corbusier, 1927; Stadtarchiv Stuttgart
172 Le Corbusier, 1927
173 Tecta, Lauenförde; *Festschrift Firma Honold*; Le Corbusier, 1927
174 Le Corbusier, 1927; *Zwischen Kunst und Industrie*, Stuttgart 1987
175 Le Corbusier, 1927; Graeff, ed., 1928
176 Tilmann Buddensieg, *Industriearchitektur—Peter Behrens und die AEG 1907–1914*, Milan 1978.
177 Heinrich Zille, *Das grosse Zille-Buch*, Gütersloh, n.d.
178 *Die Wohnungswirtschaft* (1926); *Blätter des Deutschen Roten Kreuzes* (1926); Hilberseimer, 1927
179 Stadtarchiv Stuttgart; *Die Form* (1927)
182 Heinz and Bodo Rasch, 1981
183 Nachlass Reinhold Stotz, Wuppertal; Oscar-Heinitz-Archiv, Neuhausen/F.
184 *Die Form* (1928)
185 *Die Form* (1928); Graeff, ed., 1928
187 Akademie der Künste, Berlin, Nachlass Scharoun
188 Akademie der Künste, Berlin, Nachlass Scharoun
189 Akademie der Künste, Berlin, Nachlass Scharoun
191 Akademie der Künste, Berlin, Nachlass Scharoun
192 Akademie der Künste, Berlin, Nachlass Scharoun
193 Akademie der Künste, Berlin, Nachlass Scharoun
200 Felix Schuster, ed., *Schwäbisches Heimatbuch*, Stuttgart 1941